THE MIND, BODY, SPIRIT, *And* STORYTELLING

God's DNA Bloodline—In God We Trust

Hakeem R. Jelani

Copyright © 2023 Hakeem R. Jelani
All rights reserved
First Edition

NEWMAN SPRINGS PUBLISHING
320 Broad Street
Red Bank, NJ 07701

First originally published by Newman Springs Publishing 2023

ISBN 978-1-68498-884-6 (Paperback)
ISBN 978-1-68498-885-3 (Digital)

Printed in the United States of America

THE MIND, BODY, SPIRIT, And STORYTELLING

God's DNA Bloodline—In God We Trust

"Perspicacious Intrinsic Knowledge Of The Enigmatic Psycho-Spiritual Divine Noumena. We Know Almost Nothing About The Light Of Intuition. Divine Spirit Insight And Understanding Of Purification From A Hypnotic Slumber. Awaken To Hear The Trumpets Sound Of The Clarion Call For Imperishable Validated Saved Souls Caught Up As Merkabas/Chariots Hover, Foretold As A Prophecy Endtime Sign Revelation Forewarns Of The Psycho-Spiritual Manifestations Shall Come Forth Waiting A Time When The Bible Prophecy Of Dread Is This Preeminent Ascension. The Reveal Of The Human Harvest."

Hakeem R. Jelani

Enki's Royal Bloodline Of God Fusion
Created His Crossbred Children

The Creator God Was Enki. Not Spurious Subterfuge Or Truthiness. The Bible Says That God Came From Heaven. The Anunnaki Enki, God Of Wisdom, Science, Magic Built The City-State Eridu In Sumer, Mesopotamia.

The Old Testament Bible Genesis Narrative, Chapter 1, through 11

And The Anunnaki Ancient Astronauts Hypothesis

—— ANUNNAKI ANCIENT ASTRONAUTS ——

ALIEN GOD ENKI's DNA GENE CODE EDITING
& FUSED THE CROSSBRED BLOODLINE

"Religions Sophism And Mass Deception Play"

ANNUNAKI ALIEN GOD'S EARTH MISSION VOYAGE, IT'S THE OLD TESTAMENT CHRISTIAN BIBLE ON GENESIS IS NOT THE HOLD STORY!

*"Might The Divine Ether Of Spirit Insight Be
Rational And Irrefutable Knowledge Standard"*

Cape Sounion Temple of Poseidon, Athens, Greece

The Perspicacious Insight Of Nous Atop The BenBen
Capstone Of Egyptian Religions Precept
These Words Of Expression Of Divine
Reverence For These Stately Sage Prose

AVANT-GARDE PROSE COLLECTION
---

*Missing From The Old Testament Holy Bible Genesis Narrative
Is About A Seminal Event: In God We Trust. These Revelations
Of This Assertion Is The Light And Fire That Will Brighten Your
Vision. The Spirits Of The Life Force Energy Will Demystify Those
Old Disturbing Tales Of A Spurious Falsehoods Concealed The God
Enki Genetic Manipulation Of An African Female's Mitochondrial
DNA Code Of Anunnaki Alien Astronauts Hypothesis
Is Indicative Of The Truth And Purity, Per-say!"*

CONTENTS

Introduction ix

Chapter 1: Alien Gods & African Gold Mines 1

Chapter 2: Life, Light, Love, Peace, Honor; The Eternal Sacred Nature 176

Chapter 3: Spring, Summer Leaves Die In Autumn 207

Chapter 4: Enchantress Femme Fatale Beguiling Eyes Drew Me Nigh 218

Chapter 5: Breathe Air of the Invisible Wind 309

Chapter 6: Nature's Wildlife Survival Lottery 316

Chapter 7: Muse By New Age Candlelights 327

Chapter 8: Earth, Spring Time, Birds, Butterflies & Fireflies ... 333

Chapter 9: The True Measure Integrity And Your honor 338

References 347

INTRODUCTION

Those Who From The Heavens Came

This introduction is purely about the missing link between the Old Testament Bible Genesis narrative tale that was translated into this religious New Testament Bible Genesis story that has been permeating an ecclesiastical perpetuation of the spurious attempt to conceal information regarding the alien god's who came to the Earth on board their shiny, bell-shaped UFO/AUVs. The implication being that they were intrepid ancient astronauts who were the vanguard of this seminal descent from heaven landed an alien spacecraft down on the earth plane of Summer, Mesopotamia. Following the ancient astronaut theorists hypothesis, more questions about the AUV/UFO phenomenon in conflation to the Old Testament bible Genesis scripture. Fits my overall premise as a conjecture that argues that extraterrestrial as an Olden times Anunnaki as the alien gods from the sky. Asserts to be the real true story behind the Bible Genesis creation myth. As a logical and rational person I also contend that the extraterrestrial Anunnaki were custodian and rulers. Their Anunnaki from the sky I contend is actually that fits the Old Testament Bible story of the genesis. Which lifted the original translations of the alien who came from the sky and landed on the earth plane. This would have been entered in Enki's daily log book record to give important information about the Anunnaki clans who became the first custodian of planet earth. Consider this as a codex of the Sumerian Bible was the Old Testament codex. that was edited and rewritten by the Roman Emperor, who ordered the holy Bishops to mislead humanity by perpetuating an intentional falsity to establish the New Testament

Catholic Church that was edited and rewritten by the Roman Emperor. He ordered a council of Bishops to condense the Bible, which would effectively mislead humanity to believe a false religion. And it has been perpetuated a falsity by establishment of the New Testament Catholic Church theology. Their ultimate aim was to create the structure of Western theology, with the death of Jesus Christ with the Catholic Church of God on earth that elevated a deception. And by the way here's what I mean is: I think that it marked the separation of church and state as a concept in the modern day religious belief that shine a spotlight on the truth about the vanguard flight from planet Nibiru's that was the crew of the titular alien race of ancient astronauts. They have wittingly and intentionally facilitated the words of the Bible without acknowledging that which is true about the origin of religion. What this alludes to truth and subjective perception of the creative expression as *avant-garde* prose. Whereby the instrument of inspiration turns into storytelling when the spirit of intuition reveals a lost ancient civilization and nature of God is the wisdom. The sapience of your spirit elucidates insight, which shall leave little doubt as to the omission of the identity of God which the Old Testament Bible genesis narrative recounts.

Whereas the image and likeness is intentionally missing, and very vague, giving this thread underlying the single most important evidence about the gods known as Anunnaki titular gods Anu, Enlil, and Enki represent, raising the question the real reason why the biblical genesis story clearly omitted details of the gods of Heaven anthropomorphic identity and description about were and the means by which they came from the, viz., "those who from Heaven came." Where did they come from?

Were they actually extraterrestrial aliens god? Who were the Anunnaki alien gods? Why did Hebrews and the Greeks translators of the original Anunnaki Sumerian Bible not identify who came from the sky? And why did god create homo-sapien sapiens. Why is this a mystery gods about storytelling, which is inextricably linked to the predicate assumptions posited as my examination of a mystery gods.

The amorphic extraterrestrial beings who came down onto the Earth plane? Their actual history and the biblical version. There is sufficient reason to believe the archaeological evidence that is linked an ancient astronaut's race descent is responsible for fashioning a crossbred human bloodline that fits nicely into the Old Testament Bible Genesis narrative. The background here is an incredibly fascinating story of the Old Testament Bible, Genesis narrative tale was intentionally edited out.

This is to say that much had been concealed about the Anunnaki alien race astronauts of heaven. Largely indicative of what seems to be a spurious invention. Here let me stop the spin and try to unpack a conjecture with respect to the relevance to this claim that god came down from the sky. Which is a view separate from the New Testament Christian Church religious precepts. Meaning that which is a probability of an actual historical event. One which dovetails nicely with the modern research findings and analysis that posited the controversial views of the ancient astronauts theorists hypothesis contend the Bible was written about an intelligent race of extraterrestrials.

When intelligent logic and reason apply

Try to discern what is true about the things written as religious storytelling as an incomplete historical context that raises salient questions about why the ancient astronauts hypothesis is rebuffed as poppycock. Assumptions that are aligned with archeology, anthropology, discovery and findings are scrutinized, analyzed, and digested facts, separated from fabricated mythology. We can interpret this information as available for future generations to share and discuss from a modern retrospective a vignette that presents a concise description of extraterrestrials (https://www.kemet.org/about).

So the intelligent question takes a closeup analysis of "Those who from the Heavens came." Today we know that the Old Testament Bible, Genesis narrative tale pertains to the ancient world events. Much of this historical information is simply not true if you don't objectively interpolate the ancient astronauts theorists hypothesis. This is the dirty little truth that would potentially unravel the theological foundation of our faith and confidence in the Bible storytelling, and destroy the moral and structural underpinnings that have been teaching truthiness as the words of Jesus Christ as gospel in the pews of an organized religion. So let me be clear about this assumption of extraterrestrial alien titular gods who called themselves the Anunnaki who came down from the sky (Heaven), or planet Nibiru. There is no strong evidence to support, any arguments against any of the ancient astronauts' theorists with audaciously espoused compelling arguments equates to a logical and reasonable notion which conjectures the missing elements of this too story we are not being told about:

"Those who from the Heavens (sky) came". These were ancient astronauts who came down from the sky on board some advanced aerial flying AUV/UFO spacecraft. Which, by definition, would be indicative of a highly intelligent alien race, who called themselves the Anunnaki. Is this an assertion that is not likely to be credible?

Consider the underlying premise with which you question everything you have been taught and, ponder the fundamental assertion with which I interpolate that these Anunnaki were the titular god Anu, Enlil, and Enki who was a brilliant god and the chief medical doctor who, successfully manipulating the DNA biological code and fashioned the first Homo sapiens sapiens Adam. Royal elite god Anu lowered the first royal kingship on planet Earth at Enki's city, state, of Eridu. The Anunnki King Anu gave his son, Enlil the elite title of Lord of Supreme Earth commander.

He was the god associated with the eponymous Garden of Eden. These are the gods who taught humans the art of warfare, metal working, mathematics, science and astrology psycho-spiritual science of the wisdom of the Kemet occultist practice of spiritual meditation as the gods of Heaven. A longstanding presence of the Olden Times, so-called shining ones, long before the Europeans established Jesus Christ at the epicenter of a Western blind faith religion (https://y-jesus.com/lp/0-real-jesus-ttn/2/).

Once upon a very long time ago

Let's use our imagination to excursively put ourselves back in the ancient times of the Olden Times of the gods who descended on to the earth plane. Now think about these opening lines from the Old Testament Bible:

"In the beginning was the word, and the word was with god, and the word was god" (https://www.biblestudytools.com/bible-study/topical-studies/how-in-the-beginning-was-the-word-explains-the). The anecdotal history of the Anunnaki arrival is the re-edited version of their story which begs the question: What is truth over truthiness? Because the biblical genesis doesn't record any of what is the conjugation of a seminal historical event. Scribes of the Anunnaki recording their mission earth voyage produced a voluminous account of their deeds from the time of holy book codex bible was constituted into the eponymous new world order transformation of the genesis narrative tale was re-written. The truth is that we can speculate about these titular gods seminal event that occurred in ancient Sumer, Mesopotamia a very long time ago; which is clearly a incredible moment in history if you were standing there among those indigenous earth man's tribes would have been all been awed when they watched Enki and his fifty man crew walk out of their ancient UFO spaceships. So they came from the sky and landed.

Ancient indigenous Sumerians people had initially feared the sight of that magnificent shining AUV/UFO spacecraft as it was slowly landing in the indigenous tribes of Africa's first world culture of the land that is mentioned in the Bible Old Testament as Sumer, Mesopotamia.

Of course if we were living during the time of the Anunnaki gods of the planet Nibiru, you would have been one among those who watched as the Anunnaki extraterrestrial spacecraft slowly descended from the sky and land their large, bright, shiny, bell-shaped flying spacecraft carrying the great Royal Prince Enki's and his fifty man space traveling astronauts crew as it landed down in ancient Sumer, Mesopotamia. Yeah, you would have observed this Anunnaki flight slowly landing the first titular alien gods UFO flying spacecraft. an ancient astronaut crew slowly descended onto the earth plane. Enki was the alien god who was the commander of the first ancient astronaut leader of this advanced UFO flying spacecraft. They were the first extraterrestrial space traveling astronauts. They arrived by traveling through space on a vanguard mission earth voyage from a distant higher orbital plane galaxy. And that is what the Bible alludes to as heaven, meaning they came down to earth from their home planet, Nibiru. Translation of Anunnaki means: "the people from the sky".

Or shall we say, extraterrestrial alien gods who were a race of highly intelligent alien beings. This book is written as an exegesis with the modality of speculation assertion, derived from the various eclectic sources of information, which is the fundamental predicate revealed as a compendium that focuses the lost ancient occult learning and teachings of the divine mysteries of the Anunnaki psycho-spiritual knowledge of sacred initiation of the Kemet religion of the divine *Netjer* deities. Within the modality of the gods is to acquire knowledge and wisdom without speculative assertions, which is derived from the eclectic sources of information. The fundamental predicate is intrinsic to the overall compendium of information that focuses on the true story of the Old Testament book of Genesis narrative tale. These are the titular alien gods that the holy Bible Genesis scriptures refer to as our holy father and creator in heaven. Meaning an anamorphic god of Heaven. Well then I have a different analysis in respect to an extraterrestrial alien god figure.

The conjecture here is that the missing element of biblical Genesis creation narrative. But dare we say that the story of the Old Testament was a pivotal point from the true history of the Anunnaki alien astronauts' mission earth exploration voyages enterprise? What is alleged as the modern era view of the biblical narrative is derived from this assumption that the old world was founded by the Olden Times extraterrestrial ancestors gods who descended from the sky. This belief is an assertion according to the decision taken by the quorum of the governing council board members chaired by the sky god, Royal King Anu, the Anunnaki's ruler of Nibiru.

The discussions were about how they could best resolve matters pertaining to planet Nibiru's loss of its ozone atmosphere. Its atmosphere spurred the heated discussion as they sought to find an effective solution that would seal up the slow leaks causing the loss of its atmosphere. And this is precisely what throws a great flood light on this backstory that is curiously contemporaneous with the Biblical story. We juxtaposition elements of the archaeology and anthropology discovery and findings and glean insights from has been referred to as the ancient astronauts theorists' hypothesis.

Planet Nibiru Elite King of Anunnaki

Many neophytes offer their conjectures about them as the eponymous gods of the Bible tale of Genesis. My understanding is a corresponding view with which fits nicely: ancient astronauts concur with an action undertaken by the elite Nibiru's King Anu (supreme) lord god of Heaven. What was hidden or missing is the element of truth. Much of what is missing is clearly connected to our modern UFO phenomenon, is no longer misunderstood will lend credibility to the contention that the Anunnaki King of planet Nibiru took the decision to send the vanguard crew of ancient alien astronauts to the planet earth's plane was by the consensus as a quorum of the Anunnaki council board members who had all concurred on the solution that gold from the planet earth was required to patch up critical leaking of Nibiru's ozone atmospheric liner.

Finally they all concurred that a vanguard fiftyman astronauts exploratory mission earth voyage flight would descend to the earth plane was initiated. It's the beginning flight of the ancient astronauts who were the alien gods who descended. Of course the Old Testament Bible Genesis narrative only alludes to God as a mystery tale about: "those who from the Heaven came," This is the speculative assertion, revealing shocking evidence which has been hermetically concealed to refute the assertion of the ancient astronauts arrival and establishment alien gods as those who from the Heavens came to land on the earth plane. Information which was long since been hidden by the ancient rulers who were behind the Western world religious grand scheme of controlling humanity. The premise being to distort history and cultivate a hidden agenda to control the social and religious aspects. But is this the hidden truth, as an logical pragmatic assertion given that most plausible assumptions. Ostensibly, consistent with the Genesis narrative.

HAKEEM R. JELANI

The Old Testament Bible Genesis

The Old Testament narrative has been examined through a modern prism as the Ancient astronauts' theorists. And its hypothesis is a very plausible and highly speculative as a likely predicated backstory. Which raises questions about this substantive theory is faced with plenty of criticism and skepticism. Is it quite possible that there's some secret truth that would shine a light on the anecdotal evidence that would expose the shocking cover up of the missing connection to the original custodian of planet earth? It is likely to maintain the status quo that cultivates a preferred element of a contrived set of accepted anecdotal religious blind faith.

To avoid any disillusionment about the biblical genesis narrative of this true seminal historical event that is about space traveling ancient astronauts. This story is incomplete without interpolation of the Anunnaki's alien gods presence as the essential element that fits nicely into that which is missing from the Bible. The face of the etheric light Anunnaki alien beings were the gods of Heaven, elevated to the status assigned to the highest of the divine all prevailing life force energy, meaning what? To make sense of our existence in all of its permutations of esoteric metaphors of divine fire and light. To this we unconsciously equate the words of the holy Bible Genesis with the New Testament religious teaching by the Church canons of Christianity, and creative doctrines that the works of theological bishops was a Roman Catholic invention of god as Jesus Christ (https://www.prweb.com/releases/2013/10/prweb11201273.htm).

All of this is clear to me. So allow me to express my limited spiritual understanding that conveys a fundamental shift in my intellectual worldview that in many aspects conflates personal realisms and perspectives of mankind's who seek clarity follow the paradigm shift as the light of consciousness awareness of divine infinite creator as the god we trust.

So as it goes, please allow me to elucidate with logic and reason, for the esoteric great truths are hidden in the disciplines of spiritual science and philosophy which was written about the grand architect of existence concealed, or locked the incredible ancient written manuscripts from eons of Anunnaki gods and intentionally caused a misdirection play.

Religious schemes to undermine and dismantle the original precepts and the principles of deference to African/Egyptians learning and teaching of the Anunnaki alien gods worship of African Kemet psycho-spiritual science daily practice of sacred contemplation in daily meditation were upended by the Christian faith practice of the New Testament was to bring the on the new world western interpretation of the original Orthodox gospels teachings.

The Hebrew and Greeks bible translations

These versions of the Bible were subjective translations and became the Catholic religion's new edited copy of their religion. An action ordered by the Roman state government, which was accomplished by the twelve Bishops who interpreted it and elevated it into prominence as the preeminence of the Catholic New Testament transformations of the ancient Bible translation, had facilitated as the blind faith religion, to this aim organized church Bishops successfully took hold, and solidified their sinister scheme through the creed and religious rites and doctrine to which they establishing moral authority was inculcated and brutally forced on to those who had defied the laws, in many cases those who voiced opposition, they were convicted of heresy and put to death.

It was a shameful period of time in history for those folk with conviction were deemed to be an affront to the Romans' Catholic doctrine of the new world order. were considered crimes against god. It took a toll on the newpublic psychic perception of a religious truthiness, meaning a manipulation of the original teachings of spiritual science was hijacked by ancient rulers. Bishops edited the Bible from the original psycho-spiritual sciences of the alien race. Their action planted roots for the blind faith scheme that instituted the rapid rise of the New Testament religion. The Christians religious precepts, including the mistranslation of scripture into the new condensed Bible, priests arbitrarily perpetuated and promulgated a new world religious precepts, including the mistranslation of scripture into the new condensed Bible, priests arbitrarily perpetuated and promulgated their religious precepts, including the mistranslation of scripture into the new condensed Bible, priests arbitrarily perpetuated and promulgated their skewed versions of the biblical scriptures of a blind faith religion of truthiness. This truth I allude to is about this incredible monumental seminal event of an ancient astronaut landing on Earth. Returning to the exegesis of the Old Testament Bible Genesis narrative tale, and just perhaps most people would concur with my speculation about the ancient astronauts as alien extraterrestrials.

Yes, I am inclined to concur with the modern archaeology and anthropology findings as material evidence and historical findings and scriptures conflate the relevant stories of the biblical events, which seems to confirm that the gods were a group of advanced alien space traveling race beings. And my juxtaposition isn't any clearer than that which is alluded to by the Bible, that says: "Those who from Heaven came". When analyzing the meaning of the words that were written we are convinced that this was a real historical event about the Anunnaki race of intelligent alien ancient space traveling astronauts. Might the truth be revealed about the origins of the alien avatars gods, according to the genesis said they descended from the sky (Heaven) to colonize the Earth plane. Which is the piece of truth that is missing from the holy Old Testament Bible account of the Anunnaki alien gods who arrived on the planet earth from their planet Nibiru. Which is a story of the most incredible fairy tale. Considering that it's most crucial element—the predicate background story is cleverly lifted out from what seems to be the perfect fit into the ancient astronauts controversy that inserts the interpolation of the greatest deception. Which raises the question about why there are critical limits regarding the obfuscation as to biblical creator gods profiles by revealing precisely who were: "Those from the Heavens came down to earth.

This book is a paradigm shift from the truthiness pervading the social complex perception of biblical history. Conversely, I elucidate with the modern perspective of the ancient astronauts theorists hypothesis that connects to the relevant anecdotal evidence and research findings that is missing from this historical event. Which is to interpolate a widely controversial assertion with respect to the modern phenomenon of UFO/UAVs. The so-called debate on the ancient astronauts theorists hypothesis. And any reasonable person would have to conclude that the origin of our understanding and teachings of the biblical holy scriptures was copied from the original codex, the Hebrews lifted and passed down their translation of the Sumerian's Anunnaki Bible. With mistranslations, learning and teaching regression passed on into each ancient past generations were arbitrarily altered. It became an inherent cornerstone of the many nuances brands of religion transformed into this Christian reinventing of the story of Jesus Christ. This was the ultimate underlying misdirection play. Because the true story is a paucity, without the *interrogative* of the full backstory regarding the biblical genesis narrative tale. As we know, this is a controversial subject Matter. Which often sparks discussion and spur a conversation makes one think beyond your comfort zone by raising questions about what you have been taught. There is God the creator and his human creation, right? But, ostensibly, this is a conversion that focuses on the validity of the biblical genesis scriptures, which seemingly fits nicely with the views that posits the modern ancient astronauts theorists hypothesis elucidating the notion that undermines and dismisses the ancient astronaut's earth presence.

Therein lies the rub

The truth turned into the Bible as a mystery tale has been perpetuated by the church as a spurious religious narrative It's a truth concealed behind their smokescreen of truthiness. Which seems to be a misdirection played by New Testament church teachings of Jesus as a blind faith religion. It cleverly dismisses the notion of an alien race of Anunnaki being, those who came were the titular gods of the Old Testament Bible genesis. Extraterrestrials, ancient astronauts. The New Testament author's fabricated and promulgated story of the a new Christian Jesus Christ. The aim was to supersede the Old Testament Bible Genesis as an advanced intelligent race of ancient astronauts; as alien beings who came from a higher plane, and a different constellation orbit. Whereas, skeptics may ask whether such an assertion is conjecture devoid of substantive evidence is far-fetched and hyperbolic.

Though it's arguably contentious, it sharply contradicts the holy Old Testament biblical genesis narrative, and is conspicuously silent regarding what is meant when it says: "Those who from the Heaven came". Which has to do with Bible Genesis fundamental underlying narrative tale of the Old Testament, but it has not given us the truth about precepts that undergird the phenomenon of the modern extraterrestrials, juxtaposition to the ancient origin of the Anunnaki alien beings as this spacefaring astronauts race that colonized and seeded civilization and kingship as the human social complex derived the backstory that is conspicuously missing from earth nascence of the Olden Times gods from a higher orbital plane. Which makes this book that shines the light of truth about the alien god's presence making no sense except for creating a mystery tale alluding to hiding the true identity of these extraterrestrial astronauts.

Here's your invitation to achieve the knowledge standard is an open invitation to discover the anecdotal details that are curiously missing from the Old Testament book of Genesis, chapters 1 to 11 (https://www.biblegateway.com/passage/?search=Genesis%20 1-11&version=KJV). This is an objective perspective interpretation and speculative exegesis. Views which take a critical look back into the true story and the underlying implications of the ancient alien astronaut theorist controversial hypothesis analysis as it relates to "those who from the Heaven came". When we understand the importance and significance of this statement. So, well then, it's quite obvious as to why folks should digest what and consider the underlying motivation for organized religious establishments to obfuscate or conceal the real sinister purpose for hiding the truth? Duch things have come into the modern world and have been exposed as secrets. They don't want this truth revealed. Because the real true underlying linchpin. We all of the grenade pin would expose the fundamental hidden truth about the origins of religious allegories perpetuated as the words of god. My friends, can you handle this and the implications of the consequences if the truth comes to light? This is the long held secret of the god's gambit. By their hidden hand they remain hidden away in order to subliminally inculcate and push their New Testament paucity. Or a misdirection or a deception, should concerns folks to consume and digest and discern the truthiness and with respect to a profound objective view and personal understanding. To spur folks to contemplate and discern the truth from the religion of falsehood; and pooh-pooh truthiness that has hidden identity profiles, and acknowledge that the big deception. Because the Bible is a convoluted collection of Hebrew and Greek translations of the Anunnaki Sumerian recorded accounts after they were living on the interior, ancient astronaut theorist's hypotheses about the human being endued with the seed essence began with Royal Prince Enki's creation.

It's the most logical and reasonably speculative view, as well as a paradigm shift, given that it is an assertion that indicates that the alien Anunnaki gods arrived circa 450,000 years ago.

The real truth began in the in those days

When the ancient scriptures were written to give the beginning account that marked the arrival of the ancient astronauts' arrival on Earth. Is the Bible a story of the Anunnaki who were extraterrestrial visitors to the earth mission establishing the presence of the olden time Anunnaki alien clans. Ancient astronauts who the biblical narrative says were, "Those who from the Heaven came." Within such a context, the conjecture and assumption is based on the application of a reasonable person's standard of rational intelligent knowledge, logic, and reason that obfuscates the identity of the old alien astronauts Anunnaki titular gods who descended from heaven.

What is particularly important is that the incursion was the beginning of the original version of the truth about an alien construction of ancient and modern civilization on the earth plane. Whereas much of what fits into what seems plausible is logical is curiously omitted from the written Genesis narrative. This is not a contradiction. But an observation that brings clarity to the nascent that the period is indicative of the truth that pervades intrinsically and inextricably to a fundamental foundation of knowledge and symbolism of the mystery school of ancient Kemet principles of scared psycho-spiritual religious teaching was carried out in the Egyptian initiation ceremony and the original Anunnaki Sumerian Bible Genesis narrative creation myth.

What written in the book is an incredible historical event that seemingly, is the story that is not a myth. Which is closely akin to the modern ancient astronauts theorists hypothesis is a speculative assertion. Whereof I have in common with other awake thinkers in light of what seems quite incredible when considering the views of the religious blind faith denyers, meaning that they have an inability to *gain say* the modern hypothesis. This is the underlying confirmation of the truth over truthiness. Which is based upon contemporary archeology and anthropology discovery and findings.

Substantive information about this is revealed in fictional books written by several prominent authors. Notwithstanding the holy Bible book of Genesis narrative tale is inculcated as the true word of God is still being propagated as God's religion.

Worship an invisible god of Heaven

Let's be clear about this. We all have been taught from childhood to pray to Gods of the Old Testament Bible books of Genesis narrative tale. Now would you be taken aback by the reevaluation of the olden times event, that is, a modern version, by scrolling back through the uncurated story? To reveal its pervading falsehoods that underlie this long standing cultivation of what is logically determined to be a very implausible truthiness with intelligent logic elucidate truth about the Bible creation (https://biblehub.com/library/maspero/history_of_egypt) story dovetails nicely with alien gods. Here is what you need to know to educate yourself about what has been the missing elements that are obfuscated and excluded from religious established Church denominational teaching of the Gospel of the blind faith religions. Let us use common sense and ponder why the Old Testament Bible Genesis is short of revealing any significant details regarding who, where, and how "those who from the Heaven came" were? Might such omissions have been efficaciously intentional in order to create and push the mystery of truthiness to conceal and pervades their red herring to inculcate the misdirection play.

Perhaps, just maybe with logic and reason lead us to reveal the truth that conflate with the modern ancient view posited by the astronauts' theorists' hypothesis about the Anunnaki's extraterrestrials aliens as an advanced race of man-like alien god figures acknowledge truth that is the scriptures written in the Old Testament Bible Genesis is largely the story about the Anunnaki clan's space traveling alien astronauts who descended from their own home planet orbital deep space planet, Nibiru. But there's a more significant missing element, with respect to the important narrative tale that must be interpolated into this story that is long overdue. First off, with the proper perspective, using intelligent logic and reason we concur with the ancient astronauts' theorists' hypothesis arguments that claim the Anunnaki alien gods UFO spacecraft came down to earth from a higher orbital planetary and landed in ancient Sumer, Mesopotamia.

Which was the landing zone that marks the epicenter of where the Genesis narrative says that God created the world in six days and rested on the Sabbath day. What I assert here is that the truth about those who came from heaven had a defined mission purpose. The Old Testament book of Genesis narrative tale is a perpetuated, long held hermetic secret that was exculpatory to the biblical Old Testament genesis narrative.

To posit my assumption regarding the identity of the Anunnaki extraterrestrial alien god, meaning: Those who came from Heaven were the old time's titular gods. These ancient alien Annunaki astronauts descended from the sky and were the original custodian gods of Mesopotamia. I submit to you that, it's perhaps reasonable and presumptuous to presuppose that they were the custodians of planet earth who were likely worshiped by the indigenous tribes, which was the case for the Anunnaki alien gods who descended would have been venerated as the so-called, shining ones! Ostensibly, subsequently, the *de facto* precursor gods from the sky (Heaven) came were intelligent alien beings.

These precursor gods applied knowledge to construct civilizations with many significant contributions by these ancient aliens astronauts' influence spread throughout ancient and modern generations of the children of god identity was derived from the African consciousness. Is there sufficient historical and archaeologist corroboration, which has been validating the questions by citing reference to their research discovery. Which have produced evidence that fits the ancient astronauts theorists and the Old Testament Bible, Genesis creation narrative—meaning the Anunnaki god Enki was the god who was a commander of an ancient spaceship carrying the initial fifty man astronauts crew and the Igigi labor workforce that built Enki's eponymous city of Eridu in the Southern region of Sumer, Mesopotamia. His brother was Enlil.

Lord of the Earth commander

Their father was King Anu and this trio profile, fundamentally dovetails nicely with the new age Western Romanization interpolated the rise of the Christianity biblical teachings was transformed into a religion of blind faith; and the state, to appease the occult religions embrace Catholic Christianity by the acceptance of occult festivals, by which the worshiping of pagan events became very popular, annually celebrated, holidays that fundamentally inculcated the falsehoods. The truth is lost, *ipso facto,* these actions were the cause behind the reworkings of the original sacred principles of the ancient Egyptian-Kemetic divine spiritual science philosophy. Much of it was transferred into precepts that are recognized in the modern religions' symbols of other brands of religious teachings and learning is convoluted.

Few people in our universities have apprehended an understanding of the discernment of nature profoundly. Meaning the true meaning of the enigmatic *noumena*; which transcends beyond what knowledge we have been taught or can understand is limited to social consciousness awareness. Having a limited mental clarity and to strive for enlightenment and insight is that which is endured by intelligent discernment, using logic and reason. A salient, close up, predicate that brings you a fresh approach by applying objectivity.

We have little awareness of the preponderance of the archeology and anthropology evidence that shows that every ancient and modern culture's population believes and prays to a divine being. People from every walk of life make no distinction whatsoever between the number of alleged UFOs, or extraterrestrial Anunnaki extraterrestrial ancient astronaut theorist's hypothesis, and yet save from speculation, the fact remains that: the development of our existence. The gods' presence on the Earth's interior began about 450,000 years ago, long after landing in ancient Mesopotamia. Anunnaki aliens established themselves as the Lord gods from the sky.

Their many contributions harken back to the Sumerian gods descended from the sky. Assertion I elucidate is consistent with the Ancient Astronauts Theorist's hypothesis with relevant anecdotal details given in the Bible version fits their assumption nicely with the Anunnaki Royal prince Enki's account of the creation of his son Adapa with the specificity that is revealed in the "Seven Tablets of Creation"!

Primarily, suffice it to say that the ancient astronauts theorist hypothesis, seemingly, aligns rather nicely with the missing anecdotal details curiously fits into the monumental Old Testament Bible Genesis tale narrative lead to a speculative assumption that conjure up alien UAV/UFO as graven images and no description of an extraterrestrial event of a spacecraft landing event. Anyway, therefore, I have an astonishing take on the Old Testament story about the Anunnaki and the Old Testament Bible. You can't begin to comprehend the genesis story without consideration of the Anunnaki as those ancient astronauts who came down to earth. Fundamentally speaking, I'm eager to tell others about the Anunnaki ancient astronauts as a race of alien beings. Meaning I believe this to be the true identity of the biblical gods. Whose deeds dovetails nicely with this association of and full acknowledgement of: "Those who deliberately omitted essential elements of the whole backstory, I mean why is this backstory conspicuously mute? It's neither taught by parents, in schools, nor has there been the focus of religious discussions in order to rebut such assertions.

How can we repudiate the ancient astronauts hypothesis as folly?

Truth is always fundamental to the knowledge standard of integrity—and it is the value where enlightenment is above reproach. This is a salient point to consider, and perhaps the future church congregation. And that which I mean to say: that adults need to know about this.

An account of the genesis narrative from a different perspective looks at "the god we trust" worshiping, no matter your preferred brand or religious learning and teachings that mostly pleases their spiritual consciousness. I have very mixed feelings about the construction of religious spiritualism as a fact or a popular fable. This is certainly not specious, meaning it has a false look of truth or genuineness. And so there is more to this we have to examine the Old Testament biblical tale with objective logic and reason from an intelligent person's standard.

Expose' of the Primordial Truth

My friends let me be clear, are we not the living individual children and direct offspring and the divine children of the intelligent, ineffable, Infinite bloodline of the Creator lord; Enki? Physical manifestations of his extraterrestrial physical image likeness? A unique homosapien sapiens individual with subjective experiences. To each individual *personality,* are behavioral characteristics that are unique. That is your own personal stories that tell about life experiencing the peregrinations without obfuscation; it is your tremendous psycho spiritual reality. We analyze the Bible Genesis narrative tale as an exegesis? Intuition to imbibe knowledge with insight, logic, and reason leads to the Anunnaki ancient astronauts, who were the titular Gods of Heaven. The Anunnaki were not the universal Infinity existence of God's *noumena* of the *ubiquitous pleroma.* What is the assumption that the personification of the Anunnaki, and not the all pervading, ubiquitous, infinite nature of the *Noumena,* which is of the unmanifested metaphysical of the mystery of universal consciousness of the divine geometry of the grand infinite creator God of earth material phenomenon of the reality that rules our physical and spiritual world realm. That which is of grand consciousness awareness of beingness is a spiritual identity of the self in material world reality. Our psycho spiritual intuition resides within the light force energy that animates the mind and body complex! Whereof the Anunnaki aliens were titular god personas, infused into the African consciousness through the great Royal Prince Enki. His personification aligned with the symbolical assertion of the universal divine. This nature of God's manifestation as a symbolic depiction of the universal Shakti spirit. The Anunnaki African wisdom of the divine principles of the *Shetaut Neter of Kemetic* precepts of secret societies and spiritual science mystery schools ancient Kemetic Egyptian lodges learning and teachings in the house of life.

African-Egyptians Kemetism spiritual science

Ancient initiation into the secret knowledge was first taught to the priests, who gained knowledge of the Kemet philosophy of humankind's exifidelity and the substrate creative life force energy that is fundamental to the principles precepts of logic and reason inherent in the ancient. To this acknowledge wisdom, and insight into the astrology and metaphysical spiritual sciences of God's persona permeating the divine creative cycle of nature.

What is true is that every evening when I imbibe a transition of sunshine yielding as dusk is the time when sun goes through the turnstile into the quiet comfort and peaceful solace of the surreality of nighttime. It's a dichotomy much unlike making good or evil. You see there are always several choices and decisions we can make that justify our actions. The discernment is of both logical and reasoning by an innate intelligence endued by the divine wisdom of the *Neberdjer,* which is the gift of free will consciousness awareness to think.

My moment of transformation was the mental clarity and impetus that compelled me to question just how probable and plausible to believe that it's not such a risible notion is sensible if you interpolate the modern views of the ancient astronauts hypothesis, juxtaposition to the Old Testament Holy Bible book of Genesis.

It's a subjective perspective compiled from several translated versions that don't acknowledge god as the Anunnaki Enki concerning salient intelligence or according to logic, reason, and insight about "Those who from the Heavens came"! What might this shock you to become motivated to change your paradigm to from pushing a falsity? Was it an intentional sinister scheme to inculcate a religious precept, which has steadfastly fostered the teachings of religion from the Holy Bible. But is it really a misdirection which I contend that there is a missing element of this storytelling. A different viewpoint albeit a controversial assumption. What I will tell you in this exegesis postulates that the biblical god of the Old Testament Holy Bible is an axiomatic view of the ancient astronauts known as the Anunnaki elite Royal Prince Enki/Ea. He was the first of the alien gods, which is what established him as the biblical creator god of the genesis narrative tale, with respect to those who descended from heaven and fashioned the first crossbred primitive worker who was fused with god, Enki's own Anunnaki image which began the Old Testament Bible story of the delineation of the African consciousness awareness of the homo sapien sapiens. This is to say the Hamites direct the Anunnaki alien bloodline of children of Enki (God). This is the dirty little secret that the religionist doesn't want you to know about those who come down from the deep space planet Nibiru?

Well then, you are about to learn the purveyors of the African-Egyptians. They were initiated into the secret knowledge of the mystery school temple of the high spiritual science Kemetic region of the logos. The knowledge principles of religious philosophy before biblical mythology came to prominence as Christianity Biblical story. Would it take you aback with surprise to learn that the most significant components of the Bible (Torah), meaning that it's "a paucity of information". Because what is curiously missing is the nascence; meaning we don't have any fidelity with respect to the uncured chronicles of who exactly where: "Those who from Heaven to earth came?" But, of course, I know that there is misinformation that is intended to rely on the gullible mind of the ignorant low information folks to effectively maintain their status quo deception. This is not a stretch of your logic and reason. So, as in life there are numerous truths that those of you who just can't fathom this notion of what is seemingly the plausible scenario.

Of course, this is a controversial subject matter which prompted me to elucidate these thoughts in an effort to spur others curiosity about the piece of biblical Genesis narrative. There inextricably connected to the Anunnaki alien ancient astronauts ancestors, were inextricably and irrefutably can be told that the Old Testament, Chapter 1 through 11, is consistent with god having the possessed a capability with which dovetails nicely with an advanced race of spacefaring alien astronaut persona as the Genesis narrative tale myth. Our humanity into existence, is inextricably tied to an extraterrestrial alien royal bloodline delineated from the Kemet-African and Hebrews of the Old Testament biblical historical account, the chosen crossbred children of Enki/Ea. Whose persona dovetails nicely to Enki's cult of Egyptian Osiris and Isis mythos. But how many folks know that the eponymous name of Africa was *"Akebu-Land"* of the blacks, before the arrogance of a Roman named *Scipio Africanus* changed *it* (Psalms 49:11)? Whereas, *Akebu-Land* translates into the (mother of humanity) or *"Garden of Eden."* The biblical genesis spiritual wisdom precepts of African consciousness awareness was derived from the original ancient teachings and learning about Spiritual wisdom came into the Old Testament Bible Genesis narrative tale was transliterated into the New Testament as western Christianity, and Hebrew religious beliefs emerged from African-Egyptian [Kemeticism] cognates, the beginning of the god/goddess religion of Osiris and the sister-wife Isis (https://www.stewartsynopsis.com/africans-who-wrote-the-bible). Ostensibly, this dovetails nicely into the evolution of the transitioning into the change in the history of the phenomenal world of the African conscious reality was, marked by the Western European view establishment after the reining Rome's empire collapsed. The period was in flux with the aim of hijacking and exploitation of Christianity, a conversion and transformation into the conversion into modern precepts. The growing popularity of the Christian religion caused a very swift rise in blind faith in the gospel of Trinity of Jesus Christ.

Mistranslations of the original Old Testament

From ancient codex as Anunnaki's Sumerian Holy Bible book of Genesis narrative was written to establish the record archive of the African Egyptians' Kemet Anunnaki Sumerian Bible deeds attributed to the ancient ancestors' sacred worship of psycho spiritual science—and not religion, but universal nature as the creator god of Heaven. That was a pivotal period in clinical history that had diverged from African Kemetism precepts into the transition into blind faith and devotion to religion. Might this be the dynamic progression marked by the subjugation of the eastern spiritual science which is now the prevailing teachings of modern religions. Which have done nothing to buoy up principles rooted in logic, insight into holy wisdom, and learning and teaching others the metaphysical laws of divine nature.

This notion that is of the reality of duality in aspects of individualism was imparted by Royal Prince Enki's biological DNA genetic manipulation created a crossbred homosapien race. This view is for you to imbibe the anecdotal details regarding the Anunnaki Royal bloodline.

The ancestral genetic material delineate connection is descended from the Anunnaki alien Royal Prince Enki's seminole creation of human origin Seminole event of the creation of the first human Adapa, or shall we say Adam. Most Bible scholars neither acknowledge Enki nor do they concur with the notion that he was the god figure associated with the being the Sumerian called the shining ones from the sky. Which I agree with the idea that they were the god figure associated with the Sumerians story.

Why is any of this important for me?

My friend, this book is about, it points to things that are relevant and essential to understanding the storytelling that god we trust, was the

THE MIND, BODY, SPIRIT, AND STORYTELLING

motivation for me to write about in this book in which I point these things out is quite remarkable and indeed most relevant.

Whereof, the Bible doesn't elucidate in profound anecdotal details about who were, by being vague by never acknowledging the identity of "Those who from the Heaven came" and became the presence of the first custodian alien lord gods arrived heaven to the earth plane. This is view of the ancient astronauts theorists hypothesis that speculative assumption has interpolated the missing evidence that these intrepid astronauts crew built the first city-state in the indigenous Africans that was established in Sumer, Mesopotamians used as a reverence, which was with respect to attribution and the deeds unique to the Anunnaki god Enki, the father of the genetic DNA bloodline derive the existence of a crossbreed homosapien sapien race. The Bible announces that God created Adam (man) and Eve (woman). And yes, we get it! But in terms of why or for what specific purpose raises the salient question about motivation. Why did the writers of the Old Testament Genesis intentionally decide not to elucidate this bit of specific anecdotal information? Was this not relevant? And the most critically important anecdotal evidence of the historical facts. Only the missing volume of the historical pages, that they kept them secret, for there is so much truth to know.

The Ones Who Do Not, Are Curious Seekers

Yes, indeed! My friends believe in the Genesis narrative as the words of god we trust but ask nothing about where the story is about the advanced alien beings, the so-called Anunnaki ancient astronauts. Is this the plausible version or should we simply consider the speculation as poppycock? Nonetheless not many of the skeptics have been subjective views on the matter of the ancient astronauts theorists hypothesis. With it arguments that are those of the contemporary scientific rather than theoretical. In fact, people who embrace the blind faith aren't quick to *gain-say* the objective assumptions posited as the modern viewpoint espoused by this exegesis. So to get beyond the suppression of credible sources information is the use of the misdirection play by the seduction of blind faith religions. What is meant by this comment requires a curious minded person with a bit of intellectual logic and reason to understand that the fundamental prerequisite for an evolution and transformation, is an action by which your eyes become open to the blind faith teaching and learning espoused by the modern church denominational theology. The light of spiritual science wisdom is to find truth and analyze the Bible conterminous with qualifying historical research findings. Therein lies the piece of missing information that is the fruition about the original extraterrestrial elite anamorphic race of titular alien gods behind the book Genesis tale.

The Bible with its secondhand accounts is certainly regarded as one of the greatest truthiness stories of the past events of the ages of history. It hides Enki from us, the critical reason why god created humans. Why, for what purpose, and how he genetically fused his DNA fashion by process of biological manipulation. Specifically, speaking on point, the Nibiru King Anu authorized his son Enki to clone a hybrid human species. That is to say a new Homo sapiens sapiens as a primitive worker who was to be illiterate and a lifespan devoid of the Anunnaki's secret longevity. Homo sapiens were expendable to live for no more than 120 years. Anunnaki elite council of the voting members granted Enki the approval to produce a sterile primitive worker race who would be humble primitive workers we homo sapien sapiens we began the arduous journey towards becoming the ancestral bloodline of the creator god (Enki/EA), meaning our connection to those who came.

Let's face it. The Anunnaki titular god Enki was to fashion a race of *subservient* primitive workers to perform the hard work required to extract the gold from dark deep South African gold mines in the great Zimbabwe landscape of the Southern region of Africa (Akibu lands). Enlil is the god of the garden of Eden. The first to discover that his half-brother, Enki had violated the command leadership councils prohibition by surreptitiously manipulating the DNA genes sequencing fashioned the first Adapa (Adam). The eponymous first man created, said to be imbued with knowledge by the Anunnaki god Enki, with consciousness awareness to copelat sexually. And that was what made Enlil angry in the garden of Eden in Havilah, East

THE MIND, BODY, SPIRIT, AND STORYTELLING

Africa, according to the Hebrew and Greek Septuagint Bible. What is clear is that the Bible doesn't elucidate, insofar as the affirmation that simply says he is the creator god Enki (Ea). This mysterious god persona doesn't allude to anything that is relevant to and specific about the god mentioned in the holy Old Testament scriptures that obfuscates on the anecdotal details regarding the god of who came and became the custodians of the earth by their diffusion city-states. Since the Anunnaki, Royal Prince Enki's initial mission, Earth voyage settlement, the Anunnaki alien clans began to wage bloody territorial wars among themselves after their King Anu. He was the divine personification of the sky, earth and ruler of Anunnaki most imminent god of Heaven decrees and had authorized Kingship to be established on planet earth. The King of Heaven/Nibiru actions would mark that decision was a seminal inflection point, established kingship demigods to rule over earth human https://www.britannica.com/topic/sacred-kingship/The-king-as-priest-and-seer). The earliest signs of kingship was found in Sumerian mythology in Mesopotamia which had been traced back to Uruk, circa the fourth millennium BC, dovetails nicely with ancient city-states written about in the Old Testament Bible Genesis.

You should know that the Anunnaki extraterrestrial alien beings were titular gods who instituted secret societies and religion to maintain a system of control to govern human behavior. The takeaway is that they were not the sacred ubiquitous *Shetaut Neter of divine Nebigbjur*, which is simply the product of philosophical teachings of the religious gospels of the holy biblical that derived from Enki/Ea's; the secret mystery schools of the priestly class were taught secret occult knowledge, magic craft working of sweet, seawater, and lake water, fertility, semen, magic, of Enki/Ea (god) mischief. Whereof Enlil was associated with bringing the *eponymous* Noah's flood myth (https://www.joshobrouwers.com/articles/evolution-sumerian-kingship/). But wait! Yes, indeed there's much more to consider about Enlil's personality. Enlil is the Sumerian god of the air and wind; known as *Yahweh, Ellil, or Nunamnir* to the later Akkadians. As well, Enlil is among what is like a trinity or tripartite with the elite members of the Royal council pantheon of gods. This meeting was chaired by the Supreme king Anu, the highest deity of the sky, and Enki, was the god of wisdom and freshwater. The King Anu ruled the pantheon of the gods (https://www.afrikaiswoke.com/sumerian-anunnaki-gods-divine-kingship/)

When examining the findings of archeology, anthropology, and paleography, the discovery of old ruins has revealed significant results by modern researchers and scholarship in ancient biblical history. Archeology and anthropology discoveries revealed important lost information which dovetails nicely with the missing links to the Anunnaki ancient astronauts theorists mission earth voyage; which fits with the assumption, curiously exposing an event, in the context of the Bible's narrative tale about "Those who from the Heaven/sky came".

This context is bolsters with a reasonable person standard of logic and reason lends significant credibility and clarity to this substantive assertion by the ancient astronauts theorists' hypothesis is inextricably the missing evidence that is discernible that ancient astronauts presence on earth, and as a question regarding biblical teachings of the genesis narrative, religionists obfuscated, to maintain the well-entrenched ecclesiastical body's status quo history of the church as gospel body of religious education. Which does not interpolate the true Alien god's African bloodline ties that cannot be denied the link to the Anunnaki Royal elites Enki.

He was the titular god who fused his DNA image and likeness through an ancient indigenous African-Egyptians female's genetic DNA codes, which harkens back to the predynastic ions of the custodian, who spurred the Coptic and Hebrew black African-Egyptian and the Ethiopians tribes who descended from the Enki's Anunnaki DNA genetic manipulation. Egyptians migrated out of the Nile Valley settlement in the ancient Sumerian lands of Mesopotamia (Iraq). Anyone who is interested in transparency.

Well then I think that we can Agree that the Anunnaki were ancient astronauts aliens' presence on the earth, which is the logic and reason identity fits nicely within the religious context with credibility and the dichotomy between humanity and the biblical Genesis narrative tale. It buttresses the Ancient Astronauts theorist's hypothesis.

THE MIND, BODY, SPIRIT, AND STORYTELLING

This hypothesis is essential information that doesn't obfuscate about the identity of the Anunnaki aliens gods who came down from the sky in a large, bell-like, shining spacecraft that landed on planet Earth. Before the commander, Royal Prince Enki (a.k.a) creator god. He was the flight commander of the first fifty man crew of ancient alien astronauts slowly descended and safely landed in ancient Sumer, Mesopotamia. Curiously, the Old Testament biblical genesis is a truthiness, meaning that it's a paucity that obfuscates by rejecting the ancient astronauts theorists hypothesis that derived from the Egyptian mystery schools and the house of life.

Without question, the real truth must include the specificity and anecdotal detailed information about the Anunnaki alien gods' presence on the earth 450,000, long years before the modern Bible genesis narrative tale mythos was written. This is the underlying speculative profile of the Anunnaki ancient astronauts hypothesis. An Anunnaki alien gods presence that is bolstered by the discovery of ancient Sumerians cuneiform clay tablets have revealed missing pieces of ancient historical records of the Anunnaki alien influence behind chronicles of the creation of Adam and Eve Enki and Enlil involvement in the involution and evolution contributions to the Sumerian, Mesopotamia, spread into the indigenous culture societies of African-Egyptians, Indo, and primitive cultures of the emerging world of civilized society new age development.

The Spread of Anunnaki Bible Genesis Narrative

Learning and teachings of the extraterrestrial alien god's presence were behind the emergence of myth postulated in original Bible mythology. With respect to this point, people will come to identify with truth about those stories of the Hamite who occupied Canaan circa sixth century BCE, began the enfoldment of the ancient Yahwistic tradition coming from the ninth century BCE (Finch, 1991), and the Elohistic is the eighth century BCE, and the priestly is the sixth century BCE (Buttrick, 1984; and Finch 1991).

Think again as you evaluate the inner workings of the underlying character's profile of the premier avatar of the Hebrew and

Greek Septuagint Bible book of Genesis narrative tale. It's an incomplete book that was carefully assembled by the powerful rulers. Top Roman Catholic Bishops at the Vatican and the emperor's of the Roman state, who selected and rejected certain religious texts from the ancient religious *apocryphal* writings as the western orthodox Christians holy Bible.

Which was ostensibly an intentional scheme that inculcated perpetual falsehoods as a misdirection play. The genesis creation neither discloses nor does it acknowledge these as the deeds identifiable with the present of Anunnaki as a race of extraterrestrial aliens and ancient astronauts. Hence the Bible only makes cursory references to god, and this is unmistakably very noticeable indeed as it fits nicely with the ancient mystery. Which is without a description; having no logic or reason associated with a fundamental presupposition, it is simply a sensible notion that points at: "Those who from the Heavens came." For your erudition, this is relatively straightforward; you need to know that the Bible Genesis doesn't allude to this truth. But it was the beginning of the Anunnaki gods arrival from heaven is the predicate backstory, which is missing from chapters 1 through 11. Whereof, the relevant specificity and anecdotal details about the Anunnaki alien nascence is missing. Here's this story about the Anunnaki extraterrestrial aliens who the Bible Genesis narrative refers to as the god of Heaven. Whereof this is the identity of those ancient astronauts who were from the mysterious missing planet Nibiru creation without a proper predicate or the backstory. This book is speculative as well as a theoretical perspective written in the context of prevailing paradigms, which is interpolated for the erudition and discerned with sage logic and reason. Explore this exegesis with objectivity and to understand my underlying overall premise.

Which is to make folks think with a different paradigm of intellectual audacity. Perhaps you may appreciate the content without being unconsciously biased or myopic. Wherefore you ponder whether the Bible Genesis is the incomplete story written as a mystery. But it is largely the story about the Anunnaki ancient astronauts' theorists' hypothesis, conjecture that they landed on the earth. Let's face it. With mental clarity and curiosity of people who recognized their agency and personhood ancestral connection to god. To this I elucidate the truth for your understanding consciousness is aware of our existence within this illusory dimensional realm of the reality and surreality duality. Fact is, we know that religions have not offered this version of the truth about god. Thankfully you can select and purchase compelling books that provide a thread of information that gives insight into the pieces that are missing. A complete body of knowledge for anyone to digest. Books that speculate with conjectures which argue with compelling anecdotal evidence that the archeology and anthropology discovery. The discovery of archeological and anthropology findings dovetail nicely with providing religious teachings with corroborating information. Which can now be viewed as a legitimate truth about rituals and sacred teaching of the wisdom of the spiritual science of the alien gods who the Old Testament Bible speaks of as: "Those who from the Heavens came"! Or shall we say that they were a vanguard crew of advanced intelligent alien beings that history into the light of god, as mythology. Which is connected to the ancient astronaut theorists hypothesis. A different view about those who came down from a higher orbital plane [Nibiru], or shall we say: Those Anunnaki ancient alien astronauts who were on a mission earth voyage. Yeah, let's be clear, according to Mr. Zachariah Sitchin, who said they were from the twelfth planet from Planet Nibiru that operates on a deep space elliptical orbit!

Planet Nibiru Anunnaki Council of Anu UFOs

First off as my reasonable point, please allow me to propose this salient question: Did you know that a very long time ago the Anunnaki alien god's ancient astronauts descended down from a higher plane orbital galaxy system, which was the alien gods of Heaven. Or shall we say planets [Nibiru] Anunnaki clan's had most likely descended from the sky by the direction and authority of the Supreme King, Anu. The supreme lord god sent their ancient astronauts down to earth, after discussing the matter of finding an abundant supply of gold was decided by the *quorum* of the Nibiru's twelve elite Anunnaki's council of the voting board members who had concluded the discussions. During the discussions and arguments, they voted to resolve the pressing matter regarding how best to patch up critically potential catastrophic tears that caused dangerous leaks occurring in the Anunnaki's planet's atmosphere ozone liner. Interestingly, after all the arguments and discussions were ended they reached the consensus to dispatch an exploratory advanced astronaut crew, commanded by King Anu's Great Royal Prince Enki (Ea), to spearhead the first Earth Mission voyage enterprise. The goal was to pilot a spacecraft down to planet earth to verify whether the mineral gold could be extracted in large amounts to justify constructing a full-scale gold mining production operation. Enki/Ea operation would transform it into monatomic gold particles, put it aboard the fleet of alien UFO spacecraft that would be orbiting above the earth orbit. These alien UFOs (flying disks) were bell-shaped flying spacecraft orbiting the earth and waiting to be loaded with gold that would be shuttle up to the dark side of the moon's surface. From there on to the planet Mars before being transported back to their home planet Nibiru. This was the plan laid out by a quorum of the meeting of lord King Anu's members of the Royal Council, who unanimously voted in favor of Enki's mission Earth voyage.

Accordingly, the mission Earth flight commander Enki, (god) led this biblical vanguard mission which was conterminous with the biblical genesis narrative story. An assertion that posits my belief that the Old Testament holy Bible story is, in fact, about ancient astronauts from the planet known as Nibiru was begun with a bold Earth mission purpose of which the vanguard crew had ventured out into space.

Like our NASA astronauts had a specific goal and mission purpose to execute this bold plan of action in order to exploit the earth gold mineral resources which would be shuttled via an Alien Anunnaki space flight to planet Nibiru. I have interpolated my first logic and reason from a different perspective; my scope as a narrow exegesis with mental clarity and fill in the missing pieces of our past and ancient history is for folks who want to fill in the hidden pieces from this and other information subject matter books. Folks learn about this most incredible story that is certainly not a myth but a revealing look at the most astonishing anecdotal details. Information that presents insight into this convoluted religion is closely akin to adults having blind faith in the Bible with adults being inculcated—wittingly, as the naive *parochial* level of truthiness and folly as conscious awareness. Christianity is a perennial fairytale as a biblical Myth, meaning the God Mythological narrative tale. Okay then. With specificity might the benchmark of truth be the measure of clarity?

Truth will always correspond with the curated, immutable genuine—not spoofed, altered, or fabricated a spurious false reality as a misdirection play. Which was the scheme to construct a modern religion with the church as the foundation of organized theologically to propagate control of the consciousness awareness, by definition of humans worship. Spiritualism, therefore, was the dichotomy and the antithesis of one's own intelligent knowledge, sense and discernment that lead to mental clarity. Humankind freewill and intuition of the spirit self, meaning that individual must believe that order and balance in the spirit will liberate your mind from the elites' philosophical world false dichotomy and the actual true identity between what exists as the false reality of convoluted distortions, misinformation, confusion. I present the logic and reason that will introduce insight that will enlighten your mind. If that's you, you are not alone! So the question is: are you prepared to be shocked with what I believe are the missing pages that have never been included in the so-called, religious, Holy Bible manuscript text selective translation.

Much of what underlies the Anunnaki's extraterrestrial story of the Old Testament Bible Genesis chapter one, I say that, was wittingly excised and lifted from the original alien's ancient Sumerian Bible text codex, completely rewriting the original Genesis account. Readers about the Ancient Astronauts mission earth peregrinations, revealing what the religionists don't want you to know about this human bloodline ties to the Anunnaki titular Gods descended from the sky in shining, bell-shaped flying spacecraft! What is asserted here is my personal views that have been infused with logic and reason, which underlies this writer's understanding of the Holy Bible Genesis and the ancient mythology that delineated the Hebrew and

Greek Septuagint version of the original ancient Sumerians biblical genesis narrative story of god.

We all have a story to tell from the human natal through the adult life peregrinations. And so too when I will tell you that a very long time ago at the beginning of the earth, thousands of years before the modern version of the biblical myth came into mainstream existence. What exists perpetuated today is the twisted versions of the mistranslations of the Old Testament Bible Genesis narrative tale became God's Creation of the world story with much of the truth hidden.

To this point once a very long time ago, on the alien planet Nibiru. The king and all the elite members of the council assemblyman discussed the pressing matter regarding how best to repair a slow leaking of the planet's damaged atmosphere. They finally agreed to a solution to the serious matter concerning the leaks and dangerous tears and large holes in planet Nibiru's atmospheric ozone protective liner caused slow leaks.

They agreed that they would need to find an abundant source of the material gold on the planet earth. Yeah, Lord King Anu was the supreme Sky god of the Anunnaki race. This was a ruling council of the gods and as a quorum voted, unanimously concurred, and King Anu appointed his son Royal Prince Enki. Commander Enki was responsible for leading this vanguard fifty man astronaut crew that descended from the planet Nibiru. The mission purpose was to establish a gold mining production operation on the earth. What I interpolate is a foundation as a proper predicate that decouples those whose controversial speculative views and assertions have misled. My description is neither recondite nor convoluted, but my explanation that analytical in an attempt to give some clarity to the pervading human consciousness awareness that you have been misled by the purveyors of false illusions, which is closely akin to the biblical version; and the Old Testament Bible as a convoluted fairy story tale Myth. I am wholly obliged to write this book to raise the point of view to shed light on what seems to be the most concerning salient question: of which gods mentioned in Genesis holy Bible scriptures a (false illusion)of the dichotomy.

THE MIND, BODY, SPIRIT, AND STORYTELLING

So for your elucidation of *nous,* with logic and reason, it's my understanding that the complex can be revealed with clarity diverges from understanding the entrenched truthiness, by which we acknowledge the identity of: "Those who from the Heaven came" were the Anunnaki alien astronauts gods.

Although I am not clairvoyant, at the same time, I am one among the many folks *conversant* with a controversial phenomenon, interest in extraterrestrial ancient alien Astronauts theorists hypothesis; where the scholars conflate their premise to argue that it dovetails nicely with the Old Testament Bible narrative story of the god of Heaven. To this, I'll only admit that this is consistent with my erudition of modern archeological and anthropological discovery and education of important historical information.

It diminishes the full revelations that obfuscate the information on the Anunnaki alien race. This is a consequential book on a phenomenal subject matter that I anticipate to be both inflammatory and intriguing. My friends the ancient astronauts theorists hypothesis is inextricably linked to extraterrestrial alien race who called themselves the Anunnaki, and they called their home planet Nibiru, which was ruled by the king Anu who was the elite supreme sky god who sent His sons Enki and Enlil to the earth.

Let me be clear about the premise. I know that some folk consider that ancient astronaut hypothesis to be the paradigm shift that rebuff the conventional established Christian religion of god, but not the modern church theology which dismissed the controversial that position posited by those who are proponents of the contemporary views and assertions that posited the aliens gods behind the AUV/UFOs phenomenon. We advance the opinion gods behind the AUV/UFOs phenomenon. Advancing the notion. We are advancing the notion of an alien race of extraterrestrial gods from the biblical text that says they descended from the sky. The gods who descended and landed a shiny bell-shaped UFO spacecraft on the Earth's plane. It is not far-fetched for anyone who wants to stretch their intelligence to ponder the notion. Why do we believe, but not question whether the Bible is in fact the actual word of God? It's not reasonable to think adults believe the Bible Genesis narrative tale of the alien gods story as a Mythology.

The Bible story is the composite of selected individuals of the clergy who combined ancient writings from the original apocrypha text manuscript of the ancient ancestors of the Anunnaki ancient astronauts who scribes recorded their historical epoch from the time of the gods descent. Because it's likely that the Bible is the reworked version of the actual story about the Anunnaki. And let's face it: the identity of these extraterrestrial alien beings is what curiously never acknowledges who they were. When in fact the Ancient Astronauts Theorists hypothesis dovetails with what is the missing anecdotal details part biblical about them must be connected to genesis their nascence in the ancient Sumerian cuneiform clay tablets Bible manuscripts, which certain books were copied from and later became to be a condensed version of the Hebrew and Greek Septuagint holy Bible book genesis narrative creation Myth.

Only a fraction of the Gods Apocryphal manuscripts archived records were copied, and carried away by the Hebrew high priesthood of the adapts from Ur of the Chaldeans. Historical documents of the information about the Anunnaki as the titular biblical god persona.

What seems to be a rather problematic assertion that is a the ancient astronauts theory as an assertion predicated on whether Genesis was an actual event involving the modern AUV/UFO phenomenon, just perhaps, could there be some connection to the Anunnaki titular Gods who descended from Heaven as "Those who from the Heaven came?

Of course this hypothesis has clarity that it can be construed as plausible using the reasonable person standard, based upon logic and reason which is necessary in order to interpolate the missing anecdotal details that are curiously missing from the Bible Genesis narrative tale. There is an underlying truth in this convergence of the Anunnaki aliens presence which the Bible Genesis creates an incredible historical event of misdirection and truthiness. Do you ever think profoundly as to why does not the church wish to have the full story exposed to the adult public world community?

THE MIND, BODY, SPIRIT, AND STORYTELLING

Which seemingly is quite obviously circumspection, is it because of missing evidence that suggests it be included, and viz. they simply removed aspects of the Anunnaki alien gods' arrival. Steadfastly, they hid this in the favor of the genesis fairytale, which lacks clarity and credibility. And they have been perpetuating what is a falsity, which parallels the narrative events of the Anunnaki gods' presence as they were the intelligence custodian god on the earth, right?

Why have we not been given the objective version with specificity and anecdotal detail information? We've never met. But as someone interested in the subject matter books that are not a brief synopsis. These are the books that provide an in-depth profile of information about the Anunnaki race presence and their tremendous contributions to the development involving these Olden Times space traveling ancient astronauts from the planet Nibiru. It's not complicated, indeed I say that they were not unlike our NASA space astronauts who have flown from earth and returned home from the sky! This is more than a comparison of my speculation and conjecture. Because my logic and reason comports nicely with as well as a parallel to NASA, and more aligned than disjointed discursive thinking about the contemplation that encapsulates the biblical story, but as a actual significant seminal events that the Old Testament holy scripture described as a myth, we unpack the story telling truthiness and misdirection. Which treated the bible genesis narrative like fabled fairy tales, instead of profound analysis based on intellectual logic and reason by revealing facts about god (Eki) as father of creation.

My fundamental presuppose dovetails nicely with similar views of published books about the Anunnaki alien presence. Here on earth fits the biblical god-figure tie into the Old Testament Bible, that obfuscates and excludes the Anunnaki Sumerian Holy Bible manuscript original story about these Anunnaki extraterrestrial beings material presence was curiously, and intentionally culled. Which delineates a tale with many critically important elements that clearly excludes the Ancient Astronauts theorists hypothesis in favor of the misdirection depicting a falsehood in church religious mythology.

What is presumed to be missing from the biblical manuscript, and what I interpolate is a paradigm shift in the way to teach about the truth beginning when the Anunnaki alien astronauts reveal their identity as ancient gods will explode into the public consciousness.

Which I aim to provide you with the mental clarity and insight that will make you think! I'm setting this table for a psychospiritual erudition of knowledge and wisdom that will be for your understanding of the ascent with enlightenment of mind/body/spirit complex overall consciousness awareness as a retrospective insight. Ancient Anunnaki alien astronauts descended from planet Nibiru were the earth mission voyage into the illusory realm of the material world reality existence of the reality of spirit's consciousness awareness time space continuum.

Heaven from my personal knowledge concurs with the proponents of the modern ancient astronaut's theorists hypothesis which dovetails nicely with this quote: excerpt from the Hebrew and Greek Septuagint and the KJV Bible in chapter 1, Old Testament Genesis narrative tale of the creation Myth.

Speculatively, we can in fact elucidate on these words that refer to the Anunnaki as: "Those who from Heaven came." According to the author Zachariah Sitchin suggests that the Sumerian records reveal that around 445,000 BC says that 50 *Anunnaki Ancient Astronauts* landed in Mesopotamia to mine the abundance of gold from the Persian Gulf ocean waters.

The Anunnaki had ventured from their Planet to Earth (Ki) because This I assert to be plausible, given the innate level of visceral human curiosity. I stake my flag pole with fundamental knowledge of ancient astronauts' theorists' hypothesis, which I'm just guessing that you will too after you finish reading this explanation. Here's the skinny: I accept this modern premise about the out of Africa and the ancient astronaut theorists' hypothesis because they seem very plausible. Which is to say logical juxtaposition to a reasonable person's standard of intelligent findings. Which underlies my speculative views, which is an exegesis, claiming that the Old Testament Bible Genesis narrative about god's creation Myth is in a real sense be conflated with the speculations and the conjecturing of theories of the ancient and the presence of UFOs referred to the African Kemetic Egyptians worshiping the Anunnaki alien astronauts as historical god alien Ra. The African-Egyptian sundial is symbolic of Ra's chariot. He was represented flying across the sky as the sun god Amon, Ra!

This was the time during the rise of the New Western world powers of the Roman Empires. And their influence transformed the world of blind faith religions with the Christian symbol of the cross and the invention of Jesus Christ as the god of heaven. We wittingly pray to the crucified Jesus Christ persona as the holy Trinity, meaning what? That the organized religion was established and venerated as an *amorphous* Father, Son, and holy spirit complex. Which, efficaciously superseded the old religion of psycho-spiritual science philosophy of African, Kemetism was persecuted, suppressed, and forced the occult religions to go underground to practice their faith out of fear of death as a theological heretic opposed to the new world order's inculcation of a popular blind faith Catholic fellowship worship of Jesus Christ. Meaning the deception by transforming and suppression of the Anunnaki gods Old Testament historical geneeGenesis original extraterrestrial Sumerian Holy Bible history of the ancient astronauts. This is my fantastic tale which began on the planet, and there was a quorum of Council board members present as Nibiru's Royal King Anu were mired in the discussions about what would be the solution to the problem related to an urgent matter that requiring an abundant resource of the mineral gold on planet earth. And realizing their desperate need to locate and mind gold, the King decided, and a vote was passed to dispatch his great Prince Enki to the planet earth to establish a gold mining production operation.

So pardon me if this conjecture is an abomination to the status quo paradigm of thought, but my assertion argues that "Those who from the Heavens came" were ancient space traveling alien astronauts who purpose was the Earth Mission voyage to excavate the mineral gold thousands of years before the Old Testament Bible was written. Which raises a curious question about people who have never heard anything about planet Nibiru or Enki, let alone these titular gods as an advanced race of space-faring extraterrestrial beings from the cosmic orbital cycle. These alien beings were the Olden Times Anunnaki alien ancient astronauts. They were the custodian Gods who came down from their home planet.

It is the modern paradigm which seemingly designates the alien's UFO/UAVs that have been reported in our air space for years. Speculation about the gods, there seems to be a conflation with the arrival of the Anunnaki race as the ancient astronaut Enki and these words from the Bible and attested to by residents of ancient Mesopotamia: "Those who from the Heaven came!" Although the theory is plausible. Indeed, and of course, usually we need not rely on having a panel of expert research scholars to discuss the speculative merits of the practicality of the Old Testament genesis versions of the circumstances surrounding the believability of an ancient astronauts alien got as "those who from the Heavens came down" and actually landed in ancient Sumer, Mesopotamia, in the modern day country of Iraq Persian Gulf region. There are corresponding folks with a specific interest in this. Still, plenty of skeptics mingle with fellow-minded folks who are not yet willing to get on board modernist knowledge lifeboats. These are not seekers of truth passengers who write books about the historical evidence that make people think at a higher level of consciousness with intelligent logic and reason for mental clarity. The knowledge sense that is with respect to the so-called constructive teachings of the holy scriptures of the Old Testament biblical tales book of Genesis. Most likely the nascent of human beings is in fact the greatest truth is the complete specificity and anecdotal evidence, and because the Bible version does speak to the deeds of God who came from Heaven. Curiously, he is not given to proclaim Enki as the Biblical creator god of Adam and Eve, or to acknowledge the Anunnaki as extraterrestrial alien gods. Which is closely akin to the genesis narrative tale. This according to the speculative view of how the story unfolded into the mainstay of organized religious teachings of spurious truthiness.

I was reading this book about the erudition of knowledge and learning the anecdotal details about the story of the extraterrestrial alien Gods. Whereof it's an exegesis that bolsters my premise as main arguments. To this point I interpolate my assertions in the biblical context of the historical biblical narrative with rational logic and reason to spur others curiosity—not to denigrate or castigate and discard the Bible Genesis. Only that I wish to embellish with logic and reason to bring the light of knowledge to brighten your vision of those who are fiercely cling to believe the many ecclesiastical orthodoxy religious that is the words that most pleases their *psychospiritual* African consciousness, meaning blind faith new Testament age paradigm that can have a positive. Faithful devotees adhere to blind faith religious teachings of the new age savior Jesus Christ precepts, Christians believe are the actual words of God.

With insight comes the logic and reason that the light of understanding this enlightenment which fits into this is the premise that supports the out of Africa hypothesis. And if it's true, might these extraterrestrial ancient astronauts aliens were titular gods? Perhaps their earth mission voyage was facilitated by the conveyance of the extraterrestrial UFO that landed in ancient Sumerian, Mesopotamia. Conjecture means that indigenous primitive tribes would have observed the ancient astronauts' the Anunnaki Civilization from the landing and establishment of Earth Station 1. Which was built in the *Sinai*, was destroyed by the god Enlil had ordered the destruction of the Sodom Gomora which caused the great destruction of Mesopotamia, while the area's Babylon were untouched by the devastation of the nuclear blast and the fallout from the evil wind that kill humans, livestock, and vegetation (Genesis 19:24).

This action preceded the Anunnaki departure from the earth after the conquest of Babylon by Cyrus The Great. when they watched Nibiru's ancient astronauts who came. Of course, let's face it. I guess that there is going to be seething criticism and push back from the Christian faith adherents of religious fidelity fellowship with Jesus Christ as their God and Savior. Some people have gone so far as to rebuff the ancient astronauts' theories sharply. However, there is a large number of people who are convinced otherwise.

Seekers of the *nous* are staunch devotees who have been enlightened with wisdom and can discern the truth from the truthiness andlies. Having the ability to discern and comprehend the fundamental elements state have been missing is perhaps the connection to the original custodian Anunnaki, extraterrestrial ancient alien astronaut gods Enki's African bloodline descendants (https://www.nairaland.com/4891533/how-enki-created-homo-sapiens). Blind faith and devotion by adherence to the god of Heaven. The key point here is that they have wittingly withheld and concealed these uninformed people who might develop the will to turn away from the allure of this material life. Free will we are endued as spirit embodiments as humankind with conscious biases and awareness to apply logic and reason to make choices. Therefore, meaning a common medium of the mind, body, psycho-spiritual energy complex. That I am awakened to live as animated an individual separated unit as a living soulful spirit physical embodiment. A consciousness awareness having free will to do good or evil deeds is a human being's choice to take action is directly tied to the *Kundalini energy when engaged in daily meditation* as a reflection and the purification of the mind looking into the self to achieve perfect harmonic balance with the *Nebebigjar*. This unity derived from the Intelligent Infinite Creator God's *Ruach* [breath] is the source of life, pervading within us as his spiritual existence. Likened to the breath and the wind I inhaled and exhaled out the nostrils sustaining the universe my mind/body/spirit complex.

Life-giving energy is the common medium of the intelligent cosmic universe and the human mind/body/spirit complex. And this is the story that is believed to be the written word of a god of creation. And perhaps if there is one recognized truth.

Well then, shall we acknowledge that all individuals are the living individual souls that exist as a unit of transient embodiment of mind, body, spirit complex endured by nature of the one intelligent Infinite Creator Of pervading and sustaining the universe. Human beings as a mind, body, complex of the creative consciousness. Pervading in the material form of our existence by the lifeforce energy of the divine infinite light of the metaphysical, ubiquitous, intelligent, infinity.

The living sources of sacred spirit effervescent as the harmonic vibration confluence of the sun's bright rays of the sun is symbolic of the Egyptian *ankh* is the talisman omnipotent rays possessed by the luminous divine sunlight energy. I am so thankful for the blessing for this beneficial life source sustainer of the *Shakti* spirit of a universal grand cosmic harmonic wave force energy vibration. We need to establish what is true and what is truthiness for mental clarity

THE MIND, BODY, SPIRIT, AND STORYTELLING

and perspective according to yourself and your personhood. If you are a thinker—like me, I am betting that you have wondered about god and religion. Meaning what? Like you have questions about the authenticity of the Old Testament biblical genesis narrative? Or perhaps you have had some level of incredulity. But that's quite expected of one having the tendency and courage to become a sagacious neophyte who understands the mystery of the Anunnaki extraterrestrial aliens, through curated accounts written in the original Anunnaki, Sumerian *apocryphal fur* to an advanced civilization. They possessed an advanced knowledge with those who used sophisticated technological knowledge of quantum mechanics, astrophysics and cosmology, and astronomy to allow their astronauts to enter into and navigate the aerial spacecraft that travel through the solar system.

An alien race whose pilots deployed these advanced, sophisticated aerial spacecraft. To this, I presuppose that would qualify the Anunnaki to proclaim their nobility to assume that lofty mantle of the Gods. They came down from Heaven and became the custodial gods of planet Earth. Ostensibly, they would have been original custodians of this globe. This story is irrefutably more than an esoteric hyperbolic speculative assertion deemed to be the truth about the Anunnaki clans of the ancient astronauts persona. The Bible is silent about this curiously missing insight, presumably hiding this relevant aspect of ancient astronaut's nascent life, which is essential for those who seek to discover the absolute truth. Because learning about reality is the knowledge standard that twists up the *Kundalini* into the *psychological* affinity of the mind, body, and spirit complex into the *ataraxis*. This place is the nous to discover a bloodline that harkens back to Anunnaki-African consciousness awareness of the living nature of our beingness is with the Royal bloodline that connects to a shared DNA. Some people pray in humble worshiping of god in total deference to whatever church religious teachings in the Bible Genesis they believe is god's word. But can't fathom, conceptualize.

Our understanding of Enki. Is this speculation raising fundamental salient questions to be settled in the mind of religious academic scholars; and do you concur with their views that Enki was the genesis narrative tale creator? Did He fit this scenario profile of the god of wisdom and magic who was capable of a manipulation, re-engineering, which fused His own Anunnaki alien Genetic chromosome DNA codes with the essence of the female DNA, and fashioned a new homo sapiens sapiens harkens back to the African consciousness awareness from the first human form of Adam and Eve. Enki was the god who imparted his sacred teachings of the Anunnaki's temple house of the secret knowledge initiation rites that was through the priesthood teachings. They learned about the secret societies of the occult *gnosis derived* from spiritual science; which developed the African-Egyptian [Kemetic] Religion theology precepts. What I mean is that the Anunnaki's alien beings descended from the planet Heaven (Nibiru); and viz., the original Gods who came from Heaven. The earth custodians is a premise that dovetails nicely with the true specificity and anecdotal evidence, saying that the Anunnaki alien beings who landed in ancient Mesopotamia was the original precursor god Enki taught spiritual science principles of wisdom through the mystery schools of Africa had become the epicenter of higher knowledge of the metaphysical universe!

Let's face it, many people still prefer to pervade the Bible falsehood truthiness. The truth that undergirds this speculation is the proposition put forth by irrefutable logic and reason that is the fountainhead of knowledge which is the foundation of spiritual science. The original teaching and learning call forth the codes of spiritual energy flowing up the *Kundalini* to animate the mind/body/spirit complex from the light source. Might this process have been true? Enki's crossbred creation facilitated the human DNA bloodline of the *Australopithecus africanus,* which is now an extinct species of *australopithecine* which lived from 3.67 to 2 million years ago in the Middle Pliocene to Early Pleistocene of South Africa. The species has been recovered from the cradle of humankind according to Sterkfontein, Makapansgat, and Gladysvale [https://en.wikipedia.org/wiki/Australopithecus africanus]. We must come to see your original spirit self as the essence in the mirror is the chi, the light of the spirit *shakti* (power) that animates, it is an outward reflection of the psychospiritual human material form of the god self we see as one's image looking back in the mirror. The genesis is of human

THE MIND, BODY, SPIRIT, AND STORYTELLING

consciousness awareness. To know thyself as an individual separation from creation to live by the soulful spirit of total mind/body/spirit complex as a human form of identity of the physical form of a male or female unfolded embodiment; and the energy essence endowed as an individual separation from Infinite vainglorious Creation.

The reincarnation cycles around since the beginning of human's primordial evolution of consciousness awareness; the knowing of the physical human embodiment. Enki the creator was a teacher of the secret sacred knowledge, in the discipline of the psycho-spiritual world visual reality is of the thoughtful apprehended by our subjective thoughts. It's the sensate view of human existence, unique to every person who comes forth by day and goes forth by night.

We look forward to a quiet night of restorative sleep when we lie down and close our eyes. When the sunshine transitions into the sleep cycle of nighttime tranquility. Unfolds the canvas at dusk as the time for the sun to disappear beneath the west coast horizon. It is when we lay our heads on a fluffy pillow and fall asleep. A soul embodied needs rarified air that I breathe when awake and asleep. When the symbol of the god's sunlight force of energy acquiesces to the moonlight cycle, often it's a time when I find myself realizing I was gazing up hoping to catch a shooting star zoom across the night sky. Sunlight begins to rise to ascend to apex everyday and noon slowly becomes an animated series of the recursive prodigious, unframed, excursions in the dreamweaver's night odyssey entertainment. Another morning sunrise to see fresh dew covering trees leaves and wet grass. Sounds of birds meld with a river that gently serpentines stream as it meanders the mountain hillside dals and through open meadows. Warm sunshine climbing above the eastern horizon shoreline.

There is life giving light force energy with the brilliant rays aglow that is likened to the sun that sustains the universal material reality. Light from the Sun journey across the blue sky towards the daily descent below the Western ocean view horizon Shoreline subsides into the spacetime continuum transition turns into dusk to darkness. Curiosity about history is remarkable and fascinating. When the modern intellectual scholar's discovery fits the Bible Genesis narrative tale for many ions of real historical events. This is the allegorical myth postulating the genesis beginning as a clever contrived allegorical storytelling, and the invention by the Church Bishop aims to operate in the name of Jesus Christ. Modern religious institutions have for year's perpetuated the story of Heaven. neophytes examine it as a retrospective transitional reflection back in time.

Try to think outside the old church paradigm views we were all taught as gods religions. Delve deep into Anunnaki extraterrestrial ancient astronauts theorists' hypothesis to examine the Myth in terms of an ancient world nascence with there seemingly a common context respectful of the modern UFO phenomenon. When olden time gods were the original custodians of planet earth.

Yeah they were the Gods who were intelligent extraterrestrial aliens began their cultivation and unfoldment of civilization in the dynamic field of the space and time continuum. Might this have been an event of monumental shock and awe! People who can't fathom or acknowledge the truth have no sense of logic and reasonable expectations to deviate beyond their religion's status quo ante and are likely to be inflamed with *cognitive dissonance.* When it comes to an understanding, like the pawns in the game of chess, ignorant and less informed people are maneuvered by whims of their material psycho-spiritual carnal desires that those know nothing of the true purpose of their beingness. They are the lost souls who lack understanding of the mysterious, powerful allure of the key players in the world of flesh.

We are the malleable peons in a global world of human pawns manipulated by the cabal of secret societies and the influential elite game players who are of the world of control. A two-party divided government system struggles between the political right and left flanks of the electorate who promulgate truthiness by their promises. Both political parties vie for ultimate power and control over the people epitome of a partisan *quagmire* recalcitrant opposing ideologies.

Once upon a very long time ago, from the deep cosmic Galaxy were the extraterrestrial aliens who called themselves the Anunnaki. Let's be clear, the Holy Bible book of Genesis, Chapter 1, is intentionally obfuscating in the context, which is inextricably linked to

THE MIND, BODY, SPIRIT, AND STORYTELLING

the African Egyptian Kemet people o. Where the God, Ra of the Royal Anunnaki bloodline of the Olden Times Prince Enki spearheaded the Egyptian priesthood Temple houses of sacred teachings and learning of spiritual science wisdom. Temples of priesthood were referred to as the house of life. Secret societies originate from Enki's *Serpent Brotherhood* of sacred wisdom teachings of the principles of ancient secret knowledge of the African kingdoms.

To this reasonably salient point, I attempt to elucidate, with speculative assumptions and conjecture, that it is not the Apocrypha. Still, personal beliefs are given as an explanation postulated using logic and reason, as a different opinion and perspective with emphasis given to the individuals who have been taught by spurious misdirection promulgated as the mainstream church religion's truthiness. Whereof, from Greek meaning "to hide away") in biblical literature, works outside an accepted canon of scripture (https://www.britannica.com/topic/apocrypha). The history of the term's usage indicates that it referred to a body of esoteric writings that were at first prized, later tolerated, and finally excluded, and never mentioned that the Anunnaki were: "Those whose home planet is Nibiru. A Holy Bible Genesis narrative is not a clear delineation of a truth to tell us that the Anunnaki were likely an advanced alien race of extraterrestrial alien ancient astronauts. My conjecture conflates this missing evidence that was culled out of the Bible Genesis narrative juxtaposition to the biblical creator-god, Enki, with the primordial idea of an extraterrestrial alien race.

Black African Egyptian, Kemetism was the religion of the indigenous African origin of the Hamite cultures syncretic civilization that existed in lands of the blacks female Mitochondrial DNA. By this scientific genetic manifestation process Humankind came in to existence by Enki's biological genetically modification fusion of DNA chromosome code, we are inextricably linked to the Anunnaki House of elite Royal Prince Enki's contributed Y-Chromosome genes which precipitated the DNA bloodline of the human children of God as according to what the holy Bible. As this is what the words of god/Enki alluded to in Genesis, says in the creation of Adam/man: "Genesis 1:27: "So God created man in his image, in the image of

God he created him; male and female he created them." Meaning He created humankind in His image/likeness. Shall I say that it fits quite nicely with the context of the salient quotes about the Anunnaki alien gods Enki and the revelations about: "Those who from the Heavens came"!

Yeah, and my friends, nothing is any clearer because it dovetails nicely when digested and combined with their real underlying salient purpose for coming to earth. Mr. Zecharia Sitchin has written many thrilling books that are a deep dive into how the Anunnaki extraterrestrial alien beings came from Heaven to earth to extract the mineral gold resources through a large-scale production operation. Enki was to transform it into a monatomic particle for logistical shipments to the home planet Nibiru! The Anunnaki alien gods have been recorded in the original ancient Akkadian and Sumerian cuneiform text translations of the Old Testament Bible Genesis, ostensibly, is i. e. the historical accounts of the *noumenal* world of the Anunnaki Olden Times Ancient Astronauts alien beings who descended from their home planet Nibiru onboard of advanced technology aerial piloted vehicles UAV/UFOs. Which I postulate to be the God of Heaven, known as the immortal Ancient alien Astronauts hypothesis.

Much of what we have discovered predates this as an actual historical event. Not a Myth which conflates to a conscious religious truthiness or a fairytale. The reality is that the Bible book of genesis is much more than a contrived narrative tale or a myth. But an incomplete misdirection play because it lacks the mental clarity and continuity in confluence the story, which is akin to being discredited over the information that has been missing specificity and anecdotal details necessary to support the underlying predicate being put forth.

This book addresses a subject matter from the apprehension of the modern ancient astronauts theorists hypothesis, which dovetails nicely with the biblical genesis narrative tale in all of permutations; and let's be clear that this is not a Myth. Now try to be unequivocally open minded when you conflate the Anunnaki alien race who have ostensibly were an highly advanced alien space-traveling ancient astronauts titular deity.

THE MIND, BODY, SPIRIT, AND STORYTELLING

Which the Bible is intentionally circumspect, by saying: "Those who from the Heaven came"! Might it be better if we understand that the generic reference to Heaven establishes that god/Enki, who was son of Lord King Anu, the most high god of the Olden Times Anunnaki alien of the primordial age when: "Those who from the Heavens came" down to the earth were ancient astronauts who piloted a spacecraft, which was a sort of advanced ancient technology; meaning a sophisticated flying spacecraft, which we call a AUV, or UFO. Well I presuppose that they are the descendants of the Anunnaki, whose ancient ancestors were the deities known as those from Heaven came. The Mesopotamian people revered them as the gods from the sky, who were referred to as the so-called shining ones who landed their bell-shaped spacecraft in ancient Mesopotamia.

Yeah they were the extraterrestrial alien gods who descended from planet *Nibiru*, they called their home. If you will indulge your creative senses, let's try to re-image the retrospective of this ancient historical event as seminal; and as a proper predicate, the truth can now be revealed. Greater discernment requires specificity and anecdotal details about extraterrestrial alien Annunaki titular Gods from Nibiru's mysterious planet.

Which is why we have to examine and digest the story with intelligent logic and reason, meaning that I am inclined to concur with the ancient astronaut theorists hypothesis as entirely plausible. It's hard to refute the ancient astronaut theorists' hypothesis, when you conflate it to a speculative UFO phenomenon.

The identity of the Anunnaki as "Those who came from the alien planet Nibiru had long been obscured from the light of ancient African-Kemetism religiosity and philosophically sacred hermeticism. perception of that underlies this aphorism: "As it is above; so it is below!" The causal chain of life experiences is coefficient with what the mind believes. Biblical history is convoluted; ergo, meaning the story of God is *nebulous*. Whereof in the book of Genesis narrative tale says nothing of substance about those from the Heaven who came, where they were from, why they came, and what was the purpose for coming to the Earth. Let's face it. The ancient astronaut theorists hypothesis to whom I give proper acknowledgement and thanks for their intelligent perspective as it is intricate to the substantive information I allocate in this exegesis I postulate throughout my excursive pages. Illusions of which I suspect will cause incredulous folks to arbitrarily reject much of the views that say: Indigenous earthman's ancestors trace their roots to the Anunnaki Prince Enki/Ea the biblical precursor god of Adam--man! Which is inextricably irrefutable because it has its nascent dovetails nicely with the Bible Genesis narrative tale. Events of the biblical history alluded in the Genesis narrative were coterminous with Anunnaki Royal Prince Enki's homo sapien sapien genealogical bloodline ties to the Hamite Kemet ancestors ().

It's the indigenous African consciousness that is a languishing identity that exposes the image and likeness which is the true hidden face of our ancestors' story which dovetails nicely with modern organized Christian religions. That is the template of the biblical gospel has inculcated the acceptable and prevailing paradigm and the Anunnaki Royal bloodline ties to the indigenous African female heritage derived from the hybrid homo sapiens sapien Adam and Eve. It's a connected story derived from the original descent of the ancient astronaut's historical settlement event in Sumer, Mesopotamia. It's certainly not a Mythose! But it's a different perspective juxtaposition to the Old Testament Holy Bible book of Genesis creation Myth. This subject matter is regarding the unmasking revealing the esoteric to expose the real truth over this long standing delineated and closely held pervading of truthiness. With logic and reason rewind back to the Anunnaki titular Gods of Heaven; meaning the great father Royal Prince Enki/god the creator of the earth and the crossbred Adam and Eve's species, a.k.a. the Homosapien sapiens hybrid bloodline childrens of god.

Might we expose the lie versus the probable historical epochal period event, which was ostensibly an ancillary upshot to the Anunnaki mission earth voyage purpose? What is curiously missing from the Hebrew, and the Greek Septuagint, as well as the KJV Bible narrative tale is ostensibly is like an adolescent fairy tale of The creative God of heaven persona as a cosmic divine mythological tale.

THE MIND, BODY, SPIRIT, AND STORYTELLING

This interpolation is to embellish the Genesis narrative account, to interject a rational and intelligent assertion, using logic and reason. What I mean is that there's a juxtaposition to the creator as an alien god from the planet Nibiru! Which is compelling as a paradigm can be the rub for a different kind of thinker who follows the out of Africa ties to the Anunnaki of planet Nibiru. And shall we say that these beings were likely the ancient astronauts who were "Those who were from Heaven came!"

What is the story of the Bible is a book that is anemic with respect to some important anecdotal details. Fundamental questions are crystal clear: Anunnaki ancient astronauts who came to the Earth were from a highly advanced extraterrestrials race. Or shall we say that they were the titular gods.

The Old Testament Bible Genesis storytelling.

Whereof, the biblical teachings about the titular Gods beings in the context of these Mythological accounts is the real truth about why: "Those extraterrestrial alien astronauts descended from Heaven? This is the necessary information that is material facts that isn't written in the biblical narrative tale that is a perfect fit for a mission earth voyage to the earth, it was commanded by the Nibiru elite Royal Prince Enki. The voyage earth mission commander of the Anunnaki's astronauts who were extraterrestrial alien gods from their home planet Nibiru.

Bible Genesis Garden of the Eden narrative says that, while taking a leisure *paseo* God called out for the Enki's Adam/Adapa and Eve to come appear before Him from hiding and queried. They both had covered the genitalia. Enlil knew then that His half brother Enki had given Humankind the gift knowing their nakedness Thus, Adam (Adapa) Eve had acquired the capability of consciousness awareness.

Which was a gross breach of and transgression of the Anunnaki council law that forbade humans. Enlil is confronted by Enlil for endued humans with knowledge: humankind as a crossbred primitive worker, Enki, imbued with consciousness awareness equate to the knowledge of the self that occurred one day in the garden, in the

Eden, according to what is written in the bible Genesis Garden in Eden, North Eastern Africa. Where the the river Pison (in Araxes) winds through the African people's landI Kush and Ethiopia. Probably Grecian Colchis, in the northeast corner of which was in *Havilah*, Africa. God the Anunnaki Royal Prince Enlil's consternation with his half brother Enki further strained their sibling rivalry. Whereof Enlil castigated Enki in a pejorative context; and denigrated Him as the serpent mentioned in the context of Adam and Eve narrative tale after them frightened and reluctant to appear naked before their Lord God; who with knowledge they had become consciously aware of their own material body was naked. Yeah they hid from Enlil who saw they had acquired the knowledge of their nakedness.

What is known about that event is that He assigned as the deeds of His half brother, Royal Prince Enki, a.k.a, (Ea), was known as the *serpent god of wisdom*. Enki was not a talking serpent, but he was indeed guilty of the god who created and taught it to both Adam and Eve transgressed Enlil's law that forbade humankind to possess knowledge and longevity secrets of the Anunnaki (symbolical of the gods). Enki breached and imbued Homosapeins sapien of the Anunnaki alien gods law that forbid the crossbred humans from possession of the Anunnaki's sacred roots of the knowledge sense and the secret of longevity. Why? Because Enlil and the other astronauts feared that this would allow humans to possess the capability to one day become a threat to the gods of the Heaven federation of galaxies. To some day rise up with the arrogance to develop atomic energy weapons that have the potential to destroy civilization on the planet earth. The Anunnaki Enlil didn't want to open up this godlike persona; because of God's knowledge and longevity, Enlil forbidden to human's to per take of these fruits reserved for the Anunnaki.

Enki's deed caused the brothers' relationship to become further polarized over actions of Enlil intelligence he imbued the homo sapiens sapiens' ability to know themselves. Humankind was created to function as the Anunnaki gods' obsequious naked primitive workers. Enki had transgressed Anunnaki god's law, which made Enlil angry enough to denigrate His brother by uttering a serpent epithet at Enki.

THE MIND, BODY, SPIRIT, AND STORYTELLING

Enki had surreptitiously transgressed the Anunnaki Enlil who was lord of the earth command; of which Enki took the unilateral action that Adam and Eve had forbidden the nature of the alien God's consciousness, aware of knowing of their nakedness. The Royal Prince Enki's word was the Anunnaki law on planet earth, accordingly The crossbred primitive worker Adam and Eve transgression was acquiring the knowing of their own nakedness, indicating that Enlil knew that this bold transgression was the mischief of his half-brother Enki taught them the forbidden knowledge of good and evil deeds. However, Enki permitted them to partake of the Anunnaki life of longevity. Enki's primitive worker. Adam and Eve had spurred this *imbroglio*.

Well then, my friends, this was not the beginning of the Bible story. And not adults know that Royal Prince Enki/God was the creation god action Myth that dovetails nicely with what is written in the Hebrew and Greek Septuagint holy Books. On the earth surface Enki fused His Anunnaki genetic DNA essence linked humankind to the gods family tree roots. Meaning the knowledge of conscious awareness and a life cycle of existence extends no more than a life cycle up to one hundred twenty years. Yeah. Who knows whether Enki genetically edited and manipulated His biological DNA genetic code sequencing with an African female's mitochondrial DNA chromosome codes, was fused into the biblical genesis narrative of the Old Testament creation story. I assert that there is plausibly, seemingly, credible information revealing Enki's mischief was the biblical version of the *Enuma Elish, Seven Tablets of Creation)* is the Mesopotamian creation myth.

The significance here is that this correlates with the Bible Genesis. The actual creation Myth ascribed to Adam and Eve. Enki's obsequious primitive workers.

Or is the whole story mere poppycock. The real question is whether we accept the notion that the Anunnaki are alien beings who were ancient astronauts from their own planet Nibiru or Heaven. With a simple divination from old prevailing paradigms of a biblical perspective, let's instead apply logic and reason. The aim is to get intelligent people to think about blind faith. To speculate as a perspicacious spirit with the free will to discern what is logical and plausible with all of the *permutations*; meaning, that the Bible is a convoluted condensed story, that concur with modern-day Ecchomentical church religious teachings. Of course, you know that Enlil used his authority to banish them to live outside of his personal garden landscape in Eden.

Enlil was the god who was so angry with his half brother Enki who was there in the Garden of Eden, in the scene in which the Bible Genesis narrative tale, ostensibly, misidentified Enki a serpent. Owning to Enki/Ea proclivity to inhale in mischief behavior. He was the god of mischief. His action antithetical to the Anunnaki elite council's law on earth was transgressed. This willful breach of the convention was typical behavior of Enki was the god of mischief, wisdom, freshwater, science and the arts of esoteric divination and magic working. Which qualified him to be maligned and deemed totally responsible surreptitiously Enki genetically modified the biological DNA chromosome codes genomes of an indigenous African female homo-Erectus biological essence created the crossbred human homo sapiens sapiens. Enki committed a crime against the Anunnaki law, when he endued the forbidden knowledge, which he gave Adam and Eve to have the capability to procreate sexually To actually perceive themselves with consciousness awareness! His mendacious scheme to populate planet earth with his creation of the earth plane with intelligent *obsequiously* faithful homo sapiens.

Enlil was angry and confronted His brother Enki—the character described in the Genesis narrative tale of Adam and Eve, who referred to Enki, the creator god of wisdom, magic, and mischief, denigrated as a serpent. To understand this point, you should know this: Enlil was the god Yahweh; and Enki was the creator god of the crossbred Adam/Adapa and Eve.

Yeah, the knowledge revealed to modern human beings to intelligence that has acquired the forbidden knowledge to follow the footsteps of exploring the constellation galaxies with the potential to threaten Anunnaki. Meaning what? Humankind's advanced knowledge has long been the focus of astrophysics science and advanced electronic technologies.

THE MIND, BODY, SPIRIT, AND STORYTELLING

Which is why the Anunnaki believed that Humans would one day be the extraterrestrial alien beings over many eons. We know too well that our medical field logo depicts a modern caduceus figure; and is it not true that the symbol of a coiled serpent is closely akin to the Kundalini? Egyptian perception represents the coiled energy twisted upwards serpent power spiral point of two snakes coiled around a rod. What a curious conflation about a serpent, a pejorative term twisted up by the euphonious biblical narrative Genesis, like a fairytale myth of Bible truthiness. Why has the church been afraid to reveal this to us as adults? In these pages, I elucidate my thoughts on a paradoxical view that must reconcile with modern archeology and anthropology discovery. A composite picture of our history is the theory of the ancient astronaut Gods. Hello, my friends!

I am Hakeem R. Jelani. You don't have a reason to know about me as a published literary author. What I will tell you is that I am a thinker who is in pursuit of knowledge as an adult when I began to cultivate my passion for nous. This is what has inspired me to write this chapter book for others who I share this social consciousness awareness of our secular, political, and religious construct. Without personal knowledge of the evolution of the human condition as a collective unity, the polarizing struggle against our overall dependence, we are all witting pawns in powerful rulers' decisive political systems.

The nation state and religious institutions that preach the gospel of Jesus Christ salvation; meaning that they pervade the blind faith and devotion by adherence to the truth. From the earliest time of our archived historical account, the ruler's have argued over different points via political positions, and a promise to solve issues. While the can be echoed face today into the psycho-spiritual as the church institutions have failed the honestly fulfill its role of providing some people with much sought after quiet comfort and spiritual solace; and let's face it: it may be a the right time for people of this world to find enough common ground in earnest discussions about who we are. Where did we come from which requires having the will to think outside of the old world paradigm status quo. Thanks to mass deception, the purpose of this book is to allow others to pique one's curiosity.

To help spur others who lack knowledge and understanding to be awakened from the ways of the witting blind faith following the Christian religion's doctrine of truthiness. Will we awaken our consciousness and break free from a detached hypnotic mental state of ignorant folks. Particularly if predicated on those who have likely never heard of the so-called Ancient Astronauts theorists hypothesis.

The book manuscripts, I intimate psycho-spiritual assertions of my thoughts as my innermost paradigm for others to read and ruminate the information I elucidate in this book. I concur because in the field of modern archeology and anthropology the discovery of biblical findings.

To digest the truth from the missing pieces of lost information revealing critical evidence found at ancient dig sites has dispelled many long held objections and arguments to the ancient astronauts theorists hypothesis. Which proves that there's more to their perspective and assertions, that is predicated on modern researchers who have put together information that will brighten one's understanding about the Anunnaki alien gods as astronauts conflation to the African-Egyptians, as the Kemetism developed psycho spiritual religious sacred principles of wisdom is intricate to the biblical history of ancient gods. Plausible stories with my interpolations into the holy Old Testament Bible. The UFO/UAV as well as other related anthropology and anthropology researchers modern discovery and findings.

This subject matter exposes insight and aims to present an opinion from a different perspective in order to make people think about the deeper historical aspects of the story of religion. And yes, there is a lot more to the underlying hidden story than what is inculcated as the historical true beginning of Anunnaki alien's Old Testament Bible Book of Genesis narrative tale with logic and intelligent reasoning, and examine its historical context. We suspect that folks will appreciate this book as the beginning of your erudition of a different perspective with the specific anecdotal details information that will brighten up your intelligent mind's to contemplate a paradigm for your greater insight, knowledge, and understanding. Here's where we provide the logic and reason, whereof information will let you be the judge. You see I am not asking you to believe anything that

THE MIND, BODY, SPIRIT, AND STORYTELLING

is imparted to the content of this book. Because first off, what I am telling you folks is that I think it is important for you to know who and what I am conveying here.

Now, as-it-goes. Let me see if I can pique your curiosity and get you to concur with the modern authors' ancient astronauts. Those who accept the ancient Anunnaki alien gods' hypothesis will love the book. While some people are predisposed to object to the elucidation of the Anunnaki aliens as the biblical gods. Oh, there's this speculative assertion claiming that those who came down to extract the material gold from the Earth were actually a fifty man crew of ancient alien astronauts, extraterrestrial under the aegis of Nibiru's elite King Anu. His first born son Enki was the spaceflight commander who spearheaded the vanguard mission Earth voyage to establish a gold mining operation. And yes, Enki is the creator god of the biblical genesis narrative tale that is ostensibly the nascence of the Anunnaki alien African story.

Curiously, his son Enki (Supreme Mission Flight Commander) who was the god who was never acknowledged as the god that created the first Anunnaki city-state and earth station one, which established a settlement for a full scale base of operations on earth surface in "six days" to begin their mission purpose assignment of conducting the gold mining production operation on earth.

At least this is consistent with the most informative story of the Bible according to Zechariah Sitchin books regarding this subject matter topic. We know that Lord King Anu came down from Heaven accompanied by Prince Enlil, which marked the time in the epoch when Anu bestowed total power that gave Enlil the title of "Lord of the Earth Command." As such Enki was angry with his father who he felt had demoted him; after all, Enki was the Anunnaki who was: "Those who from the Heaven came". The god the Bible Genesis narrates the deeds, synonyms with the specificity and anecdotal details in genesis chapter 1. In the Bible Genesis narrative unfolds in the pages of the Holy book, in Chapter 1, ascribed to the anamorphic titular god, the Royal Prince Enki, as we acknowledge the creator God. To be clear, King Anu had looked past Enki by giving total authority to the supreme commander of the two hundred Astronauts on earth; which was given to Anu's youngest son Enlil who had been in control of all of ancient Sumerian lands in Mesopotamia and the lofty title: "Lord of the Earth Command." Enlil was the God whose deeds were synonymous with Hebrew and Greek Septuagint holy Bible book of Genesis narrative; and counterminance with the Old Testament Biblical Adam and Eve banishment from the garden in the Eden! Don't just take my words as gospel, only that I seek to deliver the logic and reason that is put forth to make people think!

With free-will you can have an open mind as you consider stepping out of your comfortable paradigm closely akin to the falsehood misdirection. The Bible Genesis narrative is a Mythological patchwork of truthiness. Yeah what a convoluted and misleading story written about Anunnaki alien beings' historical peregrination which conceal the identity of: "Those from the Heaven came"!

But in the Holy Bible, Genesis it is curious why this perspective was not revealed in Chapter 1. To this I presuppose that the elements of truth, it was truncated from the Hebrew and the Greeks Septuagint to maintain the mystique of god and religions.

Rulers by the initiation of the priestly class sacred brotherhood learned from the Anunnaki in the 445,000 million years ago have been hidden away. Organized Church religions inculcated Christianity as the western European view, which they plagiarized, edited into the twisted manipulation, and reconstituted it into a falsehood that doesn't comport with the original Anunnaki, Sumerian Bible ancient text manuscript sacred spiritual science wisdom teachings of the African, Egyptian-Kemetism philosophy. The learning and teachings that existed long before either the Hebrew and Greek Septuagint holy Bible tale of the eponymous Noah's Ark flood Myth. What can anyone do except I suggest you read Zachariah Sitchin and William Bradley books. Informative and valuable as cross reference sources interpolate insightful information and knowledge about these Anunnaki gods with clarity, suggesting that they were alien ancient astronauts!

One cannot avoid such an amazing conclusion consistent with the scripture of the Old Testament holy biblical creation narrator regarding the extraterrestrial Anunnaki aliens as advanced alien gods.

THE MIND, BODY, SPIRIT, AND STORYTELLING

In particular, the book is about the fundamental underlying credence inherent in the Annunaki as the alien god's presence in the biblical Genesis narrative tale. is the story written about: "Those who were from the Heavens came!" So let me now invite readers to examine exactly why this assumption is curiously, and conspicuously absent. The content of this book is symbolic of the nous of the individual personhood.

My spirit energy has caused me to shine the light of wisdom upon the misled. The knowledge standard for In to inspire the greatest blessings of the benevolent seekers to scrutinize, or rebuffed as a falsehood. I elucidate my salient points as the enthusiasm of truth over truthiness. Shine and focus the light and discover the meaning of: "In God we Trust"! Revealing and unraveling millions of years to deceptions; the disclosure of long-lost historical footprints to false misleading transliterations of truthiness. This emergence of the new age of science, technological advancements, and use of lost historical information has constructed a precise account of the gods and human continuum of the timelines of evolution.

With this in mind, consider the interpolation of the concealed or hidden specificity and anecdotal details that; now then, if you will indulge me here, just perhaps you can imagine a prevailing paradigm view that shine the spotlight on to: "Those who from the Heavens came" were extraterrestrial alien ancient astronaut crew of titular gods from planet Nibiru came to the earth from another star system seated on board a large, bell-like, aerial UFO spaceship! Yeah, what has been taught as the words of god, organized church religions teach as the gospel written by the jealous amorphous creator God in Heaven.

It seems more likely that the Bible doesn't make any references which correspond to Enki's personna. Preferably the Bible has detached Enki's from the deeds that were clearly aligned with the characteristics of the Anunnaki alien astronaut—Infinite Creator!

Readers will come to the point of view about a fascinating subject matter, which is intriguing. After all much of it is written by other fictional authors. As a subject matter, I concur with what is found in published views and books that have been published by a host of modern archeology discoveries of lost historical information. And to this, I elucidate the parallel story as a segway that swerved into these logical assumptions and is remarkable. It bolsters the biblical genesis as my overall salient points. Yeah it's quite consistent a limited scope undergird the premise of the predicate.

This excursive erudition of the knowledge that efficaciously intended to brighten up your spiritual and intellectual vision and spur curiosity. Curious absence is deference to the relevant questions regarding the archeology discoveries that clearly proves the missing specificity and anecdotal details information that elevates our level of the mental clarity about the past that discredits the prevailing falsehoods. Understanding that many people have simply got on with the inculcation of church religions.

The holy Bible gospel scriptures many folks still prefer to worship whatever religion and teachings that pleases them. Whatever Christian denomination they deemed to be the most pleasing to their consciousness, awareness of the animorphs son of god's blind faith religion!

Meaning that they never raise valid questions. Questions that challenge the truthless. With questions is that ask about missing pieces of the Book story of the Genesis narrative tale of the creation.

There is still many unanswered questions about the identity of the God mentioned in the book of Genesis God's human Adam and Eve as primitive worker image and likeness; and do we question God's means of a UFO aerial spacecraft when "those who from the Heaven came" down and colonized the earth during a mission earth voyage to determine if sufficient deposits of gold could be excavated and shipped back to their home planet's to save it from further leaks that was depleting to their planets dying atmosphere!

Of course, questions remain to be answered about these Gods who were from an extraterrestrial higher plane of the constellation orbit. Which Heaven is where: "those who from the Heaven came" descended down upon the terrestrial surface. Certainly, I would say these are just some logicall, important and salient questions about underlying the biblical genesis narrative that never imply the motivation and the purpose for god to come down and have been miss-

THE MIND, BODY, SPIRIT, AND STORYTELLING

ing from their fairytale genesis narrative tale. Whereof, a true story has yet to be told because it fits rather nicely into the modern phenomenon of UFOs flying and hovering in the firmament. Within quantum mechanics their UFO spacecraft quickly accelerate, zoom upwards and vanish!

Let's juxtaposition this interpolation to push a narrative tale that talks about the modern ancient astronaut's hypothesis as the alien God is the Royal Prince Enki. The first of the extraterrestrial Anunnaki alien astronauts who successfully travel down upon the earth surface on board an advanced UFO spacecraft. Let's say that there's a parallel nexus which clearly overlaps with this Old Testament Bible Genesis narrative tale. Two versions of the same old specificity and anecdotal details about the Adam and Eve creation story.

This book is a speculative exegesis that concur with the ancient aliens ancient astronauts theorists hypothesis. The custodial extraterrestrial god. Might we examine Europeans Holy Roman Empires Christians Church Orthodoxy. We are delving into this story that venerated and elevated Jesus Christ and his mother Marry as the divine venerated personna into the worship of Jesus Christ as the son of god. Which is curious as the Egyptians and therefore being closely akin to the African female DNA bloodlines ancestor, delineated by the creation of Adapa/Adam's homosapeins sapien personhood is about the eponymous "Tree of Life" story. that was lifted from the religious priesthood of the African-Egyptian cult of Kemeticism, worshiping of the Mother Goddesses Isis and Osiris, son of the sun Egyptians mythological god Ra, Osias, Isis, and Horus.

Elements of this Egyptian religious story found their way into the Christian religion and were stretched into the new European paradigm of the western Christian perspective. Our modern discovery of the Anunnaki, Sumerian Bible history narrative, corroborated by the specificity and the anecdotal details are revealed in the *Akkadian* language.

There's a real historical past, which was written about the Old Testament book of the biblical genesis is not hyperbolic. Why? Because the god Enki was the creator of AdamaAdapa and Eve, which is undoubtedly one of the most enigmatic conundrum, that was an actual revelations about alien ancient astronauts are at the center of this event described in great specificity and anecdotal detail of Enki, Anunnaki creator of epicenter of the creation of humankind. The "Book of Enki" tells us anecdotal details about how He achieved the creation with which the specificity and anecdotal details can be confirmed by checking out the *"Seven Tablets of the Creation"* Babylonian tablets!" Much of which is well founded and quite logical and irrefutable and intriguing. Shine the light of truth and knowledge as we unpack this perspective of fictional prose. Information for which is inculcated as the neophytes enlightenment.

This I imbibe from the biblical story as an erudition of my speculation about establishing a knowledge standard of the Anunnaki alien gods conflating the Holy Old Testament Bible Genesis narrative tale reveals the ancient astronaut foreign identity of the God/Enki. His ancestral bloodline underlying this Hybrid Slave Race, Enki's manipulation of His biological genetic code of *Lemurian* DNA fashioned with a black African female, Eve's DNA, and the Anunnaki DNA alien god! The primordial life essence of creation of homo sapien sapiens derived from the African mother Goddess mitochondrial DNA genetic code is this nascent that dovetails nicely with the biblical tale of the first Adam (meaning man) and Eve (woman). Indigenous African female genetic *mitochondrial* DNA Enki extracted and fused with His Anunnaki DNA.

Therein lies the story of Enki's process in which the archetypal humankind had been fashioned on the earth's surface; not by the dust of the ground, but by genetic DNA manipulation of biological code sequencing process fused the Anunnaki DNA imprint came to the physical likeness of God/Enki, is what the book of the Genesis, narrative says. But is it the actual truth?

Might this be that dirty little secret that religious institutions don't want you to ever know about! They fear the consequence of telling the truth may facilitate the unwanted financial and moral backlash that would insure that, blind faith hyperbole would be flipped from this long standing mendacious misdirection play. Some folks don't want to discover that falsity in religious theology doesn't want the church to Christian institutions to tampered with—Even if the falsehoods are turned right-side-up. They are still intellectual denyers of the human nascent of the Intelligent Infinite energy of the Creator, God. So the basic knowledge is concealed from society. With intelligence, logic, and reason, we can discern what the truth or falsehood is. I am of this notion that the extraterrestrial alien being Enki is the personification of the biblical God. An automorphic alien who sat out from His home planet Nibiru onboard a UFO spacecraft.

Although this assertion is not mentioned in the religious holy book. Why is it not a plausible consideration; and I believe that it doesn't require some far stretching of one curiosity, wherein today's modern-human beings understand the scientific imagination as it can mirror the illusion of perceptions that some folks minds can not fathom the notion of an extraterrestrial man like alien god personification. Was Enki the actual god from Heaven; and if we concur here that the Anunnaki were an incredibly advanced aliens race of intrepid skilled ancient astronauts who piloted an UFO spacecraft which descended down from the constellation orbital plane on an Earth Mission voyage raised the salient question is about: why?

Ostensibly, does the biblical genesis narrative tale not speak of God in the context of plural God as (ancient alien astronaut commander Enki) "Those who from the Heaven came down." Think about it. Why does the Bible's reference to the deeds of Enki, the Creator God, is intentionally referred to as god—within the Bible Genesis narrative, Chapter 1, as the God Enki who was the Earth Mission voyage Commander of the first fifty Ancient Astronauts crew of Anunnaki slowly descended to the Earth's dark and murky flooded landscape. Nevertheless, Enki's crew safely landed down on the earth's interior plane. He was sent to the planet for a specific purpose to carry out exploratory research as the Earth Mission voyage commander. Enki was a brilliant scientist and chief medical director, whose purpose was to set up gold mining production operations.

Why would the actions and contributions not assigned to the Bible Genesis obfuscate on the Anunnaki identity as the ancient alien gods Mythology.

While in a speculative fiction *troupe* at the Infinite Creator is the highest nature of god that permeates all things that exist! To understand this Bible creation narrative means that we first accept the truth that God is Enki. That God was the Anunnaki's chief scientist and the mission chief medical doctor.

Enki's father Anu, who was the supreme king and lord god of Heaven or (planet Nibiru) chose his own son to be the commander of an *ad hoc* mission earth voyage of astronauts crew of skilled Anunnaki to descend from planet Nibiru. His assignment required skilled workers and academic scientists who could perform the soil samples analytical tests to determine whether there were ample deposits or to indicate the presence of the material element of gold on planet Earth. Enough to establish and produce an abundant amount of gold deposits of the mineral resources gold to establish a gold mining production operation near the modern country of Iraq's Persian Gulf. Because the gold production wasn't sufficient from the; eventually, the Anunnaki relocated operations to southeastern Zimbabwe, Africa.

There is quite amazingly convincing evidence of abandoned gold mines in this region. Extraction involved arduous physical work in dangerous conditions inside of the Earth. Anunnaki *Igigi* was assigned to carry out this heavy toil for thousands of earth years without relief, eventually disgruntled! The Anunnaki *Igigi Promethean* labor workforce bore the heavy toil without any significant relief from the hot deep African gold mining operations on planet Earth.

They were a servile labor work force that performed this task year after year in the sweltering heat of the Southeastern region of Zimbabwe would foment up as anger that soon turned into outright rebellion against their Anunnaki overlord and master Enki. Eventually this condition was the circumstance that provoked a full work stoppage. This rebellion was effervescent by the malcontents that erupted into the worker's rioters who destroyed their tools.

They refused to continue working without having some measure of relief that could satisfy their demands. Anunnaki ruling elite Gods had great discussions regarding this dilemma; an untenable situation that impacted their mission purpose and principle objective. Such a serious matter was to be considered a high priority by the Anunnaki's Supreme Lord God Anu.

THE MIND, BODY, SPIRIT, AND STORYTELLING

He convened his Ruling Council of the Anunnaki Gods to find a solution that would *ameliorate* and eliminate the *Igigi* workers list of grievances. As all options regarding this dilemma and objections erupted into heated discussion. Yeah they were hoping to reach an amenable solution to the elite god's problem was a high priority to placate the Igigi would agree to in order for the mining operation to resume, without a hitch! Without no further disruption in the gold mining operations, work resumed in the greater, southern region of Zimbabwe, Africa. Enlil's solution was to prevent further work stoppage, Enki would seize this as His opening opportunity to create a new human species.

The representative quorum convened to debate their available to save their planets ozone option was to concur with Enki's proposition. Upon all concerns of voting members' objections He had satisfied.

Everyone was in accord when the heated discussions and arguments were settled with consent. Council members had reached a final solution with voters unanimously approving Enki's creation proposal with two *provisos*, that forbid human beings possession of the Gods longevity, Enki had knowingly denied to his crossbred humankind. Enki hybrid primitive workers He surreptitiously imbued with *knowledge*. This fact is irrefutable because it says this in the Old Testament Bible.

What is written in the Bible does not comport the ancient astronaut theorist's reasonable hypothesis, is inconsistent with the thinking person's logic and reasoning, which must dovetails with the backstory, and aligns with the assertion that god came from the sky and created Adam and Eve. A race of extraterrestrial beings who were the original underlying religion tied to the teachings of the godhood mystery religion of the image and the likeness of a divine being. I propose that it was achieved by manipulation of biological DNA chromosome genetic codes manipulation by genetic editing. An assumption that is an intelligent perspective that conflates logic and reason; to apprehension and muse.

It's a viewpoint that shreds and deviates from the sophomoric fullest folly of the Bible, claiming that creator God simply formed humankind from the material dust of the earth! My fundamental presupposition is that it's poppycock, whereof it's most improbable and comical at best. Whereof it's much more likely to be credible thought to believe that the elite Royal Prince Enki was the serpent God. Might we concur with Enki being the god who blatantly violated the conditions set forth by the twelve ruling members of the Council's mandated decree; given as a conditional set of agreed to terms.

However, Enki's idea was always to carry this out without deference to, anything but to imbue His primitive workers with consciousness awareness; meaning what? Humankind was actually created by God—but not from the dusk of the ground—but while living on the Earth plane! Enki's proposal ignited plenty of fierce debate among council members; without objections they reached a consensus. Whereof all of the gods concurred and amicably they had discussed the creation as the most viable option to mitigate further work stoppages and to avoid further violence voted to allow the god Enki to fashion a hybrid primitive worker. You see, the mining production operation was under the direction of the Royal Prince Enki, original Earth Mission voyage. The purpose of mining gold on the earth was specifically mandated by orders of the supreme Nibiru's King Anu, who sent His son, Royal Prince Enki, who was the leader of the mission earth voyage flight commander. He led the first magnificent crew of highly skilled architects, geological survey scientists, medical and biological scientists who descended into the earth's surface. Those who came descended down from the firmament are consistent with the biblical genesis.

All of those who came with Enki were the Anunnaki alien gods who created the first foreign constructed city-state on the earth's surface and named it Eridu ("home in the far away").

These alien beings descended and became the earth's custodians. The Earth Mission voyage was the purpose to build a large-scale gold mining production operation that could be established for excavation for logistical shipment could be actualized. At least this much we can discern according to this assumption, meaning that the God of the Genesis narrative tale, I presuppose was in fact the deeds of the Royal Prince Enki! Anunnaki titular gods who busied himself with a bold scheme; and a perfect opportunity with which he cleverly manipulated the Anunnaki's ruling council of the Anunnaki Royal elites ruling family. The deeds of these alien titular deities have never been identified as the biblical gods as alien space traveling ancient astronauts, but why have the religious authorities have wittingly perpetuated a biblical mistranslations which propagates a persona, of religions which cloaks the biblical narrative tale that makes no mention of the Anunnaki as: "Those who from planet Nibiru (Heaven) came" down to colonize the earth's surface to mine the material gold. Which was this was the cultivation of their mendacious scheme that was the gods contrived story of a fanciful religious myth. Which would account for why there's not a reasonable explanation that explains why no one is aware of "why" God created Adam. It was because of their disgruntled *Igigi labor* workforce.

Over the years, performing this dangerous work, this became a moral problem evolved into discontent with the harsh conditions they endured. These gold miners had instigated a labor work stoppage. For Enki this was a fortuitous event when Enki addressed the council of the gods was his opportunity to present his theoretical proposal as a solution by creating a primitive worker by genetic manipulation of the Anunnaki and the indigenous genus *Australopithecus* earthman's biblical DNA genetic code. Enki was very clever, being disingenuous in verbal arguments that were rebuffed and ridiculed.

A persuasive discussion about this topic cannot refute faulty unsubstantiated arguments concerning Anunnaki alien gods' knowledge and longevity. Royal Prince Enki convinced the council members who approved Enki's scheme that it would be his opportunity to become the biblical god of the book of Genesis. Whereas His executes a deceitful mendacious scheme to establish Himself as the supreme ruler of the planet Earth. Efficiently mendacious scheme to create a race of homosapeins was by DNA genetic engineering. The biological engineering process of in vitro fertilization took place. This allowed Enki to fuse the indigenous African female's Mitochondrial DNA genetic code. Which was combined with Prince Enki's likeness and imprint of the creator using his own DNA Y-Chromosome fashioned primitive Adam.

This is the truth about the creation of Adam / *Adapa*, occurring otherwise, to bring forth the homo sapien as a crossbred human species of god? Then, just perhaps, might it be somewhat plausible to rationalize that the gods who came down from Heaven had a specific mission and purpose traveling to earth, and authorized Enki to create the new crossbred primitive workers. Right? To estapublish a human slave race of obsequiously obedient, humble primitive workers to perform as the servant to those who were from Heaven came from the Anunnaki's home planet, Nibiru—Heaven, they established gold mining production operations on their mission earth voyage to fulfill their primary objective to mind the mineral gold.

Hybrid primitive worker labor force by genetic manipulation of the indigenous African-Lamerian hominid female's *mitochondrial* DNA sequence code, crossbreed homo sapiens life cycle was 120 Earth years. When all of the objections material questions were raised, discussion, and answered everyone concurred.

We know that Enki had successfully convinced voting council members by addressing each of their objections. Unanimously, they approved the Enki solution which was a pivotal watershed moment of the alien Creation Adam/Eve which spurred the spontaneous genesis garden of Eden event that transpired in the Bible. According to the Bible Genesis tale a crossbred hybrid race came to fruition!

With deference to the eclectic sources of information put forth about the Assyrian's *Enuma Elish,* known as *The Seven Tablets of the Creation.* It was written on Cuneiform clay Tablets. Briefly, might I all remind you about the details in Enuma Elish comports with biblical the creation Myth about human beings who came into being as an afterthought, incidental to the Anunnaki as an auxiliary purpose to be primitive workers in life time of serving the gods, as their creation. The Bible alludes to in the book Genesis. My most profound and salient point, viz., revealed by written descriptions of the ancient *Enuma Elish*, cuneiform clay tablets; meaning the "eureka" moment for the archeology discovery during excavations from beneath the Royal palace of *King Assarbenipal's* palace library, archeological discovery vindicated the *Holy Bible* creation story. A event that dovetails nicely with the original ancient cuneiform text script, and both of the Hebrews and Greeks Septuagint Bibles are derived mistranslations into the Holy Old Testament Bible book of Genesis, chapter 1.

It became necessary for the Anunnaki council of the twelve gods of the council of Nibiru to convene and discuss the letter of the rioters' tumult and chaos. African gold mining production operations to be curtailed. Members of the Anunnaki Council unanimously of the senior gods concurred to an amicable plan to be reached on Enki's proposal which had authorized Him to carry out His genetic manipulation procedure for the creation of humankind; the homosapien sapiens, as a crossbred primitive work race.

Accordingly, Enki had manipulated the situation. Enki convinced all the voting members' objections that his primitive workers would replace *Igigi* labor workforce; and they concurred because the yoke of the heavy toil must continue forward without delay. African gold mines contentious work stoppage was this critical matter of a disruption revolt. Gods' labor force created a dilemma of sorts. Enki seized his opportunity as a green light to initiate a mendacious scheme to successfully fashion His hybrid primitive workers. The editing of DNA codes of the African female *Anthropithecus* DNA Mitochondrial genetic biological code with His Anunnaki image and biological alien likeness.

Consistent with dovetails nicely with the Holy Old Testament biblical narrative that says that God/Enki created Adam, meaning homo sapiens sapien while on the earth plane. Irrespective of what it says in the Holy Bible Genesis, we are the essence of the personhood, and the humble servile primitive worker; and biological, genetic genealogy, DNA code spurred by the Anunnaki titular god Enki's manipulation of His Y-chromosome; fusion with the black female mother (Eve) progenitors DNA. It's a story written about the ancient Anunnaki, extraterrestrial space-traveling astronauts, gods and the primary question, the Bible version; as it seems to be a persuasive argument. That Enki had fused the Anunnaki alien Y-Chromosome admixture with the edited indigenous African female's mitochondrial DNA genetic code was contributed.

This female African hominid species contributes to the biological genetic fusion that facilitated the success of Enki's hybrid homo sapiens sapien, as the Anunnaki's Royal genetic bloodline! Created in the image, or likeness of the alien God Enki. His genetic ancestry bloodline roots infusion with a hybrid African chronology. Let's just say what this means: Enki is the Anunnaki mastermind behind the scheme to create a primitive worker! Enki was the god who had perpetrated the genetic fuse to engineer His own Y-chromosome with the indigenous African female's mitochondrial DNA genetic code is the Genesis connection.

The Holy Biblical Old Testament scriptures explicitly claimed he fashioned Adam in his own Anunnaki likeness, an anamorphic imprint. (https://www.linkedin.com/pulse/igigi-servants-anunnaki-james-g-davidson! Of course I assert that this hypothesis dovetails the written account which is alluded to the Old Testament Bible story. Intentionally, dancing around the actual aspects concealed by the invention of Mythical storytelling.

What underlies the human creation story. The most incredible true story never to have been told until this explanation unfolded. Presciently, perhaps there's much more to this than a convoluted biblical tale. Were there some *shenanigans?* With machinations they have covered up information by concealing the extraterrestrial alien Anunnaki identity and likeness of the eponymous creator God, Enki? Okay! If this was true, then let's examine who these Gods were that came down from heaven came to earth from above so we can try to understand why God "created hybrid homo Sapien Sapiens, Enki's Adams and Eves. An episodic Bible Genesis narrative tale; and Enki had persuaded the confederation of the elite Anunnaki council who unanimously concurred to allow Enki to create his primitive workers.

With their *imprimatur*, Enki moved forward with his machinations and sinister schemes created crossbred sapien sapiens, with intelligent conscious awareness; might this be the dirty little secret that the church doesn't want us to ever know about. The Holy Bible Genesis tale only alluded to god and his creation fairytale, and the relevant specificity and anecdotal details they conceal from the ancient and modern homo sapiens-sapiens who were derived from

THE MIND, BODY, SPIRIT, AND STORYTELLING

Enki's genetic manipulation, extraterrestrial alien god Enki (Ea) said he created Adam and Eve. Look! I know exactly what you're thinking right now. You are saying that this guy has lost it! But you might not be quite so sure about any notion that this is poppycock. Because I am going to question everything that you have ever been taught as you come to grips with the intellect of your spirit Chi's that is intrinsically inherent and the impetus which is associated with one's capacity to gather information.

We synthesize the empirical archaeology and anthropology findings using intelligent logic and reason and weaving it into the context underlying clarity and conjecture takes form in this essay as an exegesis. Now shine the light on what does give an appearance of omitted information about Anunnaki gods as extraterrestrial alien astronauts. To question whether there has been a clever coverup of sorts regarding the greatest story that has ever been perpetuated in the history of the church! Was this a far fetched egregious misdirection to foster a mystery God notion to contemplate with logic and reason. A priesthood invention of the holy church Bishops and fathers of organized New Testament religions. What is to me not a far fetched genesis tale in reconcile with the out of Africa, dovetail nicely with the ancient astronauts as alien gods. Folks who rebuff the promise have been the detractors of such a speculative hypothesis, would argue that they have been straight-up dead wrong. I am betting that by the time you have digested why I assert this, well my friend, you are going to concur on the merits and substance of this hyperbolic premise. Certainly this book is in no way intended as an affront to the established religious faith of others faith. No not at all! Nevertheless, my perspective is going to shock the prevailing paradigm.

Keep reading and learn about the creation story of the holy old Testament Bible is an actual historical truthiness that conceals critical information about the nascent activities of the Anunnaki titular god Enki.

The Bible Chapter 1 writes that He/God came down, and so I presume that this was by some advanced sophisticated aerial UFOs spacecraft that had landed on the earth for the first time with this vanguard ancient astronauts fifty man intrepid initial crew of construction engineers, professional scientists. The skilled artisans came prepared with the blueprints; and so according to the New Testament holy book of Genesis narrative that they constructed the first city states on earth. Anunnaki aliens were the custodians titular gods and goddesses who were the builders of biblical names of the first city-state civilization on the earth in six days. A creation story that fits Enki's DNA manipulation, a medical procedure that facilitated the means by which he fashioned prototype crossbred homosapien Adam and Eve; He had fashioned them by biologically genetic manipulation of the DNA chromosome codes.

Well then, my friends, it's not so far-fetched to one's imagination to believe that God was (a.k.a) Enki, who was after all was, a brilliant medical doctor, a scientist, and biogenesis. Enki was the highly qualified to be a creator god who possessed the skills necessary to manipulated, modified, and engineered the fusion of His Anunnaki alien biological DNA, Y-chromosomes code with an indigenous African female's hominid X-Mitochondrial DNA genetic codes of an *Australopithecus africanus* species of African to fashion the creation of humankind that spurred the likeness. Or God's alien image of the Anunnaki Royal Family Bloodline; and the descendants of the Nibiru Royal Prince Enki, son of the Supreme Lord god Anu of the planet Nibiru, meaning Heaven! We have this venerable line with which is that of the Old Testament Bible narrative connection with the Ancient and the African genetic ancestral Hamites as children of god! The creation event was described in the *Enuma Elish. And* embellish in chapter 1. We must acknowledge that the Bible Genesis is the translated version from the original ancient Holy Bible book. Which existed long before either the Hebrew or Greek's Septuagint Bible's truthiness fits the *Enuma Elish* digest, which was a firsthand eyewitness account.

So might we acknowledge the erudition of this as a more than a silly notion because the phenomenon Okay, then, given that we do, except the Bible is the words of the Anunnaki alien gods who are the ancient astronauts orders was the earth mission voyage to exploit the earth for its abundant mineral gold resources. Having the credibility accompanied with the standard of a logical thinking person's;

and devoid of mythological *sophomoric,* that is fostering truthiness without consideration of empirical archeological and Bible history to bind together aims to bring clarity. The consciousness awareness is understanding.

We are all imbued with the spirit energy and with the light force of confusion and ambiguity of the religions paradigm of Heaven and the earth is divine enlightenment. The scriptures read about from the pages of the holy book. Much of which is revealed doesn't conflate religious teachings, meaning that it diverges from entrenched learning/teachings of African Egyptian-Kemetic spiritual science principles. Spiritual wisdom pertaining to consciousness awareness of the immanence of the south and the luminous divine within as the spirit of our physical localized self beingness in human form. Several published authors' such as Edward Bruce Bynum, Ph.D. ABPP have written books on this subject matter. Which seems credible and quite plausible in the biblical context seems closely akin to: controversial modern-day scholars ancient alien astronauts connections to the UFO phenomenon (https://www.linkedin.com/pulse/igigi-servants-anunnaki-james-g-davi). I elucidate in this book as speculative fictionalized tropes.

Some folks, however may poo poo my premise as far-fetch; and others say it is an opaque underlying paradoxical storyline that seems to fit nicely with the truth about the Anunnaki, Sumerian Gods genesis creation narrative tale's nexus that dovetails with the out-of-Africa hypothesis, saying that it underlying view fit nicely with the Anunnaki, Sumerian Gods genesis creation narrative tale's nexus that dovetails with the out-of Africa hypothesis. Anunnaki ancient astronaut theorists postulate that the hypothesis suggests that they were the space-traveling ancient astronauts from planet Nibiru! This theory is quite fascinating. A curious notion that our preconceived biblical worldview is or can be said to consist of falsity and misdirection plays away from the truth about the Anunnaki: "Those who from the Heavens came"!

Have we all been deceived and misled? Particularly concerning the creation of the human race, juxtaposition to the Bible Old Testament anecdotal detailed. Therein lies substantive evidence that exposes religious organizations. Modern free thinkers have been asserting real archeological, anthropological, and biblical historical discovery of ancient cuneiform clay tablets from the past, which dovetails adequately with the ancient astronaut theorists' hypothesis. Let's simply agree in principle on pragmatism, using intelligent logic and reasoning as you examine the underlying premise presented in the context of what I assert as a different perspective. Because the information in the controversial book, not poppycock but thoughts unfolding the *consciousness, intuition* and ideas and fictional troupe. One that you are reading now conflates archeological, anthropological, meaning that the Anunnaki, *Enuma Elish, Seven* Tablet corresponds with the creation Myth. Discovery of the ancient information from books published by prominent authors who have written a manifold of compelling books.

These subject matter books are packed with pertinent biblical historical archeology discoveries and findings that offer a vivifying perspective which paints you a shocking picture that fits nicely as a critical piece to a revealing biblical tale about the Anunnaki aliens. Can you digest this convoluted narrative tale with mental clarity? Then what I will tell you is about unpacking the missing pieces of the eponymous Holy Bible Genesis narrative details long before Noah's flood. Now is the time to know the truth about oneself as Children of God. Let's say that today there is this fascination with the UFO phenomenon is speculative conjecture I wholeheartedly concur is likely valid. Nevertheless, the most critical element that is not disclosed in the Bible Genesis narrative, which obfuscates, and wittingly makes no mention of Enki and his intrepid vanguard spacecraft traveling astronauts descent from sky came down from Heaven is the likely scenario involving Enki's crew of ancient astronauts alien gods from their home planet, Nibiru.

To this, I posit that my semi-fictionalized prose that raises salient questions surrounding the greatest truth or a cleaverist truthiness has influenced everyone in our lives! The enfoldment of the missing pieces of the pages of our human history long lost past primordial periods; an interconnected ancestors link to an aliens' cre-

THE MIND, BODY, SPIRIT, AND STORYTELLING

ator of humankind. What I posit here will resonate with those who are rational thinkers.

Those who are unbiased folks who are seekers of rational well founded knowledge. Because, if you will indulge me I aim to lead you into greater clarity; and common interconnectedness. Often there are those folks whose myopic views constrains them from thinking outside the box; and they have a neejuck reaction to any paradigm shift in the face of empirical evidence. They will reject the postulated credential's of modern findings when juxtapositioning to what is written about in the holy Bible religiously. It might have been written to be the Anunnaki clan's genealogy records to ensure the most critical episodes of the story of the archived book Genesis of the alien god's primordial presence, which I would contend was removed from the original Old Testament holy Bible book of Genesis narrative, which is incomplete and replete with truthiness! Simply put, the truth is missing the most fundamental volume of the hidden anecdotal detail concealed and left out of the Old Testament Bible Genesis religious book manuscript. One's spirit nature is the animated actions of the ubiquitous light force energy of humans, who are the consciousness awareness embodiment.

To all the nascent is your natal date born as a lifetime as a child unknowing when it ends. Consciousness awareness is withdrawn until initiation into the next *palingenesis*. Are we not talking about human beings as the bloodline descendants of extraterrestrial Anunnaki alien gods mentioned in the holy book genesis narrative tale Myth about: Those who are the childrens of gods; meaning that we are all to be judged. One's life deeds weighed against Ma'at ostrich feather determined whether it is pure and have been dutifully obedient is carried out after the soulful spirit has cycled through life. And when one's life cycle shall come to a full stop, everyone will succumb to nature's recall and rebirth cycle of life because the beginning is always assured that it ends in the same place and a date uncertain of a determined date or time reality. And when the measure of time will cease to go on counting the years we have come to crossroad full stop at the red light. To lie reposeful in silence as piece comes at the quiet comfort of sleep, until another great awakening to again the embodiment of spirit animation is gifted the salvation when the righteous one's obedient in the name of Jesus the Christ will enter Kingdom we have been inculcated by ecclesiastical Protestant and Catholic Christians biblical Gospels, dogmas, canons, and the holy religious creeds of Jesus the Christ. Therein lies the rub! When we question: Is the Bible a misdirection, fairytale, or clever truthiness? Secularist governing rulers at the very beginning of the history of the royal line of Kings were powerful rulers from the earliest arrival.

Enki, the Anunnaki alien God's spaceship, and his fifty-man ancient astronaut crew slowly descended from Heaven. The Bible narrative mentioned the landscape was ancient Sumer, Mesopotamia. But from a psychological standpoint the landscape was ancient Sumer, Mesopotamia. But from a psychological standpoint we speculate, knowing there is still some key anecdotal evidence yet to be discovered. The value of the lost history remains, missing pieces of the puzzle may never be found. We therefore realize that there are still many folks out there who are not inclined to take a sophomoric and clouded by a myopic view of God and religious beliefs. I get it! Absolutely, I mean no disrespect to the true fulcrum of anyone's life experience. No, not at all. My own insight is a psychospiritual purpose as I discover and unpack the missing piece and learn.

While unknowing of any past lives and deaths cycles in the reincarnation of many blessings of anual events. Neither can we know what our present future events will unfold—only that it will come into being one day at a minute of time passage in the present time! It's lucky that the randomness of the dynamic field of the space and time continuum of illusory world reality is the thoughts apprehended by our subjective thoughts diurnal big picture of decisions, actions, and life-changing random events. Whereas the folly-like fairy tale is a retro perspective myopic revelation that dovetails the Old Testament Holy Bible, Genesis narrative story. Which is a convoluted, discursive, nuanced reconciliation with the true light to shine on the anecdotal details of the alien Gods! This means, we need to take an unbiased look at the extraterrestrial alien God, Enki. Is he a titular ancient astronaut? This is the context with which assertions seem rather unequivocally fascinating! And as such, any prevailing

THE MIND, BODY, SPIRIT, AND STORYTELLING

paradigm shifts away from the truth about the notion of this modern anecdotal dovetail, I interpolate the speculative assumptions which ostensibly alludes to the Anunnaki connection, meaning what?

Might we weigh the vagueness of chapter 1? We have to be open-minded and scrutinize objectively and digest these words: "Those Who Came to earth; and as it is a probable consequence of their intelligence, certainly—and humans beings are capable of venturing out into space, we are mirroring our ancestors as we are now able to navigate the frontier of space exploration, it is understandable that we are the genetic adventurous DNA essence of Enki's Anunnaki fusion with indigenous African female ancestors alien crossbred bloodlines. adventurous curiosity. bloodline impetus behind fictionalized accounts"! Ostensibly, logic and reason is from the intelligence of the mind. Perception is the presence of mental clarity that manifests the state of cognitive development as having the spiritual consciousness to think! Our sense of greater understanding is free of unconscious bias. Or have we allowed our minds to be inculcated or influenced by the ignorance of lies, which pervades our social culture as poisonous biased troupes! Millions of people constitute the plethora of dalliance of the individuals who are living lost souls humanity. People have misled them into the hedonistic social lifestyle in a material world of wickedness.

Widespread iniquities inclination folks towards self greed, a propensity for evil lust for material wealth. Humankind, motivated by their carnal nature and unconscious mind that is devoid of spiritual knowledge. It originated with the Hamites, *Kemetic spiritual* science was the original learning and teaching that has yet to be taught to malleable witting pawns who have a limited understanding of the worldly economy that is so closely akin to skilled moves of a master chess player strategy.

We are all living life as the everyday world as we see it, is our uniquely shared experience people who have been preyed upon. Those who have been deceived are the victims of the global, political and religious orders, unholy alliances with the corporate media, global corporations, and religious institutions.

Whilst ordinary people use electronic digital communications information flow. There is a complete body of UFO, Anunnaki alien gods, authentic ancient astronauts, theorists' hypothesis premise representing a biblical, archeology, and plethora of anthropology information that is widely available revealing the good and bad deeds that contributed to Anunnaki and humankind's storied genesis and ancient history. People are informed about the all-seeing eye of a mendacious, malevolent hidden hand of evil forces mucking up the pure hearts, stealing the liberty and freedom of humankind who are devoid of knowledge! Indifference with dalliance, they are the missled, low information folk who are the witting pawns; those without the light of wisdom and insight are the primordial nascence of god-spirit (likeness of Enki) and this is the biblical genesis tale is chronicles that evolutionary account of the past eons. We hope that this your curiosity and helps to unlock the missing piece of the convoluted distortions of the world as a unfoldment within daily temporal reality. There is a truth within the scope of this: "out of Africa black mother goddess is tied to the Anunnaki ancient astronaut extraterrestrial alien God, Enki. The evidentiary information congruent with the historical roots dovetails nicely with the modern UFOs theorist hypothesis alignment with the Bible (Psalms 104:3). Christianity supplanted the ancient Kemetism sacred spiritual science philosophy.

Anunnaki, African-Egyptians spiritual science philosophy was taught in ancient mystery schools learning and teachings of *Shetaut Neter* meditation practice of *Smai Taui*. A mental Yoga practicing the physical exercise postures meant to enhance meditation and physical flexibility. The unity with the luminous divine *Neteru Netger*. With intelligent logic and reason is the wisdom and insight to recognize and understand the what is the true understanding of the ubiquitous pervading unity of the living nature of the light energy of the human existence endued by the all pervading spirit of Infinite Creator as the *Noumena*. The cause of the light of spiritual science is sacred wisdom principles is our God.

This book unfolds information which the establishment Church is likely to rebuff as the fountainhead of falsity. However,

THE MIND, BODY, SPIRIT, AND STORYTELLING

a plethora of reference sources replete with archeology and anthropology discovery insight. Yeah, let's face it! Often ta visceral truth is undermined, and was just as applicable hundreds of thousands the page years of archived pages of historical record information lost to the archived history traces back to the Olden Times extraterrestrial Anunnaki alien gods epoch that has long been omitted from the original biblical Genesis narrative tales conflates with the biblical manuscript ancient codex; *ipso facto*, which means that the redaction was intended to remove the Anunnaki gods identify has been a sinister scheme that deceived us for year, ab ovo. They became the custodians of the earth and the contributions to humankind, we know that this makes no acknowledgment of their presence. Only the curious students are apprised of this suppression because their identity is the missing anecdotal details of their history—not merely a Mythological construction; of an identity tone excised from the landscape of the biblical story about the alien gods of Sumer, Mesopotamia. To take on a myopic view of the future without understanding, insight, clarity, meaning clueless theology perspective. Archeology and anthropology discovery revealed historical findings that reconciled with the Bible's Genesis narrative dispels incredulity, fiercely held arguments that cannot be debunked as poppycock.

There's an original Anunnaki, Sumerian Bible text manuscript. Of which aligned the ancient gods were not fallen Angels; and the evidence suggests that they were extraterrestrial space faring alien astronautWhich seemingly aligned with the propositions that support the ancient astronaut theorists' hypothesis. Does it mean that the phenomenon story of the human creation is irrefutable if it appeared in the context of information available in the subject matter books? The theoretical views and the material evidence that harkens back to the ancient civilizations written about in the Hebrew and Greek Septuagint holy Bible book have been validated by the discovery of cuneiform clay tablets. Which is filling in the gaps with findings that go beyond any mere speculations; and that is because there is a plethora of books. Fictional accounts have written about the subject matter. Which provides a significant insight into historical anecdotal details that is revealed by research Scholars archeology and anthropology research discovery and findings.

.Relevant findings that dovetails nicely within the premise of the Olden Times Anunnaki alien gods contributions to the genesis tale, which was written about in the Old Testament biblical book of genesis narrative tale. It's much more than a Mythology; where I contend is a paucity and a narrative tale that fits nicely with the neophytes, archeologists and anthropologist modern discovery, and provides the scientists findings aligned with the African the presence of the Anunnaki ancient astronaut hypothesis descent from planet Nibiru. Perhaps plausible because it is rooted in the mental cognitive disciplines of intelligence, logic and with reason. Yet we still have some folks who are always skeptical, but without having equal curiosity about what is posited as the truth, perpetuates a truncated view of the Old Testament Bible genesis religious narrative tale. This exegesis interpolates an assumption about the Anunnaki Sumerian Bible; the truth about misrepresentations of historical information. From reading a series of various subject matter books that is a common synthesis of this phenomenal subject matter underlying this exegesis.

What is the truth? We can only speculate about this event to reveal the totality of the genesis narrative tale. But this is not an assertion of absolute certainty. Nevertheless, I am compelled to shed some light of knowledge with a spotlight by calling your attention. Anunnaki were the titular god figures, shall I dare say, they were ancient space-faring extraterrestrial alien astronauts, which the Holy Bible noun is the word God. I postulate this exegesis that which is irrefutable according to archaeology evidence and not hyperbolic god hides as a mystery identity, which is presumably the elite Royal Prince Enki's as the Annunaki Genesis Earth Mission voyage enterprise of the alien ancient astronauts of the sky.

This specific objective purpose was to locate, exploit, and extract the gold from the planet earth. The purveyors of the religious truthiness narrative tale; and they will physically recoil in their rebuff of the Ancient Astronauts theorists hypothesis—because they don't want you to know that the creation of humans was fits nicely into this hyperbole that Anunnaki who came from Heaven were in search of gold, and because of their *ad hoc ancillary* need of a large primitive worker race spurred Enki to create homo sapiens sapien to facilitate the endeavor, to carry out their end purpose. This underlying need precipitated why the crossbred primitive worker transformed into the hybrid cognate bloodline of which the Bible refers to as the children of the alien Anunnaki.

African Hamite black people perform the heavy toil inside of the deep African gold mining production operation. This was what spurred the Anunnaki alien gods to authorize Enki to create a human society of common consciousness on the earth plane which is the Mythos of the biblical tale twisted away from the African Kemetic consciousness awareness of the psycho-spiritual wisdom of Western Europeans Christianity.

The ubiquitous harmonic vibration pervades the cultural milieu social complex around the world. For example, organized religion and secularism have been abusive and eriguan in its *megalomaniac*. They asserted their free will caused some of the most violent and heinous acts that history reveals their sanguine brutal wars, was a period of unspeakable human cruelty.

Ruthless aggression they attacked in order to destroy free will was the method by means of armed warfare for power and control. They erected a Stella to proclaim their conquest and thanked their god they elevated with acknowledgment. An explanation acknowledges the Anunnaki alien Gods' contributions as a bold retrospective onto world reality within the context and scope of Anunnaki God nascence of the biblical account: "Those who from the Heavens came"! To demystify the twisted precepts of the indoctrination of the Western religious creeds with doctrines and canons, they systematically undertook a transformational schema. What is taught defines the archives of things that we have been programmed to accept as the truth about our social complex of the illusory world reality.

Now then, what was written to represent a manifold of long years ago is a selection of the so-called words of god. The story is strewn together as this transformation into a narrative Mythological tale of misdirection play and truthiness; and this religious machination. Might the truth be acknowledged that the African-Kemetic spiritual science was supplanted by secularist rulers ambitious strategy, which was to shift religious teaching into the Western world view of the Christianity, paradigm into the spurious theology by the twisted manipulation via the transformation of the Roman Catholic Church falsehoods. When holy Bishops' became the preeminent religious authority was raised to the status of the facilitator and purveyor of conscious biases.

Let's face it. History was flipped by a dominant racial phenotype who took possession of the old world order by military incursions. Yeah, transforms established the new western civilizations world view; and it was achieved by the kingdoms that created imperial rule, and elitism controlled by the sword with impunity. Or shall I say, it was with audacious acts of sanguine violence, as engaged in territorial conquest. It was in this mode of operation that he committed wholesale plunder and plagiarized the eastern Kemeticism cultures of the spiritual science philosophy principles, the epicenter of the African psycho-spiritual consciousness awareness learning and teaching knowledge of nature. While it took years to systematically subdue neighboring city-states with weaker military mighty armies with impunity, they set out to systematically subjugate and cement themselves as the ruling power. Without guilt, sin, and fear of god's retribution, the whitewash of the African personalism religions of the *Kemetic teachings of Thoth (Diop, 1991)*, the spiritual science of European Christian fused with the indigenous African-Egyptians religions during the slave trade (Tylor, 1871; Spencer 1885).

Priority with the imperial government's new world order of Emperor Constantine I. His benevolent social embrace of Christianity as the preeminent Catholic religious church was his scheme to game the people.

The real true account was flipped on its head; manipulated into the transformation and subjugation of the African-Kemetic symbols and a synchronous introduction of their new world order via a plagiarization by repressive actions to subjugate the African-Kemetic original Egyptians/Nubians teachings of the Kemet spiritual science religion that had preceded Western Christianity. Western Christians Church preaches/teaches/learns about the original Anunnaki's

THE MIND, BODY, SPIRIT, AND STORYTELLING

Sumerian Bible. And the truth about the events of the time lapse of the eons of the infinity from the pages of the historical time continuum. And my friends, I hope you can appreciate it.

Let me interpolate and enfold my thoughts about this very convoluted story that conflates an assertion which is about Enki as the Anunnaki extraterrestrial ancient astronaut; and the alien gods progenitors custodians who had been the Old Testament Bible Genesis history event (http://blaksimba.com/the-unlearning/). Whereof, critical element seems to be curiously missing the most important anecdotal details of the Hebrew and Greek Septuagint version Genesis narrative scripture. It's a story about Anunnaki extraterrestrial alien god Enki's vanguard Earth Mission voyage. Let's face it. "Those who came from Heaven" landed on earth cir. 1700 BCE. My question is this: Why would this material information omitted translations be lifted from the Black-Head Sumerians text account. Whereas the Hebrew and Greeks Bible story was intentionally misinterpreted as the Mesopotamia Anunnaki Sumerian Black-Head ancient manuscript codex.

God, Royal Prince Enki was the personal Deity and son of the Anunnaki Supreme SkyGod from the deep space planet Nibiru; the so-called Heaven. These extraterrestrial aliens' arrived from deeds deployed by a vanguard UFO fiftyman ancient astronaut vanguard astronaut crew. These space faring astronauts who were the first custodial settlers who came down on the Earth Mission's voyage, fits the Bible Old Testament Genesis narrative stories tale. Perhaps the Hebrews and the Greeks Septuagint Holy Bible versions, had some larger knowledge about: "Those who from the Heavens came"; and ostensibly have comid-transliterated the version, is guilty as charged. Now, hold on there!

Wait a darn minute here! Yes, I know that it was evil, and despicable to unfathomable! What plausible reasonable decision would be justification to "blotch" out all evidence of the Anunnaki ancient alien astronauts' established physical presence with historical contributions to human culture.

Might that have been a deception to conceal the Anunnaki's Royal Prince, Enki? Could this have been an action plan to erase the identity of the amorphous race of the extraterrestrial aliens gods? The Old Testament biblical book of Genesis to invent the book of Genesis as a Mythical storyline about the real UFO. Ancient astronaut's theorists hypothesis postulates!

Was this because the pertinent specificity and anecdotal details provide information that dovetails nicely with substantive arguments. How is the truth being unlocked by the modern Archeology discovery and findings that are being revealed as relevant lost information.

Which I might point out has some connection to an overall theme about the story of the ancient Anunnaki Astronaut; and, meaning what? That truth is about the acknowledgment of the extraterrestrial alien Anunnaki gods actual presence and contributions with respect to the Olden Times gods who descended from their planet Nibiru. A western version contrived became the Christian church religions which diverged away from the original ancient spiritual teachings of the priesthood spiritual science religions precepts about the nature of metaphysicalism. She instituted a transformation toward Christianity.

This religion was hijacked by evil rule whose aim was to mislead people into a spurious centralized theological perspective. Whereof, not a mention of the Hebrew, Greek, and KJV Septuagint, published Bible's Genesis chapter, 1 through 11 narrative tale, which does not reference in their scriptures that does not obfuscate with clarity, only that they all have omissions of significant information. Truth is that which underlies my fundamental query about the creator god of Heaven's purpose, ancillary to the motivation for coming to the earth; this lack thereof specificity and anecdotal evidence suggests the intent to create a mystery to convey this hidden identity of the Anunnaki astronauts: "Those who from the Heavens who came." As Such, this is written in the context of the original story.

Okay, it is hardly a far-fetched notion, because it's the missing material information that reconciles nicely with biblical Genesis, meaning that the deeds attributed to those of God, corresponds with Enki as this alien creator God! How curious and fascinating the world of organized religions is, whereas we are missing the true extraterrestrial alien beings arrival; as the original custodian of earth, ipso

THE MIND, BODY, SPIRIT, AND STORYTELLING

facto, a event to mark the building of the first city-state Eridu in the ancient Mesopotamia landscape of the black Sumerians in six days!

This is what is alluded to in the Old Testament Bible. Here might we interpolate the beginning of the Enki/Ea as the central character to highlight truth into a story that has earmarks of a mystery tale that is spurious, meaning that serious and relevant specificity and anecdotal details, raise questions about. I am curious to know why this is so glaringly obvious.

This is a speculative assertion that puts a spotlight on the Bible historical event that is presented in the genesis Western European context which pervaded this rewrite of the Anunnaki ancient astronauts origin into the religion of truthiness. For what purpose and to what sinister *mendacious* scheme to establish powerful ecclesiastical, blind faith religion of the ineffable creator!?

Yeah, perhap that is because the purest elements of the highest truth are unassailable according to the ings attributed to the modern work of prominent archeology, anthropology, Bible historiography researchers. Over the year's many authors' books became the catalyst for writing about this quite remarkable and rather intuitively fascinating topic that accounts for the sale of subject matter books worldwide. Full of information that is just the tip of a huge body of works by wise scholars and published authors. Therein lies information elements. Might we read the information corresponding to the Kemet spiritual science philosophy reinforcements of the original Anunnaki alien creator God Enki. Extraterrestrial ancient astronauts mission earth voyage flight commander was assigned to the Anunnaki Royal elite Prince Enki/Ea (the god of the Bible) who was the leader of: "Those who came from the Heaven came" they were the Anunnaki from planet Nibiru.

Ostensibly I apprehend, is an acknowledgement that if the *Enuma Elish* (Seven Tablets of the creation) is consistent with the book of Genesis, then the extraterrestrials DNA imprint of God/Enki(Ea) is an inextricably royal blood/indigenous African female ancestral DNA connection to the creation of His Image!

Certainly, we can simply apprehend this to be unequivocally clear that we have opened up a Pandora's box; and what is about to be unpacked is likely going to set some people's hair on fire! Let's continue to delve into the religious Church Old Testament Holy Bible narrative to obtain the real discernment from the Bible Genesis creation story, along with the research ings of modern scientific discoveries in archeological, anthropology, paleontology, genetics, biblical religious history contributions. The fundamental presupposition that is a controversial hypothesis is hardly alone in the presence of advanced academic research reference sites or intellectual and spiritual principles. My excursive prose is being revealed here to make folks think. Because the subject matter is inextricably tied to the Old Testament Biblical Genesis; and in terms of history perspective with emphasis on the Anunnaki alien ancient astronauts the Royal Prince Enki/god as the original custodial titular creator God, and His affinity with the African, Kemetic-Egyptians.

Historical information is derived from the biological genetic ancestral bloodline through a black African female mitochondrial DNA code, which Enki fashioned His Anunnaki biological DNA Y-Chromosome gene and fashioned the first homo sapiens crossbred Adam/Adamu. Truth about this is exclusively very convoluted in the Old Testament Bible. It is largely a patchwork of a much more voluminous 4, thousand years old book about the past eons of the extraterrestrial aliens' ancient manuscript codex. To be clear you should learn about the extraterrestrial alien gods who deeds are wittingly obfuscate the identity of the Anunnaki alien gods who came down from Heaven (Nibiru) have established as human hybrid homo sapiens sapien is the Royal bloodline ties with these children of Enki. You will most assuredly find that which elicits the hidden truth of the nous. The unfoldment and influence of extraterrestrial alien God of heaven brought civilization into a culture of intelligence in aspects of kingship, astronomy, architecture, and spiritual principles and ideas in a culture that was an example of learning and teaching. Boldly attempt to focus upon the core contribution of this missing truth about this African biblical history of creation Myth which is to unravel the intentional misdirection away from the fundamental biblical historical truth was written about a manifold of the black and Royal African Kings who became powerful rulers—the mighty men of renown!

These African tribal kings were the pawns of the Anunnaki alien race that became the mighty men of the Old Testament. Deeds attributed to them are conspicuously mentioned in the holy scriptures. Also, the Sumer, Elam in Mesopotamia were black (Van Sertama & Rashidi, 1990). The available versions of the Old Testament Bible Genesis narrative are best understood from the Anunnaki ancient astronauts' hypothesis is straight up not a convoluted truthiness.

Then from a fresh, unbiased perspective, unpack and unfold the development of the alien Annunaki origin custodians titular ancient astronauts Gods and the African nexus! A delineated history will harken you back to our excellent ancestors' history is the bloodline ties to the Anunnaki as the Old Testament titular alien gods who came down and built and developed civilization on earth. This Anunnaki elite Royal family bloodline is the origin of a power of kingship that was derived from and delineated through all of the family fused with the DNA of the Anunnaki family roots. It's not a far-fetched notion or any stretch of the spiritual enfoldment of fervent consciousness awareness, not of the conjectures of imagination. Particularly when assertions align with the primordial evidence. Which is corroborated by the empirical evidence that can withstand the scrutiny can't be rebuffed or discredited.

In the light of modern archaeologist and anthropologist research scientists revealed findings. Empirical evidence is shored up by religious teachings and academic scholars' credibility. Whereof the Bible Genesis and contends conflate modern day science archeology and anthropology discoveries, seems to support the Anunnaki Ancient Astronauts theorists premise.

Which has often spurred some skepticism and arguments with iased against the mainstream research findings! However, of course there are still some folks who have rebuffed the claim that the Anunnaki were the ancient astronaut alien Gods. The hypothesis they do not equivocate; because of their unconscious biases and close adherence to the canons of blind faith religions prevailing paradigm; which I say they are without logic and reason. Steadfastly they cling to their blind faith religion and the New Testament biblical gospels and denigrate the Old Testament book of Genesis is silent about the Anunnaki with respect to the notion of an ancient astronauts alien gods from planet Nibiru: and yet as detractors they have no idea about who, why, how; they prefer to perpetuate the Myth. That is to say that God created humans as it is described in the Genesis narrative tale. What was written seems remarkably hyperbole, which means that it is a flawed story which doesn't give the clear delineation of truth anything regarding what steps God to bring the grand creation events to a successful conclusion. This episode of chapter 1, enters lock with, shall we say Enki/Ea's mission earth voyage: "Those who from the Heaven came"; did they come from Nibiru, meaning what?

Was the creation an timeline epochal event; or a speculative proposition interpolated on intelligent logic and reason. Might this be the clouded truth—or the impetus that undergirds humankind genetic creation is credibility genesis without revealing the anecdotal details. A plausible premise that is not a contrived fairytale rooted in discursive religious truthiness that was written the truth about this ancient historical Anunnaki events.

The Roman Emperor, Constantine I, malevolent scheme is seen as the catalyst behind the transformation of spiritual learning/teaching associated with Western European's Christianity Catholic and Protestant theology.

Whereof the occultists pagan religious holidays and festivals celebrate convergence via the Original Nicene Creeds of 325 and of 381. Revolutions began with Western Europeans' interpolation of misdirection plays. Which supplanted the original spiritual teachings of the African-Egyptians Kemetism spiritual science religions was toppled. Egyptian-Kemetism human spiritual consciousness of spiritual principles. A new world order of religious thought emerged by the powerful imperial government authority that unfolds by the new transformation and synchronicity which has found it wise to be enjoyed by the church and state precious religious Christianity world reality. Yeah this began the rise of the Western prism; which supplanted the African social culture of the spiritual science consciousness! Now, this is a book that I have written to enlighten and spur curiosity. To know as you follow the light that leads to teachings and learning about the planet Nibiru Anunnaki, the ancient astronaut's Earth Mission voyage. To discover what prompted the alien titular Gods to descend from Heaven. With frequent reports of human abduction and physical sightings of advanced large bell UFO spacecraft appearing in the sky, it is not a question whether aliens exist. Because others are convinced that they have been making their presence known. Perhaps this is another mission Earth voyages in the modern world, to once again, extract earth's gold minerals. What is patently revealing is that the Bible book of Genesis creation narrative is not a myth; meaning that it is, however, ancillary to the true story of the Bible that dovetails nicely with Anunnaki and Enki's mission earth voyage as an ancient astronaut hypothesis is real.

It's important to know that humankind is due to the decision of the Anunnaki to allow Enki to fashion His archetypal hybrid homo sapiens species of the Adam (Man) as the archetypal *Anunnaki-African* crossbreed. The prototype hybrid was created as a servile primitive worker of the God's. This work was the Anunnaki Royal Prince Enki, the god who manipulated biological DNA genetic codes successfully fashioned in His own likeness! Primitive workers, Enki, fashioned them to perform the dangerous work needed to extract gold from inside of the dangerous African gold mines in the southeastern region of the Great country of Zimbabwe, Africa. An ancestry thread is linked back to the god Enki. African goddesses are the nexus of the alien god Enki's bloodline explains the meaning of the phrase regarding: "god's chosen peoples," which is inextricably tied to the extraterrestrial alien Enki's crew: "Those who from the Heaven came"! God's image and likeness—an assertion predicated and in accord with the primordial mitochondrial DNA African black mother bloodline, is derived from the Anunnaki Royal Prince, Enki/EA.

You see, Enki was the firstborn son of Anu, Lord and Supreme Sky God, King of extraterrestrial alien beings called themselves the Anunnaki. Curiously, what did our ancestors witness hovering in the skies? Now ask yourself this question: did a UFO space-traveling race of ancient alien astronauts from Heaven—the planet Nibiru (Planet-X)? Seriously, did the indigenous primitive tribal people. This was a moment when the ancient Sumerians people of Mesopotamia had witnessed Anunnaki's alien beings land a large bell shaped, bright and shiny UFO coming down from Heaven to the earth?

Enki was the Elohim creator of the Old Testament Bible Genesis narrative tale. Royal Prince Enki, son of the Anunnaki supreme God of Heaven, Lord Anu, was Enki's Father. God of mischief, water, science, magic was the chief medical doctor of biological, genetic science field of DNA manipulation.

Enki's genealogy team combined their effort with Enki's leadership successfully fused Enki's *Anunnaki Y-chromosome* and mixed it with the indigenous African hominid female black mother was the Genesis which created the cult of the Black mother goddess figure. Europeans worshiped an emphasis on Jesus Christ with fervor with reverence for the *eponymous* "*Black Madonna,*" and the "*Black Virgin*" cults of Egyptian sun God veneration of Ra was worked from the original African-Egyptians Kemet Osiris and Isis son Horus.

We see the correlation between the venerated African Egyptian religion cult of Osiris, Isis, and their son, the falcon god Horus. This transliteration was a translation adopted into the Western world. Still, the reverence and worship were charged into the image of the white Virgin Mother of Mary, son of Jesus Christ, New Testament. The western transliteration theology inculcated as their Savior emerged in the zodiac age of Pisces. A rise in the power and control of church and state was elevated into prominence by the Romans Emperors. Thus establishing the Holy Roman Catholic religious teachings of Jesus Christ emerged.

A New age World of Christian Religion Faith Took Hold

And out of the religious theology of the Eastern Orthodox Christianity several *scions* of the Romans Catholic faith, including the Protestantism reformation fellowship of the the gospel teachings of blind faith religious was the invention of the western world

THE MIND,BODY, SPIRIT,ANDSTORYTELLING

transformation from spirituality became the modern Christian gospel of the Trinitarian faith in Christ Jesus Europeans transported the religious teachings of the New Testament Bible. It Marked this new age beginning of the Christian religion dogma and creeds and sacred doctrine deemed to be the words of the god who resides in Heaven is illustrative of a widespread whitewashing and denigration of black Kemetism. the Christian's religious philosophy had supplanted. Now let's continue to delve deep into the transformational rise of the new age world of religious paradigm of a captivating slight of the ruler's misdirection.

The new world order of Europeans' global power of the empire, which introduced a spurious blind faith, holy devotion through the holy mother Mary, western worshiping of the original Black Egyptian God cult of Isis, Osiris, and their immaculately conceived son, the Falcon god *Horus*.

Our African Unconsciousness, which was the Black Origins of the African Psycho-spiritual science of the naturalist Mysticism (pg. 70). This is in terms of this connection, the same applies to the Osiris and Isis had a tremendous influence. Egyptians-Kemetic spiritual science. The Bible makes it clear that spiritual science of esoteric wisdom principles of modern philosophy, has been flipped to the Greeks of Western Europe.

There are lots of clear and well qualified examples of hijacking of the Hamitic people identity of African, Kemetic-Egyptian and Nubians presence that was *conterminous* with black characters. Western Europeans denigrated and plagiarized their wit deeds were not mentioned in the gospels of the New Testament Christianity; and the canon law of a New precept as a Holy Trinity doctrine vistages of white Jesus Christ established by the Catholic Church gospel. If you will, please harken back to the aforementioned Anunnaki alien Gods Enki. Anunnaki was a brilliant genetic biological scientist and Nibiru's Chief medical doctors edited and manipulated the genetic DNA codes of an indigenous African female DNA genetic code, which was fused with Enki's own Anunnaki DNA with this African *Australopithecus afarensis* female's mitochondrial DNA chromosome genes. It was mixed in a hard-baked sterile clay petri dish to become fertilized. Those fertilized embryos, Enki's team would place them inside the female Anunnaki birth mother's womb she carry to term and gave birth to Adam.

This means that the creation was associated with Enki and his biogenetic team members finally fashioned the first Adam as a crossbred prototype Homo sapien-sapien upon the earth. This is the meaning of the Genesis narrative tale account of the biblical story about God's creation Myth.

And African is the territorial tribal region of the ancient Hamite lands of the Nubian ancestral Cushite peoples of Enki's bloodline and the roots amidst the creation of Adam and Eve, of the Bible garden in the African lands known as the Eden. According to the storyline of the Old Testament Hebrew and Greek version Septuagint Bible, this fits into the Bible Genesis Chapter 1. This speculation seemingly demystifies the historical biblical story's misleading truthiness. However; the ancient astronaut theory is a speculative assertion, it can demystify the Bible Genesis narrative tale with a different perspective with respect to this conjecture. That is essentially a primordial historical biblical codex, and the concealed legacy of the Alien god's presence from the Anunnaki alien planet Nibiru/Heaven. Accept this hypothesis means to acknowledge that we are the children of the Bible's creator God, Enki. Yeah! If we interpolate anecdotal evidence, revelations of material nature are essential to disentangle from, ostensibly, the inculcated consciousness of misdirection of deception.

This was a zeel fed by the inclination towards the blind faith religion impetuous! Of course, it is my salient point: discussion of the discovery I defended here with conviction. The theology is a coalescence of various ecclesiastical religious teachings of this mystical God of Heaven. Somehow I think that they should be revealing that the discovery of lost ancient cuneiform clay tablets gives you significant weight and the credibility to posit the notion of an ancient astronaut's theorists hypothesis. Notwithstanding the juxtaposition to the Anunnaki Sumerian Old Testament Genesis Bible, the original Genesis narrative tale corresponds to the archeologist and anthropologist scientist research discovery.

THE MIND, BODY, SPIRIT, AND STORYTELLING

This book is a biblical fiction that encapsulates many research archeologists are published authors. Their informative books include subject matter consistent with the author, Zecharia Sitchin's writings that put forth the Anunnaki alien gods' contributions. The emphasis put the focus of my thoughts convergence, conflating the ancient astronauts theorists' hypothesis that scythe with alien extraterrestrial alien gods and the modern UFO phenomenon fits nicely with the premise of my controversial exegesis.

A different perspective of the biblical Genesis narrative tale. I interpolate the Anunnaki ancient astronauts, as the extraterrestrial alien gods who came down from their own Planet-X the Heavenly planet Nibiru. The distant home is far away, from which the space-traveling ancient astronauts descended from a higher constellation orbital plane. As I acknowledge, it is consistent with the gog of the biblical genesis, saying that in six days God created the earth; which is largely consistent with Enki's claim that He built, the first city-state settled on the earth surface in Mesopotamia circa 450,000 long years ago before the Bible story of Noah's flood event. Yeah they were the first custodial Anunnaki, they were the primordial titular, man-like, god figures which spearheaded our holy Bible religious history of their machinations, of their good or mendacious deeds committed actions and significant contributions. To their so-called deity, the believers praised their personal god whom he worshiped.

Whereas the Bible story is pervasive truthiness, devoid of important specificity and anecdotal evidence. Truth is everlasting standard that is stronger than the conveyance of paucity that unfolds in fairy tale version of the event of the Anunnaki descent into the ancient land of Sumer, Mesopotamia circa 5000-3000 BCE; Egypt 3100-30 BCE; Elam 2700-1539 BCE; Indus Valley, 2600-1900 BCE; and Phoenicia, 1550-300 BCE. Each of these places. I could see myself; a soulful being looking around, admiring the fidelity this unfamiliar. Epoch and aware of the chronicles of the Holy Old Testament biblical versions of the past ions of past remembrances. The Hebrew and the Greek Septuagint Bibles, beginning with Chapter 1. Anyone who is still mentally tapped without discernment to understand has probably come to reconcile your *own spiritual consciousness biases.*

You steadfastly cling to the lies of the deceivers being; meaning all of the lies that have been expressed a stereotype about the negroes that says: The Hamite race's ancestors added nothing to the advancing African civilization. Well then, might I say: this attitude just might best be advised from this toxicity by becoming a prize of the plethora of subject matter books that fill the shelves of public museums and many colleges and universities library bookshelves. It's quite easy to select from a plethora of available information regarding the subject matter books available for your erudition and knowledge about the Anunnaki Sumerian god Enki.

His contributions, no doubt influence, is the nexus of the truth that is coming into the light revealing facts. So let's be clear by raising our consciousness to a higher level to learn about the underlying motivations for the Anunnaki's identity, meaning interpretation of about what is behind the words written the Old Testament Bible Genesis narrative tale we put focus on historical fact regarding "those who came" from the Heaven who came fits nicely with the scenario that is a Bible Genesis narrative that has been hidden. critical evidence that depicts a stolen historical scene of Anunnaki alien ancient astronauts presence and Enki purpose which was to mine the mineral gold of Africa. Notwithstanding the references to the African female cult of Osiris and the Mother Goddess Isis of the Kemet spiritual science principles of the ancient temples of the original mystery schools of Africa. Indigenous Female's African mitochondrial DNA genetic code fusion with the Royal bloodline and its ties to an alien Nibiru/planet-X, Anunnaki aliens god Enki spurred a new hybrid African royal Hamite human species fashioned in the image and likeness of the Anunnaki extraterrestrial foreign god of our African Ancestors.

We should not overlook the initial presence of the Anunnaki alien as the god we trust as the Royal Elite Prince Enki. Whereof I contend he is the titular god's personage. But as to the truth many people will simply follow whatever brand of organized religion that most pleases their conscience. Which we know as the Bible is not the full development of our spiritual storied beginning, is a paucity that is woefully condensed biblical storytelling. And it is a misdirection that is not only incomplete but, also intentionally a false transliterated by religious perveyerinto to a spector like god of mystery: "Those who from Heavens came"! To be clear, the question is why Hebrews, Greeks, andfable? Whereas, I posit the critical Old Testament holy Bible Genesis narrative story was sanitized.

Anunnaki's identity, I presuppose, is best understood by comprehending the underlying meanings behind these admonitions: make no graven image of the gods. Could this be why the high priest has completely culled the Anunnaki extraterrestrial aliens' titular gods' physical identity and their activities from the Sumerian Bible? Which they wittingly created a convoluted Bible, consisting of the cherry picked version, culled from the ancient Anunnaki Astronauts Sumerian Bible manuscript codexes.

With conscious bias many ancient religious teachings were excluded in order to present only the specificity and anecdotal details fosters a misdirection away from the true identity and story of the Anunnaki extraterrestrial alien, Enki had scribes copied into the original historical manuscript. Neither His visage nor the alien *Nomen* cultivated in the storyline revealed in the Chronicles about the Anunnaki beings who were the custodian God from the planet Nibiru. Might this have been by mood of an advanced flying UFO spacecraft that facilitated the vanguard Earth Mission voyage!

Does it not seem pretty curious and suspicious that they would leave out these speculative intriguing details from the Hebrew and the Greeks Septuagint versions of the Holy Old Testament Bible Genesis narrative.

Have you asked yourself that salient question yet? You should if you have not done so! Simply put, my friends: Why on earth would those purveyors of organized religion omit this most relevant anecdotal evidence? Perhaps eclectic ancient manuscript codex was plagiarized in order to publish a condensed holy book of the transformation, which was the impetus for the New biblical story to underwrite the Christian gospel religious teachings manipulation of the prayerful bon hommes of the planet Earth.

My friends, I know, I know that this is a dodgy subject matter. Is it possible that I am straightforward and spot-on? This book is about a rather controversial hypothesis as an explanation. In this excursive manuscript collection, I postulate this exegesis as literary fictionalization. Much of what is written about in these many pages, I have to credit the kudos to all of the information written by published authors for my emotional indulgence as a writer. The important takeaway is that knowledge of things that occurred as timeline historical events represent the pieces of the global civilization in distance transformation. The aim here is to introduce some very compelling ideas to bring some logical reasoning to some intriguing insightful assumptions for the erudition of knowledge with mental focus and clarity of thought. Nevertheless I respect that it is going to be off-putting to some religious people of the blind faith theology.

But of course, there are many other views and opinions that have been argued and debated by scholars and theologians; the Ancient Astronauts theory perspective is not settled. Is it not true that we all have some levels of unconscious bias against this information that is seemingly rather closely akin to having given in to an entrenched short-sightedness! Well then, my curious friends, here in this book. I hope that you will be the judge, meaning what?

That truth is by way of the knowledge light. The nous is scattered in the achievement of the monumental amount of pages of our ancestors' golden age of history for your erudition. If you are still with me, good. Now are you ready to discover the face of the hidden one; or should I say: the light of the luminous divine nascence which is of the true definition of intelligent knowledge, insight, and spiritual wisdom spiritual science wisdom philosophy, that teaches the understanding about the image and likeness of the Ancient Anunnaki and African–Egyptian (Kemeticism) the asterisk peoples genealogical Mythological tale about the all too familiar biblical troupe. I interpolate my understanding of the African-Egyptians philosophy of religion as the teaching of the original ancient mystery lodges Kemet traditional spiritual science of sacred wisdom principle teaching has become a dichotomy between the western conventionalization of the eastern religion.

Whilst this is the story of our history. Without ever mentioning anything about decisions concerning the ancient empire rulers who undertook aggressive actions to subjugate other social cultures.

THE MIND, BODY, SPIRIT, AND STORYTELLING

Subsequently reconstructed the African Egyptian Kemetic spiritual science consciousness. Teachings knowledge in the ancient mystery lodges to the occultist initiation into the sacred brotherhood of the traditions that was created by Enki as precursor Anunnaki gods of wisdom, which was imparted to the black descents of the Anunnaki Royalbloodline ties to Enki delineated from Enki's genetic DNA manipulation of the crossbred Adams in His own image/likeness. Accordingly, this Bible story is the driver of our organized religious old genesis narrative: It's fundamental to blind faith Christianity plagiarized transliterated versions of the Bible. Which elevates the amphomorphic white image of God. Which I conflate the precepts as being polarized and twisted away from the out of Africa, the ancient astronaut theorist hypothesis. What does that mean if we come to accept the truth that the Anunnaki aliens who descended to the earth were most likely ancient space faring astronauts, right? Were they an advanced extraterrestrial titular god who came from Heaven [planet Nibiru]?!

If that is the question, then might we speculate as to authenticity to raise the arguments as an essential salient point about whether these beings are titular Gods; saying that these Anunnaki were space faring ancient astronauts. Perhaps organized religion has been the wittingly concealing the real truth about these highly advanced alien beings who arrived on earth 450,000 years ago and established a presence, and built the first city-states of *Eridu* in Sumerian hands of Mesopotamia.

This was the accomplishments of the creator god Enki, which is curiously missing from the Old Testament holy book of Genesis. Meaning that they possessed the infinity and knowledge light waves energy force of one all pervading luminous divine spirit. But they were not the actual Infinite Creator of *Shetuat Neter*.

The longevity and knowledge and contributions, indeed, was akin to the persona of an *amphomorphic* god figure, but these alien beings were not the true God of material creation. According to the definition of the luminous divine spiritual insight consciousness awareness and clarity of my endowment of god's gift of sagaciousness.

Some folks are anesthetized by their lack of knowledge and have been wittingly seduced by the indoctrinating into a well-intentioned religious fellowship of the faithful whose fears have been compelled to pray and look for their salvation in the sky.

To learning/teaching of truthiness and the creation narrative that achieved its supreme by rejecting the spiritual science philosophy of nature according to the Law of One, Infinite Creators sacred wisdom of Kemetic principles. A fulfillment of the spirit with the daily prayer in the practice of the discipline of Yoga meditation is to be humble in acknowledgement and praise given to the highest glory of the universal spirit Noumena of God.

They are unconscious of the body of conscious biased lost spirits that is anesthetized by the powerful and effectiveness of the establishment of constructs and hypotheses that speaks of the ruler's religious sophistry.

In writing this book, various other authors published subject matter material. Archeology and anthropology discovery and findings that help curious-minded people to wake up and imbibed the information that affect our mind/body/spirit complex. A provided an inspirational insight that encourages others to read authors of books. Writers whose works have been an extraordinarily invaluable treasure trove of insightful subject matter books. Lots of information about the historical epochs' contribution of the Anunnaki valuable influence after they came down from Planet-X, or Nibiru will fascinate you!

Might the existence of our past life epoch have given us some sense of clarity? And insight into this retrospective of experiences? I direct your attention to the publication that are the compelling facts references to the archeology and anthropology discovery of compelling information. Much of what is compiled in the volumetric pages of the intellectual research scholars is recorded in the library archived of the past ions is connection to the missing story written about the Anunnaki extraterrestrial alien god's presence biblical is the true history, as it corresponds with the archeology and anthropology findings, which dovetails nicely with the Egyptian interview book: "the Ra, Law of One." A paradigm shift away from the methodological perspective into the unfettered realm of thoughts and the oniric primordial state. Which proposes that logic and reason, equates with what is revealed to us in books *"by Ra, an humble messenger of The Law of One."* Principles of knowledge, which is about humankind learning / teaching others about that comprehensive plethora of sacred spiritual science. It was derived from credible evidence that is remarkable!

In a respectful two way spiritual communication, the interviewer asking questions that was answered by the Egyptian god Ra through a human instrument was the conduit that facilitated this communication. A transformation which took place was recorded during the "Ra Sessions". A decorum from a two way dialogue with the Egyptian Pharaoh, god Ra, "an humble messenger of The Law of One". Such is the paranormal two way interviewer which facilitated this telekinesis through the prone female instrument. The covered naked female body lay still beneath the white sheet in a recombinant stasis which facilitated the communication conveyance as the interviewer transcribed his copious notes of the exchange dialogue with Ra went off without a hitch!

Which the entire conversation can be gleaned from the interviews transcript. It's quite a compelling book posits the anecdotal information which manifests an extraterrestrial alien god who identified himself as Ra prior to answering each specific question—every time! In other words, the associated facts concerning the past, various events, and circumstances are involved in analyzing Biblical history from an evidentiary viewpoint.

The interest is to be of service to other beings. The aim here is to awaken the mind of the misled and the uninformed bons homme, as this is a coming-of-age to the actual story by this very modern reading activity. Substantially speaking on point, I communicate wisdom to be in the service of other people that are my humankind embodiment; my other-selves. To which my purpose is to learn and tell the truth! I have weaved together important information coalescence and dovetails nicely with the specificity and anecdotal details.

Now let's relate to key reference sources to help make sense of the patchwork of written books. Very good collection of books to acquire and describe the facts and evidence to make folks think. To discern the truth from truthiness; with their own mental *conation* develop analytical insight, intelligent logic, and deductive reasoning. Try to ponder whether Anunnaki extraterrestrial alien beings are inextricably the biblical Elohim Gods. It's about the Aliens beings who fashioned their Anunnaki genetic DNA codes imprint/likeness.

Let's face it. Is this not consistent with the knowledge based archived information regarding the historical context of human creation? What I'm talking about is the distortions of spurious Mythos presentations in the Old Testament biblical genesis narrative! No, not at all. Might I direct your focus towards the logical and reasonable insight; discernment of discovery of the missing evidence historically fits nicely with the Old Testament Bible Genesis as a realm of truthiness and unpack and unravel story about the Anunnaki aliens Gods from planet Nibiru.

Dare I venture to tout this genesis story of Enki's as the god personna, as the biblical author of creation? That is to say that it was by his knowledge of the science of biological manipulation that he fashioned the first genetic DNA code, he created humankind as a primitive workforce with his infusion of the alien DNA bloodline children of god. The merit is that modern archeology discovery and findings of biblical history references is *coterminous* with speculative assertions that underlie facts that fits nicely within the anecdotal evidence of Royal Prince Enki? Perhaps, you will come to understand the story is about the ancient astronauts who were the personification of titular Gods from planet Nibiru/Heaven.

The I lightened free thinkers whose fundamental premise remarkably parallels the Old Testament Genesis narrative tale. To be curious is to equate the Anunnaki Ancient theorists hypothesis with the Anunnaki as a perfect fit to those deeds mentioned in the context as an interpolation to the god identity the genesis, Chapter 1. Otherwise it can be considered that the story is incomplete. Is the Bible myth a truthful tale! What is composed in these pages dovetails nicely with the Bible is very convoluted and lacks these assertions. Most importantly, many books comport with the totality of the specificity and anecdotal details of the Anunnaki's God true identity;

THE MIND, BODY, SPIRIT, AND STORYTELLING

"Those who from the Heavens came" is intentionally vague, misleading, Machiavellian, and disingenuous. To say this I must admit that because a schema was seeded by the ruling class to inculcate people's consciousness, as the purveyors of organized Christianity were established to maintain the religious control system by placating people's fear of judgment after death is a troupe of religion's simplicity!

Well, because it was never about the Elohim/Gods who were ancient astronauts who piloted sophisticated bell-shaped UFO spacecraft, right? Yeah, the specificity and anecdotal details. Interpolation of modern discovery has contributed material information from the lost knowledge about our lost historical pages. Now modern archeology and anthropology discovery and findings are helping to provide material information into the ancient world's events that are proving real clarity into the irrefutable evidence.

Which is bolstering the ancient astronauts theorists hypothesis and exposing the falsehoods with the most critical information. With clarity we can rebuff the conscious biases. This is beginning to unpack which is certainly revealing our ancestors. A hidden past that is the connection derived from the Anunnaki alien presence of titular Gods. Why is it that the Bible Genesis narrative makes no mention of the true story about the Enki/Ea the Anunnaki, more specifically… the Old Testament Bible was written as a mystery, which is the missing element of regarding these ancient astronaut contributions of the Anunnaki clans historical corpus of the ancient chronicles of ancient astronauts alien god Enki's landing on the planet Earth 450-thousands of ions ago in that harken back to Sumerian, Mesopotamia. Now then let's begin to unpack and take on this arduous task of trying to fit together the missing piece of lost history, juxtaposition to the chronologically original storied past events. Among the community of people who are interested in the UFOs phenomenon.

Whereof I postulate with a serious fervor, I have read many books about Anunnaki god. But where did These titular gods come from? How and by what conveyance? Curiously, just perhaps, we are certainly weaving into a similar future that parallels the accomplishments in space dovetails nicely with the imagination of the ancient astronaut theorists' who postulate a hypothesis.

Assertion here is my way to concur and convey my own personal thought on this controversial hot button topic: saying that the alien entity known as the Anunnaki and Enki were, ostensibly, the ancient extraterrestrial alien Gods in the Bible as "Those who from the Heavens came"! Yes, you heard that right! Folks reading this book will know that which, I strongly believe, does sound at least somewhat plausible. And of course they, like others, possess the free-will of spiritual consciousness. To reject my revisionist assertion as skeptical, or may rebuff the notion as folly. That's okay Because the Holy Bible Genesis creation narrative has presented this primordial event as a mystical fairy tale that is willingly inculcated on the mind/body/spirit complex of the social culture through religious beliefs continues today, unabated.

At the same time, it is promulgated by and anchored down by modern theology organized misdirected falsehood teachings. And where this is largely truthiness, because it has fueled humanity's curiosity about God, and where, and by what means of a transport conveyance with which God manifested and created the world and humans. Is this where the Anunnaki Enki, UFOs, DNA, connection first became known that humankind are the eponymous children of god's Royal elite; the bloodline of the Anunnaki alien gods, by means of Enki's genetic manipulation, via vitro insemination of an African female's *mitochondrial* DNA code. To undertake this kind of medical procedure, Enki decided to contribute His biological genetic Y-chromosome DNA codes, which he had to manipulate the genes strands in order to limit the capability of the crossbred homosapiens phylogenetic as a new type of human race in His own likeness, or image. Yeah, this is consistent with Bible Genesis, in Chapter 1. Yet there is no mention of the Anunnaki alien gods' missing. With only the abstract words about: a God of Heaven, saying that "those who from Heaven came". It's rather clear that this is not at all descriptive and lacks information that should have painted a more visual context of this monumental event of gods; and meaning Enki. Information that bolsters the underlying premise of the ancient astronauts theorists' controversial hypothesis. And just do others who are seekers of knowledge truth, we believe the biblical version of religionists narrative is incomplete!

Whereof that old familiar prelude to every story, the biblical text doesn't acknowledge these Anunnaki as ancient astronauts alien beings who were likely: "Those who from the Heaven came" in my salient point. The latter came from the alien planet Nibiru. Is this not the most fascinating introduction to the Anunnaki God's intrepid journey of the Earth Mission exploration by a vanguard of ancient alien UFO space faring astronauts. Of course, this is not the Genesis narrative that we have all been taught by organized religion. No! Not at all. But as an adult, you will be eager to grab hold of this persuasively plausible version since the controversial 1947 UFO crash in Roswell, AFB, New Mexico. Interest in flying saucers spurred the increased sales growth of bestselling, releasing the famous book the Chariots of the Gods!

My book presents a synthesis of sources of controversial assertion regarding the modern view of the origin about the ancient astronauts theorists hypothesis. An eclectic collection of information books published about this subject matter by authors like Mr. Erich von Daniken. His book spurred this enthusiasm and curiosity about the extraterrestrial alien beings as the ancient astronauts' original custodians, and humans worshiped these strange beings as their deity! His wild assumptions have inspired a social complex conflation with the mainstream interest in the UFO phenomenon into unconscious bias sophistry.

What if Erich von Daniken is right? Without any conscious biases and reservations, perhaps this explanation is essentially just a segway by spurring others to reexamine the old paradigm. Because what we have been taught like specificity and with anecdotal details in order to push misdirection to be transformed into organized church religion. Widely available in bookstores will fill in the gaps and help put the ancient astronauts theorists hypothesis in perspective for curious neophytes to fathom. Yeah this can be fundamental to your understanding through learning from the pages of volumes of informative subject matter books, stores, and online. Perhaps curiosity will inspire others to learn more as we unravel the twisted truthiness towards a gateway of spiritual understanding that this ancient astronaut's theory, not a conscious bias of hyperbolic troupe. Yes, I know, I know that this sounds incredibly far-fetched! Especially people who have chosen to follow them. People have free-will to reject or to worship whatever god of religious teaching pleases them to fulfill the spirit's unconscious biases. Why not? Have we not been endued with the inherent gift of free will Shakti spiritual consciousness awareness of the Kushite Kemeticism. Individuals living embodiment, with a soul, endowed with our freedom of choice, meaning what? Yeah, it was the new teachings/learning the Christian religion of Protestant and the Catholic, the proclaimed and so-called the creed of the holy Trinity of God (https://asiasociety.org/education/shakti-power-feminine).

The crucifixion of Jesus the Christ by order of the Roman Empire ruler, Ponchos Pilot, has been misled into the web of the Catholic and Protestant Gospel of the New Testament Bible Canon Law emerged into blind faith denominations who promulgated promise of life after death through religions which constitute worshiping by the blood of Jesus the Christ as a personal divine savior in Heaven. The precepts of this Holy Trinitarian theology where we can witness before God for salvation through Jesus the Christ crucifixion! Respectfully, I denounce unconscious bias and allow you to perceive this as the judge! Followers are keeping faith with their ecclesiastical fellowship steeped in the theology of the anamorphic god and religion of blind faith truthiness. On the other hand, shall we say sophistry of misdirection? Yeah it's despite this, falsehood and reworking of the African Egyptian-Kemetic original spiritual science religion. It came to fruition when the Western religious doctrinal teachings were the means of achieving God's salvation.

Church bishops established the New Testament Bible that introduced the Catholic Church Holy Trinity of a personages of God in the anamorphic crucified Jesus the Christ. Jesus Christ was venerated by people. Thus the New World Order transformation into Roman Catholic Church worshiper's of the institutions of blind faith religions. Emergence of church precepts has inspired many to identify with the falsehoods; and it came to fruition from ancient wisdom of the African-Kemetic teachings. Efficaciously and surreptitiously the secret hands of evil powers have long ago been flipped by occultists.

Their purpose is to maintain their manifold scheme of total control of human consciousness awareness. Therein lies the rub: A powerful cabol network of pernicious bankers, is the hidden agenda of secret societies that have inculcated their racial bias, ever since the creation of the Anunnaki, Enki/Ea fashioned his crossbred homosapeins on the planet earth. It took hold beginning with the whitewashing of African images and began the depiction of the tall, long hair, blue eye Northern European image.

Yeah they invented the New Testament Jesus the Christ was a Roman Catholic introduction of the holy Trinitarian as God's light of salvation through the teachings and the blind faith religions worshiped Jesus the Christ as the Christian's doctrine of the divinity Trinity as Father, Son, and Holy Spirit energy. New Testament Christian religionists theology, twisted by the western Catholic Church bishops, took up the task without a license, they plagiarized and reworked into the holy scriptures of gospels, and dismissed the fact that the original sacred Bible learning and teaching a more rational perspective of the biblical genesis narrative tales.

History is written about the original story of the creation myth of the Kemetic philosophy African consciousness awareness of Egyptian-Kamit religion. Yeah it's sacred rites rituals and spiritual symbolism, as they about the Goddess Isis, Her consort the Pharaoh Osiris's *immaculate* birth of the Son Horus, which was synonymous with Mary's immaculate luminous divine birth of the Christ Jesus.

It's the original African, Egyptian-Kemetic Cult religion of the spiritual science principles derived from the tale of Isis and Osiris, Europeans twisted into the New Testament Holy Christians embrace of the so-called pagan religion. It was closely akin to, shall we say: a bait and switch from the spiritual science of the East to a Western religion, philosophical teaching and learning about the luminous divine knowledge of the spiritual science of Kemeticism. Transformation was a complete separation and departure from the Old Testament religious focus, delineating this ancestral lineage of African Egyptian-Kemetism which was promulgated as Christianity (https://www.rightamerican-future.com/articles/satanic-rituals-and-child-sacrifice-ex-top-ban).

There was the learning/teachings of the ancient priesthood of the temple God RA attempted to educate the Kemet people the psycho spiritual science teaching in the sacred halls of the initiation through priesthood great temple houses, by the learning and worship of the *Neterue*. Humankind's salvation through the humble and prayerful seated meditation to be in everyday communication with the Infinite Creator through spiritual science religions. For many years we have recognized this dichotomy between the theology of spirituality and Western European Bishop religions theology. For many years we have recognized this dichotomy between the spiritual science and the church religion with its rigged holy doctrine of Jesus Christ as savior as the theology of Trinitarianism derived from the original African Egyptian-Kemetic teachings of spiritual science teaching/learning of the sacred philosophical wisdom life-guiding principles of the pervading energy. The universal infinite, intelligent creative that imbued Adam (Adona) with his DNA essence.

This sagaciousness awakens in the conscious mind of the thinkers and the neophytes who have emerged in search of the truth that is being revealed. Well-read folks who have acquired enlightenment via a seeker's knowledge. Seekers of wisdom as a discipline of spiritual learning/teaching of the Egyptian God Ra's principles of the spiritual science philosophical harmonic cosmic balance. This fundamental principle of the great natural acknowledgement—to love your neighbors as your other selves with empire and compassion; to live and experience the universal oneness in conjugation and endued with the divine all unity as a living separation from the intelligent energy of the infinite Creative spirit that animates life below by the luminous divine crystal light force energy that is the ubiquitous bringer of esoteric occultists transportine gateway into the crossing of cycles.

The way to luminous divine salvation of the one Intelligent Infinite creative energy, the soulful spirit of science teachings of the *Shetaut Neter spirituality philosophy*. According to the Infinite Creator's Law of One; meaning unity of one love of life, light as on an individual's humankind embodiment of mind/body/spirit com-

THE MIND, BODY, SPIRIT, AND STORYTELLING

plex. A collection of optimistic worthy human souls becoming God's blessings of the shall ascend and incarnate into the fourth density of the higher level of spirit's is a sense of conscious awareness.

This moral judgment after death weighted the life measured as good/evil was balanced. An accounting of the service to oneself in service to god demonstrates selflessness in service to humankind. Selfless service as acts of goodwill to other human entities for one's salvation will be caught up into the Heavens by the infinite intelligent Creator, Adona.

Understanding the past epoch as a nascent that winds back to 450,000 years ago marks the Anunnaki history. Curiously, do you concur with the Ancient Astronauts hypothesis? So far as you can see, it could stretch the credulity of the imagination. So come on let's think outside of the status quo ante! The ancient alien Gods bloodline ties to the African-Egyptian ancestors of the Royal Prince Enki's DNA. The creation narrative tale is this human, and Anunnaki is a primordial connection with extraterrestrial alien's Gods. Ancient space travelers came down on an Earth Mission to acquire gold. They came from a higher orbit and established civilization in the landscape of Sumerian, Mesopotamia. Enki/Ea's ancient astronaut crew touched down.

To be clear, let's face it. This is the modern consensus view espoused by the neophytes of the Ancient astronauts theorists hypothesis. Which puts forth this controversial assertion as the real truth about the Bible story that began as the historical narrative that was mistranslated into the pervading a misdirection and deception. Which is closely akin to the promogating sophistry which spurred this exegesis of the Hebrew Old Testament Genesis narrative tale. Meaning that the true story is about the Anunnaki ancient alien Gods. And this Priesthood that teaches people to worship upon the altar of falsity.

They were the conveyance of which the esoteric knowledge teaching/learning of the extraterrestrial alien God's Law of one spiritual science wisdom and meditation practice of Kemetism had been means that facilitated principles of enlightenment. Humankind is a separate unit of animated material from the all luminous divine essence of the life/love/light religious philosophy of spiritual science to the ordinary people before Christianity supplanted the ancient mystery religion. This transformative emerging conveyance influenced twisted spiritual paganism teachings that were to appease Christianity's faithful followers.

Have you ever pondered why rulers push the truthiness of omission. Why is there no reference to God's as animated Anunnaki alien beings, their physical presence after they came down on board the large shiny bell-shaped UFO, chariots of the Gods, which was a spacetime of this *anachronistic* history of biblical event's fits nicely with the ancient astronauts theorists hypothesis context?

We can presuppose logic and reason by juxtapositions, of archeology and anthropology discovery. The findings correspond to the ancient astronaut theorists assumption that the UFO phenomenon. It is likely that modern AUV/UFO's have extended ancestral ties to the extraterrestrial Annunaki Olden Times titular gods that the Bible says came from the sky. My friends, religionists will never reconcile this perspective of the Bible, Chapter 1 reference which says that the Anunnaki were: "those who from the Heaven came." fits nicely with the anecdotal evidence, posturing this modern conjecture, juxtaposing the Holy Old Testament Bible against the ancient astronaut theorists' hypothesis. To the Anunnaki race, the man-like titular god personification of the Anunnaki race elite Royal Prince Enki/Ea came from the planet Nibiru. He was the Old Testament God of the book of the Bible, Chapter 1, Genesis narrative.

The vainglorious Heavenly Royal Prince who was Commander of the Earth Mission voyage of that event when God/Enki/Ea and His fifty man crew of ancient astronauts were vanguards of who came down upon the earth plane. What the Holy Bible has concealed it alludes to is not explicitly said written in chapter 1 is quite cryptic and generic.

God is the creator—not Enki/Ea as the *nominon* creator who most likely has been the god "who was from the heavens came" to the earth as an ancient astronaut; yes? Which is according to the original ancient historical narrative, the information that was lost due to translations.

THE MIND, BODY, SPIRIT, AND STORYTELLING

Now try to apprehend that alluded to in chapter 1 is a reference to *Eridu*, which was the first city-state settlement that was created in ancient Sumer Mesopotamia (Iraq). Wherein we know that *Eridu is* translated to mean: "home in the far away."

A recovery of the outdated information is being rediscovered by modern archeology, and anthropology discovery from Iraq site excavation depicts the development of the god Enki's genetic engineering methodology of the Bible *Enum Eilish Seven Cuneiform Tablets* of the creation story about Adam and Eve. Enki/Ea had by manipulation edited lines of an African female homo Erectus biological DNA genetic codes, contributed with Enki/Ea's own Y-chromosome was African mitochondrial DNA code. African Homo erectus.

She was the indigenous female species that had contributed the biological *Mitochondrial* genetic DNA chromosome, was edited by the Royal Prince Enki/Ea genetic editing facilitated by the fashion successfully created the crossbred prototype "primitive worker, He named Adapa." Though surreptitiously He imbued Eve with the tree of knowledge of consciousness awareness of their nakedness; but denied them the possession of the gods longevity with the providence of a 120 year lifespan and was expected to live for a limited number of counting earth years. He accomplished this through artificially in vitro insemination, which requires a process of combining male and female biological genetic constituents of the reproductive system as male/female DNA samples. The *eponymous Enuma Elish,* "Seven Cuneiform clay tablets lend credence to the Old Testament Genesis narrative Chapter 1, is the story about Enki / God used sterile clay petri dish to fertilize DNA Chromosome to fashion the Adamu/Adam in His Anunnaki image and likeness! God created/fashioned the race of human primitive workers!

In other words, in *vitro fertilization* of the genetic life essence provided by indigenous *Anthropithecus* African female's mitochondrial DNA was fused with Enki's own Anunnaki DNA codes. To this salient point God created the hybrid homosapien sapiens crossroads Anunnaki/African bloodline of the gods. Incontestable as that is the biological editing process of this DNA genetic research genetic manipulation of DNA genetic codes, which Enki fused his Anunnaki alien imprint of the Gods, on earth, was successful as the creation event by which the Homo sapien Sapien races proliferated upon the illusory temporal reality of the African consciousness. Which is according to the book of Genesis. My friends, herein lie the rub: this modern speculation undergirds this exegesis as my salient point to raise a divisive argument/debate. Interestingly enough, despite modern archeology and anthropology, some people who will read this book are going to agree with my view, and I expect it to be the case here.

Nevertheless, we see that, on the other hand, some folks will have a different view with a visceral reaction to this *cpus exegesis*. At the same time, those with insight will be more open-minded. Seekers of wisdom, knowledge, and spaciousness. They will be inspired to do their research to discover spiritual science wisdom subjectively. Christianity and spirituality philosophical precepts diverge. The Roman Empire, under Constantine I, separated from and embraced Christianity and created falsehoods. This certainly is true, at least as I believe it should be.

Mainly it's about the learning/teachings of the spiritual science of the metaphysical Intelligent Infinity as our actual Infinite Creator, Adona/God! Or they are, conversely, having a belief in Christianity. Might we say that this is spurious exploitation of those people who are woefully ignorant or uninformed? The truth is that our free will, consciousness, and perception are the spirit that causes our actions. We can assume that people are inclined to always believe in whatever religion concur with their cognitive bias precepts about defining God. The universal metaphysical nature of the luminous divine Intelligent Infinite Creative lifeforms energy. The most personal spirit is the devotee's guiding spirit energy. Thus we are blessed with Free Will. There was this Kushite-Kemetic African consciousness awareness which exists together as both in the enfolded human beings with the inherent ability of the capability of exercising the *moral balance,* which speaks to an individual's actions with logic and reasoning as good or evil deeds. To apprehend the knowledge of the extraterrestrial Anunnaki clan's commander was the royal prince Enki spurred

THE MIND, BODY, SPIRIT, AND STORYTELLING

by the divinations of African-Egyptian learning and teaching sacred spiritual science principles of wisdom insight.

To this you should know the true origin of yourself as a mind/body/spirit complex of the personhood of the storyline and the turn towards spiritual science of the Law of One love. My thoughts align with spiritual science as god's ubiquitously pervading consciousness awareness harmonic energy vibrations as the intelligent meditation in scent with one infinite Creator god, Adona! We are individuals separate units of universal streaming intelligence. Human beings endowed by Creative Infinity imbues all with the life force metaphysical harmonic pervasive presence of energy waves vibrations that are the luminous divine living spirits of God. The existing presence that permeates through psyho-spiritualand and astrophysical the dynamic field of the space and time continuum. It's the god spirit within us that causes our human decisions and our actions; which is responsible for all deeds of good or evil is derived from our individual free will of consciousness awareness. Being aware of the material and the ephemeral evidence, my perception of a compendium of the present and for the remembrance of the treasure of the intrinsic part of the mysterious spiritual mind, faded me into the akashic realm field of surreality.

Like space traveling astronauts the truth can echo and awaken the imagination into the excursive realm of nirvana of anachronistic places, my spirit travels in a space-time dream state without sounds. The steady coursing sensation is the soothed ceaseless rain I can hear clearly in the *forenoon* pelting the ground before the sun at dawn appears and bright stars have disappeared. Slowly disappearing as the present space-time continuum emerged with the coming forth as the sunshine rises to bring forth the light source of the vaingloriously luminous divine providence.

Unknowingly the illusory spirit energy causes all actions on rhythm cycles to manifest pervasive expressions in the natural evolution through the millennia of the future present and past life of the time-space continuum. This is according to the biblical history which writes about Kushites deeds and their teachings of the sacred mystery schools teachings of their magi priesthood spiritual temples of learning. Africa was where the mystery schools of spiritual science religions principles were taught sacred wisdom and meditation.

Was this the twisting and turning away from light energy transformation of the empirical world's new age epochal reality? Peregrinations on a winding pathway to illumination and the gateway into the blessed one who shall be the spiritual living fruit of the souls of the human races who are devotees caught up when the harvested spirit essence of the revelation time revealing the initiates unity with the luminous infinite Intelligent entities.

First is to learn/teach the ways of goodness over evil; and being in the service to the self; and in service to other-selves which is according to the Law of One. The philosophy according to the Infinite Creator of mind/body/spirit complex. The intelligent infinity of the creative consciousness awareness of the space-time continuum; and, polarized delusional fictionalization evocative speculation for the erudition of one's knowledge. Albeit a topic that aims to be controversial to wake folks up! Seriously, search for information that dovetails nicely with the modern ancient astronaut's hypothesis.

It's your understanding that transcends the *noumenal* of the hidden, meaning exactly what tha? That only those who possessed the curious-minded neophytes will wittingly seek the nous! So might our purpose in life be to be in assistance to self, learn/teach or minister wisdom to the entities that are our other-selves?

To meditate and ruminate upon pure thoughts that bring solace and minister the love of the spiritual science and philosophy of luminous divine sacred wisdom in life and love for the One Infinite Creator's Law of One love. Yeah, I accept that the Anunnaki were ancient alien astronauts. Yeah, an advanced extraterrestrial space faring alien man-like Gods who possessed sophisticated advanced knowledge of science and technology facilitated the voyage of: "Those who from the Heaven came!" Ostensibly, Anunnaki alien beings would have been the first custodian Gods given that the Bible tells us that God came down from Heaven—meaning what?

He descended from the home planet, they called Nibiru. What this tells me is that an advanced alien race arrived and established civilization among indigenous tribal cultures as the gift of the gods after Nibiru ancient astronauts landed down on the planet earth. The mission purpose was to operate a large scale gold mining excavation production operation in Africa's South Eastern region of great Zimbabwe (Zachariah Sitchin).

The Royal Prince Enki was the tspear's tip, being very instrumental in the initiatives that conferred God's knowledge of sacred writing and spiritual rites of the rituals Hetaught to the priesthood.

The enlightened initiates a secret class of tribal African-Egyptians (Kemet) bons hommes into the order of the anonymously disparage Serpent Brotherhood philosophy Initiation into the elite. Was this the actual genetic royal bloodline tied to aliens Anunnaki DNA blueprint of the homosapien sapiens fashioned race of African Hamite hybrid descendants, Hebrew/Greeks Septuagint Bible book of Genesis narrative tale?

God Enki was the founder/creator of the serpent seed the Father, Homosapien-sapiens, extraterrestrial alien bloodline ancestors of the Anunnaki secret initiation into the Egyptian serpent brotherhood. Original custodians of the social, cultural tradition of the Royal Order of wisdom teach/learn spiritual science. Intelligent insights taught from the Bible Hamite/Cushite African people narrative tale events about the African-Egyptians (Khemit) *Shetaut Neter*. The Western Roman Empire Christian religion superseded spiritual science and deemed it to be the pagan cultist religion.

Therein lies the rub: the aggressive whitewashing of the black Kemetism spiritualism social culture's influence and historical impact was vicariously attacked and systematically disparaged, vilified, and intentionally hidden away, and their physical identity a ribbed from the the pages of the Hebrew and Greek Septuagint, Old Testament Bible books scriptures. What is missing is what alludes to the Anunnaki alien gods on the Earth 75,000 years ago—is the real nascent of Anunnaki: "Those who from the Heavens came"!

Were the Anunnaki corporal beings or were they *amorphous* extraterrestrial ancient astronaut space-travelers? In form, manlike beings. But certainly not the *One Infinite Creator of this universal cosmology of metapsychics*. Whereas at this point, what I will concede to agree on is to acknowledge that these extraterrestrial Anunnaki alien beings were from an intelligent race of space-traveling astronauts from a higher level of density orbital of existence. Sophisticated advanced race in intelligence of mind/body/spirit complex.

Those who came down to the earth came aboard a UFO spacecraft for the specific purpose of establishing a large scale mass production gold mining operation. There was this imperative to produce steady amounts of gold deposits from the planet earth that would be transported to their home planet Nibiru in the monatomic particles of the asset mineral was critical to facilitate the necessary disbursements to help patch up the tear's in Nibiru's cosmic atmosphere. One can see the parallel as the earth atmosphere is experiencing the same issue as the Anunnaki aliens Gods who descended from Nibiru's Earth Mission voyage.

Whereof space exploration Heaven. I could say more on this, my friends, but I think you get the salient point of which you can digest and reach beyond mere conjectures. To unpack and evaluate the practical assumption about what the Bible narrative is telling you about this is truthiness. It's about this primordial common parent stock derived of the African spiritual science principles of wisdom, which is derived from the original ties to the Anunnaki alien gods Enki's DNA Y-chromosome code, and humans as the connection that was derived from a black hominid—the which is the so-called mitochondrial DNA code and the black mother goddess of humanity, ostensibly, links back to Eve! Surely, my friends, you catch my point! The titular god Enki safely landed in a large, shiny, bell-shaped spacecraft in ancient Sumer, Mesopotamia, of the interior Earth plane (Goddess/Ki) terrain of the modern-day country of Iraq!

Yeah it was a maverick idea embraced by prominent authors Zachariah Sitchin and others, whose hypothesis suggests that the biblical genesis narrative is not a Mythological tale. Written the Anunnaki original Sumerian Bible manuscript codexes we are likely to learn about events transcripts of the events that we have never been told are about the deeds of the Anunnaki's astronauts appointment of the of knowledge Priesthood mystery schools as the temples of learning and teaching knowledge of wisdom and yoga meditation and the Indian spiritual had recorded and maintained archived material that

THE MIND, BODY, SPIRIT, AND STORYTELLING

was available to the Hebrew Abraham from the ancient city-state of Ur, Sumer, Mesopotamia.

Abraham from his home city of Ur, traveled 700 miles to the borders of present-day Iraq, another 700 miles into Syria, another 800 down to Egypt by the inland road, and then back into the biblical land of what is known then called the land of Israel in Canaan. When Abraham strode upon the stage at Ur, he was by Semitic reckoning already a man of 75 years old. Is it possible Abraham studied from the original sacred Anunnaki Sumerian Bible?

If true, might he have internationally omitted certain fundamental information by excluding the Anunnaki gods when he traveled from the city-state of Ur in Mesopotamia? Could this have been manipulated by the Hebrew priesthood into the biblical church religions of today. Which, to a great extent would have been the embellishment and the truthiness took hold.

What we do know is that religious teachings have many dance around by nature's shifting breeze of divergent theological, Mythological religions that preach God created Heaven and Earth as humankind precepts. At the same time, my views concur with wise Scholars, particularly Michael Telling's book, as the Annunaki were responsible for introducing the concepts of money, finance, and debt to human societies. Author David Icke believes that the Anunnaki were titular (imposter) custodial Gods who today continue to be active within human affairs tied to organized religion. Secret societies initiated members maintain this as the proxy sock puppets, operating in plain sight from their appointments to exclusive seats of high profile power positions. Like the black and white Knights on a chess game board, as key players, they have the imprimaturs to use the means of their position to influence to impact the global narrative; in other words, the banking and financial wealth and economic system. One's which is endemic to the major sizable multinational business corporations operating behind the curtain—away from the public scrutiny. These entities, as humanity, manipulate political, corporate, and financial power empirically worldwide. He explains that these beings exploit humans and feed off collective fear. Mr. Icke calls for a disconnect from mainstream media's Orwellian entertainment that triggers fear and anxiety of being in a hypnotic state with a panic attack. Of which, as you can agree on the other hand, respectable academic research scientists find the articles written by the academic scholars who publish their literary works. Scholarly research has been peer reviewed and published by academic professionals who are prolific authors in the academic disciplines of history, science, theology, archeology, and anthropology. Where there is an irrefutable perfect fit is the Bible narrative tale juxtapositioned to natural history and the pervading psychology inculcation of religion.

There is a preponderance of irrefutable historical evidence corresponds with the maverick ideas that say the Old Testament Bible God of Genesis is the ancient history of the Anunnaki extraterrestrial alien God: 'those who from the heavens came to earth," or the Anunnaki.'! Yeah, I am saying this is most likely not conjectured! Yet this salient point is: Are you getting any closer to discovering the whole truth? Is this revelation simply more than we can fathom! No, my friend, this is not a foolish notion of some fantastic speculative assertion. It's undoubtedly not hyperbolic poppycock—devoid of archeological and anthropological discoveries, modern-day scientists' findings dovetails nicely with the biblical genesis narrative tale. Which Is why the ancient astronauts theorists hypothesis is neither a simple hypothesis that can be refuted, nor quickly rebuffed, rejected, discredited outright with flimsy logic and reason that are untenable faulty arguments.

These are folks who are blind faithful zealots who are not inclined towards free thinking with intelligent use of logic and reason, to presuppose the Anunnaki were not extraterrestrial beings. Anyone who would argue otherwise, and meaning that they lack creditable logic and reason, without a foundation or any intelligently justified standing.

Those who have no logic nor reason to refute empirical evidence that is deemed hyperbolic sophomoric poppycock! I now refer you to Arthur Gregg Prescott, M.S., founder, and editor of In5D and the Body/Mind/Spirit complex. The Anunnaki Gods' from planet Nibiru were original custodians of planet earth; and these earth settlers had established a God-like presence on earth 450,000s of years

THE MIND, BODY, SPIRIT, AND STORYTELLING

ago. Anunnaki and the achievements we acknowledge their deeds in totality, and the actual presence and contributions to humankind as the true face of the biblical god's identity, which has been concealed as the ancient scribes into the Sumerian Bible book, the nascence of Anunnaki alien gods presence in the Sumerian, Mesopotamia Biblical genesis codex.

This was the ancient Sumerian text from which was the main source of Hebrew and the Greek Septuagint chroniclers. Selectively did not copy any information about the Anunnaki aliens; and instead, they created the mystique. By inculcating the generic term "gods" pertaining to the Old Testament Bible. The book of Genesis narrative is incomplete, it was the Annunaki settlement and presence, curiously lifted out. Why is this missing? Does anyone disagree with the specificity and anecdotal details of the Old Testament Holy Bible book of Genesis narrative dovetails nicely with the findings of archeological anthropological discovery information? Olden Times scribes of ancient demigods. The King's deeds were carefully recorded in cuneiform writing on soft clay tablets, which was hard baked we're archived; and today, the recovery of the Assyrian King's Enuma Elish has revealed a window into the ancient history that was recovered from the cuneiform clay tablets unearthed, revealing details of the Anunnaki and the stupendous anecdotal evidence which the ancient scribes transcribed the Royal Prince Enki's Creation!

God's deeds of the human creation story corroborated the extraterrestrial alien presence as being those whose ancestor of the olden times Anunnaki ancient astronauts crew of fifty aliens: "Those of the elite Royal Anunnaki Bloodline of the titular god. Ostensibly, they were the immortal alien gods who descended from the heavenly constellation and built city-states in the ancient biblical land of Sumer, Mesopotamia.

The latter came down and landed their shiny bell-shaped spaceship descending onto the earth plane of the southern region of Sumerian, Mesopotamia. Enki, the Royale Prince of the elite Anunnaki vanguard alien astronauts, initial fifty man space flight crew Earth Mission voyage.

Yeah, let's assume here that this is the truth about what had happened one the earth hundreds of thousands of years ago in the land called Sumer; the modern day country of Iraq. This is the target landing zone where the first extraterrestrial alien God's UFO spacecraft successfully came onto the earth surface and landed in ancient Sumer, Mesopotamia. Commander Prince Enki's space faring adventure had a mission purpose to locate and establish a productive gold mining production operation and extract the Earth's material gold resources, began cir. 455,000 BC (https://www.afrikaiswoke.com/anunnaki-in-world-civilization-history/).

This is according to author Zecharia Sitchin. These are excellent books and a must-read for anyone curious about Nibiru's Royal Family of King Anu and His sons Enki. He was the flight commander of the initial Earth Mission voyage. His firstborn was Enlil, for whom Lord King Anu gave him the lofty title: Lord of the Earth Command with authority over all of the Anunnaki alien activities of clans stationed on earth.

They are central characters in machinations behind the Old Testament Holy Bible books of the Genesis narrative tale. The salient question is why is the Bible curiously propagating an incomplete history of a sophomoric version that is devoid of specificity and anecdotal detail. It is simply opting for a childlike fairy tale snapshot as a retrospective insight to understand the underlying story of the creation narrative tale. An assumption that reconciles truthiness with archeological site discoveries and findings has revealed monumental missing pieces that give a more excellent glimpse into corresponding elements of clarity and perspective on biblical history.

Why is it that the Bible version is an obfuscation? They have concealed the real story, which is closely akin to the obfuscation about modern-day UFO sightings in our sky, about an astronaut crew creating the first colony settlement on the earth in six days! The Bible doesn't write about these intrepid Anunnaki Attributions: deeds owing to: "Those who were from the Heavens came" is according to what was written about in the Holy Old Testament Bible omitted this in favor of a mythical god from the sky. Wherein the conjecture I posits is to simply given some context and character to the word

THE MIND, BODY, SPIRIT, AND STORYTELLING

god, which I presuppose was the Anunnaki alien Royal Prince Enki. The god figure that was the commander of the first skilled fifty man ancient astronaut crew who descended from to earth voyage flight, consisting of a crew of architects, builders, scientists, and medical doctors were the vanguard of those Anunnaki alien gods who came down to become the custodians of planet Earth; as the Chapter 1 alludes to; it was Enki who built the first city-state on the earth, named it Eridu in Sumer, Mesopotamia. The question that remains is whether He could create the earth in six days is hyperbole!

These extraterrestrials founded a settlement colony on Earth. The Bible Genesis says that God, meaning Enki, came down and was a custodian creator god who established civilization in ancient mesothelioma, long before and after the Great Noah's flood event. According to (Teg Gregory, April 17, 2019) saying: "The Sumerian civilization developed in the Persian Gulf, growing to strength at around 4–3,000 B.C. The 'Plane of the Land of Shinar' is the territory which, after 2,000 B.C., became called Babylon. Greeks named this region Mesopotamia (land between the two rivers), most of which lies in the modern state of Iraq (thejackofclubsclub.com).

Yeah, it's a story about the extraterrestrial alien races. And in the southern Africa interior is the ruins of Enki's gold mining production operation of the Anunnaki: "Those who from the Heaven that came" from another planet. They had a mission purpose which was to locate and extract the earth's gold mineral resources and ship the monatomic particles back to their home planet Nibiru; ergo, the nascence of the biblical tale of religions. The Anunnaki alien gods were the titular Gods from another planet. Whereof, Enki, was commander of the ancient astronaut's flight; and to this point: the Old Testament Bible Genesis narrative tale is about the so-called Adam/Eve creation myth. Humankind conscious awareness has the visual perceptions of the external empirical illusory world reality. At least according to what we have read in the Hebrew Bible Holy book of the Genesis narrative. I say you have the concept of free will.

The infinity of the intelligence truth for yourself and to know that God fashioned the human race in His image/likeness. Anunnaki alien gods' presence on earth spurred the storyline delineations as the

Old Testament biblical genesis hubris narrative of the creation Myth that does not fully go into the plausible truth about why humankind's experience in this eternal life is finite; the life force energy is a spirit of the mind and body animation by the living nature. Not the storytelling and worship of anthropomorphic personage of Jesus Christ, as the holy Trinity derived from the Anunnaki, Kemetic-African Egyptian god Ra's, Life/Light/Love trilogy complex. According to the gods Law of Neteru!

This may sound incredible, and it is undeniable because I understand to be the truth about the Sumerian Gods. The chronicles of the ancient Sumerian Kings list, contains the names of the rulers of the gods' bloodline ties to Anunnaki extraterrestrial ancient astronauts who came down from Heaven; they were the gods who the indigenous tribes of earth worshiped as their king and preferred lord god. I can imagine the awe of the manlike titular Anunnaki alien Gods arriving aboard a giant alien spacecraft, which is referred to as a UFO, as a *Vehmanna*. They have also been described as flying Chariots of the extraterrestrial alien Gods. These space vehicles were piloted by the elite Anunnaki alien gods aboard a UFO spacecraft whose descent facilitated their Earth Mission voyage from Nibiru. After landing on the Earth interior plane, the Enki crew set themselves to create a gold mining production operation in the Persian Gulf of the Sumer, Mesopotamians. Enki's and his intrepid fifty-man ancient astronaut crew successfully built the first settlement city-state called Eridu (https://www.bizsiziz.com/the-history-of-the-anunnaki-the-14-tablets-of-enki/).

According to the Old Testament, the Holy Bible was created there in six days—rested on the seventh day. Anunnaki alien god/Enki's vanguard fiftyman ancient astronaut crew successfully built and established the first City-State settlement in the interior region of Sumer, Mesopotamia, located in the modern-day country of Iraq. Later a decision to relocate their mining production operation, by Supreme King Anu, who directed His Son Enki to relocate to the southern region of African lands of Zimbabwe where gold deposits were abundant.

THE MIND, BODY, SPIRIT, AND STORYTELLING

Enki's Father granted the Hamite African territorial lands of planet Earth to Noah's ancestors. These descendants establish their identity as the great African Kingdom of ancient *Kushsite people,* Egyptian (Khemet) black dynasties of the Nile Valley civilizations. Which included the new Indus Valley Asian territory. The nascence of Bible genesis eponymous Hebrew Old Testament Bible vague Chapter 1 Genesis narrative tale.

To a great extent, misdirections that are closely akin to a bit of religion's spurious truthiness that has been shrouding the absolute truth to propagate their twisted version of the original identity of the ancient astronauts as extraterrestrial aliens with ties to the Anunnaki Royal Prince, Enki!

The son of Planet Nibiruan Supreme Lord/God Anu's, a genetic blueprint of the Anunnaki royal bloodline is shared with the alien Creator God Enki / Ea God's family tree! And meaning what? One Love in unity with the light, learning/teaching the fundamental principles of truth-telling!

Answers that demystify are neither this biblical narrative tale nor a Myth and reconcile with the speculative ancient astronaut theorist hypothesis. My exegesis concurs with the ancient astronaut hypothesis. Spiritual science is juxtaposed to the Hebrew and Greek Septuagint Old Testament Bible Christian religion. A premise asserts that the Anunnaki were the old time's extraterrestrial alien Gods of the Holy Bible: "Those who from the Heavens came—as it is most likely to be the way it happened 450,000s of years ago!

I don't even know how a logical and reasonable thinker can take issue or disagree with the speculation. And quite frankly, let me honestly say, I don't know! Nevertheless, it is merely a semi-fictional account that seeks to tease perspicacious minds to salient questions with contemplation see the perspective that will likely inspire some. While I suspect that at this point, my speculation is going to inflame others, and that means folks who are incredulity skeptical about this.

Do they not realize that without a scintilla of doubt: I concur with the ancient astronaut's theorists' hypothesis, on the evidence revealed through the modern historical archeology, anthropology, and Bible records of anecdotal dovetails, which fits nicely into the Old Testament Bible Genesis narrative tale.

What can be said about this to-days, has connection with and access to modern leviathan of archeology and anthropology discovery of relevant information posited by scholars as research scientists, who corroborate knowledge findings point to the Anunnaki presence, and although it occurred in history, it is a truth that is still hidden, behind the well established religious institutions paradigm that sustain its mystique. Which is the best well kept that can shape one's view of god as the human apprehension of the ephemeral state of the mind/body/spirit complex with understanding of our reality as the transformation cycle of life to death human consciousness. Accordingly the real reams of information is not suppressed; it's widely available for the erudition of knowledge. Anyone seeking knowledge shall ultimately a plethora of subject matter books;, this interesting question remains: Is there life on other planets with sophisticated advanced races of alien beings arriving from deep space, cosmic constellational houses were the planetary bodies, and billions of bright shining imperishable stars galaxies resting against the darkest of the cosmos subtle harmonic rhythm space-time cycle.

Yes! And that is why I have the will and opinion to apply logic and reason to comprehend the premise postulated by the Ancient Astronaut's Theorist Hypothesis. Well then, my friends, there's no better empirical evidence than *irrefragable biblical* history! Ostensibly, the big reveal of archeological and anthropology discovery information. Current evidence dovetails with the correlation with the bible history and the ancient astronaut's theorist's premise. Not only is this visceral assumption speculative, but it's realistically probable and very likely that Annunaki Gods, "Those from Heavens who came," were from the highly advanced extraterrestrial intelligent alien race! Accordingly, it is safe to say that the Old Testament Bible book of the Genesis narrative tale is implicit. Whereas, it seems that many aspects of 'In the beginning scene in Chapter 1. I surmise that there is this intentional effort to keep critical important anecdotal details as misstatements and omissions hidden. Whereas their have been some extraordinary researchers whtoday who are desperate to discover that information exists which defuses the genuine evidence behind the mystery. Anunnaki God, Royal Prince Enki's story fits the mysterious modern UFO phenomenon, which conflates the ancient chariots of the gods with the contemporary ancient astronaut in the same context of the ancient astronaut's theorists hypothesis. Meaning that an advanced alien spacecraft landing in Sumerian, Mesopotamia, just might be the fact missing from the book of Genesis, Chapter 1.

However, with our inherent intelligence, logic, and reason it appears to me that the biblical Genesis makes more sense, unless we are honest and dare to interpolate the specifier and anecdotal details which acknowledge the Anunnaki As the god as Enki and the idea of the Ancient Astronauts theorists controversial hypothesis fits into the Old Testament Bible Genesis narrative with which corresponds to the eponymous Genesis creator God Enki. Whereas the Enki's event involving Anunnaki Mission Earth voyage must be promulgated as the true primordial Gods mentioned Bible Hebrew and Greek Septuagint holy religious book of Genesis Narrative tale. This of course is a modern assertion which says that the religion's proponents of an organized status quo theology have intentionally avicated. and obfuscated the delineation of a well entrenchment falsehood deception in order to implement misdirection of misleading poppycock.

Modern skeptics dismiss this in favor of the incredibly incredulous ancient astronaut theorists' hypothesis because religious truthiness rejects the research archeological, anthropology, and Bible historical discovery and excavation of the empirical evidence! I concur with the ancient astronaut theorists, who speculate that the ancient astronaut beings who came and were those who walked upon the Earth were extraterrestrial aliens known as the Anunnaki. And whose home planet was Nibiru or (Planet X) Heaven.

Then why is this curiously missing, whereas the Bible Genesis doesn't mention conveyance of the god's aerial UFO Chariot of the Gods dissent via spaceflight? But why is it missing? I don't know about you, but, I'm inclined to concur that Anunnaki is an ancient astronaut god who landed on earth in the Sumerian, Mesopotamia landscape of modern-day country Iraq. It is worth noting that the old astronaut hypothesis is changing the conversation about contemporary UFOs sightings in our skies.

Perhaps UFOs piloted the Anunnaki titular gods' ancestors in the earth's air space. Then, might the God Enki and his fifty-man crew of skilled architects and scientists build the first settlement city of Eridu. According to the Bible Genesis, Chapter 1, God's narrative proclaims Enki/God came down. In six days, the existence of everything above and upon the Earth plane, the Bible says He God created our physical empirical world of illusory temporal, temporal reality! I aim to interpolate the luminous divine creation of the universal cosmic order of the metaphysical and physical material reality derived and imbued by ineffable One Intelligent Infinite Energy! To this wild assumption, please permit me to elucidate that archeology and anthropology modern discovery spurred this exegesis is materially and substantially consistent with the eponymous Old Testament Genesis. Which is not hyperbole or sophomoric truthiness. Why? Because fundamentally speaking, the perception of my understanding of modern archeology, anthropology, and the physical Bible history. The confluence of important research information has dovetailed nicely with insight, logic, and reason have, ostensibly, a validation of the Genesis narrative is a strong argument for ancient astronauts' theorist hypothesis! We need to carefully consider this to be a rational and plausible analysis or an explanation of the Bible; Genesis lends genuine credibility to the evidence.

Which identifies Enki's first-hand account of the creation procedure applied to fashion Adam/man and the female Eve. With recent modern archeology, the discovery of the event is inscribed onto the "Seven Cuneiform Clay Tablets of the Creation, narrative!" This is why much can be gleaned from what seems rather apparent that the Anunnaki were extraterrestrial alien Gods.

We should know that it was Enki who was the UFO flight commander of his fifty-man ancient astronaut crew that had safely come down from Heaven on a shiny bell-shaped UFO spacecraft. Why might this piece of Genesis, Chapter 1 curiously missing or hidden!

Might it not be true that the Anunnaki Royal Prince Enlil, the Lord of the earth command, was angry that His brother Enki had

THE MIND, BODY, SPIRIT, AND STORYTELLING

broken Anunnaki's law that forbade Adams and Eves to acquire the alien god's knowledge and longevity! So might perhaps this be true about the distortion of true depictions of these Anunnaki, titular Gods who came down from the a higher plane of planet Nibiru? That they were the original custodians Gods who colonized the fertile fruits of the Earth's plane.

Whereas the Bible has referred to as the land called Sumer, Mesopotamia the race that built city-state and civilization after they safely landed on the Earth among the Sumerian Black Heads *Dravidians* like people who worship Enki as their Infinite Creators! Was this anamorphic? Royal great prince, the God mentioned in the Old Testament biblical genesis story, was an Anunnaki God? Ostensibly to recognize the identity of astronauts who arrived and landed in the olden time's Earth Mission expedition voyage to earth.

We must ascribe to Enki's and other Old Testament, recognize contributions made by the same Anunnaki space-traveling ancient astronauts. This god's presence among the indigenous earthman roots is derived from the ancient Chronicles pages of the gods original Anunnaki, Sumerian Bible, Genesis narrative fits the profile. That a space-traveling extraterrestrial alien god Enki descended from Heaven.

The alien astronaut vanguard crew landed in Sumer as the flight commander of an ancient astronaut Gods arrived on a gold mining production operation set up in the Persian Gulf! These beings were titular Gods and, as mentioned in the opening narrative, translations turned into Bible's book of Genesis, Myth of Chapter 1.

Or is this a farfetched and outrageous bit of hyperbole nonesense about the Anunnaki Enki, King Anu, two Sons Enki and Enlil. Full of adventures with misdeeds as evidence of inevitable conflicts and enter action between Anunnaki siblings that played out as a biblical narrative tale.

Let's say that upon a time in the beginning of the Anunnaki, Enki was God! The Flight Commander from planet Nibiru, and it was Enki who was the leader at the tip of the spear of the vanguard of the Earth Mission. Yeah, Enki was the titular God: "those who from the Heavens came"; were an ancient astronaut who was the flight commander of the first group of 50 intrepid ancient space-travelers who in six days! This audacious fifty men ancient astronaut crew built and established a settlement colony on the vast interior Earth plane in the southeastern land of Sumer, Mesopotamia, located near the pure fresh waters of the earth.

Which is congruent with what corresponds with Genesis narrative tale is irrefutable and par for the course. The Anunnaki family Royal Elites deities had their bloody wars as Kings with legendary exploits, earning them fanciful titles that identify their particular City-State and political power as a symbolic mark of the evil Beast. Global indigenous peoples misled; and so we worship the anamorphic manifestations of titular gods.

Modern theologians quote Bible history as a metaphor as God's own words. Accordingly, throughout humanity over the eons the scribes of the rulers have recorded their deeds; evidence of their actions and views proclaimed they were justified by their personal Gods had inspired them.

Their actions fulfilled their responsibility in a literal, physical, earthly sense in the past, present or future. They ruled over as God/King of their conquered city-state kingdom territorial lands. Bible Genesis narrative tale is the translation and twisted falsehood of omissions of the Anunnaki: "Those who from the Heaven came down from a higher plane landed on planet earth were extraterrestrial ancient alien astronaut who came down from the outlying mysterious Annunaki from Nibiru/Heaven [Planet-X].

Yeah, now let's digest that fantastic account with logic and reason. I presuppose most people are unfamiliar with the Book of Enoch, which alludes to and delineates the Anunnaki alien God's genealogical. The bloodline of the identity type of the extraterrestrial alien Anunnaki: "Those who were from Heaven came."

Yes, my friends, we face a shocking truth about Enki/Ea, the extraterrestrial alien God figure? Does His persona conflate the biblical genesis narrative story. If you accept the notion that, think for a moment, what are the chances that He manipulates beings with His own Anunnaki alien bloodline created the crossbreed Homosapeins His own likeness/image; as obsequious servile labor.

THE MIND, BODY, SPIRIT, AND STORYTELLING

His purpose was to fashion primitive workers to do the heavy backbreaking work to extract the mineral gold from inside of the great country of Zimbabwe, Africa, African gold mining operations. And to achieve this, Enki successfully genetically engineered the Nibiru god's bloodline to the Anunnaki's Royal Family Tree using a fusion of his own biological, genetic material code with an indigenous African female homo Earectus DNA code Enki/Ea edited and fused with his owe Anunnaki image/likeness; he successfully created crossbreed Adam (meaning man); the Homosapien Sapien earthman with the Anunnaki likeness/imprint. The Bible never identified Enki as the God of wisdom, saying God/Enki had created the first Adam/Man in His image/likeness.

The inference is that they are intentionally deceptive—but why not omit the specificity and anecdotal details about the motive and process that reveal what we know about has been hidden. Well then, my friends, might we all pause and ponder the Anunnaki account in the context of God's creation of human Adam and Eve. Enki was the creator god of the Homosapien-sapiens crossbreed by genetic fusion of the Anunnaki Royal Prince Enki DNA, which would enable Him as the father who manipulation of Anunnaki alien biological DNA genetic code with mitochondrial genetic DNA code, fashioned modern human hybrid as a race of primitive workers while living in the Earth plane of Africa! Yeah! These alien astronauts came from Planet-X, Nibiru. Those who came to the sky established colonies and built city-states settlements, religion, education, agriculture, arts and writing, and other significant elements of civilized social administrative governments. Their contributions marked the advancement of the ancient civil society's cultural development and evolution that sprang from the Anunnaki Enki. Which is about the Bible Genesis creation account written as Adapa and Eve narrative; essentially, it was the epicenter of humankind according to the Bible, and it is the place with ties out of the African-Egyptian Kemeticism psycho-spiritual consciousness emerged. The Bible is identified as Hamit peoples' land, which the Greeks derived from a translation called Africa. It was located between the Tigris and Euphrates Rivers. The original inhabitants worshiped the Anunnaki and their demigod ancestors through a hybrid bloodline of the Gods (Book by Nick Redfern). It's as much about the initial connection to the titular God of the planet-X, Heaven Bible.

The known physical history of the Ancient Astronaut UFO, the human race, was created by Nibiruan, the Royal great prince Enki [The God of Creation]. In the presence of the Anunnaki's astronaut alien God's mission, initial aerial Earth voyage gold mining production operation in southern East Africa, Great Zimbabwe.

Enki set up this deep gold mining production operation. A fact that corresponds with the specificity and anecdotal details of the ancient astronaut theorists' chronicles about this predicate that harkens back to the Anunnaki, Enki's Earth Mission voyage. Which are the critical missing elements of the eponymous Holy Bible Old Testament, Chapter 1. My explanation raises a fundamental salient question as to why this information is curiously missing from the narrative of the KJV, Hebrew, and the Greek's Orthodox, Septuagint Old Testament Holy Bible book of Genesis narrative elucidating the Bible story in chapter 1. The ancient astronaut theorists' premise that level of credibility corresponds with an Anunnaki presence, that advanced planet Earth civilization for the bons hommes human experience. Meaning that according to Rudolf Steiner, who says: that "*Lucifer* incarnated in a human body during the third millennium before Christ, and that *Ahriman* will likewise incarnate in the third millennium after Christ, we are currently entering [http://www.doyletics.com/arj/landarvw.htm]. How can we be better prepared for the coming events of this New Testament Bible Book of the Revelations that is predicted to come to earth (Ahriman); which will be praised by the people as the return of the one known as Jesus the Christ; or gods.

We must balance both the attributes of Ahriman and the attributes of Lucifer with Christ as our guide and companion. The Influences of Lucifer & Ahriman is the evil spirit in Early Iranian Religion, Zoroastrianism, Zurvanism, Lord of Darkness, and Chaos, and the natural source of human confusion, disappointment, and strife. Feb 10, 202, only that the God of the Bible says: "those who from the heavens came to earth," or the Anunnaki." And in the beginning, before the earth was in form or before fresh reflective waters were separated from the ferment above the surface of the landscape. Well then, might I presuppose this image of some physical, bell-shaped, bright shiny UFO spacecraft might have come down and was hovering over and looking at the massive flood waters that covered all the surface of the planet Earth?

Might an intelligent thinking person consider the certain speculative aspects, surmise that perhaps there is more than a curious passing through that modern humans would use knowledge to eventually evolve into a race of man-like gods that rebuild their tower of Babel, to reach out into deep orbit in search of a creator?

An advanced ancient space-traveling astronaut, titular God' was the creator of humans, Adapa/Adam and Eve's narrative tale of a garden was this idyllic landscape in Africa East of the Eden. The Bible Genesis illustrates this eponymous contiguous duality cycleas good over evil is of the free consciousness awareness.

Human beings are not subordinate in their churlish behavior. Yeah it's the example of Adam/Eve disobeying Anunnaki Enlil, the appointed God of the Earth Command. So as the narrative tale unfolds into the extraterrestrial alien Royal Prince, Enlil's law, his brother Enki is the creator God denigrated by Enlil using a *derogatory reference* to a Serpent for giving the Adam and Eve consciousness awareness—to know of their form being naked. Enlil considered this criminal act of defiance against Anunnaki law. You see, Enki was tasked with developing a prototype servile race of "obedient primitive workers who would be tasked to perform the grueling gregarious heavy labor as the replacements for the Anunnaki's *Igigi* workers.

Ergo, the harsh working conditions had spurred the *Igigi* workers to staged a labor revolt. They were disgruntled over their work conditions inside of the deep African gold mining production operations located in the Southeastern regions of great Zimbabwe, Africa's.; expelled Enki's bloodline Adam/Adapa and (Tiahma) Eve from the garden land called Eden. Enlil is the God who is equated in the biblical story as a serpent.

Why was this action considered a blatant transgression, a violation of Enlil's law that forbade humans from acquiring the Anunnaki alien beings sacred knowledge and longevity proscribed. What this narrative illustrates is that there were some unintended consequences which came to fruition, surreptitiously by Enki's DNA genetic manipulation. The bottom line was that Enlil was angry to discover that primitive workers had been consciously aware of their naked body! This is simply to knowledge of themselves.

The means of having free will to be more than the Anunnaki's naked servile primitive worker slaves, which ment they could one day be as the alien gods who came to earth from from Heaven! You see, Enlil's word was the law on planet Earth.

Anunnaki we're not of the one all-true vainglorious Infinite Creator God is the *Nebebigjur*. While on the other hand manlike titular gods from Heaven fashioned a crossbred Adam were space-traveling alien astronauts.

Their earth mission voyage was about to unfold after their UFO spaceship completed a successful, safe landing onto the Sumerian plane of ancient Mesopotamia. In these pages of this explanation, allow the waves of your thoughts to harken back to the fantastic remarkable space-traveling ancient astronauts presence in fits the ancient biblical empirical world of Anunnaki extraterrestrial aliens landed in Sumerian Mesopotamia.

Well then now, in these pages is my semi-fictionalized look back into this remarkable and shockingly speculative assertion of this quite controversial opinion about the Biblical Old Testament book of Genesis narrative tale written to be a perception of the Anunnaki storied account: "Those who were from the Heavens came"! Hereto the assertion posits a premise that the Old Testament Bible narrative tales are very cautious.

Whereas religion says nothing about Enki, the ancient astronaut titular creator god of the Old Testament holy book of the Genesis narrative story about the Anunnaki, references to, "Those who from Hewere came". It is the nascent biblical creator god from another celestial planet called Nibiru. What is written about this in the Bible book chapter 1, is the eponymous genesis narrative. The juxtaposition can conflate this with the ancient astronaut theorists hypothesized. Saying that the Anunnaki alien God identity in this context is

THE MIND, BODY, SPIRIT, AND STORYTELLING

consciously omitted from the Hebrew and Greek Septuagint version of the Holy Bible book of Genesis narrative tale about "Those who from Heaven came "!

Anunnaki were a sophisticated space-traveling race of intelligent beings from their home planet they called Nibiru. The anamorphic man-like titular Gods who were: "Those from the Heaven came" landed down upon the earth's interior plane and walked among the indigenous people who were perceived as God! Although astronauts' primary mission was to extract the gold from the earth. And Enki was the creator God who taught humans with forbidden knowledge!

The intrepid Anunnaki titular God Enki is the God mentioned in Genesis chapter 1. Look! Let's be clear about the story of the biblical tale and the Anunnaki alien Gods who descended from Heaven is a seamless fit within the Biblical nascence!

According to the Anunnaki Gods Enki, as the persona of the biblical Genesis narrative tale. To a great extent here is my salient point: alien astronauts were: 'Those who were from Heaven came were the extraterrestrial beings who landed their aerial spacecraft on the interior earth plane of Sumer, Mesopotamia.

A perilous space voyage traveling across the dark cosmos in search of gold for their home planet, Nebiru. King Anu, the Supreme Lord and sky god of the elite Ruling house of Anu, was a clan of extraterrestrial aliens from a higher level of orbiting the cosmic constellation of distant Galaxies. He, in consultation with other elite ruling council members, occurred in their discussion of the critical agenda issue and had great consternation and concern about the need for significant sources of gold resources that was required to patch up tears and the leaks in Nibiru from dying atmosphere.

All of the members of the elite Anunnaki ruling council board members unanimously voted to assemble the earth mission voyage for gold as the critical solution to patch up the increasingly large holds and tears was causing Nibiru to lose the planet's atmosphere. The King decided to send his eldest son Enki (Ea), who became the first ancient astronaut commander, to land a fifty-man crew on the earth's surface.

Yeah! An alien piloted UFO spacecraft was successful in manipulating the rocket ship into and through the constellation celestial bodies and landed on the Sumerian interior plane of southern Mesopotamia. The Old Testament Bible Genesis story of god from the plane of the Heavens marks this auspicious nascent of the religious narrative tale that hides this truth! That alien gods who came to mind for gold also brought civilization to Earth bons hommes. Yet, this is curiously, never taught! Why? Because this is seemingly the real true story has not and will not ever be permitted to be taught as truth over falsehoods. Today there is a body of evidence available in books. For the curious folks who seek to explore further. You should consider reading widely to broaden up your understanding in the context of the Bible religious teaching to obtain credible information that will reveals information that con allow you to expand your knowledge to go beyond the constriction and rigid ecclesiastical paradigm views as a dichotomy between psychospiritual and psycho religion; the consciousness awareness precepts, in respect to prayerful devotion to God.

Try to read with newfound unbiased predisposition, and you will appreciate having greater clarity and the insight to analyze assertions about the ancient astronaut's theorists' hypothesis. Much of which dovetails nicely with the Old Testament Bible Genesis narrative tale. What is was the historical connection between the Anunnaki aliens and the ancient astronaut's hypothesis. What is written in the pages of numerous subject matter books. All of which provided valuable information as a source reference material was instrumental in my understanding, context development of this explanation of deeds and contribution to civilization. Much of which pertains to African-Egyptian Khemit spiritual science of meditation acquires further development of the self spiritual complex. Which is using learning and teaching others the pathways towards the wisdom principles of religious philosophy Law of One; to learn to service the self, to be of service to our other-self entities of the human family to live/love/life. And love is the purpose of individuals that is a common medium of mind/body/spirit's complex as a separate unit from the luminous divine Infinite Creator of universal existence. Such was the arrogance of the western Europeans demonstrated a visceral lust for wealth by imperial power; they combined with Catholic religious beliefs that supplanted the Anunnaki Enki's African Egyptian Kemetism principles of spiritual science religions of Serpent Temple of the secret societies learning and teachings of the occult religion of the Anunnaki, who seeded the Royal Kingship practice on earth by the Nibiru Sky god Anu (An), which to impart the wisdom philosophy of spiritual science of *shakti* of Heaven. European subjugation paved the way for their ability to maintain total control of the unsuspecting poor ignorant folks' consciousness.

The beginning of the new twisted empirical world transformation from the African-Egyptian influence of the Anunnaki bloodline of the God/Pharaohs of African people's Kingdoms. Evolution into the modern face of truthiness, abusive, the false teaching that coincident with the jumpstart the new rotation cycle in accordance with the zodiac new time period; and this was during the age of Pisces was ushered in the time/space was the ruthless transformation that took place under the twisted version of the Christians.

Religious doctrinal canons ecclesiastical trinity which propagated a of many churches denomination and Jewish synagogues to perpetuate various misleading religious education pervades falsehoods. Let's take a close analysis as we look at the Anunnaki in the context of the beginning of the Holy Bible story, according to speculation. This book is to make sense of this nascence of an Hebrew, Greek Septuagint Bible's selective and subjective versions of the God into the Christians' religions, meaning exactly what? Anunnaki alien God's presence on the as the Bible Genesis creator got Enki/Ea as the who landed a spacecraft down to earth in ancient Mesopotamia. Clearly, he had also visited both the Mesoamerica and African-Egyptian lands. Clearly a story written about the Anunnaki extraterrestrial alien beings Earth Mission voyage historical event, as it seems inextricably linked to the arrival of the Enki's landing his UFO spacecraft in the plane of Sumer, Mesopotamia; and subsequently the astronauts crew of aliens inevitable contribution to the indigenous cultures of Africa, India, and Mesoamercan continent long before Christopher Columbus voyage hyperbolic discovery of America.

We must ask ourselves if this is attributable to the Anunnaki Gods contributions, as merely to these beings as the original custodians—as being consistent with the ancient astronaut's theorist hypothesis story of the Anunnaki alien Gods influences on the primordial indigenous people's mind/body/spirit social complex.

Which is inarguably the smoking gun that underlies the significant ings of ancient information, which corroborates with the Bible history of material is an acknowledges that the postulated ancient astronauts theorists account concur, that extraterrestrials alien Gods influenced has ties to the humans creation story were connected to the the narrative of the Bible writes about God: "Those who from the Heavens came."

It was the Anunnaki extraterrestrial alien beings who referred to the planet Nibiru as their home in Heaven. Zachariah Sitchin and some modern astronomers have referred to it as the Earth's missing tenth Planet-X, it's not some fanciful far fetched notion. No, not at all!

However; it's very significant in my observation and eruption of facts. These archeological findings are rather remarkable—if in fact it is true it is rather remarkable that modern astronomy discovery focuses the spotlight towards this incredible story of the Bible history; and, identify the gods from heaven as an historical biblical event. It is important to note this as we try to deconstruct lies and establish truth over truthiness. might it also threaten to deconstruct the status quo blind faith Christian doctrine, cannon, and religious creed?

My hypothesis is available in most major retail book sellers or for convenient purchase order from home at online merchants. A plethora of important facts and relevant anecdotal information is revealed to intelligent thinkers with clear logic and reasonable perception of things that recognize transcendent god as nature.

Whereas most of the biblical and historical evidence subjugation reveals the shocking. Material transliterated into other languages has often been taken out of the spiritual science context. Their aim was to disparage the mystery wisdom.

THE MIND, BODY, SPIRIT, AND STORYTELLING

Enki was the god of initiator into the Serpent Brotherhood, custodian of the African-Egyptian Kemeticism science wisdom, cultural religious tradition of teaching/learning the spiritual science philosophy inherent in what was taught by the Anunnaki Royal Prince Enki/Ra.

Whereas the original account according to the archived records as the Anunnaki-Sumerian Bible Genesis which is speculative fiction claims that the original history that is missing the original Anunnaki presence is stored in halls of ancient astronaut hypothesis that an extraterrestrial aliens race. Might it have been confirmed that the Anunnaki were the alien Gods who descended from Heaven?

These beings are connected to the Hermetic corpus of scientific and esoteric Anunnaki, Sumerian Holy Bible Genesis narrative story! Became the Western/Eastern cultures subsequent misstatements and omissions, loosely written translations. Western Europeans arose from their usurpations, by means of hijacking and the whitewashing out of Africa's Egyptian-Kemetism sacred principles of the ancient mystery schools of the African EgyptianKemet spiritual sciences of priesthood wisdom of the Anunnaki alien of planet Nibiru. As the original custodian of the earth plane, might it be plausible to speculate, with some certainty, that these extraterrestrials decimated their knowledge by teaching it to the indigenous African-Egyptians/Kemet tribal clans? African *Hamite peoples* genealogy has roots conned with the branches of Anunnaki alien gods and lords of planet Nibiru's Anunnaki house of the Royal Prince Enki's descendant is tied to the biblical extraterrestrial blood genetic roots—derived from the Enki/Ea; He was the creator God of Adam/Eve, and His halfbrother Enlil was the of the Hebrews Yahweh, theSupreme Lord of the Earth Command. Original anecdotal details account recorded in the Anunnaki's Sumerian Bible manuscript text was the source material from which the Old Testament Bible, Genesis, translations misrepresented the identity of the Anunnaki, the mystery god of Heaven.

So we should pay attention to the true truth and try to make sense of Anunnaki ancient astronauts theorists hypothesis as it conflates to the chronicles of the biblical genealogy, which relates and connects with Enki and the biblical narrative tale of humankind creation. He was the eponymous god who edited the biological DNA of the indigenous African female tribal with Anunnaki DNA and fashioned a genetic bloodline African connection with the Egyptian *Khemit* peoples of the African territorial lands written about in the Bible Old Testament book of Genesis narrative tale. The word Khemit refers to the African-Egyptians, which means black people of who are those mentioned in the Old Testament Bible Genesis book has delineated a clear distinWhich, shall we say, and agree corresponds to a particular identity type; tribal peoples predominantly from territories located in Africa were inextricably consistent with the Anunnaki alien presence in Africa.

This was the indigenous black lands of African people. Anu in an effort to petition the geological region of the earth, the Supreme God the planet Nibiru, the most high Lord of Heaven, and those of his kingdom included the Anunnaki who were aboard the UFO spacecraft that landed and built the first civilizations on earth down to earth. As the Supreme Sky God, he sent his son Enki to rule all African lands to Abraham's grandson Ham (Hamites). Mesopotamian ancient Sumerian landscape he granted to the Middle East (Sumerian, Mesopotamia) territory, Nibiruan Supreme Sky God Anu bequeathed to His son, Royal Prince, Enlil as territory to rule. King Anu, the Lord god of the Heaven and the Earth, came down to the earth surface to settle all of the perpetual sibling rivalries over territorial claims that caused conflicts to erupted between the Anunnaki clans living on planet Earth—before the great eponymous Noah's Flood of the Old Testament transliteration of the Hebrew and Greek Orthodox Biblical narrative tales! This was regional territory Lord Anu bequeathed to His son, the Royal great prince Enki, after Anunnaki titular Gods had returned to the earth after the tremendous retelling of the eponymous Noah's flood had receded.

This is the nascence of Anunnaki Sumerian Bible original Genesis narrative. This was the land of the blacks bequeathed to Enki/Ea descendants. His fusion of His Anunnaki DNA fused with an African indigionist female mitochondrial DNA was fused genetic bloodline of Adapa (Adam and Eve), ancestry bloodline, derived from the Royal great prince's Enki's monumental creation narrative

THE MIND, BODY, SPIRIT, AND STORYTELLING

event seems entirely plausible to proponents of the ancient astronaut's theorists hypothesis.

Christian faith does not incline to that the Holy Old Testament Bible Genesis narrative tales have its development to a historical account about Africa ancient history, of which the Bible is derived from which chapter 1 is the Bible Genesis narrative tale. However, was that intentionally, it would seem to be rather curiously been minimized to mitigate and downplay out of Africa the theoretical paradigm.

We know that conscious bias is the reason for the whitewashing of black people's identity in biblical narratives not given acknowledgment to black African consciousness through the indigenous females. The ties that are inextricably linked to Enki, an extraterrestrial alien creator god of wisdom and magic who contributed to building the earth station settlement of Eridu in six days! Which is more closely akin to the true history; not hyperbolical after His fifty man ancient astronauts crew descended from a higher cosmic constellation of planetary orbit of Nibiru. The Supreme God of the Planet Nibiru resides in the distant deep space higher orbital plane. Royal Prince Enki genetic engineering of His crossbred human species on the earth landscape had become quite a troubling affair; meaning that Enki deed spurred the ancestral bloodline ties which is inextricably connected to Enki and His own father in Heaven. The Supreme Lord of the sky/Heaven was the Anunnaki King Anu! The Royal elite Anunnaki is the supreme king of Heaven.

The father sent Enki on the Earth Mission voyage to verify whether the mineral gold deposits were of an abundance of mineral resources to establish a large-scale productive operation on the earth. It was the purpose and explained precisely why there is substancI and these creditable true words: "Those who from the Heavens came" down and colonized the lands of the Earth indigenous bon homies! Are you a victim, if you are willing to believe without doing research; or because you don't concur with this hypothesis? Ancient astronaut's theorist's premise is neither a silly notion nor is it some spurious hyperbolic poppycock! It's the presumption, put forth with logic and reason because it's predicated, according to Biblical and historical the ancient African-Egyptians, learning/teachings of Kemetism. Extraterrestrial Anunnaki aliens taught the natural spiritual science sacred principles of the Gods (Netjer). The Infinite Creator is an essential deity to a Kemetic religious tradition. Enki was the creator God behind the team of alien scientists who worked to unlock the mysteries of the biological DNA genome, and the venerable God to be worshiped by Sumerian and the Egyptians God *Atom Ra* was honored by the people in Heliopolis. He imparted the sacred principles and rituals teaching / learning as sacred rites through forms of the religion's esoteric initiation ceremonies.

These Anunnaki installed on Earth the rules of the Royal Kingship, which they brought from their home planet Nibiru. This is a known physical history of these Anunnaki as the titular gods instructed royal court scribes to enter the affairs of rulers' accomplishments into the daily Hall of records about the *Anunnaki Sumerian Bible*. Which is the understanding of sacred knowledge, that which we know was denigrated, maligned, suppressed by various empirical mighty armies. During its history, Egypt-Kemet was invaded or conquered by several foreign powers, including the *Hyksos*, the *Libyans*, the *Nubians*, *Assyrians*, *Achaemenid Persians*, and the *Macedonians* under the command of Alexander the Great.

Oftentimes this is what has always been said: "To the victors goes the spoils"! To my salient point, this excursive exegesis speculation that fits nicely with the ancient astronaut's theorists premise! The aim here is to interpolate a speculative assertion of the identity associated with the Egyptian-Kemetic roots. Sumerian who called themselves the Black-Heads. The city-state governors and ruling Kings led mighty armies to reveal the Prasanna and countenance of the Gods and their demigods.

They used powerful armies against other city-states and subdued and relegated them to their subordinate status as vassals. Rulers who waged war to accumulate and consolidate their authority resorted to the violent use of wars would eventually be defeated by a new emerging city-state that demonstrated the same behavior, to be defeated was a trend that played out through eons of records of humanity, exemplified by a violence history of cruelty. The impulse of and aims

THE MIND, BODY, SPIRIT, AND STORYTELLING

to cause actions destabilized the order of humanity by utilizing the armed force exemplifying their inspiration. The malicious activities brutal behavior perpetuated by the seat of the power ruling elites inculcated their pervading truthless aggression. Which was without provocation. Kings rule the lands they claimed and defended by means of their own authority; these evil depots lusted for greater material wealth was never satiated by their victory.

Continued their campaign to acquire the treasure's and amassed bountiful amounts of gold, silver, jewelstones, and vast tracts of the landscapes as their conquered possessions. Kings led their well-equipped military armed forces into bloody battles to consolidate their power and control over city-state god/kind's defending military forces. Audacious Warrior King's attacked territorial neighbors with murderous evil intent by violently carrying out massive, armed forces trained campaign with ruthless aggression they killed and conquest in the name of their god of worship and glorified him as thanks for their military victories.

Victory from their campaigns was acknowledged and archived by the scribes, with their accounts proclaiming their overwhelming and undisputed supremacy over enemies sovereign lands, and stolen chattel property. There were many wars fought on earth between different clans of the Anunnaki aliens to seize control of the earth landscape.

They constantly fought each other; and, these wars were also fought by the Anunnaki Olden Times ancient astronauts descendants! They were the mighty men and the fallen angels mentioned in the Old Testament Bible, as described in Genesis 1:26 and Genesis 2:12-10. The information about this derives from the conversation during the council of the Anunnaki. In the beginning of the "word", per the Old Testament Bible note that it was the royal prince Enki who said: "Let us create primitive workers in our image/likeness to perform the heavy work required to mine the earth gold deposits in the Eden (https://www.afrikaiswoke.com/). Their aim was to conquer the regional lands of neighbors' by means of warfare to establish ambitious rule for themselves as the undisputed Kingdoms aimed by violent acts of warfare.

Throughout the eons, they have claimed this bloodshed was carried out in the name of the unmanifested, anamorphic Gods of Heaven. History records reveal the destruction by every means through human warfare. The genesis teaching of the glorification of the ancient astronauts dramatically began with the God manifold creation Myth. With events which is the delineation of deeds that we attribute to the extraterrestrial alien beings known as the Anunnaki's Earth Mission voyage of titular gods from Planet Nibiru. Royal great prince Enki, and His fifty man astronaut crew that came down from Heaven unfolded into the eponymous Old Testament Bible narrative tale of Genesis Chapter 1. Anunnaki alien creator Gods *Enki* and Ninhursag built the first city-state settlement after Enki spaceship came down and landed on the Earth interior plane of ancient Sumer, Mesopotamia. Chapter 1 of the Bible, says: that, in six days, God created this base camp on the earth and called it Eridu, meaning *"Home in the faraway"*. Which is located in the modern-day country of Iraq. According to ("The Adapa legend and the Biblical story (of Adam) there are fundamentally as far apart as *antipodes.*" When the story of *Adapa* was first rediscovered some scholars saw a resemblance with the story of the biblical Adam,[9] in such a connection as Albert Tobias Clay.[11] have rejected this connection; however, potential relationships are still (1981) considered worthy of analysis (Andreasen, Niels-Erik (1981), "Adam and Adapa: Two Anthropological Characters"(PDF), Andrews University Seminary Studies (Autumn 1981), pp. 179–194 Sanders 2017, p. 52) Adapa would have been the adviser of the Mythical first (antediluvian) ruling king of the city state of ancient Eridu. The first king whose name appears on numerous versions of the *Sumerian King List* (SKL). He was succeeded by *Alalngar*... The SKL states that Alulim's name appears on the Sumerian King List (Alalngar) as *Adapa Alulim*. In the context of this exegesis argument that undergirds the presumption of my thoughts that is in accord with the controversial modern ancient astronauts hypothesis. Whereas every assertion made in this book is the fundamental substrate, echo my conjectures.

Others may construe their own views and opinions of my interpolation throughout my personal assertions in these many storied pages. Nonetheless, despite the number of tertiary sources of information, there is the resistance from skeptical folk of different thoughts and feelings about this subject matter. Why would anyone want to suppress, and not seek to flush out the plethora of information that is our enlightenment with various sources of compelling information sources. It is seemingly nothing more, or less *perspicacious*; and just a twisted view towards erudition of knowledge. This means that to fit together some evidence of the discovery. That it is to shine the light of truthiness; that it is so clearly identified as erroneous falsehoods or deceptions. And so much so that I have been compelled to write a semi-fictional tale of a historical event that raises questions about the Bible and the History of Anunnaki. Whereas this heroic history worshipers of God celebrated truthiness, they elevated and glorified their brutal conquests.

What marvelous as well as disgraceful moments that have transpired over the past eons of the historical evolution through the millennia and involution over many epochs. The historical timeline delineated from the Paleolithic nascent is inextricably linked to the Ancient Astronauts' theorists hypothesis.

The Anunnaki were the proclaimed *de facto*, precursors of alien custodial gods of the planet Earth. And as humans, we owe deference to them indeed for inventing the written languages; they also taught humans the art of weapons-making arms for conducting bloody warfare that facilitated and perpetuated conflicts of aggressive behavior between neighbors fighting for over territory that has occurred throughout many years of human existence. We are endowed with the free will of consciousness; I can choose to do either good or evil actions. It's inherent like Homosapien; Sapiens can use knowledge to develop deadly military weapons they put up upon their neighbor's territory claims of sovereign autonomy. These aggressors waged many destructive campaigns of conquest and established a delineation or warfare through the annals of ancient/modern history. There are hundreds of thousands of years of historical evidence of irrefutable past misdeeds that are unforgiven. This was criminal conduct with many examples of ambitious, ruthless, mendacious kings who led their armies on unprovoked brutal and bloody campaigns and carried out the indiscriminate acts of killing the innocent men, women, and children. With impunity they carted off wagons of stolen property, such as farm animals, chatelal and lands, and in chains marched thousands of their people away under the fetters as unwitting human slaves who fates was sealed by the owed their fealty in service to their conquering rulers city-states. Such as it was in the old middle and new millennium was the struggle to gain power and control as alpha kings became dominant imperial kingdoms is notably a common behavior throughout the story of the biblical and human beings history. [https://www.worldhistory.org/eridu/].

Which claimed victory in the name of their chosen deity; with the sinister motivation of greed, many conflicts and wars were fought in the name of their preferred god, whom they trusted would bring them tremendous material wealth and an entire treasury. While sacking and torching religious Temples and *razing* real property to ashes, and brutally raped. Defiled women, appropriated farmers' livestock animals, and captured thousands of human beings. Captured prisoners were unceremoniously put to death. While the army was defeated, its citizens' population had been ingloriously dominated by the victorious warrior Kings who put them under a yoke. Ancient astronauts who were the living player's in the personification of the Anunnaki alien gods; and the story of the Old Testament Bible Genesis Narrative tale.

The ancient history records and the Bible described secession of wars between rival emperors. Kings who waged warfare were bellicose in the aftermath of a bloody conquest, and corrected large commemorative stela for their own self aggrandizement.

Discover the missing pieces of long lost pages, and reinstating the enfoldment of important relevant information to shore up and bolster the scope and perspective of the confused who will read other books about the Babylon, Akkadian, Assyrians, Mede Persians, and the Greek Macedonia wars under Alexander the Great will learn about how they figured prominently in the Bible, with respect to how Kings, and the religious hierarchy and their priesthood line exist in the ascendancy of the conquering Lion of the princely tribe of Judah had fallen captive, yield to the authority of powerful rulers armed forces.

THE MIND, BODY, SPIRIT, AND STORYTELLING

The fate of local vanquished territorial neighbors was crushed then brought under the King's mighty army of conquerors of neighbors. They were fueled by the actions of their schemed and evil deeds sacked city-towns whose king was forced into surrender—in total humbling defeat agreed to pay annual material monetary tributes to the victorious Kingdom Royal treasury.

People had their lives were relegated to a life of poverty and irrelevance by kings who aspired to gain huge wealth by aggressive their warrior cult is the historical chronicles: Truth telling physical history of the book pages we read the history of the rise of Kings who with trepidation saw their once-great umpires powerful army defeated by a powerful rival Kingdom conquering armed forces brought them bin the need to defeat.

History of wars between neighboring city-states went to war against each other, countless populations and civilizations were subdued and the city-state governor, or King was chained and led away is bondage. The real fact of history: ancient wearing clans would often force the losers to become the victor's obsequious free labor force. The slave of war a victorious invader (*"My people are destroyed for the lack of knowledge" (Hosea 4:6)*).

Anunnaki Kings of Mesopotamia fought wars, to conquer and claim neighboring city-states territory to enrich themselves and build powerful empires that are mentioned in the Old Testament Bible book of Genesis.

There you can read the chronicles of bloody military victories in words on a large stone stele erected to proclaim the deeds from times and areas of hubris King's words, the scribes inscribed into the archival records was final, according to that account. Of particular note, such as a successful military campaign conquest.

They were boastful and would give their own god praise for every victory memorialized by carving the king's words into the face of a tall garnet stone obelisk. And thus in a manner that glorified brutal pure power, aggression and vicious campaigns of ruthless savagery. A victorious Kings, aproclaimed his own greatness from the works and their military victories. With which they praised their deeds as achievements, scribes of the king recorded their deeds in resplendent specificity and anecdotal details according to their wars of conquest and battlefield destruction.

They gave glorious thanks to a particular Anunnaki alien deity of whatever god for the amount of the bountiful cache of booty was bountiful, and considered to be the blessing of God., consider their deeds the gift from God who had given a successful conquest by the will of and the gracious hand king praise their city-state God, who rewarded them with the treasure they obtained by sheer force of their armed military warfare conflicts. Yes we can read about the deeds recorded on the ancient King who fought protracted wars to claim their rule over the entire regional territorial lands of their neighbors through deeds of armed aggression. This was a seditious lust to acquire a powerful and control system was a race to gain financial wealth from building a strong military empire using force and religion to over human mind/body/spirit complex. Without provocation, they were spurred by their inherent vicious greed.

Which was the motivation to destroy neighbors' city-state settlements, razing their homes and businesses by burning them to the ground—with impunity after all there were no repercussions or recriminations!

Ostensibly, without any scintilla of compassion, all whilst operating in accordance with the indecorous so-called "Golden Rule." conquering armies proclaimed themselves to be great Kings.

And these Royal Kings give praise to acknowledge their chosen city-state deity whom they worshiped, giving them a bountiful blessing in war booty. With their lack of amoral and depravity and the lack of deference to this *aphorism*: "To love thy neighbor" was rebuffed out of hand as mere folly. It's an old *aphorism* that is spoken; and seemingly, seldom adhered to in deeds! Given the number of *gregarious* innocent villagers who watched brutal killings of willful intent carried out by ruthless armed aggression!

Their deeds were chronicled and archived in the halls of ancient historical records library professionals, temples had carefully left use a plethora of information they delineated as the sources revealing evidence with which was written down.

THE MIND, BODY, SPIRIT, AND STORYTELLING

This historical account reveals that the Anunnaki had a presence in the African lands with which ties directly to these extraterrestrials' alien connection. Why does the Bible book of the Old Testament, Genesis narrate this truthiness, meaning that it obfuscates to avoid revealing the specificity and anecdotal details of ancient astronauts' presence and identity? Here's my fundamental premise: This fundamental to the knowledge standard of the ultimate truth that is inarguably intricate to the pieces which fits in with the demystifying the ancient backstory of underlying of the old world religions that supplanted the African-Egyptian priesthood Kemetism spiritual science symbolism of the Sun Disk was the representation of the Aten Ra. This sacred symbol of worship tied to the learning and teaching of other mysteries of Kemetism embraced as the Law of One Love in unity with the divine philosophy of god' wisdom principles!

The African wisdom of consciousness awareness through the moral principles of spiritual individualism, unselfish love of God's ubiquitous universal nature. This is the true lost identity: the persona of "Those who came from the Heavens were the Anunnaki alien titular gods that established civilization upon the earth.

Therefore might it be assumed that the indigenous human beings were taught to worship them as the god of the firmament? Because there's plenty of information that was never included in the Hebrews and the Greeks Septuagint translation, which they appropriated their own version of the original Genesis narrative of the Chronicles within the account of the Anunnaki ian Bible. This is echoed in the ineffable Book, Enoch; it is pretty easy to understand the identity of astronauts' pre-flood earth visitations. In the Bible book of Genesis did not elaborate on the Anunnaki aliens as being: "Those who from the Heaven came" were alien entities which had come down to earth from their home planet Nibiru. Well let's face it! The Anunnaki, the titular Gods and the ancient astronauts of the Heavenly higher orbital celestial plane!

This I supposition dovetails nicely with the a sophisticated advanced race of man like space-traveling ancient astronaut's is a perfect fit for this hypothesis about Anunnaki: "Those who came down sat on board of advanced sophisticated flying chariots of Anunnaki alien were titular Gods came down from a higher mysterious planet called Nibiru/Heaven, or some astrologers have called it Planet-X! The prevailing opinion of highly regarded scientists and researcher archeologists and anthropology findings of well-known proponents in the latter half of the 20th century who wrote numerous books or appear regularly in mass media including Erich von Däniken, Zecharia Sitchin, Robert K. G. Temple, Giorgio A. Tsoukalos, and David Hatcher Childress.

Why are the pages of the Bible silent about the missing conspicuously glossed over or lifted out of the Bible? Is this the truth as recorded in the original Old Testament KJV Bible is the original Anunnaki, Sumerian Bible is the story of Genesis, Chapter 1. And as you and I know that there's no acknowledgment of the Anunnaki alien Gods—as ancient astronauts from the planet Nibiru: "Those who from the Heavens came!

"The Anunnaki gods' history was derived from the African-Egyptian [Kemetic] consciousness; Europeans intentionally lifted their true withheld from Chapter 1.

We question the Hebrew and Greek Orthodox Septuagint transliterated version of the Old Testament book of biblical Genesis narrative tale. Which would seem to be truthiness! And learning to teach others about the Anunnaki Sumerian Bible original text. Why is this information not the most critical revelation point not regarded as unnecessary to the specificity and anecdotal details, which I convey here should be relevant; Right? Would we be worse or better off than we are today?

The Church must be inclined to learn/teach others about this story; the whole primordial truth that doesn't wittingly omit and seek to hide the distortion of the fundamental facts.

To acknowledge and redress the blatant mistranslation perpetuates the falsity! Because the Holy Bible Genesis narrative interpolates the Anunnaki story and the Bible, interpreted into the deeds of Royal Prince Enki.

It takes a different view on the presence of the Olden Times Bible Genesis storytelling. It explains why they came down to the earth plane, which is in respect to this overall premise, reconciled with the personage of a race of ancient astronauts' as a modern assertion that suggests, speculation that ovetails with juxtaposition to Christianity. Now go beyond false religious doctrinal cannons and religious creeds necessary to redress the truthiness. Might I say that sufficient archeology and anthropology research dovetails nicely with modern discovery. Unearthing of missing ancient recorded information is irrefutable!

This book propagates my interpretation about Anunnaki ancient astronauts as titular Gods of Heaven. With clarity I surmise that: These Anunnaki were the extraterrestrial aliens, who were the ancient UFOs, who were Earth Mission voyagers who built and established a gold mining production operation in the southern region of the Great Zimbabwe Africa Southern. Clearly some people are still too blind to acknowledge our very existence. What seems to be the most important and plausible truth. Ostensibly, that's if the real truth is too frightening for you to see that we are all living spirits of the mind/body/spirit complex of the soul's embodiments. The light is of the god in use that we seek the nous. Notwithstanding that which underlies the biblical teachings pushed by the organized church gospel religious rituals of theological teachings from the book of Genesis narrative. Will you continue to stake your soul upon the vapid and spuriously pervading of a contrived narrative tale that preaches the same old regurgitation of the ecclesiastical church gospel troupe? Awaken my friends because here's the story about god that lends a much more astounding paradigm to the great Royal prince Enki/Ea as the creator god of the Bible. He built/created his base camp six days after their UFO spacecraft landed in Sumer, Mesopotamia. It was there that he also built the first ancient alien spaceport, and carried out his earth mission to establish a large-scale gold mining production to embrace the disciplines of the ancient psychic-spiritual sciences of Kemetism by his own study of ancient Egyptian religions of Shatuat Neter philosophy. The daily practice of spiritual meditation which was popular in Eastern African, Persian, and Indian cultures. While there is sufficient evidentiary information, what is troubling about this is that the neither the schools nor the churches attempt to elucidate about the influence which was the inflection point of the turn toward the Western European hegemony of Christianity that took hold in the ascendancy and direction which was the defining shift that diverged from the African, Egyptian (Kemet) traditional cultures religious mythology precepts. We know that Enki's ancient gold mining production operation was widespread throughout the entire southeastern region of great Zimbabwe on a large scale (http://sakshizion.com/?p=1673). My aim is to disseminate the information presented in this book and become a catalyst to your own search for the real truth.

Take your own personal journey by discovering a plethora of different sources of relevant information that will enlighten your curiosity and learning and teaching truth that is important in logic and reason. Whereof finding the righteous pathway to away from the misguided mental state of disillusionment. With understanding the spirit, intution and not truthiness. My exegesis of biblical creation seeks to provide knowledge. My friends, as you read or listen to this book you are holding in your hand right now you are learning the light of nous. In one's adult lifetime being inspired by assertions elucidated in this excursive exegesis will cultivate the mind. To know of thyself curious minds must live the awakening state of conscious awareness and spiritual enlightenment through yoga meditation as a free will thinker. Being synced with the sacred intelligent energy of the creative life force, harmonic balance and cosmic order in unity with nature's law of one. To follow the positive over the narrative. To represent a dynamic personality that exemplified confidence and the proper decorum in every aspect of the individual personhood devoid of misdeeds to gain the elite status of the corrupt rulers who covet wealth by any means to control humankind liberty and freedom.

To study the Bible with an objective perspective and avoid the allure of the blind faith religions misdirection and truthiness. A critical subject matter, which I say, is about clarity and understanding of the untruthful religious and spiritual, concerning the Holy Bible book of Genesis Chapter 1. The elucidation for you who want to read this content may change how you think about religion and extraterrestrial aliens' earth visitations. Because you learn the unexplained truth regarding the advanced race of ancient astronauts.

THE MIND, BODY, SPIRIT, AND STORYTELLING

Whereas the Holy Bible Tales narrative is the Gods of the Old Testament Bible is devoid of the real story, which I assert that the Old Testament Biblical Genesis narrative account doesn't mention the Anunnaki of Infinite Creators Law of One; that is the lead humans being into the application of God's Principle of one unity is about the fire that brings forth by the light, and life of one love; to be in self-service; while in service to the spiritual entities other-selves of humankind.

My learning/teaching of wisdom, knowledge, understanding the nature of the hidden one are all true mysteries. The biblical historical events fit in this astronaut's theorist's speculative premise. It's Not some false notion devoid of inconclusive evidence that can debunk the prehistoric origin of the African-Egyptians spiritual science preceded the Western Christian religionist invention of Jesus Christ (http://sakshizion.com/?p=1673). We should try to keep this in mind that the original image of Jesus, not as a blond, blue-eyed Christ, who the Bible is clear in when reporting that Jesus Christ had "wooly hair" and that his feet were the color of bronze" (Revelation 1:14-15). Therein lies the essential question: Why is it not acknowledged in the chronicles of the organized church canons, doctrines, and gospel teachings? An ancient original codex manuscript prior to the Hebrew and Greek *Septuagint* holyBible. We all can examine published evidence of these Anunnaki alien gods who came down seated onboard the large bell shaped flying UFO spacecrafts.

The chariots of the extraterrestrial alien Gods came down from a higher cosmic plane, descended on the planet earth 450,000s of years ago.

Did you know that there is plenty of evidence of this lost historic tale of the Bible? Yes, that which they refuse to flush out helps to perpetuate a fairly in order to deceive. Perhaps this information was excluded from the Bible in order to intentionally foster and perpetuate a misdirection as a falsehood. Perhaps the ruling elites went so far as to willfully manipulate the original ancient codices, by selectively excluding the critical and relevant material information from the original ancient Anunnaki ties to the African Egyptians-Kemet psycho-spiritual science principle of the esoteric religious mystery!

What other reason why the religious leaders conceal these facts that point to the ancient astronauts Yahweh's presence.

Does the historical Bible fit the profile of Anunnaki, extraterrestrial, and their influence on the contribution of these titular Gods? Why is it that the revelation about the truth lies in the book of Enoch? Of which I discerned that the Bible book of Genesis Chapter 1, clearly doesn't show that the Anunnaki, the Royal great prince Enki [the God of wisdom espoused Ra, a humble messenger of The Law of One; meaning what? Learning/teaching others about the lack of love in common with our society as a whole unity, meaning what?

Simply that everyone would largely benefit humanity if this could be instituted as a universal the overwhelming fundamental precepts embraced by the earth's *bons hommes*; in service to one's self, while being in service to all others! Enki was appointed the Earth Mission voyage commander. In this instance He and the fifty man crew Astronauts lifted off from planet Nibiru: "Those who were from Heaven came"! Down they traveled and successfully landed down on the Earth's interior surface.

His father Anu was the supreme king of the Anunnaki clans on planet Nibiru; and viz., gods of Heaven. Simply put, he sent these ancient astronauts to earth to confirm whether the material gold was sufficient enough to conduct a large-scale gold mining production operation could be feasible to send: "Those were from Heaven came "! In case you don't remember, this seems to allude to God's true identity, suggesting an oddly enough, speculative notion that can be reconciled to the conflated nexus that comports with the ancient astronaut theorists' premise.

That seems rather remarkable is that what is not being regarded as the most relevant important question. Why is it that there is a pervasive trepidation by some who are in the establishment ruling class who object to the historical, archeology, and anthropology discovered information?

Might we presuppose that the significant and detailed account of the Anunnaki Earth Mission voyage space log books contain the information that was intentionally left out of the Hebrew, Greek, and the KJV Septuagint versions of the biblical history intention-

THE MIND, BODY, SPIRIT, AND STORYTELLING

ally removed from chapters 1, by the church bishops whose aim was to create a holy book to seduce the minds of the low information human populist with a contrived narrative tale.

The primordial presence of the Anunnaki description and identity had been co-opted and replaced with the term God. Our past is inextricably delineated from the extraterrestrials; and with clarity and understanding—the truthiness about the Genesis of the Bible is the story of the Chronicles, the auspicious event of the arrival of ancient alien astronauts the Bible says: "Those from the Heavens came" were likely from home Planet-X, which has they called Nibiru. To which I say: Why would they perpetuate the false teachings of an apomorphic God?

The personification of Jesus Christ as humankind's salvation has misled millions of blind faith-wittingly religious followers! Simply because the empirical evidence is undeniably revealing that they were likely to be from an advanced, sophisticated alien race of giant man-like extraterrestrials aliens.

I assert that it was ostensibly the titular God who descended and landed a bright shining spacecraft upon the earth planet seated onboard a large, bright, shiny, strange-looking UFO spacecraft, which was a fifty man astronauts crew of sophisticated alien beings.

Yeah, the hidden identity of those extraterrestrial ancient astronauts who piloted their bell-shaped aerial spacecraft descended from the planet Nibiru/Heaven. Yeah, let's say that the Bible Genesis narrative, beginning with chapter 1, is obviously telling a falsehood of omission without acknowledging. The truth about the nascent of the Old Testament Bible genesis has been hiding from you. Hiding the truth about Anunnaki extraterrestrial alien influence.

The Anunnaki titular Gods imparted many wonderful contributions. Which was likely written by ancient scribes and the deeds of the Olden Time Nibiru presence covering up information about an Anunnaki clan of alien astronauts; an extraterrestrial foreign god on earth remains hidden away from the light of truth. Ancient astronaut Gods have been prominent in the original Anunnaki, Sumerian Bible manuscript.

Let's say that curiously my divergent exegesis is describing this fancifully fiction is a speculation about Romanized Christians Catholic religious teachings, mentally handicapping generations to follow external empirical worldwide embrace falsehood and truthiness. One that appropriated the original Kemetism knowledge of the African-Egyptian Mystery spiritual science of the learning and teachings of the sacred wisdom of the Law of One love, they manipulated philosophical expertise and religious principles of the Anunnaki Seven Tablet of Creation!

Yeah, this is a divergence from spiritualism. Being caught up in a distortion of established organized church religious systems, many faithful and knowledgeable followers aim to serve others; learn/teach about the love of Jesus Christ's death and resurrection. To me this was a witting action by the clever machinations contrived by the empirical powerful church and state in their grandiose aims to inculcate their misdirection. Of which archeology and anthropology research discovery/ings dovetail nicely with the anecdotal details of the ancient astronaut's theorists' assumption. Which has long been transformed into a narrative mystery tale.

While Chapters of the New Testament are silent and content to pervade the gospel of Jesus the Christ truthiness!

Curiously, the Anunnaki gods' storied history and contributions was surreptitiously plagiarized, usurped, and stolen from the African ancestral genealogy was transformed by the Westerrere surreptitiously plagiarized, usurped, and stolen from the African ancestral genealogy was transformed by the Western European's spurious identity. Ancient space-traveling astronauts who were the titular Gods of aliens in the personification was the African-Egyptian Mystery spiritual science of the sacred principles learning and teachings of the *Kemetism* religion of the Law of One. The bringer of the fire that brings forth the light of life force spirit energy of the all noumenal and phenomenal material world of the universal existence of the present state of the illusory reality.

The all infinite wisdom of the Law of One love by The RA Material; Book 1, pg. 106). Thereof, the nascence of the Anunnaki alien gods is not a mythos; but the a historical presence which is the

THE MIND, BODY, SPIRIT, AND STORYTELLING

true story of the extraterrestrial UFO, or shall we say the ancient astronauts custodial titular gods who the established civilization throughout ancient Mesopotamia 450,000 years ago, according to modern researchers findings conflates with the old Testament Bible, African-Egyptians apocryphal and canonical Christians texts. Ancient texts written after the Olden Times Anunnaki's god's contributions spurred by the Royal Prince Enki's personification as god. It's an assertion that fits into the Old Testament Biblical Genesis narrative storytelling, ostensibly, omitted the contributions ascribed to deeds of the, Anunnaki as an aliens extraterrestrial manlike Gods from Nibiru had presence that began in ancient Sumerian land of Mesopotamia; and this assertion is a perfect fit with the historical records, respecting the extraterrestrial ancient Seven Tablet of Creation. To which the book of Enoch alludes to the Annunaki Genesis narrative that connects to the Enki bloodline which point the Anunnaki imprint, manlike, titular Gods. Their attributions to our understanding is a very perfect fit to the much Old Testament Bible Genesis narrative tale of ancient astronauts monumental Earth Mission destination is the story that is not included in the Bible genesis as the extraterrestrial alien race of the Anunnaki Gods.

Ancient space faring astronauts who were on a EarthMission voyage to extract the much needed mineral gold. What spurred them to come down from a higher plane came down to earth seated onboard a large, shiny, and bell-shaped advanced UFO flying spacecraft landed in the southern region of modern day country of Iraq, is ancient Sumer, Mesopotamia. But the old Testament Bible genesis narrative is intentionally a brief synopsis that is curiously missing the specificity and anecdotal details information I just alluded to is the ancient astronauts theorists hypothesis, which is with respect to the gods presence conterminous with alien gods is very clear. It was a space traveling mission flight commanded by the great Royal Prince, Enki landed his UFO and began to mine gold from the shores of the Persian Gulf waters. It was determined to produce insufficient gold output. Later it was determined that Africa's Southern region of great Zimbabwe possessed a rich abundance of the mineral that they could mine and extract from the earth. The assertion specificity and anecdotal about the alien Gods motivation to extract gold is undoubtedly very irreparable! as the allure dovetails nicely with the value and power of gold resources can be traced back to every primordial social culture. That list this information is relevant because it corresponds to the archeology, anthropology, biblical genesis that is the perfect fit with the speculative premise that is postulated by the esteemed followers who ascribe to the theory that the Anunnaki initial fifty man crew of ancient astronauts descended from Heaven were merely the titular Gods from their home planet Nibiru (Planet-X)! Christians organized church religion created and inculcated this twist into a popular convergence of a false *luciferianism* narrative. It has been blissfully willful as its articulation fosters the worship of the Gospel teachings of Jesus Christ through a doctrine of prayer through blind faith.

It has been and continues to be a priority for a majority of the earth's inhabitants who are living in the faithful fellowship of organized Christianity. Well then, shall we say that it's okay that some of you do not concur or believe that: We are getting much closer than the skeptical comatose people think. Well then, my friends, you are wise to question everything that you have been taught! At the same time, others who have awakened from a dystopian state of religious inculcation foster the impulse to follow the teachings of the consciousness of church misdirections away from spiritual consciousness awareness. That which is the most significant material religious truthiness, or a speculative ancient astronaut hypothesis! My premise that say that as the presence of the extraterrestrial Annunaki came here in chariots down had brought civilization fits nicely with the original coherent vision comports with the Anunnaki, Sumerian Bible cuneiform clay tablets provide information written in the ancient Akkadian and Babylonnian language. The valid account of Genesis pred on the "Seven Tablets of the Creation" is the source of the Hebrew and Greek Septuagint Holy Bible narrative tale that has promulgated mistranslations.

The actual ancestors of the Anunnaki the Royal great prince had instructed their scribes to write it down as an account of the original record of the Anunnaki's Earth mission voyage of the Anunnaki.

THE MIND, BODY, SPIRIT, AND STORYTELLING

Extraterrestrial alien beings descended from Heaven to land on earth via their bright and shiny UFO spacecraft!

My friends, let's consider this hypothesis plausible, amplified the amount of archeology and anthropology discovery. with the empirical biblical genesis, meaning this is speculative fiction; as conjecture this is about a different perspective of biblical history. Raising the curiosity of civil entries that plagues society of ordinary consciousness. Whereof, the unbiased African consciousness awareness of self and becomes thus a pivotal epicenter of Enki, as the figure is aligned with the entrenched Genesis narrative. Thus, in retrospect he was the personality that fits into the Anunnaki from his arrival on and mission purpose for coming down oowon't the Earth plane to extract, which was the mission. And as mission creep always necessitated a need for a change of planning of unforeseen, the need for primitive workers was authorized to fashion a crossbred primitive worker race sacred mystery schools of the occultist (hidden). These wisdom keepers of God's teachings they imparted have roots in African Kemetism. This knowledge and understanding, is tied to the metaphysical spiritual science taught as the initiation into the temple priesthood serpent brotherhood founder (Enki). And this was origin of the Adam and Eve story, which was derived from the ancient African consciousness awareness of human ancestors delineated through the roots of the family tree from the *aegis* of the Anunnaki titular Gods mythology that never elucidate a connection to Enki as the biblical creator god figure wisdom and knowledge teachings of the Royal Prince Enki. With which wisdom principles were seeded before the paradigm shifted into the Western European age of the Christian religion seized and became the predominant ruling seat of a new world order. By the cross and the sword, efficiently they supplanted the old world order.

All the while they killed and conquered other nations by the blood of their ruthless aggression, the autonomy of spiritual science, the history of the killing of blacks, and others, shall we say was closely akin to a raging wildfire spreading; and viz, this vein of consciousness has indeed spurred the neophytes' curiosity the Egyptians nous—the *Shetaut Neter* philosophical wisdom principles according to the God Ra's Law of One as a unity that must be redressed in the subjective context from the perspective of the luminous spiritual divine nature of sacred principles. That is a fundamental substrate consciousness that is our common medium of the mind. learning/teachings of consciousness awareness in self-service, and the service to entities of our other-selves. The ancient cultists mystery religious teaching and learning the spiritual science philosophy. Of course, there is much controversy over the ancient astronaut theorists' assertion that is predicated on their assumption, which dovetails nicely with the out-of-African and Anunnaki god Enki's alien royal cross red genetic bloodline. What is seemingly the big secret that is withheld from the Old Testament holy book Genesis scriptures is revealed in chapters 1 through 11, is the obfuscation on the treasure of archeological discovery and historical finding about: "those who from the Heavens came" true identity were. But it is an irrefutable folly of unconscious bias to ignore the parallels of the Bible and simply rebuff the glaring amount of the African Egyptians religious symbolism. True is that the story of God in the modern Gospel scriptures is a conflation that is undeniably, closely akin to the fundamental truth. But it has been manipulated into the whitewashed versions of the modern day Westerners Christian Gospel religions, doctrine and creeds truthiness dogmas. To learn/teach the incredible truth will rival the falsity of the archeological and anthropology findings.

Discovery of the evolutionary timeline is helping to complete the Bible Genesis narrative tale which is slowly taking hold in the social culture, which says that mystery spiritual science is becoming mainstream civil society, unlocks the ancient wisdom of the Law of One love of bon homies mind/body/spirit complex.

However, I am very uncertain about the Anunnaki Sumerian Holy Bible Genesis narrative. Nevertheless, still, many unwise people carry on being impervious of and devoid of logic and reason have no understanding; viz., and, *ipso facto* have not evolved towards conscientious mental awareness. They ignore that truth, which underlie the dynamic forces of the all pervading universal grand intelligence of life giving infinity, which is the nature of God as a sustainable presence existing in the everyday world as we see it, is our uniquely shared experience and everywhere in all material forms.

THE MIND, BODY, SPIRIT, AND STORYTELLING

We are all derived from God as an animated free willing spirit. The *Shakti* of a pulsating harmonic energy vibrations that causes our actions. To understand for elucidation of the esoteric wisdom principles brings forth knowledge of the Anunnaki's Kemetism religion of the ancient sacred spiritual science mysteries of the luminous divine nature of the God principles of religious worship. The vainglorious luminous divine light, which is the nascent. For we all separate individual units of human beings from the universal Infinite Creator. The seekers of knowledge and wisdom are as one with the Law of One love! Might we as humankind bring forth the correspondence of sacred wisdom principles edifying words of the Egyptian deity Ra, words revealed as He speaks them in a *telekinesis* manner is revealed to us in "The RA Material; Book 1, pg.106". Within this context Ra communication as the voice of the Infinite Creator, *Adona*.

The universal ubiquitous energy most high Gods of the primeval universe are the metaphysical luminous divine *Shetuat Neter* of the great *Neberdjuer*! Well then, my friends, might we be missing the most important anecdotal details, seemingly lifted from the mentioned or ancient book of Enoch. This orthodox Christianity created the blind faith religions paucity as the truthiness of a holy Bible's Genesis narrative tale. But the mind must be open to the mind/body/spirit self is a magnificent living complex. To be consciously aware is to be awakened, and my thoughts are one scent clearly in with a pure heart of luminous divine unity of infinite creator through a daily meditation to further development of the spiritual complex consciousness awareness. While at the same time, my purpose is simple. I am a humble messenger. Human, soulful spirit embodiment of consciousness awareness. For me this I say that I aim to serve myself and to serve other humans because I am just trying to wake people up!

Okay! We must help to bring others into this knowledge, insight, of the mystical, spiritual science of the sacred principles of ancient spiritual, intellectual wisdom of the Law of One love of the Law of One mind/body/spirit complex as individual units of bequeathed separate being of the universal cosmic luminous divine *Netjer*. Might I speak vivifying words of logic and reason, learning and teaching principles of actual spiritual science seated meditation, being one separate unit from the Infinite Creator of the luminous divine *Shetuat Neter* of the *Neberdjuer*! And this is for the people who would be remiss, foolhardy, derelict, and unwise *Dennison* that have been detached from and misled by the spurious away from responsibilities have been jettisoned by the earth's bon homies. For we all are disengaged and distracted by empirical worldly things of the perceived consciousness concrete illusory temporal reality.

Yeah, the home of humankind failed to learn to follow the way of sacred moral principles. To teach and live according to the Anunnaki comprehension of the Law of One love; to squire an impulse to learn/teach truth. Individuals living in unity as individual souls separated from the luminous divine cosmic universal, metaphysical is the spiritual harmonic vibrations. The esoteric life force waves of particle light energy forces streaming into the earth. The *Shakti* spirit is luminous divine intelligent energy that pervades ubiquitously, and this according to the Hindu teachings, is a powerful goddess who represents feminine energy. A dynamic force moves by the universal light energy of div intelligence causes actions. Well then, my friends, you must keep an open mind. Let your intelligence discern truth and the pieces will bring you to the fire that brings forth light of life and brighten up your understanding and lead you towards the sacred parlance. Why is it that this is missing chapters from Bible Genesis narrative creation tale: A monumental distortion of naivety between what is spurious ecclesiastical Christianity dogma and truthiness espoused as the words of the one actual infinite creator, god *Adona*. Or shall we say that it means, my lord! Biblical church religion with re-workings of Anunnaki inspired Kemetism custodian of cultural tradition by Western canonizations rites and rituals lifted from the African-Egyptians spiritual science philosophy was replaced with a mass transformation. By denigrating the learning/teachings of sacred wisdom of the Law of One love principles of Neberdjer. Which in itself is a juxtaposition for contrasting doctrines of God, the archetypal Infinite Creators.

Yeah, it's the archeology; anthropology discovers that this fundamental substrate reveals a plethora of biblical and historical facts dovetails nicely with ancient Sumerians, Mesopotamia site excavations of unearthed empirical evidence. Findings which correspond with the speculative and specious arguments, suggesting that the ancient astronaut's theorists' hypothesis dovetails nicely when the Old Testament Bible Genesis narrative tale, which is conflating the biblical historical to Anunnaki Sumerian Bible. What seemingly fits the missing specificity and anecdotal information, written by temple priesthood scribes recorded in thousands of Babylonian and Akkadian languages of the Anunnaki extraterrestrial Alien: Those who from the Heaven came. "And this should be the most important point that a thinking person may determine to be curious! Yet I respectively propose a fundamental speculative assertion based upon my logic and reasoning and understanding, my friends, please permit me to indulge you further as I postulate this exegesis. Of which is this fundamental presupposition, ostensibly, dare to raise such a salient question as this: Why has this information been deliberately omitted, hidden, or rebuffed as a ludicrous notion of just folly?

Might I dare to say: Genesis is a spurious paucity that has impacted the public's social and global Church of God through an entrenchment of this schema of organized blind faith religious worshipers; those who a falsehood. While behind the scenes cabal machination of the secret societies is operating as a hidden institution of a media system that is organized for controlling the unsuspecting bon homies.

Their proxy corporate sock puppets in accord with large numbers of Multimedia marketers, and intimate communication is the instruments they use with technology innovations, and thereby they efficaciously manipulated to gain massive wealth from having influences over the social, economic, political, financial, religious sovereignty of church and states? What does it mean?

Well, I guess what I'm saying here is that the ecclesiastical Christian religions have all been preaching and teaching the same *troupe*. Preachers of the, shall we say, the words of God they promulgated through the Church fathers congregations. To say that the voices of church Catholic Bishops, Protestant Preachers and Deacons are propagating false teaching as the Christian Holy Gospel through the salvation of the doctrine of the religion Trinitarian creed of Jesus the Christ. I guess a salient question here is whether we have descended spiritualism as an alternative means towards personal knowledge and salvation through precepts of the Law of One theology in our search for truth! Certainly we should query and seek answers regarding the historical things that date from the earliest biblical period, and gain the truth story chronology that is revealed in the discovery of the ancient documents. Those things recognized by archeological and anthropology, revealing the Homosapien-Sapiens nascence was *coterminous* with the intelligence of the ancient astronauts' possession of advanced knowledge of conscious temporal reality;, self-conscious awareness of beings in the original custodians of earth. I imagine with a *sapient* mental perception and speculation that in the past and this present time/space continuum is corresponding with UFO Anunnaki gods: "those who from the heavens came to earth," or the Anunnaki."; meaning the extraterrestrial alien titular God Enki.

The ancient astronaut traveled down and landed on Earth. Being born with the inherited free will as self-determination and consciousness awareness with the intelligence of thoughts to cause the animations of our spirit's actions. Having been endued with free will, positive, benevolent good deeds, or the adverse mendacious machinations of evil acts by choice of consciousness inspired impulses manifestation thereof spurs the inclination to lust after the material things that perpetuates an evil lusting after power and control. It is symptomatic of the syndrome of the world capital economics system of the elite ruling cabal hidden hands of secret societies.

The wealthy elites who advocate paradigm shift towards the proliferation of this end-times March towards the *Luciferian* globalism new empirical world order. A digital based IT legacy system, derived from the Anunnaki Gods of Heaven demigods. Yeah! A new age of transportation of status quo ante; the heritage of humankind's known historical biblical events are orchestrated by: "Those who from the Heaven came" to the earth surface from another planet; their story dovetails nicely with the anecdotal details of the ancient astronaut theorists' premises. Here is the exegesis that interpolates my views on what I believe is the truth.

THE MIND, BODY, SPIRIT, AND STORYTELLING

This is to posit the missing chapters specificity and anecdotal details, I assert that the fundamental substrate that underlies the biblical genesis narrative story. The extraterrestrial alien who is inextricably tied to what was written in Hebrew/Greek Septuagint biblical scriptures, Genesis chapter 1 says Anunnaki we're: *"those who from the heavens came to earth," or the Anunnaki. down to earth came"*...

Okay! Here's where I want to point out that the Bible comments mention that Enki and His brother Enlil were the Princes from the House of Anunnaki, the Nibiru Elite Royal Family supreme God Anu the Sky God of Heaven. The Heaven to earth mission was authorized under the *auspices* of the Nibiru's King Anu, assigned the task to His son, Royal Prince Enki who was appointed to command the first Earth Mission voyage which was to confirm whether sufficient deposits of the material gold resources that would be sustainable for the establishment of an vital industrial base of gold mining production operations on planet earth.

Gold mining production took place initially in the Persian gulf waters; and due to its low output a more vigorous production output was the catalyst which drove the decision to extricate the plentiful amount of gold from the deep and African gold from mining production operation in great Zimbabwe, Africa. UFO shuttle flights were used to ferry flights of monatomic gold to the moon, to Mars, on to planet Nibiru where it was dispersed into the dangerous hole a that was causing leaks in their planet's atmosphere.

These Anunnaki took on the task to establish their presence on the Planet Earth in writing. And being curious and careful not to elucidate my perception, these beings were: "Those who from the Heaven came" from to create the earth in six days. Without alluding to the specificity and anecdotal details about the Anunnaki Sumerian Bible nascence narrative source information, I interpolate logic and reason that assert that this is the fundamental truth about the religion narrative tale of these manlike extraterrestrial aliens, who were the titular God is the alien Anunnaki extraterrestrial being who descended from planet Nibiru [Heaven]. In the context of this explanation, there is synergy between the Bible Genesis narrative and the juxtaposition with the ancient astronaut hypothesis, which raises questions about the God of the Bible may seem a bit *spurious*.

Archeology and anthropology discovery and research can't be rebuffed because the evidence fits the ancient astronaut's theorists premise, which dovetails nicely with speculations. Anunnaki alien gods as ancient astronaut's hypothesis credible or sophistry. To rebuff the false teachings of secret machinations which therein lies the rub: the derivation of the biblical religion and cultists spiritual teachings and the truth is a perennial historical and religious debate without either side the winner! While ecclesiastical proponents inculcate the doctrinal canons of Christianity empirical worldwide with misleading truthiness.

Conversely, spirituality is the essence of the new age consciousness awareness learning/teachings that posits an assumption that conflates with the pathway to the One Infinite Creator of intelligent energy of the luminous divine. Evidence of archeology and anthropology discovery by putting pieces of the Bible historical information with the Genesis narrative tale.

New revelations about the nascence of the past history and Anunnaki Gods advances this ancient astronaut Gods hypothesis. Saying the Anunnaki extraterrestrial alien race was: Those who were from Heaven came to land down onto the earth's interior surface! Accordingly, this corresponds with the original Sumerian Holy Bible text account from which we know that the Hebrew and Greek Septuagint holy Bibles translations were derived. But curiously makes no references to or mention that the titular Gods descended from Heaven were manlike Anunnaki, giant [alien beings] were ancient space-traveling astronauts from their home planet Nibiru. This isn't some implausible conspiracy theory. That's not it's; not even close! Far from it! Because in terms of the original their ancient cultic practices and theological reflections there was no disbelief in the worshiping of the living beings; *"Those who from the heavens came"*. This quote was written and translated from the Anunnaki Sumerian Bible Genesis narrative tale. It's the inflection point of nascence about the Anunnaki alien beings; so-called manlike Elohims who were said to have descended from above is an incredible tale recorded in the

THE MIND, BODY, SPIRIT, AND STORYTELLING

Sumerian biblical text, which made references to them as the "shining ones".

My friends, substantively, I elucidate on point, because, let's face it. This exegesis is a speculative assertion that is most credible, plausible, the probability that dovetails nicely to fit the information missing and left out of the Biblical book of genesis narrative—chapter1. But why? Primordial story about God and humankind is the underlying history and the concealed mystery of the Bible has come face to face with the modern ancient astronaut hypothesis, which says and believes that an intelligent Anunnaki race of extraterrestrial aliens were: "Those who from the Heaven came down to the earth" were from Planet-X, or Nibiru. What does this assertion mean? Well, first off this comes down to your concept of religious beliefs according to what you think about this exegesis. Which is an approach my intelligent the bible, modern archeological, anthropological discovery and findings—compared within an analytical application of what seems plausible, logical, and very rational. Herein lies a judgment of my unconscious biases; it's a belief in Agnosticism!

Let's try to carefully examine here just what undergirds my *perspicacious wisdom.*

"Agnosticism is the view that the existence of God, the luminous divine, or the supernatural is not known or knowable with any certainty. If the question is "Does God exist?", "yes" would imply theism, "no" would imply atheism, and "I'm not sure" would imply agnosticism—that God possibly can or cannot exist. (Wikipedia).

Now ask this salient question: Can you conflate the Old Testament Bible? Indeed this is the assumption and the foundation of the ancient astronaut's hypothesis! Using logic and rational thinking debunks a hyperbole allegorical genesis narrative tale. Concerning alien, man-like, extraterrestrial Annunaki ancient astronauts who are the strange extraterrestrial Gods. Despite everything you think you know to be the truth. Why do so many people acquiesce to religious truthiness? Have we Not? Indeed public attention has made the ancient astronaut's hypothesis a plausible theory.

The fact is that this has credible and obviously substantive regarding these salient and posits questions that asks: Was Anunnaki alien existence as the biblical Gods of earth intentionally erased, scrubbed, and lifted out the: the developing history of the Old Testament book of Chapter 1, Bible Genesis speculative premise? Maybe there are some who disagree with this. Yes. But now then, skeptics? Of course, we know now that there are still those folks out there who vehemently disagree with such a curious exegesis! Nevertheless, I elucidate my perceptions to make this mention, that I am saying that Anunnaki extraterrestrial aliens Gods were the ancient astronaut entities—UFOs that landed marked the beginning of the Bible story. It corresponds to the initial lines of an alien presence on the planet Earth which began in the southern region of ancient Sumerian, Mesopotamia. We can juxtapose that this fits the Genesis storytelling with the irrefutable finding of anecdotal details revealed in the Bible is a perfect fit, with which the ancient astronaut's theorists' premise alluded to an assertion I postulate the explanation. Relevant, irrefutable information dovetails nicely with the empirical ings of modern archeology and anthropology discovery of ancient scribes records found at excavation of unearthed historical dig sites in the region of the Persian Gulf Southern, Mesopotamia, and in southern eastern region of great Zimbabwe, Africa resides the evidence of megalithic ancient ruins of gold mining operations.

Might we assume that this is the development? Which seems odd because it raises the salient question: Why is not the comprehensive storyline, right? aspect had been concealed to a that deceives religious blind faithful followers. All the while they have been misdirecting the believers with a smile, wink, and a nod, the organized Church fathers seemed to be withholding the truth about the Anunnaki Sumerian Bible narrative tale.

Now allow me to put forth and this quarry which I raise this salient and essential question: why would there be a reason for the Old Testament Genesis not mention of the specificity and anecdotal details about the Anunnaki alien gods who descended from Heaven (planet Nibiru)? The obfuscation and lack of full disclosure is closely akin to the denying that UAVs and UFOs are not true. Which is the reason for the conjectures about the extraterrestrial presence of space travelers vehicles in our sky; and the speculative view behind the mod-

THE MIND, BODY, SPIRIT, AND STORYTELLING

ern ancient astronauts theorists' hypothesis conflation to alien beings as gods symbiotic relationship with crossbred humankind, primitive workers who were genetically created by Enki. Aunnnaki's fashioned them on the earth surface to carry out an ad hoc auxiliary, specific mission purpose to be of and obedience to serve the gods as their free manual labor work force. Of course this happens to be contravention to what is revealed in the Old Testament, Genesis Biblical narrative. Which simply makes no mention of it; and gives a cursory statement that says God was looking down at the earth's surface at the mingling of waters. Came down and created the earth in six days!? Okay, are you kidding me?

It sounds like hyperbole is an understatement! I can't and don't buy this simple insidious fairytale. Then might we conflate this to a mythological *talisman?* While many people have done their due diligence and have been awakened to this folly of a blind faith teachings of the truthiness. People are becoming knowledgeable about this historical Bible narrative tale. Simply by reading and learning the truth about the nascence of the Biblical genesis is the Anunnaki alien, as titular Gods as the ancient astronauts. To analyze the Old Testament biblical genesis narrative, and simply apply fundamental logic and reason that comports with the Ancient Astronaut hypothesis. Those who have perused the Anunnaki Sumerian Holy Bible manuscript codes. The ancient recorded text accounts in the language of the *Arkkadian, Babylonian, and Assyrians* Royal Elite rulers of ancient Mesopotamia. The Anunnaki were alien titular Gods who were: "Those who from the Orion group from heavens came" the elite rulers operate a control over humankind by bringing into the people increasing negative influence of Yahweh (Enlil). Those whose aim was to manipulate and enslave others on an Earth Mission voyage were the space-traveling ancient astronauts. I interpolate a speculative assertion, saying Anunnaki extraterrestrials were these Royal elite aliens who were titular Gods.

Yeah! Those who from the heavens came to earth," or the Anunnaki. Down to earth came down the titular gods of Genesis. Yeah, ancient astronauts UFOs were extraterrestrial aliens who descended from Heaven (Nibiru/Planet-X). Where the Anunnaki alien ancient astronauts who landed and inhabited planet Earth before the eponymous Noah's flood and the creation fit into the debate that has rejected UFO connection as poppycock. to What seems quite obvious is also curiously obfuscated, bolsters religion the Bible does elucidate is the existence of the Anunnaki, olden times Gods the Anunnaki's earth mission voyage in their search for gold and their earth mission voyage.

The God (Enki) manipulation of the Anunnaki's gods royal DNA gene code when he fashioned his own biological genetic code essence with an indigenous African female Homenoid. He set up the Annunaki deep mining dark gold mines production operations after his ancient astronaut's colonization of the lands of Sumer, Mesopotamia. deities were extraterrestrial aliens who piloted their bright "shiny" UFOs from their home planet, Nibiru (Planet-X). People who had first contact and most likely welcomed Enki's and his fifty-man astronaut crew of ancient astronauts; this was a vanguard Earth mission voyagers who extracted and processed the abundance of the Earth deposits of the elemental mineral gold from the southern region of tribal people of great Zimbabwe African homelands. Whereas, Lord Anu appointed his son Enlil with authority to rule as Supreme Lord Anunnaki gods. And as you can imagine that this would become a touchstone issue between the two brothers. What you see here is that Enlil's word was final; and his law forbade Enki's crossbred homosapeins-sapiens purpose was to serve the Anunnaki as a primitive labor force. But Enki as the creator God had genetically modified their DNA profile with the *elixir* of knowledge—but not longevity. Yeah this set the epic cinematic drama that played out symbolically as the Anunnaki forbidden fruit of knowingness was exposed in the Bible tale of Enlil's Temple Garden in the Eden. It is also called in Genesis the Garden of Yahweh, the God of Israel, and, in Ezekiel, the Garden of God. Adam and Eve's crime was that they were consciously aware of their own being; and their crime was that they had acquired the Anunnaki alien forbidden fruit of knowledge: knowing of their own nakedness. Being confronted with Adam and Eve for being blatantly disobedient, Enlil vituperates His brother Enki's mischief (aka, serpent) who was guilty of defiance of

THE MIND, BODY, SPIRIT, AND STORYTELLING

the Anunnaki illicit of knowledge and longevity. Which He had *surreptitiously* violated by a witting decision to imbue crossbred homo sapiens sapiens genes chromosome, and it was Enki whose fusion of DNA gave the Adams free will consciousness to know of things and their own sexuality. And the choice to choose to do good or evil.

This is a story of ancient space-traveling; the astronaut's crew's maiden voyage conflates the primordial ancient Gods Enki's creation procedure. Modern biological DNA genetic scientists have replicated Enki's DNA manipulation of genetic chromosome code sequencing procedures, in the same manner that was used by Enki to fashion the crossbred Adam and Eve's bloodline of the Royal House of the Anunnaki alien race.

Lord Anu, Enki, and Enlil's story begin to unfold in Chapter 1, of earth primordial history when they successfully come down upon Earth (Ki) plane. And this is believed to have happened; and the missing lost Anunnaki story of the extraterrestrial astronauts' peregrination was to exploit the African rich gold mineral resource. This event was the birth of the ancient astronauts. When upon a very long time ago the Anunnaki, a race of extraterrestrials from planet Nibiru descended from the higher plane of the orbital constellation, the first ancient astronaut UFO fifty man crew of Mission voyage to conduct its large-scale gold mining production operation, meaning what? These beings were on a mission, of which alluded to this historic monumental account in the Old Testament Holy Bible book, Chapter 1, which tells those who have read Genesis can surmise, with logic and reason this interpolation is whether or not it is plausible, do you think or believable the Anunnaki were anything other than sophisticated extraterrestrial aliens: "Those from the Heaven came"! Right? Anu was the Supreme God of the Nibiruans Federation's ruling Council of twelve elite judges unanimously voted for Anu's son, the great Royal Prince, Enki (EA).

He was the commander of the first earth mission voyage; the leader of a fifty-man crew which means he is the god of chapter1, Genesis narrative tale! Respectfully, I elucidate that this was a of the Anunnaki gods initial gold mining primordial enterprise. This aspect of the Bible story is curiously missing from the religious teaching/learning not *coterminous* with what was written out of the Old Testament Bible book of the Anunnaki alien gods of Genesis Mythology. Ostensibly, an important piece of the anecdotal ancient astronauts' Anunnaki alien presence is curiously never acknowledged in the Bible chapters 1.

Why is this? Might we have been better served with the real truth of Enki's Earth Mission voyage? It appears to be a perfect fit in which archeology specificity and anecdotal archeology, and collection of the Bible historical text seem to dovetail nicely with modern findings. Anunnaki alien Gods as ancient astronauts theorists have been writing about is being exposed; and, the shocking information that had been the hidden mystery of the olden times Mythology of the gods is finally getting revealed to the public. It is perspicaciously, the folks who are the seekers of nous can discern the truth about the *eponymous* creator God of Nibiru being conflated with the Genesis narrative tale of Chapter 1, were the Anunnaki, anamorphic, man-like alien titular God: "Those from the Heaven to earth came." But it seems curious that the Old Testament biblical genesis narrative.

Curiously, speculations alluded here are about the anecdotal details regarding the vagueness of teachings of Chapter 1, Genesis narrative tale. That the creator Anunnaki titular God was from the extraterrestrial alien planet Nibiru. For might we the Royal great prince Enki's personification, which I concur was the voice of the Infinite Creator God figure that proclaimed the beautiful events of The Holy Bible Genesis narrative tale of Chapter 1; who I presuppose was the extraterrestrial Anunnaki aliens astronauts crew of: "Those who from the Heaven came down from a higher cosmic plane. The Anunnaki alien gods begin their Earth Mission gold mining exploration, led by the elite Royal Prince Enki who was commander of the initial earth mission voyage. Yeah this was the nascence of the transformation that was ostensibly the genesis narrative tale that underlie the truth about a maiden enterprise spacecraft commander of that first space faring ancient astronaut crew. Yeah, Enki was the titular God who built the first colonial settlement in "six days" after they "came" to land down in the interior of Southern Sumer; and the Bible records that the creation god, Enki and other of clans members build and established independent territorial city-state settlements in "six days!" This is what was in keeping with building a safe camp site after these extraterrestrial ancient astronauts who "came" to land in the Southern region of the Sumerian Mesopotamia interior earth plain [modern day country of Iraq].

Well then, my friends, might I employ you to consider delving deep into the Anunnaki years in ancient Mesopotamia if you have chosen to follow the teachings of a deception that has been kept under wraps by political and religious church perceptible illusory temporal reality of blind faith truthiness!

Curiously, hark back through history and conjugate the specificity and anecdotal details, with the real evidence; meaning with respect to the modern archeology and anthropology excavation of buried scientific evidence. That is revealing the fact that the Anunnaki, Sumerian Biblical text is historical and relevant, because it is irrefutable that it is missing from the biblical Genesis narrative story—curiously, it doesn't make sense if you never mention the Anunnaki! There is the purpose of God's mission/earth voyage peregrination. Which is to the ancient Chronicles of the Annunaki Genesis Biblical narrative is the chronicle of the history written to establish the Anunnaki Aliens account of Enki's epic cinematic dramas delineated account of the creation claims fits nicely into the assumption that the Anunnaki extraterrestrial aliens from Heaven/Nibiru's ancient astronauts theorists premise that a giant manlike titular Gods arrived and landed in the olden time's God.

In point of fact, Yahweh is the God Enlil. The god in the Bible is referred to in common parlance as the god of the Christian religions. Hebrew and Greek Septuagint Bible holy translations, dressed up in the guise of the Testament conceals the hidden truth about the Anunnaki alien gods identity by dismissing and ties to this highly probable salient point that conflates the Bible ancienn astronauts presence, where these extraterrestrials are always mentioned as just got. Sounds like an attentional action to curate the ancient astronauts' nascent, of the personification of this extraterrestrial titular God that landed down in the southern region of the ancient land of so-called blackhead Sumerian people of Mesopotamia (Iraq).

It is an account with which references are relevant to the Anunnaki Gods from the planet Nibiru (Planet-X). The extraterrestrial race nature of the man-gods. The Holy Bible Genesis narrative says that in Chapter 1, the God from the higher plane from Heavens was: "Those who from the heavens came down" onto the planet Earth's interior plane of ancient Mesopotamia.

This likely referred to an advanced extraterrestrial alien race of large man-like titular gods, who were ancient astronauts. They were the extraterrestrial aliens who piloted their sophisticated aerial UFOs spacecraft. They were planet Nibiru's space-traveling ancient astronauts who maneuvered down through the asteroid belt, entered into this safe crossing between the planets Mars and Jupiter, and landed a spacecraft on the earth from a deep space constellation of celestial orbital bodies and shining stars. This was the most critical esoteric specificity of these anecdotal details are missing from chapters 1, the premise is to interpolate the ancient astronauts theory as a presupposition which dovetails nicely with the Old Testament. The Hebrew and Christian Bible Genesis narrative transactions delude religion as an air of mystery and truthiness; they promulgate to the malleable with the false teaching of dogmatism. For sure, we can all have a different opinion about this, right? Ignorant of the spiritual science fundamental mystery learning/teaching of one actual Infinite intelligent infinity of the Natural Law of One, one unity of mind/body/spirit complex, if you follow my drift? Let's face it! We can handle the truth about immutable empirical evidence about the Anunnaki extraterrestrial alien infusion and the UFO/AUVs existence and their influence in the evolution and involvement in planet Earth social complex in modern cultural, social construct and ancient astronaut God.

Those who came down and settled in the land the Bible calls Sumer, Mesopotamia. My purpose in writing about this book is to wake up and spur folks away from the misconceptions and the sophist falsehoods! This hyperbolic *exegesis* represents an attempt to a view with the intent to add clarity and understanding about the convoluted narrative tale of genesis. Albeit from a different perspective, it's a rather incredible endeavor, which was a misleading fal-

THE MIND, BODY, SPIRIT, AND STORYTELLING

sity. To elucidate a paradigm compendium of the Anunnaki alien "knowledge standard" that debunks the religions precepts of truthiness. Particularly how one chooses to synthesize God and about the understanding of what we have been endued with free will, to believe is facts of omission regarding the assertion I posit here.

The Anunnaki Gods and human history alludes to Chapter 1 of the Bible narrative tale is not a fairy tale story or a Myth! No, not at all! It's inextricably linked to the specificity and anecdotal details that are curiously missing this assertion that the Anunnaki astronauts' alien god Enki is the most important part and significant aspects that dovetails nicely with the Old Testament Hebrew and Greek Septuagint holy Bibles. This missing anecdotal detail is concealed from the content pages of the Old Testament Bible genesis Chapter 1 narrative tale. So you gotta ask yourself what would be an acceptable reason not to acknowledge that God's presence on earth was Enki, an ancient astronaut's Anunnaki God's presence was hidden from the bon homies physical history of the Holy Bible.

It was this most evocative natal nature which marked the beginning timeline that harkens you back inside of the Anunnaki IFO spacecraft as it slowly descended; and they were actually: "Those who from the Heaven came…" down onto the Earth plane under the Great Royal Prince Enki leadership. This mission earth voyage was under the aegis of His father, the Supreme Sky God, and Royal King Anu, who was the lord of the Anunnaki clan had commissioned His son commander to land down upon earth with his intrepid fifty man crew of Nibiru's extraterrestrial alien ancient astronauts. This speculation is inextricably linked to the Bible Old Testament Genesis narrative tales, which the biblical text curiously objectifies God, and without giving any identity of the extraterrestrial Annunaki as being: "Those who from the Heavens came!

The most obvious salient question is why? Was this not a significantly pivotal point of the evolution and evolution of the revolution that changed the life of the people on the planet Earth? When every event had begun! The focus of our attention is not a question about who I am. No! Absolutely not. Because you are now about to ponder something that will excite curiosity, being inspired by the introduction, as I am awakened and attuned to the harmonic resonance vibration with my other selves.

Hello my friends

My name is Hakeem R. Jelani. And this book is my exegesis on the Old Testament Holy Bible. What is written may shock you or amaze folks who have been inculcated and anesthetized in the blind faith religious beliefs that we all have taught to believe is the gospel truth. Of course I expect many of you, who are skeptical, averse to the ancient astronauts theorist hypothesis, a new paradigm shift from what we all have been taught as to think about UFO sightings, given the fact that the "Church and the global nation-state. Why is it that these Anunnaki alien gods' presence on earth, Genesis only mentioned as an abstract word as God.

In Chapter 1 of the holy Bible Genesis narrative they make no attempt to give the true backstory of just gods as an Anunnaki ancient alien astronaut, likened to a young child's simple fairytale about "those who came down from a higher plane of the cosmic universe. What I posit here is to conflate Genesis and the Anunnaki living on earth dovetail nicely with the UFO/AUV presence flying around in the Earth. Which says that they were the ancient alien astronaut entities who were Anunnaki! "Those who from the Heavens came" were extraterrestrial alien astronauts who became the titular creator God of the Old Testament Bible Genesis narrative tale. We never heard of this account as young children while in the church Sunday school class lesson. Teachers of these classes do not know anything about the Anunnaki (God) who were: "Those who from the Heavens came down"! Yeah! Okay, then, my friends, can you think of any reason God admonishes His auspices monumental creation Event on earth would say: "Make no grave images of the Gods? Might this be truthiness? After all, might we simply speculate as to why, or just refute o, some of this might seem fanciful.

Whereas such as it may be untenable as it relates to biblical archeological anthropological research studies, publishing peer review is not sophistry, but it is bolstered by fundamental logic and reasonable analysis consistent with the controversial ancient astronauts hypothesis. It depends on whether one might simply dismiss this premise as sophistry and truthiness is considered to be the indefensible argument. The peer review of mainstream archeology and anthropology on the presence of extraterrestrial aliens; and human space exploration is more than a historical and religious vigorous debate, it means that God and UAVs/UFOs are real. NASA's scientific minds' plans include the exploration and conquest with human settlements on distant planets.

The human ideals to achieve in the future world adventures involving NASA's mission goals to colonize the planet Mars and the moon, dovetails nicely with the Anunnaki ancient astronaut mission Earth voyage enterprise Genesis. We pre suppose then that this hypothesis is the actual truth, which is about the nascence derived from the source information. To this, I can say that the Hebrew and Greek Septuagint Holy Bibles genesis Gods. The Anunnaki were the extraterrestrial alien's ancient astronauts race from planet Nibiru [Heaven], the home of the extraterrestrial aliens who called themselves the Anunnaki: "Those from Heaven came" to earth is what Hebrew and Greek Septuagint Holy Bible writes, which doesn't allude to and due to the mistranslations.

The truth about this is revealed on Sumerians thousands of cuneiform clay tablets, the four-thousand years old *Seven Tablets of the Creation* were unearthed. And we have the ancient Egyptians Pyramid text manuscript known as the Book of the Dead. Gives a first-hand knowledge of what is written as an account of old astronaut presence among the indigenous people of Mesopotamia, revealing that these giant alien beings came to the Earth from the mysterious (planet X), or Nibiru. Their preeminent status was fused into the early ancient cult-like religious primary is the full power of the consciousness—Catholic Church teaches us that blind faith Christianity is the pathway to the salvation of the luminous divine Kavod. The archetypal promise through doctrinal canon laws and creeds religion.

Whereof; the misdirection away from the learning and teachings of the ancient metaphysical mystical spiritual science of sacred meditation was supplanted by the paganism religions of falsehood where inculcated. And as such, using your mental freewill consciousness awareness through logic and reason questioned everything that you have learned. As you will come to discover where truth clarity converges and aligns with speculation, about the Anunnaki Gods of the biblical genesis narrative is historically relevant to the ancient astronauts theorists hypothesis. Which I say dovetails nicely with the emerging challenges we face in today's perceptible illusory temporal reality; as the juxtaposition of information uncovered and excavated by archeology and anthropology discovery presence in the context of modern culture. Protestant ecclesiastical church pastors perpetuated church piety, taught through theological worship, teachings of goodwill, benevolent, worshiping of Christianity like God's blind faith religions. Ostensibly, it's a religious teaching that has misled the church leaders as witting enablers blind faith Religious simplicity of the Echomentical church Gospels troupe to promulgate and misled a society of common consciousness unsuspecting bon homies. The New Age Christian Bible book and blind faith religious zeal for the teachings of the words ascribed to an *anthropomorphic* alien god of the sky (Heaven). The doctrine and dogmatic creeds was pervaded throughout the social culture of humankind. What I will tell you is that this was materially ing people by omission away from the Old Testament about the intimate perceptible illusory material consciousness temporal reality that followed after the vanguard fifty man crew voyage of extraterrestrial Anunnaki, spearheaded by the Missions the Royal great prince Enki.

Yeah, the Earth Mission Flight Commander scenario is conveniently missing. Why? And why is this curiously left to The ancient astronaut to elucidate this Bible Genesis narrative is convoluted episodes of Nibiru Anunnaki space-traveling ancient astronaut: "Those who from the Heavens came" from a higher solar planet landed; they taught the mystery spiritual science of seated meditation, they don't teach this as the convention of ancient mystical spiritual science of organized religion. And the words that are fake to a dishonest degree of *dodginess* that misled people to diverge into worshiping Christ, lookHeaven as the gateway into God's salvation. What I am to posit here, though it's speculative, is most probably and likely the absolute truth about the Anunnaki, which dovetails nicely with the convergence of the ancient astronaut's theory.

My friends, that is to say we are learning of the past. With knowledge, a sense of wisdom and power to break free from the fetter operating in the guise of evil deeds pervading through the illusory reality by means of mendacious deceptions. Manifestation of mendacious evil fetters underlie the lust for wealth, power, and dominant control in order to rule and dictate the human condition and behavior. Their sinister misdirection is the personification of the accumulation of wealth and power! Hostile powerful rulers used the force of arms to supplant the sacred principles of African-Egyptians. Kemet-African psycho-spiritual science religion was unceremoniously denigrated, efficaciously up-ended, and plagiarized to bring forth the Westernized twisted falsehood New Testament version of the Christian religion Catholic and Protestant church doctrines, canons, and creeds; this was the fountainhead of which a manifold of ecclesiastical denominations of the blind faith religions infused a spurious misdirection. They targeted those who are unwise, ignorant, uninformed bon homies. With the interpolation of the teaching of the doctrinal of Christianity teaching of the blind faith religions Gospel of Jesus Christ (http://sakshizion.com/?p=1673). Which doesn't advance the actual teachings of the original sacred principles of Kemetic complexities of ancient mystery spiritual science.

The learning and teaching of our divinity unity with the natural Law of one philosophical wisdom of the Law of One love of the Law of One love sacred principles. To this point, my friends, are you ready for my thoughts on a Subject matter presented for the erudition psycho-spiritual African Kemet philosophical import of sacred knowledge and wisdom were supplanted by the Olden Times alien Annunaki god rooRoyal Prince Enk insight. Because the Bible Genesis narrative has been abbabout obfuscation and dismissive of the modern claim of the ancient astronauts hypothesis is a theory that searches for psychological import of truth. Well, here it is! The truth pervades understanding the Bible Genesis narrative. Religious tenets of Christianity are never going to or embrace the ancient astronaut theorists' premise. A hypothesis that conflates ancient alien

UFOs (titular Gods). Perhaps the Bible is this contrivance to conceal the Anunnaki Sumerian Bible text account of the extraterrestrial aliens, who were the manlike titular Gods figures who were "Those who from the Heaven came." At least, according to the anamorphic alien beings known as the so-called "Shining Ones"! Anunnaki aliens descended from the ancient extraterrestrial astronaut from Nibiru or Planet-X. Which concurs and comports precisely to what appears in original codes of the *Anunnaki Sumerian Bible* hypothesis. Thoughts of which may come to your own perspective might therefore be, rather seemingly conflicting after you finish reading this controversial book. But that's okay, too, because we are just trying to make you think about the subject matter. Those who don't agree with the ancient astronauts and the Africa hypothesis never will consider this exegesis as anything more than a truthiness. Yeah you are correct if you have already guessed that this book is clearly to postulate the elucidation of the erudition of the archeology and anthropology discovery of revelations found at ancient site excavations. Nevertheless, neophytes hold these views, which concur with the controversial eponymous "Ancient Astronauts theorists premise.

Of course curious minded seekers just might presume that canvas of the ancient Anunnki and this is an intertwining nexus; meaning all things that come into existence is endowed with a hidden purpose to experience, and to learn and teach others the psycho-spiritual knowledge of the unity of a common benevolent journey of this illusory world consciousness we imbibe of the luminous divine light/life/love spirit impressions.

Words expressing the changing evolution and transformation over eons of consciousness awareness is to experience the temporal reality. Which means to enrich the mind/body complex with the negative and positive forces. Material and spiritual distortion and the polarity of harmonic vibrations. Yeah it's the unity of the Earth bon homie's understanding of humankind's entire existence, dynamic metaphysics of the luminous divine Law of One living *Netjer*.

The nous must be taught to defuse teaching and learning by the mystical, spiritual science of daily meditation to feed the mind/body/spirit complex discernment for the Earth's *bon homies*. Encourages

THE MIND, BODY, SPIRIT, AND STORYTELLING

and inspires others' philosophical understanding which seek meaningful studies towards the learning/teaching of humankind to pursue God's mystery of unity, to spur themselves to seek out the intellectual, spiritual truth. Then might my understanding spur my others-selves to pursue a life of learning and teaching others to seek knowledge, insight, and the wisdom of nous; the spiritual science of actual monad energy that my spirit intelligent flow of the life force energy animates enliven the avatar physical mind/body/spirit complex unity with the in mediation state with a luminous divine spiritual nature of God.

This is by the wisdom of the Law of One love teachings towards learning the way to the initiation into salvation. And this is what is the mendacious truthiness that conceals the true connection between the Anunnaki Sumerian tablets and humankind's nascene is critical to the eponymous Holy Bible Genesis narrative story of the Adam and Eve creation. Might this be the absolute truth?

Therein lies truth regarding relevant facts and the important piece of the Genesis, which has been missing, conflates untold anecdotal details, and question why none of the organized prominent established Churches have been unwilling to concur with an speculation about what is seemingly plausible, perhaps, also quite logical conjecture that the story of the ancient deities were Anunnaki extraterrestrials—the rulers twisted into a mass deception—or dead I say falsehood religious storytelling! written information about that has been archived, stowed away in and closely guarded to prevent the truth from being exposed to human scrutiny. Which seems to be quite a plausible notion.

Suffice to say that the Anunnaki were the elite pantheon of titular gods from planet Nibiru. This is what the holy Bible Genesis obfuscates and pushes false narrative of truthiness. In the biblical book of god, Enki was a carefully crafted narrative without a predicate backstory. The specificity and anecdotal details about a physical place description of where, how, why: those from the Heavenly bodies purpose for descending down to the Earth landscape. Particularly what motivated the god/Enki to create Homo sapiens sapiens.

Enki was the commander of the UFO spacecraft that arrived and landed safely on the earth with His fifty-man ancient astronaut crew. The God that established city-states' settlements in ancient Mesopotamia. Archeology discovery stirred speculation on a Biblical tale. So where does the truth lie? With today's archeology discovery we have access to enough information to question what we have been taught to be true. So ask yourself: Why exactly is the ancient astronaut alien god's presence missing from the Old Testament Bible Genesis narrative silent about this? Because for me, the nascence of the Anunnaki's Sumerian Bible codex makes the most sense to elucidate the nous.

That fits nicely with the anecdotal details about why and how the Nibiruan Anunnaki, chief Medical Doctor, Royal Prince Enki/god created humankind as a primordial servile race of primitive workers to mine the earth's deep gold mining operations. A medical scientist in the field of Biological DNA genetics. Enki was the god of the wisdom of the Law of One love of the Law of One love and magic; and a member of Planet Nibiru's elite council of Anunnaki extraterrestrials aliens. Yeah this is the backstory to the Old Testament Holy Bible book of Genesis narrative: began the story written in the holy Old Testament Bible Chapter 1 through 11. Both conspicuously and curiously there are missing pieces of information that are judged on to be very relevant anecdotal details about the Anunnaki alien gods of the sky. The evidence in the Old Testament biblical narrative nexus is slowly being revealed, revealing a delineation from the original nascence of the Genesis tale is not so recondite! Because without the organized church religious teachings of the fanciful, ordinary people would not have been misled. Or, perhaps, we have been hoodwinked! Because what many of us have been taught as the words of god have been skewed in condensed version with predicate backstory of the Anunnaki ancient astronuattauts presence has been removed from the Old Testament biblical genesis narrative, which is incompatible with the story written about Enki's the vanguard exposition had come down to earth was to fulfill the Earth mission voyage under commander Enki's and his fifty man crew of ancient astronauts who were the original custodians of planet earth. The *eponymous* God-like figures are the key players in Old Testament Hebrew Holy Biblical Genesis, Chapter 1, narrative drama! Which began with the creation story. This version seemed to be a false reality as the modern ancient astronauts are on a mission that parallel the ancient astronauts theorists' premise. That is to say that a dichotomy is insofar as the truth lies in this religious truthiness!

Which seems to have had a fatal effect on the Earth's *bonhomes*. But there is one original account! Yeah, I posit that Anunnaki's original Sumerian Bible text recorded the nascence account. The relevant desperate for information on the genesis Gods. These missing and irrefutable evidence reveal evidence that they were *ancient space-traveling astronauts*.

The historical facts notwithstanding archeology discovery of the Sumerian Bible Genesis narrative. Curiously this book presents a view of what seems to be missing anecdotal details about God.

Historical pages written in the Book of Genesis revealed God's personna according to the Hebrew and Greek genesis narrative account is a truthiness because objective evidence about this was disclosed in the original Sumerian Holy Bible, contains a set of facts that the Anunnaki were extraterrestrial aliens—the Anunnaki titular Gods was an advanced race from their home planet, that they called Nibiru: "Those who from the Heaven came down" and landed on the interior earth plane. Planet-X, shall we call it, Nibiru alludes to the earth solar system so-called missing tenth orbital planet according to Zachariah Sitchin is referring to this mysterious Planet-X [Heaven]! But is there evidence of a missing the tenth planet? Some astronomers think so and might the conjecture of the Anunnaki alien's ancient astronomer theory fit into the context of the Old Testament Bible genesis narrative tale is not a Myth. It is suspected that the discovery of this mysterious tenth planet that seems to work the Mythological Heaven mentioned in the Holy Bible Genesis narrative says does not allude to that which would add clarity and insight into the image of the Anunnaki Anu, his Royal princes Enlil and Enki as God; meaning, what? They hide the fact that there is an argument that supports the ancient astronauts theorist fundamental hypothesis assertion that the Anunnaki were extraterrestrial aliens titular gods: A advanced intellect race of sophisticated space-travelers, whose space exploration was much the same as our own NASA preoccupation and aims to visit other planets as they revisit places where the lord and King of the Anunnaki clan from the planet Nibiru searched 450,000 years ago. Anunnaki extraterrestrials would have been the alien beings who piloted large, bright, and shiny bell-shaped aerial UFOs. They have been careful not to make mention of them in the Old Testament Bible, Chapter 1, Genesis narrative tales about: "Those who from the Heaven came onto the earth. Modern archeology discovery has provided significant historical evidence.

Important empirical historical archeology and anthropology discovery and findings, giving the knowledge and insight from perception of the external empirical world of the ancient Anunnaki walked among the humans as their god, as were ancient astronaut custodians of the Earth.

They were the gods who from Heaven came down to earth from a higher orbital density plane to achieve their mission purpose was to extract the mineral Gold, which ultimately they discovered that Southern Zimbabwe East Africa was largely rich with vast amounts of gold deposits. Which dovetails nicely with the ancient astronauts who were the Olden s biblical Genesis narrative. It's much easier for folks to corroborate the rich sources of desperate information on development connecting humankind to Enki; and my fundamental presupposition is that we can unpack some of the missing or lost anecdotal details about missing evidence, which alludes to the Anunnaki ancient alien astronauts who present seem credible evidence.

The nexus between the missing, the concealed, the truthiness, and the truth exposed to the light by the scientists' scholarly knowledge of archeology and anthropology. And then only to provide the erudition of the acknowledgment of the Anunnaki titular God (Enki) was the eponymous Infinite Creator mentioned in the Bible story of the first chapter of the Old Testament book of the Genesis narrative! What seems entirely plausible to me is that in Chapter 1, we are left to apprehend that God was a mysterious figure speaking and calling things into physically perceptible illusory temporal reality. What would seem to be a bold attempt to create a religious doctrine of dishonesty which was the means of misdirection? To cut away from the original narrative story about the Anunnaki: Those who from the Heaven came from (their home Planet) Nibiru and landed on planet earth. Planet-X is the tenth planet that is missing from our sun's orbital solar system.

Truth must be revealed, giving what can be discernible from historical content. With much respect due to the scholars who have been showing to everyone. Modern discoveries of thirty-thousands of Akkadian records of hard-baked ancient Cuneiform clay tablets alluded to the deeds of the Anunnaki revealed that they had been the custodian deities during gods, presence on Earth dovetail nicely to the Ancient Astronauts Theory. Whereas it was written and seemingly fit the objective and subjective analysis of the Bible Historical epoch of times. With the archeological and anthropology researchers, scientific scrutiny has been occurring and this conflates with this overall premise [https://www.britannica.com/topic/idealism]. Anunnaki beings that colonized Earth were from Nibiruan, and Enki proclaimed himself the Infinite Creator God!

As such, He is inextricably tied to the evolution and involution homo sapiens sapiens nascent, which is alluded to in the Hebrew and Greek Septuagint Holy Bible narrative tale epoch, which means what? The omissions are curiously remiss by not referring to the Bible God of creation was a man-like extraterrestrial aliens space faring (UFOs) who "came down" and landed a UFO spacecraft in ancient Mesopotamia.

Well, my friends, the Anunnaki Sumerian Bible is the most incredible truth! The facts are significant to the material facts derived from the original Old Hebrew/Greek Biblical Genesis narrative tale. The Anunnaki presence proved to have been titular Gods. Yes, these Gods were worshiped as luminous divine city-states deities as the rulers over the so-called Sumerians (blackheads). And no matter how entrenchment of some conscious biases the common ancestor bloodline arch back beyond the Holy Bible.

That is because the Anunnaki extraterrestrial alien gods were the original custodians, and is most notably connected to those who taught the mystery of the knowledge to the ancient Egyptian. This means they are likely Enki, as a precursor race of beings who implemented the original creation Myth about African hybrid Adam and the prototype female Eve homo sapiens existence! Simply try to deny that it is not a compelling story related to Nibiru's ancient astronaut god's when Enki UFO spacecraft arrived was a great Anunnaki race: "*Those who from the Heaven came*" spurred the nascent and the Genesis of the gods, they likely landed in Sumer, Mesopotamia was the Earth Mission voyage.

Curiously, the suspect is why transformations of the Hebrew and Greek septuagenarian Old Testament Holy Bible Genesis narrative are careful not to reveal evidence of the *Anunnaki Sumerian Bible Text*. We have never learned that this subject matter should become an exciting priority to unravel this long-standing truthiness of sophistry. Seemingly, a falsity to mislead the earth *bon homies* into the integration of Christianity and Paganism into a Roman Catholicism version in favor of the Westernized from New Testament perspective view as the religious establishment Church importance of blind faith dogma twisted African Egyptians psycho spiritual science teachings of ancient Kemetic mystery school religious institutions. This sacred knowledge was the understanding of the occult, (hidden) religion of the initiation rites of the priesthood. This was promulgated through Hebrews and Greeks priest and Bishop's interpretations, or mistranslation of certain Bible scriptures. spread as Orthodox learning/teaching which the Roman Catholic influence affected the schisms in the western Christian Churches religions doctrines and creeds. But no matter that the facts support archeology discovery.

The organized church denominations will neither willingly reconcile nor reveal the holy biblical Genesis tale. Yeah it's a contrivance that is the concealment of the Anunnaki extraterrestrial alien narrative titular Gods who were those giant man-like beings who came here in chariots from planet Nibiru [Heaven], or planet-X. Anunnaki spiritual narrative is revised into today's three external empirical world religions. The UFOs phenomenon of today dovetails nicely with the old astronauts' theorists hypothesis; that extraterrestrial intelligent beings landed on the earth's surface 450,000 years ago. The Anunnaki were the custodian gods who descended from above, and that these beings' presence began many years ago in Mesopotamia, the land of the Sumerian (blackheads) peoples. The organized reli-

THE MIND, BODY, SPIRIT, AND STORYTELLING

gious institutions don't want churches to conflate the status quo with teaching psycho-spiritual science philosophy, which dovetails nicely with modern research archeology discovery and findings.

To prevent speciousness from being reconciled with biblical false teachings/learning about Anunnaki. Presumably, these manlike aliens were teachers of the spiritual science principles of sacred knowledge. precepts was taught to the African-Egyptian as a mystery science of wisdom principles of African-*Kemetism* Law of One. According to the Egyptian mystery and the Bible Genesis is an incomplete truth; with the most important details missing from the pages of the original Anunnaki Sumerian Bible promulgated by Genesis Chapter 1 through 11. A provocative essay was written which might help spur learning and teaching of the mystical wisdom of the Law of One love in self-service. Meaning, it's important for us to first serve ourselves. While we aim towards higher service to one's other-selves, meaning what? That we are to possess a heart of moral spirit and observe the divine principles and laws of nature's empirical world. The mystery light of the occultist knowledge brings clarity and understanding. The compendium of the primordial knowledge derived from this the Anunnaki, Royal Prince Enki was commander of: "Those who from the Heaven came"! Their bell-space spacecraft arrived and landed upon the interior earth plane in the southern region of ancient Sumer, Mesopotamia were the ancient astronauts. Okay, the extraterrestrial alien God's. But could this be truthiness, or just perhaps the ancient astronaut theorists hypothesis is indisputably true! Given that the modern archeology and anthropology research discoveries have corroborated the material ings that dovetail nicely with the Anunnaki Sumerian Bible manuscript!

The Anunnaki titular Gods came here in chariots to the Earth. We're aliens from planet Nibiru, a historical discovery missing from the elite Royal Prince Enki's initial earth mission voyage critical gold mining mission operation. The Anunnaki ancient astronauts' fifty men crew safely arrived above Earth, then slowly landed down and established civilizations throughout the Sumerian interior plane's landscape. An enigmatic event which is most curiously noticeably absent from the Holy Bible, Genesis chapter 1, narrative tale.

HAKEEM R. JELANI

My salient question coalesce with the Old Testament Biblical book of the Annunaki Genesis narrative anecdotal details in Chapter 1, fits archeology discoveries and the ancient astronaut premise. These findings correspond with the genesis tale of ancient narrative. These are the footprints of the extraterrestrial Anunnaki alien God's presence on the earth's physical plane of human history, owing to their mission and purpose. Why this is speculation is missing; because it's devoid of anecdotal details and fits nicely with the creator God of the Bible in ancient Sumer, Mesopotamia. Now let's face it. The truth is being revealed to you and me by scientists who have accurately carbon-dated artifacts from the past, corresponding to Genesis, suggesting that the ancient creation Myth points to the exceeds the Old Testament Genesis narrates and Chronicled in the Babylonian tale of the *"Enuma Elish, Seven Tablets of Creation."* It gave the Old Testament Bible Genesis narrative legitimacy. The discovery gave credence to the findings of the modern ancient astronauts theorists hypothesis.

introduced this Bible story with conjectures and speculation with an assertion that the Anunnaki Enki (EA), is the creator god of the Old Testament Bible Genesis is about these intelligent extraterrestrial alien race who came down from the sky, and this is the essences of the religions are elevated! Most likely the so-called Gods who landed down in the earth interior plane of ancient Mesopotamian.

And being typical of all families, disagreements spurred sibling rivalry. Our modern archeology discoveries have corroborated the biblical opening lines we can believe. As such, it might ring true as the development of the missing pages reveals the face of Anunnaki extraterrestrial alien beings. Titular gods had arrived and landed on planet Earth 450,000 years ago. The Anunnaki extraterrestrial aliens Gods colonize planet earth. These biblical gods came down and landed from an advanced race onboard sophisticated aerial spacecraft in ancient Mesopotamia. My friends, you might want to ask further questions about whether the Anunnaki was an alien race that made significant contributions to the evolution and involution of humanity during their epoch of time during the Olden s Gods 450,000s of years ago.

THE MIND, BODY, SPIRIT, AND STORYTELLING

Might the Anunnaki alien gods have been the original custodians who established civilization in the interior earth plane of ancient Mesopotamia? Yes! For those who are unfamiliar, well then this is the true story with which I elucidate the a delineation of the irrefutable views of the alien gods and the biblical creation myth according to the connection with which was derived from Enki's creation of of crossbred homosapeins sapien human races on earth—thus the truth about Christianity account that was cherry-picking and rebranded into the New Testament version of the origin sacred wisdom teachings of Kemetism. The evolution of spiritual science wisdom spurred by the Anunnaki, Enki's secret societies of the African-Egyptian mystery schools occult (hidden) knowledge of the ancient temples priesthood serpent learning and teachings of African consciousness awareness transformational understanding through meditation. Which imparted and advanced knowledge of the esoteric to the transformation into cultures of civilization. These valuable cuneiform clay tablets that were unearthed in the ancient library of *King Ashurbanipal's Royal Palace compound* located in *Nipper* in the modern day country of Iraq, which was called Sumer, Mesopotamia. Significant theological, biblical genesis narrative nascence of Christianity. With empirical evidence, archeology and anthropology discovery represents the missing anecdotal details that reconciled the original Anunnaki presence.

These scholars are able to validate certain historical facts and references accurately matched to the historical timeline of the Old Testament Bible story. Events of the past, modern archeology and anthropology discovery, meaning what? Ancient astronauts theorists hypothesized; it predicates conjugate clarity to discern what is obfuscated in the context of the genesis narrative is incomplete—because the Anunnaki presence is absolutely inherent to the overall historical facts and evidence of modern archeology and anthropology research discovery.

No! No! Not at all. Why? Because much of what is written about the Anunnaki extraterrestrial alien beings, suggesting that there's some truth to the theorists hypothesis; whereas it's a very compelling retrospective that frames the assertion that the Anunnaki alien gods theory fits quite nicely with the proper contexts: meaning that "Those who from the Heaven came" is not a Mythos. The ancient astronauts' storied adventure was excised by biblical translations, meaning that religious bishops intentionally perpetuated a contrived religious misdirection.

Which validates the Old Testament book of the Annunaki Genesis narrative tale, revealing a culture juxtaposition to Anunnaki alien Gods walking the earth in Mesopotamian Account. Which details the genesis narrative events of the was written on cuneiform clay tablets known as the "Babylonian Seven Tablet of the Creation" was found at *Ashur, Kish, Ashurbanipal's* library at *Nineveh*.

The excavated hard-baked cuneiform clay tablets found at ancient sites. Locations are mentioned in the Bible, dating back to a very relevant monumental connection to the epoch of time revealed that the Anunnaki extraterrestrial Astronauts scenario is consistent with significant biblical known events [1]. Archeologists excavated a treasure trove of 30 thousand Sumerians cuneiform clay tablets, and from underneath the Assyrian King, Ashurbanipal's Royal main palace temple complex, his ancient library was located in Iraq. Inspire curiosity and spur consciousness to get at what is accurate against what is spurious. This is central to the inspiration for writing a chapter book that might convey this reconcile to the retrospective that is my learning and teaching others about the love of the lights of the ubiquitous spirit of the Netjer and of the metaphysical cosmic nature that is revealed—One all Infinite Creator's Law of One, the pervading animating manifestation of the spiritual science of infinite Creator.

The all-unity of the love pleroma is inspired by free will and imbued with consciousness awareness to live by the Law of One intelligence of the infinite energy from the spirit of God. The expressions of love are words that in the Greek language are: *Eros, Phila, and Agape*. And like human emotions, feelings are quite visceral in all relationships. I love you all and I thank you for letting me share these eccentric creative harmonic streams of my mind/body/spirit vibrations of the Infinite Creator, Adona!

THE MIND, BODY, SPIRIT, AND STORYTELLING

I certainly appreciate that by the same light of the Intelligent Infinite Creator's Law of One's vivifying words resonate with the unity of mind/body/spirit complex. Rejoice for the peregrinations while learning to be a soul in service to humanity's other entities; the other selves of the creative energy, Adona—God! The most extraordinary bonds we cultivate in the universal human family.

There's plenty of folks who read and quote from the Bible thinking that they have answers. While others think that it's the truth but (they have know idea)! Well then my friends, stay *loving* in the *light* of the time/space continuum. I bless you all in the name of the Infinite Creator!

Ancient Astronauts Mined Africa's Gold Anunnaki's Mission Earth Voyage, And Humans

The Anunnaki Sumerian Bible Old Testament Book of Genesis, and how much of what the organized religious institutions have been teaching is sophistry? Or, dare shall I question, elucidate about a *malicious* truthiness! But there is a growing mainstream of neophytes in search of the hidden mystery behind the Mesopotamian and African-Egyptian [Kemetic] art of spiritual science where you may find the empowerment and enlightenment of and meaning of true life experience and understanding of the true illumination of the Gnosis.

We are all the living embodiments of the luminous spirits, sapient beings; and the seekers who espouse support of the controversial ancient astronaut theorists hypothesis. Meaning that logic and reason conflates archeology and anthropology discovery and historical research. The information dovetails nicely with misleading religious distortions in the Old Testament Bible book of Genesis truthiness! But is this curiosity somehow a falsehood? The translations of the Holy Bible, humans, have perpetuated as the actual words of God, mentioned in the mistranslated Hebrew Old Testament Bible Genesis narrative? Might I say that without a doubt attaining a deeper esoteric understanding of what we now must learn about the past historical facts as a preceptor of others by the erudition of knowledge is luminous divine wisdom of the Law of One love derived from Low of One mystical, spiritual science sacred principles?

Human beings synced to the universal cosmic harmonic balance of nature religious unity. I beheld the one true God is dwelling as a soulful spirit; and my intelligent energy which animates my mind/body/spirit complex spurs human beings' churlish actions and behavioral impulses consciousness awareness. Having free will to make excellent or wrong decisions is being aware of your actions as a cause and effect relationship as we are interacting in the present time is constantly evolving and transforming into the past vault of remembrance, our transient life events are the illusory reality.

This is just a snapshots of human consciousness, awareness of the curated experiences of the spiritual peregrinations, and cycle events of the spinning planet of the darkness to the daylight to darkness turnstile duality, which passes through every second into historical archived moments of transient episodes of the timeline of the life cycle continuum—from death, resurrection, life comes into light.

We visually perceive the manifestation of daily reality of the temporal world in measure of real-time material form. Mysteries hidden from the ancient past biblical history and the modern examination from the prisms of archeology and anthropology discovery and findings, juxtaposition to the controversy surrounding the ancient astronaut's theorists hypothesis speculation that the Anunnaki Royal elites were the alien Gods: Those who from the Heavens came from Planet-X, shall I say the missing plane Nibiru! That is to say that they were ancient Gods, space astronauts who came down from Heaven to Planet Earth. The real story of the Old Testament chapter 1, veiled the Anunnaki presence, was about the ancient astronaut's extraterrestrial alien God's presence on the planet earth's surface.

There seems to be no pmissing anecdotal details about this topic that can no longer remain hidden mysteries of the Infinite Creator is the intelligent energy of the creative infinity. African Hebrews Bible Story telling of the Old Testament Genesis narrative tales. Which speaks in terms of an historical context with respect to the Olden Times Anunnaki alien God of ancient Mesopotamia. An identity truncated and hermetically concealed from the beginning of the alien god's departure from the Earth after the conquest of ancient Babylonian kings Cyrus the great's victory over the king of Babylonian.

Thus mistranslation of purveyors of misinterpreting Kemetic teaching/learning about natural principles of the luminous divine philosophical, spiritual science of God from the original Anunnaki/Sumerian Bible. Knowledge and wisdom taught by the Anunnaki

THE MIND, BODY, SPIRIT, AND STORYTELLING

God of wisdom and understanding, Enki led to the cult of ordained priests via the sacred initiation ceremonial ritual and rites of the spiritual science precepts of the Law of One love. Enlightenment of salvation became tenets of African-Kemetic *Coptic Egyptian-Kemetism*, with Western Europe Greek transformation and the suppression of these indigenous religious beliefs as their original ideas and teachings about *Amon-Ra's Law of One* (Diop, 1974; Jahn, 1961). Of the practice of ancient mystery spiritual science through the daily inward reflection of meditative state. By the inward reflection becoming sync with the universal spirit of the generous spirit of God rhythmic, harmonic unity of vibrations for total mind/body/spirit balance of the cosmic metaphysical

We expect the faithful to learn and teach others by revealing the specificity and anecdotal details about Anunnaki learning and teaching about things of knowledge that were derived from the ancient astronaut's theory. This premise interpolates a countervailing storyline, and *ipso facto,* this explanation will help the bons hommes mind to finally break free from the constraints of misdirection and truthiness, meaning what? And without the balance of sacred principles to guide folk through the gateway of intelligent infinity, we will be filled with the wisdom of the Law of One! Yeah, to funnel a humble life into the light of love in service to our self and our other selves is to follow God's philosophical Law of One. Meaning to teach/learn about the pathway to salvation through meditation. This is not by the religious teachings that comports deceptions with imparting that practice of Zen which focuses on meditation and intuition Principles focus on achieving enlightenment through spiritual science religions teachings and learning about the mind, body, spirit complex.

That is to say, by means of the African-Egyptian secret ritual sciences of Kemetism as the cult of Isis, and Osiris sacred knowledge principles taught to priests, such as wisdom of astronomy, mathematics, medicines, was understandably mastered the ancient mysteries. Might it be true that these fields of intellectual knowledge be traced back to the Anunnaki alien god Enki's and the African indigenous hominid Female DNA connection to the arrival of this sophisticated UFO space-flight, as it fits nicely with the ancient astronaut aliens

Enki was likely the god of the Old Testament Holy Bible narrative of the Anunnaki as the extraterrestrial alien gods.

The presence of intelligent Gods mentioned in the pages of the Holy Old Testament Bible on Earth [2]. That which seems to be a truthiness because it lacks the whole truth! And isn't it true that we possess cosmic law of the forces of one's free will to choose worship and or follow the religious ecclesiastical teachings espoused by whichever spiritual teachings we adhere to as the words of God? But is this the most pleasing truth, that unsuspecting people are less inclined towards the mystery spiritual science of seated meditation? Instead, they opted to embrace the Christian faith, religious teaching of paganism and Christianity. Kemetism teaches the sacred religious principles of mind/body/spirit unity with the Netjer and the God's Law of One unity with the universally harmonic vibration unity with the cosmic pleroma. Egyptian of the priesthood learning /teaching the spiritual science Law of One. Ancient African-Egyptian knowledge of spiritual wisdom principles the Anunnaki Enki taught the spiritual science religion of the African Kemetic bloodline lineage before the imperial Rome hegemony rose to efficaciously elevated the primacy of the Roman Catholic Church.

Such an incredible paradigm. A cultural shift away from the African-Egyptian spiritual cult wisdom derived from this learning teaching of this spiritual science philosophy and principles.

They subjugated and unceremoniously erased and denigrated them exported to Western European powers retelling of intelligence contributions. African black peoples consciousness awareness. The fNew Testament transformation emerged into Christian gospels of the western interpretation and perspective came forth a different perspective of religious precepts teaching merged twisted into the age reworked versions of the cult of Isis and Osiris mysteries. A pivotal moment gave rise to the contrived Romans New Testament Christianity; and thus, hegemony of the holy Trinity came into existence under the direct influence of the powerful Catholic Church Roman Papacy. Few individuals dare oppose or question the ruling elite's authority faced severe consequences for defying the Catholic church religious edicts, and as the predominant western Church, because elements of the pagan occultism practices were adapted and embraced by Imperial Rome.

Christianity established the ultimate non-spiritualist religion, with the Vatican Papacy as god representative (https://www.kemeticcenteredliving.com/blog/kemetic-spiritual-science-basics-for-beginners).

The punishment of anyone who challenged the new testament Canon law they deemed to be heretical and a threat to the established papal Catholic Church doctrines and creeds. The Church order of Bishop and the new priesthood often punished anyone who they found guilty of carrying out violent abuses towards an accused, which was a sharp departure from the mystery cultist wisdom principles of the Kemet teachings of spiritualism. People who feared persecution were forced underground fearing punitive repercussions. Western religious views supplanted the philosophy of the Law of One spiritual education of knowledge as the teaching/learning of Romanized Christianity, inserted their strict instructions as a religious doctrinal creed.

They put forth organized church religions as a schemed as the will of God with prescribed religious ritual, rites, canon laws cemented and vested in the biblical books of the New Testament Christians holy Bible. This is the blind faithful religion through confession of sins and prayerful worshiping of the apomorphic Jesus Christ as the living God of Heaven. God's personification, is the gospel which the church authority praises as the Infinite Creator is lost in the shameful history of the church.

The new age rulers hubris and arrogance was mendacious, as they pervaded and entrenched Christian Orthodox prescribed teachings of the falsehoods precepts as god's house of religious traditions and thoughts, which was the elevation an cementation of their misdirection into the ordained instructions for vainglorious theology of the ecclesiastical formation of a blind faithful Gospel of truthiness; away from the true universal spirit nature of god's Kemetic Sky god Ra, who was the purveyors of the esoteric wisdom of spiritual science secret through the learning and teaching of the sacred the divine Law of One universal Al Infinite Creator of the harmonic logos pervading life force energy; that which provides and sustains the material existence of our reality. All physic and metaphysical noumena, having a fidelity with the constellation orbital around the glowing sunshine associated with the luminous sacred divine light force energy element burning fire! One truth I aspire to embrace by my spiritual insight and wisdom; and not that of organized religious belief in the one all merciful God unity of one true monad Law of One love of the great *Neberdjer*.

My friends, perhaps the steadying of archeology and anthropology, but the significant focus on the facts which are a convergence of an intersect dovetails with the linguistic tropes. Or perhaps to be appreciated, shall we say that the biblical genesis narrative purports to say nothing about the ancient astronauts! Nevertheless, it is a highly credible and fascinating hypothetically rational speculative premise. The old biblical gods and their presence in ancient Mesopotamia. Archeology discoveries are responsible for giving credible evidence concerning the extraterrestrial alien Gods, and that is to say: certain assumptions can be gleaned from the source ings of the archeology dig sites, and that the anthropology study and discovery is revealing that the speculation about the Anunnaki fit ancient astronauts hypothesis is a perfect fit the Genesis creation narrative tale: "Those who from the Heaven came down to earth came "!

Yeah just perhaps the Old Testament Bible narrative tale is a plagiarized truthiness, of the African Egyptian, Kemeticism Isis and Osiris initiation Mythology; which was manipulated into the truthiness tale of the Bible story into a religious beliefs that is closely akin to the original truth story about the Anunnaki alien god Enki as the first extraterrestrial ancient astronaut who descended from Heaven the earth plain of ancient Sumerian, Mesopotamia. This assumption has parallel to the Bible Genesis narrative that curiously omitted this important anecdotal detail. That which the Anunnaki Sumerian Bible genesis narrative was the developing and original illuminating accounts of the positive historical records, which dovetails nicely with the Enuma Elish Seven Tablets of the ancient Babylon Sumerian Biblical books of the Genesis Story. Yeah, unearthing the hidden mysteries details of our story is, in fact, my friends, it's largely an alien attribution that is derived from the ancient astronauts theory.

THE MIND, BODY, SPIRIT, AND STORYTELLING

It is parallel with earth man's and his scientific advancement towards deep space exploration is closely akin to UFOs presence in earth air space. And this is to say that the Anunnaki Sumerian Bible narrative is not antithetical to the ancient astronaut theorists' premise. It is no longer convoluted; we can now expose people to what seems perfectly logically plausible and responsible. The information is about the eruditions, which is being revealed to the curious archeology and anthropology research discovery and findings of lost ancient cuneiform clay tablets and the translations.

Evidence that supersedes the falsity of misdirections that the churches' religionists believe diverge from the complexities of ancient mystery spiritual science Law of One luminous divine primal wisdom of the Law of One love with a light heart of transformation through the African-Egyptians Kemetism spirituality. What is the meaning of spirituality science meditation?

Might there actually be a supernatural power? Gods and demons wagering to win humankind's souls; and, if true, are they somehow involved with the surface illusion of manipulation of the mind/body complex of the human entities free-will to do good or evil deeds? According to Hinduism Buddhism of Sanskrit [from the Sanskrit māyā, from mā 'create'], that which exists and having the power by which the personhood of the earth bon homies are of the mind, body, spirit complex of the material world universe living manifestations; we are all the embodiments of the transformation of the bifurcated world societies. Which is a common mediate of our individual psychospiritual empirical world phenomenon. To this, *Māyā* is also a spiritual concept connoting that which "is constantly changing and thus is said to be of the essence of spiritually unreal *pleroma*" (opposition to an absolute), "concealing the true aspects of the spiritual science principles of the temporal reality" [https://www.lexico.com/en/definition/maya].

Religion theology of the teachings of the Luciferian falsehood that promulgated the sense of the external empirical world illusory temporal reality has become the current impulse of the mainstream contemporary culture of human society has emerged in the subconscious mind of the faithful blind faith religious teachings of the New Testament books of Christianity.

Okay! Now might I direct your conscious awareness to this salient fact that Christianity was a twisted version of the African-Egyptian mysteries, which they denigrate as the occultists, while very knowledgeable about the nascence of the mystery spiritual science wisdom teaching of the Egyptian God Ra's Law of One? Yeah, Kemetism was taught and learned through the sacred initiation into priesthood fellowship with extraterrestrial Annunaki race extraterrestrial alien beings worshipers. Romanized by doctrinal dogmatic creed of truthiness, which misled the blind faith Christian faithful worshiping Christ as humankind's salvation.

Particularly, genesis narrative tale that dovetails nicely with the UFOs speculatively ancient astronaut premise with respect to the extraterrestrial alien Annunaki Gods who were those came here in chariots down from planet Nibiru's [Heaven] consistent with tale of holy Bible Genesis narrative; that is to dovetails nicely with the elite the Royal great prince Enki [the prosonna of the biblical creator Gods who descended from the higher plane's constellational cosmic orbital existence.

They had landed an alien spacecraft in Mesopotamia with a fifty-man crew. The Bible alludes to this in Chapter 1, Genesis narrative. According to the opponents of the ancient astronaut's theory, they believe this theoretical assertion to be improbable, while scientists think that it seems plausible.

The purpose of this exegesis is to pique the latent curiosity of anyone who is a skeptic. And whoever is skeptical--perhaps you should question why you have reservations about this topic with curious concerns about being misled by blind faith religion falsity?

Yeah. and what say you? Are you inclined to concur with this vivifying ancient astronaut's perspective as a practical matter, with understanding may harshly critique the thesis. Many folks are pretty unfamiliar with the Anunnaki extraterrestrial aliens controversy.

Nevertheless, the ancient astronaut theory (definitely) is very arguably compelling, plausible as the Sumerian Bible text juxtaposes against the objective logic and reason. Truth can never be rebuffed. That the extraterrestrial and UFOs phenomenon is most likely intimately connected to the ancient astronaut's hypothesis.

So then, I would argue that the Bible book of the Old Testament Genesis is false because it hides the evidence of the Anunnaki presence as mentioned in ancient Anunnaki Sumerian original Holy Bible accounts. These aliens were the custodian titular gods who seeded civilization's spiritual teachings on the surface of planet Earth.

The ancient astronaut who descended from the higher plane and established civilization predicted the absolute truth and enlightened folks whose consciousness was aware of the jejune misguided. But salient questions remain: Did an advanced race of extraterrestrial intelligence alien beings possessing sophisticated knowledge travel via flying spacecraft descend from a high plane of the constellational orbit. This was the job of the "Watchers". A functional role performed in support of Nibiru's ancient astronaut we are acquainted with from the Old Testament Bible genesis narrative. Was this some kind of ancient orbital space station? Of course, the Bible also tells us that god (Enki) built or created the first outlying alien city-states settlements community based settlement in Sumer, Mesopotamia. These beings were the titular gods who came to earth from their own home planet Nibiru! They were only space-traveling ancient astronauts who came here in chariots from their home planet Nibiru [3]. As humankind's ancestors had perceived the anamorphic Anunnaki Lord King Anu as supreme Sky God in Heaven, His sons, the Royal great prince Enki and Enlil, both were worshiped in Mesopotamia in the personification deities deeds were permeated and pervaded among the Sumerian people as the perceived to be beings chariots of flames arrived from a higher plane of the cosmic orbital cycle; the so-called "shining ones"!

The presence of extraterrestrial aliens who were a sophisticated race with many attributes, e.g., the God Enki as the earth creator God of water, genetic science, magic, mischief, and wisdom of the Law of One love: The God of the Olden Times Anunnaki, who Commanded the first fifty man astronauts crew of UFOs from the planet Nibiru: *"Those who from the Heaven came"* they worshiped: saying that the Anunnaki were: Those who from the Heavens came …meaning what? The original Bible Genesis narrative is Anunnaki's presence in Mesopotamia; the template strand is the epoch of the extraterrestrial known as Annunaki, Anunna, Ananaki, other variations of deities who appear in the ancient Sumerians' Mythological traditions Akkadians, Assyrians, and Babylonians [4].

They were an advanced race of space-traveling ancient astronauts descended from their home planet Nibiru, or as some have called earth's missing *Planet-X*. Genesis narrative reads that they were "Those who from the Heaven came down to earth came down onto the earth interior plane...the titular Gods from a higher constellation orbital plane. To assume assertions over the biblical genesis narrative storytelling, buttress the modern premise of astronaut extraterrestrial aliens beings as the *Anunnaki* were likely the original custodian gods. And they probably colonized planet Earth 450,000 years ago and after the initial landing in *Mesopotamia*. I am saying that religion's theologian will never reveal that aliens seeded the temple priesthood with sacred teaching of spiritual meditation. Bring purity of the heart within unity with the harmonic vibration of the mind, body, spirit, insight complex balance with divine *Shetaut Neberdjuer* Kemetism philosophy--esoteric consciousness. These titular man-like God figures were the extraterrestrial aliens' space-traveling astronauts. The custodian of the earth who taught the primitive indigenous earth man initiates their priesthood sacred temple spiritual worship of the Gods of Planet Nibiru secret knowledge of the ancient spiritual wisdom of the Law of One love of the Law of One love teaching of the mysteries. To become minister to the souls of those who are common folks devoid of the pathway toward spiritual meditation and the worshiping of the Infinite Creator God of Heaven. But still there are and are people who are devoted to their Christian faiths that most pleases the agency that reconciles their own council with God's truth. They consider and dutifully accept the Catholicism and the Protestantism Christian church theological precepts by worshiping Gods in the personification of their savior Jesus Christ, who has been proclaimed the savior and redeemer Jesus Christ as follows:

> ..."*The religious devotion has been taught as the gospel of truth constitutes millions of faithful human followers who worship the Christian Bible*

> as the words of the God of Heaven according to the ancient rituals, doctrines creed as Cannon Law by blind faith church religion. Yeah, people are attracted by the belief in worshiping God in personification in the Trinity of Jesus Christ as their luminous divine nature of the savior. The Name Of The Savior Is Yeshua HaMashiach; It Is Not 'Jesus Christ'!! According to the English Bible, the name of the Savior-Son of Elohim, the Highest One, is Jesus… Instead, it was deliberately introduced into the Holy Scriptures by some being of evil intent!! May 6, 2014… (*http://sbpra.com/ChrisBapuohyele*).

We must recognize that uninformed people are content to be misled because many are disinclined to seek the available information—if they would read widely! Yeah. Let's face it: they wittingly behave in the manner of blind sheep being led astray by this religion of falsity. The leading Church denominations. Members of the congregation have settled into social fellowship within their consciousness and, through the Gospels, adhere to the truthiness; some people say: that God hears the prayer without the learning of the ancient esoteric sacred religious mind/body/spirit avatar complex unity.

For it is true that people today embrace Gospel religious sects that propagate a misdirection away from faithful spiritual providence and salvation. Humankind nascence and rise of occultists complexities of ancient mystery spiritual science, of seated meditation, was about teachings and learning about The Kemetism esoteric spiritual ancient wisdom of the Law of One love and understanding of sacred principles of sophistication of the old mystery spiritual science of meditation the Romans Emperor embraced, superseded, and consolidated the Kemet teachings, which was the transformation of Africa's spiritual occultists wisdom of the Law of One into the Christian church religions. The rigidity of learning and teaching of sacred principles was derived from ancient esoteric schools, which elements of paganism embraced and then incorporated into the foundational ethos of Christianity's adopted the doctrinal religion cannons of the new Westernized Empirical blind faith religionist theological: a Holy Roman Catholic dogmatism. Doctrinal creeds and canon teachings of the faith were called into question by a German Bishop. And He said: "*I cannot and will not recant anything, for to go against conscience is neither right nor safe. Here I stand; Ican do no other, so help me God. Amen.*"

The words which inspired seek teach several new theological religions of ecclesiastical and evangelical implementation of the interpretation, as the Protestants Church began teachings of conservatism. Therein religious Church doctrine of the Holy Trinity Creed [5]. The Protestants' impetus is owing to Martin Luther "who is the German professor of theology, priest, author, composer, Augustinian monk, and a figure in the Reformation. Luther was ordained into the priesthood in 1507. He rejected much of the pagan teachings and practices of the Roman Catholic Church; at that particular moment, he disputed the view on indulgences [Wikipedia].

Let's face it.

The truth about ancient astronauts, the Anunnaki titular Gods, of materialization of alien UFOs phenomenon intermittently uninvited external manifestations, perhaps is a misunderstood bugaboo. Gold was an abundantly available resource in the southeastern region of great Zimbabwe, Africa.

The Anunnaki were an advanced race; we call the ancient astronauts who arrived in ancient Mesopotamia. What was a voyage with a specific mission: to mind the earth's material gold resources. To process the gold into monatomic gold particles. With available and steady resources of gold shipments from planet Earth.

The mineral gold was critical for saving the Anunnaki's home planet's from the destructive damage that had been occurring in their home planet's ozone atmosphere and was required to effectively patch up and seal dangerous holes in Nibiru's loss of atmosphere. A space faring event *coterminously* and *inextricably* fits into most logical and very reasonable missing Anunnaki presence made many significant contributions towards humankind, which we now know was intentionally excised from the Bible's book of Genesis, Chapter 1. But what exactly does my exegesis mean?

Here's my book that posits a plausible premise that a paradigm shifts away from false religious deceptive truthiness teachings of Christianity's truthiness. While my purpose here is to impart logic and reason with which spur the *bon homies* to be victims of the misdirection by the church authority, religious truthiness. That they perpetuate an incomplete story about the Nascence of the Holy Bible Genesis narrative. To the ancient creation Myths is a salient point. Reconciliation with which is the juxtaposition of spiritual erudition. Yeah archeology discovery dovetails nicely with the synergy of an ancient alien extraterrestrial being perceived as a titular God. Yeah, those Anunnaki': those from Heaven were ancient astronauts, alien gods of the planet Nibiru's missioned earth voyages, with which their purpose was not to create Adam and Eve. No! Not at all, which was incidental to the actual priority was to mine and excavate earth's gold resources. Yeah it was the purpose of this advanced alien race that was known as the Royal-Elite Anunnaki; the original custodians rulers' who with them knowledge and system of the and state. Anunnaki aliens were the original and custodians, ancient extraterrestrial space-traveling alien astronauts were not Gods.

Extraterrestrials who came from Heaven

I am betting that the Old Testament Genesis tale allows you to glean that they were from advanced, men-like beings, from the planet Nibiru. An advanced vanguard of the Anunnaki Olden times titular Gods, the Sumerians called them the "*Shining One*". This was the initial ancient astronaut crew that had been launched from their home planet Nibiru (planet-X). Just perhaps it's logical and presumptuous to conclude that it is true that the Anunnaki earth mission voyage was not conjectures, and not storytelling—as some would have us believe. But what if were historical events; and then ponder the likelihood of intelligent extraterrestrials as being ancient astronauts who came was led by the great Royal Prince, Enki. Is it possible or unfathomable to accept that they likely landed in Sumerian Mesopotamia.

Their mission was to land down on the planet Earth's surface interior plane to locate and mine gold deposits by establishing a production operation and transforming it to monatomic gold particles. To expedite gold back to the Anunnaki's home planet Nibiru where it was needed to patch all critical holes to prevent the loss of Nibiru's atmosphere. These Anunnaki established their presence in ancient Mesopotamia and were cemented as the original custodians of the planet Earth.

These aliens were the earth's titular Gods of the indigenous people of the earth. They were the precursor beings who established their presence by creating the first civilization by building great important institutions that would educate the public well being. And as the powerful Gods on earth initiated the order of the god's initiation into the sacred wisdom of esoteric mystery, spiritual science and religion of priests temple worship through the ordained holy priesthood; that through seated meditation. Priests as God's personal appointed Holy ministers who were ordained to teach the law of one love of the ways of people about the African-Egyptians *Kemeticism, luminous divine* spiritual wisdom of the Law of One love and reward is the salvation after death, that luminous divine spirit again realignment is retained until the natal of my rebirth from the 369 transportine initiation; as my spirit essence bypass cold motionless death of the fleshy body when the soul of the Gods luminous divine intelligent harvested me from the *recombinant* state of quiet comfort resting in solace I reside buoyant in Heaven with the Infinite Creator in stupendous peaceful and harmony! It's this series of holy ceremonies, rituals, and sacred rites; they do not know the true luminous divine nature of the hidden Kemetic ancient spiritual science teaching/learning about being unity with the *Infinite Creator's* Law of One principle. Whether this was achieved while the titular gods the Royal great prince Enki carried out the gold mining production operations in Africa's great Zimbabwe. From there transport the mineral in sufficient amounts back to planet Nibiru. The Infinite Creator God of Heaven wisdom of the Law of One love while living on Earth taught the priesthood sacred principles of spiritualism Law of One.

THE MIND, BODY, SPIRIT, AND STORYTELLING

The light of complexities of ancient mystery spiritual science creative sacred principles of unconditional love imbued by the most high nature; luminous divine spirit consciousness awareness of meditation. Pernicious sinister fetters underlie the evil ruler's aims to mislead and deceive civil society of common consciousness. Rulers maintained the status quo ante of a system of centralized global political and influential religious and global monetary economies (that is, the wealth system) of power-driven by the Eagle's fiat currency system. But might such a system be it a manifestation of the material monitory form of slavery? Which humankind becomes deceived with the fascination with the materialistic. Divergence from the meaningful purpose of spiritual simplicity: to live in harmony, always loving, living, and to meditate upon perfection, raising our consciousness through the pathway of spirituality science, within profound greater insight into a prayerful seated meditation. And with an air of purity preaching about the Holy Spirit to lead towards personal providence and salvation. With integrity, we are not trapped and held captives in the machinations of the financial debt systems rut of high-interest rates. Of which it's everyday consumers who use their plastic credit card debt drive the economic exploitation of the civil society at large; as I refer is the invisible hand of the cabal mechanisms to maintain control the hidden hand of the deceivers of global elites, the powerful system of state governments tied to the central banking system. It's a whole substrate financial credit/debt financial banking system managed as the external empirical world comprehensive banks system operates at the behest of Anunnaki cabal's player's machinations.

Yeah, they are still the powerful players who are behind the world's economies and they exercise their control ever since the so-called empirical world of wealthy drug dealers. The distributors and purveyors of the empirical worldwide illicit drug dealing supply chain networks operated by powerful cartel's who perpetuate addiction, physical and mental health issues, sueside, homelessness, and death. This insidious deed is prevalent among the youth in every social community's culture, and it has shown no signs of being eradicated.

Is it not the allure of the commercial world of big profit business enterprise economies involved in this global network of institutional powers, and their amoral player's with sinister motivation they seek to achieve the means to gain capital wealth. This was by whatever means they deemed to be necessary was motivated by greed. It was ultimately for the lust to acquire the material gold, was a rush to accumulate vast wealth, quickly became a driver for those evil purveyors who are in the illicit drugs traffic enterprise that is killing people.

They are the facilitators who are devoid of benevolent goodness of moral turpitude. Drug dealers who by their actions wittingly deal in the retail distribution of recreational poisons. Which facilitates what can be defined as pure evil deeds personified criminal activity caused by those purveyors of all harmful commodities; the legal tobacco, alcohol, and all dangerous illicit drugs. The enablers have consigned scores of people to a miserable life, one that is closely akin to spiritual enslavement! This is inarguably a consignment to a dangerous psychological of self-imprisonment, to ing life in a meter of social deprivation. A consignment to an inevitable slow death by suicide!

Evidence is there throughout the visual empirical world at large. The truth is hidden by the evil deeds carried out by the powerful secret societies' elite cabals, who are the ruling class network machinations! Globalist plots aim to use the elite communication media to control and enslave the social consciousness narrative for their manipulated purpose to determine the desired outcome of empirical world events. Efficaciously, to bring about a new empirical world order by means using digital electronic technology to assert absolute control as the new empirical world order of electronic system innovation in aspects of the modern financial, economic, and political elements of social engineering to impact in life-changing ways of human autonomy. Actions of evolution away from their pathway towards the mystery of spiritual science sacred principles for humankind is the wisdom of the Law of One love. This is learning and teaching the knowledge of the agreement of the Law of One luminous divine spirit of consciousness, awareness among hearts and souls of people. People who first serve themselves and to serve others. To forsake the lustful nature of materialism all and lust desire for wealth and power. It's not a concealed hidden mysteries system. It's a well-entrenched monitory web of the underlying, mendacious evil deeds has connection to secret societies and fraternities of brotherhood bloodlines. Global power of a growth system of globalization was spurred by the Western model. Its machinations' to construct a capitalist economic power system as a blueprint. To maintain ultimate central control of the institutions of religion in worship of Gods we trust; and by the state of capitalism. Misled by blind faith, religious doctrine is taught as God's Word and promulgates the words "In God We Trust." Indeed, this is simply incredible! The two faces of *Janus* are not a hidden mystery hand—it has existed in plain sight, and it manipulates as the ruler's invisible hand of these decisive mendacious deceitful actions. The elite rulers aimed to achieve and maintain the status quo ante.

The mission Earth voyage was undertaken to acquire the mineral gold; the creation of human beings was an ancillary necessity, requiring Enki to fashion primitive workers to serve the titular gods of Heaven.

Yeah, those who seek to enlighten themselves are to those who possess the gold. They write the laws that facilitate accumulating unbridled material wealth and power moves on a monopoly game board of economic capitalism.

This is not a conspiracy theory, my friends; it's this well-crafted and established system of the perpetual falsity of illusory material consciousness fortunate winners, and let's face the reality: there are many unfortunate losers in life. And like the neophytes and adept of the wisdom of the Law of One love. Perhaps you, too, will want to learn/teach others to gain a sagaciousness for understanding nature; the spiritual inspiration of luminous divine sacred principles is God's Law of One love.

Wake up people!

You are deceived and misled from knowing of the discernment of truth. Be open-minded and engage illusory temporal reality and know thyself. For it is pertinent to know that we are all of the one luminous divine mind/body/spirit social complex. Among the human experience of living in the society of common consciousness there are some *inscrutable* and skeptical people who are ignorant and uninformed. Such as I contend are blind faithful followers who worship the god of the false organized Church religion's theology.

I thank you for your interest, illustrated by the conscientiousness in taking the time to digest the subject matter of this exegesis expose'. Whereas my imagination, our eyes were blindfolded by Priests and Pastors is closely the Pharisees of the biblical genesis, they were deceivers for the organized Church's religious transformation divergence away from the philosophical wisdom of the Law of One love of the sacred teaching of the original spiritual nature of the universal luminous divine nature of the Monad.

Which was the true precepts and teachings of the Egyptian [Kemet] God Ra's spiritual science wisdom of ancient religion. Which was taught and imparted to the Anunnaki followers (Enki's), had chosen to be ordained a priest of the sacred Anunnaki serpent brotherhood order of the initiation. And thus, totally entranced by the visual relics of the pious holy men who seized the heritage of Jesus Christ. Proclaim themselves vicar's of God! Elevated themselves as the central authority that represented a Catholic Church doctrine and canoes, by usurpation by the establishment of the Western and Eastern European religious thoughts, by undermining the wisdom teachings of Kemetic spiritual science. All the while they preached the words of an amorphous god, they proclaimed the power of a living God in Jesus Christ in Heaven had vested the Gospel of Jesus Christ the Trinity of God, in blind faith.

Yeah, people have allowed themselves to be deceived by the religious words spoken by purveyors of organized religion. Pompous religious shepherds sounding like pious holy men, wearing their long colorful pastoral raiment, and to their congregation preach religious *jeJune* religious teachings about Jesus Christ. Our perception of his nature as the Gods of the Trinity doctrinal creeds as the theological words of God. Through faith, prayerful worshipers seek supplications, forgiveness to atone for sinful behavior. Worshippers are the savior god in Jesus Christ, those who wear a gold chain and the Christian Cross and on Sunday sit in the congregation to atone for sinful behavior. At the same time their derogation, abstain from sacred principles and spiritual teachings of the luminous divine *Kavod* that does not follow the pathway towards human beings' luminous divine salvation. The congregation's millions of witting blind faithful followers listen to the prayerful sermons by church preachers, who proclaim that the Bible teaches us the words of God! Some Mythological God from Heaven; and from behind a podium with an air of holiness, they speak loudly about the Gospels of God with eloquent words that are stirring.

Yes, they sit in the Sunday church pews hanging on every word; they listen intently as if they heard the inspirational sermon as a fulfillment. They denigrate the sinful behavior of evil and the wicked for their transgressions.

Why have they not incubated the Law of One sacred philosophy principles of learning and teaching luminous divine wisdom of the Law of One love insights? Devotion to be in a personal relationship with the prayerful unity with the spiritual nature of God by daily meditation. Which is the path towards achieving one's salvation. These sacred principles lead to the wisdom of the Law of One love is the unity of the mind/body/spirit complex. Our common origin is the deeper meaning of the mystery that underlies the Kemeticism of ancient Egyptian wisdom. That knowledge was conveyed by a cadre of esoteric secret society ritual and rites, the brotherhood bloodline initiation into the Temple priesthood. Of which the version of Western Christian religion usurped Osiris and Isis into the Bible narrative of Jesus Christ and their transformation into a symbol of a performance in which the wholesale thief of the Egyptian Ankh was a symbol of life. Whereas the Christian symbolized the religion of death and resurrection of Jesus Christ.

No longer a symbol of life; it was changed to represent the death/resurrection of the Virgin born Child in the personage of God; philosophy of the teaching/learning/practice of the spiritual science through daily meditation. To think that you and I as the earth's bon homies consciousness awareness, we might understand and come to teach and learn about the *Neberdjer*, sacred principles of African-Egyptian wisdom of the Law of One love of *Shetaut Neter*. Which is derived from pages of the original ancient Anunnaki Sumerian Bible text, written on the soft and then hard-baked cuneiform clay tablets. The translations of extraterrestrial aliens' words recorded, reveal insight into the epoch of time; and ancient ceremonies of the titular God's holy rituals and luminous divine rites and sacred spiritual wisdom of the Law of One love through the priesthood initiation via formal daily meditation teaching of the scientific principles, teaching/learning of psychological ministers. And to which let me draw your attention to this point, meaning what? "If you have ever wondered about the age-old burning questions concerning the human race: Who are we and where did we come from? Where are we going? And where does the truth lie with which to give up the answers we seek? Well there are plenty of we'll write subject matter books for your erudition.

These are very credible published authors that put forth the known physical history of the archeology, and anthropology context to pique the curious casual reader's interest. This is revealed in Michael Tellinger's book: The *Slave Species of the Gods*. What is written here is the point of view intended for people who want to learn from becoming enlightened. Yeah substantive information intended for your erudition of knowledge. I speak to you as you are all the children of the most high intelligence Infinite Creator.

I presuppose that there is so many confused people who walk among the societies of humankind, some will find that the discovery of the hidden consciousness awareness, you will too will conflate these words with the UFOs, extraterrestrial aliens beings are the original Anunnaki custodial titular gods: "Those who from the Heaven came." were ancient astronauts who true identity resides in the ancient pages of the Anunnaki Sumerian Bible *Appocrefer* is the source of the historical texts, meaning the original story which the Hebrew and Greek Septuagint Bible Genesis narrative was transliterated into the modern interpretations of the Old Testaments biblical truthiness. And still few religious people today have had an inclination to examine the folly.

THE MIND, BODY, SPIRIT, AND STORYTELLING

Honestly, why are people fascinated with the Bible narrative tale of Chapter 1 through 11? This book is a gripping read for the curious folks who are ambivalent about the story gravely vague descriptive words of the Old Testament Bible description of god seems to parallel the persona of the Royal Prince Enki; ergo the anamorphic creator god who was a brilliant scientist, who possessed the intelligent knowledge required to facilitate the process of performing the genetic manipulation and editing and mixing of two different DNA in a "clay" Petri dish for fertilization and insert into a segregate Anunnaki birth mother. This was likely the process that had been undertaken by Enki because he was a research laboratory scientist in Africa where Enki fashioned/created the first crossbred primitive worker—Adam/Adapa.

This gives anecdotal details within a scope without apprehension using the quintessential application of your own logic and reason with the relevant information contained in the ancient Babylonian Seven Tablet of the creation Myth description; as the eponymous *Enuma Elish* texts comports with the relevant information which indicate that Enki/god creation of homo sapien sapien, was much more than a Mythological, contrived biblical narrative tale.

This is to introduce others to the much-maligned ancient astronauts theorist hypothesis. This is: "…a gripping read that you'll be excited to share with friends'" [6] [7]. What does this mean? The Recalcitrant ensconced bench sitters and the deceived are devoid of knowledge light of the Ancient Astronauts Theorist hypothesis. The profound understanding specifically, the discussion about the biblical genesis narrative and the alien UFOs phenomenon. And just for a brief period of your marvelous life and existence as a great heroic journey, my friends, have you ever wondered about why the Bible Genesis narrative tale, Chapter 1, is vague?

They *obfuscate* and are well entrenched in their theological dogmatism that denigrates the ancient astronauts theorists premise. The theologians prefer to distance themselves from some folks who believe the anecdotal details; the facts point concurs with the ancient astronaut's hypothesis. Certainly it is necessary to revisit and redress the omission of genesis narrative. To examine the nascent epoch of culture of the Anunnaki race Nibiru elite the Royal great prince Enki's did in fact fashion [his] own likeness (DNA) he had created, or fashioned His/the "Children of Gods"!

The Biblical story of Adam (Adapa) Enki fashioned by genetic engineering by manipulating of the sacred hermetic principles in the process of ordering His Anunnaki DNA genetic material code with indigenous African female DNA code, which was fertilizer in a can't petri dish and, then inside of six Anunnaki birth mother's womb they carried to full term; and thereby created the first crossbred homosa-peins-sapien being on planetEarth. Curious enough, was this fiction, Myth, or fact?

It raises the salient fundamental question of whether this is an actual book: The Hermetic Code in DNA, written by the author, Michael Hayes because he puts forth a hypothesis. I propose a point of view which concurs with intelligent logic and reason in accord with an ancient astronaut's hypothesis. Whereas it's rather a theory that is consistent with my elucidation that is parallel with the Anunnaki race, the extraterrestrial pilots of alien UFOs presence seems to be connected to the Old Testament titular Gods of the Bible! Enki was the Earth Mission's chief medical doctor. Enki, as a biological, genetic scientist, used his advanced biological knowledge of genetic DNA, successfully manipulated His own Anunnaki DNA essence, and mixed DNA of the indigenous African female hominid species. Genetic DNA codes had fashioned the first crossbred Adapa/Adam (Man) and Eve the (Women). This was to be the nascent of humankind, by DNA genetic engineering. The original spark plug for human civilization and homo sapiens sapiens existence and free will evolution, by the Anunnaki's Enki creation of a primitive slave labor workforce. Simply put: To slaves who were cloned to perform the dangerous work inside the deep African gold mining operations in southern Zimbabwe as the replacements for the free-up the young Anunnaki *Igigi workforce* from years of performing the heavy grievous toil inside the deep dark gold mines located in the southeastern region of Great Zimbabwe, African.

If you are starting to follow the events of the Holy Bible narrative book of Genesis, you see Enki's hyperbolic achievements, of which the genesis says references of God. He is the creator of Adam. He was fashioned [created] in His biological research lab located in the African the Southern region of great African land of Great Zimbabwe. From the "dust of the African ground" at His scientists laboratory: it was there Adam and Eve came the emergence of the *Homosapien-sapien* as the first hybrid Human beings: "Those came here in chariots out of Africa" ...The Anunnaki were there mining the mineral gold from the planet earth dark continent--rich with the exotic species of animals, another valuable resource; to include diamonds.

Still, it was while the Anunnaki race was living as the settlers who brought civilization to the earth's interior plane. This was a monumental event. Enki's purpose was to create a crossbreed human beings primitive that was needed to extricate and an obedient primitive worker who would be servile in social personality traits. How do our spiritual essence spur decisions and actions that make us all individually unique? And how is it that we don't know that it is our own spirit that is the cause of the actions of my spirit's intelligent energy? Actions and behavior as conscious bias influence what we believe to be true, good, or evil determine the way we think define religious attitudes.

Our assumption, whether they are my intelligent logic and reason to concur with or denounce the notion of UFOs, conflates the Ancient Astronauts Theorist hypothesis into a history bible book narrative that Chronicles the premortal story written about the Anunnaki alien as the God as an ancient astronaut from a planet-X/Nibiru.

My friends, could any of this be true? After all, what would be the rationale to perpetuate truthiness, right? Well, to have knowledge, wisdom, and insight is to be understood that you are engaged with the sage of the Infinite Creators Intellectual energy field of light of the spiritual science.

You are attuned to enlightenment; as an individual spirit embodiment of mind/body/spirit complex can walk upon the external empirical world temporal reality and experience the personification of principle against amoral deeds of perspicacious lusting after material wealth. Whereof humankind's inclination lacks the decorum of obedience, failed to embrace, never espoused the Law of One love principles of life/life/love!

It will change the trajectory of your view of a lifetime living in the perceptible illusory temporal reality. So let's think and recently meditate upon thoughts that bring solace on whether your *sentence* corresponds with the Law of One? That life exists in the material time/space continuum is "Everything" that you see before and around you from the moment of your beginning, is ultimately this surface illusion connected within the time/space dimensions! Yeah, you and I are ordinary, separate entities of the mind/body/spirit complex, having free-will consciousness. Not the ways of the *Lusifatian's* agenda (https://www.frontiersin.org/articles/10.3389/).

In an empirical world of the visual, material, and metaphysical complex. That there are many substrates of *cognitive dissonance,* with wave fields of discordant, cacophony of streaming of various noise distractions. The experiences of life enfoldments pervading distortions, pinging dissonance, collides on human entities' mind/body/spirit complex. With manifestations of the psychological reality of the material world illusory reality and the surreal realm of the consciousnesses thoughts. Humankind has been coming into the full possession of their power of irrepressible consciousness awareness.

The true spiritual teaching of universal harmonic unity vibration with the luminous divine nature of mind, body, spirit complex synthesis of the luminous divine wisdom insight derived from the Anunnaki and humans fusion of life/death/reincarnation spiritual science transformation cycle of life experiences, death, burial, and rebirth into a new objective reality empirical world incarnation of consciousness awareness of visual perception.

My friends, regarding this subject matter, I propose to you this serious question for you to take a moment to ponder this salient question: why does the Bible description obfuscate, it's exasperation, which is vaguely as is closely akin to truthiness. Whereof I postulate is predicate that the story seems to be a little misdirection or a falsehood, wittingly contrived into the mysterious prosonna god. It's convoluted; it lacks full disclosure without providing substantive anecdotal details that can be analyzed to make the recondite—simplistic! Which leaves out critical material information regarding the scope and context of facts which is missing from the Old Testament, holy Bible book of Genesis narrative tale is a seemingly convoluted invention. Ostensibly, devoid of clarity, logic, and reason. Despite the *eccentricity* of one's inclinations of humankind, we pray to God for blessings through faith in the Christian gospel of Jesus the Christ as our savior; our luminous divine salvation!

Whereof the material and the spiritual essence of the lives and deaths cycle through separate incarnations.

Meaning that spiritualism is the lighted gateway crossing, and the pathway to salvations. The harvest is of the Infinite Creative energy that reclaims and recycles human souls from the material embodiment. Esoteric nous resides in an unselfish heart of compassionate heart, to be weighed and found light against is the imbued with the spirit of love. Best benevolence deeds in unity with the spiritual nature—by the mantle on which one zeal is a bond by the faithful fellowship, but to learn truths and to teach others to be in service of the Infinite Creator the spiritual science religion philosophy. Having embraced valuable principles of and worshiping God in daily prayerful meditation inspired with humility, a pure heart, and a spiritual mind body complex, ultimately be sent to consciousness awareness in quiet comfort and peaceful solace.

Whereas some overzealous folks might have objections without the clarity of insight and understanding of the human mind/body/spirit complex. The all unified and synthetic transformation as a condition of being;psychological, social, and moral predisposition towards religious teachings and the character and personality that is our factual spiritual self-identity distortions of an individual's cosmic law of the forces of one's free will spirit's is the personality that is our behavior type and self-identity. What motivation for or manner of truth about which lies makes one responsible for our conduct with human life and time?

Look, my friends, it makes sense that there's no other way to say this…but it is rational that we take stock of human behavior. To judge whether our actions are justified. Because intrinsically the pulsating spirit is the cause that my spirit's intelligent energy animates every action. Where humans endued free-will to do either good or to do pernicious deeds? By extension, our spirit causes the mind animations to take action. Yet there are those with their *insouciant* attitude and distorted bad behavior without the admiration of the nature of the common unity of the essence of complexities of ancient mystery spiritual sciences of *Neberdjer*.

It's the pervading spirit of the intelligent infinity illusion entities of the natural creative principles and the human beings free will and self-subconsciousness. Because the spirit is the cause of human decisions and actions, albeit benevolent and pernicious evil actions pervaded within the power of free will consciousness. What does this mean: that it is the human spirit that causes our animated action. Then might we ponder why or whether this is why we pray for our providence and salvation?

Well then the truth is this, my friends, we are all individual units of spirit separation from this living all-pervading luminous divine entity; the cosmos all universal *Monad*? With which we wittingly pray to Kavad of the highest *Kavod* of Jah (Yahweh); the Hebrew term for God: "'I am, which indicates: the eternal empirical world life and time continuum of nature). Humans of the Infinite Creator preying in person prayerful worship, meaning: acknowledgment of self-awareness in connection with this empirical world mind/body/spirit complex.

The empirical world life and time of the cosmic law of forces of one's free will consciousness in obedient unity with God. It's in every sense of the Law of One spirit according to sacred principles that teaches spiritual meditation; through the occultists esoteric rites and ritualized *sacerdotalism* soothing and calming solace that heals and transforms negative energy inner anger, anxiety and into positive energy and helps soothe the soul and enlivened the spirit and strengthening of relationships. Which is mentally cathartic in maintaining a Salubrious balanced relationship with the psychological mind and body life's overall well-being. It's this dynamic inherently pulsating resonance connection from the all ancient creation Myths. But actually we are talking about the nascent age of the ancient astro-

THE MIND,BODY, SPIRIT,ANDSTORYTELLING

naut from millennia ago. I am one among a growing neophyte who are peering into the ancient history of our origin; and at antiquity. Looking back eons to Trying to learn and teach others the absolute truth about trying to untwist the psychological truthiness into a proper context.

With which sophistry is the focus on the Old Testament Hebrew people's original Anunnaki, Sumerian genesis tale narrative that fits nicely with archeology discovery consistent with the ancient astronaut'. Yes we can only ruminate about our past incarnation, knowing we can peer back into a history, like the turned pages of the books read. We must learn and teach the fidelity of being in service to our self-knowledge, being as other-selves [8]. The purpose of this book is to interpolate desperately for information on what is undisclosed, hidden from the Old Testament Bible Genesis Chapter1.

My conjectures according to the ancient astronaut theorist's premises. Let's face it, much of the credible analysis of the biblical text written in the language of its original or earliest available form ["Jan 6, 2021l].

Look. My friends, do you think that this scenario is logical and plausible? If yes, shall we focus attention towards extraterrestrial UFO phenomenon? A non nuanced retrospective of Sumerian Bible narrative tales [9].

Here's a synopsis excerpted from the publication Britannica that says: "Humans have long pondered not only how we came into being of an of surface illusion ary space of the perceptible illusory material consciousness temporal reality; but also consider why humans are form bare witness to my natal's living nature. Each person is an individual endowed with the polarity of luminous divine nature of the spark of radiant. Our qualities are assigned by the planetary constellation that is the "House of Life". It corresponds with the Zodiac signs; meaning the personal characteristics assigned to each of the twelve months of the earth calandra that corresponds to the chart of the astrological zodiac profiles. Divinity of the universal Monad, *Neberdjer imbued it as* a vivified mind/body/spirit complex of human life and time existences.

Well then, my friends, we know that: "the earliest Greek philosophers focused their attention on the origin and nature of the physical external empirical world; and later philosophers have theorized about the nature of knowledge, truth, good, evil, love, friendship, and so much more. Philosophy involves a systematic assessment of all aspects of human existence upon the plane of human For it is so important to note that we possess the gift of free will and intellectual logic, and reason. Having been endued by the Infinite Creator, human civilization possesses the inherent gift of cosmic law of free will spirit energy that causes humans animated actions. Individuals have a responsibility to use their own intelligence as a memory complex.

The mundane vagaries of life are according to the reality of logic and reason, spurred by the Law of One and the principle of *Neberdjer*. Human intellectuals' transformation using sophisticated scientific knowledge and advanced innovations in biological science and engineering technology leads to the invention of the digital age of high speed computers, the internet, NASA space flight is about human beings ability to enter advanced space flight exploration. For year's NASA has launched rocket ships from and safely returned to planet earth. Our research scientists have been using advanced knowledge in biomedical genetic research studies to save lives and create clones. The ability to manipulate electricity and atomic nuclear power weapons develop to be used for both energy and military application. To create electric self-piloted commercial airplanes, advanced innovative self-driving passenger motor vehicle cars, and instant external empirical worldwide wide bandwidth wireless cellular and landline telephone communication devices.

These are some innovations created by human beings in every field of scientific technology with which our ancestors' ignorance never possessed knowledge of such achievements. And most likely it can be said that the acquisition of the forbidden knowledge is a double edged sword; and it's because humans' application has been used and, more often abused as a means of evil brutality. As progressive advancements bring huge leaps into the affinity with the supreme deity is illustrative of the biblical Genesis tree of knowledge allegory.

THE MIND, BODY, SPIRIT, AND STORYTELLING

This is a semi-fictional illuminating account of the positive historical records, that is a storyline retrospective about the Anunnaki search for the earth's precious mineral gold resources. Is this the story that hasn't been written about the Gods connection with the sightings of modern UFO space faring ancient astronauts explorers who descended down from Heavenly planet of Nibiruan, their UFO landed in Sumer, Mesopotamia. Mesopotamians referred to the Anunnaki astronauts as the "shining ones" of the Heavens; and they worshiped Him as their god. The so-called ancient Sumerians Annunaki, alien deity/Gods from their home planet, Nibiru.

From the Heave they came down and landed their UFO spaceship, and in six days God/Enki and his fifty man crew built the first city-state settlements on earth correspond to the Hebrew and Greek Septuagint versions of the Old Testament, book of the Holy Bible book of the Genesis narrative tales. Which says He/God, or shall we say that the Nibiruan Royal Prince, Enki/Ea, meaning the God known to be *Yahweh,* the Bible, Chapter 1, declared that in six days God says that He built the first city-state of *Eridu,* after the bell shaped sky-craft lands and established a settlement colony on planet Earth. He was originally worshiped by people as their patron god of the city of Eridu, but later the influence of his cult began to be embraced throughout the region of Sumer, Mesopotamia; and this reached into the Canaanites, Hittites, and Hurrians land. Extraterrestrial alien Gods foothold in the region of the Sumerian, Mesopotamian civilization and cultures?

They possessed highly sophisticated knowledge and became the original custodian race to settle down and colonize all across the idyllic landscape after they called down from Nibiru [Heaven] 445 thousands of years ago! Is this not hyperbolic? It's possible in my conjecture to say: (1) The so-called Middle Eastern belt of the African continent has been significantly prominent in the Biblical Genesis narrative tale of the Hebrew and Greek version of the scriptures in chapter 1, Old Testament biblical mistranslations. And (2) the mistranslations of events revelation. Saying that it was the Anunnaki's original Sumerians Bible account of the "Seven Tablets of Creation".

This evidence gives us anecdotal details, which was written about these extraterrestrial alien beings, "Those from the Heaven In the Garden came here in chariots down onto the earth'". Yeah, Eden is the epic of time period of the Olden s Anunnaki (titular) Gods (Enlil and Enki), who were the two principal the Royal great princes from their home planet Nibiru involving the issue of (Enlil's) policy of forbidden knowledge. From the Christian Bible Genesis scriptures is the narrative episodic scene when Enlil was strolling through His beautiful garden landscape and discovered that His brother, Enki, the creator of Adam/Adapa and Eve had been given the knowledge of conscious awareness of their nakedness. Which was countervailing to the Anunnaki Law of Enlil, who was the Lord of the Earth Command. He castigated and denigrated Enki/Ea as the serpent for His breach of the Anunnaki titular God protocol that forbade Enki's crossbred homosapeins-Sapeins the acquisition of knowledge and longevity—of which Adam and Eve was given given the of consciousness awareness of their own mind/body/spirit complex, with understanding of their naked bodys. Enlil became angry when He realized that Adam and Eve had been given the Gods forbidden fruit of the nous/knowledge was indicative of Enki willful disobeyed Enlil's law that caused His action to expel and banished Enki's eponymous Adam and Eve from the land located in Havilah. They were sent out from the *paradisiacal* territorial land identified by the Old Testament Holy Bible referred to as the Anunnaki God Enlil's Garden in Eden. These are the territorial lands that are mentioned within the Bible book of Genesis (Book, The Gods of Eden, written by William Bramley, March 1993).

The identity is unknown to the chronicle of the contribution to the African-Egyptian, Coptic Kushite people's historical ties to Noah's Hamite Africa tribal bloodline ancestors. We can speculate as to why Enlil's vituperation towards his brother, the Royal-Elite Prince Enki. Enlil's pejorative aims to denigrate Enki for these transgressions. Enlil conflated Enki to a serpent; and this is the reason for expelling Adam and Eve, Enki's had fashioned as "crossbred primitive workerRs" by genetic manipulation of the DNA chromosome codes—after all, Enki was the commanding of the Earth Mission voyage, chosen because he was Nibiru's highly skilled biological scientist and chief medical doctor who was recognized as the most qualified to lead to carry out the Anunnaki Gods from Heaven had a mission purpose to find and extract gold, became the first group of ancient astronauts established the first city-state of Eridu on the earth's in Sumer, Mesopotamia.

Just as significant, Enki was the *eponymous creator god.* In the Bible Genesis narrative, *maligned as the serpent; the geo-special boundary* assigned to the African *Cushite peoples Eden* (Havilah) (Genesis 3:23-24). The Bible states in Genesis 3:21 that God made Adam and Eve coats of skins and clothed them. From the episode, Enki (God) did not abandon them; and it was the punishment that the crossbred Homosapien had been left to become self-reliant, to build their shelter, the sowing of their foods, meaning to live outside of Eden was a punishment. An illusory temporal reality check.

We might do as in today's terms, tough-love; a kind of valuable teaching moment for blatant acts of disobedience. But other than that, we know that Eden was this place equated with paradise [10]. Now it would become their responsibility for daily survival skills by manipulating nature.

Adapt and use knowledge to build protective shelter, hunt, and kill wild animals for food and clothing. To domesticate farm animals for livestock to provide a daily basis subsistence. The physiological higher order of survival needs to be safe and secure. The only burning question is where did this event take root?

We know the Holy Bible says God (Enlil), He was Supreme lord god Anu's son Enlil. Enlil expelled Adam and Eve from Eden. Indeed He knew that his brother Enki (a.k.a. the Serpent god of wisdom and mischief) became conscious when the third eye was opened, and the self-image in the illusory temporal reality is perceived! Transgression of the Royal Prince Enlil law Enki's crossbred homo sapiens sapiens. Enlil had forbidden knowledge and longevity to the human beings.

Possessing the sacred knowledge and longevity was deemed strictly reserved for Anunnaki. We already know from Genesis the scene that transpired--replete with the anecdotal details of this episodic event; Right? So here's what I will tell you regarding the important salient point of my *exegesis* is that: This Bible event and the wider narrative had its nascent when the elite the Royal great prince, Enki commander of a fifty man crew landed his ancient spacecraft that traveled from Heaven down through the crossing of the planet Mars and Jupiter to successfully land in ancient Mesopotamia.

Extraterrestrial beings were the titular Gods of earth who had arrived on scene. They came from planet Nibiru to extract the mineral element gold. In the context of the discovery of planet earth, which connects to the rich abundance of material resources of the African gold deposits found in the Great Zimbabwe gold mines was seminal. Enki relocated to Africa, and there, he resumed his gold mining production operations. This tells us that God has bequeathed the African territorial African lands of Ham and Cushite (Ethiopian), tribal lands as the grandson of Noah's, and the ancestral people. In several books of the Bible, the one mentioned in Genesis 2:10-11, but does it seem odd to you that Genesis makes no mention of how God came down to walk in the eponymous Biblical garden in the land of Eden. While the other place is thought in Africa, it says it is in Genesis 10:7; Havilah [11].

This story is about the Hamite people's ancestors' territory in African homelands that the Anunnaki Supreme SkyGod of Heaven and planet Earth, King Lord God Anu, the father of the the Royal great prince Enki and Enlil bequeathed the regional idyllic landscape of the African continent as his kingdom.

In the Southern state of Great Zimbabwe, he established and operated the deep gold mine production excavation operation. The truth about the Anunnaki Enki revelation: at least this is what we have learned from 200,000-year-old sites fits the Sumerian descriptions of the dovetails nicely with the ancient astronaut's Prince Enki's African deep gold mining production operation of the Anunnaki presence [Michael Tellinger book: Temples of the African Gods].

He and other biological, genetic scientists successfully manipulated DNA to fashion Adam (Man) and Eve (Woman), the disobedient primitive workers. According to the ancient Sumerian Anunnaki Bible, The Anunnaki Bible: The Sumerian texts is the origin of the source and translations of the Judeo Christian Bibles. Enki uses two biological DNA genetic codes to fashion the creation of His crossbred Adam (Man) and Eve (Women). This is what was recorded in the Anunnaki Sumerian Ethiopian original ancient orthodox Bible text version of the "*Book of Enoch*" that was of critical importance. Also, the "*Book of Giants*" [Angels/Watchers] includes the "*Seven Tablets of Creation*". Genesis Chapter 6 through Chapter 9 reads the source material from which the Hebrew and Greek Septuagint Bible Genesis narrative tale was omitted, and mistranslations occurred.

Therein lies the true purpose: Those Anunnaki's earth mission voyage is the nascence of biblical genesis God of creation Myth, archetype primitive worker Adam and Eve were the precursor prototype *Homosapien*. A crossbred species of Adam (Man) was fashioned by Enki to become the *obsequiously* obedient servile labor force of the Anunnaki titular Gods. The Anunnaki alien gods needed to find a means which would release the rebellious *Igigi* labor worker force from having to continue to perform the heavy backbreaking work inside dangerous deep and dark goldmines of the southeastern region of Zimbabwe, Africa.

The Royal Prince Enki is the god first mentioned in the Old Testament Bible book of Genesis; meaning that after he safely landed in ancient Mesopotamia, His architectural engineers used the blueprints to construct used city-state settlements [*Eridu*] in six days which established a base of operation during the initial mission mission voyage. He was appointed to lead the voyage under orders, give by his father, Nibiru's King Anu who commissioned Royal Prince Enki as the flight mission commander of a vanguard fiftyman ancient astronaut crew, consisting of skilled engineers and scientist construction specialists for building a space station spaceport for the shuttle astronauts spacecraft landing platform in order to facilitate the transporting of gold excavated from their gold mining production operations.

After all, the goal of the Anunnaki presence and purpose was inextricably linked to having a successful steady and efficient gold mining production operation source for shipping back to on planet Nibiru. Specifically, to release the *Anunnaki Igigi* from the backbreaking laborious and grievous toil they had performed to extract the gold from within the deep African gold mining production operation. Yeah this is the mendacious sinister scheme, with which the Royal great prince Enki had planned to seize to present his solution. He proposes an ultimate solution and convinces the council of the Anunnaki to agree to allow him to fashion a primeval race of hybrid primitive workers. Workers who could carry out the heavy toil inside of the hot, deep, dangerous African gold mines. Efficaciously become replacements who could perform the heavy backbreaking work that would free up the rioting *Igigi* of their grievous labor inside of the gold mining production operations which offers the best solution. To this Enki's ambitious proposition was accepted based upon the promise to fashion them without the cognitive knowledge and the longevity of the Anunnaki aliens. But Enki had His own purpose and to the task of the DNA codes manipulation of natal nature a prototype homo sapien sapien human, Adapa or Adam the female Eve according to the Genesis narrative tale.

Enki crossbred Primitive workersAdams and Eve spurred *obsequiously*, and Not so obedient crossbred primitive labor force! Yeah. He spurred discontent among these workers who refused to continue this work if they were not granted some kind of relief.

Enki's elaborate initial purpose persuaded the Anunnaki Nibiruan Ruling Council of the Twelve and they authorized the creation. But the Royal great prince Enki had his personal reason for the earth to propagate with intelligent Humankind. The crossbred Adam(s) would worship him as their spiritual God as a servile, obedient primitive labor force. Undergirding the proliferation of the Adam (Adapa) and Eve explains why Enlil (God) prohibited them from acquiring the Anunnaki's sacred knowledge and exclusive possession of longevity. This scene was in Havilah, with which the Bible narrative tale associated with the garden in the land of the Eden, mentioned in the Book of Genesis (2:10-12), is a reference via this hyperlink [12]. We are clear why the titular God (Royal prince Enlil) *vituperates* His mischievous brother Royal-Elite Prince Enki for giving His crossbreed Adam and Eve "knowledge, meaning enlightenment of consciousness awareness like titular gods."

THE MIND, BODY, SPIRIT, AND STORYTELLING

The Anunnaki preferred the Enki's crossbred homo sapien sapiens were cloned to be primitive workers whose purpose was to serve the Anunnaki as their obsequiously obedient primitive workers. This point, folks this is what you need to know is why the Anunnaki the Royal great prince Enlil was the titular Gods who was Lord of the Earth Mission Commander; and what was decreed could not be canceled. With great respect to humankind's possession of the gods' knowledge, we are without longevity, as Enlil feared that humans' beings possessed this propensity for evil and violence as an innate inclination to one day challenge Nibiru's Anunnaki race Supremacy. That humans could threaten existence by destroying life on the earth with nuclear warfare and powerful dangerous weapons. And the Anunnaki god Royal great prince Enlil's original fears of humans having possession of knowledge was a realization when humans entered into an age of nuclear warfare—not peace and god's will. God's prophecy points to the *apocalyptic* end times clash between earth's powerful evil forces who shall enjoin the final battle at *Armageddon*. And as it pertains to the revelations associated with the subjective matters of this speculative exegesis; well, I'll just let you use logic and reason on the nature of evil.

Whereof this is the equation some equate to the Holy Bible book of Revelation.

Then the subject matter of this exegesis, however not a discussion about God and the human beings end war. We have been misled away from *Kemeticism* spiritual teachings of universal luminous divine meditation with the sacred rites and rituals of *sacerdotalism* worshiping service towards universal spirit understanding. The elite extraterrestrial alien beings who were living on the earth, were not the luminous divine monad of the *Neberdjer*; but they were those who were from the higher level of the constellation orbital cycle, and descended from Heaven and introduced sacred wisdom principles of the Kemetism *al-chemical* laws of nature. Although in philosophy, ritual theological religious teachings. Academic discourse has intersected with conducting their own curious inquiries about how human beings came to be. Bits of discovery of lost information has been published in the journal and books from the ancient astronaut's theorists enfoldment of their quite controversial subject matter researchers' discovery and analysis of information which revealed the critical insightful historical and biblical information that providers substance and credibility to the conventional view of religion from an intelligently well informed perspective. And as such with your eyes open using logic and reason you shall enliven the senses of your divine spirit reveal the clarity of true enlightenment. Space flight is already advancing towards space exploration, which is now neither some far fetched, conceivably it's a notion that is neither considered impossible, nor is it improbable.

Modern human beings are expected to achieve with intelligence! Today astronauts, like Mauro's Bigino's research, attributed to the Vatican's findings, which seems to be a confirmation of the ancient astronauts theory. It's this premise that inspired the curiosity of the *neophytes* and those adept to profess an unconventional perspective with which to seek a convergence theory regarding the ancient astronauts, gold, Gods, and UFOs as the alien Anunnaki on earth; and what does it mean? In context of the Rome's Vatican researcher, Mr. Mauro's Bigino, speaks to the thesis with understanding that the Bible Old Testament narrative ancient creation Myths, story is an illuminating about this small group of Anunnaki space faring astronauts who descended from planet Nibiru were extraterrestrial.

The home planet of the titular Gods of Heaven planet most profoundly mysterious (Planet-X), as such, I feel quite strongly in saying that I'm justified in my thoughts on a hypothesis that puts forth this as an exegesis. For wisdom of the Law of One (love) and knowledge is the insight when one has enlightenment. Thus it has long been said that out of the darkness. Without the clarity of your spirit, you are devoid of the wisdom discernment, there is a lack of purpose and understanding of the biblical falsehoods.

That which deception is mired in mind causes the deleterious effects that confuse the mind of humankind. For the nous of consciousness awareness of our life purpose, in ignorance can not learn or teach others to embrace the Enlightenment of the principles philosophy of the spiritual science Christianity of misdirection, which does not lead one towards the spiritual science nirvana of light and away from the spurious organized religions of truthiness that propagates a gospel of the blind faith religions falsehoods. And, my friends, then might folks appreciate this as scholarly erudition? This is my exegesis and is not as empirical unearthed.

It's informative in so far as what we read and study of the Bible Genesis subjectively as this immense and valuable retrospective; viz., a glimpse back in historical context juxtaposition with archeology and ritual theology. To allow us to uncover the missing anecdotal unearthed about the ancient past history. Okay, then. With all that we seek understanding, owing to scholarly researchers diligently monumental comprehensiveness, we can examine whether or not the biblical genesis narrative tale is credible.

Such folks who are capable of discerning what is true and is the most interesting and reliable unearthed for a connection to archeology discovery can be reconciled with the Old Testament Bible book of Genesis creation narrative.

There are actual artifacts that bring this set of the most monumental facts that dovetails nicely with the ancient astronaut's theory. They assert that it was an incredible historical event about the alien Gods, humans, and all life on earth (http://www.mesopotamiangods.com/enki/). A study and practice of the psychology of ancient spiritual science and blind faith religions undermines how humankind long speculated about its existence; its origin seems to suggest that this scenario fits into what is a quite able possibility.

Whereof acceptance of the facts advances with acceptance of the speculation about an advanced extraterrestrial alien race hypothesis that fits into the ancient astronauts theorists premise, saying that from a higher plane. The earth orbital solar system constellation precessional cycles is associated with the cosmic the twelve signs of the Zodiac house wheel in circumambulation through each epoch of the zodiacal houses in processional orbit around the life sustaining sunlight energy. To which the Ancient Astronauts Theory posits the hypothesis saying: they were not Gods. So might we say that they were extraterrestrial alien beings who lived on earth 450,000s of years ago. High above the earth's surface, I saw a murky and dark chaotic landscape without the bright Eastern sunrise. These assumptions assert that the Anunnaki were space faring astronauts (UFOs) who had arrived from the planet Nibiru. This consciously is not recognized in the biblical Old Testament Bible Genesis narrative account that began in ancient Mesopotamia many years ago.

Today there are a lot of religious people who profess a belief in the holy trinity of Jesus Christ for their salvation. Okay. But some people don't believe in the ancient astronaut theory. Many are convinced that alien extraterrestrial beings. Might the Anunnaki alien gods be behind the modern UFOs phenomenon in our sky? Yeah, and I contend that they are related to those who from Heaven came, is closely akin to the biblical genesis narrative story chapter 1 through 11 identity of the God of religion.

Research on this topic has been dominated by public interest in the ancient astronaut theory. And, what I would tell you, my friends, is this thing, which seems to be fascinating, raises the salient question about what is the true purpose of all of these strange UFO sightings? Of course, the speculation about the intentions as well as their motivation is naturally well founded as a curiosity; right? And I contend that these modern extraterrestrials were the ancient astronauts, an advanced extraterrestrials alien race called the *Anunnaki*, said to have arrived from planet Nibiru or (planet-X). After all, perhaps there is a connection between the increasing incidence of modern UFO sightings and human abduction.

At the same time, it seems to be a plethora of people convinced that there is a compelling argument about the ancient astronauts and the contemporary evidence, which seemingly conflates the Bible Genesis narrative that is cryptic and equally obfuscating by never mentioning that the Anunnaki were: Those who from the Heavens came! Never acknowledges the missing elements of the relevant information about alien extraterrestrials as an advanced race. as the so-called gods of heaven descended and landed a bell-shaped AUV/UFO on the surface in Mesopotamia. Titular Gods came here in chariots down to the earth plane. Yeah! Those who arrived seated aboard some sophisticated flying spacecraft piloted by a crew of ancient astronauts. Their Flight Commander was a member of Nibiru's Council of the Royal Elite, Prince Enki (Ea).

Enki was the son of the High Supreme Sky God, *Anu* [King of Nibiru/Heaven]. Ruler of Anunnaki was in heaven, and his presence was the nascence of the biblical genesis narrative while living on the planet earth. If this is the truth, then I say: Might these intrepid extraterrestrial alien beings, in fact, came down from a higher level orbital cycle of the constellation of planets and became the first custodian race of planet Earth solar system elliptical orbital rotational cycle with its 2,160 cosmic rotation—one Great Year, which equals 25,920 years of the zodiac wheels annual precession cycle movement through each of the 12 houses of the zodiac signs that = 2,160 years. This event circumambulates around the brilliant, radiant glow of the Sun marks either the current or forthcoming astrological age, depending on the method of calculation (https://en.m.wikipedia.org/wiki/Age_of_Aquarius).

The ancient astronaut theorists contend that these were the titular Gods seeded by their Royal Kingship and complexities of old mystery spiritual science of Kemetism, wisdom of the Law of One love principles.

The teachings of the African-Egyptian secret societies mysteries ceremonies, rituals, and rites initiation into the Temple's priesthood bequeathed from the Anunnaki titular Gods. With their advanced knowledge, they used scientific technology, piloted sophisticated aerial UFOs spacecraft to descend from their home planet Nibiru, built city-states on earth, and constructed monuments of palaces and temple buildings, and excellent strategic landing spaceport sites at specific locations inside the Mesopotamian interior earth plane, viz., in Africa, Indus Valley, and the ancient Mesoamerican cultures.

These extraterrestrial alien beings' Earth Mission voyage was to teach humans civilization, ostensibly learning religion. An affinity with the biblical gods from the cosmic constellation as the titular biblical gods who descended from Heaven (planet Nibiru).

The biblical Genesis narrative recounts in the epoch of cultural, historical societies built across the earth Mesoamerican interior plane of ancient Sumer. The indigenous peoples of Eridu. Enki was elevated and given reverence as the city-state deity. He was given such an honor and accordingly, Eridu worshiped the Royal-Elite Prince

Enki as their preferred Anunnaki city-state deity as the luminous divine personna as their lord luminous divine, with esteem and reverence as was customary for the royal prince of the most high elite Sky God, King Anu. The Supreme Lord from their planet Nibiru, as the personification of the Gods of Heaven first born son, was the great elite Royal Prince Enlil who he had given the title of lord of the earth command. Never mind the fact that it was Enki who was the first Anunnaki to land down in the land of the Sumerian plane of ancient Mesopotamia; and according to the book of Genesis Enki had been the god figure build the first city-state settlement on earth and named it Eridu, this He did in six earth days!

You express an opinion or debate whether these anecdotal details can rebuff the assertion that UAV/UFOs were not the actual conveyance of astronauts' spacecraft of the Anunnaki: "those who from the heavens came to earth," or the Anunnaki." and landed in Sumerian, Mesopotamia. This is the biblical land of reference in the Hebrew Israelite Jewish people's ancestors.

The name Šinʻar occurs eight s in the Hebrew Bible, in which it refers to Babylonia. This location of Shinar is evident from its description as encompassing both Babel/Babylon (in northern Babylonia); Erech/Uruk (in southern Babylonia). Anunnaki extraterrestrial aliens (Titular Gods) were instrumental in the civilization's cosmic evolution, and involvement in the custodial development of the historical line was significant in its cultural progression. A book about this Royal Alien Anunnaki and the African Genesis narrative revealing the gods bloodline of material proxies. The sacrificing of spiritual values for power, knowledge, material gain. our ancient historical progression had influenced the external empirical world; and *ipso-facto* the titular gods unpowered human civilizations.

Within modern society of common consciousness there's a growing fascination with the UFO maniacs' enthusiasm for information regarding sightings. Is it intimately connected to God? The UFO phenomenon is quite curious and very fascinating, which spurred credible subject matter books regarding the ancient astronaut theory as a hypothesis. Many publishers and authors have fueled the speculation about the Anunnaki as titular Gods.

THE MIND, BODY, SPIRIT, AND STORYTELLING

The extraterrestrial beings that came from an advanced civilization; and after they had landed, they were likely worshiped by superstitious indigenous peoples of the idyllic interior landscape. But curiously enough, we know that the Bible book of Genesis narrative conspicuously mentioned Anunnaki ancient astronauts nexus. Seemingly having faith in the persona of an anamorphic god *Talismanic* manifestation. A God from Heaven! In the Old Testament Genesis narrative tale is about God. But what if it's a true story about the Anunnaki titular Gods as ancient astronauts? My view is that with ruminations using logic and reason of spiritual wisdom of the Law of One love and let's pause. To speculate about this salient burning question: did this advanced civilization was established by the Anunnaki Those. The latter came down from their home planet Nibiru. The flight Commander, the King's Royal Prince, was appointed to lead the Enki. Successful space travelers from deep space, the higher-level plane of the orbital constellation.

The clan of ancient astronauts or the ancient Sumerians called the *epithet*, about the Anunnaki: "the gods who came from Heaven;" Enki (Ea) landed their UFO spaceship in Mesopotamia.

This was the first small group of Nibiru's Anunnaki extraterrestrials space-traveling astronauts who were anamorphic alien gods who settled and became the titular gods of the ancient Sumerian peoples of Mesopotamia. There are folks who concur in logic and reason to believe the Anunnaki were the god mentioned in the Old Testament Genesis narrative storytelling about "those who came from Heaven came." Or shall I say, that the God of Genesis was the Royal-Elite Prince Enki who is mentioned in the Old Testament Bible narrative of Chapter one. To this point, I interpolate the fact that Enki was Commander of the Earth Mission Voyage via a large UFO flying spacecraft with an initial fifty man alien astronauts who were those who came down from Planet Nibiru and had successfully landed in the Southern interior plane of the land of Sumer, Mesopotamia/Iraq. Enki was the God who had superb leadership, built and established the first city-state, Eridu, on the sixth day and rested on day seven, and became the first Anunnaki Custodian God to create a civilization in ancient *Eridu*, Mesopotamia.

As an intelligent and advanced extraterrestrial race they possessed advanced, sophisticated knowledge in biological, genetic science, which the Royal great prince Enki used to manipulate DNA successfully. It has been revealed that the great royal prince, Enki fused His Anunnaki DNA with an indigenous African female's DNA codes and created Homosapien-sapiens, Adapa (Adam), and Eve! He was successful in fashioning crossbreed Homo sapien-sapiens, the Adam and Eve! What then does it mean? Well my friends, just in case you don't remember this fact, Enki [God] proclaimed God—as the Infinite Creation of Earth civilization and human race of crossbred Homo sapiens.

Yeah, Enki was the God of wisdom principle of the Law of One love and magic whose deeds correspond to the Anunnaki deity Enki as the narrator of Genesis Chapter 1, mentioned in the Old Testament Holy Bible book of Genesis, Chapter 1, seems to be alluding to God hovering high above the Earth. An observation of Enki's intrepid fifty men vantage astronaut crew, the Anunnaki alien God who looked down upon the murky dark waters that covered flood Earth (Ezekiel 1:14, And the living creatures ran and returned as the appearance of a flash of lightning). The Bible says that He separated the waters from the freshwater! Or might we consider the claim as a hyperbole narrative account? Did God arrive onboard an AUV/UFO spacecraft? Not by feathered wings like the birds. No, Not at all! Most likely the real truth is that they were the Anunnaki extraterrestrial aliens.

Okay but the spacecraft hovered above the planet; holding their position while observing the terrestrial Earth and observed the landscape prior to them landing their sophisticated aerial UFOs spacecraft. Then as the waters slowly receded, the land emerged before Enki's UFO spaceship descendants and landed in ancient Sumerian, Mesopotamia earth plain.

This likely was the most plausible scenario. Which is inconsistent with the KJV *sophistry*. As such with some sensory motivation, as a thinker who seek spiritual wisdom, the soulful spirit in me that inspired me with the nous and the passion to seek greater learning, and with the will teach others my understanding of knowledge and wisdom, this book is the product that let others be their on analysis and critical judge of my controversial views for your own eruditon of knowledge.

Of which I say that it does raise a rather intelligent question about whether there is any truth in the ancient astronaut's theory and whether there is a direct symbiotic connection to the Anunnaki Ancient Astronaut gods who came down from the so-called Planet-X, Nibiru [https://www.biblestudytbehavior]. Is this consistent with the Egyptian Sky God Ra, philosophy of learning and teaching the sacred principles of the "Law of One Love.

We are all supposed to contribute to humanity in benefit of our other selves as a benevolent social deed for one's who first serve the self and demonstrate the selflessness love by being in common service as part of the spiritual unifying fields that binds humankind to the cosmetic infinity's harmonic vibrations light/life/love spiritual infinity. Yeah, and all the while, NASA and the federal government have been documenting our activities; and secretly we are being monitored by the watchers. Using electronic communication technology, our privacy rights are being ignored with impunity.

My friends, facts lend credibility and substance regarding the presence of extraterrestrial aliens and UFO spacecraft can't be denied: "Those who were from Heaven came" ostensibly the Bible never alludes to God in terms of an alien race of beings; not of astronauts and UFOs. Nevertheless, these are substantially desperate for information on aliens as being the original creator God/Enki was likely settlers/custodians of the earth. And I presuppose that the case of lost files containing the mission reports logs are unsubstantiated. Modern secret documents of witnesses' statements had claimed that they experienced an abduction encounter of themselves being examined onboard a modern UFO when they had been taken by alien extraterrestrial spacecraft. Are these the ancestors of Olden Times Gods? We know that despite the overwhelming facts, the federal government has been keeping silent about this incredible amount of empirical evidence. This evidence suggests that the UFOs phenomenon is much more than mere *poppycock*! Let's face it. While the more expansive government is grudgingly acknowledging that which the ancient astronaut's theorists hypothesis is an obfuscation, and the denial of any original Anunaki alien astronauts connection to the term chariots of the gods referred to the modern sighting of UAVs / UFOs—despite a growing number of actual sightings on air traffic radar monitors in our air space for years have become more frequent. So at which point will these beings be acknowledged as those who from the Heavens descending from the Earth's sky is alarming and problematic? And although is a subject matter that is being taken seriously some people my not be convinced are the AUO/UFO skeptics about a possible nexus with which suggests that the Anunnaki Sumerian Bible narrative tale corresponding to the seven cuneiform clay tablets of the Bible Creation found in the ancient ruins unearthed by the ancient Palace library of the Assyrian King Asurbanipal's Royal palaces complex at Nipper.

It seems to be this nexus between the UFOs of today in scyn to the ancient astronauts theorists premise; ergo the Anunnaki: "Those who were from the Heavens came down." And my friends, by what means or modify convalescence might know the God (Enki) had when He came down onto the earth surface from the sky, according to the Old Testament Bible book of Genesis narrative tale. And might we assume it's highly likely to be a curious connection herewith the truth if it dovetails nicely with anecdotal details written in the original Anunnaki Sumerian Bible genesis narrative ancient text. Therein we are likely to get the truth. It starts there and then we can understand what the ETs/UFOs' intentions are. They were the titular Gods who were the original custodian race that colonized and brought civilization to the denizens of planet earth. We can not simply dismiss this phenomenon!

Well then, my friends, what I will tell you about this Bible book of Genesis narrative is that the ancient astronauts' theorists' premise is that a hypothesis is not hyperbole or poppycock! UFOs' presence is real but with respect to what their intentions remain uncertain. Nevertheless, a national security issue that raises the level of curiosity of humans is an alarming priority that may pose a grave threat to human beings. But for now humans remain captivated and intrigued by UFO phenomena. This is what I have to say about this: that there is nothing new; extraterrestrials, alien UFOs. They have been visiting the earth since the nascent of the ancient astronaut of the Holy Bible, Chapter 1, saying that God came down from Heaven; Human beings became inextricably linked to ancient astronauts, original custodians.

Royal Prince Enki (God) was the keeper of the blueprint used to colonize and create the establishment of the first civilization in the interior Earth plane of ancient Mesopotamia. And like modern NASA's mission control center. Likewise, the Anunnaki's mission control center was akin to the NASA's (Watchers) platform orbiting high above earth, equivalent to Anunnaki Igigi (*Watchers*) mentioned in the Old Testament holy biblical Genesis narrative. What I will tell you is this: the so-called 200 renegade *Fallen Angeles (Igigi)* were none other than the infamous Anunnaki gods. These agents were disobedience which we remember from the Bible Old Testament Genesis. My assumption dovetails to what is written in the holy book? It mentions this as a truth but, by omission they are careful to never link alien gods as ancient astronauts. Which is the missing anecdotal details event, while curiously treating the possibility of this in the same manner as the Book of Enoch", which was left out of the Old Testament biblical narrative tale! Perhaps we might speculate that these 200 hundred extraterrestrial aliens Igigi were the ancient astronauts who deserted their space command assignment on board the mission voyages platform that was orbiting high above the earth Anunnaki's communication platform.

The religions of ancient space and present are narrative stories about the earth's density, light/life/love of the One Infinite Creator, Adona! This is a disconcerting apprehension of the human existence embodiment of the material form as a mind/body/spirit complex. Imbued by the Infinite Creator. One individual separate unity is the spirit's free-will conscious awareness to perceive life as a human experience. Our purpose is simple: to live and learn to serve oneself; while serving others as a human social complex. One positive life unified by one empirical worldwide love according to the Law of One conscious unity. Our conscious free will spirit seeks to achieve the purified heart of compassion devoid of the evil Seth. And in common, they all seemingly preach guidelines and judge different kinds of social human personality behavior.

Above the most inherently personal. And in prayerful daily meditation, spiritual providence as blessings is endued from the highest Infinite Creator God of Heaven and the Earth. And is it our spirit that causes human beings to wittingly worship Christianity's doctrinal creed of blind faith in an apomorphic God gift of luminous divine nature that offers the path to ultimate providence and salvation [13]? This underlying common theme of this exegesis is directed on organized religious teaching/learning of spiritual truth. Whereas chapter 1 the Bible book of Genesis is a narrative tale about the Anunnaki clans who were space-traveling ancient astronaut explorers, which according to the well-known published author, Zecharia Sitchin's books, estimated that the Anunnaki's first earth incursion had occurred around 445 thousand years ago is referred to as the ancient astronaut theorists premise. And that the Anunnaki were the extraterrestrial entities that were the titular Gods; the *apomorphic, alien race who were the key players of the Holy Olden Times Gods who arrived from their home* planet, Nibiru (so-called Planet-X)!

It is an assertion that is credible but not plausible regardless of the archeology and anthropology discovery of the anecdotal details that fit nicely with the Anunnaki *Sumerian Bible* narrative tale of ancient creation Myths. Whereof the true genesis narrative facts about Anunnaki extraterrestrials presence of earth is written in revealing that in the beginning the Anunnaki (Royal Elites), Enki and Enlil were the protagonist and antagonist; the animated manifestation of God and Satan representing the duality of good and evil personas.

These god figures were the so-called Olden times Anunnaki clans whose children were born on the earth. As it is within generations of Anunnaki, influence as the Gods of human beings, had prompted a struggle between them which evolved into wars of many bloody conflicts over territorial claims that precipitated fighting against each other by means of conquest to establish their power and control for many generations following their clans UFO chariots initial earth mission voyage flight when Enki UFO arrived on earth from the Anunnaki home planet, Nibiru. They were the intelligent custodians of the earth plane, where the Bible alluded to them as the god who created the "Earth" in six days. This took place in the ancient Persian gulf region named Sumer, in Mesopotamia. Modern astronomers and scientists speculate that the ancient astronauts came from Nibiru; and they say that it is likely the Earth solar system's missing tenth planet.

Travels in an elliptical orbit around the Sun astrological houses constellation solar cycles every 3,600 years through the zodiacal cycle orbit (M. J. Evans, Ph.D.; book: Zechariah Sitchin, Extraterrestrial Origins of Humanity) as humans titular Gods on earth. My friends, it is instructable to our logic. Homosapeins genetically fashioned by Enki imbued humans with the teaching, the learning of the Anunnaki complexities of ancient mystery spiritual science of meditation. The ultimate test of humanity's cosmic law of one consciousness of the universal cosmic spacetime perceptible illusory of our temporal reality. Are we not all living entities of the universal infinite creator of all pervading life force energy. A rectitude that is a visceral pernicious evil. There is not a shortage of scholarly arguments about this salient observation.

You see, a luminous divine God spirit essence resides inside the human body. Perhaps this is the cause of all animated human beings' actions—in the end of this scene! But perhaps the perspicacious curious-minded neophyte are truth seekers who have unpacked the so-called Pandora's box! Through the contemporary researcher's a plethora of irrefutable historical information has been discovered corroborating evidence that lends credibility to the highly disputed ancient astronauts theorists hypothesis (https://www.jstor.org/stable/23244960). New knowledge of the lost historical account of historical accounts, is the result of archeology and anthropology discovery findings revealed insight about the biblical religious and the psychospirituality teaching dichotomy; and meaning what? Fundamentally speaking the truth about aliens as the ancient astronauts god's is the erudition of knowledge is published in many authors who have written subject matter books given context that fits into the Bible genesis narrative tale. I believe a juxtaposition to the archeology discovery and findings reveals a treasure trove of the hidden mysteries truth with which underlie the missing anecdotal detailed evidence about the Anunnaki Earth Mission intrepid space-traveling voyagers.

Real results of credible unearthed research that are compelling in support of points of historical relevance are tremendous. My friends try to connect with the historical threads that run through the Genesis narrative regarding the ancient astronaut theory.

Being notably aware of many astonishing archeology discoveries and material ings. Information of past known physical history of the is relevant because it puts the lost ancient records from the historical epoch of times, in reconciliation with the biblical genesis narrative account.

The missing facts and these evocative prose are controversial. Meaning, we know very little about this ancient astronaut theory; extraterrestrial space faring aliens scenario. According to Hebrew Bible Genesis God [Enki/Ea], the ancient seven cuneiform clay tablets reveal empirical evidence that Enki had successfully manipulated His own biological DNA genetic code with an indigenous African to create a primordial crossbred servile human species as the Adam and Eve. Yeah, Enki declared that He created an obsequious primitive labor force. The Anunnaki came down to earth because they had a specific critical purpose; and it was to extract gold from the establishment of the African gold mining production operation Enki constructed in the southeastern region of great Zimbabwe, Africa. My friends, are you among the misled and deceived, willingly obedient blind faithful followers—misguided followers of the purveyors whose earth mission voyage was not to create a race of primitive human beings as a free labor force.

Yet, we know that this event came to fruition because it is written in the Hebrew Old Testament Bible Genesis narrative tale speaks of God's claims to have declared Himself as the creator of the crossbred Adam and Eve. Ostensibly the children of God came to be by Enki's manifestation of his biological Anunnaki DNA codes which essentially means: His own biological Royal DNA, genetic essence, bloodline descent from Anunnaki alien Enki who efficaciously fashioned the homo sapiens sapien Adam [as a new human species]. Whereof the Bible version is misleading, it's rather plausible to accept

THE MIND,BODY, SPIRIT,ANDSTORYTELLING

that this event occurred while the Anunnaki were living on the earth surface, meaning what? Not—from the dirt of the earth! His brother Enlil the Anunnaki supreme god over extraterrestrial alien beings who were actually living on earth. Yeah Enlil who was the god who confronted Adam and Eve as he was casually strolling through the garden in Edin! Which is omitted from the Old Testament biblical creation narrative—and why, might I ask: the Anunnaki alien God is not mentioned? What is rather implicit is that within the cinematic storyline we are left to speculate on the event as a narrative tale!

The acknowledgement that Enki/Ea, [Ra/Osiris] in fact, were the Egyptian gods of the mystery religion of the priesthood teachings of Kemet; and people worshiping of spiritual science of the Ancient Anunnaki Biblical, which was the precursor religion that became taught as the Bible Genesis narrative tale of the creator God. And this means that Enki, the first alien commander who led his two hundred alien astronaut crew of Anunnaki who was sent down to colonize the planet on this incredible Earth Mission voyage was commissioned by Nibiru's was Enki's father, King Anu! He was not only the flight mission commander; but He was the Anunnaki's Chief scientists and medical doctor. That while on earth and in need of primitive workers to perform as servile workers, exploits the indigenous people of planet earth had successfully genetically manipulated and modified the African indigenous female biological *mitochondrial* chromosome, which He fused with His own Anunnaki alien genetic chromosome code sequencing was derived the methodology that created the crossbred *homosapeins-sapeinprimative* while living on the earth surface.

This was not done using the ground dust, but by no means—should anyone continue to believe that god (Enki) formed Adam out of clay. Yeah, and this twisted version was introduced as by modern Western European civilization to subjugate spiritual science with their manifold power and control grabs via the infusion of the Christians church religious construct that is fundamental to the doctrinal canons and creeds of the secularism of organized Church religion. Disciples of an organized religion that provided human society with a mind/body/spirit complex with lies? The falsehood of a luminous divine God and Savior in personification Jesus Christ, doctrinal worship, which refers to you as the plebeians. Accepting the holy Christian gospel teachings without questions compels us to reexamine the history of the Church with discerning curiosity. By the way, this assertion is seemingly far-fetched, although true, it's not so widely accepted as by many church leaders who are now and continue to mislead the faithful with their specious troup. It's mind blowing to think about human beings' having free will consciousness awareness.

So throughout the pages of this book, I raise questions that every young child would ask parents about God.

Well my friends, I think that the ancient astronaut theory is a speculative hypothesis that fits nicely within the Genesis episodic narrative story of an actual historical epoch of culture and its nascent. The mysteries of the cultists' wisdom and knowledge of life to death cycle begin and end in the same place.

Chronicles of the Monumental Creation Event

To me, the ancient astronaut theory is the only vein that makes the most sense! The erudition of recent archeology discoveries, the missing, hidden mysteries, and lost pages of human civilizations historical knowledge is revealing significant findings. Their researchers work continues to uncover more significant historical material that dovetails nicely with the biblical and the ancient astronaut theorists premise.

There is absolutely no shortage of popular subject matter books that provide intriguing anecdotal detail about this interesting topic. You can purchase these books from outlet stores and online websites: I suppose that you will be fascinated with a series of published books on this subject, starting with "*Chariots of the Gods*" in 1968, written by notable Swiss pseudo archeologist, *Erich von Däniken* who claimed that extraterrestrial "ancient astronauts" had visited a prehistoric Earth. While those who find this hypothesis hyperbolic, must admit that it is intriguing. To which I suggest they go read Mr. Von Däniken's book. I think he has remarkable insight into this external empirical and spiritual world about extraterrestrial alien beings, the titular gods, with which therein it seems to be a nexus. It has everything to do with the original ancient Sumerian texts of the Holy Bible Old Testament as strong evidence [69][70][71]; Ref. to [14].

The Truth Let's all face it

Because, my friends, if you have made it this far, then stay with me because just perhaps a *caveat lector* is necessary here: Let all people not be neither *none-plussed* nor surprised to learn that recalcitrant Christians do not know anything about the history of religious in terms of origin of the Christian's Trinitaian doctrinal canons. Much of what is taught is distortion that fosters skepticism. The teaching of ideas that contradicts the Kemetic religious teaching of the Egyptians spiritual science philosophy, which reaches back beyond the scope of Bible knowledge. In spiritual thinking these are Christians. Religious people who are zealous-minded, devotees are the followers of the blind faith religions. Simply put they have acquiesced to the New Testament religious gospels of truthiness.

For them, a paradigm shifts into the spiritual science learning/teachings about God and the Law of One love. An understanding that attests to being in unity with the most high spirit is this common medium of the mind. As it is arguably quite true, and without any ambiguity, we share the providence of the universal life force energy harmonic vibrations, praying in homage for our life, though prayerful meditation infinite Creator. Neither I not anyone else fully apprehend anything of the controversy surrounding the Anunnaki extraterrestrial alien gods. Yet with spirit, insight, logic, and reason believe that a strong possibility that ancient alien astronauts came from the sky and landed down on planet earth eleven thousands of years ago. Yet, I found my perception was familiar with their presence although I knew nothing about their appearance before. Whether this was me recalling ancient astronaut theorists' hypothesis is correct, and I certainly don't know if any of this is true. But, allow me to opine about this controversy. It doesn't matter what I say, think or believe.

Through my understanding of the Old Testament Bible, chapter 1, juxtaposed to archeology and anthropology researchers discoveries of historical findings. Clearly they have contributed to the plethora of material information available for reference which prominent author's site in published subject matter books.

Which reveals to us substantial substantive anecdotal details that are closely akin to the subject of the Anunnaki alien gods that have been excised from the first version of the Genesis narrative. So wouldn't this material omission be regarded as the salient point of view and the curiosity about Anunnaki? Whereas the author, Mr. Zachariah Sitchin posits that extraterrestrial aliens, large manlike Gods, were ancient space-traveling astronauts.

His hypothesis provides a great premise which in his books fits into what is written in the context of the Old Testament Bible. Genesis' holy book narrative fits nicely into the eponymous Anunnaki Enki' seminal DNA fusion of alien and indigenous African female genetic code, which delineates the Babylonian Creation tail as the event in great detail delineating the Babylonian Creation tail as the event in great detaas seminal DNA fusion of alien and indigenous African female genetic code, delineating the Babylonian Creation tail as the event in great detail. I highly recommend you purchase his series of informative, great books on the Nibiruan Anunnaki, Royal family: Lord Gods Anu, Enki, Enlil, as the ancient astronauts: "Those who came"! The scope of this explanation ostensibly dovetails nicely with a tremendous volume of subject matter books written by the authors who are the purveyors of controversy over this ancient astronaut hypothesis. But as remarkable as it is to believe—my friends, it's not just me who is perspicacious. Others have the discernment to understand that the absolute truth lies in the perception of glaring misstatements and omissions of facts about the Nascence of the Anunnaki Sumerian Bible narrative tale. Clearly the genesis narrative was converted into a religious truthiness tale because its concealment infers that the biblical narrative story is obviously careful not to mention Anunnaki alien Gods. The identity of the ancient astronauts, the Anunnaki alien beings, have been lifted from chapter 1:1 through 11 and is by every measure called God.

It suddenly occurred to me in ruminations about the Holy Bible Genesis narrative, that I concluded that this is the missing aspect of this true story that organized church religionists don't ever want people to figure out. As the elucidation, it would seem to me is likely to be the nascence of the Anunnaki titular God Enki in the profile that connects Him with the Earth Mission voyage! The Anunnaki titular Gods from the planet Nibiru that landed on earth by means of an advanced aerial spacecraft as His conveyance.

Okay, my friends, what about the premise of this Ancient Astronauts Theory? Well, then you must please permit me to say that the empirical evidence puts the material information is plausible. You see, we believe in an alien god-man, meaning that they were an intelligent extraterrestrial race that possessed advanced knowledge. The possessed sophisticated advanced technology and knowledge of aerial spaceflight, it was highly likely the genesis. Ergo, this interpolation of logic and reason is unraveling the hidden mysteries of the Old Testament Biblical Genesis narrative. Because it was by means of the sky that ancient astronauts descended from the Nibiru (Heaven), the higher plane they came down. This was a UFO vehicle piloted by an ancient astronaut who arrived and landed in the Sumerians planes of Mesopotamia! Simply put: Most remarkable is the salient question about what it means by a highly technical sophisticated conveyance; other than by some advanced flying spacecraft about it? We all have been misled by truthiness. We are an enthusiastic body of seekers; and those who are living, se, and determined to uncover the truth about the lost and hidden mysteries, ancient mysteries of earthly historical facts concerning the identity of the old astronaut hypothesis.

It's mainly about what other people have been led to believe that the biblical story is more than just an allegory. To finally learn that what we have been taught isn't true; that the biblical Genesis version hides the real Bible truth is convoluted less insofar as: the extraterrestrial Anunnaki in Mesopotamia, the Olden s, and post great flood ties to the ancient astronauts Gods; and, their ferry to extract the gold mineral deposits out of the gold mining operations located in Great Zimbabwe.

Abundant mines by the fashioning of a Hybrid prototype crossbred homosapien primitive worker is inextricably true--not spurious poppycock (Book Ref.: The Light of Egypt by Thomas H. Boygoyne, the Science of The Soul, Vol I & II; Chapter X, pg. [80] [81] [82]. space faring extraterrestrial alien beings, the so-called astronauts titular God's presence on earth in the ancient external empirical world. According to ancient Egyptian texts, strange space-traveling space-traveling astronauts, Anunnaki, arrived in Sumerian Mesopotamia 75,000 years ago.

Their mission, they chose to accept, was explicitly an exploration-focused search for large deposits of gold resources. In one of the documents, we found a particularly interesting account down onto the earth surface interior plane. Egyptian records tell us that these extraterrestrial beings were the Anunnaki: Those came here in chariots from Heaven! God who was said to have come to Earth from a distant place in the psychic and spiritual universe.

I am aware of the anecdotal evidence copied from the original sacred Anunnaki's ancient Holy text of the original Sumerian manuscript, which the Hebrew and Greek Septuagint version of the Holy Bible translated. That we are human beings who are capable of making either good or bad choices as created Homosapien sapiens that worship Gods on blind faith in what religion that is most pleasing to us, for we have freedom of religion—no matter if by blind faith.

What matters is that your spirit enlightens your consciousness. Having a deeper understanding of this *exegesis* I implore the blind sheep to think about what is the most remarkable story that has ever been taught is truthiness. Well then, my friends, what we were prepared from the Biblical Genesis was wrong your entire adult life! But was this retelling of creation a sinister invention, and some mendacious twisting the Anunnaki presence on earth 450,000 years ago is the ancient astronauts (extraterrestrial alien) elaborate tale.

Might we surmise that the indigenous tribesmen of the earth would have worshiped these extraterrestrial alien beings as god? And might we be perpetuating this Cinematic exegesis of African/Egyptians interpolation derived from the spiritual teachings of the secret priesthood worshiping of the holy temple occultists spirit teachings of the lost Kemetism orthodox Priesthood rites and ritual theology of the archetype Kemetism, ritual and rites; learning the fidelity's instructions of the selfings of the *Neberdjer*.

Where mystery spiritual science of meditation teaches/learning about the Law of One doesn't the ignoble bon homies. The uninitiated are the blind faith religion followers of theological doctrine and dogmatic creeds that are devoid of the unverified nature of the ancient sciences of a luminous divine spiritual wisdom of the Law of One love that teaches endued unity sacred principles. as a servile primitive workers, worshiping ritual and rites of sacerdotalism, by accepting Christ (Truth) as the Romanized priest who falsely proclaimed themselves to be humble vicar's of luminous divine nature of spirit being; alien titular God as the self appointed "doctor of the human's mind/body/spirit complex."

The pious purveyors of the new church Christian and Protestant faiths religion doctrinal canons held titles such as the Roman Catholic Pope, called Holy Father, Cardinal, Bishop, and Protestant Pastors, Deacons offered their congregations their wise sermons to the worshiper who with their supplications established their religious orders with ceremonial ritual and rites according to their ecumenical churches theological religionist teachings which correspond to the canonized creed adopted and taught from the Christian Bible to be the actual gospel.

Words of the Savior in Jesus Christ the only begotten son of God—the Holy Father! But did you know that reading the Bible was forbidden by the Pope? Yeah, no one dared to question this titular holy vicar of god! Moreover, "any persons of the laity who was found to have in their possession a copy of the Bible was obligated to hand it over to the church to be burned. And that in 1536 William Tynsdale was burned at the stake—as a consequence for publishing the Bible in the common folk vernacular; meaning that the Bible is literally baptized in fire!" Enough blood has been shed in the name of god, with impunity—let your conscience be the judge of as you begin to drill down to find evidence hidden in the veins of concealed historical and biblical information.

Which has been discovered and is slowly raised from beneath the surface into the light from the machinations of the dark order that have twisted the original spiritual science principles of wisdom, and suppressed the truth about god by manipulation of religions.

A monumental manifold of falsehoods that is one hundred and eighty degrees out of phase with African-Egyptian Kemetism spiritual philosophy. The significance of this event in ancient known physical history is monumental in the battle and switch from African Kemetism. The science of teachings and learning to spiritual meditation of sacred occultists theology. The elevation of the human soul in the worshiping of the infinite Creator Law of One; the universal monad, *Neberdjer* in unity with infinity of God's luminous divine universal nature.

Whereof, the bon homies have been faithful followers of the religious denominations church doctrines and theological creeds. This event marked supremacy and with arrogance their attitude of supremacy, effectively was cemented.

A New Testament theology transformation was twisted into the religious blind faith of the Christians view of theology and correspondingly, and the New Testament Bible of the Catholics and Protestant church authority emerged as the unfoldment of God as the Christ. Our holy redeemer and savior of Heaven was proclaimed through the personhood of the crucified Jesus Christ. Theology of the new religions were pushed and defended by the Church's appropriations of the holy religious cross; and doctrinal teachings of blind faith religious worship of Jesus Christ and Christianity as a synergy of thoughts inculcated that offer the path to ultimate providence. The salvations is belief in the luminous divine nature of the spirit holy trinity of God. It was the fourth century Christian Era of racism.

This was about the fear of the black African race imagery that was pronounced in the prominent depictions, that Western Europeans had become the dominant rulers of the empirical world in which the epoch of the African spiritual science principles were stolen, and the script was flipped into the Caucasian's depictions replaced the imagery of the dark skin into white figures who now represent Christianity empirical worldwide! It's well entrenched throughout the known modern empirical world up to this present temporal reality.

However, owing to the *mendacious imbroglio*, Romans Emperor Constantine I, deception. Spuriously he proclaimed to have been told by God that he would be victorious in battle by displaying the Christian cross on his army's war banner.

That was seen as a sign that the cross would bring his army victory over his opponent's opposing army. History records in the present time/space continuum leaving a snapshot of the specificity of anecdotal detail that were written down; it's a reflection of past events. Every action takes the spirit of the human being's free will. Consciousness awareness is what allows our spirit that directs our decisions to actions that we take as animated energy beings; having free-will, is *ipso facto*, endued by the Anunnaki alien God's who settle in the Sumer, Mesopotamia interior plane.

According to the Old Testament version of the original Anunnaki Sumerian Bible manuscript Enki's Astronauts crew built the first city-state in six days, and He named it Eridu—meaning: *"their home in the far away"*! They became the custodians and they steadfastly been the Master manipulators who are hidden. Meaning that they are the invisible hands of the powerful and wealthy who are the control element of influence of economic machinations; absolute power and control of the empirical world's financial system. The new world order to bring the conflicts on to the earth, replete with the rewritten biblical new age chronicling historical events horizon will emergence into the transformation into the western consciousness mind of the European creation of empires under a secular state king as the ruling power as its authorities which embraced Christianity as the Catholic Church of god.

This was the that supplanted Kemetism mystery spiritual science of meditation. Which was the spiritual wisdom of the Law of One love teachings and learning of African-Egyptians science of knowledge of soulful meditation that was co-opting by the falsehood twisted Holy religion doctrine of the Cross of Christianity took the knowledge of spirituality and predicate thes divergence which marked the transformation from the mystery spiritual science of souls mind/

body/spirit complex into a a "'false religious doctrinal philosophy and tricked us into believing our luminous divine sacred knowledge of wisdom of the Law of One love'" [paganism as black magic madguru]. A transformation that emerged from the epoch of time evolution into the new age history of Christianity that came into prominence during the third millennium A.D. [http://www.ravshaul.com/christianitythegreatdeception/TheSpiritbehindChristianity.htm].

It was the turning point of dishonesty, which was attributed to the Romans Empire's and Pope's began a period when the Western European powers implemented their empirical juggernaut exemplified the new world order; one that emerged as an empirical power and control to exploited earth's bon homies new world order.

This is the History that speaks of oppression and social volumes about the poor who were exploited as they were deprived of human dignity, and emigrated, as economic opportunities was a reality that was truncated lift many citizens with a life of poverty, trampled and subsidized by a blind faith religion; and the promise of going to salvation in Heaven after death. A blessing given to faithful followers in services in the name of Jesus Christ; the God of the sacred providence. All the while they set about to whitewash the African-Egyptians, Khemit spiritual science by every means of deception and distortions to erase the African-Egyptians' mystery of symbology. Such as the *Ankh* of love and life, they transform into one that today became a symbol of the death saga in the Christian church worship, into a prominent religious symbol meaning death and resurrection! A transformation perverted the Kemetic complexities of ancient mystery spiritual science sacred principles of the African-Egyptian wisdom of the Law of One love teaching/learning of the mysteries of God's prayerful meditation, which was attacked, denigrated, and with impunity! Was his action endued by some means of luminous divine intervention? Neither you nor I can attest to this as the truth. I don't know if Constantine I victory had anything to do with some God' telling him to conquer in the name of the Christians symbol of the holy sign of the cross, which he proclaimed had been inspired by a visit from god.

History recorded that his army rallied on and defeated the army that was engaged in the battle, it was victory for the imperial Roman army of Constantine I. He began to openly embrace Christianity. He was very instrumental a major influence in putting forth the widespread acceptance of the social religion that began to grow as Catholic Churches authority. Dominated during the epoch the rise of was the struggle to gain authority control of Christianity after the crucifixion death of Jesus the Christ who was worshiped as the Son of the God of Heaven. With this authority a brutal persecution of those who dared will reject or renounce teachings, under fear of persecution, Constantine I forbade all persecutions in order to capitalize upon its rising popularity. While making this assertion began to suppress melded with some sacred pagan occultists' philosophy would include their holidays.

Paganism occultists theology was adapted as the Catholic Christians church authority allowed some pagan rites, rituals, including the occultists popular holidays. The authority of Christianity had cleverly begun to set forth the Catholic Church's supremacy; it was a falsehood that caused the religious schism that occurred between the spurious Western religious orthodoxy.

I acknowledge whether anyone's view can be justifiably rebuffed free from their own conscious or unconscious biases is anyone's reconciliation of the amount of curated synchronization of available information data.

With which truthiness elements are being promulgated through the religious worshiping of Christianity to-day! But here's the salient questions, my friends: could I be wrong about this, or am I right? Who among us can know; or fathom the inclination of the assertion espoused by this literary exegesis. One which may seem rather far out as I interpolate a skewed paradigm of Genesis that doesn't comport with my interpretation of the Bible narrative. Why? Well. Simply put I am convinced that *nascentism* from the intrepid ancient astronaut theorists premise.

What a supposition! It fits in nicely as missing pieces of information that are not disclosed in the biblical genesis version. Because the biblical narrative tale seems to be rather closely akin to the ancient astronauts theorists hypothesis? That Nibiru's Anunnaki were the ancient astronauts of the past astronomical age of exploration—just as NASA, are the forward looking astronauts who probably would be regarded as the modern-day titular Gods from planet earth. According to historical evidence, Constantine I, Emperor of the ancient Eastern Romans Emperor took control of Christianity in A. D. He ordered the Bishop to centralize cultist religion into a Christian doctrine. It marked a new directional transformation. Which helped to ensure that Christianity's followers were free from persecutions under the auspices of the New romanized Catholic church's authority supremacy of the Rome holy papacy doctrine of the holy trinity of God. It was born out of the consolidation of Ecchomentical doctrines and dogmatic creeds.

I say it's okay. We know popular elements of paganism and Christianity were combined into the mainstream religion. Strategic machinations of the Roman Emperor—Constinetine the ultimate opportunists. Occultist teachings of original African-Egyptians, complexities of ancient mystery spiritual science of the *Kemetism* of *Shethut Neteru Neberdjer*. This New Vatican teachings of Christianity was clearly the nascence of the Western European chronicles divergence from the complexities of ancient mystery spiritual science of teachings the universal Nature of the monad meditation). My premise raises the speculation with respect to this invariably controversial topic regarding the biblical genesis and the Ancient Astronauts Theory; it's linked to the original Sumerian Biblical historical narrative tale of the ancient creation Myth [15].

Constantine I, Fusion of African Kemet and Christian Religion

It was Constantine I, the Roman Emperor, who convened the Council of Nicaea (325 CE) to create the Jesus Christ phantom. Dr. Martyn Percy, the famous canon expert wrote and I quote: "The Bible did not arrive by fax from heaven." The Bible is a creation of man. Man, not God, writes history, and history is always from the conqueror's perspective, not the conquered. It is the elite, the most powerful in society, that define the impres-

sion of the society's temporal reality, and that is exactly what Constantine did after subduing African influence in the empirical world. In Emperor Constantine's days, the official Roman religion was Sun worship (i.e., the African Egyptian cult of Sol Invictus or the Invincible Sun). They called it the Jovian Mystery System, and Constantine was the Chief priest.

During the reign of Constantine and over three hundred years after the alleged crucifixion of Jesus, the Christian population had grown to pose a severe threat to the unity of Rome. The Christians were constantly warring with the Pagans and threatening to tear Rome apart. Constantine I, an intelligent opportunist, decided to tinker with both religions to create a monster. Constantine converted his Sun God worshipers to Christianity by creating an amalgam, a hybrid, a fusion of 'Pagan symbols, dates, rituals, and ideas, hijacked and weaved into hybrid creation of the Pagan-Christian religion truthiness. It's time to produce the absolute truth! Which rulers of the church and state have been seduced and seemingly compromised by the selfish allure of the illusory temporal reality of the material empirical world. Constantine produced a sacred entity outside the scope of the human empirical world whose power was unchallengeable by mere mortals, and called it the Roman Catholic Church. To do this, he conveyed his 325 CE Council of Nicaea that produced the Nicene creed.

The problem at the time, was whether Auset, (who was the Virgin Birth Mother in the ancient African Mystery System, imbibed by the Jovian Mystery, which was being adapted by the Church Bishops, should continue to take precedence over her son Heru, as in the ancient African Myth). In the end, God Ausar, (re-named Yahweh), retained his double roles as the Holy Ghost (misunderstood by Christians as the universal 'Spirit'), and as the human 'God the Father' in the African Mysteries, 4,425 years earlier, (who became the Christian Ghost Impregnator), of Mother Auset, re-named Mary, with Auset's Virgin Son, Heru, (renamed Jesus).

In other words, "Holy" and "Virgin Birth," were transferred to Jesus and Mary, from Heru and Auset. Jesus became born in Bethlehem and acquired higher rank than his contrived mother. He was supposed to be *her first child and to have been miraculously conceived. His foster-father was given the name Joseph, and the carpentry profession, to appeal to humility. The name 'Christ' came from the Greek translation of Christos (meaning anointed), taken from the Hebrew title of Messiah. The Bishops at the Nicaea Council in 325 CE decided that Jesus, who was supposed to have been baptized as and called Emmanuel before the Jesus Christ was born in Bethlehem in Judea. All these were happening some 325 years after the purported death of Jesus"*

(blackhistory938.wordpress.com).

What are the hidden mysteries?

It's about the treasure of ancient spiritual wisdom of the Law of One love, that is the purpose of which the erudite seekers must learn and teach others about the lost knowledge of the Eastern sacred Law of One. Throughout this book the aim was to impart information insights, philosophies, inspirational musings and wisdom of the Law of One love posits the sourced books attributed exegesis, derived from eclectic authors. Such as published prolific author, Dr. Sebai Muata Ashby's outstanding collection of good books to read, as well as many others that provide a valuable and invaluable compendium of helpful information about this spring of confluence of outrageous subjects matter, a plethora of intriguing anecdotal details regarding this exciting topic. The information in each is mind-opening; and provides a window for anyone who wants to learn the facts about the ancient physical and spiritual empirical worlds, the external empirical world of sacred principles of erudition of religious truth. Here's a brief segway to this description revealing [16]..."For thousands of years the spiritual tradition of Ancient Egypt, Shetaut Neter, The Egyptian Mysteries, The Secret Teachings have fascinated and tantalized the external empirical world. At one exalted and recognized as the highest culture of the external empirical world by Africans, Europeans, Asiatics, Hindus, Buddhists. Might the ancient convey the practical history and biblical blind faith religion?

THE MIND, BODY, SPIRIT, AND STORYTELLING

Empirical embrace of central church authority vested in the theological teachings of Christianity as the gospel of Jesus Christ, as the Trinity as the final words of God, according to the Holy Bible. The transformation imposed. As arrogant ruler's implemented arbitrary dogmatic doctrines with which became law enforcement. The aim was to concConsolidate the system of the power of the state spurred the creation of the Roman Catholic Church system in the personification of the organized central authority of the Holy Trinitarian Doctrines creeds and the creed, which the Holy Roman Emperor embraced a convergence into the central administration by church bishops and the Popes of Rome as the vicar of god. It was this Temples unholy alliance that was behind the most insidious evil deeds with acts of brutal aggression was a wave of intolerance. By any means necessary, threat against the Catholic Church religious dogma and creeds was deemed to be a harisi against the New Testament religion theology. The new age Christian religion was unlike the principle learning/teaching of sacred spiritual science philosophical of traditional African-Egyptians Kemetic focus on individualism and minimalistic values of simplicity of universal law of one unity of love. This was about the love and respect of the philosophical understanding of the living nature of the mystical *Medu Neter*, meaning the sacred, mysterious hieroglyphic texts hold the secret symbolic meaning that has scarcely been discerned or understood up to now.

With the advent of modern organized church religion we have lost an important part of our human story as a spiritual reflection of the intelligent ego construct of divine consciousness. Were these secrets of the spirit awakening to great remembrance and emancipation and resurrection? This was more than a literal translation of ancient volumes of the Shetitu Neter spiritual teaching of sacred knowledge. Was it deciphered by Egyptologists, nor could they be understood. The interpretation of the African-Egyptian complexities of ancient mystery spiritual science and the wisdom of the Law of One love is available in modern times. The alien titular Anunnaki gods of the planet Nibiru seeded spiritual wisdom of the Law of One love teaching through the Temple Priesthood. They buried the Royal

Pharaoh Egyptian Kingship on Earth after the biblical eponymous narrative tale of the great Noah's flood.

Anunnaki Enki began to advance his sacred Serpent Temple Priestly Brotherhood of the Law of One, learning / teaching Kemetism religious principles of the mystery spiritual science of Yoga meditation via the secret ritual cultists' motherhood of the serpent initiation ceremony. Gods and goddesses of the Anunnaki

Imperial authority of the Holy Roman Christendom

The predominance of the Eastern occult orthodoxy was subjectively plagiarized, and selectively edited and subjugated, translated, and transmitted in the New Testament Catholic Church religion. Spiritualism was subject to attacks by the Roman Church. Which was being taught as the word of Jesus Christ as a Trinitarian precept. Thus the truth was converted into storytelling. Enki's crossbred humans descendants were apprised, persecuted, hunted down and eliminated in order to upended with the conquest of Kemetism when the Pharaohs and Priests of the Temple worshipers was dismantled by the Imperial Roman legions was the death nail that vanished Kemetism spiritualism teachings. And in so doing paved the way for the Mosque of the prophet Mohammed, which began a new religion that imposed their rule over the ordinary bon homies who worshiped them as their keepers of the sacred creation of the (god) Enki. He was the deity of the Mesopotamia city of Eridu (Khem via black rites 17). Under the. Constantine made Christianity the main religion of Rome, and created Constantinople, which became the most powerful city in the empirical world. Emperor Constantine (ca A.D. 280–337) reigned over a major transition that spread in the Roman Empire (ref.: from Feb 25, 2019), https://www.nationalgeographic.com). Christianity for millions of people of religious worship it is a matter of blind faith, as people who look to gain salvation tend to follow whatever religious denomination that most pleases them is phenomenal, without exception.

This was the emergence into the contrivance of the Christian religions doctrinal creed and the embrace and whitewashing dogmatic of blind faith worship Jesus Christ of the Holy Trinity. Whereas Constantine I. "Writing about the latter, Miroslav Volf says: "Beginning at least with Constantine's conversion, the followers of the Crucified have perpetrated gruesome acts of violence under the sign of the Christian Cross.

The symbolism of the religionist Holy Gospel Trinity of Jesus Christ as the pathway to salvation. Ironically, the hatred towards the spiritual occultists' teachings evolved into Christianity transformation by Constantine I, who converted to Christianity was likely the turning point of this pivotal epoch of culture of religious doctrines. An intervention that marked the rise and the emerging Christianity in the New Testament Bible's teachings of blind faith was the profession of the "Second Coming!" A brand of Christianity that has its history that has been shameful in mendacious sanguin violence and corruption executed in the name of the god.

Much of the weight of religion transformation and subjugation by the power and control under the Roman Emperor, Constantine I. A mendacious sinister schema to establish religious supremacy! This was the embrace of Christianity. But was it a clever scheme in order to bring about the establishment of a centralized authority in Christian control over religion. He convened Bishops of the new Christianity and tasked them to edit and come up with a Trinitarian God, the Father; and regarding Jesus Christ as the divinity Son of God at the *Council of Nicaea*. First Council of Nicaea was a council of Christian bishops convened in the Bithynian city of Nicaea (now İznik, Turkey) by the Roman Emperor Constantine I, embraced this populous rise of Christianity incapital state government to edit the religion of Christianity of the Pope and to Romans Emperor authority when he had "convened the Bishops in 335 AD, tasked these Bishops to construct one Holy Ecumenical Christian religious of the doctrinal creed of blind faith. With the issue settled regarding Jesus and the Holy Trinity resolved the controversial matter, which answered the question regarding the nature and Divinity of God according to the Western European religious chronicles introduced their twisted reworking African spiritual science underwent a thistransformation into the western theological holy canons and the New Testament Christian doctrinal creeds.

The hijacking of *Neberdjer's* spiritual principles

Were it not for the universal luminous divine natural laws and sacred principles, could modern age humans, like our ancient space-traveling astronauts, possess the necessary intellectual insight to achieve the eponymous reverence to be perceived as and worshiped?

Gods of Heaven and the Earth. To me, this makes absolutely no sense if we believe that this apomorphic god from Heaven can call illusory temporal reality into existence. By my own logic and reason, contend that the Biblical narrative is a truthiness. Why would I say that? Because it's falsehood that doesn't make sense. However it seems probable that it's becauses of every action and behavior is the spirit of my natal living action and reactions in the cycle of living expenses until the death of my physical human form.

Since the earth was colonized by aliens Gods came and landed their flying chariots; that is to say: from Heaven to Earth, arrived from a higher cosmic density plane of intelligent extraterrestrial alien Gods. The biblical Genesis narrative story is most likely about this intrepid crew of fifty Nibiru spaces-traveling astronauts' voyage and landing on earth. And in what is the recondite sense, it seems they were the pre-flood Earth Olden Times Anunnaki Gods from planet Nibiru [18].

Some believed they were the ancient extraterrestrial astronauts of olden s Sumerian titular Gods of Nibiru (Planet-X) or Heaven. Well then, my friends, the monad is the living spirit of the *Neberdjuer;* this spiritual theology teaching of God has long been lost, hidden mysteries, hermetically concealed--supplanted by false religious education of the blind faith doctrine. That Genesis narrative is about an ancient astronaut in Mesopotamia developing.

Modern-day theory exposes a conspiracy in that the Bible Chapter 1: verses history represent the absolute truthiness; the mythology of the surface illusion of a contrived invention. So what exactly does it mean? That there's information hidden mysteries,

THE MIND, BODY, SPIRIT, AND STORYTELLING

kept secret suppressed and conceal; as the archetypal historical events of the Bible narrators of the Old Testament (original Anunnaki, Sumerian Bible) story was *coterminous* with the aliens extraterrestrials Enki's initial arrival, which described as Gods: The ancient astronaut's hypothesis. Which reveals the auspicious Golden age events on earth. The views about this are shockingly controversial, with opinions is largely discordant noise from skeptical religious folks that still pervade the teaching which inculcate a misdirection akin to mendacious deception; and falsehoods (*The Gods of Eden, William Bramley; Avon Books*). The Old Testament Hebrew/Greek Bibles is a composite of the most convoluted stories written by my different authors; and simply put of historic paucity of a conf timeline events that makes no effort to the Anunnaki as the titular God as: "Those who from the heaven came"!

There is no truer way to refute the evidence which suggests that they were any other than extraterrestrial ancient astronauts, came here in chariots here in chariots down and seeded civilization by colonizing planet Earth. yet the ancient astronauts theorists posits this missing fact that curiously intentionally has hidden mysteries the truth about the identity of the God that is voice that narrator the Genesis text of Chapter 1, a story which was written about the Anunnaki space-traveling alien race of extraterrestrial alien beings: "Those who from the Heaven came" had successfully descended from a higher cosmic orbital planetary sphere solar system. Their motivation was to extract earth's abundant gold resources.

Such is this account of an incredible story, we do a deep dive far back into the nascence of the ancient empirical external world history of humanity: When it was said and written that: In the beginning many eons ago this advanced race of extraterrestrials, manlike beings, the ancient astronauts theorists, believed that these were the alien beings who spurred many notable accomplishments whilst living among indigenous peoples unconquered landscape of earth humans earlier ancestors.

Such as the wheel, beer, farming, writing, astronomical observation, warfare, and the temporal priesthood worship to their god's planet earth before and after the great Noah's flood occurred.

Anunnaki *Igigi* aliens were the Anunnaki labor that performed the back-breaking hard sweat and and and grievous toil required to work inside the deep mining operation in great southern Zimbabwe, Africa—the mineral gold was desperately needed to patch up the hole and tires in planet Nibiru's dwindling atmosphere. Yet, this is a far more plausible narrative tale, and viz. A probable scenario consisting of ancient astronaut theory fits nicely with the eccentric eruption of facts related to archeology discovery and the Biblical Genesis narrative Chapter 1, verses. The light of the past becomes the prologue, and a treasure trove of 30,000 cuneiform clay tablets was found, which contained a cuneiform script, the oldest written language ever uncovered, dating back 6,000 years. Some of these tablets that were unearthed contained the Babylonian legend of the *Enuma Elish*.

The Enūma Eliš is the Babylonian creation Myth

It was recovered by English archeologist Austen Henry Layard in 1849 after excavating the ruins of the Library of Ashurbanipal at Nineveh. Nineveh was an ancient Assyrian city of Upper Mesopotamia, located on the outskirts of Mosul in modern-day northern Iraq. Located on the eastern bank of the Tigris River; and the largest capital city of the Neo-Assyrian Empire in the external empirical world for several decades (911 BC–609 BC), https://en.wikipedia.org/wiki/Neo-Assyrian_Empire.

cuneiform clay tablets were found in Nipper, Mesopotamia (Southern Iraq). And according to the conventional use of critical thinking, logical, and able arguments with which archeology discovery dovetails nicely with the assertion that the Old Testament biblical story is about an ancient astronaut God; meaning, what? I presuppose that these Anunnaki alien gods were, indeed, spacefaring UFOs who descended from a higher cosmic orbital plane that had a specific purpose when they launched from their vehicles on an earth mission visitation. Might this speculative assertion be plausible, meaning that the truth is revealed to those who know about the intrinsic life transformation, and examine the ancient astronauts theorists' hypothesis. With which simplifies the recondite with the clarity of introspection and understanding that these alien god's had advanced knowledge of the metaphysical cosmic universe, spiritual, scientific and sophisticated technology, is the definition of god's as a spacefaring race?

Which brings to mind the old axiom that there is nothing new under the sun; meaning that the beginnings and endings in the mystery always ends in the same place! This is my understanding of the hidden mysteries connection to the cosmic Monad, the universal all unity of the sacred *Neberdjer*. Thereof about humans and plants live animations of various forms of earth's dens matter. With humankind worshiping Christ as Lord holy veneration of a luminous divine supreme Deity worship of Jesus Christ as a personal savior.

These Western Europe churches introduced their theoretical doctrine of the Holy Trinity underlying tenets of the Father, Son, and Holy Spirit of God theology teachings of a blind faith illusion. I have been reading and digesting my analysis of this topic as my exegesis, which posits an assertion conflated to the ancient astronaut hypothesis. To try to entertain the notion that the Old Testament Bible story is clearly about the Annunaki Genesis narrative tale of these extraterrestrial beings who were apomorphic manlike titular Gods from a deep space orbital planet, they called Nibiru. And read the Biblical account of Genesis Chapter 1, ostensibly there was no mention of the Anunnaki Enki as the God of which proclaimed credit for the creation narrative event. And it was He the Nibiruan the Royal great prince, Enki was the Anunnaki God of waters and the God of wisdom of the Law of One love and magic; the God who successfully manipulated His and an African female genetic mitochondrial DNA biological codes essence.

Okay, let's accept the story that Adamu/Adam was indeed fashioned by the Royal Prince Enki—in His own image or Anunnaki likeness. Then we must also accept that the Gods of the genesis narrative tale is true, then the Anunnaki were, in fact, not god's, but they were the Ancient Astronauts who were "Those who from the Heaven came" became Earth's custodians, and the extraterrestrial aliens created the first homo sapiens sapien's DNA, genetically engineered hybrid crossbreeds beings as the Anunnaki descendents derived from the biblical myth about *Adapa* (Adam) and Eve. While living in the Earth's interior plane of Zimbabwe, Africa.

This is extremely important in understanding what seems quite indicative is that God was probably an extraterrestrial manlike ancient astronaut from the planet called Nibiru! Seems quite very plausible. To me, this theory seems to make more sense.

What is plausible is that an extraterrestrial alien race of titular gods living among humans. Confidential information was manufactured by the ambitious ruler's mendacious schemes to exercise a lust for power and influence to gain a dominant amount of stolen booty through territorial wars of aggression pervading society. Anunnaki extraterrestrial; and their Demigod crossbred humans facilitated by the spirit caused the Anunnaki alien Royal bloodline to the living form of the light source of the godhead spirit consciousness awareness. Existence is influenced by the free-will embodiment of selfish desire of sinister motivation. We glean inside our consciousness but some irrational thoughts for logic and spiritual providence. Our existence and knowledge lie in the clarity of our understanding through the daily meditation path to greater consciousness awareness about what it's likely true; the actual knowledge that the titular gods of the Bible were ancient astronauts.

The Sumerian peoples' Old Testament God, Enki's astronaut crew, landed in the ancient Persian Gulf region where the *Tigris–Euphrates* river system, the Anunnaki titular God Enki's ancient astronauts' crew is where they landed a spacecraft on planet earth. The [Bible] mentioned this as the first city-state, and Royal-Elite Prince Enki named it *Eridu, meaning* what?

Their *"home in the faraway"*! This fits the creation narrative roughly equivalent to that which is found written in Chapters 1 through 11, in the Book of Genesis [https://www.bizsiziz.com/the-history-of-the-anunnaki]. The Bible Genesis narrative tale is written about the African-Egyptian Kemetic spiritual science wisdom associated with sensory knowledge. The epicenter of human consciousness awareness scenery of ancient astronauts alien deities and the constructions of city-states in Sumer, Mesopotamia were built by the Hebrew-Israelites; who ancestors descendants they worshiped came from the

THE MIND, BODY, SPIRIT, AND STORYTELLING

Anunnaki clans, which corresponds with the Old Testament—Olden Times gods who came down from the firmament. This extraterrestrial Annunaki titular God Enki; to the Hebrew-Israelites followers he was the God Enki. This is in the biblical book of Genesis, Chapter 1. Wherein the Royal Prince Enki had built the first earth colony in six days. He and his group of aliens conquered the landscape through clan and sibling warfare. Using logic, might we assume that a spacecraft's mode of transportation conveyance [20]. And my friends, wouldn't that line of thinking be extremely ludicrous folly?! It was by sophisticated advanced space flight (UFOs), so I am betting that the initial vanguard of Anunnaki space-traveling astronauts came here in chariots here in chariots from the planet of Nibiru, I assert, landed upon the earth plane comfortably seated in flying chariots from the planet of Nibiru, I assert, landed upon the earth plane comfortably seated onboard a sophisticated, shining metallic extraterrestrial spacecraft piloted by ancient astronauts. If true, they must have possessed a higher level of advanced scientific technology, Right? After all, my friends, I'm sure that an able thinking person who should question why the Old Testament Bible, Genesis chapter 1: verses, 1 through 11 story of the Biblical God of Genesis is very silent. But were they space-traveling ancient astronauts who the Sumerian people worshiped Prince Enki as their God?

So what? The *neophytes* and spiritual seekers of truth, alludes to the space-traveling *Anunnaki* as merely the misrepresentation of the monad of *Neberdjer* (God Spirit). Advanced extraterrestrial alien beings were from planets-X (Nibiru). It has an elliptical constellation Zodiacal earth orbit.

Enki/Ea and his intrepid fifty-man crew of space-traveling astronauts navigate safely down through the dangerous asteroid belt and down between Mars and Jupiter, which was known as the gateway entrance into the *crossing* led by the commander, Enki. The son of the Sky God *Anu*, and great supreme Anunnaki *King (God)*, over the extraterrestrial alien race on earth and in Heaven.

Awed indigenous earth men likely cowering in fear, gazed upward at a magnificent extraterrestrial bell shaped alien UFO Chariot slowly descending and landing in ancient Mesopotamia.

And try to imagine yourself there with all of these wide-eyed *scallywag* tribal men. Their hearts fear that these enormously large manlike figures appear to have arrived wearing armor over their chest were the extraterrestrial titular Gods! This is the hidden mystery of the secret powers of the elite cabal mechanisms of the hidden hand of the deceivers of the orders of the organized secret societies. After all, at the apex of the social construct resides in the secret shadows, is the mysterious hidden hand that facilitates the means of control by a body of non-elected bloodline ancestors of the Royal Anunnaki Ruling Council of elite gods of homeland Nibiru or (Planet-X)) is the mysterious hidden hand that facilitates the means of control by a body of non-elected bloodline ancestors of the Royal Anunnaki Ruling Council of elite gods of homeland Nibiru or (Planet-X). The Great supreme god, King of the heavenly (sky) and the Earth (the Mother Goddess) Ki, was Anu (An), Lord and King of this advanced race of extraterrestrial alien Gods. The Old Testament Bible Genesis narrative hides this; viz., and this is critical to understanding the whole truth...

Yes! And why would the story not include the anecdotal details; to me the biblical genesis narrative is silent, meaning what? Is it not, then a truthiness devoid of the true beginning? Well, my friends, the real true beginning is clearly missing from Genesis Chapter 1. Curiously, let's be clear and respectful as we analyze my thoughts in context of this salient question: for what would the opening episode, the beginning scene, be seemingly intentionally willful, in Genesis; in the telling of the opening that says: "'In the beginning God...'"! What might it lead the curious mind to ruminate and ponder and make connections about this as a scholarly exegesis. Because the logic raises, God used the issue of the salient and a substantive, relevant question about what means or mode of the flight to descend from Heaven to as the Bible says that he looks down onto the Earth's and saw that it was this murky and dark landscape? What was God's purpose for coming from heaven to create the Earth as a planet if he arrived and observed it?

For what and motivation were at play when the Genesis narrative chose not to include anything that makes no mention of this connection to the Old Testament Holy Bible story.

This point of view is most probably the most plausible historical account about the Anunnaki, Sumerian Bible was written, and the Hebrew and Greek Septuagint biblical version was derived from the mistranslation of Christian Bible book truthiness—a religious truthiness. The Anunnaki Sumerians were the original players of the Genesis narrative story written about the extraterrestrial episodes epoch of time, that advanced alien of a small group of Anunnaki crew that arrived on earth during the initial Earth Mission voyage. The Anunnaki was the original custodian's titular alien Gods: "'Those who were from Heaven came'" down from a higher constellation orbital planet. They colonized and brought civilization to the Sumerian interior Earth planet. Enki and Enlil, the two sons of the Nibiru Anunnaki Royal King Anu, the preeminent power players who descended from Heaven to earth in flying spacecraft. And it was the Royal great prince Enki Earth Mission voyage Commander of the first fifty man astronaut crew to establish a forward base of operations in ancient Mesopotamia, land of the ancient Sumerian peoples—the "Black Heads."

The extraterrestrial man-like figure who traveled aboard ancient astronauts for Who arrived tarrying above the earth before they landed on planet Earth. Mesopotamian community had worshiped Enki as a God who piloted sophisticated aerial UFO (chariots) descended from Heaven, or shall I say: was the first fifty man crew of intrepid ancient astronauts.

I accept the premise that a vanguard of Anunnaki aliens skilled astronauts were actually those who came to earth and became the first custodians after they descended and created the civilizations on earth. And imagine them sitting onboard an advanced large flying spacecraft quietly hovering in the air above the landing target. Inside, Enki looked down at the indigenous people through the windows.

Most likely they were getting ready to prepare for the land down on the Earth to begin their mission to establish a gold mining production operation in the southeastern region of great Zimbabwe,

Africans. What an event. Of course, the Biblical Genesis narrative, Chapter 1, made no mention of this. Why is this not written about in the Holy Bible book of the Genesis narrative? This is never alluded to in Chapter 1 through 11, which seemingly reveals the creation myth without credible substantive information about the elite, Anunnaki, great Royal prince Enki (Gods). But to be clear these beings were titular gods, and not ephemeral *pleroma* that is the all pervading Infinite Creator God of the Noumena and the phenomenon of our perception of reality. Clarity is necessary at the juncture to draw a distinction between the prevailing perception and understanding that are unequivocally the fundamental principles of the spiritual science principles and the acknowledgement of the *eponymous*ly Enki personna the brilliant biological scientist and medical doctor on planet Nibiru conflate with the deeds of the biblical creator god. I believe dovetails and echoes nicely with the notion of AUV/UFOs fits the template consistent with the intrepid commander Enki ancient astronauts' Earth Mission voyage [21].

It was Enki, not the Royal great prince Enlil, but Enki who fashioned Adam as the hybrid Homosapien race of primitive workers came here in chariots into being to be the Anunnaki's servile primitive labor. To this point, I interpolate the clarity that the Anunnaki God, Enki, operated under the auspices of Royal Elite; and the Galaxy Federation Council the gods authorized Enki to fashion the first created, crossbred humanoid beings during His Earth Mission. To create a primitive worker who could be trained to perform the back breaking heavy workload and toil inside Zimbabwe, African deep hot gold mining operation.

This is the exculpatory anecdotal fact which is the true nascence of which the Biblical Genesis provides clear evidence of an intentional omission. Adam and Eve is depicted as an allegory. But not so fast, my friends! These homosapeins--Sapeins crossbreed human beings Enki's manipulation of biological genetics. The actual infusion of His Anunnaki and the African hominid female DNA code facilitated the creation of human procreation of the human bloodline children with the Anunnaki genetic imprint (image) of alien God, Enki!

THE MIND, BODY, SPIRIT, AND STORYTELLING

We speculate that the astronaut's long spiritual journey towards exploring down on the earth's surface was an ambitious undertaking to establish a gold mining production operation on earth. And to me, this story is plausible, but it is consciously missing the absolute truth antecedence, meaning what? Simply put, the Old Testament biblical genesis narrative makes no sense, and that is to say that biblical Genesis narrative chapter 1 presumably wittingly deluded the individual self-deception.

Meaning what? It lacks relevant specificity and anecdotal information, which seems deceptive. And conversely, as it stands against a reasonable person's criteria of analysis of ancient astronauts' theory, as far as the truth goes, it is an assertion that is most likely what happened: A History of the Biblical Anunnaki historical account was written about an Anunnaki extraterrestrial alien race from the planet Nibiruan. Genesis narrative is clearly a record about planet Nibirui's pantheon of twelve Elite Anunnaki gods. Prince Enki and his half brother Enlil were members. Two key players of this historical drama. It is about an advanced alien race that was capable of sending their ancient astronauts. Two siblings (titular Gods) from the Anunnaki Royal elite Kingship: Those who from the Heavens came." They struggled for supremacy control over the earth's interior plane. A hypothesis according to the Anunnaki Sumerian ancient cuneiform clay tablet, revealing the knowledge about the "Seven Tablets of the Creation Myth. They were the sons fathered by Nibiru's King and Supreme God of the Anunnaki Anu.

Anu was the Supreme Deity of planet Nibiru with his authority, assigned his son Royal Prince Enki/Ea on the deployment as the Earth Mission voyage Commander 450, thousand years ago. He arrived and landed successfully in the southern region of Sumer, Mesopotamia.

The original vanguard of the Anunnaki Oldens Anunnaki clans, perceived as great titular benevolent Gods. Those from above came from Heaven and descended and heave the say they had landed by the conveyance of advanced spacecraft. They would be considered to be the original custodians of the earth constellation orbit cycle. The protagonist and antagonist siblings are Nibiru Royal-Elite

Prince Enki. The great Nibiruan Royal Prince Enki (Ea) was the earth mission commander of the vanguard of the ancient astronauts. For this reason, we have to assume that any reference of the God of the Old Testament Bible Genesis tale, I would surmise we must have attributed to Enki (Ea).

They successfully landed in Sumer, Mesopotamia where Royal Prince Enki built the city-state on the earth, which He named Eridu. The people came to venerate Enki, and worshiped Him as their Personal God of wisdom and magic—author of the original primitive Anunnaki Sumerian Bible Genesis narrative tale account of God's presence as the custodians of the planet earth.

They had referred to these gods as the "*shining* ones" who came here in chariots from the higher plane of constellation orbit and arrived in the Earth orbital plane; they were astronauts from Planet-X (Nibiru) is indeed very plausible. Which will appeal to the *perspicacious* thinkers and raise salient questions about the Genesis narrative as a real event fits nicely with the discussion of ancient astronauts theory.

It is this template clarity by examining and analyzing the actual evidence that can bring clarity by revealing the specificity and anecdotal details; juxtaposition to the opening scene of biblical Genesis narrative Chapter 1, meaning what? Desperate for information on this is conspicuously concealing some facts that the purveyors of theological rulers know that would unravel the narrative stories, which is the Bible Genesis mystique that hid the extraterrestrial alien beings at the center of a diegetic tale of an ancient event.

It is concerning that there is no mention of this biblical Myth. Why did the Bible authors intentionally make no definitive mention of any specificity and anecdotal details about aliens (UFOs) presence in the book of Genesis Chapter 1. Reveals the shape of these Anunnaki elongated, oval shapes of the metallic appearance of space-traveling astronauts who descended—have preferred not to mention that these Anunnaki had arrived from their home planet where the *Orion crusaders* came here from the empirical world Nibiru. On board a metallic flying (AUV) chariot fifty man professional astronaut flight crew.

The omission is curiously very ing, red herring, fuels their blind faith followers of *truthiness*.

Whereof the motivation it seems was inculcation of the New Testament religion retelling of Kemetic the Egyptian psycho-spiritual science, which is nothing more than that, it confirm the notion that people will choose to worship whatever religious teaching that please them is precisely why people have been inculcated with the religions of blind faith that misleads them. It's largely a speculative exegesis to make people understand that religion is nothing more than a historical truthiness. Followers have misled humankind away from the African-Egyptian Spiritual science teachings of theology. Christianity as a blind faith religion arose and became the Predominant gospel of Christ and was spread through every part of the global had established this falsehood foothold of panpsychism temporal reality has been a transmutation religious consciousness of the total mind/body/spirit complex sense psycho-spiritual awareness (https://plato.stanford.edu/entries/panpsychism/).

While scholars analyze religious rites and rituals, ostensibly prayers follow in the common lockstep without raising skepticism; challenging questions seem very conscious. What seems to be witnessed is that perhaps the establishment acquiesced, upholding the powerful relics of the earth's evolution of transformative periods of the epoch. Meaning the learning and teaching was a misdirection inculcated to the earth's bon homies who failed to digest the psychospiritual science of the mystery wisdom teachings of the Law of One love. Which was superseded by western world new age religion of worshiping Christ as the *apomorphic* Christian cross of God, as the luminous divine savior of the blind faith religious theology.

Human beings are the god of salvation at death. The complexities of ancient mystery, the spiritual science of *Kemetism, the wisdom of the Law of One love*. For me the creation story raises questions as there is strong evidence that points to the Kemetic Tree of Life Ancient Africa Egyptian Metaphysics and Cosmology for Higher Consciousness by Dr. Muata Ashby (bookshop.org). Muata Ashby is an Anunnaki crew of space-traveling ancient astronauts and the arrival of an alien, the first vanguard crew of Anunnaki's mission voyage of Gods. A Gold mining operation coterminous with the Old Testament Bible Chapter 1, we accept that the voice of the creator is the written word of God. Do we not? The advanced extraterrestrial beings from the planet Nibiru. The Holy Bible Genesis Scripture, Chapter 1, verse 1 through 11 is most probably a reference to the Royal great prince *Enki's* (Ea) as God, meaning what? This was a space faring astronaut crew sent on the earth mission voyage that was commanded and Led by the planet Nibiru's great Royal prince Enki was the commander of the Nibiruan Earth Mission voyage.

It was a fifty man astronaut crew. consisting of professional skilled scientists among the Anunnaki titular Gods came here in chariots from planet Nibiru had successfully landed down on the earth surface in ancient Mesopotamia. This event would be that material event horizon that has been what is concealed; this acknowledgment of Annunaki presence in the Old Testament Holy book of the Genesis narrative Chapter 1! The assertion that posits that ancient spacecraft landed down on the earth's surface interior plane is indeed a rather monumental hypothesis; wherein the underlying premise abides in the noumenon, which is essential to truth-telling as it's the to an attempt to demystify the truth behind the ancient astronaut theorists premise. Which seemingly interpolate a perfect fit into the Old Testament Genesis narrative that says that the Olden Times man like Anunnaki extraterrestrial alien God of the Bible story equates to a manifestation of Enki. Which acknowledges that Enki was the Creator God, the Bible manuscript written in Genesis narrative of Chapter 1.

There seems to be conveniently left out that they were ancient astronauts; and although, speculative one can deduce from Genesis Chapter 1, that the so-called Anunnaki were likely: "Those who from the Heavens came" down from about the earth celestial plane successfully landed. And this marked the nascent of the Earth Mission voyage. And according to author Zecharia Sitchin's book, *the Earth Chronicles, the* Anunnaki came down from their own distance home planet, Nibiru was for the purpose to extra the precious gold material resources that were desperately needed to save their slowly dying planet was losing its dwindling apmasphere.

THE MIND, BODY, SPIRIT, AND STORYTELLING

Those who from Heaven came to mine and extract the gold mineral resources as the underlying purpose. Enki was successful, and accomplished this mission voyage--without a hitch! Which was accomplished in the Southern Eastern region of the great Zimbabwe, African. Gold deposits were mined then transformed into monatomic gold particles and put on the Anunnaki UFO spaceships, to be sent back to the home planet, Nibiru! But is it plausible? And is this likely true? Well my friends it is necessary for some introspection and rumination. Because do I dare say that: once upon a long time ago, planet Nibiru launched a fifty-man ancient astronaut crew of extraterrestrial aliens on an Anunnaki spacecraft that safely came down to land on the interior surface of the planet earth thousands of years ago.

But How is it that anyone can think it impossible to believe in the Ancient Astronauts Theory? When our own modern cultures NASA's mission uses advanced aerial space rocket ships to achieve the aspirations to travel to the planet Mars; and that we have already reached and heave the say they had landed on the moon surface and returned to earth. Modern biological scientists researchers have used technology innovations in bio-genetics and DNA biological researchers' knowledge to discover new ways to live better in this surface illusion of earth's illusory temporal reality.

How *Orwellian* and bizarre that Nibiru's Royal-Elite Prince Enki (Ea) had successfully manipulated and fused His own DNA code He had mixed with an indigenous African female's embryogenesis development and morphogenesis biological DNA genetic code. Those fertilized embryos He inserted into six Anunnaki female birth mother's wombs carried them to full natal term.

Efficaciously, his biological procedure successfully fashioned the crossbred Adam and Eve from the womb of an Anunnaki alien female. Enki's crossbred creation was by the biblical insemination of the indigenous African female humanoid species DNA code brought in the new crossbred primitive worker homo-sapiens bloodline descendants.

A delineation of Hebrew ancestors of generations through *Adam* and *Eve's* of the Anunnaki extraterrestrials alien bloodline. We know that the means that facilitated the Enki's hybrid primitive workers was by *envitrial-insemination*, placing fertilized embryos of Enki's Y-chromosome with the African female Mitochondrial DNA essence. Enki placed inside of the six Anunnaki female birth mother's womb carried to full term; and this was described in the *Akkadian "Seven Tablet of the Creation; it is given credence in the* story telling described as an event written in the Akkadian cuneiform language, which was revealed on seven clay tablets found in ancient Babylonian's "*Enuma Elish"* account (https://www.britannica.com/topic/Enuma-Elish).

Adam (Adapa) He fashioned human beings. The biblical Genesis narrative has misled us to view it as a Mythological creator god figure. Let's face it! The material evidence has revealed that the creator was a very intelligent, brilliant scientist, and medical doctor came from planet Nibiru. The gods with a higher mental complex came from the cosmos fashioned humankind to possess the ability to think. A fashioned genetic human species created to be primitive workers as an obedient labor force of the Anunnaki's African gold mining production operation located in the Southern region of Great Africa's State of Zimbabwe.

The heavy work of gold mining was assigned to Enki's obsequious primitive workers and the server of the Anunnaki alien Gods. The primitive human creation was to use humans as the Anunnaki's alien Gods obsequious servile primitive workers as a free labor force of the Anunnaki on Earth.

Just as it was back then, even today this is the paradoxical purpose to serve God by the love and a life of teachings/learning to be of spiritual services to humanity in humble reverence and illuminated by complexities of ancient mystery spiritual science.

By and blind faith, obedience devoid of intelligence uses your free will consciousness to do good or evil. The actions of the human beings cosmic law of free will is always a factor of every cosmic involution from the nascence; and ergo, though s periods of *eons,* viz.: steady streaming onto the pages of our history. That constant reminder of this delinNations, there is evidence of mendacious visceral acts of evil devoid of sacred principles of meditative inner spirit consciousness of ultimate manipulator, the seekers whose am is to maintain the institutions of hidden mysteries hands of powerful cathode derived of the original Anunnaki ancient astronauts. The latter facilitated civilization as earth's custodians. Their system that exercises social control over the avatar mind/body/spirit complex of the earth's distortions that pings amid the planet's harmonic waves vibrates the earth density perpetuates indifference and perpetuates ignorance.

The misguided material illusory material consciousness, temporal reality, in as much as one's chosen pathway leads to the deception for the selfish greed and avariciousness, slutted after material wealth! Whilst we have wittingly behaved in the humble manner of grazing sheep, we are the novice pawns who play in this grand system that is closely akin to a Monopoly game board; a mercantile markets free wheeling individual humankind's financial moves in the economic capitalism schemes and government spending money that funds all institutions, convergence of religion, money, ruler's ultimate execution of control power.

The underlying system of global control over the human's in fear of losing the path to beings, the ultimate providence and salvation of the soul. Wittingly we pray for forgiveness for our spirit that is the cause of human beings' behavior as animated actions! Yes, the creation of the existence of homo sapiens sapiens were primitive workers created by Royal Prince Enki (Ea), who "the Anunnaki Sumerian text revealed. After all, Enki was the god with the knowledge as a skilled biological scientist and medical doctor who used his own genetic DNA codes [essence/likeness] successfully fashioned *Homosapein-Sapiens Adam* and *Eve* (Women) on earth, according to the Bible genesis narrative creation tale.

Using knowledge successfully manipulated DNA codes and genetically fashioned Aunnaki and an African indigenous hominid female DNA, Enki (Ea) had biologically fused His Anunnaki likeness into a new crossbred human species—on planet earth! The animated spirit essence of the titular God's "breath of life"!

We can now reference: "The Enūma Eliš is the Babylonian creation Myth. It was recovered by English archeologist Austen Henry Layard in 1849 in the ruined Library of Ashurbanipal at

Nineveh. As Cuneiform Clay Tablet says in the Holy Bible Genesis scripture, Chapter 1 through 11. Fact matters whenever it can turn back the light of truth that disentangles the Bible's truthiness, by concealing the truth about the extraterrestrial aliens race as ancient astronauts from Heaven; who were, ostensibly, the Anunnaki alien beings were not god. But the Mesopotamian called them the shining ones. (https://www.watkinspublishing.com/shop/the-shining-ones-by-philip-gardiner-and-gary-osborn/).

This is not simply a case of selective omission? No! Not at all, but it's a body of information that was arbitrarily deemed unimportant, as a matter of expediency and simplicity; as an assumption it lacks elements of specificity and anecdotal details about this narrative tale. Attributions important to knowing about the anamorphic alien deities, e.g. Anu, Enlil, and Enki.

My erudition about understanding the Old Testament Genesis narrative raises the salient question, for religion narrative doesn't teach us that these Gods of the Hebrew and Greek mistranslations of the Holy Bible are about Anu, Enki, and Enlil—the titular gods who descended from Heaven.

Whereof the genesis narrative failed to say that it was Enlil who was annoyed with (Enki's created) noisy human beings before the great Noah's flood. The God Anu and his son Enlil expressed displeasure with the human beings working together to construct a *Tower of Babylon* [http://www.ravshaul.com/christianitythegreatdeception/TheSpiritbehindChristia!

Why was it forbidden? Why would the Anunnaki titular Gods regarding these humans who had acquired intelligence breaking the law? The Genesis narrative mentions God said, let's go down and confuse the people's languages; *ipso facto*, a communication system called the Tower of Babylon. God had concerns that the crossbred Adams/Mankind (human races). According to the unearthed *Enuma Elish, Seven Tablets of the Creation*, there is literally no-doubt that Enki was the Earth's initial custodian, and the creator God! any past, present, and future actions regarding the historical Chronicles of humankind's endeavors that humankind could achieve, using knowledge and free will. Enlil understood that if man could use knowledge to construct such a large complex feared that they were capable of being Gods.

They possessed the elixir of the Gods exclusive possession of longevity! Yeah, we can speculate that Enlil was likely the titular God who descended and confused the people's language. Why would the Anunnaki god Enlil want to prevent the building of a *Tower of Babel*? Why were the people inspired to construct a towel that reaches high into Heaven; given in Genesis 11:1–9, it appears to be an explanation for the existence of diverse human languages (https://www.britannica.com/topic/Tower).

To this He said: "Come, let Us go down and confuse their language so that they will not understand each other's speech by fragmentation of human languages ded in Genesis 11:1–9. This notwithstanding considering allowing the Royal great prince Enki's homo sapien sapiens crossbred primitive earth man to be eviscerated by the Noah flood. Whereas in this book postulates the premise that Enki, of planet Nibiru was an extraterrestrial ancient astronaut titular God; but there is no single reference, meaning what? This is most problematic for those folks who adhere to the ancient astronaut theory.

With a fresh and open objective mind, I was unknowing of any of my own soul's past natal natures or prior cycles of reincarnation existences. The present for me to grow and learn to live and enjoy the new beginning. Your natural life exists on a path that witnessed your ancestors' nascence in the southern plane of ancient Mesopotamia. And if the Anunnaki ancient astronauts were the Infinite Creator. Dare ask the question about how they embarked from Heaven; meaning by how exactly did these great space faring astronaut's make the journey down to planet Earth. Certainly by some sophisticated advanced UFO spacecraft.

Or is it inherently, perhaps merely folly for the folks who can not phathum, let alone imagine a hovering spacecraft was commanded by the Anunnaki astronaut ancient Enki came down and landed on earth surface in ancient Sumer, Mesopotamia over the earth and slowly descending down and safely landing as the indigenous Mesopotamia tribesmen were in awe as they stood poised on the cusp of the extraterrestrial alien Anunnaki Ancient Astronauts spacecraft descended on the earth surface, they watched with a *prescient shiver* that went through everyone standing there. The Bible tale of the book of Genesis they couldn't comprehend. With clear eyes, they are the Gods who, I must say: Anunnaki extraterrestrial alien Gods certainly did not fly down from Planet Nibiru/Heaven on wings like feathered birds. But by pilots onboard AUV/UFO chariots!

The Royal great prince Enki was the commander of the first piloted spacecraft from the planet Nibiru and the leader of an ancient astronaut fifty-man crew. We have no idea of who exactly the Anunnaki was because the Bible is silent on this controversial matter regarding the god we trust?

Whereas the Bible simply leads to speculations and questions about: "Those who from the Heavens came" down were on the Earth Mission voyage to establish their gold mining production operation! My friends, will your curiosity override the incredulity and embured your sense of *perspicaciousness?*

We have neither been taught any of this in the Sunday morning churches nor did we hear it in school.

So as you listen to the premise that the Anunnaki was a group of ancient space faring astronauts who traveled from their planet Nibiruan (Planet-X). And from the Persian Gulf region and subsequently his gold mining operations in Zimbabwe, southeast Africa. I posit this insight into the spiritual external empirical world: I assert that this was an extraterrestrial astronaut who arrived to extract gold. Enki's father gave Anu the Hamite people's Akebu (ancient Africans') lands to control. His father, Supreme God of Nibiru (Heaven) and of Earth (Mother Goddess) Ki, meaning exactly what? That ancient astronauts colonized Earth. Perhaps this is more likely the real Bible Genesis story about the Anunnaki fifty men maiden flight crew who sat out on their earth mission gold mining exploration astronaut voyage from the planet Nibiru.

And now, my friends might clear your mind of those extraneous mental discordant noise distortions that pervade upon and try to imagine that these people of Mesopotamia were frightened.

It was an exceptional moment watching the tribe's families looking upward and watching the alien gods come down from the sky clouds! Awed, they huddled together as they observed the Anunnaki astronaut's pilot, bell-shaped, shiny-looking spaceship hovering above before slowly descending towards earth in a spectacular flying vessel. As I looked down from the spacecraft, the frightened indigenous primitive inhabitants of earth were looking up and pointing. I was there when the Anunnaki ancient astronauts had tarried and pondered above physical, temporal reality in awe. When I saw colorful atmospheric swirling amorphous clouds diffused all around, and changing shapes as I was moving in subtle motion across the dark constellation canvas of stars asynchronously glinting like the facets of a perfect Diamond. I slowly began to descend into the bemused indigenous humans watched in awe.

Now imagine the alien Earth Mission commander seated onboard a metallic ancient astronaut space flight. The flight mission commander Enki was giving orders as He performed his perfunctory pre-flight duties in preparation to land down on the target landing zone. He would have meticulously made an account of the anecdotal details he entered into a mission Flight Log Book. And yes, my friends, this is the very beginning of anecdotal details that have conspicuously been excised from this Bible Genesis narrative of Chapter I. With which ancient astronaut theory certainly interpolates the logic and of what is the truest thing that is a perfect fit.

If we are the truth seekers then clarity of version is that the Bible Genesis is not the whole truth! And, my friends, in all probability archeology records discovery revealed a plethora of imperial and anecdotal evidence as irrefutable ancient records have given us thinking folks--20;20 hindsight, meaning what? That we accept the premise that the ancient astronaut's theory posits. Recently 30 thousand cuneiform clay tablets were excavated from the ancient site and ruins have produced a large cache of discovery of historical *Sumerian, Akkadian, and the Babylonian* ancient clay Tablets. Which is of the titular Gods.

Their deeds were always recorded in every detail regarding the Anunnaki alien gods Enki and Enlil time on earth as I have exposed accounts of the ancient astronauts' critical earth mission voyage. Perhaps it's a true story that seemingly dovetails nicely with my interpolated premise that is merely speculative. Anunnaki in ancient Mesopotamia were space faring ancient astronauts (titular Gods) from planet Nibiru.

Of course, according to the discovery of strong ancient evidence about the astronaut theorists: The first period of Anunnaki activity began before the great Noah's eponymous deluge event that was recorded in the Bible genesis narrative tale Myth.

Biblical history did not acknowledge the alien Anunnaki as Olden Times extraterrestrial aliens Gods from Heaven. Are we not talking about the identity "Those who from the Heaven came" were led by the great Royal princes Enki.

They are the two Royal Princes, sons of planet Nibiru's Supreme High God King Anu, Lord who was not the god mentioned in the book Genesis Chapter One. As an assertion I contend that there is sufficient evidence, which clearly support a hypothesis that some advanced extraterrestrial aliens deployed technology in the distant past, and accordingly with that knowledge, and human astronauts advancement in into space exploration, and understandingly, I am all in with my supporting the ancient astronauts theorists speculation hypothesis. Saying that the Anunnaki were the titular Gods from planet Nibiru (Heaven). Biblical writings have been excluded the most essential beginning to the greatest storyline anecdotal details; and that they have been willing to perpetuate the misdirection without ever mentioning the story about Nibiru's 200 intrepid Anunnaki ancient astronauts space-travelers that came down to the Earth surface by means of a sophisticated UFO spacecraft, 445,000 BC.

Did these Anunnaki the aliens astronauts; and the beings who were those who built the first city-state Earth settlement civilization in Sumer, Mesopotamia in six days after their arrival on earth to complete the gold mining earth mission voyage under the flight mission Commander, Nibiru's the Royal great prince Enki the God of wisdom of the Law of One (love) and magic and a member of the Confederation of interstellar Council of the Royal-Elite had sanctioned the vanguard earth Earth Mission voyage. Enki was the appointed mission Commander that led the fifty man crew of intrepid ancient astronauts crew that came from the Heaven to land a spaceship that came down from Nibiru and landed in Mesopotamia. The god who built the first city-state and named it Eridu in ancient Sumer which was *Edin* or *Earth Station 1*.

My friends How hard is it now for you to believe why Sumerians worshiped the Royal great prince Enki as the Sumerians God [19]. It was Enki who proclaimed that He built the first living settlement on the earth after the Anunnaki titular God successfully landed in ancient Mesopotamia where He also built a spacecraft landing port in the city-state of *Eridu [https://www.external empirical worldhistory.org/eridu/]*.

Thus, it is understandable Why He named the first earth city state settlements in Sumerians lands as *Eridu* in southern Mesopotamia. Because its name meant *"the home in the far away"!* The names Enki and Enlil are synonymous with ancient peoples of Mesopotamia who were the Sumerians race who recognized the beneficence of the teachings of the Anunnaki, and as earth indigenous peoples, they ded themselves the Black Heads. While they called the Anunnaki (titular Gods) "the "Shining Ones"! Okay according to the researcher, Mr. Runoko Rashidi, London: Karnak House, 1992, pg. 69). First off it is relevant to know:

> "*The founders of the first Mesopotamian civilization were Black Sumerians. Mesopotamia was the Biblical land of Shinar (Sumer). The Sumerians left no doubt it has a germ of truth about how they viewed themselves racially. The Sumerians called themselves sag-gig-ga, the Black-headed people. Sumer was the crossroads of the lands of Asia, Africa, and Europe. While Sumer was not a homogenous society, the Blackheads of Sumer were politically and social dominant. (Introduction to the Study of African Classical Civilizations.*"

What we know is that John Baldwin wrote this:

"*The early colonists of Babylonia were of the same race as the inhabitants of the Upper Nile.*" (PreHistoric Nations by John D. Baldwin, New

York: Harper & Brothers, 1869, pg. 192); and the key is knowledge of the Sumerian people's identity, the scholarly scientist's research: *"'my intelligent the statuaries and steles of Babylonia, the Sumerians were "of dark complexion (chocolate color), short stature, but of sturdy frame, an oval face, stout nose, straight hair, full head; they typically resembled the Dravidians, not only in the cranium but almost in all the details." (A Study in Hindu Social Polity by Chandra Chakraborty, Delhi: Mittal Publications, 1987, pg. 33);* and, just so that I leave no doubt that is clearly aligned with what the Bible Genesis is about the dark peoples of the ancient world before the rise of Western Europeans Christianity plagiarized.

It's unequivocally the overwhelming use of the Egyptian African-Kemetism teachings of *Isis, Osiris* and their son *Horus* transformation of the Myth, into the Hebrew and Greek Septuagint holy Old Testament Bible Genesis narrative tale. To examine your understanding of the Anunnaki God Enki contact with the indigenous people. Which is alluded to in the prosonna which is associated with Enki arrival and landing of his Spacecraft down in the ancient Sumerian landscape.

He was a corporeal alien being; and not some Mythical god with wings. He arrived as the commander of a UFO. This earliest ancient contact was in Western Asia. It was in the Sumer, Mesopotamia, where he built Eridu, as later the cultures of Babylonia and Chaldea became the names and places mentioned in Genesis Chapter One. The Sumerian civilization, which ruled the southern portion of the fertile Tigris/Euphrates River Valley, sprang up around 3000 B.C. and lasted until about 1750 B.C.

This is genesis narrative story began

It was Enki, the Anunnaki god of Heaven (planet Nibiru), the Genesis narrative, who created civilization from the murky earth frontier post. His ancient astronaut crew spacecraft had safely landed. Now then, my friends, do you feel like the narrative creation story of Genesis is a truthiness, meaning what? Well then, might I postulate an unconventional paradigm view that presupposes that biblical gods and UFOs' sightings own the connection that has since been excised from the opening scene of the Old Testament Genesis narrative? The modern biblical religious teachings have come face to face in this collision with the ancient astronaut theory.

The Holy Bible is intrinsically a truthiness with which some omissions and facts dovetail nicely with plausible archeological and anthropology discovery researchers' findings. And previously, my friends might I elucidate my erudition about this fundamental presupposition: saying that perspicacious neophytes are the seekers of the knowledge, wisdom, insight of the Law of One love sacred science of the *Neberdjer*. God as is so mentioned in the pages of the Holy Bible book. An *Old Testament Bible* is most probable, is notably compelling about the *Anunnaki* ancient astronauts. The extraterrestrial traveled to the earth from their Planet-X; the aliens came here in chariots from the higher plane.

Without a scintilla of doubt, there is absolutely not a scintilla of reservations with respect to what my assumptions being positedhere.

You see, my friends, I am a simple and humble spirit of all Intelligent One Creator God of universal Unity. Let me make this salient point: on the merits of spirituality, I can certainly say that I am a believer in God; and a seeker whose aim and purpose is to propagate Ra's Law of One.

To assert this is the missing piece of information that is quite plausible to say unequivocally that the Old Testament Bible Genesis narrative is derived from the Anunnaki alien beings descent from the sky as ancient astronauts, and not the eternal nature of the one true divine spirit of the most high creator of the Noumena of the universe existence. The manifestation of things of the phenomenal world of the cosmic spiritual mind of the Logos, or the ineffable monad that is the all-pervading embodiment of the *Neberdjer*. This is to assert that these alien beings possessed advanced, sophisticated knowledge of technology and science to send their ancient astronauts to land on planet earth; viz., they were manlike, titular god figures. And in their form, the spirit essence of the one All cosmic universe with which they possessed an external manifestation.

Knowledge of earth illusion of true illusory temporal reality, they told indigenous *Sumerians* and *Mesoamericans* primitive tribal earth man that their home planet lies among the cosmos vast constellation. Some might think this specter of God as the ancient astronaut's theorists insist that the Sumerian Gods of the Old Testament Bible, Chapter One, Genesis narrative.

Might we interpolate we have UFOs in common today; and do we not have an unhealthy fascination with this alien phenomenon? This is telling, is it not because a trustworthy amount of information is being revealed about these anonymously visible sightings, I think is not of religious teachings. Just perhaps this incredible nexus is a red herring which has converged into the human consciousness. Curious sightings aligned with ruminations about this are becoming more of an than being rebuffed as folly.

It all comes into focus, using logic and reason of spiritual wisdom of the Law of One love and reason of free will consciousness; the luminosity of ancient astronaut theorists enlightenment. My friends, if you search deeper you will eventually discover where the real truth lies. Truth about the historical record of the empirical worldwide story we have accepted as notable events. Facts seen may not always be pure, but often distortion applied with motives and willful intent to mislead the public.

Whereas, things are carefully hidden away, often curiously turning back into the pages of history, in our modern time that which was hidden away is shown as the big lies when the spirit of God reveals the falsity in the brightest light truth. What is taught as the fact doesn't necessarily fit into spurious logic and reason? We must concern ourselves with spurious evil ways of deception and lies; the seeking truth is to uncover the hidden mysteries truth; it should matter in every adult's life; viz., Roman Christianity religion perpetuates a truthiness [http://www.ravshaul.com/christianitythegreatdeception/TheSpiritbehindChristianity.htm]?

The genesis personage of God is apomorphic, with manlike characteristics. We are left to speculate about this and interpolate our minds' perception that alien beings had this incredible advanced scientific knowledge. Their presence had a tremendous influence over the actions of the indigenous earthman's human affairs.

Take a moment to apply logic and reason to learn whether you have been *innestitized* with their sophists' teaching of truthiness. Why is it that they wittingly excised the Anunnaki aliens from the extraterrestrial ancient astronauts contributions, which should be conflated with the original Old Testament, Anunnaki Sumerians Holy Bible which correspond with assertion that the Enki as the Earth custodian God from the planets of Nibiru. The ancient astronauts; meaning that He was God who had led a fiftyman crew that came down from Heaven and built the city of *Eridu* in ancient Mesopotamia.

Christian denominations are eager for it to be exposed to modern-day transparent scrutiny. We elucidate this erudition as a speculative assertion about the Old Testament Bible, saying that the Genesis narrative tale is not a mythos. It's most likely to embellish historical Anunnaki, extraterrestrials' events involving alien gods who were ancient astronauts. Incredibly, the eccentricity of ancient astronaut theorists' interpretation of the biblical narrative. Antithetical longer ignoring the will to adherence to tropes.

To have the will to escape from the churches well establishments of the conical religious institutions by the ecclesiastical purveyor, falsehood theological, doctrinal religion creed. It's the embrace of the new age of psychological religious doctrine that teaches the church gospel of blind faith Christianity. The fundamental complex presupposition is that most problematic for the establishment is to deny any connection exists, meaning what? We suspect that a parallel existed as in the olden times UFO ancient astronauts connecting to the present sightings of UFOs, is the most likely ancient alien; meaning that they were the Anunnaki alien beings who were actually the creator god Enki.

He commanded the first fifty astronauts crew who were the first custodians Gods to make contact with the primitive indigenous earthmen, who worshiped the Anunnaki who successfully built the first city-state around 50 thousand years ago. These people were the frightened witnesses to the Anunnaki ancient astronauts' arrival when they landed in the interior of the earth plane of southern

Mesopotamia that were not Infinite Creator Gods of the Intelligent Infinity. Human beings worshiped them as their servants, as much as today's faithful modern humans believe the Holy Bible Genesis narrative. You have only to decide whether or not you believe that God who expelled Enki's, *Adam* and *Eve*, from his *Garden in Eden*, was *apomorphic*. With the erudition of archeology discovery of ancient cuneiform clay tablets containing the Bible Genesis narrative of the creation Myth.

My friends, might those who have a curious mind raised a salient question about the episode that recounts the *garden in the land of the Eden* scene: To pause now and reflect on Why had God, Prince Enlil, the supreme Anunnaki (*Lord of the Earth Command*) objurgated his half-brother the Royal-Elite Prince Enki. Who *secretly* fused His biological essence successfully fashioned an remarkably intelligent prototype genetically manipulated *crossbreed* human race of Adam(s) and Eve(s).

What we do not know about this is that the Gods Enlil had forbidden Enki's Adam and Eve to know if their body was naked, meaning what? To deny humankind to be awakened to their spiritual conscious awareness!

Enlil (God) was furious and called Enki the Serpent

Enki undermined the decree that prohibited the fruits of knowledge and longevity, exclusive to only the Nibiru, Anunnaki Gods secret elixir. He had ordered that Humanoid crossbred earthlings be forbidden from any possession thereof; the restrictions of knowledge and longevity; viz., ensuring that Humans would remain the primitive servile obedient labor; and, they were worshipers of a titular Nibiru's Anunnaki Gods of Heaven and over the people of the planet Earth--in perpetuity. Enlil's fear was that humans having acquired knowledge would elevate to one day be in common with other Gods. The fear of the possibility of humans having a very long life was why Enlil banished Adam and Eve; they could be challengers to the Gods.

His brother Enki was the (*God of wisdom* by knowledge and application *of the Law of One love; is the creator god of the Serpents*

Priestly Brotherhood) who disobeyed His brother. And it was Enki (Lucifer) who beguiled His crossbred Homosapeins—Eve with the concept of free will consciousness awareness; a discovery of and focus on Her self-awareness; the knowing of herself being—naked!

Yeah it was the knowing of sexual pleasure, (knowing of sexual intercourse) Adam became aware of nakedness! Prince Enlil, Lord of the Earth Command law, forbids Enki's crossbreed Homosapien to have the Anunnaki knowledge and longevity. Now you no longer have to wonder why—because my friends, I am betting that you too know why! Right? Because I am compelled to convey this exegesis as a substantive discourse about blind faith religious teachings which is most likely going to put some folks off. But it's not okay to carry on spreading falsehood if the Bible Genesis narrative tale is untruthful.

Let's face it! Is the Old Testament Bible Genesis narrative tale, ostensibly missing critical elements?! It seems so incredibly insidious and rather spurious. This is why the Anunnaki extraterrestrial alien astronauts fit the more contemporary Scholars' theoretical erudition of human intelligence. To apply logic and reason for your erudition of knowledge of archeology and anthropology research discovery and findings. I aim to establish a paradigm shift, with which to spur deeper understanding with clarity. Truth says that this spellbinding tale is more than a mythological tale. Yeah, let's delicately set the story for us to take a clear view and digest this material information that an extraterrestrial alien Gods Enki (fashioned) humankind while living upon the Earth. Babylon creation is about the ancient biblical *Enuma Elish*, Anunnaki gods from Nibiru (planets-X).

These Sumerians worshiped Prince Enki as their God of the Nibiruan Anunnaki Royal DNA bloodline. For, my friends, let's face it the titular god Enki successfully fashioned His likeness upon the earth surface by fusion of His own biological (image/likeness) with the DNA of an indigenous Humanoid, African female's species genetic codes; viz., and Enki then placed the manipulated DNA engineered fertilized embryos into six sterile clay *Petri dishes*.

He placed them inside of six Anunnaki female birth mothers' wombs, facilitated the Enki process, which he and Nyngazida had successfully fashioned Adam/Eve Enki while on Earth in the

Eastern region of Great Zimbabwe, African gold mines! That "... the vast majority of humankind--85 to 90 percent--is Rh positive, which means a person's red blood cells contain an antigen directly connected to the Rhesus monkey. This blood antigen is known and has been called the Rh factor." Is this the smoking gun that unravels what is quite an intriguing perspective that is a strong argument for confirming the Anunnaki aliens Royal elites bloodline that traces back to the book of Genesis and of course, the ancient astronaut and the ancient humanity out of Africa original Diaspora. I highly recommend you to read author Nick Redfern's book, *The Bloodline of the Gods: Unravel the Human Blood Type to Reveal the Aliens Among Us!* An archetypal genetic manipulation of the crossbred prototype Adam who was raised and trained to the Anunnaki's garden in the land of Eden, the naked African-Egyptian Hamites.

Yeah, it's a very fascinating story about those who were assigned to work in the titular God, the Royal great prince Enlil's Temple compound of his beautiful glittering cultivated garden. From which Adam and Eve were two of Enki's, human hybrids Adam and Eve, the Anunnaki Prince *Enlil*, was the Lord of laws issued by him as the Anunnaki's Earth Mission Command. Enlil was furious that his brother Enki had given humans knowledge. Enlil and the other members of the Anunnaki ruling Council considered Enki's actions with which he had given his hybrid homo sapiens sapiens the "knowledge" of consciousness awareness—knowing of their nakedness! Thus, the consequences of Enki's transgressions was considered a blatant violation of the law that foreboded any of the Adam's from the Anunnaki gods exclusive possession of their longevity and knowledge. What has followed from Enlil and Enki scene as it relates to the Bible story of the *Garden in the Eden* is the eponymous genealogy of Anunnaki hybrid Hebrew's roots that is a conspicuous connection to the Bible Genesis narrative; the royal bloodline, which has delineating ties to the extraterrestrial alien which, ostensibly has a history that is sourced from and extends to a primeval African FemalesDNA! indigenous had been inseminated by Prince Enki for thousands of his future generations, including the Biblical Noah.

This is the Holy Bible story book of the Genesis narrative. Then elite Anunnaki alienated the great royal prince Enki. In full disclosure mode, might I alluded to the incredulity, by daring to say that Enki was the brilliant biological scientist; and it was His team that successfully genetically engineered the indigenous African hominid female mitochondrial DNA code, mixed with Enki Y-Chromosome DNA codes facilitated the Gods eponymous creation of the first Homosapiens, Adam/Adapa (*man*), and Eve woman. And as this story unfolded they were punished for disobeying Enki's brother, Enki's warning.

Enlil was the supreme commander and Lord of the Earth Command, meaning that His word was final on all matters pertaining to the Anunnaki.

Not the spirit of the Infinite Creator of the universe. Enki is acknowledge the brilliant scientist who fashioned his image likeness on Adam while serving as the Anunnaki's chief medical scientist and doctor which is to say that Royal Prince Enki fashioned humankind embodiment via DNA manifestation. This was auxiliary, and was likely considered as mission creep; and so out of need such deeds had to be done by Him to accomplish the initial specific purpose of the mission: which justified the creation of the *obsequious* obedient primitive workers. The obedient servants of the Anunnaki who were living on the earth. And it was the [Infinite Creator] God Enki, the brother of the Royal great prince Enlil. Enlil was the Anunnaki god who had confronted Adam/Eve during that eponymous Garden in the Eden episode that transpired long before Noah's Flood. Refer to: (https://www.quora.com/Is-the-Garden-of-Eden-in-the-Bible-actually-located-around-the-modern-day-Iraq). The Anunnaki biological research scientist and the chief medical doctor, the Royal great prince Enki, had secretly modified and manipulated her Anunnaki genetic DNA physica code imprinted [the Anunnaki's genetic blueprint of the Anunnaki royal bloodline is shared with the alien Creator God Enki / Ea], or shall I say: "God's likeness," What does this mean? Enki is the biological Heaven father and the precursor of the Homo sapiens sapiens. Scholars have known that evidence supporting the out of Africa theory is unmistakable, because there is sufficient information about the eponymous Anunnaki creator god Enki, the ancient alien who was the commander of a fifty man astronaut crew, the book of Genesis creation narrative story says God was "Those who came down from Heaven (the cosmos). Then the Bible story about the creator on earth is unmistakably a crew of extraterrestrial aliens gods who established civilization settlements after Anunnaki ancient astronauts landed in Sumer, Mesopotamia (modern day country of Iraq) in the Persian Gulf region.

What is also written in the page's of the Bible is this, seemingly incredible creation of the human race, meaning that ancient primordial humanity began in Africa! Elements of this story are aligned with the specificity and anecdotal detail evidence, which is obfuscation by this wittingly, attempts to conceal and mislead humanity. With what we know about the creator God / Enki has been curiously relevant and has been inextricably linked to his manipulation of an indigenous African female homenoi's DNA code, He mixed it with His own Anunnaki alien DNA Y-chromosome genome. He fashioned a new human homo-sapien sapiens; a crossbred ancestor who are the biological Hamite children of God [Enki]. Fact is that ninety percent of the global population are intelligent, but are asleep and totally oblivious of UFO information.

You should know the truth about the Anunnaki extraterrestrial alien godEnki/Ea (God) creation primitive labor force! Enslaved people were assigned to perform the heavy and backbreaking work inside of the deep hot African gold mining production operation located in great Zimbabwe, Southern Africa. So if you are still asleep, wake up now because the truth is about the exposure to the actual story; this posits insight into the external spiritual empirical world, and your conscious awareness is human beings' enlightenment. Let's agree that the annals of the beginning of relationships between the ancient astronauts' initial Earth Mission landing were probably a space-traveling alien race who were the *Anunnaki*--who were titular Anunnaki gods of the fringe outside of the sun orbital solar system.

Yet, given this fact, skeptics are adamantly reluctant to admit that there is strong anecdotal evidence of these yearly reports of the ancient and modern-day visitation. Perhaps the UFOs' presence is manipulating affairs through the means of human proxies. Words of the Bible Genesis and the New Testament are the means of the religionist catalyst for the inculcating the spurious gospel teachings of the Christianity as a blind faithful theological truthiness. So is religious teaching a spurious truthiness.

Did you not know: that African-Egyptian ancestors carried and wore an *Ankh;* it symbolized Life or the Eternal Life (key of life). The Coptic Christians accepted it as their holy cross. The Ankh is a symbol that broadly represents the merging of masculine and feminine energies; it was said the spirits possess the telematic power to heal our mind by penetrating the consciousness of the individual mind/body/spirit complex.

The learning and teaching of *Neberdjer;* the principle of the Law of One. Then the rise of Roman Catholics' religious creed that took hold with the consolidation of paganism and Christianity became the theology. That image is symbolic of the Egyptian Ankh; and the symbol of life, underwent a transformation into the crucifixion cross that became the Romans Christian Holy Cross which is now the symbol of Jesus death! It had long been represented as the spirituality science which was overlaid by the Rome Catholic Church of a Western European imperialism.

Which commenced to the actions of whitewash of the Blacks heritage spiritualism African-Egyptian Kemetism religious teachings. Under the Romanized embrace of Christianity the African-Egyptian design of the original *Ankh symbol,* Romans reconfigured it as the Holy cross symbol to represent death and salvation through Jesus Christ.

Simply put: The Christian worshiping of the blind faith religion doctrine according to a new New Testament religion Trinitarian dogmatic creeds of through Jesus Christ's resurrection and the promise of salvation. Blind faith religion became the pathway to Heaven. The transliteration and melding of paganism and the occult were merged into the powerful Christian religious teachings of Christianity as ritual theology. With its crucifixion symbol of the cross, the figure supplanted the Egyptian spiritual theology symbol of the Ankh. With this emerging new world order.

What followed would come to be known as the constituted twisted world reordered by the western European imperial rulers dictatorial authority, having the powerful synergy with the control through unity between government institutions that created Christianity as a religious appeasement.

Often aggressive kings invaded their neighbors' terrestrial lands and enslaved them with willful intent to consolidate their power and influence and sought to accumulate vast wealth as an empire builder. This was a cause that destabilized and controlled the world by military armed aggressive actions that totally dismantled, destroyed, and systematically sought to upend the predominant African old world hegemony. The rise of the new world order paradigm signaled the demise of glorious black African dynasties consciousness that was derived from the olden times rulers names that are mentioned in the Holy Old Testament Bible description of the ancient Mesopotamia landscape of the civilization established by Enki was the god who built the first original city state of Eridu in Sumerian; This was indigenous homelands of black African *Hamites* tribes. Let's acknowledge that the Bible Genesis alludes to the racial identity of the black genotype, which the Bible is replete with references to the black hamites and Semitic cultures is quite indicative of what is evident in the Old Testament book of Genesis. Africa is the home land of the ancient Egyptian-Kemet peoples. Bible history is remarkable. It's this historical story that effervescence is ostensibly, inextricably rich with elements of an African hegemony. I presupposed that this advanced civilization came to flourish under the defendants of the Anunnaki alien Enki; after all He was the immortal god of sacred knowledge and esoteric wisdom and magic. Which was transmuted through the initiation of the Serpent Priestly Temple rites and rituals, as the learning and secret teachings of the mysteries principles of the sacred psycho-spiritual science of the hidden, knowledge, wisdom, and insight that is associated with the ancient-Egyptian, African and Indus *Khamit-Kushites* culture. The great peoples' influence inspired the social, cultural, and social complex throughout the external landscape and defended the mighty armies of aggressive world empires' and eventually subjugated African spiritual science consciousness. This theological psycho-spiritual discipline; which mirrored the realm of (Heaven) was free from unconscious bias of the closed-minded views of racist white supremacy views [23]. We know that the Egyptian Ankh was the key of life symbol, used to represent the word for "life" and, by extension, as a symbol of life itself. Christianity dogma, rites, and rituals of the priests aligned worship and ignoble educated people who fear God's allowed the temple priesthood class and the temporal Royal-Elite King elite to rhetorical sermons to take advantage of the ordinary people who were compelled to pray to avoid the vengeance and loss of offer the path to beings the ultimate providence and salvations from God after death.

The actual means of the mysterious spiritual teaching of human predilection towards daily medication and wisdom of the Law of One love sacred principles were denigrated. The fact is this: Western Europe appropriated from the African-Egyptian spiritual teachings of Kemetism science they reworked. It was an attempt to erase the supremacy of Eastern spiritual mind/body/spirit avatar complex of the wisdom of the Law of One love teaching and learning with which was derived from the esoteric sacred knowledge of the God Ra's; teaching and learning about the Law of One love.

This was a priestly priesthood, temple worship enshrined as the principle of luminous divine Kingship, religious ceremonies, rites, and the teachings through Egyptian Temple priests. Sacred wisdom Law of One love of self and our other selves in fellowship in God's service on earth.

Anunnaki Initiation of the Egyptians into Enki's Serpent Priestley Brotherhood establishment of secret societies tied to African-Kemetism. With which the it's symbolism and sacred spiritual symbolism ancient teachings underwent a mendacious transformative destruction. And rise of Christian religious worship of the martyred death of Jesus Christ.

His crucifixion was to become a focus on the Son of God's death and miracles resurrection. So allow me to put forth these unconventional conjectures. All I am saying is: extraterrestrial alien beings who were the original custodians of planet earth were ancient astronauts from planet Nibiru.

To any person who has not yet become familiar with the UFO phenomena, the sightings, and the abductions, I say you must come to assume that they are likely ancestors of the Anunnaki. As a significant number of records have documented the thousand and thousands of these credible sighted UFO entities reported sightings. People are trying to figure out whether these are the original God of the Bible Genesis narrative with which some refer to as a fanciful Mythical tale. So let's face it. Likely, the ancient astronaut theory is, most importantly, not a truthiness or the folly of speculation.

I, however, on the other hand, presuppose some extraterrestrial race indeed colonized planet Earth; aliens from a higher density level who posted advanced, sophisticated scientific intelligence knowledge. Accordingly, I prefer not to poo-poo the curious claims of modern-day UFO/UAVs sightings in our air space; I think that it is relevant because they are the Anunnaki God Enki (Ea), their ancestors related to Royal Prince Enlil (the Hebrew Bible God Yahweh) will soon appear on the second mission earth voyage; but this is to begin the prophecy of the Harvesting of individual moral souls when the planet Nibiru will pass through their planets 36-thousands years elliptical orbits is expected to create constellation disturbances. You see the events prophecies of the Biblical book of Revelations loom, the Anunnaki UFO/UAVs visitations will be revealed as the Olden Times Chariots of the Anunnaki alien gods. Might the Anunnaki alien Gods return to reclaim this planet and exploit humankind for their own benevolent or mendacious purpose? Will they elevate the faithful followers of modern church religions who bend their knee witting; and serve the gods in loyal obedience to the original custodians lord gods who will reclaim earth and the earth obsequious primitive workers? Of course, in juxtaposition to the ancient UFOs phenomenon, biblical text dovetails with events toe into UFOs appearances throughout history. Christians and other religions will never address this UFO bugaboo! Right? And might this indicate that they intend to reclaim this planet? We all must now think about this because everything postulated in this explanation is most likely akin to the true story about the Anunnaki titular [Gods who descended from Heaven] might be connected to the contemporary UFOs' presence visitations commonly known and not some new external empirical world phenomenon.

But is this not true? No, indeed! Not even close. We must connect the past to the present-day reports of UFOs sightings to be strong evidence of an actual genuine extraterrestrial visitation. The fact missing from Genesis creation of Adam and Eve has been this secret: Enki the Anunnaki (God) of mischief and wisdom of the Law of One love was a brilliant biological scientist. His knowledge of genetic engineering by fusion of His alien DNA bloodline mixed with the DNA bloodline of an African female genetic code produced the crossbreed Homosapien Adam and Eve. Details about this human creation you can discover in the: "*Seven Tablets of Creation*" description is an irrefutable account according to the Royal great prince Egas was the biological father of Adam.

This was Adam's physical DNA taken from his rib with which Enki had fused to fashion Eve. They were assigned to work as *subordinate primitive workers inside the Lord of the Earth Command's Enlil's eponymous Garden in the place called the* Edin. They were primitive workers of Enlil, the Supreme God, or the Anunnaki as the Supreme Earth Mission Commander. Enlil's two crossbreed humans, Adam and Eve, are primitive workers in *Havilah's garden in the land of Eden*. As a curious student neophyte of the ancient astronaut theory logic, let's think. The idea of extraterrestrial aliens as the original settlers; they contributed for thousands of years. Please don't take my word. Visit it [24]! Mortal humans have been suspicious of UFOs visiting earth.

Do you acknowledge that the Anunnaki alien beings were UFO entities conspicuous visitation? The exact Anunnaki immortal titular god figure of the Judo-Christian biblical narrative tale is god? What if these UFOs are astronauts from Nibiru who were the ancient astronauts? These alien custodian settlers were the first Nibiru Anunnaki astronauts who had successfully landed a spacecraft on Earth and built an advanced civilization. [25]. The *Igigi* aliens were in the habit of the Nibiru's twelve members ruling council; mostly, they were in the *humble* labor of the extraterrestrial authority gold mining Earth Mission voyage initial vanguard.

An ancient astronaut mission earth voyage theory ties into our emerging further, and my friends, I have to remind folks to read: "Book of Enoch. We know that Enoch was the grandson of Noah who had walked with God as it was written in the Ethiopian original Holy Bible. Here as in the *Book of Enoch* mentions the watchers (Aramaic iyrin) angels dispatched to Earth to watch over humans (https://en.wikipedia.org/wiki/Watcher(angel).

They soon begin to lust for human women and, at the prodding of their leader Samyaza, defect en masse to illicitly instruct humanity and procreate among them". The Bible refers to their moral turpitude, identifying that the Igigi ancient astronauts had become the infamous eponymous Watchers. I interpolate that they were manlike aliens who descended and landed their ancient astronauts spacecraft on earth. The truth is about the Anunnaki ancient astronauts. In other words God's mode of conveyance was facilitated by aerial spacecraft from planet Nibiru. Yeah it's an outrageous thing to conjecture. With logic and reason it dovetails nicely with the premise of the modern day technology that NASA is parallelling in its own sophisticated advanced space exploration of the deep space cosmic frontier adventures into planetary constellation with human astronauts pi, on board of a sophisticated NASA-like space rocket ship. Anunnaki astronauts piloted spacecraft while onboard their orbital space station. The watchers mentioned in the Bible book of Genesis are the narrative of the great Royal Prince, Enki, and Enlil, who were the sons of the Supreme God of the Planet Nibiru.

Anu was the God of the Sky/Heaven and the Lord God of the Anunnaki in Heaven those who He sent to the planet Earth (Ki). The Anunnaki clan's Anu sent on their Earth Mission voyage to extract Earth's gold, Enki's relocated his mining production operation to the Southeastern region of Africa's great land of Zimbabwe, which was bountifully blessed with the mineral gold for the mining production operation. And in Great Zimbabwe, Southern Africa, the Abzu [26] discovered many productive resources. This is was where Enki successfully fashioned Adapa/Adam Man) And the Women Even as His prototype Seville crossbred Homosapien-Sapien as primitive workers to perform the and grievous toiling labor required to extract the mineral gold deposits from the deep and hot mines, which was to help facilitate the transportation cargo shipments of gold that were ferried by space flight to the planet Nibiru via shuttle spacecraft orbiting high above the Earth was a "Space" command vehicle mothership communication command platform that was under the control of the Igigi—the Bible called them the Watchers [27].

It's an uncanny parallel that's closely what human progression NASA is mirroring to-day! Human beings are followers of the ancient astronaut direction; we are reaching out to explore beyond earth. Now ask yourself: Why is it that NASA's scientists are applying an aerial space technology knowledge mission to travel and land manned spacecraft on a mission to colonize the Moon and Mars? My friends might you concur with as evidence of humankind behaving in the manner of the all-knowing—monad? The modern human race is attempting to break away from our stewardship and the surrounding environmental responsibility to love and care for earthly life's existence. Why are NASA's scientists motivated to venture off the earth to explore the vast constellation of planets?

Whatever the reason, the aim was to reach out to unlock the hidden mysteries of deep space travel and exploration. What concerns me here is curious: zeal to explore the region's of the space frontier, ipso facto, extraterrestrial UFO entities that have been studying humankind's progression and how we are thinking since the Anunnaki Gods destroyed the cities of Sodom and Gomorrah and confounded humans language for attempting to construct the eponymous Tower of Babylon [28].

And yet, in the interior earth plane, the earth's surface illusion of illusory material consciousness is temporal reality—too many people are clueless adults asleep walking through this earthly existence. Maybe it's to open up the Bible Genesis and think. Then ask yourself questions about whether what I posit here, relates to the Kemeticism discipline of spiritual predilection towards daily medication. Which we might develop and come to experience the virtues of loving with a spiritual purified warm heart beating that serves in unity with the needs of the earthly *bons-hommes* of the universal *Nebebidjer*.

The god Ra's Law of One principle is teaching and learning about the monad energy vibration through the Kundalini alignment of the mind/body/spirit avatar complex. Being in total harmonic balance to think and let you be the judge, discerning what is true and what a spurious truthiness. Like myself and other folks have been taught and intentionally misled by falsehoods.

Spurious misdirections have inspired curious neophytes to go in search to discover answers which fits nicely with the plausible ancient astronauts hypothesis; meaning the truth that was curiously hidden or written out and transliterated into a biblical narrative tale; that rebuffed any notion of the extraterrestrial alien Gods as the UFO entities as being: Those who from the Heaven came" tells the story of an actually alien race of Gods who had been the custodians of their earth mission voyage under the command of the Royal Prince Enki. The Anunnaki titular Gods arrived from the planet of Nibiru's nascence in context in reference to the Old Testament genesis narrative tale. People in the modern fields of scientists set for truth are beginning to see the light! Putting missing pieces into place for clarity, filling in the gaps that expose global elite rulers' deeds.

We aim to reveal the missing elements of the Anunnaki Sumerian Bible pertaining to astronaut alien Enki and Enlil ties to the Old Testament, spiritual science, and the new age Catholic Church religious Gospels of the blind faith truthiness as specious sophistry as the authority of holy [29]. It is a very daring premise because this means I have courage of my human convictions. I think beyond the traditional status quo religion, old boundary precepts of Christianity construction of creeds and the gospel orthodoxy. Now pause and ponder whether these Anunnaki stories have a semblance of the biblical God narrative tale. The premise that fits nicely as the anecdotal detail missing from the Genesis chapter 1 through 11 narrative. Because right now the story perforce as described or is a truthiness--that needs to that: [a] The Sumerian God Enki (Ea) was the genetic scientists who successfully [fashioned] homo sapiens in His physical likeness or image [man] the [Adam/Adapa] from the dust of Earth's Interior plane; at least, this was what we all have heard of this story. We have read this incredible story and just assumed that it is true—accepting it on blind faith—then might we speculate: (1) let's agree that we're of God's likeness; (2) if an apomorphic god[s] from above created Heaven and things on earth, what means or mode of space flight transportation was the conveyance; and, (3) let's now agree to accept that this Bible Genesis narrative was the true beginning of establishment of a humans civilization on earth sprang out of the Anunnaki gold mining earth mission voyage.

To this I say that the fact is this: Humans possess a common ancestor genealogy DNA with these extraterrestrial ancestors, the human species bloodline descended from the titular god, Prince Enki (Ea). Humankind He fashioned in His own likeness; the original custodian settlers of planet earth civilization.

The titular Gods who colonized earth. My premise is a fundamental complex supposition of this incredible beginning. This book is a look at the religious teachings of organized Christianity, which perpetuates the inculcation of the biblical genesis nascence is a truthiness tale of an Anunnaki historical event. But it's never going to be disclosed, my friends. I presuppose something very critical is conspicuous life to our speculation; that inspires others to analyze the narrative. A natal nature date extended back beyond the rise of the Judo-Christian Bible version of the ancient history of the Anunnaki extraterrestrial astronauts alien race of giant manlike human beings who had successfully landed a space flight vehicle on their Earth Mission voyage. So I would think modern-day UFOs incursions have chosen to say that many years ago, primitive indigenous denizen earthmen, trembling in fear, watched manlike gods land. And given that with advanced technology, we can fly across the and above to explore vast space galaxies. And in the real true biblical narrative.

The extraterrestrial ancient astronauts' massive fiery space vehicle slowly descends; the titular gods landed. In disbelief, craven earthmen watched the alien beings arrive in the Sumerian landscape. I hope you can mentally imagine being there standing within the crowds of wide eyes bemused indigenous peoples' sunburnt bronze faces of the primitive Sumerian Earth's people who stood together, all looking and gazing up into the morning sky. With awe and genuine fear of these Gods spacecraft, they watched the landing of this bizarre-looking large framed metallic sky bird slowly descending against the sky canvas backdrop against the white clouds in subtle movement drifting crossing with the warm sunshine. And as if time had frozen their faces with fear and trepidation, they witnessed the large Anunnaki ancient astronaut UFO spacecraft as it slowly descended into the earth plane of Sumer, Mesopotamia. Archeology and anthropology research scholars' modern discoveries leave plenty of room for the scientific mindset to fit in this biblical tale *conterminous* historical information.

Indeed this dovetails nicely with the Old Testament Bible narrative tale. The presence of an advanced ancient race who possesses very advanced knowledge in the disciplines of the sciences of nature's psychic and spiritual universe. Researchers put forth information about the past that fits into the Bible historical context; which has been analyzed and peer reviewed. It's an exegesis to spur others' curiosity to take a close-up look at the alien ancient astronaut's theory. Then consider the possibility and likelihood that "Those who from Heaven came" were the extraterrestrial aliens who called themselves the Anunnaki.

Whether or not they were likely Ancient Astronauts; and not Gods! But most likely it's true that they were the original custodian Gods of the Bible Genesis narrative. Perhaps this has far reaching implications, which has been in this context as a proper predicate put forth by ancient astronaut theorists as a speculative hypothesis. So this book is an attempt to frame a reference.

Now can you visualize the agitated crowd of curious indigenous primitive tribal, wide eyes gazing up while pointing to Anunnaki's colossal UFO spaceship slowly descending from the amorphous clouds concealed by the Anunnaki astronauts who were the *Watchers*? Looking down and all of these curious frightened indigenous people. In incredible awe, crowds of earth men were watching a large and bright shining metallic spacecraft touching down on the earth surface of ancient Sumer, Mesopotamia. And like that the alien gods became custodians of planet earth. As they possessed the technological knowledge to travel across the sky.

THE MIND, BODY, SPIRIT, AND STORYTELLING

Today 32 percent of people believe, or think that UFOs are real [30]. What seems absurd today is that we have skeptics who don't believe UFOs phenomenon is connected with the ancient astronaut theorists' premise. If it's true, then, of course, had this event taken place, it would have been this very monumentally incredibly amazing diegetic or incredible splendid historical scene! The Sumerian people who witnessed the Anunnaki, manlike strange-looking extraterrestrial aliens bright shiny spacecraft land in Mesopotamia, called these titular gods as the so-called "shining ones! They would have most certainly all of the villagers felt intimidated as they gathered as the crowds of tribesmen stood watching in awe. These primitive tribesmen were the ancient indigenous people of Mesopotamia. With blathering *badinage* the tribesmen watched the Enki's alien astronauts crew land an alien UFO in southern Mesopotamia. The Anunnaki astronauts from the planet Nibiru's Earth Mission crew led by the operations mission commander, the Royal-Elite Prince Enki, or Ea, who was sent to the earth by his father, *Anu*, who was Nibiru's Supreme God of Heaven and the Earth.

The Royal great prince Enki's father, Lord King *An/Anu*, who had sent the prince to the earth. The Genesis Earth Mission voyage ended with a successful landing. No. This was Not an ordinary dreamscape excursion. Because their specific purpose was to locate and confirm the existence of the mineral gold, insufficient amounts justify Enki to be a mining production operation. The initial extraction is located in southern Mesopotamia and the Persian gulf sea of the modern country of Iraq. However, due to an insufficient amount could be extracted from the sea, Nibiru's Supreme God/King, Anu along with his heir apparent, Royal-Elite Prince Enlil came to earth and had determined that the Royal great prince Enki would relocate the gold mining production operation to great Zimbabwe, southern Africa. This tells me that Enki and his intrepid fiftymen ancient astronaut crew had in fact safely traveled through space flight and arrived down through the asteroid belt. Whilst maneuvering through the crossing between the planets Mars and Jupiter heading towards the earth surface. Above the earth surface they hovered above the target landing down on a steady approach descent and landed on the target zone.

Enki's crew were ready to land down in the interior earth plane. While on the earth's surface, wide-eyed primitive earthmen stood still. All were looking up at what to them was this large scale strange-looking spacecraft was monumental for those eyewitnesses who watched the enormously historical true illusory temporal reality. A remarkable and coherent vision of brilliant sights to behold that which is manifestly real! Yeah! These titular gods landed, and their presence was the beginning of the establishment. What we see is like the snapshot that extends far back into a plausible interpolation on the history of biblical illusory material consciousness temporal reality.

Yes, my friends, the fundamental presupposition of the objective about the Ancient "Seven Tablets of the Creation Myth is [unequivocally] most closely akin to the hypothesis that dovetails nicely with Ancient Astronaut Theory" corresponding to the hyperbolic narrator account of the opening episode we read in chapter 1, of the Holy Bible Genesis narrative account. The Old Testament Bible voice is silent.

I guess that the only appropriate question that I want clarity is: Why? Whereas the answer is quite obvious, indeed is my salient point: it should be rather shocking because so many people live out their entire adult life being misled by a spurious religion.

It may sound crazy but many adults have just accepted the biblical teachings of the church religions gospel as the unvarnished true words of god. I pose a salient question: Has it ever occurred to you to question this notion of the blind faith religion teachings and ritual ecclesiastical denominations' doctrine of the Catholic and Protestant's theological Judeo-Christian Orthodox.

Perhaps you have and that's great; because my friends, indeed too many, have not done that! But you can start right now; and let's face it, it's not enough to accept any religious doctrines that places you. Humankind is imbued with the means of intelligent knowledge of the past.

Things that are far more likely our lost ancient civilization of the mysterious spiritual science. Wisdom is insight into the Law of One love, sacred principles. Your learning, and the teachings of other individuals is the one pathway towards a Christ sweven.

THE MIND, BODY, SPIRIT, AND STORYTELLING

The space landing vehicle arrived with its crew of scientists on the missions that had come down from above. It descended on the landing point in southern Mesopotamia--modern-day country of the Iraqi Persian gulf. And in the same manner of today's NASA Astronauts descended on the moon's surface. And indeed, the Anunnaki ancient astronauts were: "Those who from the Heaven came" could have achieved the same frites millions of years ago, and came face to face with hard-bitten, fearful, primitive earthman? Yeah, a long time ago they came down to earth from Heaven. They entered and maneuvered down through the crossing Mars and Jupiter and maneuvered their spacecraft into the large and dangerous asteroid belt field. And by this means a conjecture that is fundamental to the modern age elucidation appertaining to the controversial ancient astronaut theory. Olden s Anunnaki's alien god arrives aboard the materialistic of the biblical tale. The most plausible thing about the Bible is the fact that the storyline of the biblical narrative has parallels that postulates the arrival of the extraterrestrial alien god to be no other than Royal elite Nibiru Prince Enki. The assertion being that he was the first ancient alien astronaut mentioned and delineated in the Bible's book of Genesis episode written about in chapter 1 maxes the deeds of the god of the creation myth. Seemingly, might we consider that they were "Those who from Heaven came" from above, descended down and landed on the Earth plane.

Might they have been extraterrestrial alien gods from a higher plane of the celestial orbital solar system orbital? There are conjecture and speculative views that claim they were from planet Nibiru or (Planet-X), the so-called missing twelve planets. These beings were not God living on earth some estimated 450,000 years ago. Custodians of the earth's constellation orbital system circumambulate as the glittering stars in the dark moonlighted firmament constellation orbital cycle.

According to some modern research scientists know that planet-X/Nibiru is a vast elliptical orbit for which the Nibiru a planet in the solar system is according to the Sumerian texts equivalent with 3600 earth solar orbital cycle travel in a deep space elliptical precession around the sun moves into each of the twelve Zodiac periods of 25,920 through each astrological hoThe solar system is, according to the Sumerian texts, equivalent to. Thoth is the Egyptian Ibis Headed deity in this story, created and established the 365-day solar calendar. The Twelve-months Zodiacal, like the calendar, came into use in ancient Egyptian Mythology. The Anunnaki Nibiru calendar precession cycle lasts 25,800 years, and there are 12 constellations of the zodiac.

So There is roughly a 2,150 year cycle in the twelve celestial movements. The bright stars glistening against the stars like diamonds sparkling by night 365 days a year in the Heavens; it's unlike an Anunnaki (year) which is 25,190 years.

Twelve time periods cycle through each Zodiacal constellation House orbit. Bold Speculative assertion, maybe! A question is whether Anunnaki clans were ancient astronauts, custodial gods 450 thousand years ago. Moreover, the anecdotal details of the Bible genesis narrative reflect an opening scene suggesting, *ipso-facto*, from out of the annals of the universal creation is the existence of all units of the fundamental substrate: *Neberdjer* (God's spirit essence) symbolical of the uniformed field of the manifold purified pleroma of the physical and spiritual empirical worlds manifestations.

The perception of material existence as mere Maya or illusion, but instead considers them sacred creation, the visible form of the Supreme God.' [https://www.lexico.com/en/definition/maya]. The biblical genesis narrative event in its storytelling. The curiosity and interest among modern-day Mythological scientists in extraterrestrial research interest in UFOs can likely be synthesized in parallel with the archeological discovery of ancient *Sumerian* cuneiform clay tablets. Historical records which archeology discovers evidence that put forth facts about the biblical story dovetails nicely with *Sumerian*, *Akkadian*, and *Babylonian* accounts.

The Annunaki arrived on Earth 450,000 years ago looking for minerals. Archeology discovery of ancient cuneiform clay tablets excavated from under the ruins of the Royal-Elite Library at *Nineveh*. The Royal Library of *Ashurbanipal*, named after *Ashurbanipal*, the last great king of the Assyrian Empire.

THE MIND,BODY, SPIRIT,ANDSTORYTELLING

Archeology discovery revealed a collection of thousands of ancient clay fragmented tablets. They corroborated that the Annunaki arrived on Earth 450,000 years ago looking for earth to extract deposits of gold minerals. How do we know any of this is true? Because we really don't know anything for sure. Well then, I point you to the archeology ings of facts revealed by some remarkable archeological ings that have been made as a modern discovery of 30,000 thousand ancient Mesopotamia cuneiform clay tablets found in the site ruins discovered beneath the Royal-Elite Library at Nineveh [32]. The Mesopotamian ancient city states are mentioned in the Old Testament holy Bible. And the first city-state of Eridu, Enki proclaimed that it was built in six days; on the seventh day, He rested according to the Genesis narrative tale of God's creation story.

This vanguard of ancient astronauts spearheaded the earth mission voyage, whose contribution spread over the earth's interior plane, which impacted the evolution and involution of social consciousness. These alien beings inspired and inculcated their kingship and the cult of the African Egyptian-Kemetism mystery, with the precepts; meaning the teachings and learning about the spiritual science principles of esoteric wisdom of the god Ra's "Law of One". To have reverence for love of the *Nebedjer*!

Humankind embraced a secular culture of centralized political rulers by establishment of powerful government authority and laws. Temple religious rites and religious rituals were instituted through the sacred priesthood class, education, economic commercial trade markets, agricultural farming, science and astronomy, social and moral principles were taught to the Kemetic people who learned about the Anunnaki as the temple practices for worshiping the Gods from Heaven as lord of the ancient mystery spiritual science teachings and learning of the luminous divine nature of the Ancient teachings of the occultist's sacred wisdom of the Law of One love principles. And indeed, these are the essential facts that have been conspicuously excised and conveniently disconnected from and are missing from the historical anecdotal details that fits the Genesis olden times custodian God's during the biblical events.

Which is the missing anecdotal strong evidence that dovetails nicely with the landing of an ancient race of beings influence in Old Testament gods who seeded civilization on earth in the region of Africa and Sumerian in Mesopotamia, Akkadian, Babylonian, and Egyptian archeology and biblical historical discovery and findings. But is this the real true nascence? To connect the elements of a perpetual falsity with which traces back into the storied beginning of Nibiru *Annunaki* ancient astronaut crewmen Earth mission's voyage commander *Enki* (Ea) landing in southern Mesopotamia.

Then in six days, Genesis writes that he (God) built and established *Eridu* as the first permanent city state settlements on Earth *"home in the far away"*. Wait a darn minute here, is this the meaning of *Eridu*—oh! All of this has something to do with the whole arcana of the original storylines in totality. The nature of humanity's evolution and the extrapolation of human beings on earth over many eons.

Then I posited this salient question for the curious-minded neophyte who has ruminated on that concerning the biblical narrative as a historical event.

Or is it perhaps the real true story derived from the original ancient astronaut theorists hypothesis. It's an assertion predicated on the modern evidence related to a biblical statement which says declare the presence of god's as *"Those who from the Heaven came"*! Therefore this hypothesis dovetails nicely with modernism. Ancient astronauts theorists' hypothesis assertion extraterrestrial aliens' custodian gods who established Earth civilization were worshiped as the gods, And given that I am not a philosophical or theological subject matter expert or a scholar, I'm not declaring that this Ancient Astronauts Theory is true. Absolutely 100 percent not at all! This is a scintillating topic for others like minded people who ponder why this Bible story is a paucity of the real nascence of the ancient astronauts account; and it is indeed a rather curiously seeking the process that unveils the path to consciousness awareness—with which man is taught to fellowship in blind faith. To be the slavish obsequious obedience primitive workers. The underlying fundamental presupposition that blind faith inculcates a truthiness. Truth is religious institutions preaching the complexities of the ancient mystery spiritual science teachings and learning about the Law of One. The practice of *Shautu Neter* towards daily medication wisdom of the Law of One love principles of the *Neberdjer*. To bring the mind to penetrate self-consciousness of the empirical world of thinking/body/spirit avatar complex into a personal unity with the *Neberdjer*. Our spiritual essence is but an incredible separation from the *pleroma* of the harmonic cosmic universe. Knowledge of the sacred principles that are being taught to achieve a purified heart. That one's soul is judged to be righteous according to the teaching of African/Egyptian Kemeticism.

So now let's frame thIs the body of work in the annals of organized religious zealots. Meaning folks who don't want to put the material information into the proper context seems curiously visceral; and intolerance towards the spiritual science principles of nature of creative infinity with Christianity. All world religions were guilty and complicit in perpetuating acts of gratuitous violence and brutality. What a shameful history of violence, and crimes carried out in the name of the church, viz., those committed under the holy bishops central authority during the New Testament Bible, invented by the Roman control of the Papal state, after African-Kemetism philosophical principles of spiritual science were destroyed and subjugated. With a transformation derived from the original ancient mystery spiritual science of the ancient sacred wisdom teachings of the Law of One love. Which was superseded with religious sects like *Yahshua (Jesus), the relentless persecution of conceivable brutality.* Heresy was considered a high crime according to pious rulers of establishing a Romanized Catholic falsehood religious doctrinal edits and rituals creed. We know that the actual Bible symbolic of spirituality and occultism, the origin of the Christian religion, was stolen from African/Egyptian Kemet-Cushite [33]. We seek the actual real truth. What if this insidious evil took control in the mind of the elite cabal mechanisms of the hidden hand of the deceivers of ancient Anunnaki rulers.

The *Holy Romans Emperor* had a sinister scheme to proclaim the Pope as vicar of the gods in Heaven.

His was to embrace Christianity; claiming that while awaiting during the epoch of time of culture of AD 332. Permit me to redirect you to what are undisputed facts with which it is hard to *fathom* the bloody despicable crimes committed against citizens by the power of the Romans Church. Five examples of these scurrilously criminal acts of evil deeds perpetrated on humankind by religious authority and secret societies with influence that have been occurring across the four thousand years period of human civilizations. It is by no means an exhaustive list of examples of arrogance and ruthless aggression by the Catholic Church institutions perpetuating the worship of the ecclesiastical gospel doctrine teachings of Holy Trinity.

Where citizens witnessed the following examples of the deeds that are guided by flagrant actions that can be construed as evils carried out by the authority of the Christian's Church, history revealed evidence that isused the religious bishops ordered the killings of innocent people who were persecuted and condemned to death by the most despicable punishment is irrefutable. According to Church documents, 20,000 heretics were slaughtered in and around Beziers and the town burned to the ground.doctrinal authority.

Following links references to blatant examples of irrefutable ruthless aggression imposed by religious dogmatism, by rise of religious authoritarian zealots who carried out many sinister killings. Deeds that were very wicked, criminally abusive actions, which were put upon weaker neighboring countries; and justified as they claimed was sanctioned and blessed in the name of the God of Heaven follows:

- https://www.ancient.eu/Cathars/
- https://www.google.com/amp/s/www.history.com/.amp/topics/middle-ages/the-knights-templar
- https://www.google.com/search?q=the+inquestion&ie=UTF-8&oe=UTF-8&hl=en-us&client=safari
- https://en.m.wikipedia.org/wiki/Christianity_and_colonialism#Background
- https://www.christianitytoday.com/history/issues/issue-51/heresy-in-early-church-gallery-of-malcontents

THE MIND, BODY, SPIRIT, AND STORYTELLING

So can we agree on the historical chronology? The history of Christianity has much to atone for the many despicable crimes committed in the name of religious teachings by a religious ruling authority. Noticeably so, and of course, we must never forget about the *Inquisitions*. The intent was to maintain Catholic orthodoxy in their ruling kingdoms and replace the Medieval Inquisition. This kind of evil behavior was sanctioned by the Protestants and Catholics Church as justified in the eyes of the religious authority and claimed in Jesus Christ. This irrefutable evidence points to the three different manifestations. There was a Catholic Inquisition, Roman Inquisition, and a Portuguese Inquisition.

No matter how you view the history of the church, violence is there every step of the way; no matter what, one can not deny that purveyors of evil carried out evil deeds against humanity, and it was so fierce e as the rulers lusted for power and control in the name of God through organized Catholic and Protestant banner of religion. The people being illiterate have *become* anesthetized by their preferred blind faith religion.

Yeah, followers of blind faith falsehoods had the power to erase the history of the *Cushites*, the ancient, historic people from the tribes of Judea or Judaea, which we know about from the Holy Bible. Yeah it's about the Hebrew tribe of Judah. You see, Mr. Alexander Fantalkin, believes that this archeological evidence is for the extensive kingdom of Judah; there is evidence that exists before the late eighth century BCE is too weak and that the methodology used to obtain the evidence is flawed. Nevermind that anyone forgot that according to some current estimates, around 150,000 falsely accused Christian and Hebrews were prosecuted for various alleged offenses during the three-century duration of the Spanish Inquisition, out of which between 3,000 and 5,000 were executed (percent of all cases).

Rulers who have only their lust for economic wealth and power by means of and state seem clear to the sagacious mind that seeks objective truth. Because in the name of God, many examples of despicable very evil crimes have been perpetrated against humanity by those who arrogantly wrapped themselves in so-called words of religion, have misused the notion of religion symbolic to justify their efficacious mendacious lust for wealth, power, and religious twisting and manipulating the teaching of spiritualism. And did you know anything about the Anunnaki alien gods who had been the custodians who made many significant and quite remarkable consequential contributions involving the evolution and involutions in development of our human civilization.

Indeed, inextricably linked to the extraterrestrial alien's abduction to-day is connected to these same titular gods? The Anunnaki vanguard established their living accommodations here on Earth in six days and "then God rested on the seventh day!" But the Genesis narrative is conspicuously very careful to excise the fact that this hypothesis specificity and anecdotal details about this from chapter 1, the Holy Bible book's diffusive excursive tale of the anachronistic period when the biblical story alludes to the events that recounts the story written about the Anunnaki extraterrestrial alien astronauts; meaning that Enki was the God who descended from the sky as the commander of: "those who from the Heaven came". Let's develop some clarity in this recondite place; and, the universal nascence of our intellectual minds that is inextricably tied into our forefathers genealogy; the ancestors' roots fashioned by the Royal Prince Enki.

Anunnaki's Chief Medical Officer, assistant to Ninmah's biological collaboration. Genetic scientists were titular gods whose pioneering genetic research methodology. They created Homosapien sapien by the process of editing and manipulation of the biological sequencing of chromosome genetic codes. Which was carried out by the Royal Prince Enki and his team of scientists who successfully fashioned the first homo sapiens sapiens Adam in His physical image and likeness at his bioresearch lab, which was likely located in Zimbabwe, Southern Africa. The nexus is this: "The garden in the land of the Eden was in Havila (Ethiopia) perhaps this was the location of the genesis narrative tale, is according to the elucidation of modern archeologist's discovery and findings about the *Holy Sepulchre in Jerusalem*, a documentary claimed. The garden in the land of the Eden, also referred to as Paradise, is the eponymous biblical garden of God (Enlil) as ded in the Old Testament Bible Book of

Genesis reference about (Prince Enki's) prototype servant (primitive workers). Feb 18, 2020.

The Bible narrative storied tale seems to be lacking, yet it dovetails nicely with the erudition and knowledge conflated to the controversial, so-called ancient astronaut theory. Thus I hereby openly predicate my thoughts here aiming to penetrate the self-consciousness of a different perception of the empirical world to spur others to discern the knowledge learned from an eclectic source of informative historical, biblical, and archeological books for personal erudition and knowledge. True analysis of religion and spiritual teachings about the annals of our past. Such as the archeology discoveries that fit within the revelation of hidden mysteries and the missing pages of biblical lines are to put forth relevant material facts about the *ancient astronaut's theory*. The magnificent Anunnaki the Royal great prince Enki established Egyptian civilization and seeded the Temple Priesthood wisdom of the Law of One (love) temple of *Sacred Serpent Brotherhood* worship of God was passed down by the Anunnaki alien demigods bloodline of the demigod African-Egyptian Pharaoh. Anunnaki titular god's installed the humans to demigods as the successor to the Anunnaki's Kingship to rule over the *plebeians.*

This was true in both Africa and America's indigenous cultures. Tribal ancestors were taught to recite the spirit of the oral traditions and luminous divine sacred rites. It marked the telling of stories about the nascence of extraterrestrial alien beings who were "Those who from the heaven came" where worshiped as the perceived Gods that had departed from Heaven after they landed on the planet Earth and had helped them.

Ancient alien beings who told them that their home planet was in the sky or Heaven. On Earth they arrived on the mission and began to extract gold. Thus this spurred the nascence of gods and human contact and beneficence relationships. For me it's very plausible that these extraterrestrial beings had to have possessed the scientific knowledge required to have been capable of manipulating biological DNA codes to genetically fashion the first crossbred human species Adam (man) and Eve (woman), to be the obsequiously obedient servants to the *Anunnaki* titular gods. The ancient astronaut crew came to land safely and built civilization as the custodians of the Earth's interior landscape. And, here, too, these extraterrestrial alien beings possess advanced levels of physics and scientific geometric knowledge of the vast solar system Zodiacal cycles orbital cosmos. Life of every human being is a microcosm derived from the universal *Neberdjer*. And so here too, we are all born on Earth with a level of consciousness. Knowing of luminous divine nature is my spirit-energy that causes my animated actions of beingness.

To think that we exist in the mind/body/spirit complex embodiment to live in a physical world of religious confusion! Religious institutions that praise their and minister to their followers according to the learning and teaching of Judaism, Christianity, Islam, Zoroastrianism, and Buddhist monks adhere to devotion to primeval precepts like Hinduism, Taoism, and Confucianism. There are many forms of religious worshiping the luminous metaphysical *noumena* god of the sky.

The heavenly constellation of spinning orbital residing the most significant evolution is an incomplete story of our existence on Earth was lost. And because there are parts to that voluminous corpus that are missing. And so I take the liberty of mentioning this assumption here to declare my understanding with respect to: the Bible for the erudition of knowledge which I interpret as a historical perspective. However we know that this tells us that we should worship God but make known graven images of gods countenance. If you have read the Bible's Genesis narrative—as I presuppose that you did, and perhaps like me you still can't forthwith make sense as to why. In this respect, it is the hidden mysteries mystique of religious teachings because we are devoid of clarity that has led to many scholarly debates about the God's missing element that is an incomplete biblical history has been transliterated into a convoluted religious story ostensibly mislead and deceived folks with the blind faith Christianity, which inculcated the premise of salvation through the religious teachings of blind faithful precepts. My friends, the nascence of the Anunnaki aliens ancient astronaut theory presents the hypothesis that exposes people to a more plausible intelligent perspective, albeit may seem rather subjective and a far flung notion, when juxtaposition to the biblical status quo ante theology of the well entrenched religious body mainstream complex.

Archeology discovery evidence is about revealing the relevant facts as material history information of substantive strong evidence—to raise probative questions that challenge the original Christianity paradigms. Surely you would expect some specificity and anecdotal orthodoxy. All pages lead to reveal organized religion concealing the truth about the Anunnaki extraterrestrial aliens as the titular God of Genesis.

Forging proper speculations for the fact-checkers into archeological discovery of cuneiform tablets, the *Emerald Tablets, Enūma Eliš* Babylonian creation myth. And there is to *Al-kimia Hermetic* light of initiation into the Egyptians Pharaoh's mystical sacred wisdom of the Law of One love.

Initiated into the priestly teachings of luminous divine spiritual temple brotherhood of the fellowship through secret ceremonial initiation rituals and rites of the sacred pyramid Egyptian-Kemetism worship, there was this reverence for the Enki, who was deity behind the *temple of the feathered serpent god worship*.

My friends, let's face it. Much about what is written in translation of the Hebrew and Greek Bible have been spreading the religious truthiness, with respect to the Anunnaki, extraterrestrial aliens, and the biblical creator god was the Royal Prince, Enki. The church denominations are never going to acknowledge or wittingly concur with these paradigm views.

Yeah, the Bible Genesis narrative doesn't declare any of the specificity and anecdotal details espoused as the Anunnaki alien gods and therefore does not concur with the archeology and anthropology discovery of ancient historical evidence. In fact, they have rebuffed this acknowledgement, notwithstanding the empirical ties to irrefutable recovery of the African-Egyptian (*Kemetic*) spiritual science of the *Corpus Hermeticism* religion cuneiform clay tablets found at Nipper, buried beneath the library of King Ashurbanipal's royal palace complex grounds. This has significance, as it was an incredible discovery of ancient sources revealing credible context material evidence, which has references to its historical nascence of the Genesis narrative. Which is clearly an old allegory that omitted any mentioning of the backstory of the Anunnaki identity as earth's titular gods figures, seemingly implies that the ancient astronaut theory understood that the book of Genesis narrative tale is much more than simply conjecture. Yeah it's about these extraterrestrial (manlike) aliens who were most likely the original custodians of planet Earth 450, 000 years ago from a planet they called *Nibiru* (heaven)!

This is why the Bible truth is about this arcane historical nascence. Because our planet ancestors interacted with these titular gods. Well, then are you and me right to question whether the Holy Bible Genesis is a truth? Much of the events of the epoch history the ancient scribes carefully wrote down what they witness from the earliest time of Mesopotamian, Arkkadian, Babylonian, Greecian, African Egyptian, and Mede Persian ruling kings whose deeds are the archived record *cache* buried cuneiform clay tablets. The conquest of wars they carved into stone *obelisk* announced the king's account. According to the king's desire to advance a positive narrative tale that would represent his legacy. Whereof it was more often a skewed biblical historical context that was the most pleasing account. Whereof in the Bible Genesis narrative, the translations failed to mention: Those who came would have likely piloted a large shiny bell-like flying chariot when they arrived from heaven, down to the Earth's interior plane and landed in the southern ocean of Mesopotamia. They were the so-called *Anunnaki titular* gods, the shining ones from our Earth's solar system missing tenth Planet-X; or planet *Nibiru* (heaven) by renowned author Mr. Zachariah Sitchin.

Whereof Zachariah Sitchin and other fictional authors have postulated that extraterrestrial ancient alien gods; and they were a race of large, manlike, ancient astronauts. When Enki came down from their own home planet Nibiru is a higher plane of an elliptical channel or density of cosmic orbit. In the Hebrew Holy Bible chapters 1 through 11, the book of the Sumerian, Annunaki Genesis biblical narrative tale is the event that is ostensibly historical, edited to make it dovetails nicely with the irrefutable premise of the ancient astronauts theory that posits gods as an advanced race of extraterrestrial aliens. Sophisticated alien beings descended from a higher level of constellational orbital above earth's interior plane. My qualified position is specific and substantive, compelling as a logic and reasonable assumptions and speculative assertions.

I have heavily relied on available books that were written on this controversial subject matter topic. Books that were instrumental as a plethora of source reference, and to the information I needed to write prose have been so instrumental in a meaningful way to allow digest their formation and integrate the relevant information into a compelling fictionalized predicate aim and focus to make folks think. There is a growing number of curious minded UFO enthusiasts who have embraced the body of historical and biblical researcher's information about an ancient view of astronauts' theorists' premise, the *Anunnaki* arrived above the surface of earth aboard advanced spacecrafts sky birds, spacecraft was piloted by the titular god Prince Enki. Anunnaki alien gods were likely to have traveled down from planet Nibiru, orbited the Earth solar system, and "hovered over the target landing zone seated onboard these so-called *'Shining One,'* bright metallic spacecraft. The question here is whether or not the creator god Enki's astronaut crew separated the mingled fresh waters from the Earth's moving oceans waters that covered the vast surface of the earth. And in the beginning divided the sky into darkness to light and cultivated vegetation, and animals in six days". What is omitted here is that the biblical narrative references a deception that keeps the Anunnaki true identity as the ancient astronauts under wraps in favor of a mood of the fanciful! We should understand this in context of whether it was possible or improbable to have occurred as the Bible creator paucity, an actual historical event.

Does not this sound rather plausible that god (Prince Enki/Ea), a vanguard crew of fifty space faring alien astronauts, were responsible for the establishment of the first settlement on the earth's surface in Sumer, Mesopotamia's marshy landscape in six days! Which corresponds with the biblical Genesis conflating with the Anunnaki great Royal Prince Enki being the deity who claims to have constructed the first city-state of *Eridu*, (means: their *home in the far away*, the juxtaposition, according to the *Nibiruan* calendar which is the counting of the days of the year in Sars/years. To this significant distinction,

I elucidate information that is for your erudition as a fundamental interpolation: that posits the idea that Nibiru's Lord King Anu had given the lofty tilt of mission Commander to elite Royal Prince, Enki, or (Ea) and his skilled crew ancients astronauts who spacecraft slowly descend towards a landing target zone. I submit this semi-fictional assertion that the written information revealed in the books of notable and prominent distinguished published author, Zechariah Sitchin.

He published many very informative books, such as *The Earth Chronicles,* that posits thirty years of intensive research into the *Anunnaki* extraterrestrials from planet Nibiru, or heaven. A richly enigmatic exposé to put forth a speculative exegesis, meaning what? Combining my perspective with modern biblical history reveals lots of important material information from the archeology and anthropology research discovery and findings. And a common conjecture about ancient and modern space-faring ancient astronauts, with the biblical genesis narrative truthiness. Saying that the God of the Bible chapter 1 is the narrative tale seems to be the true story that was written as a chronicle of Enki's historical account of the Anunnaki extraterrestrial alien beings who were in fact the nascence of: *"those who from the Heaven came"* to Earth by means of their advanced sophisticated UFO flying spacecraft. Those whose manlike appearance was *coterminous* a titular God (Enki); it was he who biologically fused his own Anunnaki genetic DNA codes and successfully put the Anunnaki imprint upon Adam (man) and Eve (woman) and created the first crossbred Homo sapien sapien, which Enki created to establish an obedient primitive labor workforce of servile obsequious workers who worshiped the Anunnaki as a titular god by means of editing and fusion of his and that of an indigenous African females mitochondrial DNA codes manipulation in a sterile clay petri dish.

The discovery of the ancient Anunnaki Sumerian Bible text that was found at an archaeological dig site revealed a glimpse into the ancient: *"Seven Tablet of the Creation"* narrative about alien beings which means what?

1. The shining ones indicate that Enki was the god who commanded the Earth mission voyage
2. This was the space mission enterprise exploration authorized under the auspices of Nibiruan god Anu
3. Enki's mode of travel was via an advanced spacecraft and a fifty-man crew of highly skilled architects
4. His crew likely consisted of builders, technicians, scientists, and biologists
5. Beginning with chapter 1 narrative tale the scripture of the Bible's book of Genesis says that god/Enki hovered above, he was looking down at the dark and murky primeval waters that covers the landscape
6. Suggest He observed the surface from above the ground, and his description says that it's waters were mingled and that it was murky, chaotic without form

After the spacecraft safely landed in the southern Mesopotamian region between the *Tigris* and *Euphrates Rivers* of the modern-day country of Iraq, in six days. Whereof the Bible Genesis scriptures make no mention of ancient alien astronauts, spacecraft landing on the earth surface in Sumer Mesopotamia. Which curiously and intentionally missing anecdotal details information about who came down from Heaven and built the first City state settlement on earth. It's quite concerning why this achievement of the earth creation myth has dismissed the notion that it seems plausible to speculate that Enki was the god who built the first city state in Mesopotamia, which he named Eridu, meaning: *home on the car Away*. Conspicuously this relevant material is interestingly left to the conjecture and speculation, meaning what? That the ware ancient astronauts theory assumption is most probably the absolute truth that has been missing because it will expose the mendacious sinister falsehood. of organized religion.

A series of ecumenical councils convened by successive Roman emperors met during the fourth and fifth centuries. NBut

Christianity continued to suffer rifts and schisms surrounding the theological and Christological doctrines of Arianism, Nestorianism, and Miaphysitism. My friends, this is most important to become awake; and understand being of the spirit essence, the specificity and anecdotal details of another quintessential truth. Ask yourself why religion prefers to have blind faith followers? An acknowledgment of Enki's and his first fifty-man extraterrestrial ancient astronaut crew was *coterminous* with the modern-day UFO is not a new phenomenon. This seems to say that they were a crew of ancient astronauts the indigenous tribes perceived to be gods from the sky. Perhaps it's understandable that these indigenous earthmen were frightened and acquiesced to worship these strange large manlike *anamorphic* figures, higher dimension luminous divine beings that have come down from heaven and who brought them advanced knowledge to all tribal peoples across the lands before and after the great *Noah's flood*.

Yes, let's all face it: extraterrestrials seeded this planet's landscape, and built colonies, cities and kingdoms they established on planet Earth. These alien beings were the original custodian titular gods of Heaven. I guess the salient question is whether the flight crew of ancient astronaut theory is indeed true. And if they were these extraterrestrials, Anunnaki aliens came down from the sky/Heaven to Earth. I presuppose that we might say that Royal Prince Enki's initial deeds and attributes entitled to the unique mantle of being the first amorphous custodian of planet earth.

As the custodial titular god of heaven used their knowledge to colonize the landscape, by building a cultural civilization across Southern *Mesopotamia* interior plane, dynasties of ancient *African Egyptian* culture's advanced civilization. Its modern day location is the country of Iraq.

Enki was the mastermind that possessed the construction blueprints used by Enki's crew to construct Mesopotamia's first sophisticated city state among the indigenous tribes. This is an incredible work combining facts and fiction in its own literary storytelling in order to upend the conventional narrative trope. And so, it's in this recondite sense to tease the people's curiosity which awakens contemporary free thinkers to study the footsteps of humankind.

THE MIND, BODY, SPIRIT, AND STORYTELLING

Okay, let's face the truth. So are you ready and willing to learn/teach others what is ostensibly closely akin to what is likely the real truth? Curious neophytes, are you awakened, open-minded, and truly inspired towards knowing that truth is about the Law of One? To be humble and wisdom minded in nature of the *noumena* mysteries' esoteric symbology of sacred expression about the Egyptian god Ra's pervasive Law of One teachings and learnings about the spiritual science principles of the occultists' *Kemetic* philosophy teachings of the nature of spiritual science sync with the souls divine luminous cosmetic universal harmonic balance of *Neberdjer*.

Human beings can ascend to higher levels of spiritual priority between birth and one's death; several years, endured from God as life on the Earth plane. An irrefutable consensus has been raising the public interest in this ancient astronaut theorist's UAVs/UFOs hypothesis ever since the 1947 incident, when the government and military were behind a cover-up that denied a flying saucer crashed at Roswell,. Obstinsively, the phenomenon is largely due to the increasing number of archived government files containing secret, inaccessible documentation confirming a increase in the reported number of these strange AUV/UFO flying vehicles that have been identified by people who are indisputably to refute as mere poppycock. Could what folks have been witnessing have a correlation and connection to those Anunnaki alien gods who descended from heaven and landed in Mesopotamia years ago and modern times? The Royal-Elite bloodline of alien demigod rulers of the titular gods' genetic roots.

This genesis connection links back to the *Cushite Egyptian* Pharaohs. The premise is that the *Anunnaki* were the *ancient* astronaut's demigod proxies who were installed as the Hamite people's of African dynasties. Demigods were the bloodline descendants of the Anunnaki, great Royal Prince Enki with his accomplished team of biological scientist and medical doctors, their genetic manipulation of DNA successfully created the Adapa/Adamu as a new crossbred Homosapeins sapiens on the planet Earth. Enki was the extraterrestrial alien flight mission commander of the first Anunnaki clan voyage crew that came down and created the first mission to Earth to establish an exploration base of operation that built an outpost settlement on another orbital planet. Genetically he successfully modified an indigenous Homosapien species' natal Adam and Eve. Meaning that Enki was the god the Bible Genesis narrative tale that did not say Enki was the creator god; or that he fashioned his own genetic DNA image/likeness, or imprint was his manipulation of biological DNA genetic code sequencing, caused the actions which created the crossbred humans Adapa (Adam/man). Remember that the Bible is devoid of the specificity and anecdotal details which the supreme Nibiru's lord god Anu's council of the federation of planetary galaxies commissioned Enki with the authority to initiate a creation of primitive humans as a servile race, and it was successfully brought to fruition out during the earth mission voyage is the biblical God of the Bible's Genesis creation story. Civilization owes much acknowledgement to the original custodians being extraterrestrial, manlike Sumerian gods of wisdom of the Law of One love and magic. And before the great flood his father Anu (An) Nibiru's Supreme God of the sky (heaven) and the Earth (the Mother Goddess), Ki and King of the *Annunaki, Nibiru royal elite* Prince Enki (Ea) and Enlil. Anu the Anunnaki, came down to the Earth to settle sibling disputes between his sons Enki and Enlil was settled as a *trialogue* agreement, Anu would resolve the matter of their clan rivalries over territorial land disputes each son was granted as their possession. King Anu came to Earth and listened to all of the siblings arguments, and decided that they would each draw lots. Each took their turn in which Anu would remain the lord of planet Nibiru, with all of the Hamitic peoples' land going to Prince Enki and Enlil receiving the Semitic people's land. So it was a final decision that settled terrestrial integrity distribution.

Author Zachariah Sitchin says that these ancient astronauts' key players were King Anu and his two Royal princes, Enki, and Enlil, the gods that descended from the sky, or shall we say heaven. They were those who descended from Nibiru, a *trialogue* of elite Anunnaki who agreed to divide up the Earth into four regions. Such as is the Egyptian Nile Valley Region which fell under the control of Egypt's chosen Anunnaki ancient astronaut god, Enki/Ptah (the ancient astronaut theory goes on further to claim that Enki/Ptah drained the flood waters and constructed dykes in Egypt to establish the Nile valley civilization arose, which was likely influenced by the Anunnaki alien astronaut imprint and established Egyptians ancient dynastic Kemet culture.

It was to be agreed that straws would be drawn to determine the status of regions each would rule. The results were as follows: (1) King Anu remained the god of the sky (heaven), (2) Lord King Anu made the sibling rivalry toxic because he made his first born son Prince Enlil Supreme lord god of the earth Command; and (3). Prince Enki is actually the personification of the biblical god of heaven earth because his deeds conflate nicely with the speculative views regarding the ancient astronauts theorists hypothesis. This was after the great Noah's flood. A fundamental presupposition is that there is this human and Anunnaki, Nibiru ancient alien bloodline, which is derived by a biological genetic DNA codes, with which delineates through the god Enki (Ea,) had manipulated his own Anunnaki genetic code's DNA with that of an indigenous African female. Enki carefully inserted germinated embryo cells that were fertilized in a clay petri dish; Enki carefully placed them inside six healthy Anunnaki birth mothers' wombs.

The scribes recorded the deed by the Royal Prince Enki, which gave a written account of the creation process that was a matter of the archetypal creation of Adapa/Adam (Man), which is the anecdotal details information regarding Enki Anunnaki likeness/Image was accomplished at Enki's African biology laboratory which was located in great *Zimbabwe,* African were there remains many abandoned gold mines. Of course, the Bible's Genesis creation story does not reflect this connection.

The synopsis of sorts alludes to a geographic location: the African kingdom *Kemetism of Cushite* people's lands of African *Hamite people, i. e. Canaanites* and *Cushites* racial phenotype. The snake logo became very influential in early human societies of both hemispheres. A brotherhood dedicated to the spiritual discipline of the purest attainment of spiritual freedom and the highest plane mental clarity. The brotherhood of the snake opposed the enslavement of spiritual beings, and, according to Egyptian writings, it sought to liberate the human race from custodial bondage. They figure prominently throughout the book of Genesis creation narrative accounts about the Hebrew tribes of the Bible's old testament; they, after all, are the blood descendants of Enki (Yahweh's), chosen people. These are the bloodline precursors descendants of the human race who were carried out of Africa as human livestock.

Black African Hebrew tribe of Judah humanity where victims had their individual dignity and personhood stripped away as buyers' and sales contracted the deed of purchase in a faraway land in slave bondage. Black who became unwitting victims of King of African empires were facilitates involved in the sale and transportation shipments of chained human slaves commercial cargo. Black bodies tightly packed together, into the hulls of large merchant sailing vessels engaged in the diaspora of African Hebrews.

The slaves sales market for buyers and sellers at the major foreign ports auction-houses; for contract sale of black Africans to the highest bidder. Which set the stage for living in the slavery conditions of the brutal plantations's lifetime in bondage (Genesis 15:13) https://www.biblegateway.com/verse/EN/Genesis%2015:13. The indignity was teal and perpetuated on a global scale with arrogance and evil and powerful wealthy men deemed it lawful, and justified as god punishment for the Hebrew sins against God. Really! Was the complete story of the book of the Old Testament mistreated, or arbitrarily manipulated?

Or perhaps we pause to revisit the epoch during the Byzantine emperor Constantine I, which was a vision in the sky that convinced him to suddenly embrace Christian. Which marked the transformation of the new religion away from spiritual science. His conversion elevated orthodox Christian into a religious church authority, as well as the western Roman Catholic Church authority of authoritarian bishops and the pope rulers.

Ergo these actions were manipulated by himHis actions in history spurred the new religious teachings of Christianity, church edicts that converged paganism and spiritual occultism into the orthodoxy worshiping of new age Christian theology. This sinister act was that the do-gooder impulse spurred up from the ruler's aims at self-interest, and not to minister spiritual teachings of true love and salvation in the service of the ordinary people's public *beneficence* to the human understanding of their own consciousness awareness.

What we know is true comes to us from AD 77; the public was brought to submission by the religious authority of church brutal manipulation and *usurpation,* which twisted into a New Testament Roman Catholic spiritual teachings of blind faith Christianity. It was mendacious and audacious; adoption of Christ became the mainstream religion, the embodiment of Christianity, and the reverence of the Cross in the personification of Jesus Christ as Christianity's new age doctrine and creeds emerged as this blind faith religion of falsehood came to fusion under emperor Constantine I convened church bishops in 325 A. D. First *Ecclesiastical* council in a transformational, one religious consciousness. He exploited indigenous primitive Australopithecus cultures as a fused element of paganism with the Christian religions into the Christians Church of St.

The Roman pope's supreme authority shrouded Peter of the Apostles of Jesus Christ. "Insofar as historicity is concerned, Christianity was a product of second temple Judaism and first century Roman values. Whereas the cultic practices surround the Mesopotamian Gods Enlil and Enki far predate the origins of Christianity." If you want some valid information go visit https://www.reddit.com/).

The deception is undergirding a blind faith belief by worshiping Christ as the way to salvation after death! Holy Church fathers had proclaimed themselves to be the endowed vicar of the crucifixion of the Christ, Jesus. This *inauspicious* event would signal the emergence of the old spiritual beliefs into the new external empirical world order. Throughout the eons of time there is a compelling urge to gain total power and control over human beings through whatever means deemed possible, whether it's taught via religious vestiges of the Old Testament's initial biblical Israelites, the Jewish seed of Abraham, authentic peoples' ties to the sacred occult teachings. My friends, please take note of the brutal persecution, war, and territorial conquests by the Romans emperors' embrace of a state sanctioned religion. This transformation of the Kemetism occultists (hidden mysteries) African/Egyptian spiritual teachings of the *Shetaut Neter* was the reworked whitewashed Christianity religious teachings stolen from the original black peoples of the Hebrew people's lands of the biblical narrative story. With the Romans in control of the ancient external empirical world in AD 325, this falsehood emerged as the rulers twisted the Bible's history.

They set out to systematically whitewash the Nubian African images from black to the European white Jesus as the Son of Gods is the mires of a stupendous truthiness. With impunity, they taught the new religious Gospel teachings of the Holy Trinity. With deliberate intentions this was a mendacious scheme to institute a falsity. The institution of a religious order to establish control of the popular religious African optic set of Christianst was embraced by kings who seized their opportunity to create wealth after the crucifixion of the Hebrew, Jesus Christ segwayed into the Catholic Church authority to create a stream of wealth, power, and control. The deviation of a monumental complex consequence marked by irrefutable oppression; with the effectiveness of the overall population spurred by the migration of the Israelite or Canaanite Jews had sought safety, poured into the interior plains of Africa, the Nubian peoples' territorial lands. For might this holy book of the Bible Genesis narrative account, the curse of African Israelites (blacks) escaping the Romans persecutions had left the territorial lands of *Canaan* and retreated into their Hamitic ancestors' lands where were captured by the blacks, Arabian, and European slave traders.

The nascence foretold by Enlil the Anunnaki, Lord of the mission Earth command, or shall we say god *Yahweh's* black Hebrew people of the *Israelites* tribe Judah. Yahew, god's so-called people were captured, chained, sold to the buyers of European slave trading company's. Africans were tightly packed into the hull of cargo ships during the insidious inhumanity of the years of the trans-Atlantic slave trade. Black people became victims of this commercial sanctioned global enterprise of unspeakable evidence of gross genocide. Herein began the diaspora of black Hebrew bodies taken from their ancestors' homeland who lost racial and tribal identity. This was indeed the beginning of the Christian European chronicles of whitewash and the interpolation of religious falsehood. A transformation of the tribe of Judah who were fleeing into Africa to the Romans persecutions, and they were then sold as chattel into a life of bondage in strange lands. A terrible future awaited those who survived the middle passage, tightly packed in close quarters laying body to body in crowded conditions of slavey diaspora of commercial merchants' trading vessels carried loads captured African.

They were savagely chained together and shipped to various parts of the world aboard slave ships that departed from the African western shores to lands across the Atlantic as nonhuman slaves cargo. Such fate that came to fruition was the yolk of the African Negro Hebrews, we're the *biblical Jew's* capacity. The African tribe of Judah was scattered into many nations' lands as free manual labor (Deuteronomy 4:27 K J V; Genesis 13-15; Jeremiah 15:14). As with any valid identity, there is always much scholarly erudition of the facts that was not respectable of will, and evil intention challenges history. I respect other points of view. Which my mind thinks outside the box. Well, it's because there is but one thing for certain: most people who are faithful followers of religious teachings and biblical ritual reject this notion of Afrikan/Egyptian spiritual wisdom of the Law of One love as pagan mythology.

Yet these are folks who would deny that the eponymous chosen people of God are people of color, right? For who would go so far as to straight-up conceal facts and be misled by deception by ancient astronauts. Whereas biblical Genesis narrative is inextricably the beginning of this hidden mystery truth about Prince Enki's fusion of his DNA. He fused it with the indigenous African female's species with his alien DNA, which spurred the Genesis creation story. As the Nibiruan chief biological scientist, Enki successfully genetically fashioned Adam (man) as the crossbred human son *Noah,* viz., and *avo vobo* is the Anunnaki Royal Prince Enki's is tied to African nascence, by the genetic engineering of the DNA chromosome bloodline that delineates a fusion of the indigenous females Mitochondrial DNA connection with the Hamite. They became victims of European interlopers invaded and conquered long before the Roman Europeans in

77 AD. What followed was their actions to transform the spiritual teachings/learning of spiritual occultists' Law of One.

They were instrumental in recasting and mistranslating the holy book, purposefully excised by the rise of the brutal Romans hegemony yoke of oppression and their reworking of *Kemetism* righteousness teachings. It was truncated and denigrated by the Romans' Catholic religious orthodox reworking of the sacred wisdom of the Law of One love.

The Bible book lacks *instituted Christianity, devoid of the proper acknowledgment of the Sumerian Anunnaki as the extraterrestrial alien* connection. Of which giant manlike ancient astronauts' presence on Earth has long since been viscerally silenced by the new external empirical world emergence in the annals of AD millennial external empirical world's order. A conspicuously distortion of biblical Genesis 1. Ergo, indigenous ancient Sumerian tribe members wittingly worshiped Enki as their city-state's titular god.

It was founded in circa 5400 BCE. It was thought to have been created by the great Royal Prince Enki (Ea) by the Akkadians, and was worshiped as their local god of fresh waters. Enki was the god of the wisdom of the Law of One love and magic (among other attributes), with deities such as Anu, Enlil, and Inanna (July 20, 2010, (https://www.ancient.eu/eridu/).

The original olden times custodial settlers, presence of Enki ancient astronauts landed in Mesopotamia, and built the first city-states of ancient Mesopotamian. Biblical Genesis is a truthiness because it is missing the real true nascence; making no mention of the arrival of ancient space-traveling astronauts being d as the Anunnaki's alien beings who were the original custodian's settlers. They were lage alien extraterrestrials who had advanced knowledge, then I would presuppose that it stands to the inclination of human scientist fascination beings behind NASA efforts to explore other distant cycles of the planet solar systems cosmic space exploration of planets beyond earth surface. Yeah. One could support such as being closely akin to the ancient astronaut's theorists hypothesis of old gods: Those who from Heaven came from the sky reconciled with Sumerian cuneiform clay tablets have revealed, meaning the African spiritual science principles conflate the theology that undergirds the Egyptian sun god Aten Ra's practice of one love in fellowship. A fundamental adherence to embrace the learning and teachings of the esoteric wisdom principles of the conscious awareness of the psychospiritual nous of the cultivation of inner peace, quiet comfort, and spiritual solace that resides in your mind, body, spirit complex as it is god's temple of the brotherhood of being initiated into your spirit consciousness unity with your Godself.

The priestly temple of the secret society was derived when the Royal great prince Enki created the first homo sapiens sapiens. It was by fusion of his imprint; it was his manipulation of the Anunnaki and African female's bloodline that spurred the temple of the serpent brotherhood of the sacred initiation! This is a spurious deception and pernicious Hebrew and Greek Septuagint mistranslations of the Anunnaki's original Sumerian Holy Bible is not the whole story.

Do we call it into question? The titular gods of the Bible story doesn't provide the real narrative tale of the extraterrestrial aliens' presence in ancient Mesopotamia: they were the *Anunnaki* of planet *Nibiru*. So might this exegesis about the archeological discoveries reveal strong evidence that these extraterrestrials were indeed the earth's original custodian settlers of our planet? The olden time gods who were the ancient astronauts alien Gods featured in the Bible Genesis narrative tale. How do I say this is absolutely true?

Well then, what? The Genesis narrative event when Anunnaki aliens from the sky came down is the story that is missing from the Bible and doesn't allude to Enki's mission purpose. Their underlying intentions were simply interpolate ambiguity to postulate a hyperbolic perspective air of mystery that is devoid of any specificity and anecdotal details of clarity. Only the statement that began in the beginning God created the earth in six days? Did it not speak that these were the words of the God of heaven (planet-X, Nibiru)? This planet has a far-flung elliptical orbit, according to the astrological observations charts concurs with the ancient astronaut: those who from the Heavens came" down on the Earth mission voyage. It was a fifty man astronaut crew that descended from the higher constellation orbital plane to establish a gold mining production on Earth.

Royal Prince, the creator god who built a civilization on the Earth's interior plane of ancient Mesopotamia, in the land of Sumer. Those who called themselves the Black Heads. The Anunnaki race told them they descended from their home planet, *Nibiru*.

These extraterrestrial beings used their advanced superior knowledge of science and technology to initiate a man's space flight spiritual journey to Earth. And from their home in the faraway and above the Earth orbital plane, were the space travelers on an Earth mission voyages. Anunnaki titular gods, their presence had been apparently seen long before the eponymous biblical tale of Noah's flood event! Long before these alien beings had established demigods as rulers, their precursor demigods were the Pharaonic dynastic bloodlines of African-Egyptian kingdoms. The earth mission voyage with which the Anunnaki Supreme Gods of the planet Nibiru assigned to his son Royal Elite Prince Enki. His intrepid fifty-man astronaut crew were to journey through the asteroid belt, land on the Earth's surface to determine whether the planet contained sufficient quantities of material gold, was converted into monatomic gold particles and shipped back to Nibiru.

According to Zechariah Sitchin's account, the Anunnaki Enki's mission required the construction of a landing spaceport platform on earth. The Enki astronaut construction project included skilled engineers who, according to the master blueprint, built the first city-state settlement. And began the task of mining gold from near the Persian Gulf. Only discovering that gold was found to be insufficient, and the decision was taken to relocate the production operation was moved to the Southeastern region of great Zimbabwe, Africa, where the production supply of gold deposits was extracted from the gold mines, Prince Enki/Ea operation was full speed ahead. Ancillary to his primary mission objective and underlying purpose, he established his biological genetic research scientist laboratory. The creation of Adam and Eve was fashioned in the African landscape.

What seems quite certain is that in the beginning, at birth, is a journey to find the luminous divine pathway toward the sacred law of one love, learning and teaching the Egyptian Kemetic spiritual science religion of daily calm meditation. A gift of life entity separated condition that is the underlying substrate of earthly existence. That Enki's DNA genetic engineering imbued homosapien Adapa (Adam) with his anunnaki image and likeness spurred the ancestral bloodline of the elite pantheon Royal prince Enki by manipulation of His ties to the indigenetic DNA codes he fashioned with the DNA genetic codes of an indigenous African female facilitated the creation of a new Homosapiens race inside of a sterile clay *petri-dish*.

Under Enki's leadership, the direction was facilitated by his biological, genetic skilled medical research doctors and scientists. All of whom were instrumental in the embryonic genetic manipulation procedure in the creation process and procedures that fashioned Adapa (Adam/man) on the earth.

What took place created crossbred human beings who were to serve the Anunnaki gods as primitive workers, a slave species to carry out the manual labor that came to fruition by Enki's in South African research laboratory in great Zimbabwe, Africa. This team of the Anunnaki scientists fashioned the first Adam (man) while living on the surface of planet earth--and not from the dust of the earth.

What seems clear to Enki, is that he possessed the requisite knowledge of having the medical knowledge profile of the god of creation. Because he was qualified and recognized as the chief medical officer of planet Nibiru. His father Anu sent the great Royal prince Enki to lead the vanguard mission earth voyage to verify and confirm whether large quantities of gold deposits was sufficient to fulfill the steady requirements needed to save planet Nibiru's dwindling atmosphere. Given that Enki was Nibiru's god of water, semen, wisdom, magic spells and chief biological, scientists, and medical doctor on planet Nibiru. His tale of Adam's creation on the earth he had documented in the *Seven Tablets of the Creation* text records this monumental nascence, giving the anecdotal details about how Enki had successfully fashioned his *Adam(s)* and *Eve(s)*, the prototype crossbreed human on the planet Earth's interior plane. Creator of human beings as the alien gods' primitive workers. The Anunnaki's alien god Enki fashioned humans to replace the *Igigi* gold mining free labor workforce that had been performing the heavy backbreaking toil of demand to excavate gold from inside the hot deep mining production operations. Prince Enki was given command of the operational task to extract gold from the Southern land of great Zimbabwe, Africa. Whereof archaeological discovery of seven ancient cuneiform clay tablets revealing the inscription of a biological crossbred indigenous hominid female human ancestors' *African* and *Anunnaki* biological alien DNA code has roots are derived from the extraterrestrial alien titular gods from the home planet Nibiru (heaven). For learning about this you must read the Book by Zecharia Sitchin: *The Lost Book of Enki: Memoirs and Prophecies of an Extraterrestrial God.*

And you will also want to accompany the volume to The Earth Chronicles series that reveals the identity of humanity's ancient gods. Zechariah Sitchin's series of informative books explains why these Anunnaki gods descended from their home planet Nibiru to the earth plane of orbit, genetically engineered Homo sapiens sapiens. The truth revealed in this revelation has spurred a plethora of informative books that will blow your mind! But at the same time I can not believe that many adults know nothing about the ancient astronauts theorists hypothesis. We have never been taught this insight into the *eponymous* Anunnaki, Igigi, and UFO alien who was a god that came from Heaven and had a half brother, Enlil is not mere folly or poppycock.

Yet the truth is always rooted in logic and of the curious neophyte. My beloved family and friends understand why (1) Constantine and the bishops of the Council of Nicaea (325). The centrally placed and haloed emperor established the doctrinal creed. He was introduced by the Bishops who attended the Council of Constantinople to define the nature of Jesus Christ an (381). A religious transformation became the mainstream debated divinity, during the AD 325 and 381 Bishops at the council of *Nicaea* introduced a Catholic Church New Testament, Bible, teachings of western theology with Jesus Christ as the *de facto* vicar of the God of Christian religious rites and ritual. It seized absolute authority and became the movement's *de facto* spiritual consciousness arbiter of god with the power to condemn heretical views of what they deemed crimes against god. Many unjust decisions taken in the name of god's came during a disturbing period of extremely volatile means by evoking Christianity as a philosophy of god's religion was promulgated as blatant truthiness.

Roman Catholicism Religionist Faith Supplanted Spiritual Theology

The central Roman Catholic papacy authority organized religion and decreed blind faith and intolerance; a shameful period of what brutality can persecute opponents of the age twisted interpretation of new religionist theology. Note that in 325 AD, religious Bishops were convened by the Roman emperor, Constantine I; to forge/formulate the one Bible of Christianity.

This convergence of the spiritual cult theology allowed Christianity to embrace the popular belief that was acceptable to the ruling authorities of both religions and the power of Rome. Which was tantamount to being an appeasement, had been the mendacious scheme that cemented the Catholic faith and the Protestant faith inculcation of a New Testament tradition, which even deviated from the eastern philosophy of Orthodox Christianity had been transformed into the spreading of the gospel doctrine of the blind faith established as a foundation of organizing religion through the crucified personification of God as Jesus Christ! Israel Jewish and Christians. A history of organized central religion authority emerged from its despicable crimes against humanity that had been sanctioned by the pope's of Rome. So guilty of carrying out a ruthless killing of innocent people who were sentenced to death for acts of heresy against the power of the church's authority (https://www.medievalists.net/2011/08/in-her-voice-the-destruction-of-the-cathars-in-languedoc/).

I'm repulsed by the many evil machinations of humankind, those folks who profess themselves to be doing the will of their God in heaven have been guilty for committing audacious crimes of evil and violent actions against humanity. The pages of violence against humanity historical archive reflects the senseless acts of gratuitous sanguine killing of innocent people to be falsely accused and in the name of God's convicted and sentenced folks to death for blasphemy or religious heresy if they had dared to speak out against Christianity.

Or had refused to follow in the worshiping of ecclesiastical religious teachings of the church's gospel doctrine according to the Roman Catholic and Protestant dogmatic canons, creeds, and Holy doctrines as infallible. They received a public punishment demonstration or activity with which they deemed to be blasphemy or heresy. What was done in the name of God is unconscionable, a mendacious evil lust for wealth and power and control of humankind by religious misdirection from spiritual meditation worship of God!

Organized Religion Centralized Authority

So, my friends, I wish you a warm and gracious good day to indulge in a calm cathartic peregrination. To apprehend these creative prose comes alive as my creative psychological imagination.

Diegesis of Ancient Astronauts Titular God

But it's important that I introduce myself. Hello, my friends! I'm Hakeem R. Jelani. And of course, you don't know me, but this is my *non-diegetic* explanation of Genesis narrative historical event. First off, there's two things you should know about me: (1) I am awakened and a seeker of spiritual wisdom of the Law of One love, sacred principles that provides insight into the spiritual external empirical world; and viz., meaning having the clarity of understanding of the recondite and esoteric sacred mysteries. To discern truth and knowledge with which derives a manifestation of sapience wisdom of the Law of One, sacred principles' endued enlightenment with consciousness awareness. (2) I am attuned in my thoughts that seek to be in harmonic balance of mind/body/spirit complex in life through meditation using logic and reason in the way I think. (3) I'm not a religious zealot who is dogmatic, but I seek the erudition of actual knowledge.

Yet it's appropriate for me to tell you that I am a thinker whose eyes are no longer blinded by the scheme and truthiness regarding the ancient biblical gods of the biblical genesis narrative. I am awakened. I am a fellow neophyte who gives thanks to the infinite eternal intelligent infinity—the infinite creators spirit you who are so gracious enough to reveal that we have a common curious, inquisitive mind to seek the wisdom of the Law of One love of knowledge about: the Anunnaki alien gods were ancient astronauts who descended aboard advanced spacecraft in ancient Mesopotamia. The current UFO phenomenon makes this a seemingly credible speculation about this theory. Yeah, this particular moment, if you consider that NASA is planning to venture into deep spacecraft astronauts pilots will soon travel to the planet Mars and beyond into the outer reaches of the vast cosmic frontier. I deeply appreciate the information about these subject-matter books. I am forever grateful and forever indebted to them for their stellar published books about the extraterrestrial AUVs/UFOs.

Now that you have made it this far! This says that truth and wisdom resonate with clarity in this state of spiritual intuition as the enlightenment is the light in harmonic balance. Whereof wisdom and insight is your logic, reason, and understanding of your existence in God's empirical illusory external world reality. Living at peace and from the extraneous daily distortions cloud your judgment. My overall purpose for this book is to inform those misled. The people whose life is mired in a web of willful distortions are disconnected and competitive vibrations of the mind/body/spirit avatar complex teach/learn of the *Neberdjer* universal intrinsic and monad Law of Oneness, as it pertains to this explanation.

It's surely nonfiction. It's of course written as evocative prose that aims to inspire controversy concerning Christianity and dovetails with the modern view that seemingly harkens back to the eponymous Ancient Astronaut Theorist view for the reader's curious ruminations, juxtaposition to alien UFOs viz., alien Anunnaki titular gods!

Bible Genesis Gods And Alien Astronauts Anu, Enlil, And Enki

This is a semi-fictional *diegetic* storytelling that presents a reexamination of the nascent story of the biblical tale; the natal nature of human life, speciality of the surface illusion of oneiric love; and esoteric of light within an external empirical world of convergence and divergence. To allow the readers and the listeners to enjoy this manuscript as an imaginary poppy, ostensibly composed as evocatively creative semi-fictionalized entertainment for ruminations. Themes about one's very own life of the everyday world shared experiences. Those excursions that are replete with the missing anecdotal details. This is an exegesis on the Old Testament to target folks who are genuinely curious about this external empirical world illusory temporal reality. First off, I know that you don't know me. But, with spiritual intuition I elucidate for the erudition of knowledge about deep spirit intuition that is consciousness awareness.

This Is Quite An Extraordinary Topic

Stick with me on this my friends. I am Hakeem R. Jelani, a thinker and a neophyte and I was born in America. To be clear let me say that many years ago I was born, died, and incarnated here on the earth. A time of that was austere for blacks descendants of the diaspora, save for the story told to me a my six siblings, I know not but a fraction of the social economic constraints of the living conditions of the constricted oppression of the blacks sharecroppers who suffered from the southern conscious bias of the Jim Crow laws as my remembrance. Only that it was somewhere in the past, completely buried and lost only to receive my new animated mind/body/spirit complex. It's all of the achieved records of my primordial nascence of my spirit essence of a natal in transformation into the life peregrinations through manifestation and reincarnations. The re-awakened to experience the present time space continuum to live, learn/teach others in service to the spirit of the ubiquitous Infinite Creator. The god of the all divine pleroma endued this gift that is my mind, body, and spirit complex animates me with the lifeblood of the divine light force energy to fulfill my life purpose by the power of the all ubiquitously most high's energy that is the cause of my actions as a physical embodiment. Human material entities as a conscious level of the sensate view as human existence in the time space continuum of

THE MIND,BODY, SPIRIT,ANDSTORYTELLING

intelligent energy of the universal infinity, viz., the all illusory and material consciousness.

The spark of my soul is this living spirit of nature; it was April 1952. It was eighty-seven years after the American Civil War, between the union of states of Northern and Southern states. History as America's bloodiest war that ended enslavement's brutal oppression of Enki (gods) chosen black peoples of Hebrews in a strange far away land of the American homelands, to include the negroe shipped from Africa for four hundred years. To this fact I have witnessed my own awakening. I am not unlike so many of my race whose original identity was eviscerated by Europeans machinations, to denigrate and suppress other nations' cultures, history description refers to them as aggressive invaders whose powerful military forces erased the Hebrew ancestors' family roots through slavery. Such as it was the recording of the genesis of my peoples; it came to represent this shameful prior in which the indigenous African-Hebrew peoples experienced. By the continuum, I emerged into this period as a new child embodiment on my natal date. For my remembrances of my past life history truncated every past experienced illusory.

Now in the presence to live with my new life purpose to love and to be loved by others in this illusory world reality of life time/space continuum. I seek genuine heartfelt love and tranquil life experiences of joy in nature's beautiful bucolic rolling countryside vistas of thick forest canopy of inner peace solace, with tranquility and quiet comfort of mental harmonic balance synced with the Infinite Creator as a unity spirit vibration. To understand the unique spiritual beginning by means of incarnation into the cycle of life. descended into the space continuum; that it is true that humans have all been born naked, like others who are reborn into the animated body as a unique individual human soul embodiment. The incarnations of spiritual essence alive in the new material period in an embryonic state; in birth and *peregrination into* death throes upon the interior Earth plane. A blank page upon Anunnaki, Sumerian Bible chapter 1 delineated from the beginning of the extraterrestrial alien who came from the sky to earth, that monumental event is not a myth; it's the incomplete story known as the holy book of Genesis which should be regarded as history of the ancient astronauts earth landing in ancient Mesopotamia. Within this original Bible text known as the *Enūma Eliš* Babylonian creation myth, that is the *Asher Hassus*.

The full measure of fidelity in judgment of one's life purpose: learning to fulfill your purposeful life! This to love one's self and to be loved by our other human selves. That to know of myself as a person born to live beneath the vaulted blue and white skydome. Living every day, breathing in the pristine breath of air that flows is this magnificent effulgent warmed by sunlight, by day beginning when the sunshine rises and moves westward amid the atmospheric clouds of crepuscular soft clouds standing against the blue sky canvas drifting above the earth. This illusory depicts a manifestation of the visual *anachronistic* material space beneath the metaphysical evolution of time and space reality. Religion was a blind faith theology teachings of Christianity. The sons and daughters born of mother and father are living shepherds of god through this world, as the spirit of the individual's personhood comes into existence by the usual way. An incarnation beheld by lovely parents.

To learn the understanding of life's purpose whilst I experience all of these things of my ephemeral illusory. Life in its straightaways is replete with blind spots that twists and turns along the pathway towards the death throes of God's harvest.

With the sentient clarity of spiritual principles of unity; the morality of Infinite Creator's Law of One. Existence is the Intelligent of the Infinite Creative flow of the life force energy that manifests my mind/body/spirit complex as the embodiment of corporeal human form. The gift of nature with the free will consciousness to cause my avatar to animate, influence, and experience the distortion of my actions. My evolution and involution as a human being, living in the Earth's interior plane within the perception of the illusory temporal, temporal reality.

Yeah, my spirit spurred every action of force energy via free will as a consciousness awareness awakened by the spark of this epoch of incarnation into the world to live. By the circumambulation cycles through the twelve zodiac houses, cosmic manifestation at the time. The labor of my Mother was a physical form of mind/body/spirit

THE MIND, BODY, SPIRIT, AND STORYTELLING

complex born under the time cycle sign of Taurus the bull. A time/space to mark the date when I came forth into the life/love/light present time-space continuum cycle. My gift of life and my parents whose purpose was to shepherd me towards my peregrinations from my birthplace in the Southern State of Jackson, Tennessee, of the United States of America. The living essence of my form was delivered to live together in a two parents' home. It was born in this illusory reality by the hands of the midwife, I emerged from the embryonic development and morphogenesis state.

Whereof my frail infant human body was delivered, my tiny body was born then wrapped in a blanket and placed in my mothers waiting arms. Souls come into this mystery life not by a living myth, of or by the Isis and Osiris gods of Egyptians spiritual science, wisdom of the sacred spiritual priesthood.

Yet I have acquired the god's knowledge through learning and teaching the luminous divine Kemetic philosophy: meaning a belief in the God Ra's "Law of One" in the Yoga meditation that is the way. It had a significance, meaning denizens born on the earth. And might this be the most accurate thing about life that we would want to know? That life's embryonic growth began as an embryonic fetus developed in the womb, until the light forced energy. A beautiful life to experience many things before leaving the dead cold lifeless body when it stiffened from the rigamortis of melancholy of the death cycle.

Evolution into the perception of temporal reality of the changes from the epoch of times of the eons is history. Everybody is turning around and twisting upwards in the cycle of measured time in the light of day and the darkness of night to live by the Sunlight! With symphonic wave vibrations, a melding cacophony of noise distortions by the mind, body, and spirit complex.

An all inclusive unity of the human social complex. From the date of my birth, there was a spark that caused me to wake up and grow in the solar days and lunar nights of restorative sleep to awaken the mind/body/spirit complex. Rested in subtle motion until awakened from God's law of free will. I am of the present time-space, alive; the annual harvest death recalls my soul from the Earth. I am like any other human individual separate of animated human units from the one infinite creator, imbued life by luminous divine *Nebedjer*! According to the African-Egyptian Kemeticism Spiritual science principles of intelligent infinity of the Creator. Knowledge that we are all of the one cosmic unity, human individual units as avatars, reflective of the intelligent *Nebegdjer* of God. A store that is promulgated as religious theology which teaches other human entities. God created a myth without any *coincident* connection to the Anunnaki god Enki! His manipulation of his Anunnaki race DNA biological genetic code with an indigenous African female's genetic DNA codes, which Enki fertilized in a biologists sterile clay laboratory petri-dish. These fertilized embryonic cells were the essence of two life forms. God placed it inside of six Anunnaki Nibiruan female birth mothers' wombs. Enk's procedure worked when Adam was and Even took their first breaths. On the African landscape, in Enki's biological genetics laboratory the anonymous Adapa (Adamu), the first prototype homosapien sapien was born. But the manner in which the major religions have been promoting this event pushes their false narrative as if Enki (god) scooped up some clay and simply breathed life into it to create an animated man. It's a blatant falsehood; and it should buy the mind of a child, because like me and others, have been anesthetized by this blind faith allusion!

The natal nature of a chosen peoples disobedience! Those who were found unfaithful did not know of the learning/teaching about the fidelity of the self sacred principles and wisdom of the Law of One *Nebedjer*! From my adolescence, I was in search of this pathway to higher blessing through means of prayerful meditation. And not ever knowing what one's meaningful life purpose is to live to become like *Marjhru meaning a pure warm heart* and teaching the ways of the infinite creator. The spirit of all is one unity of mind/body/spirit complex in harmonic balance. Yeah. My essence had been withdrawn back into the third level of the density of humankind who seek salvation. To experience temporal reality until I sojourn and enter through the gateway of my death cycle into the *akashic field*, into the Egyptians *Halls of Amenti*. An entity that is no longer the embodiment of my human physical form, material image that folds my soulful spirit essence lives on.

Though seemingly bemused, I am alive and asleep and dreaming. The body is imbued with my animated spirit essence to enjoy the beingness until the coming of human harvest from the imaginary realm of existence. And my body lies still and empty in a sublime recombinant state of inner peace, quiet comfort, and solace. In rest, free from life's daily frivolity, devoid of dissertations and distortions. I saw that light and walked across transportine entrance straight into the ephemeral dream space through the luminous gateway glow of the bright crystal lighted dimension of the excursive surreal realm. And to my delight a treasure of the most marvelous of sights was a material world of illusion as everything visible seemed to appear before our eyes everyday under the skydome dome of the grand architect of the universal garden of Eden. Long before the time for the eyes depictions of a beautifully biosphere of my refractive vision of the mind streaming episodes of colorful artistic displays of an illustrative parlance for the intelligent energy duality, of the illusory reality and surreality. So let me say that I am appreciative that you have tuned your ears to allow your mind to freely imbibe up the philosophical theological expressions of my literary creative trope and *metromania*. Twisting perception serpentines through luminous chapters or levels of psychological storied entertainment. Now get ready to open up the mind's discipline to attend your ears with learning and teaching the spiritual discipline of the *Neberdjer* spirit complex alignment with the *Shetaut Neter spirituality philosophy*.

You are about to become scent into the infinite creator's law of one, uniform intelligent infinity of the soulful spirit's *pleroma* of luminous divine metaphysics. The excursions and experiences of love, conscious life of experiences. Where you are about to enter into the mind's space and drift on a journey into the anachronistic realm of oneiric illusory temporal reality. My soul sojourns alive amid experience, going hither and thither via the third eye into the psychological streaming odyssey of dreams episodes. A realm of the creative dimensions of entertainment is an external empirical world of imagination that has become my new labor of my heartfelt love.

HAKEEM R. JELANI

We are all unique living individuals, a and fleshy human entity with curious-minded freewill thinkers; each individual is inviting others to share their understanding of spiritual wisdom and science philosophy and guided by the positive energy of the divine life force animated as a conscious human consciousness in total inner peace with mental harmonic balance in quiet comfort and peaceful solace. A silent moment in calm and prayerful meditation from the temporal reality time-space continuum into the inward spirit dimensions of divine *pleroma that* permeates the sacred realm of the dynamic cosmic universe.

The psychological religion of the *Neberdjer's* Law of Correspondence apply to the ancient Egyptian spiritual sacred principles of contiguous duality cycle reflects the cycles of the radiance the effulgent sunlight that rise in its rotations of daylight and darkness turnstile of the terrestrial temporal reality as mind/body/spirit complex, animated activities of my conscious and unconscious state oneiric illusion of daylight activities and going to sleep at night fluidly dreaming illusion of heartfelt prose titillation the rhythms of the waves sound vibrations as a psychological transformation into streaming visual animated of dream episodes.

To be awake to the *permutations* in sync with the facets of learning about the material reality forms of disciplines. We are individuals who navigate through the polarity of reality and surreality as the life spirit essence, which lies the cause behind decisions and actions. Neophytes who seek to become one with the ubiquitous infinite intelligent creator god of all existence above and below. Each soul is born as individual separate living entities of the highest intelligence. Always humble and pure at heart. Being of a free mind without turpitude or world's indulgences and embracing knowledge, understanding, and wisdom expression of evocative prose; and imbibe Kemeticism teaching for others erudition of knowledge.

For you are about to experience the knowledge lifesaving principles of Kemetism to achieve a warm loving heart and mental harmonic balance. Meaning that innate application of the introspective and extrospection who understand our manifestations is by divine spirit energy syncs with the luminous divine universal cosmic harmonic waves vibrations. All luminous divine things unbounded, the reflections thereof we observe in many forms of my creative expressions.

The deep thoughts of my intuition unfolds this sensory enlightenment, with clarity of thoughts devoid of unfettered psychological consciousness biases that must be purged from the human mind, body, spirit complex. That essence of life is the spirit that causes negative and positive actions and deeds as consciousness awareness. free will, and with discernment of foresight to break from the psychological bondage of negative and live a positive journey with a pure heart. And while thereof being in illusory temporal reality. To be alive your spirit is a separated unit of god. To know of the true inner spirit life force energy, recognizable as a physical form of living material substance that streams as *oppopee*. It's therefore fitting that thank you for spending time reading or listening to these words as my deep spiritual intuition reveals this creative fiction. The empirical external world curiosity. Please permit me to say this: I am tipsy with ease and feeling blessed by the high spirit of the one universal unity of divine creation. To be as humble as I am becoming inspired by the wisdom endued by the luminous divine all *rubric,* which is the spirit of avant-garde *prose* conveyance of these confabulations.

The melodiously conjugated poetic rhyme prose verses of invariably the effervescence of expressions of nature dictation of the embryonic stem of the source of life, which comes forth to live by the light force energy and love our other selves, are the conversant with the universal unity vibration harmonic balance with unity and love for all individuals of the human families' tree of life!

Sentimental prose and semi-fictional illusory perception

Notable examples of the creative depictions of every day or mundane serendipitous nuisances events in aspects waxing the everyday world shared. This cognitive perception of Earth's daily illusory temporal reality and the illusory of ephemeral illusory temporal reality. A purposeful Life and to follow the will of the spirit journey seeking a purified heart of the mind, body, and soul. To appreciate life and love the infinite Creator's benevolent gift to find happiness and providence and salvation. This magnificent parlance is subjective interpolations with confabulations of subjective encapsulation within the cerebral moods.

You are letting me take you along the way with the confluence themes that perfectly meld in sync with the unity of sagacious consciousness awareness and perception of illusory depictions. The ineffable visions of unbridled thoughts and behaviors of sentient human beings as individuals living units in the interior plane of the living illusory temporal reality of earth's luminous divine is that of which all humans beings are uniquely separated from the grand all divine essence that is streaming consthe universal creative entertainment. It's this magnificent pleroma of creative illusory visions streaming oneiric realm. Enter into the lighted gateway of the dream dimension of the mercurial realm is the sleep cycles into ephemeral night dreams of the psychological mind space. Where our bodies lie resting in a *recumbent* state as the mind apprehended beautiful illusory episodic depictions. Three magnificent, beautiful marble water fountains were centrally placed to complement the landscape of the colorful arrangement of that featured in this magnificent palace courtyard that was idyllic with flora and white doves, and ducks roamed freely in this magnificent world; and it was a perfect beautiful place. It was extraordinarily so perfect to see it in nature, displaying an omnifarious *biosphere,* including all different varieties of stupendous beautiful lush garden landscaped courtyard view landscape of colored flora.

It was quite illustrative of divine intelligence of the seeds *efflorescence* in as a microcosm of the intelligence that is nature's milieu cycles of new shoots bursting into the light to grow by sunlight. The air felt cool, and I could smell hibiscus, roses, jasmine, cherry blossoms, sunflowers, daffodils, and magnificent willow trees displaying various shades of lush verdant summer landscapes and postcard-worthy fall colors. Bushes meticulously pruned with noticeable perfection.

A breathtaking display of flora arrangement of contrasting beautiful colorful flowers with captivating contrast arrangements with

THE MIND, BODY, SPIRIT, AND STORYTELLING

meticulous care that demonstrated a high level of artistic perfection. I admire this beautiful courtyard of this stupendously well-maintained garden vista was fantastic to apprehend. Such a magnificent place where I imbibed vistas and smelled those aromatic scents essence flowers effervescent. I beheld the natural effulgence that grew there. I tarried for a moment, then meandered to observe those delicate leaves swaying as if they were simply dancing with the majestic to see as I sensed the motion. I beheld the most colorful courtyard that was an extraordinary exemplar display of fauna and flora of nature's breathtaking beauty growing alongside the white limestone surface winding pathway. I walked there and thought about this beautiful scenery; I was besotted and unaware and telling myself, don't let this place get to me. Don't get caught up in this surreal place. Seemingly, though, it occurred to me that I was alive in this place—totally free from my body's physical bondage. This reality is heavily laden with financial woes derived from our monetary markets fluctuating economic uncertainty, and the irreversible runaway government deficits, higher inflation; and individual's personal irrepressible credit card debt bondage syndrome. Families today, of every means, are headed for a very *unpropitious!* There's this high probability of vast waves of potential social decline. The *hedonistic* manifestation of depravity pervasive within the social culture, political parties amid the volatility of the external empirical world economy. This is exceedingly problematic, for I am inviting the universal listening audience to indulge in these cathartic *ataraxia.* For I have genuine respect and appreciation for folks who are fans of my extraordinarily creative *avant-garde* prose collection.

Yeah, indeed this is an incredible fabricated work of fiction. What a fantastic psychological symbolic depiction of separate individuals' souls who shared a common human experience in a social collective. It is the sunshine of the forenoon that marks every unit of time we live as a spirit embodiment surrounded by I communicating with nature in its positive and negative life force energy that pervades through this cosmic universe vibrations. psychological efflorescence manicured the garden's milieu of *flora* and *fauna.* Each morning and evening diurnal and nocturnal illusory reality and illusory temporal reality—frames of days and nights within cosmic harmonic waves frequency.

The sun is our life-giving luminous divine radiation of nature. With which sound vibrations predominates and pervades as the life-force energy of the universal cosmic consciousness awareness. A starry realm of space illusory temporal reality.

Living consciousness awareness of the cosmic natures of harmonic unity of spiritual vibrations is intune with humankind; that spirit essence that causes our actions animation. Effects spurred by the human spirit, an individual unit of separation from the universal Infinity's Law of One cosmetic consciousness awareness. The material manifestations, visual form within the realm of this living illusory temporal reality!

The oneiric illusory temporal reality is pellucid. To live is to experience the surface illusion of daily illusory temporal reality perceptions of life's physical excursive experiences in the material things in the terrestrial realm. Buoyant by the third eye subconsciousness, my spirit caused me to drift into nirvana's magnificent places with sublime fulfillment each time period episode and the subtle rhythms pervading on all sides set the mood amid the aromatic herbs of scented pervading subtle psychological enchantment my sensory envisaged. To enter into the realm of the starry arch of this psychological perception. To which I crossbred the transportine crossing of beauty and splendid animation, someplace of unimaginable wondrous scenes. It was so bizarre, like a vivid dream. As I was thinking, I sensed myself panning around this place that was like a desert oasis, as if I was physically there, mingling among others who were all like avatars.

They were engaged in friendly social conversations, with badinage on all sides. I observed and was delighted with the enfoldments within the stupendous storied narrative. Thereof my subconsciousness beheld the most incredible exhibited luxury, and great wealth and prominent class were on full display of glamor. While tightly curated, subtle lilting arrangements melded and pervaded harmonic vibrations of sweet, melodiously soft rhythmic tunes that soothed my soul and enlivened my sensory perception. A visual scene with which my third eye has imbibed a full look at wondrous visualizations. Yet unknowing that my body lies asleep dreaming, devoid of the excursive illusion of the oneiric surreal realm where spirit energy was the cause of this animation is of subconscious awareness. The unselfish cognitive thoughts, spurred my spirit's to cause the subconscious to delight in the *melliferous* wondrous tranquility of my *excursive peregrinations*. I felt captivated by my physical separation from my body. My soul attuned and purged from the vagaries of the corporeal body of evil toxins that underlies the pervasive negative wave vibrations. A new state of beautiful calm spirit external empirical world as the diffused sensory. In a recumbent state of dreaming you have crossed the transportine dreamtime excursion through the pathway to escape from the *earthly dross* of daily frivolity, and *viz.,* your ears are attuned to imbibe things in quiet comfort amid colorful, melodiously beautiful, the rhythm s expressions in the cycles of musically soothing, lilting soft jazz mellifluous tunes buoyed my spirit essence likened to nirvana mirthful touch of inner peace abound. Where the inner spirit came over me as I paused and slowly took a small sip of a neat tincture of Cognac, as it enlivened my mind, soothed my soul, and delighted the senses. A magnificent entertaining quintessence and flora and fauna titillates the mood with a pleasant touch. I was buoyant with the rhythmic sound of my heart beating. One conscious unity of the soul pleroma, into the harmonic vibrations inspirational waves. In this field, intimately transcendent within this spirit unification. To know oneself as a material physical human embodiment that is animated by your spirit that causes our actions by day, and by night, when the body lies resting in a recumbent state of peaceful sleep dreaming in a different dimension.

The human body lies calmly sleeping and resting in bed, dreaming, as our playful spirit is the cause of the third eye acting upon the mental perception. Sensational images of enchanting visualization animated scenes of artists' beautiful mercurial soulful spirit essence that apprehension the *anachronistic* places in quiet comfort, solace, and tranquility nestled in the captivated my serenity vision. This one night I embibe amorphous clouds setting low as if touching the high mountain ranges. It was a wonderful breathtaking vistas of nature. I behold the majestic scenic views as l appreciated with reverence.

You walk fields of the surrounding forested hills, snow-capped tall mountain ridges listen to the trickling rushing waters that traverses the beautiful and colorful vast landscape of the foothills and pastoral valleys, and with awe I appreciated the value of my spirit consciousness awareness and beheld as a remarkable surreal captivating canvas picturesque beauty of nature's bucolic biosphere. Yet all around me as I stood there in my six and twelve posture, watching branches of the leaves swaying as the weather was calm and breezy within the tranquil existence by being amid the forest of nature's tall grass and a tangential cool breeze that touched my face.

I was there enjoying the beautiful spirit energy abounded in nature's season, transitioning green leaves into rustic dead leaves that had withered up and floated from the branches of forest trees. Seemingly dancing back and forth whimsically to the subtle breezes.

Another dimension of space-time delusion is the minds-escape psychological thoughts streaming the episode's perceptive reality. Life events and going inside excursive surrealism, wandering spirit dream odysseys. This is about the light, love, life, and the Egyptian spiritual teachings of theism. The unit essence of the pleroma; the soul as a luminous divine human mind/body/spirit complex.

Which is symbolic of the infinite unity with the *Neberdjuer*. The complexities of ancient mystery spiritual science of the *Shetaut Neter* leads one toward luminous divine salvation after the death of the human body. All forms of the material realm are in sync with the great cosmetic all-perfect unidentified encapsulated illusory temporal reality of the existing cosmic psychic and spiritual universe and order. As such, we have a cosmic law of free will souls endued with energy in this multidimensional diurnal cosmic universe. The universal principle of duality is the illusory reality of light, and darkness cycles amid the spinning balance in the three-dimensional daily space is the dent of the material, aily space is available on days and nights. I appreciated the true beauty of the creation of fulfillment of this divine spirit essence is the cause of my animated soul's living life force energy, adrift and imperceptible sync with the dreamweaver odyssey abounding in the *oneiric* blissful canvas of my surreal unconsciousness illusory state. I tarried until slowly, the darkness began to fade into the dawn before sunlight brought forth.

We are all children of the sun's brilliant rays; we are bathed in the vainglorious worm and life-sustaining orb of yellow, the daily effulgent sun rising into the sky. This gift of life is the material external empirical world's illusion of illusory temporal reality. Feel this intimate sense of emotions; *viz* to indulge by entering upon my formative mind space of subconscious tranquility. Letting one's imagination explore the underlying portraits that is the nature of illusory temporal reality. For it is true, like Adam and Eve, all humans were embryonic animations of physical manifestations; a soul embodiment born as naked sentient corporeal beings. Our purposeful journey towards the purity of love and the light of the living experiences of love, a sense of quiet comfort and solace.

Graciously serve God on the interior plane, provided by the Infinite Creator of life to all people. To learn/teach others to understand oneself is the sacred luminous divine wisdom of intelligent fidelity to infinity—ubiquitous perennial consciousness awareness of the divine mystery.

Your perception is always inclined to subjectivity in a framework of imperialisms; thoughts residing within the constellation's display of life's days as the diurnal binary pattern of oneiric nocturnal and daily illusory temporal reality of sunshine. A symbiotic relationship with its beautiful milieu of the luminous divine surrounding of biological lattice structure array that is the thread, which in a common medium of the creative intelligence and personalism is unique consciousness awareness endued to each individual, unit as a separation from the supreme intelligence of the Infinity Creator of all existence. With knowledge and understanding we all love to share in the common medium of the collective conscious spirit of humanity. Therein lies the esoteric perspective of the mental faculty of the dynamic mind/body/spirit energy complex. Things animated create our illusory world reality is a depiction of the material and the *sensate* of the human existence of beingness. Living beings' underlying substrate. Accordingly, as per the ancient Egyptians, an imaginary astral external empirical world's illusory levels are the episodic unreal temporal reality. Where harmonic vibrations resonate and pervade life waves of esoteric three dimensional terrestrials and celestial space. Perception of illusory temporal reality manifestation of vibrantly unframed visual depictions of the wonderful creative scenes of luminous divine creation. The psychological breathtaking iconic *oneiric* paradisiacal unity of existence.

A beingness of the luminous divinely inspirational state of the unawakened without remembrance, of being in the surreal state of the dream perceptions. It's such a very magical dreamscape for I to experience the excursions into this *splendid insouciance realm of the enchantment* are lost. Though I was there and had entered into the rhythm of the night. Whereas the mind unfolds in the oneiric dream visions that takes you inside a diffusion of the psychological *anachronistic* places where the relativity dimension is devoid of space-time. Wonderfully dream of vivid episodic scene unframed images of the streaming consciousness bold and recursive mercurial scene showcasing the magnificent fantastical sweet *oneiric* depiction. This life of ease, I felt it while I was laid-back inside oneiric visions within the subconscious psychological state. This magnificent voyage of the spirit *pleroma* of mental complex pinging away entered into an *anachronistic* higher plane of earth's orbit, an amazing precession's dimensional external empirical world odyssey dream travel.

My mental complex perception was keenly acute. My soul was unmanifested within this mercurial dreamy state. While my physical body was manifested resting in a suspended *recumbent* state. That physical selfishness of my being's subconsciousness was resting and dreaming. My soul separated from my own creative unity of existence. I was freewheeling and drifting away amid these psychological, multidimensional weblike lattice structures of intersections of human traffic that took me up into the higher dimension of space and illusion. Excursions inside the mercurial realm going here and there drifting into *anachronistic* scenic places with rhythmic tunes pervading with every strong or gentle wind that blows. And feeling buoyed in this dimension of imperceptible motion. Everywhere my ears attend; and as my spirit consciousness awake, curiously, my thoughts imbibe breathtaking, miraculous depictions. I have experienced this beautifully soothing, melodic music unfolding tranquility of paradisiacal unity of creative expressions of my perception inviting me hither and thither. Deeper I drifted into the realm of the framed surreal.

The akashic state of subconscious mind and matter. Illustrative of a transient oneiric illusory of this *anachronistic* perception, adrift and streaming in the time-space continuum revealed depictions of lovely places I don't remember. Where *residents of this three-dimensional* objective unreal temporal reality cosmic escape from the weight of daily *reverie*!

My spirit has attended my ears and eyes gleaned around; as I drifted and entered into the anachronistic realm of surreal poetry. Indulge your perception with my diffusion of creative delusion. It's the titillating thoughts that spur one's emotions. Beautifully poignant is becoming visually recognizable. Indeed, creatively poignantly written prose apprehension of illusory world reality. and the A seductive field of every temptations as we struggle not to go beyond moral reproachments that pervades the diurnal orbiting Earth's illusory reality. Many thoughts reside animated by human beings' luminous divine lifeblood. It flows through veins of everyone's beating heart of human beings magnificent creation—the beginning and the ending of physical life and rotating cycles are in the same place.

This beautiful visualization of the reality of the material existential imperial physical world in the solar orbital spinning around the Earth's axis pole, 365 days are passing days and nights in space-rotating into the lunar processes cycles. Magnificent cosmic universal *paradisiacal* life of this imperceptible motion of luminous divine consciousness awareness. My real perception passes from daylight into another *twilight* that fades in the maze of the *oneiric* darkness. I behold the beings of the one who truly exists as *Shetaut Neberdjer*.

For what is life but perhaps some grandiose destination; and like you, I drifted away descending across and through the terrestrial sky dome. I journeyed beyond this ful earthly dross plane of material human existence. This magnificent vision for the curious minded to imbibe a full sip of such ruminations. Let us peek inside of the perceptive mind and feel the quiet blissfulness, conscious awareness of comfort, and solace. For it is the nascence is the beginning through the time cycle of life rejuvenations until the new natal incarnation.

This involution is the creative which is written for the folks who may feel somewhat ambivalent, indifferent, and anyone who is not a huge fan of fanciful narrative prose. Those perfectly symmetrical circular waves ring expanding outward quietly pushed by nature's energy force life cycle of harmonious distortions and synchronicity. The material's lyrical illustrative perception of the natural rhythm ebbs and flows.

All can experience the material and spiritual everywhere; you see and hear the confluences of sounds of a beautiful surrounding environment to admire and appreciate the blessings. Across the world, in many places, are large and small sculpted stone mountain peaks towering upwards stretching into the majestic clouds is nature's skyline. The views within the living nature are the places of rocky shorelines, calm and violent ocean waves, sunny days and stormy weather impacts upon this spectacular planet with ocean waves that ebbs and flows that crested upon the sandy beaches. Its wondrous and cathartic sound inspires me to write visceral evocative prose of mental creativity, and inspires me to create a gloriously subtle depiction of my perception of dimension within the psychological mindscape. This effervescence constriction reflects manifestations of psychological creative spiritual animation. The profound intelligence of existence as an animation of material of harmonic vibration of the spiritual *laws of correspondence.* A contiguous duality cycleabounding into the narrative scheme of ephemeral life journey pervading as a creatively higher plane (https://www.mindbody.com). The introduction to fanciful inspirational creative storied entertainment to pique one's curiosity. Prescient *oneiric* epic dreams as your spirit apprehended the perception of stories pervades the humankind's mind. To meditate and imbibe up the wonderful cosmic radiant bright warm sunlight that bathes and sustains God's *bon homies.* Whereas the objective material illusory reality buttresses the surreal realm that I envisage spirituality, subjective luminosity pervades as subconscious entertaining animation as the confluence of spectacle psychological pellucid dreamy depictions within anachronistic fanciful places. I have vague or no recollections of the transcendental illusory temporal reality going beyond the boundaries of daylight to darkness, the physical illusion of a living canvas.

Your soul adrift in the realm of *oneiric* mystical episodes of the *Akashic* plane pervading cosmic energy fields' by the subconscious awareness. A magnificent midnight mystical psychological brain wave. When my mind is drifting towards these shifting scenes. The gentle pellucid air surrounded me. I stood there admiring and immersed in a setting that delighted me with clarity of sub-consciousness perception. My ears attend to the harmonically balanced melodious magnificently jazz music arrangements pervading within this *anachronistic* episodic place. Good cheer and subtle flows of easiness accentuated a lively mood unbounded. My physical projections; my spirit being a personification someplace within the anachronistic space-time continuum. The spirit is, seemingly, in subtle motion and feeling buoyant traveling beyond terrestrial world dualistic dimensions. Like the mercurial spirit that is animated during the dark canvas of the lunatic night light turns motions, which causes the low and high tide waves into subtle and violent ocean waves that push towards the earth's shoreline. Heavenly cosmic bodies that turn the spindrift into the waves that crest onto the sandy beaches ashore is the immutable force and power of the ubiquitous earth, air, fire, and water that is nature that causes the wind caused wind blown sprays of rimple waves to crest ashore. Slow soft winds, the yellow flames that flicker, it's the incredible ambiance. Mesmerized in this shimmering yellow candlelight pervaded. And in this invitingly demure view, I was compelled to glean around within this fantastic splendor. My mind is freely drifting toward the crossroads, that manifestation of this quantum physics, a fleeting moment of the mercurial vision streaming this *oneiric scenery of tranquil anagnorisis.*

Freewheeling scenes entail knowledge-creation that both illusory reality and surreality is the underlying lattice structure that is the fundamental substrate of the mind's deep spirit intuition of the mind's apprehension and intelligent perception. Are we alive and traveling through space and illusion within this transformational state of some *anachronistic paradisiacal* simulator in an illusion of illusory temporal reality by the creation of visual encapsulations? If you are willing to indulge a literary free will.

Who am I to dare to entertain interpolations as a diegetic of the psychological imaginary speculation about a life-altering journey to represent the biblical nascence for others to ponder. Of which, thoughts and conjugated delineations of the biblical olden revisited in the *ataraxia* that is the tranquility of the mind in quiet comfort and solace. To relax and recently meditate upon thoughts that bring solace on the brilliant religious teachings of Christianity's religious crystal light of providence and salvation. A beautiful quiet time together, a psychological delight in the tranquility of purely vivid imagination, a peaceful realm that exists within a creative mind shaft visual introspection. Now come peer inside your higher state of consciousness and enter the teleportation which transcends beyond the material objective illusory realities into a surreal existence. Break away into nirvana excursions traveling into otherworldly dimensional space odyssey; and being free from the external world illusory reality of streaming inhumanity; the financial greed and lustful material desires, and the diseases that cause physical pain, and death. To escape into episodic scenes replete with joy and solace. Letting your *Kundalini* converge the conscious state elevates to the superconscious illusory temporal reality. Ascend as you are drifting away, going deeper into a subconscious state of epic stories flow with delightful anecdotal details. Experience intimately dramatic visions and the salubrious fresh air as a backdrop to the introspection of the deep spirit's intuition and understanding our human behavior and life purpose. Tenuous vivid expressions of comfort. One's psychological mind goes beyond *conscious* illusory temporal reality into a *nebulous* turnstile. There shines a bright brilliant white glowing practical light wave with me glinting inside of this magnificent crystalline passageway across in through the transportine Stargate secret portal. It was that I entered into the gateway tunnel of the radiance, to see the candle flickering as my essence aspired to ascend upwards to seek the light of my initiation and the intelligent infinity of the universal cycle of earth's space-time continuum.

THE MIND, BODY, SPIRIT, AND STORYTELLING

Within this flash of my spirit consciousness awareness was animation of my actions within this splendid realm of streaming *oneiric* mystical illusory atemporal reality. The titillations of entertainment for the audience of listeners to transcend the illusory existence of the light and nighttime duality turnstile between physical realm reality, into subconscious pellucid surreality *oneiric* state of sleeping. The dichotomy between material illusory temporal reality and mercurial luminous odyssey. Excursions wax by the full moon against darkness of night. Excursions waxing moon in twilight. It was my spirit self. I felt very buoyant and very aware of being one's objective conscious self relaxed and awake as my body was asleep and resting. On a higher celestial plane, I see beautiful scenes on all sides which enliven my peace of mind as my spirit energy was animated; it drifted to an unknown destination. I was relaxing on a sky-boat. Quiet subtle in this tranquility. Colorful lights in motion felt myself aboard a fast *Vemana* that ascends and descends down into *anachronistic* places, drifting hither and thither in space and far beyond the Earth's illusory temporal reality into illusory temporal reality. In my mind, the spirit of psycho-spiritual imagination streaming creative episodes of unframed illusory temporal reality.

This universal *Akashic* field depicts anachronistic places. My psychological thought waves of this cognitive mind space have opened up the mysterious pathway way into the lighted crystal gateway arch portal. The esoteric eponymous *transportine* gateway crossing into the labyrinth of the elevated dimensions.

Therein lilting, mercurial sounds residing in me imbibed by this unbounded stupendous showcase with contrasted elements of different shapes and amazing colorful flowers and plants bathing in the warm rays of sun lighted through the amorphous clouds subtle imperceptible motion. Every perception pervaded that pleased my mind, the host of new majestic visual illusory temporal reality. And the living spirit essence actions animated the corporal human embodiment on the decision we take. Humankind's existence unfolds from a natal into the world of the living beings, endued by a universal frequency vibrations as a *mellifluous* voice. Parents' joyous smiles enjoined the tears of the quiet presence of all of the two families' long lists of ancestral life trees.

Subconscious mind meandering, peregrinating spiritual essence with my self-awareness as the physical and psychological unity of spiritual free will embodiment. The subconscious mind is a meandering peregrination. I suddenly felt myself drifting *asynchronously* into beautiful anachronistic places, confluence as entertainment of the dream episodes in a different dimension. My spirit me go hither to thither, only to reappeared someplace amid the people of past eons from the olden gods time period going through the transportine Stargate sign of the crossing, for I to enter the gateways transportine pathway that opened up the splendid interdimensional surreal realm excursive dream odyssey. To this I say that I planned to go there. Yet the transformation intertwined with my thoughts conjugated this confluence of my spiritual vision for which I imbibed the paradisiacal psychological journey into anachronistic places. Although my mind/body/spirit essence was separated from the *geosynchronous* orbital cycle of the time measures. For, in reality, daylight and sunlight start to fade away and, in turn, enter the cycle of dusk, and we see the darkness of the night canvas for all to fall asleep in the dreamscape peregrinations unfolded. With Free wheel my spirit compelled me into remarkable *anachronistic* places far afield of the present time space continuum. Where nirvana resides on all sides of the surreality of the wondrous things in perfect harmony balance. I remember that it was hard times But we were very happy and full of high-minded dreams of future happiness just eating a meal in those days. We were filled with life experiences free from the drugs induced altered state of consciousness awareness. Within the quiet comfort and peaceful solace, without any cognitive measure of the spacetime continuum and away from everyday daily activities. Going beyond the physical restraints of the terrestrial blue and white skydome of Egyptian god Nut. I was an avatar of animated spirit adrift amid the lively soulful spirit that was gathering other avatars of human entertainment until the light of dawn closed into the cover of the darkest night. The wonderful cycle in real time comes when lunar light glows in the overnight sky, and in turn will yield to the sun rise in the Eastern

THE MIND, BODY, SPIRIT, AND STORYTELLING

shoreline horizon. My essence of mind/body/spirit complex ready to rise again from a restful night of restorative sleep. I am no longer awake, but dreams as my spirit cause is taking a *paseo* into the wondrous surrealism that abide in the translucent streaming episodes of the dreamweaver's amusing entertainment. My eyes have relaxed as my spirit separated from my body. I entered into the transportine archway crossing towards the vortex, and meandered buoyancy and felt appreciation of life of freewill. And to my delight eased into and touched down in the space time illusion after I fell asleep. My spirit intuition for I to experience an anachronistic voyage countdown and liftoff in the dreamspace travel through the peregrination of the sleep cycle. The tranquil feeling of being asleep in bed, while the spirit entered the social halls of splendid palaces covered with gold. Where the air felt pleasant and exceedingly comfortable. Atemporal scene of purity in an existential realm I invsaggested without a chronology into anachronism, where time didn't matter to me. Some place separated from distortions of the earth's external world; and there I walk among others psychological surreality; and the soul of myself is animated someplace within the realm of the other side of the *Noumena*; which is the cycle in manifestations of consciousness awareness realm of the duality. The separation from reality when we enter into the gateway crossing through the turnstile dimensional cycle of coming forth in the period realm of sunshine and in turn going forth into the lunar light turns up the rhythm ocean with ripples sound; and the scuds of the salty sea water that is the serenity that comes as a dynamic refreshing sensation when subtle waves crested ashore, with the rhythmic waves was cathartic. Beguile by this mysterious elegant lady whose lips were covered behind her satin veil, peered at me with seductive eyes. It was as if we were tuned into an aura of harmonic waves vibrations.

    I don't want to escape from the imaginary dimension of the Earth's surface. The empirical world is a unit of illusory temporal reality separated from the psychological state of daily cycles of existence. To rest is being free from daylight frivolity *hebdomadal matutinal* animated routines. And the perception of the illusory human experience is the life existences and daily *pabulum* experiences random challenges and responsibilities.

And so, my friends, let face these spiritual theological peregrinations upon the earth crystallized interior plane creative illusory temporal reality. Exit is the time to awaken from ephemeral night dreams, refreshed. For life is truly the delightful moments by which every morning I inhale the breath of fresh air into my lungs. I inhale and exhale the rustic beauty of my controlled breathing for I to escape into the unbridled blissful inner peace, with the quiet comfort, and solace in yoga meditations. The ataraxia of spiritual spirit complexes into a symbiotic state of Yoga meditation, a cathartic sense of mental focus, and harmonic balance. Expressions of the sentimental pierce the beautiful spirit of nature's biosphere. To take a glimpse of the creative physical episodic illusory temporal reality. To loosen up, relax, and enjoy as you imbibe mental solace and entreat the sensory emotions.

Adrift with those warm feelings, replete, and redolent of the most imaginative. Surrealism's temporal reality is like the mystery of the dreams episodic scenery visions. The exclusion of the dream cycles is dissolved without *remembrance of* the past flitting of dissipation of the surreal metaphysical ethereal cycle into the *Akashic wave field previous.* Subconsciously everything conjugated into transmutative scenes of mercurial illumination. This is such a lovely and wondrous union that is to be a common medium of the sensory. Imparting knowledge of the Kemet spiritual science principles connected to nature divine effluent of the Infinite Creator. The mind's free will in an inner external empirical world, the spiritual consciousness of human faculty, and the psychic and spiritual universe is a pathway connection to the cosmic universe's ephemeral metaphysical surreal dimensions.

Streaming themes of the ephemeral. Which I speak of was a corona that brightly shone forth to sustain life upon material illusory temporal reality. I awake by day my corporeal body lies in bed resting in a recumbent state. My eyes are closed and will open with visual perception. Things of great knowledge have been revealed to me in a material existence. Nature is magnificent in all aspects to behold

THE MIND, BODY, SPIRIT, AND STORYTELLING

in reverence to intelligent infinite creators. All that our eyes can see and experience felt real in humble appreciation being amid the harmonic wave vibrations spurred my love embrace for brotherly love. Might your body's *kundalini radiate with luminous divine vibrations* of waves. A sensory vision of marvelous depictions; your subconscious awareness enters into the realm of the higher plane of supreme creative existence. Within a recondite scene of psychological visual perception like framed portraits of spiritual theology consciousness. Behold, I am entering the captivating luminosity pervading through a higher radiance of mindspace.

This is being in the most idyllic of supreme tranquility and depictions within the mind's creative sensory a psychological enchantment. With such great felicity buoyed by the underlying lifeblood of the Egyptian god Ra's Law of One. Our mind and body *Kundalini* energy aligned with the divine harmonic vibration. The daily forenoon quiet time of yoga meditation feeling the nirvana on a higher plane of consciousness awareness. And no longer feeling those woes of or mundane work-a-day weight of this external empirical worldwide *reverie*. Let the subconscious mind jettison your daily emotional stresses.

Being detached and free from the bonds of daily vagaries; which is derived from social degradation and volatile economic woes that pervades within this quintessence of cosmic creative harmonic vibrations. The living things of a symphonic are universally reality incredible divine nature. Within luminous divine harmonic frequency light practical waves are derived by the lifeblood.

Universal cosmic unity of sync to and morality dovetails nicely to the precepts of spiritual theology teachings of the *natural laws*. Humanist idealism is cultivated by wisdom of the Law of One love. And enlightenment is endued to thoughts and behavior. The guidance of unwavering sacred principles and form underlying each human spirit's free will actions is tied to the cause and effects is the manifestation of our conscious free-will. Or, just perhaps, life is about the idea of having free-will consciousness awareness apply to us in some curious measure. Where our own choices allow us to make wise choices. Decisions that will delineate outcomes that will shape our events that are positive, or negative self-destruction. Everything has a default endgame of potential negative or positive consequences.

Might it be derived from consciousness awareness; the consequences for decisions or actions to do good or a maelstrom of evil deeds. A mental complex of the psycho spirit essence as an individual separated human being, that is a common medium of the mind, that is a creative lattice structure. This realm of illusory reality of *ataraxis* meditation. The sound of nature breathing as the wind is ebbing and flowing sustains my mind/into the distortion of harmonic waves vibrations. This takes the negative details and magnifies those details while filtering out all positive aspects of a situation. Allow your subconscious mind to dream into the esoteric realm. This magnificent place of dazzling tranquility. Amid dreamers, the spirit unwinds to saucy mellifluous lilting jazz tunes that enliven the spirit of nature's fresh pleroma of heaven. The folks in intimate conversation and the amusement of playful *badinage* and peals of laughter as I gleaned around to admire and appreciate being in such an wonderful *asynchronous* of this *asynchronous* stupendous fanciful place with all the opulence, to which I was very unfamiliar to me.

I drifted into nirvana when I was looking around in this delightful place full of lively good cheers and it felt so right that night. The mood was mellow with the ambiance and aromatic fragrance of jasmine flora that enlivened the space of merriment. All around me people were smiling; children were playing romantic lovers held hands within this *anachronistic* epic scene; tranquility abounded amid people's confabulations were full of *shivoo*. There was this aura of joy amid the hightone and merrymaking that was the lucerne dream scenes I imbibed on all sides. Let your imagination apprehend the excursive surreal realm. For many, both the sensory visions and beyond the temporary ephemeralness and the permanent objective illusory temporal reality. Two faceted universes exist beyond night and day, three dimensions experiencing spiritual growth development devoid of daily healthiness that causes human stress. Why, surely we must, at times, realize this blissful feeling, happiness, the peace that equates to the mind, body, and spiritual alliances in perfect vibrations of harmonic balance that comes from within your unity

THE MIND, BODY, SPIRIT, AND STORYTELLING

with the personal consciousness. Yeah, to be relaxing the body, I was freeing my mind as I drift off and sleep buoyant and dreaming of wondrous *anachronistic* places. In every scene of my envisage, it was delightful, as if material things seemed surreal, for these are scenes that are unfamiliar. Deeper I go as I am drawn there in this realm of calm beingness, compelling my spirit's essence onward towards the state of beautiful ascension into a higher level of esoteric spiritual state of consciousness awareness into a dimension of nirvana.

I had entered the state of my subconscious mind that was a *kaleidoscope* cloud, seemingly, floating within peace realms of the time and space continuum. The perception of these swevenly-like visual reflections.

To be calm in meditation and to focus on the marvelous things of streaming subconsciousness *effervescent* into surreal wonderful oneiric depiction of the blissful ataraxis state of buoyant peace and tranquil sleep, where the hollows of dream vision are beyond the mere empirical world material density. Readers attuned to these creative psychological prose.

To bring you a sense of quiet comfort and calming solace. The mystery of the ephemeral dreamtime idyllic excursions streaming visual depictions as wonderfully perceptions interpolations of beautiful enchanting episodes of luminous divine peregrinations' of the vainglorious realm of surrealism!

And as I am aware of my own being, it is not independent or exclusive to the providence that is in need of the brilliant arrays of thermodynamics sun energy the orbital cycle through twelve zodiacal houses' orbital earth rotations circumambulating processions around in the *uni-solar* and *lunar-solar* equilibrium turnstile. The fiery radiance of the lifegiving material presence is a luminous divine *Nibizbijur* (nature); and the cycle of the all-pervasive consciousness with the evolution cycle of the cosmic constellation universe. Life, the *Al-Kemia* mysteries universal great intelligent life of the monad creationism; of the luminous divine providence. The sun sustains humanity and flora and fauna of the Earth's beautiful *milieu*. The existence of embodiment of the spirit's illusion of illusory temporal reality.

HAKEEM R. JELANI

Now sit still and quiet your mind and loosen up, letting your subconscious bridge the *kaleidoscopic* inner workings of the temporal reality devoid of the earth's time-space illusory temporal reality. Your mind slowly apprehends an illustrative narrative. Seamlessly to escape from the daily dregs of the external vagaries, of life mental shackles, to pervade through the fantasy realm nondescript vision, going far beyond the external empirical terrestrial world dimension. Take a glimpse inside your own mind space while never realizing that subconsciously, I was asleep and in bed dreaming. These inner workings are of psychological dreams; the fantastical external empirical world dimensions of elegance and enchantment will take you into the anachronistic psychological tenuous places within the surreal external practical world dimensions! And yes my friend, in light of this discursive preface, I am profoundly honored and sincerely very grateful to have been inspired to write this book. Mostly appreciative of others who devote themselves to digest and reflect on the literary exegesis of my avant garde prose collections. Again, I flash back into the mental illusory gateway crossing into the dream state odyssey.

Wherein the all magnificent is the place where all creation arises from the luminous divine unity of infinite spirit pleroma derived into existence, each living spirit is the separation into visual tas perceptions; illusory scenes where the consciousness awareness en the vainglorious unity with the cosmos of this volumetric time-space continuum.

Magnificence elixirs of many ebulliently streams of very beautiful clouds of wonderful colors were on all sides of this marvelous surreal realm is an escape from the pinging noises of earth distortions into the dream excursions. The gateway crosses into the secret stargate portal. I entered into the subjective perception of the luminous constrictions. Diffusion of this *avant-garde prose collectio*n a deed spirit intuition that reflects the scenes of enigmatic mystery religion that transcends ordinary consciousness awareness from which all creation resides. Everyday frivolity into the *spiritual light, love,* and *life's* luminous divine *spirit* pervading during calm meditation in sync with the mind of the universal light of nature's beautiful vistas! My energy of mind/body/spirit complex was in harmonic balance. You and I will begin a life journey of excursive prose. A beautiful profundity it is: *"said humankind's emergence from its self-incurred immaturity, our lazy and cowardly submissiveness to the blind faith in dogmas and formulas, e.g., political authorities.*

For enlightenment, He proclaimed humanity must Dare to understand" (Mr. Immanuel Kant).
Kemetic Religion (Shetaut Neter) "Neterianism"
The philosophy, history, and teaching of Ancient Egyptian spiritual theology and mysticism (https://www.egyptianmysteries.org/what-do-neterians-believe-in).
Muata Ashby (June 13, 2014).
(https://www.egyptianyoga.com/category/kemetic-religion/).
Kemetism religious path of Shetaut Neter,
Study of the wisdom of the Law of One (love) teachings (Rech-Ab), Devotion to God (Uashu), Acting with Righteousness (https://www.egyptianyoga.com/41/), and Meditation (Uaa). Neberdjer provided the Shetitu, the spiritual theology teaching written in Medu Neter (hieroglyphic scripture) so that the Shemsu (followers) might study the wisdom of the Law of One (love) teaching of Shetaut Neter. The two most critical Neterian scriptures are the Pert M Hru and the Hessu Amun, and the most crucial Neterian Myth is the Asian Resurrection. By the practice of the disciplines of Shedy, I will discover the Shetaut (Mysteries) of life and become Maakheru, Pure of Heart.
I will become one with God even before death, give you the spirit of the supreme peace, abiding happiness, and fulfillment of purpose, and promote peace and harmony for the external empirical world.

Mentions of the word line one might recognize and agree that fundamental complex biogenesis understanding of science points to a salient truth are this visual duality being; both reflect the recognizable existence of things of both animate and inanimate resides within the preparatory laws of Nature, which is to saying man, as a higher expression, only, of the same universal *"biguine life,"* contains the same. *The Light of Egypt; Or, The Science of the Soul*
(Thomas H. Burgoyne)

Forbidden Knowledge and Longevity: God (Enlil) Expelled Adam and Eve

This book is the introduction for your ruminations on the question why Enlil *was flummoxed* when his brother, Enki (*lord of the Egyptian secret society of the serpents priestly brotherhood*). Enki was cursed, and vilified for surreptitiously, Enki had informed Eve with the forbidden truth, about the knowledge sense of her consciousness awareness, to know of her own human nakedness. The gift of her consciousness awareness. which he knew when he hatched a scheme to defy his half-brother, Enlil's, who was the lord of Earth command, mandate, and strict rules to the contrary. The ultimate act of spite was the blatant action Enki took to teach Adam and Eve, which was without fear of backlash if they would be found to be intelligent beings.

This discursively written representation represents a bugaboo's with which the ancient astronaut theory is a controversial interpolation of the logic and reason for mental clarity regarding the garden in the land of the Eden narrative tale. Wake up with me and move away from the anesthetizing fetters that inculcates the paucity of mental confusion. Awakened to the eruption of enlightenment and learn about a past remembrance of the epoch that harkens you back into the olden period by spiritual meditation, and feel the ataraxia of the inner peaceful mental harmonic balance, with quiet comfort and solace.

The evolution and cosmic evolution of human purpose and mental complex identity predominates with a purified warm heart and consciousness awareness imbibed with love and synchronized with *Nebergdjer.* Hermetically sealed *Akashic* records of the luminous divine universal monad.

This was my spirit unity of the mind, body, and spirit complex a the synthesis of the harmonic vibrations of the all-pervasive infinite and unity. The fulfillment of humankind's purpose is your spiritual journey to take decisions and actions. Enki's DNA code was *surreptitiously* fused into the African Royal bloodline in the narrative tale described in the Enuma Elish, Seven Tablets of the creation of Adam and Eve after the descent from heaven to the planet earth. Replete

THE MIND, BODY, SPIRIT, AND STORYTELLING

with Enki's awakening of their consciousness awareness, it was revealed in the eponymous Old Testament Bible tale of the Genesis Garden in Eden reveal that luminous innovative scientific advancements of the human spirit knowledge of themselves as a sexual spirit of the embodiment of mind, body, and spirit complex. A fear that human beings could pose a real potential danger to established order, meaning knowledge and longevity of the gods if they acquired the same capability of exploring interstellar orbital space travel into the deep frontier galaxies. Some folks have asked this salient question: how is it that the Bible Genesis narrative tale makes no mention of ancient astronauts? And yes, it's a very good question considering that our NASA scientists are seeking to establish human colonization of Mars! After all this future endeavor, is it not at all a far-fetched pipe dream, but rather practical and not different from what the ancient astronaut theorists' hypothesis contend, right?

Human beings could one day, undoubtedly become capable of deploying their own spacecraft from their modern-age NASA sends man-piloted vehicles from earth into outer space orbit and safely returning to Earth. Might, somehow, curious humans adventure beyond the moon into the cosmic deep space frontier constellation much like the Anunnaki alien astronauts who came from planet Nibiru achieved.

The space traveling astronauts from a distant planet of Anunnaki ancient astronauts came from Nibiru.

And isn't it ironic that in the biblical Genesis narrative, the king Anu appointed his son Enlil, the lord of the mission command. He was the god who had explicitly forbidden humans to possess neither *knowledge* nor the gods' secret elixir? for longevity. Yes, today's human astronauts have been operating NASA's space flights, and so on will carry out deep space ventures to colonize the planet Mars. Is starting to sound much in the way of the Anunnaki, right? With our modern astronauts, as scientists have traveled on the NASA space shuttle, they have conducted tests in space which is not a silly notion that harkens me back to the Bible Genesis eponymous tale of Enki's *Adam* and *Eve* creation narrative. Was this an elaborate record written about an actual historical event that occurred after the Royal Elite

Prince Enki (founder of the serpent brotherhood. Oh, and there's this his half brother Enlil had besmirched, when he called Enki a serpent in the Garden of Eden, he knew it was Enki's mischief because he had surreptitiously disregarded the forbidden law of the Anunnaki council's approved mandate when he fashioned his likeness/imprint on an indigenous African female homo-erectus Earth species. Their approval was made clear that the creation of crossread humans were forbidden from access to the Anunnaki clans' sacred knowledge and longevity. His fashioned cross breeds were created by the Anunnaki to serve as a prototype primitive workers!

He defied federations law which caused Enlil, authority to enforce discipline and control under his reign of laws that fell under His charge. Nevermind that his brother Enki found ways to subvert Enlil, as in the case of Adam and Eve, which was exemplified in the eponymous episode that was quite revealing as the scene unfolded in the Bible Genesis narrative tale of the Garden of the Eden. He became conscious of self-awareness as an affront to his brother, the Royal great prince Enlil's command decreed. The consequence caused Adam and Eve to be expelled from Enlil's private temple palace in the *Garden of Eden. Some claim it is actually* located in the Cushite land of Africa known as Havilah. The Bible record mentions as follows:

In one case, Havilah is associated with the garden in the land of Eden, as it is mentioned in the Book of Genesis (2:10--12): A river flows out of Eden to the garden, and from there it divides and becomes four branches. The name of the first is Pishon; it is the one that flows around the whole land of Havilah, where there is gold; 12 the gold of that land is good; bdellium and onyx stone are there [1].

In addition to the region ded in chapter 2 of Genesis, two individuals named Havilah are listed in the Table of Nations. The Table lists the descendants of Noah, who are considered eponymous ancestors of nations. Besides the name mentioned in Genesis 10:7–29, another is mentioned in the Books of Chronicles (1 Chronicles 1:9–23). One person is the son of Cush, the son of Ham.

The other person is a son of Joktan and descendant of Shem. The name Havilah appears in Genesis 25:18, where it defines the territory inhabited by the Ishmaelites as being "from Havilah to Shur, opposite

THE MIND, BODY, SPIRIT, AND STORYTELLING

Egypt in the direction of Assyria and in the Books of Samuel (1 Samuel 15:7–8), which states that King Saul smites the Amalekites who were living there, for King Agag, whom he took prisoner [38].

The Hamite African people

Those whose sons and daughters are the bloodline descendants of Noah's ark. But I bet you didn't know that Royal Prince Enki gave Noah the blueprints to build that submersible vessel in order to save his human *progeny* from the eponymous great flood. Or did you know that Enki (the creator god) fittingly defied his half-brother Enlil. The plan was to allow his human beings to be swept away by the catastrophic deluge (https://www.ntd.com/noahs-ark-blueprints-extracted-from-ancient-babylonian-relic_302258.html). Let me be clear, it let them all die was Enlil's master plan which is a detail that is not alluded to in the Old Testament Bible genesis tale narratives tale. It's credence must be objectively weighed and interpolated in consideration of the modern ancient astronauts theorists hypothesis, with respect to the biblical genesis story to arrive at what dovetail rather nicely with extraterrestrial alien Anunnaki clans as: "those who from the heavens came", had descended to the Earth, was lead by the titular god Enki. Their mission was under the *exegesis* and *plenipotentiary* of the Lord supreme god Anu's two sons was in possession of the African peoples' home lands allotted to Hamites: Egypt (Kemet), Kush, Put, and Cush extended across the eastern region of Africa. And according to Enki's brother Enlil, the supreme titular god of the Genesis narrative, was angry when he realized that Enki had spurred Adam and Eve to disobey him. Immediately he realized that Enki had given Adam and Eve awareness of their nakedness! The Anunnaki supreme deity Anu was Lord over the Anunnaki of heaven and the Earth. The supreme god Anu appointed his firstborn son Enki with the command of the first voyage to Earth exploration mission to verify whether insignificant gold was available to patch the damaged holes in Nibiru's damaged ozone atmosphere. Then mined, processed and converted into a fine *monatomic gold particle* that could then be transported by means of their fleet of advanced

UFO vehicles that would be loaded into hovering spacecraft on to the planet Nibiru, with the first stop over on the moon then on to Mars waystations. This was a command oversight responsibility of the Royal Prince Enlil, who was the god *Yahweh*. While Royal prince Enki was the brilliant creator god who used biological sciences to manipulate and modify DNA chromosomes to fashion a new hybrid homosapien sapiens.

And he was the eponymous god of wisdom, mischief and sacred geometric magic makings. But what is written in the Bible about the creator God/Enki, seemingly doesn't mention the identity which fits the description of: "Those who from the Heaven came" equates to the biblical Genesis gods identity of the chapter 1, obfuscate by wittingly suppressing the Anunnaki as ancient astronauts extraterrestrial alien gods. The manipulator of the mitochondrial and Y-chromosome biological DNA codes. Enki was the Anunnaki alien god who successfully fashioned a crossbred human species upon the African interior Earth plane! He was the god denigrated by his brother, and the lord god of the Earth command was angry enough to disparage Enki with the *prerogative* of the snake for intentionally disregarding his decree that humankind was forbidden to partake in the acquisition of Anunnaki knowledge—consciousness and self-awareness!

The ability to know of their nakedness, and the free will consciousness to think about our actions is a spiritual journey, for with clarity and understanding we choose good over evil actions and deeds. Enlil preferred to deny the primitive workers knowledge; they were considered the same as the animals. Let's assume that it is axiomatic. Whereof modern human beings' share the Anunnaki-African Kemet bloodline consciousness awareness. This requires a medical procedure that to be performed by a brilliant skilled medical procedural protocol that was *efficaciously* performed by Enki, intended to manipulate and modify the biological genes sequence of an indigenous Homo Erectus female mitochondrial DNA code and fused it with his Anunnaki DNA, Y chromosome.

Yeah it's the hidden mystery religion, which Enki taught the priesthood through the house of life, which was perpetuated via the secret societies' teaching learning of spiritual-scientific knowledge.

THE MIND, BODY, SPIRIT, AND STORYTELLING

That which sacred rites and rituals were taught in the initiation, was passed down from the Anunnaki is delineated as the development of our modern astronauts of earth-man's space flight accomplishment achieved milestones through human astronaut crews could one day achieve the capability construct and launch advanced spacecraft from the earth and safely reenter the geosynchronous orbital with aid of the flight mission control to land them on the moon, explore the surface, and successfully safely lifted off and land their space shuttle back down onto the terrestrial planet. NASA scientists are advancing toward deep space mission explorations, and their skilled scientists possess the requisite knowledge to conduct geological surveys and exploit astrological cosmic universal space-age technology. Space science, as well as biological engineering, are in parallel with and underlie the missing anecdotal details information that is undisclosed in the genesis narrative tale! Enki was successful in reaching the farthest planetary sphere stars galaxies?

Here's the good news: you and I are a microcosm of a universal volumetric scale; individual units of spirit consciousness awareness. And yes, let's face it. Many people might not consider the biblical Genesis narrative to be this monumental event, which is actually not a fairytale or a myth, but it's a seminal historical description about the ancient astronauts created civilization after arriving, they landed near the Persian Gulf of Sumer ancient Mesopotamia. The Anunnaki deployment to earth were inscrutable intelligent space-faring astronauts. They possessed an advanced knowledge of the cosmic galaxy of orbital planets and stars. The salient question is this: Might the Royal Elite Prince Enki and his biological genetics team used their knowledge to fashion aliens, and the indigenous DNA manipulated an indigenous African female's essence fashioned to fashion a prototype crossbreed (Adam and Eve) Homosapien, humans? Is this the connection that humans are tied to the Anunnaki ancient astronaut astronaut God's likeness?

Let's face it. Human beings have been fascinated by this innate desire to adventure out from the surface. To follow in the footsteps of the ancient gods; to discover another habitable life, sustainable outer empirical world planets. And like the Anunnaki alien gods, through space exploration, conquer the farthest outer reaches and tame the vast cosmos space frontier.

The predicate for such lofty aspirations is the fact that NASA's space technology and modern achievements fit the profile of the Anunnaki "those who were from Heaven came." We read it transliterated in the Hebrew/Greek versions of the Old Testament Holy Bible, and say that it was an actual historical event according to Genesis, chapter 1! Does it not say this? We read that the words are quite comprehensive in this nascent, meaning what?

Ancient astronauts who descended from their own planet Nibiru/Planet-X. Hardly anyone who believes in God and religions have probably never heard of the Anunnaki alien of the original Genesis narrative tale, in The context of the ancient astronaut's theorists' hypothesis about these alien titular gods' arrival of Anunnaki extraterrestrial alien beings who came from their far away distant home planet, Nibiru, space-faring astronauts flight commander, Royal Prince Enki's Earth mission voyage fifty man crews that successfully came down from heaven to earth by maneuvering a shining, bell-shaped UFO sky chariot through the asteroid belt, descended and landed in the southern interior region of Sumer, Mesopotamia.

It could be understood that God/Enki's humankind was advanced by empirical influence in civilization, not speaking about the creation of the earth, which would have been an incredibly impossible achievement in just six days, would it not? Enki ostensibly the personification of god on earth because he was the *plenipotentiary* of his father, the supreme lord god Anu; the elite king and ruler of the Anunnaki clan in heaven and of the intrepid extraterrestrial ancient alien astronauts who the biblical account say built the first established city-state settlement on the Earth plane. Which is likely to have been carried out by Enki's crew of highly skilled architects that built (created) Enki's city state, which he appropriately named *Eridu* which means "home in the far away". And of course, this is alluded to in the Old Testament book Genesis's account. Enki as their lord god. This was located in ancient Sumer, Mesopotamia. There was reverence for God/Enki through Temple Priesthood; His worship was the personal preference for Enki as the city-state deity of Eridu.

Archeology discovery revealed the extraction of quantities of gold was mined there.

We are aware UFOs today are the Anunnaki alien astronauts gods who descended in Mesopotamia; those who came in as UFO astronaut gods who exploited Earth's African gold deposits!

Honor, Light, Life, Love, In Eternal Everlasting Peace And Joy

Hi! Greetings to all my friends. Before I begin with my excursive elucidations that comport with the wisdom principles, this is to teach others spiritual erudition of my intuition derived from the nous of the living spark of the spirit that dwells as a mind/body/spirit complex. As such, we all experience things within the living reality enrolment of the personhood.

To each of us, a luminous divine spark of energy is the light of a living spirit. For us as one and our other selves, living together is a fundamental unity of the oneness with which a positive nature imbibes things of truth. It is a visceral feeling as an individual's soulful spirit is in sync with the law of one flow of the life force energy. So let me briefly pause to you all that are the seekers of the light of the truth, that you and I are the spiritual beings. As such, we are all separate individual units of the luminous divine, for I am humble and wise according to the consciousness of the way towards salvation, saved by the brilliant divine light wisdom of the Law of One love. The philosophy of the ancient Egyptian religion of the sun god Ra, the king of all the deities and the eponymous father of all creation and the highest of all human beings, is a significant complex (https://egyptianmuseum.org/deities-ra). Yeah, it's the sage life of perception, my material contributions, a heart weight found light as Ma'at's ostrich feather.

No! Not at all! I will tell you about my accomplishments. An exemplary stellar military career was for twenty-four years. Awakening, and I have opened the door and connected my glowing divine spirit fire endued with conscious awareness transformation has been an insight into the social complex of spacetime, sacred light of mind and body complex; myself, a material entity of an intrinsic unity with the infinite Creator.

Black people's original history truncated the cultural and tribal African family psycho-spiritual bonds with the higher plane of con-

THE MIND, BODY, SPIRIT, AND STORYTELLING

sciousness awareness. The fundamental truth is to seek to find the delineated tree of my truncated family roots. The original connection to my lost indigenous people's true fidelity to their ancestors. African and Chickasaw roots. Profound respect is due to the stolen family surname that was a branch torn from the tribal ancestors. The ancient astronaut alien god Enki contributed his Y chromosome with the biological genetically derived African female's mitochondrial DNA created the Homo sapiens sapiens, the ancient human ancestors' direct royal bloodline, Enki had intentionally made. And for disobedience, according to the Bible, allowing the Hebrews, God's people had been punished as a Hamitic tribe who had their African identity truncated and; with which other nations scattered his people around the empirical world was a mendacious act of social genocide. We now know the most brutal, visceral, and shameful evil ever to have been perpetrated upon humanity was atrocities committed in the name of economic profits power and wealth during the disgraceful system during the African diaspora. The enslavement of Africans being traded as a commercialized market commodity, was a schema of the Western empirical world economic powers; people are the ancestors of the Hebrew of th tribe of Judah, who fled into black Africa land to avoid the systematic attack on the flowers of the spiritual science learning/teaching of sacred wisdom principles, I interpolate is the story about the exposing the missing piece of the Old Testament Bible book of Genesis to tell the longstanding falsehood biases consciousness—in the narrative justified actions in the name of god to efficaciously denigrate black people to the social status of the victims of a government sanctioned genocide! You who have viewed those horrible directions of black bodies packed tight into the hulls of the slavers' ships have witnessed their dreadful conditions of human beings sold into bondage.

The sale of black human beings whose descendants were taken from the land of Africa to several foreign countries. Weron shackles, Africans captured and placed in the cargo area of enslaved people were shipped as black human cattle and sold to wealthy buyers of human slaves.

What is planned to me is how this enterprise conflates with the story written about in the Old Testament Holy Bible tale of chapter 1, book of Genesis. It says that God punished African-Hebrews for their evil deeds and disobedience in which all of the Israelite tribal people of Judah suf-

fered from their lack of understanding. Their transgressions were against the creator Anunnaki extraterrestrial titular god Enki. Which is written in the pages of the Old Testament's Genesis and perpetrated over many past external empirical worlds centuries of countless actions of pure and cruel evil. Don't just take my word for it; go and do some homework because it was disgusting! Try to fathom the arrogance of the powerful western nation who proffered for years from this evil degradation put upon Africans who suffered from the holocaust that happened during the diaspora: trafficking of black slaves, stolen, and sold into strange lands across the Atlantic Ocean!

This is commensurate with the historical injustices as a pernicious holocaust has yet to be reconciled and redressed. Yeah, it's the atonement for the African, Muslim, and Western rulers of the governments who participated were complicit in these transgressions that can't be justified by evoking the words attributed to the biblical Hebrew Bible Genesis. Recompense is muted by the opponents who push against any justification for reparation payment to the generations of the victims' line of descendants. They are owned pecuniary damage for the heavy yoke bestowed on one's dignity, which was a system that profited from years of being cursed, as the unpaid black labor force of the white criminal oppressors of black family roots of African tribal ancestors' truncated and lost historical identity. Lines of ancestors' forever languishing with absolutely no knowledge of their family tree roots, which is displaced from the identity.

Briefly, I reveal this snapshot of truth, recognized as a historical nugget that has ties to the plight of the indigenous people's homelands. Might I share the erudition that imparts this knowledge of al-kimia of relevant pages of the Akashic *Halls of* Records *archived for the curious-thinking plebeians who are becoming the awake enlightened minds of the bons hommes (http://slaveryandremembrance.org/articles/article/index.cfm?i).*

Are you following me? And if so, then perhaps you'll also appreciate the value of acquiring knowledge, insight, and the sense of having wisdom to be in sync with the philosophy of the great bringer of the souls into light with a purity of heart, of love and happiness. The truth is, to enter into the light of wisdom by the Law of One love and insight into the spiritual external empirical worldly life force balanced, harmonically

THE MIND, BODY, SPIRIT, AND STORYTELLING

tuned, and sync in the mind/body/spirit complex of solace. To know thyself mirror image reflection as a fundamental mystery derived from the slavery diaspora. The cargo of captured entities sold into bondage to other entities. The human beings became the victim Africans, Europeans, and Arabian races were involved as merchant traders of human cattle for in the logistic cargo contracts transportation that facilitated buyers' and sellers' transactions throughout history. The African Hebrew's bondage is consistent with references mentioned in the Holy Bible; it was the condoning of inhumanity that nevertheless shameful and archived history that has recorded their deeds, which the new age potentates crafted into eclectic holy gospels by the church religionists. wittingly mistranslated scriptures as their edited books that are biblical epochs of the Anunnaki ancient astronauts' story of gods; meaning, the Anunnaki extraterrestrial alien beings, astronauts, "Those who from the Heaven came" human beings history. And so, might this hidden secret about our ancestors be linked to the lost tribes of Africa/Israeli Jews after the death of Jesus's crucifixion? The Jewish Hebrew people's migration was to hide among the Gentile nations (2 Nephi 25:15; Luke 21:24; Doctrines and Covenants 45:18–21, 24). These were the Israeli tribes held captive and the victims of bondage, as were various other nations of different periods of conquest; examples: (1) the Egyptian captivity, 1500 BC; (2.) the Assyrian captivity, 720 BC; (3.) the Babylonian captivity, 586 BC; (4) the Persian captivity, 538 BC; (5) the Greek captivity, 332 BC; (6) the Roman captivity, AD 70; (7) and of course, the American captivity, AD 1619 is history (Leviticus 26:14–45, 26:46; Deuteronomy 28:15–68). Are they the people cursed by the Anunnaki's creator god Enki, the god of Hamitic-Israelite (Jewish) people's African Hebrews ancestral tribesmen. Humankind who were the victims of an evil commercialization for the trading of black bodies as an investment instrument that was the market value for profiteers from sales of the global trans atlantic enterprise of captured black slaves.

An estimated ten million black Israelites tribal people were African slave exported from their homeland were captured, chained, and sold into bondage, they were tightly packed into the slavers ships. They were the Israelites' lost Jewish tribe that had slowly migrated to escape persecution or death from the Roman legions. Yeah to interpolate the thoughts on my thoughts regarding persecution. Given as the truth about indigenous Moorish Israeli Jewish peoples African ancestral bloodline forefathers, which has been linked to the genetic offspring of the Royal Prince Enki (Ea) eponymous Hamite African bloodline.

Yeah, the Anunnaki aliens' DNA connection to African-Egyptian roots is delineated from the Enki's Adam and Eve creation. Here's the story about the natal of Enki's ancestors' crossbred DNA manipulation fashioning the first line of Enki and Nyngazida. The associated member of the mission Earth voyage's medical research team was involved in the successful creation of the Earth's Homo sapiens sapiens, Adam, by genetic manipulation of both Anunnaki and the indigenous African female DNA biblical essence occurs on Earth. And by this process evolves the children of Enki. Meaning that my family bloodline descended from Enki's creation.

The biblical chronicles of the Genesis narrative, traces back to the biological fusion of the mitochondrial DNA, the editing of chromosome genetic code extraction from an indigenous Homo erectus female contributor from Africa. The creation of the crossbreed races of Homosapein-sapiens, which Enki had infused them with the Anunnaki Royal alien bloodline of those who from the Heaven came Enki and his team of medical doctors successfully created Adam (Man) and Eve (Woman) in his own likeness. This is what the Bible tells us what happened was the actual events! Whereof, much of what is written in the Old Testament Bible in is about the Hebrew people can be extrapolated to the mixing of the human race. Native people lands exploited, as in the case, in such as the displaced Hebrew Negro tribes of Judah, Native American Americans, Chickasaw Indian ancestor the Moorish African, Indian, Asian, and European peoples bloodline DNA blood types. For this view; and in fact, unequivocally, the point here is that all humans share this common origin from Enki's and the connection between the Anunnaki's derivatives from their ancestors and the indigenous African female DNA manipulation, the Old Testament Bible Genesis makes very clear. The Bible narrative is the ancient historical record turned into a Christian narrative myth. But just to be clear that what is written in the Bible is not always forthright in terms of the whole truth with all of the anecdotal evidence. Lost or hidden codexes that which give us what is ostensibly

THE MIND, BODY, SPIRIT, AND STORYTELLING

the revelation of an ancient extraterrestrial origin has been covered up the real story by the original custodian gods was written on thousands of hard-baked cuneiform clay tablets have been found buried beneath the king Assurbanepal's palace ruins, discovered at Sippur, Iraq, have been corroborated the veracity fits the genealogy of information, it have been determined conspicuously, irretrievably creditable. A royal ancestry is a common bloodline that goes back eleven thousand years ago, is the archetypal Hebrew phenotype identity derived from the elite royal Anunnaki, Nibiruan Elohim the creator god Enki, and his ties to the indigenous African female. A truth which is no longer lost; it has been uncovered, it's a revealing part of our ancestors. This modern empirical worldwide learning and teaching about the positive and perniciously and evil against African Hebrew people who had been the slave sold into bondage. Yeah, I am referring to the Middle Passage! An epoch of the most disgraceful diaspora, the wholesale marketing of black people, the slave traders who participated and facilitated a total evisceration of the human story, and by doing this, they removed, confused, and abused the truth and raised up the most significant fairy tale about the Genesis creator Enki. The original book of the lost family tree of the bloodline is the Anunnaki alien gods story is the out-of-Africa consciousness theorists hypothesis that is the convoluted genesis narrative tale myth.

Now researchers have revealed written accounts onto rugged baked cuneiform clay tablets, Historically speaking people are desperate for information on this. A topic about Anunnaki ancient astronauts, as space travels, of an alien race; viz., the speculative views in books. These sources of information give the specificity and anecdotal details about contributions from both the judgment of the good deeds and the shameful and unholy facts.

The author's books serve humanity by revealing the context of the historical humankind's epoch of time. Culture written about the history of eons has been written in the pages of books that have been written with the aim of making people think. And for years, they exposed the machinations of the leaders, who were the power of the rulers. Those who use Christian religious doctrine to inculcate teaching for the purpose to control, or manipulate the psyche, meaning the folks' meditation practice involves achieving a pure heart in harmonic balance of the mind, body, spirit complex. They had this successfully caused the olden days' spiritual knowledge of the wisdom of the African-Egyptians Law of One love by practice of sacred principles in unity with the Egyptian deity AtenRa's practice through his application of yoga meditation in daily worshiping Neteru philosophical import consciousness awareness doesn't predetermine individual's destiny. And every living soul is born with a purpose. Yet, unfortunately, my family roots were upended and severed by the evil oppression owing to the mendacious Western European rulers of bankrupted kingdoms. They set out on a quest to conquer other countries and disrupted their sovereign liberty over their tribal claims to the territorial lands settled as the custodians who seeded civilization and rule on planet Earth.

Aggressive tactics and military encroachment spurned the African Israeli indigenous Jewish tribes of Judah to misfortunes to befall future destiny of human degradation for four hundred years. The evil exploitation was a scheme to capitalize from the Negroe human diaspora that built the transatlantic trade. What? Yeah, that's right.

Oh, there's this and so much that we should know a Western European's history (https://chattnewschronicle.com/african-american-history/black-kings-and-queens-ruled-europe-for-almost-700-years/) and they pulled this off?!

Yes indeed in the normal way of buyers and sellers, as Afrikan Kings and Arabian traders were complicit players. Effectively lives were upended in the name of their God, perpetrated by the evil souls of men and their sinister proxy insatiable lust for wealth. This was never ever bequeathed by the installed demigod rulers, who all wittingly executed this human tragedy was genocide. This was a preceding epoch of archived history as fascinating history revealed the despicable evil crimes against humanity. Whereas we read of these chronicles, harken back into periods of many life cycles and brighten up your vision with clarity and understanding of the present time that is a fraction of the world's broad psychological tapestry of the ephemeral thinks of the past lies the knowledge of our archived pages and anecdotal details, long before your or my human natal living breath, experiencing life's peregrinations that end at death; curtain call that will carry me home. Now before we were first fashioned into the illusion of the physical external empirical world of our spirit that causes our animated actions to enter into the life portal of the glowing lighted entrance, I walked into the ambiance arcing harmonic corona that was this light energy waves vibrated that sync with my transformation into the incorporeal spirit form of myself, the embryonic essence of the mind unwise, my spirit of consciousness. And from the realm of luminous divine nirvana, I was born and unknowing of my own self, as a vivified entity of the mercurial essence. Yet the soulful spirit that caused my spark to animate my living actions. A human life-form came into the physical form as corporeal matter. Living is the true nature of our visceral conscious awareness, the true nature of illusory temporal reality.

    And might we have all recognized our divinity as a benevolent soulful spirit at peace is sacred to providence and salvation? And might you question why it is curious that Genesis does not elucidate on the real purpose why the royal god Enki (Ea) fashioned (created) Adam (man) in his own image? Humm? He was the biological Father of the Homo sapiens, who suddenly appeared as a new race of earthly human beings. And have we not entered the interior plane of living material illusory temporal reality—into the ankh that complex symbolic radiant light? Born naked, unknowing of the mind/body/spirit avatar complex of myself, given life without the luminous divine wisdom of the Law of One, love of the hidden mysteries, knowledge of Egyptian Kemetism meditation, the ancient Egyptian path to enlightenment, and the mythology of spiritual treasures of the wisdom of the Law of One love teachings. Original esoteric teachings of the great sacred wisdom of the Law of One love of the natural laws and moral guiding principles of the warm glowing sunlight particles upon the rotation of Earth's incredible plane. All manner of material life forms, all alive is the spirit declining beautiful other self, spirits' animation living life upon this terrestrial plane. To discover the pathway toward the ancient Kemetic knowledge of Neberdjer teachings and understanding god. For all beings to develop within and learn to know thyself and achieve that equilibrium; whether the heart is pure and judged light against the ostrich feather of the Egyptian old kingdom goddess, Ma'at's sacred principles (https://www.ancient.eu/Ma'at/).

    The inward spiritual teachings of guiding sacred principles of the great spirit Neberdjer resides. And in this external empirical world, it's a multitudinous established system; you struggle to win in man's controlled powerful institutional competitive system of illusory temporal reality to survive. We are either winners or losers who will all die on some uncertain date. For by night, we sleep dreaming reposefully, you drift off to the tremendous anachronistic dichotomy of the pure mind's Al-Kimia luminous places.

Of which humanity's countenance is made in the likeness of the vainglorious Kavod of cosmic peace that is ubiquitous, uncompromised new age world order; and it's uniformity of harmonic waves frequency vibration of the cosmic universe affinities of the cosmos constellation of twelve zodiacal houses spinning time-space continuum orbits. It's about letting yourself live and loving this in the illusion of the living illusory temporal reality, learning and understanding loving with pure, unselfish heart/soul/spirit unity of the infinite creators—the human transformation upon the interior Earth's plane. All individual life as a separate unity of experiences between the embryonic miracle emanation from the nine months of the natal and death cycle. It's a material illusion of physical matter to develop the light purified heart. The human birth symbolical of sacred Egyptian Ankh is the luminous divine natal nature in eternal crystal life, light, and love. To be born is to achieve a fidelity of mind of true honor and integrity. Life being free of and from all evil machinations of all fetters that prey upon human immortality. This is my literacy original elucidation is my insightful prose serpentines with humble ruminations as a transportine crossing mental journey and enter through the gateway crossing into the psycho-spiritual realm and in humble appreciation living my life each day beneath the sky canvas of luminosity of introspection.

To enter into the mind state of the dreams, adrift, traveling beyond the restraints of the Earth's interior plane beneath a sky-dome, a band of billions of bright carat-like diamonds, sit high in the glinting starry night, dotted the dark canvas constellations sparkle bright. Perceptions of me are imbibed of things in the glories of the sun. Yeah, it's the illusory temporal reality beneath a band of cosmos lighted of billions of stars. I traveled on the physics of the vibrations of the harmonic wave, a fantastic epoch illusory reality of counting days and years on the Earth's space time continuum. Learning about the present time-space sensates the world. To be as humble as a wise spirit of the Law of One love philosophy. And yes, it's a state of existence and the inner peace and harmonic balance, quiet comfort of ataraxia and solace. Our purpose is to live, in the light spirit of love of the self and our other selves. It's true for every natal blessed as a soul born in the interior earth plane of experience. A gift from the all dynamic of being among the living by the vainglorious most high. And I aspired to greatness and righteousness. To enjoy our journey through life experiences of temporal reality in search of a purpose of love, peace, to experience solace. For into this life plane, we are all born naked without raiment and unknowing of nature; and it's a touchdown in mercurial Earth's evolving eons cosmic cycles. The life force energy is endued with from the divine spirit with freewill; and as such eschew the ways of turpitude have been vivified with the spark to do good or evil deeds. That we may be responsible for our own actions in an interior earth plane of material illusory temporal reality. A fantastic voyage begins and ends in a labyrinth of olden refractions to achieve a purified character and personality that is our true self-identity of proprietary positive moral righteousness.

We are all born unknowingly of our physical form. We enter into the light knowing nothing about integrity. At birth, we are vulnerable with no character development; to be acquired from teaching and learning, we'll soon develop our personality. A lifetime journey towards daily life experiences, every moment bathed in the sunrises and sunsets. Spiritually being alive and insync with the orbital mystical Earth cycles of the cosmic twelve constellation body of the star system of the zodiac houses which are symbolically the zodiac wheels, 25,290 cosmic dance of the movements of the twelve planets.

My angelic spirit-self is attuned to the wisdom of the Law of One love teachings of the ancient mystery schools of the spiritual science meditation on the Law of One luminous divine sacred wisdom principles.

Humankind beings in unity with the cosmic Nebebigjar sitting flexed in the lotus position. My peace of mind is achieved through daily meditation. This relaxing my focus brings me into the purity with the one all unity in sync with the divine embrace of the life forces energy for harmonic balance of sublime nature of formosity, and reverence for the universal spirit of the one infinite creator God! A fantastic intersection with sacred energy that is devoid of dalliance or real-ruminations. A speculation with a fiction is the hyperbole synopsis, diffusive thoughts effulgence of my associates with logic and reason of a well-informed pure mind. And most reflective of my perception of bright stars arrayed in the dark during nighttime, and the symbolic Solar god of Aten Ra sails across the cloud covered canvas by daylight. Calmly, I took a pause and sat down as my spirit caused me to ponder all that surrounds me on all sides. I narrowed my focus, and my mind cogitated this illusion of an anachronistic enigmatic epoch of transformation of the time space. Within the period of cycles, my soulful spirit appreciated the harmonic vibrational infinity and affinities of my fascinating rhythms of the crowded room with the great heart of the higher minded.

My soul attuned enjoin a common medium of a pure creative mind and matter coalesce. My soul being free from dredges idle earthman's nefarious evil human cognitive dissonance is the dalliance of wayward souls purveying evil deeds. Of the manifestation of my human form transported into an objective plane of universal luminous divine cosmic nature; we are all living souls on a finite transformative journey towards our purposeful life. Consciousness awareness acquiesces to the sleep state of the mind in transition is not yet awake. The soulful spirit of my free will unity, animates my separation from my fleshly embodiment of present tense escape transitions into the dreamweaver's peregrination through the sleep state. The mind confluence through the anachronistic surreal realm of space-time. Light is in my mind/body/spirit complex that causes my actions and every breath I take in the illustrative daylight reality.

Humankind's soul embodiment is an individual unit of the luminous divine separation; and, as the living manifestation, we live and experience Earth's illusory temporal reality in its garden biosphere. Human beings are the living units of separation from this universal, all pervading living source of the supreme universal Neberdjer oneness. So might it be that the luminous divine light, I have descended and was incarnated, risen into this new life cycle of the physical objective empirical external world with its cacophony of pinging noise and audible sound distortions. And for quiet comfort in the ataraxia of Yoga meditation, feel the spirit conjugate myself to enter into the serenity with harmonic balance, meaning a common medium of the mind is in perfect wave vibrations I imbibed in a different place. And you and all indeed exist as of flesh. I am in this form as a living being attuned to the way of knowing. Well, my friends, I am humble and wise as I ask you to digest this explanation, which says the truth about the Anunnaki Sumerian Bible narrative is out there for your perusal of archeology and anthropology discovery of biblical Genesis narrative creation God. People are awakening in the spiritual teachings/learning about the bon homies who are unwisely lost in the blind faith religion. Their eyes are open, and they are all alive but have no understanding of the recondite Al-Kimia (hidden mysteries) facts about Earth's interior plane.

Evolution and involution of confluence rhythm harmonic waves, vibrations of inner peace awareness and mental harmonic balance and solace adherence to the Egyptian principles and wisdom that is the Law of One love love philosophical medium to the human mind, body, and spirit complex. Teaching and learning spiritual things about psycho-spiritual science disciplines through the initiation of ancient Kemetism practice of sacred meditation. The aim of this is to gain a purified heart and mind, the awakening to know the inner self at a higher level of knowledge and wisdom. A sacred understanding of the infinity of life journey is derived from roots of the human ancestral tree, the life forces in the mind, body, spirit units of the all intelligence infinity of the divinity life source that is the one force of energy. Your soul as a unit of separated corporeal life form that is finite energy of human embodiment that is but one individual unit of the reach of the all ineffable sublime infinity of the Kavod that, ubiquitously, pervades through noumena of the intelligent universal Neteru.

We are born awakened spirits and crystallized creation in matter. It's a life journey in illusory temporal reality to learn to know myself. And for my Ka titivate toll cultivated into the beneficence as purified heart of a sense of the ataraxia state of quiet comfort and solace resting. A disparaging distortion of the precursor Anunnaki extraterrestrial alien beings, the settlers of the arcane nascence of the foreign titular gods—the original custodians of life as titular deities of planet Earth as they were revered and perceived as the immortal gods who came down from the heavens had brought civilization, religion and divine kingship to inculcate their power of God and rule on earth. Then, my friends, might there exist that invisible hand of the mendacious secret cabal quietly operating behind the scenes of the political and economic machinations that continues today? The apex of the rulers is the orchestration of hidden mysteries in the shadows that drives actions that cause the manifestation of the earth's three-dimensional countryside landscape with the air that the ripples of the meadows and fields of waves of tall grass.

Now seriously, folks, you need to think about this: Why did the authors of the Old Testament holy Bible be so disinclined to elucidate on these ancient astronauts as an extraterrestrial alien race landing? Or that on the earth's surface and becoming creators of a higher social culture that spread to many areas of the interior plane from Mesopotamia, Africa, Central Asia, Mesoamerica, and Western Europe invaders.

The terrestrial planet spectrum of metaphysical construction by the original great all-luminous divine Egyptian sagaciousness teachings of the Al-Kimia Kemetism treasures that exemplify the teaching and learning to adhere to the wisdom principles of the all unity derived from the African Egyptian solar god Aten Ra's Law of One love of the self and our other selves.

And yes, this perspective is intuitive with clarity in thought that transforms you into the constrictions that are the psychological spirit realm. In quiet comfort concealed. Human souls are born unknowingly of past eons. This lost information will leave you baffled without the objective capability to apply intelligent logic and reason, understanding religion via the conscious bias sensate modality. You see, folks are not motivated to question everything that they were taught about the Bible from the very early beginning because we were told that it happened that way!

What is a dichotomy between spiritual science and theological church religions and thoughts represents In my balanced view, what I interpolate is according to the fundamental logic and reason proposition to assert assertions that is seemingly personification of truth that coalesces from ancient Egyptian Kemetism principles of the divine sacred derived knowledge, teachings and learnings of the secret wisdom principles of the ancient mysteries schools that were sacked and razed down to the ground by such armies as the Hyksos, Hittites, Persian, Romans, and Arabian invaders destroyed! Oh, and there's this... Many of the histories of the records they stole were cautiously aimed with the intent to truncate and erase the social construct of spiritual science and intellectual knowledge of the powerful predominant African kingdoms, such as Egypt and Meroe' Kemet kingdoms (https://www.britannica.com/place/Meroe).

At that inflection point was without impunity conquering armies wittingly pillaging and plagiarizing the African Egyptian Kemet cultures that were once promulgated under the blue sky and white clouds canvas; which had existed through many eons from the began Anunnaki on the earth. Rule of the earth was begun by the creation of Homo sapiens sapiens came forth to be by Enki's creation of the human phenotype. Whereas, it suffices me to acknowledge that we all live as a human form, embodiments of the finite material mind, body, and spirit complex. Alive by the most high bathed in the time cycles of the sun heat wave energy for a daytime and nighttime of counting the calendar days of the twelve months growing old as the duality of revolving time clock that ticks away, forever streaming nonstop; and each passage is beneath the skydome cycle were the beginning and ending comes around in the same place for thousands of years. Each one is the one under the sun and long before the rise of other humanist forms of biblical historical religious teachings. A transportine descent adrift across space constriction is derived from the great Al-kimia of all unity.

Might I imbibe configurations and monumental true wisdom of the Law of One love learning of spiritual meditation teachings. Whereof all truth is sacred fountains pervading consciousness awareness. Curious erudite minds will think it wise to take a deep dive into this for a glimpse into what was found that it is a proper predicate for discovering lost historical revelations about primordial cosmic periods of the metaphysical evolutionary history of the Anunnaki alien gods: "Those who from the Heaven came." Accordingly, I was inspired to write this book I convey on blank pages. I have been inspired to tell you this story that is tied to nature's vibrant dichotomy.

Rejoice in life and love free of distortions en to the Law of One true Creator in death and rhythmic cycles into the event with providence and salvation. To be aligned with luminous divine cosmic milieus. Quality features of a gloriously grand style of the medieval architecture of the higher planes, blissful sweven into the inner realities. Birth is a cradle-to-grave religion of salvation and redemption psychological, metaphysical *law of harmonious correspondence sounds and the noise dissipation, to everything positive and negative harmonics vibrations of the Neberdjer. Ordinary people. Whom there is the collective unconscious and the amoral radical misguided confused people who are going hither and thither without knowledge of their potential or their human purpose.*

Yes suffice it to say confess that I know about this from my own journey through my youthful life. When I was at the pivottable and winding crossroad, I was unsure of which decision to make; and my future direction; I ed among the malleable seas of the aimlessly flawed wayward human souls. Emergence to life and be warmed by the rays of bright light and hear that clarion call from the beginning through the slow waning of the counting of years of daylight to darkness no more. luminous divine souls lie suspended in an embryonic fetal state. And might I ask you to permit me to say that every human soul is the unit of separation from the monad spirit of the Neberdjer's universal essence that has spurred our soul to breathe. My third eye of the human soul awakens from a recumbent state to spark nature to rise from astros metaphysical units of imperceptibility, the separation from this divine all-luminous, finite animated soulful spirit existence.

A mother's warmth is a place to sleep and grow until the natal date. From the embryonic state of my mind/body/spirit complex, I thank Anunnaki. A life of existence has brought forth the opportunity to discover that each time we have been born, we have no prior knowledge of past lifetime experiences. Each time we must fulfill our purposeful life peregrinations and awakenings to know of good or bad consequences.

Sensation of seeing starry bright lights in the darkness of night. I feel related as one with the infinite intelligent mind of the most high divine luminous light of the metaphysical nature of the all divine life forces energy; that is, the architect of the construct of existential material forms that came forth into existence. The divine life forces energy; that is to say the architect of the construct of existential material forms that came forth into a Christian religious faith theology. However, it doesn't comport with the ubiquitous grand architect of the universal construct of creator of the cosmic and material geometry spiritual life forces ell; that is, the architect of the construct of existential material forms that came forth into existence. The sensate of the external visual empirical world that came forth so that you and I might fulfill our life's purpose with inner peace and spiritual solace in quiet comfort. I am that human body and soulful light as the flame that animates us all who are the material forms transcends the time cycle continuum.

At the appointed duration the anesthetized embryonic state awakened. When our spirit animates the inert body by the laws of physics into the divine state of duality. Humankind being calm in body, mind, spirit, complex embryonic form growing awaits their palingenesia my natal date. On the interior Earth plane of old allegorical anachronistic illusory reality, which you and I were born to live, enjoy the radiance imbibing the divine spirituality of the light force energy. The most significantly important thing is transcendence involution of the soul in sync with the universal cosmic noumena.

A pure love of self is vibrant with the lifeblood of daily existence by the Kavod of the light source bathed in the light of spirituality. And underneath it all, the cheerful facade of civility lies the teachings of Kemetism precepts. We are individual children derived as separate units of mind, body, spirit complex from the divine great all, born of biological illusory material world constructions. It's a life cycle conundrum that resides impersonal to experience the material things. Truth is that all denizens of the living bio-field of the metaphysical sensate waves vibrate in manifestations of nature's units of representation, derived from two primordial entities biological DNA lifeblood blueprints (ref.). Of the Janus of the contiguous duality cycle, our spirit causes every action of human knowledge. And so in the spinning lunar cycles of nine celestial calandra moons orbits, endued by the higher of Neberdjer spirit I was born into life. My benevolent God. Oh God HalleluJah!

I am a material living embodiment in human form, a miracle spirit imbued as a human soul animated substance as a mind/body/spirit complex of luminous divine energy essence. To this I say: my god, O' HalleluJah!

We are bathed in and blessed by the light of the Monad energy force of a Neterian mercurial radiance of Sun permeating as harmonic vibratory upon harmonic life force energy from the glowing sunshine. It is sustainable and brings forth nourishment to the interior terrestrial plane bountiful milieu and biosphere. A true clarity of purpose alive within the psychological state of illusory temporal reality of to feel the love, the sense ataraxy of quiet comfort and solace. Awakened and raised into the light, I am a finite material form living upon illusory existential temporal reality beneath blue and white soft, atmospheric clouds drifting across the terrestrial sky. Blessing shall come to truth seekers in their daily fulfillment by spiritual prayer and meditation. My sensate was in sync with nirvana within perfect harmonic balance of being one unit manifestation of the universal spirit of Neter (Nebegijur). All high praise is to be given as acknowledgement of the one vainglorious harmonic balance of flame that is 's providence to sustain the spiritual essence of life of the light force energy that is the Eastern sunrise.

My eyes are closed and I am in a calm state of mind and I'm sitting in the lotus position, while my mind is relaxed and focused inward in sync with my spirit ataraxy in quiet comfort and solace. My introspection free from my illusory state of mind; as daily temporal reality is of no consequence. My spirit is now free from the redolent Neteru of flora of the fauna and flora. I am only hearing the lilting sound of the water flowing from the rock filled stream trickle down from high elevation. The majestic scenic vistas and lofty mountain ridges, and the fresh, cool, clean air to breathe, the trickling sound of crystal water flowing and serpentine through a narrow stream surrounded by a lilting majestic panoramic milieu.

The cacophony of nature sounds pervades as mental vision as I dwelled and tarried for a moment of tranquility. A sojourn in the quiet comfort, the symbol of birth, growth, and seasonal symbolic cycle of rebirth.

The wide sensational vista with asynchronous sounds as if I am my presence that was being announced. This was a wonderful time for I to breathe the fresh calm air of nature walking amid the vivid picturesque mountain chain rugged colorful landscape of plants, and all manner of trees was a visible display amid a subtle wave of gentle breezes that pervaded the of the living forest amid the hillsides and grassy dales.

A magnificent calm vistas of this volatile natural external empirical world of the luminous divine radiant sunshine upon the earth plane. Always be humble and wise as guardian that causes the spirits actions shepherd's a life through a number of counting years all the days of my given life.

Humans live in the realm of duality as a lifetime experience living within the interior plane of reality's harmonic wave/particle light energy with quiet and noise discordance. A common fundamental esoteric; and that is genuinely symbolic of the spirit of life, light, and love.

Take a close look at a mirror, and you'll see the reflection of your countenance in visual form and matter. The humanself imprint in God's own likeness. Whereof you and I are embodiment of the form corporeal matter and incorporeal a finite animated hologram?

You and I countenance reflection for all beings to see a physical lifeform; the illusory temporal reality of depicting my corporeal fashioned by a DNA code higher being? A corporeal human substance, recognize my countenance reflection? With the golden ratio my mind awakened into the light. Our past s lost and like dreams forever dissipated, unknowing of the past eons have been archived; As I may think, nothing has revealed anything of this primordial ancestral delineations of this Homo sapiens biological father and mother deep Ancient Anunnaki Anthropithecus Genesis bloodline ties to the Family roots! Yet this is theorized as the origin of Africa's of humankind. By male and female mothers womb you as I was conceived to grow until a date certain. With consciousness awareness we slowly begin to learn and wonder about things; and invariably, we are conscious of our beingness. About who we are and where we come from is always a child's most salient question. And what a revelation for you to pre suppose that the Anunnaki titular God/Enki the extraterrestrial biological scientist and medical doctor.

They claimed that He had successfully manipulated African females' mitochondrial DNA Code fashioned human beings by using his own genetic DNA Y-chromosome to create the prototype homo sapien sapiens Adapa(Adam) and Tehama(Eve) created the likeness—to honor His chosen people?

It's the storyline that we know from the holy Bible of Genesis, which we accept as the truth, unconditionally as a fact—wittingly by worship of the blind faith religious teachings in the Old Testament biblical story alludes to as such. that things of the universal cycle of life cycles and transitions from a birth into death upon this earth plane is spinning on a fulcrum axis of luminous divine equilibrium in harmonic waves vibrations that underlie a substrate of volatile primal elements pulsating amid the everyday world we see is the posited of the psychological reality and the mystery creator.

There are curious fractionalized external empirical world consciousness; what we see are glaringly discernable strong evidence of this endemic drug crisis. Our external empirical world is a chasm between those termed radical malcontents with their sense of dreadful lifestyle devoid of the status quo ante. A chasm and a struggle to bring forth a new age consciousness awareness facilities in transformations that supersede the falsehoods of those rulers aspire government's unbridled system of global capitalism and socialism—a external empirical world in which is the game of kings, bishops, the pawns are the relevant players in the monopoly system of global financial economic activity.

A global exchange market system of profit-seeking sellers of buying volatility drives the economic growth that is the lifeblood of the player's financial wealth and cash flow streams. Whilst the pawns of humanity fund the issues of their political parties partisan agenda promises. This is the syndrome, like drugs, money, power, and monetary control and enslavement or manipulation to serve the self that undergird our economic system. And in the realm of earth's interior landscape lies a scale of winners and losers. And like a chessboard a player's conscious spirit that causes our thoughts and each decision and action to take moves. A board game that is closely related to the human spirit in this real life earthly drama.

Our original custodians of planet earth are the titular gods behind their global economic and financial institutions for political and religious control over the ignorant sons and daughters of men. Ordinary people subconsciously asleep adhere to the blind faith status quote anti. Actions of the elite rulers they execute through human proxies—their witting cadres, their secret societies are the hidden hands of the secret cabals that have total control of the entire financial and economic systems.

The decision makers of a global intrinsically manifold ruling class of wealth acThey take actions and make decisions that are efficaciously and closely akin to the tactics and strategic moves in this real-life global chessboard. It's a game of Rooks, Bishops, Queens, King, and of course, *the human plebeian servants who constitute valuable pawns! Most of those who have advocated for a new age favor this elitist collectivism scheme of one-empirical world power of the globalist order.*

To gain total power and influence for control over the individual rights and the free will of consciousness awareness. To decry a justification by pious populous, moral virtues and responsible human species and the condition by pushing a narrative of misguided falsehoods.

Persistently the cloven "Janus" partisan left and right-winged political argumentative ideological views have no benefit for resolving the global social constructs of the haves and the have nots. Nor do political parties have agreed on a final solution. Are we all the living souls of the spirit dimension who must understand that we must learn to live morally pure and filled with treasures of the wisdom of the Law of One love. To learn and know ourselves as the luminous divine spirit embodiment on a life journey with conscious awareness walking through life. We are all wobbling and trying to steady ourselves on the tightrope. twenty-first-century social outlier of profane, immoral turpitude of adolescents malcontent. Paroxysms of the misled capricious is churlish behavior. To be forbidden in the likes of the wayward indecorous wayward arrival of malcontents; those who are the elite rulers over the earth.

The disruptors who manipulate through power and control of the social construct of church and state established political systems. But proprietary means of political and economics have been deceiving by every intrinsic positive and negative evil fetters through machinations.

Still we have others who reject this luminous view of the divine archetypal teachings of the origin of ancient African/Egyptian mythology, which extends from the learning and teachings of the divine psycho-spiritual science of the universal sacred Neter. Not just the belief in modern ecclesiastical religion that diverges from an rejected philosophy of the Neberdjer's spiritual and material evolution of the true life guiding sacred principles of the natural laws, aligned with the in unified spirit of the harmonic waves force energy pervades through this grand labyrinth the material and metaphysical universal macrocosm; and, this terrestrial experience in every "forms" and "matter across the earth plane. It is the home and the place where humankind was born into life to live, learn, love and to be loved by our other self as a visual peregrination. The pur-

pose is about knowing one's understanding is that insight is the knowledge standard and the gift of sagacious consciousness awareness of the in nature; and experiencing the life journey from the natal dates that is the life cycle rewinds back to our beginning. A new incarnation, another, life peregrination unfolds into the esoteric diurnal turnstyle of sleep and awakening is the cycle of counting days and nights to live in the illusory reality. With clarscentiant I felt myself attune to the enigmatic positive life force spirit pulsating the energy that causes consciousness awareness of and to experience waves moving across the water surface.

Then, might a majestic heartfelt dual soul be weighted in equal measure against the principle precepts of moral turpitude? It's a measure of service to self and to the entities of our other living selves, by the Egyptian Goddess Ma'at Ostrich feather. With a heavy heart murkiness descends from a broken contemporary social upheaval. Ours is a political intrenching cantankerous arguments/debates, left and right uncompromising two party Janus political ideas and never mitigating the human issues. When human social concerns attenuate into violent actions and. Presciently, millions of ordinary people's economic well-being is the byproduct of debt.

There's a wave of unintentional consequences which is associated with reality that is tumult from credit card overspending which spirals out of control; and it's a tenuous situation with years of economic despair spurs destruction. People are living with on clear-sightedness to turn away from their lifestyle of indolence. We are living in the status quo, the world of materialism—the Constitutional laws that stand for good order against those who are misguided and misled pawns. They are blind followers motivated by the reprehensible behavior in the ways of the evil fetters; human beings devoid of disciplined ways of Kemetism teaching of moral sacred principles of life. And with logic or these are the lost callow souls who rally in bringing forth social violence and anarchy. With dalliance they relish and revere destructive civil instability and disobedience by organizing politically motivated activism.

These indolence grifters conspire to achieve a utopian society by their grand deception by undermining the pillars of human freedom. Rogue tactics have been malcontents advocating a spurious scheme to undermine the society's fundamental complex sacred principles constitu-

tion. Whilst Socialism is the creeping Trojan Horse has infiltrated freedom loving people by incremental complex encroachment. My friends, they do not know what they aspire to open the front door by a deceptive crusade to spur socialism. To establish the redistribution of wealth as over this transformative new leviathan of the succore. The reprobates of socialism's creeping dark order contend to espouse a new age of socialized human beings, the new world order enfoldment into the coming age of Aquarius. New ages spur social malcontents who are those who eschew from the existing civil order, precursors of opposing views seeking to effectuate their views in the new-age as the new world horizon.

And it's this anagnorisis that pervades in the zodiacal house of emerging negative of shockwaves on society's external thoughts, perceptions confluence positive and negative experiences of how human beings view illusory temporal reality. The 'nescient' of the deception have been misled by the evil deeds of restless infomedics; wayward human souls, devoid of proper "mitzvah" espouse sanguin gratuitous violence by their spurious craven racism, rhetorical hatred and divisiveness. Prescient, the manifestation of misled pathological disorder. This enmity spurred social syndrome of malcontents pervading a new age agenda of new external empirical world anarchy. A new age of fractional nationalism, Socialism, and Communism pervading fiery rivalries among the trenchant unflappable churlish social right-wing, left-visceral political government debates.

These underlying hyperbolic platitudes arguments are recognisably reconcilable, unsettled ping-pong ad hominem issues of the powers of the infinite and antipathy ad-nauseam! Another of nature's creations buttresses against the metric of grand intelligent design.

All things of the luminous divine are encapsulated in my perceptions and appear in my thoughts as if on the blank pages of my life. Little of one's past incarnation is lost with the new life in sync with the divine rhythms of the cosmic harmonic dance. A social complex is a Life, the Light, and the sensual love as if a merry-go-round twisting upward on the life cycle of time. I am a state of manifestation; one unit of separation from the all vainglorious luminous divine creation of a universal great spirit. Though some skeptics may argue, disputes obfuscate the truth about this matter amid the public society's increasing consciousness awareness.

HAKEEM R. JELANI

It is becoming well informed with the biblical and historical relevance of archeology and anthropology researchers' empirical evidence that dovetails with the biblical genesis narrative tale. The ings say that we are a human species, the ancient primitive workers fashioned by the Anunnaki extraterrestrial alien, Nibiru the Royal great prince Enki, the biblical Gods figure of the eponymous—Infinite Creator God of the Old Testament biblical genesis narrative story. He arrived and landed in the olden times as Anunnaki, God of Ancient Mesopotamian history, and people who were the ancient Sumerian City of "Eridu"!

Extension the personification we call to in prayerful worshiping in faithful fellowship—as we are devoid of mystery, spiritual science, and wisdom of the Law of One love. The sacred principles of wisdom teaching/learning of the natural Laws of One Shetaut Neter spiritual light of knowledge and understanding of the Law of One love the natural existence of the Neberdjer philosophy. Of course, we are free thinkers who can learn/teach others the spiritual science of Kemetism, the original wisdom principles of the luminous divine Law of One unity derived from Life, Light, Love evolution of Shetaut Neter Religion.

In the recumbent state, alive and asleep while tethered to the cycle of the present time-space continuum, unfold as you and I for nine lunar moons. A miracle soul is resting until the natal nature; as I drew of my first life breath. Awaken from darkness into the daily effulgent of sunlight; an embryonic state into the plane of objective illusory temporal life reality.

To each a separate measure of life existence as perception to transitions of time in the illusion of the mind cycle through the quantum dimensions of duality; meaning the cycle rotation between lunar light and daylight canopy by the bright sun. A skydome of blue fluffy white clouds drifting within the life cycles imbued and synced to the illusory psychological temporal reality. Life's fertile seed resides conceived; in a fetal position in mystical and esotericism—erudition of the time and seasons; and ergo, thus, the monthly calendar.

It marked a natural birth date, a delineation of time of experiences until the full stop. And into the light of nature had begun in 1952 and born in the second shining zodiac house of Taurus alive. All human beings are held in a mother's womb. Our conscious awareness is not fully awakened to animated illusory temporal reality. From the embryonic state. We all have been asleep resting in our mothers womb until that proper natal birth date. An embryonic fetal position rests whence and whither in the developmental recumbent state of sleep. To the living, all asleep in the fetal position were born naked without consciousness. Yet as the archetypal Adam (Adapa) and Eve (woman), we too were fashioned. You, too, knew not of your nakedness; it's true of everyone! Fear of light overcame me in darkness in my recumbent state of a sense of quiet comfort.

To be clear about this, I knew nothing of this busy life of imperceptible spiritual rhythmically pulsating. And calmly, my subtle, easy rhythm beats the heart of my embryonic nascence. My human spark, the natal nature of substance, began. Into the external empirical world before my eyes were opened and before my mind could apprehend and navigate the edd and flowing through the diurnal world. Though our souls began this way, unknowingly we have been awakened from the sleep inside our mother's womb. Slowly I grew by the nine sacred moons until that was certain. The Neter enfolded my mind/body/spirit complex; protection was shrouded like a beautiful embryonic red rose until the positive manifestation of a new development came, the first birthday a celebration of life experiences and the joyful time and the intermittent moments of unhappiness. I had no memories of my previous life/illusion complex.

The joy of being alive and experiencing the light of my spirit is warm soothing rays of the majestic energy of the monad. I am awakened by this natal life force of my essence. Born by luminous divine nature. This law of free will to do good or evil deeds; of which my heart is to be measured against the sacred ostrich feathers of the Egyptian goddess Ma'at's moral sacred principles of philosophy.

To have been judged and pure with a spirit of eternal truth, the illusory temporal reality extends to several counting years. The glorious old life remembrances of the past living souls are arcane; it all has been forgotten. A realm being derived as the nascence upon the cosmic cycle of nature's new birth, life, death, and resurrection and goodness shall follow I all the days of my life. An anachronistic space on a plane of life, light, and lovely parents as guiding shepherds. Human beings' free will consciousness—the idealism of logic and reason. As perceived temporal reality. A subjective and objective mental ego and the mental alter ego confluence in the empirical world, viz., the absolute nature of illusory material reality.

A period to learn about a bygone era of the past years of eons of lost life consciousness awareness. In illusory temporal reality, I searched for the sacred wisdom of the Law of One love. Cognitively recognizable creative images; sensory synopsis of the inward spirit that causes human actions. Being alive is appreciating the subtle nuances of material psycho-spiritual visual awareness, we can imbibe the living nature in swiftly river rapids flowing streams. When the weather is comfortable and the sunshine over the earth as it moves across the panoramic milieu's beautiful natural vistas. Therein lies the effulgent sunlight I behold such animations of this soul 'is mine, body, (unity) and consciousness awareness. This principle of duality is perception. The Anunnaki ancient alien astronauts' had a presence and a connection to the Old Testament Holy Bible story.

A salient question to consider as you ponder this: Why is this predicate backstory not elucidated in the Genesis narrative account? Oh, and there's this…the African Egyptian consciousness is derived from the Kemetic spiritual science sacred wisdom principles initiation teaching and learning of the Law of One Love. Religion is the antipathy to the propagation of the religious teachings that have diverged from the complexities of ancient mystery spiritual science of the Law of One wisdom of the Law of One love from teachings of the meditation of the inward unity with the Kavod of luminous divine sacred principles that is the Nebedjuer, shetaut more net.

The purifying of humankind's mind, body, and spirit complex. To aspire to and eventually achieve Initiation is to be one with intelligent infinity! Unconditional devotion to learning/teaching about the African Egyptian Pharaoh solar god Ra's Law of One, being consistently honest, humble, and wise in our interaction with others. Living every day with a pure heart and, ipso facto, from birth, learning to love and to be loved.

People have closed their eyes. The lost souls of human society walk among us who love the light of god. We see some while others succeed without knowing of a benevolent purpose in life. First, we are one family community of souls who are all individual units of the life force solar energy. And, ipso facto, it's a clarity of the transformation, living joyful, *blissful life experiences of the life cycle, and the force energy that fades away with death.*

Welcomed into a new proprietary life full of everyday or mundane pathways to navigate the life journey along multitudinous diverse human experiences juxtaposed against the Law of Correspondence. Everyone's life peregrinations are the streaming consciousness of illusory world reality. To seek the perfection of spiritual ascent into the realm of divine salvation.

Nature's melodious lilting sounds of birds are pleasing to my innermost mental state of quiet comfort, ataraxy, and peaceful solace. The earth is spinning around, but in the embryonic state, I can't look around; and my mouth was without a voice. In silence I only sleep because I can't talk. Someone's hands spank me. I cried louder to sense my mother's warmth to comfort the first I called. This oneiric allusory is a blank page; a story is about the nascent transportine dreamtime excursion through the golden age derived from Mars and Jupiter crossing into the icons of a golden age of gods and men. There are irrefutable historical connections to Old Testament Bible scripture that fits nicely with this ancestral bloodline DNA code. The Anunnaki god Enki had surreptitiously bequeathed the Hamite tribal peoples' lands that Ham had settled, according to the Bible genesis narrative. And so our theological organized religions seem apprised of perpetuating the biblical religious teachings of Christianity's blindness faith lack makes no mention about the speculation that within Genesis, Chapter 1, eponymous storied narrative descriptive; is careful to reject the ancient astronauts as very plausible and relevant to the assertion that Anunnaki titular Gods from the planet Nibiru were likely to be the original custodian's settlers of the world Earth's interior plane. Let's accept the harmonic vibration as Neberdjer, the voice of God of all things metaphysical and physical creation is not an allegorical story about the milieu as a garden in the land of Eden. The home of Adam and Eve were the precursor Homo sapiens denizens. Enki fashioned the sons and daughters of the green vistas on earth. A paradisiacal great ancestral honor of the interior landscape of the luminous divine as a garden in the land of Eden (https://www.awaytoafrica.com/know-african-roots). *Behold with both eyes; we awaken to experience and learn. From sleep, I fear not a light of truth. Its knowledge and treasures of the wisdom of the Law of One love of Neberdjer are always resting inside of my soul. And so the Bible Genesis begins. Prince Enki (the titular god) arrived onboard a large extraterrestrial, bell-shaped, shiny spacecraft and observed the murky dark plane surface of the Earth.*

Introspection felt the clarion call to awaken to live in the earth's radiant warm sunlight, experiencing nature's universal Neberdjer. The glorious human succor of spiritual light and love. Hear me now. Attune your ears and cogitate your open mind. Let's attune and listen to the bountiful melodiously harmonic modes of wave vibrations derived from the supreme intelligence of Neter residing life, light, and love of knowledge!

Be aware, humble, and wise when you listen to learn to hear and discern in the appreciative love of your life. With the ears attending, what is truthiness, and what is the truth? To know that it is your spirit of free will which causes our actions to lead you towards a god of salvation. To live being humble and wise to the luminous divine Neteru of life flows; it's sublimely beautiful evanescent of nature's milieu replete with a scenic view and lush green dales. Stunning panoramic rolling vistas of things alive lie amid nature's quintessence.

The creative allurements of living things are framed within the melodious harmonic cacophony of Earth's interior plane's garden milieu, a myriad of various sounds melding amid the scenic landscape.

For my eyes see extensive mountain ranges where you feel the cool flowing air of the high elevation peaks with the streams of nature's crescendo of the rushing sounds of the crashing waterfall from a distance. Could feel the air touch; and I smelled and appreciated this essence of every manner of nature's flowers that covered the environment with an array of beautiful flora against the waterfall cascading down upon the pool that slowly careens as it serpentines through nature's beautiful milieu.

The wet foot trails are muddy after the torrential rain of the baleful thunder clouds has stopped pouring rain. Listen to appreciate birds chattering amid the rushing sound of the earth, water traversing through nature's animation to breach the bountiful tranquility. To apprehend this incredible scene of a spectacular windswept dense forest hollow and the naked trees all around in the little clearing had lost their lives will face the coming of the brutal, chilling cold winter weather season. Peaceful quiet feelings while on a walk through tranquility of nature's spirit and imbibe and appreciate the forest biosphere. Life is a gentle journey as in

THE MIND, BODY, SPIRIT, AND STORYTELLING

If beautiful biosphere of many sounds distortions could be heard walking upon the wet leaves amplified in the peaceful silence amid this reverence. I am still, quiet, and humble as I admire the tranquility. It's a perfect time when the transition of the dark canvas of the nighttime cycle becomes a manifestation of awakening into nature, the life force energy of sunshine. There is the presence of the Infinite Creator that sustained looking down from the drifting clouds in the sky. Serene drizzles of cool spraying mist of falling raindrops mixed with the warm sun rays that makes things grow. such are all the things in this vistas of the daily providence of the illusory world landscapes garden milieu of various colorful depictions of fauna and flora. All green grass and wild plants, colorful flowers, and large trees with all manner of rugged areas of rocky gravel beds. Touched by a moment of quiet enchanting blissfulness.

What a tremendously remarkable walk to imbibe in this cathartic scenic panoramic natural living milieu; it's so incredible! The magnificent spectrum of vibrant colors of life growing wild all across the fruited earth landscape. I am no longer asleep, but I am awake among all denizens' material form and essence, externalized upon the material plane of that animated reality of energy and form. For it's not a recondite unit of the mind complex learning to know myself! With my sacred honor, pray that all are blessed with good health and a bountiful and prosperous happy life journey.

I am a tremendous marvelous being, no longer an embryonic soul; raised from rest in the inward spiritual Law of One infinite creator, a supreme spirit monad existence is the divine essence which resides in living beings of earth. We are all one separated unity of animated avatar corporeal form of mind/body/spirit complex; endued living energy; and humankind of a luminous divine Law of One Correspondence. And so might ethereal energy waves vibrations always guide you. And by the warm calming circle of life, light, love, honor, and much-esteemed respect for all mothers and fathers salvation. We all look for our deceased family ancestors. We pray to bring many warm-hearted blessings to protect individual freedom living as a family toward the rhythmic, harmonic spirit wave vibrations of peace and the luminous divine salvation beyond external illusory temporal reality's light.

Every living breath, magnificent vainglorious blessed by the human condition replete with experience (www.egyptianmysteries.org/what-do-neterians-believe-in-what-are-the-fundamental complex-sacred principal). A glorious Praise is to Neberdjer. A humble and wise servant of my spirit awakened by actions while living each day and night in the oneiric plane's surreal illusory invisible realm of the lunar cycle of darkness. I am like you, too, who have come forth into the interior earth plane to fulfill my life purpose; and I have been learning along my journey with every day I have experienced, and dwell briefly in the higher levels of my inner peace and solace. All souls will in death return into the vast reaches with which the beginning and the ending are in the same place.

Beneficence ubiquitous unity of manifestations of sacred equilibrium. Synchronized oneiric mystic human spirit and soul of the entity enters into the dreamweaver's psychological odyssey transformation of the surreal illusory plane.

Unknowing all that is to be experienced or the purpose of a new earthly life peregrination of the transformational sojourn recombinant state of the embryonic sacred water resting in the peaceful calming of my blessed Mother with child.

My spirit is waiting for the time of the natal date of birth. The irrefutable existential essence of the objective human condition on Earth has the cosmic law of free will, conscious illusory temporal reality. As a requiem of life measure of teaching and learning to discover the Egyptian Shetaut Neter mystic philosophy (https://www.chaucersbooks.com/book/9781884564413). To know myself within and become Maakheru the purified heart. That all is God within yourself corresponds with it in nature.~ Ancient Egyptian proverb: www.instagram.com/mynzah/ www.pinterest.com/mynzah/). The wisdom that is nous of the ancient mythology of the Egyptian goddess Ma'at's judgment that weighs the heart against the sacred Ostrich feather. The Law of One love is the benchmark standard for everyone to live by the light of the one Infinite Creator. I greet all of you right now with my heart that knows love and is loved; and I have a heart that will be judged and found to be light as an ostrich feather. With the glorious most high praise given for the luminous divine spiritual wisdom of the Law of One love, might, in turn, be humble in service to the infinite Creator's philosophy. The messenger who taught the spiritual science of the Neberdjer.

To everyone, you have a life purpose. You must know it. You for a finite number of Earth year's. Enjoy it. And everyone's life journey is a cycle through a beginning that ends in the same place. with you standing in the presence of the one all infinite creator, Adonai ("The Lord")! Might my spirit be to live in this outer empirical world blessed within the light truth those who are blind shall see the ways of the keepers of the light of the living spirit of love, joy, and happiness. And as the beginning and ending cycle around as it twists upward, live every moment of each day and rejoice. For life is a great blessing for all eyes to see the divine dynamic power of love/light that brings forth to provide all that is the sustainable providence of the Nebegjure great psycho-spiritual symbols of God, Adonai. It has been so many long and dark days that loom as history has passed away as old dusty pages of records. And sure as history comes to reality for a number of year's. We are who seek to know what was full of lessons we should learn erudition of the old social complex. Relatively speaking each of us have been complacent, engaged as witting pawns of the financial credit debt cycle by default have been trapped by this yoke for years. While the elephant in our government fiduciary oversight authorities have facilitated massive printing of U.S. dollars and spurred rising prices! Why is not considered an unavailable ticking time bomb, which puts the future prosperity of this nation in total jeopardy?

America's enormous 31 trillion government's debt is an ominous market indicator that is slowly spiraling into a potential freefall. Clearly the mother of all nightmare crises is due to irresponsibility caused by years of rampant disregard of rising interest payment on the debt obligation. Which is a bubble that is going to pop; and it's the future without the means to settle this dollar driven monetary exchange currency. And loose accounting and the administration monetary policy. The policy will pivot to the electronic bitcoin currency value, which aimss to replace the volatile ebbs and flows of the dollar driven global exchange market economy. And like nature's ocean wave rises and falls, we face this intimidating uncertainty, in all of the possible possibilities with this dreadful wave crashing down. And aimlessly we are drifting in the very dangerous shark infested heavy economic ocean waves and liberatt-infested heavy economic ocean waves and liberate our fears and trepidations as we come face to face with the inevitable dreadful calamity.

Oh my lord, save us from these destructive waves of doom! This evil crisis looms as we are without recourse to divert from the impending fire. As the flame is to come against humanity! Oh, my gracious, benevolent heavenly father...Oh Hallelujah!

Summer Green Leaves
Turns To Rustic Colors Die In Autumn

The sun's light rises upward, drifts across the sky, and slowly, it begins to ascend beneath the western coast and disappears. It's that majestic reverence I yield in anticipation of the lunar tranquility as time cycles through the four seasonal transformations.

A time when the vernal equinox arrival is around March 20 and, in turn, signifies the start of the spring cycle to resurrect the new life. Again when the sunshine down from the sky bathes as the photosynthesis sustains fresh green leaves to grow up in the warm summer months. And, predictably in turn every cycle brings forth new vibrant green leaves that begin to wane into a transformation of colorful rustic pigments is the face of the autumnal period on the Earth's cycle into the fall equinox.

This fantastic season comes around every year by the time cycling the zodiac wheel marks the farmers' annual fields harvest event. And the change in weather attests to this time when cool weather arrives, and the dead leaves start to fall from the tree branches. All save for those perennial sturdy pine and spruce trees that retain their colorful green leaves. Dead leaves float down and lie scattered over the ground in August. With appreciation as my soul is blessed to live, to see, and experience the lilting tranquil transition that begins and ends during this period, the third period of the four annual seasons of the twelve calendar months. It seems idyllic and majestic as the present time of the calendar that shows the date and weeks, so too marks the months of the year. We are all living for the next day of counting towards future times that will come to be. Nature verified the spiritual cycle of life in harmonic equilibrium.

Beautiful idyllic displays of colorful arrays of material animations amid the lilting harmonic sound distortion. Yeah, it is so calming and cathartic for the mind/body/spirit complex in this quiet time for my ruminations on psychological perception. I'm at peace musing as I mean-

der amid the arborous depiction of nature's panoramic milieu. My creative sensory reflection of the forest biosphere, replete with the showcase of naked trees, echoes, and the cool fresh air to breathe, set the mood to come upon the earth's stunningly beautiful vistas astir. Appreciate the arrival of the vernal equinox, a favorite time of the four seasons, each with a distinctive renewal as time cycles into transitional periods when the weather taunts and teases—the events of mother nature.

You feel this euphoria; I briefly paused there and admired nature's breathtaking spirit. The essence was stupendous. The stunning scenery of the beautiful views of nature's majestic panoramic made me marvel at the chilling hollows of naked forest trees that have become bare from transformation. It's a transformative season that mesmerized me, and on all sides, forest trees were shedding dead leaves. I observed the windswept leaves falling all around these naked trees as they steadily shed the beautiful orange, brown, gold, and yellow-colored leaves scattered over the wet forest ground strewn about the forest landscape. Within the spiritual context of the orbital constellational procession movement with its unfolding of the birth, death, and rebirth cycles, when Autumn arrives, weather enters the season that follows summer weather; and transitions into the landscape of death. When the weather is excellent, the leaves slowly fall in the transformation cycle of the tree's life providence. It's the farmer's annual time of the harvest "fardel" when trees begin to shed their rustic leaves that cover the ground of nature's biosphere; it's the precursor season that signals winter will arrive and leaves this naked hollow scene that inspired me to go for a trek through the forest to enjoy being in the forestry milieu of transformational tranquility. Yeah, it's another autumn, the seasonal cycle of the autumn wind and rain display a cozy tranquility when the weather is pleasantly calm and the sun is bright. Yes, another year when the lush green leaves of the forest milieu is a transformation of low voices echo amid the scenic milieu. All is well in high elevation mountain ranges piedmont and the cool flowing spring water serpentining down through atemporal tranquil nature of the beautiful countryside vistas.

Farmer's busy themselves with their labor annual harvest yield when dead leaves are a precursor to the conditions of the constellations, more brumous snowy weather to come. We anticipate the beautiful depictions of this change into chilling weather, and that is to say, our third calendar season in a full spectrum of the rustic color of the time, that is, the annual harvest moon's third season.

The autumn moonlight is a transformative seasonal milieu. In this visually beautiful stunning landscape within the measure of harmonic balance, in my quiet solace, I take a peaceful walk with a pure heartfelt, visceral introspection. Yeah, I admired the beautiful rustic arrival of this fourth season. As always, infants are born into this life of consciousness to live in the earth's interior plane.

In all of living, nature's green leaves are a breath that sustains, and in your tranquility, every day, you refresh me in humble reverence. Much love is due to the rustic dead leaves in repose floating down onto the earth's surface. This majestic procession of the Law of One principle of the universal cosmic movements, nature's dance through the constellation around sunlight into the lunar light glow at night, plays out against earth's surface orbital rotation.

It's predictable as the sun rises into the sky that day, and for me to again feel ebullience with excitement to see another autumn bring an equinox change into the fall season. That time when the air is pure from the rain that washes the sky clean and refreshing pristine air is reminiscent of the olden times of the gods. That this earth has four seasonal cycles through each zodiac house travels through the astronomical signs of each appointed period. The planet's rotation around the bright solar light in the astronomical zodiac houses cosmic precession through the motions of the constellation's wheelhouse precessional cycle through twelve celestial period signs of the zodiac houses. The eternal living life is the symbolic mythology of the Egyptian god Ra's solar sun disk chariot traveling from the east across sky canvas and descending beneath the Western shoreline ocean horizon.

Sunshine rays continue to rise to energize the force, and In every turn is the cycle in the orbital journey. Sunlight energizes my spirit that causes my actions to follow the pathway that passes through the disciplines of Kemetic ancient mystery. It's a spiritual science of the geometrical cosmic astronomical cycles.

It's the zodiacal wheel of the heavenly constellations house of the cycle through the twelve zodiacal signs wheelhouses in a circumambulation *rotation, planetary bodies orbiting promenade around the bright rays of the daylight, and the dark sky canvas with a lunar glowing backdrop arrayed against billions of glinting bright diamonds. The process is Leo, and it again came moving after Cancer and the zodiac houses' rotation. The sign of Virgo transforms the leaves shades of rustic color; it's replete with withering leaves in the death throes. To fill the cool weather of the autumn season begins its transformational cycle and is a precursor to the white snow cover that will fall, and the ground will be covered with a cold white blanket for all to bundle up to stay warm. Sunlight's ascension casts warm rays as light energy cycles of the twelve calendar months of the zodiac sign circumambulate; the constellational orbit revisit every harvest moon season by the transformation of autumn. This is the most joyous time to reap the bountiful fruits as the luminous divine providence for gregarious mundane time of labor marked by the lunar cycles was shrouded in hollows of ancient tales and mystery. That held that the predictable diurnal turnstile that I presage in sync with the calendar days of the month, and the cosmic constellation professional is the calendar measure of counting days events of the peregrinations.*

This is likened to the old tales that spurred esoteric rumors and my mystery and the hallows of the transformational to the naked season. It's nature's luminous divine intrinsic spirits foreshadowing the mysterious weather specter that cycles into the third calendar, a season that transitions to the face of autumn. It's the precursor to the time which brings forth the chilly climate of frosty white snowfall. This symbolic astrological sign depicts the seasonal sojourn through the four celestial zodiac house cycles. When the time is passing down beneath the earth's western horizon the celestial time events. We enter into this twelve-period as a cycle of awake and sleep, going through the transitions and predictable four climate seasonal patterns.

Each, in turn, precedes and comes forth as autumn emerges before chilly brumous winter seasons' fall weather blankets the landscape with northern light. The barren forest changes with the frosty chilling air of the fall weather when voices echo through the tranquility signals the rebirth cycle that is the death throes of the arrival of Autumn. It always comes every year; and it's closely akin to the playground ride on the merry-go-round or the see-saw of nature's days of bitter chilly weather arrive! The

THE MIND, BODY, SPIRIT, AND STORYTELLING

northern solstice sits high in the sky; the moonlight glows in the canvas of darkness with Mother's more net nature again, bringing the cycle of death throes into another manifestation of spirit, changing shifts into the autumn season.

Another fall season is when the earth fragment brings calm winds, and the air is pleasantly cool. Those vibrant green leaves had transformed into dead colorful dry leaves that changed in color and are no longer affixed to the forest trees, slowly falling onto the earth. The wind has scattered them all over the woods beneath the base of the parent tree's form into a white blanket that covered all the dead rustic leaves covering the landscape. The rich display of lush, vibrant green leaves falls.

They no longer play host to the stout branches of the forest trees. The fall chill is in the air, and all the forest trees shed and scattered dead leaves in autumn. Sturdy verdant leaves are slowly emptying onto nature forest. Those once stunningly beautiful colorful leaves are withering; the once vibrant green leaves turned into a rustic color lie scattered around the landscape, they are now covering the forest ground beneath my feet. I admire that beautiful landscape. A peaceful sensory feeling being alive feeling buoyant and blissful in the wondrous spirit of nature. With each step that I took those fallen leaves crept underneath my feet as I enjoyed slowly meandered as I moved through the divine reverence of the naked hollow forest, its echoes the sound of my voice and I hear the dead leaves crunching beneath my feet amid the blue sun in the lighted sky with its subtle cover of white clouds sky dome with coruscating rays of sunshine turning around, and just as the glowing moon comes out and showcased that beautiful planetary canvas of and billions of stars revealed. To the cool autumn air, I watch the leaves move as they fall and cover the ground beneath my feet when autumn time reminds me of nature's Palingenesis. Spring brings forth seasonal alchemy of the transformation in the third life cycle. Might my eyes imbibed and appreciate this tranquility of earth in the chilly transformation from summer into the falling leaves ablaze with subtle rustic colors I now trampled beneath my feet. And lo, the wind scatters dead leaves, all falling from the in repose.

The colorful rustic leaves fall silently cover the ground in the autumn annual season. When dead leaves accommodate the cycle of the harvest that abides by the time cycle of death throes. To feel reverence in the majestic transformation of the green leaves that turn orange, yellow, and brown in autumn, I tarried there briefly with awe and marveled in fondness the beautiful colorful biospheres' milieu, the panoramic vistas of such a beautiful landscape. And I thoroughly appreciated the van glorious divine providence of Netjer. Personification in material form and matter, pervading as the luminous divine Netjer. The majestical seasons are the precursor of the birth of the living breath of life we live and succumb to the death throes.

The universe's cosmic all bring forth the bountiful nature cycle of life regeneration of earth's foremocity. Orbital cycles of a sustainable home breathe in the air. The stillness of the forest has been shedding withered leaves curcumin to the predictable death throes in the autumn time cycle.

Slowly one by one, the trees shred the once vibrant green leaves that had entered the cycle of death. Looking around, I appreciated every cool breath of the air and all of those beautiful rustic dead leaves that had succumbed to the transient-like cycle. The autumn annual harvest season is when the dead leaves fall on the ground. Universal cycles of creative force bring forth physical transformational beauty upon the biosphere, the snow that glistens from the solar energy; bright heat rays of the cold northeaster winter weather fourth constellations cycle of the transformational zodiac calendar year. The planets in cycle circumambulations are predictable events that come around every year by the solar lightforce energy, and each season brings an aroma was the ambrosia which pervades with the subtleness which flows as quietness is to tranquility is not a dystopian event that is real. Though nothing can ever compare to the springtime with blooming flowers and fresh smell grass when the spring moves into summertime. Before fullness of fall weather will become a precursor to the chill and cold period of the frosty season and the cold winter weather snow blanket coverup the landscapes.

Lo! The annual coming forth into the calm autumn third season of planetary four earth elements of the change in the northern snowfall falling from the cosmic constellations. The zodiac wheel representing each of the twelve astrological houses' manifestation represents an astrological, personality profile birth sign displayed as the appointed time measurement of seasons.

THE MIND, BODY, SPIRIT, AND STORYTELLING

The coming length of days on earth brings long days and nights of events that are marked by counting the year's cycles of the orbital time of daylight and ataraxis night time resting in bed. Humans live every day in the cosmic cycle of the spinning earth plane's subtle orbital motion of the rotating time-space continuum. I have been consumed by this blissful serenity of ataraxia, to feel the order and harmonic balance being totally sync with the spatial time-space illusory.

To be buoyed out from experiencing reality dreaming in the surreal mystique of the infinitely streaming consciousness touched by the cool breeze of the fresh and pure reach from the drizzle of raindrops that produces the rarefied dispensation of the foggy weather and the early morning dew. The weather patterns bring long days and short nights when we snuggle up and stay buttoned up when the cold weather snowfall. Some rue the bitter snow days and the long cold chilly nights. We see the clouds and the living breath revealed in the cold air amid the shortened daylight turn of the long nights with snowfall that has blanketed the earth's biosphere. Might a clarity of the mind be the precursor of the primordial pure divine cycle is derived from the perennial existence and the transformation of the changes to annual seasonal solstices, save the exception of perennial species of pine trees that retained their vibrant green colored leaves that survive through the fall and winter seasons. The windswept forest trees, shedding those vibrant green leaves; the dark colorful green raiment that grew by sun bathed the leaves that covered the lush sturdy maple, spruce, oak, sycamore, willow, and the tall lombardy poplar trees. The sunlight ascends higher and slowly descends towards the cardinal horizon. And like a dreamscape of visualization, not asleep but walking under the sunshine bathing my animated mind, body, and spirit complex.

Nature is alive and full of various sounds distortions and it invites with the mystical quality of tranquility of nirvana. For every precious day with joy I appreciate the cycle into this period that brings forth a beautiful day in nature's ataraxia solace. For I anticipate the sunshine as it ascends up into the sky, peaking each day at noon as it drifts across the sky towards the west coast shoreline. Light energy rays depict the milieu; therein, we can see the great quadrivium nature of the intelligent universal creative existence of the divine infinity. Acknowledgment of God's presence is the application of the four liberal arts of number, geometry, music, and cosmology. The living spirit unity begins and ends each day in the same place is a mystery of the creative Hermetic logos. In this vespertine of the dawn I watch as the sun god Ra's light descends, and the lighted sky starts to dim as daylight turns into nirvana as dawn, transforms into the curtain of darkness cloak, and tranquility of the dark mystique of dalliance of the night has come again. A colorful manifold of fallen forest tree leaves I imbibed as scattered death. By the force of the wind that blows them around, while rain-swept leaves cover the landscape that is scattered all over the scenic view, as I survey the natural mountain chains, picturesque hillside sales of the autumn vista. Trees are losing their dead leaves lying stretched over the ground beneath my feet. As reality is that we observe the lifegiving and death that surround me on all sides.

Subtle transformation was transferred to nature's environment. Briefly I tarried and imbibed the sounds of noisy birds chattering all around with their asynchronous communication. Now I continue to stroll on the bosky trail. And I casually walked and admired the crisp cool air. The air was a perfect ataraxia in the Autumn season that turns the forest green leaves into marvelous rustic landscapes, of fallen dead leaves strewn around are dead leaves lying everywhere I look. The fall season has turned those green leaves rustic, the autumn in its blanket of leaves protecting the earth's forest surrounding environment. We are all free to live in unity with full perception in humble reverence and harmony of existence that is teaming with our wonderful divine spirit and have appreciation in awe of the many diffusion of the colorful tranquility of the subtle manifestations of nature's lilting sounds amid nature's laws scent to sunshine. My ears attend to the matted bedding of ground covering the fallen dead leaves strewn beneath my feet. It's so cathartic and euphonious. It's this delightful reverence and peace with delicate leaves falling around as I inhale another breath of nature's cool fresh air. What a spectacular amusement for me to live and watch nature's fallen leaves; death has laid them low underneath my feet as I enjoyed hiking on a familiar bosky trail, feeling carefree as I loved maundering amid the hollow tree leaves that went down to the transformed landscape of the colorful biosphere of fauna and flora. The rhythm of nature is that you and I have come to life in the zodiacal cycle to revisit autumn leaves falling asynchronously as the green leaves transform into blazing colorful pigments that fall from the branches of forest trees and the dead leaves slowly float down onto the ground.

Subtle periods of cool refreshing clean windswept trees succumb to the death throes of life and shed the fruits of providence in the grip of the autumn seasonal harvest cycle. It begins with another manifestation of the spring season of naked trees bringing new birth into the rays of bright sunlight until fall is the season.

Again it has come around into the rhythmic waves of earth's four seasonal cycles. The rebirth of life as unframed incredible depictions of the living Neter is the supreme being of four mysteries. The life in space and illusion measures conflates many counting years, days, hours, minutes, seconds of every day as the long and shorthand of time cycle is slowly ticking around the clock face.

This capstone has come around as a new arrival of the earth in orbital climatic seasons in Spring, Fall before the cold, snowy weather arrives. Forest trees are virtually barren of their dead leaves. The forest scene is melodiously hollow with lilting sounds. The birds are chattering asynchronously. Such as was in a moment feeling blissful as I slowly walked with appreciation of nature experiencing my beingness. Wonderful physical world reality of the colorful landscape of fauna and flora on all sides as my sensory cortex envisioned.

The effulgence of life essence pervading through days of warm rays of god's vainglorious geo grand miracle.

Light touches upon my beingness. I was comfortable as the sun rays bathed my face in the grand luminous divine energy of nature's vainglorious one-ness in this third quarter of nature's changing seasons. The wondrous miracle of life is temporal reality. Of the seasonal life cycle, many of the leaves of forest trees in autumn become rufous by late October and have caused the forest trees shedding leaves when air is cool and therein you can hear the cacophony of a mellow breeze and the audible sound of mountain's waterfall streams fresh flowing water miles away in autumn environment echoes when trees are completely bare naked. It's my love of the air of Neter's refreshing air to breathe that permeates in such radiance that defies the immutable earth's laws of physics. The beauty of nature *and the warmth from the sunlight rays pervades the plane with the thermal energy that coalescence with a dynamic lifeforce. In a varied form is an annual rotation into four seasonal cycles as nature's hands of the constellations dance through twelve zodiac houses and transition to each of the four climates bathed by radiation of warm sun energy. Yeah, we are all blessed to be alive to see and appreciate this unframed dispensation bathing in nature's vanglorious sunlight. Cosmic circumambulation solar orbit rotations brings the seasonal event cycle from the forenoon sunrise over the eastern shore horizon.*

Snapshot of the unframed diurnal light at sunrise inspired my lively prose. Depictions of nature's milieu are ripe in contrast; vivid displays of the creative design of natural laws that transform earth scenery into the seasonal autumn milieu. It's this time of year before the arrival of the shivering cold of winter, chilly brutal weather of snow and ice in the winter season. In turn, it plays out the nascence of nature's laws. It's this all-majestic elegance of poignantly inspiring scenic landscape.

In earnest reverent appreciation of nature, I realized that it's a stupendous Eden. So existential in the most observable panoramic visuals in the private reflection. Quiet thoughts full of appreciation for good blessings; awed by all of the things that appear before me is the actual illusory mind's perception of the living temporal reality. The form and matter define earthly animated creation of the material realm. Stuff being the cycle forms natal nature to death and an interim life as human matter.

I calmly stroll through nature, revealing a forest of naked trees that have shed their dead leaves. Unframed depictions of the transition into sweven, calmness of spring season arrival. And in turn beautifully picturesque scenes of a transformation unfolding a panoramic broad view of the countryside amused me. A display of expansive vistas arrayed like earth's exotic four seasonal climatic changes. It was majestic. Peaceful in mind/body/spirit complex, in meditation elevation of the space time melancholy can't bypass the transitional cycle of the inevitable death throes. Not tarry above the sentimental touching moment in appreciation for this passing moment. I admired geo metaphysical laws. We are with the living spirit complex in harmonic balance in the wonderland of nature's all manifestations; as the storyline for all humans to experience the transformation from life into the reverence of like the dead leaves that are majestically floating down onto the earth. They will no longer rhythmically sway to the air we breathe, as we watch them fall from sturdy branches in poetic reverence. Yeah, nature's green tree leaves are rustic colors, now lying scattered all across the transitional terrestrial planet.

The illusion is devoid of relativity or the space dimensions of actual temporal reality. But on the southern horizon in the sky canvas, there is the precursor sign of the calendar to cycle into one of them. That hiemal recombinant state of the festival heat of summer, the vernal period of spring, those vibrant green leaves slowly begin their transformations into autumn's season with beautiful colors is the turning of the cosmic calendar of the astronomical rotation of the zodiac wheelhouse melodious tranquility of nature's third-quarter season of the predictable transformation. The cycle of the divine Noumena that is the cause of constellation movement that turns into equal measures as life and death, that transformational cycles are bringing chilly autumn's weather.

In the northern autumnal equinox, the sun sets down as dusk in the ataraxis of quiet comfort and solace as the night curtain comes again when the moon glows and billions of starlight sparkles against the dark night sky canvas tranquility.

ENCHANTRESS EYES
A Heartbreaker Beguiled Me Into A Psychological Seduction

Might I make a dream come true. The one perfect one-on-one… Of all my choices, she was the queen for me when she came and sat next to me—my sweetie, My one-on-one, Inamorata. My queen and the one love to put me on a pedestal. A stunningly titillating femme fatale, she seduced me into a fatal attraction. She is the lovely apple of my eye. Enchanted, I admired the beautiful femme fatale countenance! And lo! A silk filigree veil hid her perfect lips. Yes, her eyes mesmerized me into a psychological attraction. I gleaned to obtain my celestial desire for or her graceful psychological visitation. Alluringly sensual spiritual adorned beautiful eyes; Her charming demeanor buoyed me up with her perfect smile with regal panache, and playful coyness was a psychological seduction; of which, her decorum had that certain je ne sais quoi! Her style was royal, with an air of a very high tone. Her courtesy and friendliness were mesmerizingly urbane comportment. I desired to lift the scarlet veil to see the lips that complimented her comeliness. This diva's presence mesmerized my pure vision with the friendliness to command and reciprocate a mutual attraction. Her charming romanticism betokened reciprocal smiles in a love vision to give a sweven of sentimental long stem red rose blooms. She was beautiful, a wonderful vision to behold her insouciant, evocative, crush-worthy romanticism with coy, Risqué jaunty stood out, as she charmed me with limerence had drawn me nigh!

THE MIND, BODY, SPIRIT, AND STORYTELLING

The Beguiled Enchantress's Big Brown Eyes;
In The Crystal Alchemy Of Moonlight

This remembrance of that one special night of visitation as I was in the thralls of this stupendously glorious perfect female avatar. A lovely manifestation of female form. And feeling buoyant when this femme fatale had caught my eye as I entered into a vainglorious mystical dimensional realm. To my delight I envisioned the most mysterious gorgeous lady in this spectacular night in the dreamscape surreal odyssey. Bemused, I was buoyant as gleaned longingly and marveled in awe of the most beautiful, visually stunning enchantress. She was staring at me with the most extraordinarily flirtatious adorned spiritual eyes. This was the first time our eyes were fixed on each other across the room in a dream excursive odyssey—someplace somewhere unknown and unfamiliar. And this was the first time I recall that very moment when I looked, and there before me I was looking into the eyes of the most stunningly beautiful woman I had ever seen. Her voice was melodious and she had eyes that evoked a magic spell that consumed me. I didn't know that this effervescence was my excursive peregrinations of a transportine crossing of the subconscious dreamscape; and this was a one-off chance encounter. Being fortuitous for me to glean the countenance of having met the my most beautiful queen, it was the psychological beginning of what I recalled was an incredible psychological excursion when I was there in this streaming dreamscape episodes that felt so real and such a thrill and a delight, as I was present somewhere in the allusion of my creative imagination separated from the illusion of daylight reality. The world is a living vista of nature's divine providence endued to everyone who awakened into these wonderful familiar scenes with, reflections I ruminate by day, and to dream by the dark nighttime canvas slowly yield moonlight faded as morning crept into the tranquility before sunshine came shining through the window of my bedroom. A private time to hear nature's morning symphony of sounds impinge in my ears with justified appreciation of my most reflective thoughts. Comfortably, I was ensconced and resting in my quiet bedroom just musing. Slowly dawn had come again before the luminous bright rays of coruscated sunlight entered the bedroom.

And I cling to the cathartic mental image that she was right there with me remembering our time dancing all night in a realm of joyful enchantment. I enjoy the merriment of the private royal opulent of the grand palace hall of folks in convivial friendly exchange of conversation.

Such as a dream transformation living it up with her; I know it was a one in a million chance to discover that limerence as a psychological vision of myself in appreciating this tranquility.

Whereof, I was abiding with thoughts that I had envisaged that day for me to live my one spiritual peregrinations. I felt like this before in this peaceful quiet time ticking into a new sunny day. From the light of dawn till dusk comes the time of life experiences of the glorious bright light of the sun ready to brighten up my spirit that is the cause of my every action. My spirit energy was the of my transcendental meditation it harkens me back to this one night when serendipitously as I was in the surreality of my spiritual unfoldment, going far beyond my bedroom into the nirvana of stupendous glitzy grand palace hall of my emerging transformation into the ephemeral visitation. My spirit essence envisaged appears in this anachronistic place.

As I sensed myself there mingling among the social classes engaged in confabulation with each other in the comforting surrounding of this grandeur that was with stately opulence and befitting the stupendous royalty that flanked me on all sides of this grand palace hall in a different world filled with that glitzy fantasy illusion. Delight in the vainglorious light that is the pure essence of the intelligent spirit essence of life force energy of the noumena of the hermetic realm of incarnation and the dreamscape annoccult realm of incarnation and the dreamscape and the transportine turnstile of duality. Yes indeed the night time is the mystical time for imbibing the resting daylight that went down below the earth in reverence every day and, again, in the turnaround is superseded by bright moonlight. Again I am alone in my comfortable king-sized bed with no one to cuddle next to me. Again, in its most sacred providence I appreciate seeing the lucerne sunshine of the wonderful morning light force energy of the divine spirit bringing blessing with warm sunshine. Another new sunny day arises and again I will sit at my breakfast table slowly sipping my cup of coffee with a balanced healthy breakfast vital and contemplate my day that will unfold, revealing this *priori* cycle of random life experiences.

Yeah, I am aware that it's the arrival of the quiet comfort and tranquility that precedes the transportine crossing space-time duality of the daylight hours and the body lies resting for hours asleep til the awakening. Rise again as is your spirit which is the cause of another morning of breathing in this delightful invitation to live and enjoy each and every new gift of divine daylight. Again the cycle begins as the world turns from the dusk's to low light darkness transitions to evening time. As always, I turned my head to read red digital numbers on the electronic digital clock resting on the nightstand next to my bed. The lighted digital display was precisely 5:45 a.m. And as always I wish she was lying beside me. But as the sun emerged over the coastal ocean, the eastern horizon slowly ascended toward the sky with the radiant light force energy of sustainable divine providence. And before sunrise I was listening to the cathartic sound of the steady stream of the melodious raindrops trickling down my window.

All is well with my sentience as a living being of consciousness awareness conjugated mind/body/spirit complex. I'm fully aware of myself and my perception of my material form, fully aware of my quite familiar dark quiet bedroom. In ataraxia solace, asleep dreaming without conscious mental activity.

Of my subconscious mind I apprehended the glitz and glamor sense of a dynamic metaphysical realm somewhere in my spirit entering the confluence episodes of the carousel of duality which circumambulates the cycle of daylight into nighttime. I mused in deep thought before the light of the eastern horizon. That is to contemplate my life with appreciation, being thankful to revisit the dreamscape into the surreal odyssey! The consciousness awareness synced in unity with circadian rhythms, harmonic energy vibration sync within the quintessential joy of dawn horizon, yet clinging to the most incredibly vivid convoluted dream. Might eyes on her. I could feel her amorous glance at me as she was turning heads. Like a bolt of flashing lightning. She ignited a fervent desire. This magic inflection point where my dream unfolded while I was sleeping with my head lying on a pillow. Without a hint, there I was, marveling in appreciation of this *eidetic* grand edifice, with a very exotic spectacular garden landscape confluence utopian feeling like nirvana. So I dithered there to admire all of those wondrous things revealing insights of the third eye vision of my perceptions in the *anachronistic* dreamscape I beheld in the surreal realm. You see, this is my thoughtful rumination upon the remembrance of this once-time surreality when I recalled the things while in my vivid dreamscape illusory, gazing into a beautiful femme fatale enchantress's eyes. I was there searching for her among everyone who was enjoying themselves. Things I could see, I saw there and the things I felt seemed to be so real. Just spending time with her was a night of *eidetic* clarity that painted images of stupendous opulence on all sides. It was my creative illusion of which I am musing about in a relaxed state of remembrance from the dream weaver's script odyssey, excursive spiritual free-will. I am a spirit essence traveling into the dreamscape episodes. And all the while, I realized that I was no longer lying in bed when these ruminations merged.

A special lady to share a lovely night of dalliance dining alfresco as the romantic sounds of smooth string of alluring flute set the mood that pleasantly pervades the cool air of the fanciful aura of this atemporal surreal realm, replete with every manner of this beautiful *anachronistic* places. Wherein, I entered other dimensions and places redolent with the aroma of rose petals and smooth lilting sounds of jazz tunes pervading in an unfamiliar surreal realm; was replete with fantastic flight destinations.

The evoking surreal episode was quite breathtaking, fanciful, and a very spectacular creative mystical dream weaver's excursive evocative flight destinations. Within these captivating stops, my spirit caused me to meander in and among all who were milling about in the enchanting world of the surreal peregrinations while my body was still asleep.

THE MIND, BODY, SPIRIT, AND STORYTELLING

No! This wasn't an ephemeral dream. Not at all as it was incredibly vivid and bizarre in the most remarkable and pleasing remembrance I treasure this dreamweaver's odyssey which was unlike others. Somewhere I was not familiar as I was beguiled, gazing into an enchantress's adorned spiritual eyes. And suddenly it struck me that the gorgeous eyes of the *femme fatale* had drawn me nigh!

I looked to engage in conversation with this stunning femme fatale that sat next to me in this stylish grand palace hall with exquisite opulence and beautiful luxury. Fine art pieces were displayed that exemplified wealth and power on all sides of this mysterious realm. This is what I recalled in the unrestrained quintessential amazement. I was subdued by being in this sentimental emotions, kool and poised, I took in this moment briefly in the time *atemporal* cinematic drama, as I paused to watch this beautiful *femme fatale*'s delightful presence gracefully strolled toward the bar, and made her way through the crowd of lovely people who eyes was full of deep awe, gleaned as they clamored for her attention. She had come to join this scene of animated merrymaking which my spirit essence envisioned her and, I still can't let go; and I recall enjoying that sentimental vision of the dreamweaver odyssey by my free will excursive surreality creative perception rewinding my consciousness imagination into illusory reality and the visual excursive realm of the present daylight time, and the surreality of the spacetime continuum turnstile of coming forth by day and going forth by nightfall. I entered the excursive dimensions of the spirit realm intersections.

Yeah, this was not some ordinary perception of the stuff of dalliance in this dreamweaver ephemeral visions that I recalled vivid things with *eidetic* clarity. It was like a painting transformation of the mind into a streaming image in the spacetime continuum. Smooth soft jazz tunes amid the enlivened night mood melting into the soulful sensory cortex.

For in an instance this feeling had come surging into my heart; and I felt that I had met the lady who was missing in a wonderful dream that felt so very real. She and I created the perfect *alchemy* of intoxicating psychological dream fantasy. Yeah I was there. Though my body was calmly lying asleep in my bed resting and dreaming of these entertainment episodes that felt so right! Yeah, I was asleep as my spirit was wandering while I was in a recumbent state. My ears began to slowly tune into the familiar matutinal morning sounds of the conjunction distortions. My eyes have fully opened, and my mind fixed on the *anagnorisis* of light. This as it was I perceived as the animated present time-space continuum, free from the visual illusory harmonic waves of the consciousness awareness of the reality; a daily promenade into the excursive transitions to the ego state of the apprehension of the psychospiritual, drifting away into the creative realm of subconscious nirvana.

It's another morning, alive to walk again among the earth's bon homies, to appreciate being animated by an unframed transformation of the time-space continuum. Nights of my creative dreamscape where I enter into anachronistic places while my body receives restorative sleep in the quietness of the darkest night. For this was such a very special moment of the dream time illusion, I often ruminate upon before getting out of my bed. A reflection I treasure every morning when I shudder to harken back to my remembering the oneiric excursive dream odyssey, my animated spirit essence envisioned me where I was fully aware of being optimistic and delighted by with feeling great nirvana, inside of anachronistic places of such a bright unparalleled radiance glowing in a different sky.

Without saying a word, she and I gleaned to imbibe each other's countenance. There I saw the beautiful people dancing, smiling, talking, laughing, and dining in this crowded place of merrymaking amid the ambient smooth, lilting jazz music amid the peels of badinage.

I saw her and knew that she was the most stunningly beautiful woman with a lovely radiance I valued above all the others. This gorgeous lady I saw was the most beautiful woman, and she was a lady of great dignity and bearing a delightful golden ratio with the perfect female form. She was urbane and charming with a wonderful presence that I valued above all the others.

I gleaned from getting a visceral look in her beautiful spiritual eyes, her beautiful lips with a perfect smile from behind a scarlet *filigree* veil. Feeling buoyant, I paused briefly to take a moment and marveled at myself to share in the moment of effulgence, as my delight was the ambrosia for the soul in the presence of this beautiful woman who countenance of a female goddess in my space. A charming smile with a sweven-like aura. I smiled back and fixed my eyes on her seductive big brown spiritual eyes to imbibe a full measure of her beauty. I reciprocated with easy *dulcet blarney*. We were flirting with friendly affability and charm, this mysterious demure enchantment panache was with inviting eyes of mutual attraction that drew me nigh. And lo, I was beset with *basorexia* for her lips that were full; those big brown adorned eyes drew me nigh. I smiled and wondered why I had never kissed her in the moonlight, within that perfect mood of the heartfelt screenshot. Yeah, she imbibed me with those adorned spiritual eyes fixed upon me was a psychological dreamscape odyssey.

She of great beauty is still the dream vision I desire to have as the love in my life. So let's forever chill as I glean deeply inside her beautiful brown spiritual adorned eyes that measured me. Feeling buoyed, I marveled at this beautiful musical surreal dimension of the dreamscape. To my delight, I was imbued and besotted by this lovely femme fatale countenance was a beguiling cameo appearance when she came into this unframed ephemeral psychological consumed by transformation. It is a trill and a delight to enter the illusory realm dimension to *anachronistic* the enchantment. My remembrance of this gorgeous femme fatal surg from the dream state illusory back into a unity of mind/body/spirit complex had merged.

I was in a recumbent stasis, dreaming and animated encounters while I was asleep in the boundary of the bedroom. This transition from the quiet morning sunshine to the dream excursion as my spirit essence *cavorted* in a different time and place dimension.

Whereas I was amid lively party-goers. In the daylight hours, with clarity, my dream didn't effervesce into this bizarre ficto-sexual psychological love affair in real-time reality. It's my psychological imagination and delusional excursive episode of the dream odyssey, separated from my body of intangible intransigence of the dream-weaver interim nighttime script of the overnight cycle riding the *cusp* of another early sunrise, emerging event horizon to delight in celebrate the majestic horizon with ruminations of this lovely *femme fatal*.

Her radiance touched and permeated visceral thoughts. The new day slowly unfurled into a vainglorious present time-space reality! From the darkness of night, sunlight peaks, then rises on the eastern shoreline. Yeah, a brief quiet time of third-eye introspection experience the luminous of visual reflections conjugating subconscious psychological thoughts muses about the delightful dreamweaver's odyssey entertainment streaming exclusive oneiric voyage.

It was that I couldn't seem to forget spending time with her. And this quiet morning, I was not ready yet to arise and go forth into twists and turns by day that are unpredictable life experiences. Yet, I was not quite ready to climb out of bed and begin to follow my scenic early morning romantic musing routine of the anachronistic psychological dreamscape odyssey excursive of 2017. Here I am on the cusp of this new day and laying in my bed, thinking that with a bit of good fortune, as I remember I had the most vivid flashback to the excursions into an atemporal *anachronistic* dreamweaver's surreal world and be subconscious and aware. Whereof, I perceive the early existence with a whirlwind of turns of transcendent into the odyssey of good fortune she is laying in this bed next to me squeezing, hugging, and kissing. And wondering in deep thoughts as I ready myself to take on the day. Will this be the day that is to bring the providence of great fortuitous blessing for me to behold when *crepuscular* clouds as sunlight begins to turn down every hour in the power of the dawn and passing into the darkness canvas when the moon retires and all of the city street lights are shut down until the sunlight descends below the western horizon ocean shoreline.

When the noise of the present-day distortion begins to quiet down at the turn of dawn, tranquility quietly whispers beneath the glowing moon. I thank god for another day to lift my soulful *shakti* energy providence from the gods of heaven. For I pondered, this light is unfolding for me to rise and go forth as the dawn precedes another spectacular daily sunrise. To begin my familiar daily routine for harmonic balance as I sit calmly relaxed in the lotus position in unity with the *Shetaut Neter* (devotion to God). Spiritual, peaceful introspection is my cathartic meditation routine to practicing internal worship or spiritual purity through daily meditation. The practice is known as Smayua. My devotion to Yoga meditation a divine spirit reverence before I sit down to enjoy my slow sips of hot green tea, I drink with the daily balanced meal of healthy breakfast vitals.

As always I have started delineating my day with a *matutinal* moment musing in deep thoughts. I smile this morning as I was musing knowing that I was beguiled by the anthropomorphic beautiful *Aphrodite* avatar of this lovely allure of this goddess of love and beauty as she pervades my dream folly, as I admired the ephemeral vision while in *atemporal* oneiric surreal realm of a psychological affair. I envisaged myself experiencing the ephemeral realm of the dreamweaver's odyssey. And you know, it's true that I can't stop thinking about this remarkable enchantress'. Yeah this lovely femme fatale's adorned mesmerizing eyes beguiled me into a fatal attraction.

What a beautiful feeling buoyant with full moonlight memory of her seated next to me, confabulating amid distant stars that sparkled like the facets of the perfect one hundred karat diamonds were scattered across the darkness canvas backdrop.

The air filled with smooth lilting jazz streaming romanticism. We gazed into each other's eyes; it was beautiful, sensate likeness was a surreal piece of nirvana. So at this particular moment in my space, I awaken to my dream unfolding with my reflective thoughts, for these are the creative literary prose of my subconscious excursive peregrinations. I welcome another bright sunny day that spark confluences thoughts of this private introspection, I am awakened remembering this vision of her adorable spiritual eyes. It's a very evocative psychological nudity of my sensory dream, which means it's the excursive perception of the dreamweaver creative episodic scene of the ephemeral *peregrination* of the surreal realm of confluence became a cinematic animations of the minds of the streaming depictions of wondrous anachronistic places unfolding in as interim spirits envisaged uplifting and compelling.

What joyful mirth with teasing *blarney* amid lilting sounds had conjugated into this sense of nirvana I had attended to the melodious cacophony, and my spirit was chattering her up with melodious dulcet words, and we exchanged mutually charming smiles that sparked a betokened genuine capstone love supreme. With the ambiance of demure fluttering candle light fire created a romantic attraction amid the darkness; night sky canvas beset me on all sides streaming surreal visceral episodes that are my flashbacks to the remembrances when we confabulated that first night. Lively scenes, flashed as I was rewinding through the pathway crossing. Enter this place where you will see the residential streets of the community scene, where beautiful willows, colorful purple blossoms of beautiful jacaranda trees and the sweet smells of aromatic cherry blossoms alluring flora is a sensory pleasing trill and a lovely delightful experience in appreciation for the living spirit of nature.

I am awake and very much aware of everything that I experienced in this ataraxia adrift in the time-space dimension of the surreal psychological introspections into the dream travel, somewhere in time living it up before the break of dawn rises with the morning rays when the sunlight is waiting it's turn to peek above the eastern shoreline to begin with the morning sky, let's go of darkness to bring daylight. Her beauty was the full measure I had imbibed in abiding luminosity and frivolity. Her smile and enchantress eyes beguiled me, and she was gone as I woke up from this creative excursive dreamweavers odyssey into the surreal realm's sojourn. The exclusive realm of the contiguous duality cycle of my consciousness is streaming episodes of the illusory realm of surreality, in turn, into daily temporal reality is my consciousness. Oneiric scenes follow the bright sunlight rise until the moonlight disappears beneath the eastern shore horizon. And right on time the divine brightens up the sky with the sunlight to reappear in symbolical reverence to Egyptian eponymous deity, meaning the sun god *Aten-Ra's* chariot moves slowly drifted through the firmament, and somewhere unknown to me I descended low after the night canvas unfolded beneath the west coast ocean horizon cycles begins and ends in the same place that is the imperceptible time of twilight. While clouds drift high above is closely akin to earth's skydome.

The daylight enters its intersection with the western coastal horizon. In this surreal realm I slowly emerged again, into the bright

THE MIND, BODY, SPIRIT, AND STORYTELLING

morning daylight, which terminated. I was besotted and ambivalent as I sensed that I was no longer there spending time with her in the illusory state of being present, but not physically there.

I was delighted to behold this vision. Was she not the most beautiful version of the imagination? I was in the presence of a *mysterious femme fatale* that beguiled me with her lovely big bright brown adorned eyes that had drawn me nigh. She had beguiled me with genuine heartfelt fervent desire for her was my nirvana. As I felt buoyant with heartfelt limerence for her risque *jonunty*, she was my *inamorata*. She was the apple of my eye, for I desired her to become my one-on-one. My spirit subconscious mind had entered the *dream* state, adrift in my subconscious apprehension of psychological nudity of a beautiful dream illusion. I imbibe her very perfect female form that was a psychological ephemeral surreal depiction amid the mood of candlelight enchantress. She was a wonderful woman who I desired to be the perfect queen to make my dreams come true. My sweetie to be my one-on-one; a lovely vision that I desired to put on a pedestal. To effervescence into my one on one in diurnal reality. Yes, appreciate each moment that precedes the daily sunrise attests to visual manifestation of our vainglorious gifts of sustainable providence. The cult of rebirth is the symbolism of an ancient *Osirian*, of ancient African Egyptians priesthood ritual symbolism of the personification and worshiped Egyptian deity Ra chariot crossing the sky. We watch as the depiction of the daily sun's ascent begins with the rising upward in the eastern horizon. And the sun at its *apogee* is noontime, continuing its slow movement across the sky, traveling toward its daily descent beneath waves of the western coastal ocean shoreline horizon.

That tranquil feeling of the warm sun brings forth the blessings of another glorious good day to enjoy my gift of life awake to continue to fulfill my spiritual noumena excursive peregrination, my Chi's inner third eye perception in my daily meditative state. A focus to achieve harmonic balance nvisage to jump-start my daily routine experiences. This *sensation* is like nirvana, as I envisioned and experienced this unparalleled clarity of apprehension was understood as my soulful spirit being was an individual separation from the luminous divine. I am not in my physical form as I am detached from all feelings of my body, psycho spiritual consciousness being entered into a dimension of surreality.

I know that I am awakened to live in the illusory reality in mind/body/spirit complex, the catalyst for inner peace and harmonic balance. For I am fortunate to enjoy a daily providence.

My peace is pure of heart; my motivation is not a material desire. Right on time each morning comes the predictable old familiar bombastic sound bellowing announcement of the hubris country barnyard cock; when that rooster crows three times it's the morning revelry announcement. All things are synchronized with this early morning phenomenal daily sunshine rising up high and slowly moving across the sky by the life force energy as the source of divine providence.

Yeah, I felt so calm being in the state of quiet comfort and inner peace and solace lying inside of my king-size bed. Feeling blessed, knowing that I live to appreciate the value of life as a precious gift of the intrinsic creative fidelity has not come to a determinative conclusion.

The surreal realm depictions pervaded the ephemeral realm of the excursive dream; tranquility of the spirit that causes individual human units of mind/body/spirit separation. Everyone is a unique embodiment that is an animated presence that transmutates between the diurnal duality of measured units in the time-space continuum. Again, I am fully awakened and alive at this specific epoch of this particular moment to enjoy luminous inner vision's third-eye peace with mental harmonic balance. Slowly emerging is that vainglorious bright sunlight energy brings forth. Living each day acknowledges that love is a peaceful feeling like watching the sun as it slowly rises with a vibrant new light of warming sun rays to brighten up my vision. We can watch as it slowly rises in the eastern shoreline and steadily drifts on a pathway set beneath the western skyline horizon. A cycle of the infinity of the creative life force streaming manifestation of consciousness awareness. Nature's harmonic balances between duality time-space transportine adventure into the dreamweaver's constellation orbital cycle into the geometric episodes of the dimensional conventions of grand architecture dreamscape. There I was feeling my spirit essence rewinding me from the excursion of the oneiric illusory episodes of this dream folly; everything was fading. Yet, I couldn't separate from this fanciful realm of the illusion of my surreal experience.

Nevertheless, thoughts of her came forth to delight my mind as I smiled and contemplated every future sunrise of another radiant rays crossing various intersections with the coruscating bright daylight. I am ready to live *coterminous* with my true spirit-self purpose; to experience a density of the material entity's in the world in which we reside in existential reality with free-will engagement of life daily experiences in physical three dimensional space time continuum of boundary of living entity of consciousness awareness!

Humans are the living embodiment of ourselves as an individual living personhood in the imaginary realm. A living soul of the mind/body/spirit complex blessed to coexist with the immaterial and physical things to love, and to be loved by my other selves in the service to self, and to be of services that they are my other human entity-selves is in the total unity sync with the one all-pervading infinite Creator. It's a cycle of warm energy that brings forth streaming episodes and life existences experienced by humans. As animated humankind embodiment has come, life has been a present form of a mind/body/spirit complex. The human physical image reflection is the form of myself I see looking back at me in the mirror that is the same countenance that reflects in still calm water. Our dreams are streaming episodic animations.

The energy life force is an ethereal animated spirit. The energetic rays of the warm sunlight days and the luna light in the dark night sky. I sleep resting and before continuing to awaken to fulfill my life purpose. To serve myself in the service to my other-selves spirit entities to the social-psychological effect.

I am alive with the purpose to help the Earth bon homies to awaken to heed righteousness of the spirit before the trumpet sound is to announce the human harvest. Compassion, focusing my mind/body/spirit was closely akin to being a radiating animated avatar presence. Might this be true for you and me? For all the while, this Earth's surface is spinning from dusk to dawn. When again subtlety I see the night curtain come down to host the glowing moonlight. My circadian rhythm of the spirit drifts away; and enters the turnstile crossing into the dimensional realm of the ephemeral surreal space-time by cameo excursive *sojourn* into *anachronistic* wondrous places of the creative odyssey. The grand cosmic time cycle when I enter into the bright transportine crossing. Whereof in every second and minute, it ticks without a pause. Existence is to live in how you choose to spin in the daily carousel of nature's duality unfolds in equal measure of the illusory reality. Being humble and grateful everyday for the brilliant sunshine that brightens up my sensory vision.

My peregrination and paradisiacal dreaming was a wonderful experience. I felt as if my heart was light spiritual essence. As alive and calm in this realm like the most tangential concentric wave energy of a leaf or a feather that stirs up perfect waves that glide outward crest against the sandy shoreline and the rocky muddy river banks. Another repeat episode brings forth the sunrise that is on a trajectory upward before it peaks at high noon. It is slowly drifting toward the westward sailing across the blue sky that hosts light, moving to its *rendezvous* with its daily intersection cardinal horizon as sun gradually descends into the twilight dusk, sunlight asleep before it resurrects again as it ascends above the eastern horizon.

The warm radiant sunshine brightens my bedroom. I turn my mind to watch as the bright sun transformation supersedes when slowly the twilight drifts into the canvas of darkness when the sun descends low beneath the west coast ocean horizon shoreline. The night appears as the dark canvas showcases the moonlight glow. Awake and I am refreshed, wearing my night raiment as I take a long deep breath of the morning *ruach*. I am just lying in bed with my deep musing in this time of quiet reflective private thoughts, aimlessly looking up at the ceiling. Musing in deep thoughts and musing with reflections about these psycho-spiritual innermost private thoughts. Sunshine gleaming through the windowpane. As the sunlight rises I hear the thundering sounds as intermittent lightning flashes light up the window pane.

THE MIND, BODY, SPIRIT, AND STORYTELLING

I listen to the steady sound of the gentle and cathodic raindrops melodiously trickle down. In a moment of reflection, I appreciate the solace. Felt very calm and at peace as I was relaxing, and all the while I'm thinking about the femme fatale seductive unforgettable big brown eyes. I mused about her before the dawn fades away and leaves me with my limerence that is this feeling of being buoyant and feeling blessed. My quiet time in reflection was quiet comfort in a sweven, state of calm meditation. My consciousness is illumined. As I was in my avatar synced in my unity with the mind/body/spirit complex which was in calm mental reverence.

Spiritual essence animates the embryonic human body and comes into existence in the usual way, stasis asleep, growing to full term while we wait for the natal date. Born into the world Earth's plane, unknowing of any of my old prior life incarnation cycles of this soul. Although I came into this life again unknowing that my purpose was to service myself and all of the other entities of humankind. Those who have loved and lost their loved ones embrace a cycle of joy in the birth that cycles souls into time of passing away. The living material from embodiment exists in the universal duality cycle. Humankind is animated units derived by the infinite Creator in the existential realm.

My last natal date began in the embryonic sleep state of which I rested in quiet comfort prior to the day of my new day of coming forth into an incarnation of the material embodiment of mind/body/spirit, to live a finite number of counting years. Unframed animation of subjective mental illusory visions of the time-space confluences streaming wonderful illustrative material scenes of existential reality. The old empirical world epochs of the mercurial visage of truth, tranquil, lilting, pervading luminous, *sweven* like, oneiric visions.

For every new morning, the sun brings forth another vainglorious brilliant gift of life in that light of the sun rises in the east and moves across the sky is a familiar daily routine. In mind/body/spirit totality, my daily meditation alignment with the one true luminous divine of the solar radiant light waves that pervades the terrestrial interior plane. Our providence is derived from the energy that gives the life that comes forth as the daily cycle. I am synced with the *Kavod* of the Egyptian god *Aton's* bright sunrise. God of our providence is the sustainable source of all things that exists, a phenomenon of the creative vision of the material world is emblematic of the ancient symbolic mythological Egyptian chariot of Ra's sky boat as the transportine crossing symbolizes the spirit essence of god ascending above and descending below the cardinal horizon. Everyday the sun cycle of life reappears as a radiant symbolic rebirth as the morning sun brings the light until the lunar light reflects the stars onto rimping energy waves vibrating that illuminates and glistens on the eastern shoreline will peak at noon. Then it slowly began to wane into the *occidental* horizon. This extraordinary night canvas was mystical darkness waxing through this mercurial space after I had settled down and had fallen asleep, to rest from conscious awareness. My eyes closed, liken to wearing a blindfold. Slowly, I felt my spirit essence begin to drift away as I was coming back into the mental state of conscious ataraxia of the present time continuum.

These cinematic episodes depict the unframed surreal realm of the state of psychological enchantress beguiling eyes of this transient vision of folly was a fatal attraction.

Interpolations are of the illusory reality of the imagery beguiling the enchantress's beautiful adorned spiritual eyes. My *inamorata* was only my *psycho-spiritual* heartfelt d'amore. The confluence of *peregrinations* reveal such wonderful episodes of the most stupendous dreamscape. When I was in the anachronistic places of the dreamweaver realm I envisaged. This was the illustrative order of the grand utopian nirvana streaming idyllic episodes that pleased my starry eyes. A very evocative female beauty who was the most perfect visual goddess. She beguiled extraordinarily with vivacity, affability and charm. She was a lady of great dignity and bearing a very beautiful spiritual vision, a masterpiece portrait; Her beautiful countenance I beheld. She smiled through a fashionable sheer stylish veil. I could discern her full perfect lips; and wondered why we never kissed in the moonlight? I watched her apply a rufous peach-colored lipstick that complemented her lovely adorned spiritual eyes that were very beautiful and seductive. A heartbreaker that could charm and that excited my limerence. She was urbane with the decorum of the royalty on display.

She was so charming and sophisticated; and an intoxicating delightful heartbreaker! She was a treasure for my eyes to imbibe of her incredible diamond-like beauty. I felt those beautiful adorned eyes on me and I knew she was the one for me. So mysterious, with an alluring presence that *captivated* my gazing eyes. For at this moment, might I dare feast my eyes upon the countenance covered she hid behind a stylish scarlet filigree veil. The most beautiful face was the mysterious female femme fatale goddess. Her wildly seductive presence was impressively unforgettable. Mesmerized, I felt myself buoyant by ruminations with visceral delightfulness; remembrance of confluence within an anachronistic oneiric surreal realm.

The *auroras* of sparkles of the bright stars complimented the graceful presence of the *femme fatale* enchantress eyes. She was full of *charisma* and *blarney* excited the limerence of everyone whose eyes could not look away was mesmerized. When I fell into this psychological fix-asexual attraction compell me in the dreamscape illusion tranquility, which was the manifestation of *imponderabilia* insight into the most excursive transcendental whirlwind flight adrift in nirvana into *anachronistic* time travel.

The sacred halls of the subconsciousness, and all the while, my body reposed in the quintessence state of peaceful solace. Yet again, quiet contentment, I lay in my bedroom and appreciated the quiet solace. I was no longer dreaming cognitively, rewind to replay my streaming dream episode, fanciful surreal excursions and drifting while my body rested in a recumbent state.

It was these initiation disciplines, which every myopathy learns of nature's transition of the meditation into the spirit separation that began to slowly descend, and rewind back into the morning fresh air. I began with my *anticipation*. I yawned and listened to the early morning melodic sounds of nature's bird chatter. Earth is slowly spinning the rotation of the night and day time in equal measure on the melodious tune of the song as we love to hear the mockingbirds' singing are very precious moments to behold as an insightful prized reflection.

HAKEEM R. JELANI

My intimate private thoughts are a pleasant vision I beheld. Begin to go forth into another of my excursively dynamic peregrinations. I am awakened to comfort in material form and live/learn/love the peregrinations which are underlying the flow of the life force energy. It's the odyssey of the dreamweaver surreal illusory episode of the spiritual perception of consciousness awareness. Material form is my existence on duality in tangent with imaginary, and material temporal world order is the present state of perception of surreal avatars as the spirit animation living in the interior earth plane! Such is my remembrance, and my everyday reflections of the dynamic duality that turns around daily is always streaming. Asleep the spirit enters into the ephemeral peregrinations of the psycho spiritual world where you cross over into and dream dimensional realm. Somewhere on the other side of our modern world reality of the present and past time streaming episodes in real-time daily life cycle of events of causes and effects illusion, turnstile. This present time space continuum of tranquility and nirvana is pervading as the illusory of ataraxia. The measure of time that ticks continue from the darkness of night into the sunlight of dawn of every new day in the *poignant* conjunction unfolding into the web-like crystallized lattice structure.

That is a common medium of humankind's mind, body, spirit complex. We have all been blessed to live our lives in the sunshine. Indeed a mysterious, beautiful femme fatale is a psychological vision to see that the most fantastic beautiful woman I have ever seen had fixed her big brown beautiful sultry, adorned spiritual eyes on me. Our spirit essence was a mutual attraction coalescing into moonlight enchantment in the grand palace of opulence being somewhere surrounded by colorful flora and the lilting soft jazz tunes that permeated the mood amid this Tony affair which showcased splendid place of beauty and opulence with live music streaming with melodious entertainment for the night with all the fashionable party goers' who delighted themselves with a full measure of living it up in the elitist enjoying the dream odyssey. The harmonic vibration of light wave particle moon light. That ultimate manifestation of luminous divine energy that is a common unity of the mind, body, spirit complex spurs the conscious awareness upon a plurality of earth's *bon homies*.

THE MIND, BODY, SPIRIT, AND STORYTELLING

That I perceive and attend my ears and listen to a cacophony of asynchronous sounds of metropolitan cities teeming with life. Behold this dream as it is a myriad of vibrant thought waves of the steaming magnificent humankind incredible life. Behold the myriad waves of teeming magnificent humankind full of luminous divine vibrations.

There were no studio ceiling lights. The mood of merriment was palpable as those alluring candle lights flickered from the chandeliers dancing shadows on the smiling faces. Flickering flame reflected like still pools of water, I found inside of her eyes, and the glance I gleaned of her eyes was dazzling. A force of the love unity was stirring. As all life and love every gift of sunrise into the new day till transitioning into evening time where the sun sets down beneath the western horizon. Daily sun rays descend into the *solace* as it approaches the cardinal horizon at dusk to darkness canvas.

You see I knew nothing of this place of lively shivoo of the streaming episodes of cinematic drama amid people milling in the surreal realms time-space continuum of my imagination unfold in fanciful dream vision. The manifestation of my soul awakened and imbued with the sweet lilting sounds, soothing my spirit, separated from my complex. Entering through the gateway crossing where I was shepherded through and into the pure anachronistic Stargate of the surreal realm and was animated in the atemporal cinematic episodes of the oneiric illusory of the great dreamweaver creative excursions. That is the nature of the unframed beautiful portrait scene of the sounds we hear everyday of distortions of daily noises pinging that a cacophony of frivolities melded. Yeah, just another manic day amid the public commuting crowds of humankind's pure streaming as wave force energy vibration moving as a crowd of people streaming passed by folks on the pedestrian sidewalks. With notable observations, watch as the strangers' procession moves along, while the indolent panhandlers wait for the motor vehicles to stop and wait for the red traffic intersection and watch for the light to turn green. and then they slowly walk down the lanes. Everyday life of the panhandlers is busy soliciting donations from the commuters who are the drivers seated in their motor vehicles wade through the rush-hour traffic, going and coming, to hither and thither in the noisiness of the stressful discordance of the irrepressible daily distortions that ping into the ears. People walking and in motor vehicles seem sure of themselves are detached from the insipid panhandlers who slowly walk down through the lines of the waiting cars that are at a full stop at a traffic intersection; and with private thoughts and secrets, trying hard to avoid or divert eye contact.

Apprehension in the crowd waves of the visual reality of the material world of the human mind, body, and spirit complex of the living embodiment. Yeah, I felt translucent, as if I was devoid of physical form. A present lucid spirit essence amid the busy metropolitan's heavy crowd of rush hour scenes of commuters. Of all the people that passed, I didn't observe one with a smiling true face. It's just another everyday crowd of pedestrian waves of human foot traffic, and we all see them walking about in this animated hustling urban scene of curious individuals milling about in the bustling metropolitan area looking around. Some seemed to be enjoying themselves while others had stoic faces, tight lips and fixed eyes looking at the fashionable window displays. Some curious individuals casually strolling by with vapid stares passed some with notable stressed-out faces.

People are living in their high-tone material external empirical world lifestyles. Meaning arrogant elites who are living a hightone people who enjoy their jet setting lifestyles; they are all walking on a precarious high tight wire looking down on those who are the ordinary people of this commercial world of electronic and digital media enterprises that entertain the public social consciousness.

While ordinary people's daily subsistence is a labor of struggles to achieve existence in a marginal material world of success in daily pabulum life activities sustainable with fiat money and very high-interest bank issued new money plastic credit cards. Such material things reflect one's status in the social complex, a zenithal feeling of self-esteem within our beingness.

The temporal reality we see is a subset of a mind/body/spirit identity. I stood there amid the line of the bustling metropolitan concrete temporal reality, and watching, I saw the shopping mall scene of the waves of foot traffic streaming past each other. While some people stood in lines that were forming at the food court to satisfy their hunger. Patiently waiting in a serpentine queue as I observed the feckless crowd of parsimonious weekend window shoppers walking about inside. Folks mingling and passing by with plastic money is the irrepressible impulse that drives the global monetary wealth/growth economic system.

It's just another ordinary day of government debt financing and consumers' daily plastic credit card debt spending drives interest rates driven by the powerful global financial businesses and consumer structured buyers and sellers stock market exchange equity funds and bond profits and losses in the trading of futures underlying market securities enterprises systems or high risk for creating wealth. They are the crowds of pedestrians walking mingling with other human spirit embodiments of shopping consumers of the economic global market growth system. Some folks are profligate spenders that spur economic sales growth. Business owners' profit margins erosion can not escape from the Pac-Man-like emerging creeping inflation.

Daily purchases are the banker's parlor game of high-interest credit line cards that is the driving force behind the new world order economic growth system mechanism of the consumer market present world reality. In the time cycles of this workaday life of the window shopping margins of hard-working ordinary people. Families who struggle to pay down a long term monthly bank financed debt obligation to pay off their thirty-year mortgage commitment. Humankind is a mind, body, spirit, and complex of animated physical material existence as living spirit entities. For our mental health and well-being, and to appreciate the image of God's countenance as our god-self in the mirror is conscious awareness. It was not just another ordinary dream excursion unfolding into the cycle of measure of the diurnal daily frivolities. To see and experience all living beings in this illusory perception of the psychological fast lanes of the living embodiment spurred by the decision and actions of this energies' confluence stream that resides within nature's volatile material, competitive lifestyle that is pervasive amid the external empirical illusion. Spiritualism, the beingness, occurs within the material reality of human lust to acquire power and control through the economic system of capital wealth and market value and exploitation. Devoid of due diligence has destabilized the irresponsible and unrestrained lack of fiduciary responsibility because of profligate reckless printing of the American government fiat dollar currency facilitated record debt spending without a lifeline to future prosperity.

Is this not a total lack of accountability that has led us to a leveraged debt-to-income ratio, which means this is an untenable situation with an ominous consequence! Neither the taxpayers of today nor the future generations of taxpayers will escape the *tsunami* from *the incipient* yoke of the government's mammoth thirty Trillion government debt! This yoke is an insurmountable debt obligation.

Which has created serious financial consequences for future generations of taxpayers is a unfortuitous and bleak harbinger. It's noticeably impossible to pay off this loan term, high-interest debt payments, is closely akin to a real bleak future to come. What a dreadful misfortune of a stressful situation to confront this commercial calamity of debt bondage. Government profligate spending spurred this untenable, revolving merry-go-round system turning is the instability inherent in the stock market player's unrestrained earnings potential, rimpling profit and loss of the game of chance to acquire windfall profits from the sellers and buyers. The speculators hedge their bet in this commercial global economic market exchange profit and loss system which is the financial consumers' game of network activity that is closely akin to the devalued government fiat currency with which fuels the system of daily market activities inflection points with undulations of frivolous profligate deficits spending, with no default switch! Its commercial banking epicenter of ruling class elite who were most powerful players mendacious against inept *fiduciaries*. Political parties who have entrapped us in the evil yoke and bonds of slavery fetters. Whereof this irony is the paradox between the sustainable consumption and the economic providence is deficit spending mired in poverty foreshadowing stressful conditions to come. And without a miracle, there's no lifeline. The distress is the pain of payments that doesn't afford an escape hatch to open up the release from inevitable yoke. It is the consequences of high-interest rates and unsustainable government debt spending with payments obligations of wasteful Federal Reserve printing of fiat dollars!

THE MIND, BODY, SPIRIT, AND STORYTELLING

Total indifference to the temporal reality of the repercussions, which ignore a dreadful creeping calamity. The ramifications of a social government *leviathan* segway into the financial woes of default and the economic slowdown, is a collapse closing in like a giant global anaconda constricting, and killing freedom with impunity! We all live within our own personal space, replete with the earth's distortions with the materialistic vision of negative and positive human actions as the free will choices permeates the consciousness mental perception of the external illusory empirical world of good and evil. You cannot hide in the tall municipal buildings of this hubris modern day reminiscent of the olden time period Babylon, which An angered God of the Heavens called upon the inhabitants of the sky, who destroyed the tower and scattered its inhabitants. The story was not related to either a flood or the confusion of languages, although Frazer connects its construction and the scattering of the giants with the Tower of Babel the gods (Enlil) ordered the destruction.

In real quiet introspection I pass strangers from all directions within an anachronistic surreal space.

Yet it was just me, looking around for things recognizable. I sensed myself being part of the metaphysics life force energy convergences feeling buoyant and cathodic of ataraxia for tranquility had enfolded within as I was going far beyond the cacophony of Earth distortions that ping upon my unity of separation from the most high. When I awakened, I was dreaming free from discordant noise vibrations of the material reality, harmonic animations of living activities, symphonic sounds that abound in a workaday empirical world *pablum*. Another daylight cycles around into the future life of love. Commuters walking the wide paved sidewalks. I took another moment of this quiet introspection and reflected as I observed all manner of fast-moving stylish motor vehicles rolling down the black asphalt paved street surfaces. Humankind mingling together as the rich man and the poor man experiencing the imaginary world's ebbs and flows is closely akin to the vibrations of the harmonic wave consumed by the life force energy. Ordinary everyday people who are making a living with concerning issues. And all the while enduring the daily vagaries of the stressful commuters traffic time of the bumper-to-bumper waves of moving motor vehicle cars and people who walk up and down the concrete metropolitan concrete metropolitan city noise and stop and go traffic that is closely akin to the cattle herds movement during daily commuters in the bustlin world of peoples trials and tribulations. Human spirits living it up in three dimensions of this psychological material realm. And visual transformation is most like a living dreamscape odyssey of existences we face in dynamic *anachronist* places to find tranquility in wonderful perfect vistas. I was there looking around admiring everything I envisioned. I stood in rapture; awed by nature's magnificent biosphere of beautiful arrays of this fantastic garden vistas.

Yeah, I was in this area of the space-time pervasive illusion and delusional continuum was confluence.

While I was not sure of where I envisaged. Whereof I was looking around in awe and humble appreciation, to feel alive animated in the dimensional to enjoy every moment of tranquility. I was amid embodied souls and awed by the *fauna and flora*. Animated life forms surround me with the playful humanity moving about the bountiful landscape. Beautiful ordinary folks must fully awaken and walk among strangers who never courteously greeted anyone they passed without comportment or a polite smile. Poised, I observe human dalliance and decadence on display amid this crowd of beautiful people whose presence appeared in my dream. Everyone was partying. You are exemplifying great wealthy high-class stylish raiment that showcase fortuitous economic opportunities. Unlike the broken and disheveled vagabonds whose persona is akin to those folks who are the panhandlers who are like the walking dead, lifeless victims of bad life choices. It was symbolic of a human devoid of every social grace and economic opportunity. Seemingly, they are alive and devoid of consciousness and awareness of their condition; they have become the wayward and *disheveled shylocks* among crowds of commuters. Might they lift their spirit with a meaningful life purpose, and with the condition, with the mental faculty of purpose, desire, or the will to perform an action, volition. No, indeed, their aim is to prey upon sympathetic innocent humankind sitting inside a motor vehicle, pausing for the red traffic signal light to turn green. Yeah, there I sat, behind my car's steering wheel, patiently waiting as I observed them enter into the street, hustlers applying their trade walking between motor vehicles stopped at the traffic intersection's red light.

There we can witness their dalliance, their apathy, indolence, and entropy, clearly impervious to a productive life of employment; they have missed their opportunity, and much to my chagrin; they seemed to prefer to collect free-gratis donations from the merciful generosity of god's kind hardworking drivers. Twisted wayward souls slowly walk between motor vehicles at a full stop waiting to go. They wait for the red traffic light to turn green. We watch this indulgence as strategically as zombified *disheveled* panhandles slowly walk between lines of motor vehicles at a full stop waiting for the red intersection traffic light to change to green. It is a fleeting scene that showcases this lifestyle of sloth is chosen by the panhandlers. The weak scared souls who have a self actualized state of poverty flood into the bustling lines of waiting motor vehicle cars who are watching to go when the major metropolitan city-streets signal is green is the scene we revisit in every city and town major intersections. They are minimalist people who have become displaced souls among the community of the mainstream productive social complex, swimming against the waves of human material societies values. Blessings come to all of the benevolent souls with a heart of golden generosity. Being productive in the life of this peregrination elude all who have chosen to walk down through the lanes of waiting cars.

The life of dalliance for folks who chose the lifestyle of folly is confirmed when we see them all out of touch with their meaningful life purpose. What a ball of sad tears is the fate of those who chose the left over the right direction and must extricate themselves from the misfortunate consequences of the indiscriminate all consuming control system. This pathway that drives the economic grind, which is the lifeline unity in common, is alive for everyone everyday allures in the mainstreams away from the road less traveled. Instead, the adults seek a productive pathway that diverges away from the pitfalls of dalliance of the dreadful pitfalls of the slippery slope. They embrace the pathway of the vagabond; meaning that they are wayward souls who lifestyle of sloth unconscious panhandling pit stop crews. We can watch them apply who seek solicitation for money from the drivers sitting in the heavy, bustling metropolitan traffic scenes of every model of motor vehicles and the subway station astir with the bustles noise of humankind melded against the traffic waves of dalliance of hustlers, buskers was conspicuous.

Okay the excited wide eyed vacationing tourists can't subdue their rabbit amusement they are looking and pointing. I was there and watched the tourists, and saw the vagabond who slowly walked between the traffic lanes, waiting for motor vehicles holding a cardboard sign to solicit charitable donations from benevolent drivers to show compassion for humankind.

Yeah, we can witness them holding up their handwritten cardboard signs, and while it seems that they are awake, they are the animated spirits that cause our actions and constraints limitations in the physical condition of this physical manifested reality. To everyone who sleeps and our minds are dreaming, lucidly in action as we do the movement, and a somewhat carefree lifestyle of dalliance the wayward; the lost callow souls are wasting their gift of life. They are sleep-walking through life. Their emotional appeal is a psychological inspiring target to touch upon the heartstrings of the kind and merciful intelligent people.

This illustrates the profile of the lazy sloth of those whose aim and purpose is to hang on to society by clinging to dalliance; they are feeding off the responsible social culture, playing on the kindness of humankind's generous charitable contributions of the pure at heart. To eke out a life of substance, you will see them walking all day long. The red traffic signal turned red. Panhandlers began to hold up a small cardboard sign and started to walk down between the traffic lanes of waiting motor vehicle cars. Drivers are looking ahead ready to go when the red traffic light turns from red to green.

They are the maladjusted bon homies who live with a miserable lifestyle heavy yoke. They are the lost souls walking amid the productive gregarious pawns who drive the economic system as the dispassionate everyday working people. Might we all be like those who show their benevolent human spirits when they show their light hearted, too, with good blessing to be exculpated from dreadful conditions of distortion.

Will you dare cast them aside? Those lost souls walk between the cars of the nine-to-five commuters who travel by motor vehicles, waiting for the stopped traffic intersection red light to turn green. It's a rather all too familiar daily scene we revisit in every city and town. They are the ones who maneuver in and out of the street, and slowly, they walk between the lanes while lines of vehicles idle at the red traffic waiting for the intersection traffic light to turn green. The dalliance of unkempt misguided human souls flooding into the waiting traffic with their stoic vapid sad eyes eschewed their employment opportunities; meaning that, unlike another well-adjusted adult who has acquired gainful employment. Instead disinclination to an earnest means of steady jobs that would be of self-service of beingness in the human community social complex. This is the profile of those who have chosen to embrace the lifestyles of dalliance and sloth. We see the dysfunctional elements of the social complex, which constitutes the misfortune or ignorance of the wayward miserable souls who have surrendered their life and have come to face reality without a change of direction.

To apprehend the logic of the lazy, it seems they are wayward souls with no future. And what fate is there to await the walking dead, poor, and forsaken folks who in perpetual dalliance of an unredeemable social *drowse*, and humankind disheveled dreads of the civilized complex *peregrinations,* meaning those who are devoid of their life purpose. To this I think we all have apprehended this manifestation of dalliance, seemingly axiomatically closely akin to the folly of the lazy grasshopper.

What is the future for the journeyman who tarried there amid the busy, bustling metropolis traffic scene with the cardboard sign saying, hungry veteran, please spare some change! What my eyes see is such a pitiful stirring scene.

Indeed, the spirit of goodness and mercy for those who have stopped distributing alms showed compassion for humanity. There I witnessed the gratuity and gratitude of people who smiled as they gave generous benevolent blessings of the light heart compassionate people. Everyday during my commute from home, I am touched by the disheveled vagabonds who long ago jettisoned the allure of the substantive lifestyle by means or will to be productive. Instead, they have no desire to conform to the pursuit of gainful, meaningful, and purposeful social life peregrination. The unremarkable grinders exemplified faces of failure is such a misfortune circumstance! The wayward people who are living beings; the outliers living on the margins of the society of common consciousness who have no potential opportunities. They are the lost callow souls who have to exploit the system, they are living without a meaningful life purpose.

These folks are the dreadful, disheveled, *melodiously* unkempt people who flood into the street when vehicles stop for at the intersection red light. While some drivers' hearts compelled them to give *alms* to their poor fellowman who walked between the waiting car for merciful generous supplications, holding the cardboard sign as the hot sun rays baked their skin.

Their faces baked by the sun showcased vapid, sad, transfixed, jaundiced eyes.

They were the grifters who were content to prey upon kind-hearted people with generous compassion for merciful folks who wittingly give with kindness and compassion. The souls' embodiment as a human mind/body/spirit avatar complex. While we are living in a political and religious mysticisms has been an evolutionary element of the ancient and modern world illusory temporal reality bequeathed to all the time to experience life. I walked there and apprehended this place, whereof I *tarried* for only a brief moment and admired all of the things that unfolded for my enjoyment. I paused to enjoy being in the time-space of the dynamic unity of the infinite intelligent Creator, who opened my eyes to imbibe things in appreciation of the intrinsically harmonic balance of the infinite Creator's living spirit, energy pulsating waves and vibrations of love as the light. Where ordinary folks passed by another chattering into their cell phones. Aimlessly going along life's peregrination with a daily illusion of the temporal reality's epicenter with moral desires—only to survive. While some folks's eyes were fixed with a gazing into a cellular telephone screen in silence, then looking down at the screen texting; others are confabulating via their voice from their electronic voice cellular telephone. They passed by each other and hardly ever noticed that there were others amid waves of humanity going hither and thither into episodic scenes, which I entered with very stupendous opulence and grandeur. It was this otherworldly scene I envisioned while being there in some higher level of another dimension. Some wonderful and strange places I was unfamiliar with. My spirit had guided me into this spectacular place with good chivalry and etiquette, and the full displays of stylish elegance and well-dressed folks wearing the most fashionable attired people enjoying themselves. I knew that my perception was reflective of the dreamweaver's hand at play. As I realized that this is a psychological illusion of this confluence as manifestations of my spiritual beingness had carried me into the dimension of this surreal realm of nirvana. Away from the vagaries of the terrestrial urban landscape of diurnal *cacophony* of the *asynchronous* metropolitan noises upon my clairsentience. I looked around to see all the living throngs of humanity., trying to admire humanity's depiction of streaming social distortion. In every small town and city-states life plays out in this material world of glass, concrete, steel metropolitan commercial construction amid the bustling crowded traffic scenes.

Therein we have centers of tall, steel, concrete towering construction with tinted refractive glass windows that are incredibly magnificent of humanity. An unframed backdrop and a beautiful perspective against the blue sky, and the white clouds steadily drift across the calm blue sky with a warm sunlight vista. Such is the perception of the bustling animated illusory temporal reality of the busy rush hour traffic. A spectacle replete with the weekend crowds of mall walkers, shoplifters, the profligate plastic credit card shoppers and the casual window foot traffic. Ordinary people were walking, talking, looking, and window shopping walking past each other. It was as if they couldn't see me there. Yet I was there walking among the throngs of animated waves of people moving about. Within this realm of animation of Earth's interior plane of corporeal life form and matter, in spirit my mental complex consciousness awareness. There I tarry amid the animated activity of human beings streaming within the bustling metropolis skyline of wide-angle scenes of the unframed illusory reality's illusory material world construction. From every direction streaming into every facet of the interior earthly experiences of the existential realm of illusory reality. My spirit was buoyant in joyful mirth. I'm there mingling among the merrymaking with adrift in the streaming episodes oneiric with socialites.

Yeah, I could apprehend the people who walked past each other; while others were driving, some with passengers riding in motor vehicle cars, trucks, and public transient buses. Ordinary people aim to travel through the street traffic, some wait for the crosswalk green light, eagerly ready to cross the transportine dreamtime lanes and crosswalk to reach the other side. Together, they Patiently waited for the traffic green light to go across the intersection. It's a visual reflection. The animated crowds of humankind mulling about, amid the spiritual embodiments of lively souls of individuals as separated units from the mind, body, spirit complex. I am just one of the many unique units of separation from our ineffable Infinite Creator of the all universal Neter. It's just an ordinary experience in which the Sun's radiant heat waves energize the living nature. Amid the crowds of people I could see these faces of human consciousness embodiments. Humanity is the massive waves of the corporal embodiment of energetic soulful spirit living and walking, talking, and the coming forth by day and going forth by night and day.

We stand next to people in silence at the red traffic stop light waiting to go when vehicle cars wait for the city intersection red traffic light to turn green.

Drivers are patiently looking at the red to change to yellow when the signal light switches to green. Thongs of noisy daily impatient commuters, some standing others are watching for the red pedestrians walk light to turn to green. With eccentricity, might my thoughts tarry amid this illusory temporal reality of transient buses, commuter trains, taxis, stylish passenger cars? Large trucks drive through the green right away traffic signal. Pedestrians wait for their green light signal melded with vibratory sounds of the human mind/body/spirit complex, the past magnificently tall buildings.

THE MIND, BODY, SPIRIT, AND STORYTELLING

There were busy metropolis communities where the trees lined the streets that were tinged with the smell and the noise from fast moving motor vehicles and pedestrians passing other people walking on the concrete sidewalks. Some folks enter stores; others are coming out of the buildings of the commercial work environments. On display before my eyes were these embodiments of everyday people experiencing life as a daily routine activity. Nowhere to escape and hide from trivial matters of living in a concrete cacophony of the asynchronous noisy metropolis street traffic. I was seeing that we have become indifferent and desensitized to asphalt and all human activity, yet seemingly so detached from the concern of other people's peregrination, our life to love and to be loved. Happiness of being and enjoying existence and discerning the true blessings through the turns, straight aways, intersections, crosswalks, on the pathways, towards the secret Stargate portals, and turn-around life's unpredictable events. The streaming magnificently episodes of dalliance in the present time continuum. Mystery and wondrous dream odyssey, which is the transportine gateway crossing of the intermittent exclusive dalliance of the subconscious vision, inner reflection coefficient of the enigmatic spirit abiding in a different dimension of oneiric surreal realm of the dreamweaver unscripted episode's. The spirit's abiding in the enfoldment is a replete blissful calm and relaxing inner separation adrift in the subconscious mind of peaceful meditative state of solace. A deeper level of nighttime excursive odyssey of the intelligent *monads*, with which all things are derived as creative thoughts. Have you or I the quieted spirit essence of the infinite spiritual existential miracle of the universal phenomenon world.

Metaphysical noumena spirit life forces energy of the mind/body/spirit complex of the material illusion of this temporal reality! The reality of duality of action and quiet comfort and solace in the time cycle by the day and go forth by night; and all the while my consciousness awareness and thoughts turn to idle when my mind/body/spirit complex is a spiritual separation for my embodiment to lie resting in my recombinant state. We are the spirit essence consciousness awareness and the physical form of material male and female embodiments. At night we sleep to rest in a recumbent state, as the body yields the spirit energy is transported by subconscious freewill imbibed of awareness is animated by going hither and thither entering through the archway crossing into unfamiliar anachronistic places at night time. Alive with a free will spirit energy that spurs my animations to respond as positive and negative actions and deeds.

    My starry eyes delighted as the spirit walked among the animated crowd's of lively human scenes moving manifestations of the uncurated metaphysical embodiments. These were energetic spirits; they flanked me on all sides. Things I observed were quite splendid and appeared as a perfect masterpiece portrait that were very beautiful, and I was there watching and listening to blathering amid the most stupendous display of grand royal opulence and wealth, unfolded into this beautiful landscaped courtyard scene in the full lighted alchemy, revealed in full effect of the excursive odyssey dream vision I apprehended in an anachronistic marvelous dimension. Where dreaming spirit energy is the respite for everyday people's souls escape our corporeal human bodies are animated in the existential world of daylight, entering the adult playground night illusory of turning into the merry-go-round roller coaster riding. I'm going up then down on the seesaw; I dwelled among them in a present timespace continuum where the two hands of time are steady and the clock is ticketing without a pause; as reality is slowly moving around the clock face. There I entered through an energized crystal gateway portal. I looked and knew that I had entered into this bright arching vision of the gateway turnstile, and was buoyant by this remarkable transition into the interim dream vision. Episodic animated scenes of great wonderful anachronistic places were streaming. This mystique goes beyond the physical illusory temporal world reality. A wonderful place of grandeur of a breathtaking merry-go-round!

    It's a feeling of total blissfulness! Living it up in the mystery realm of surreality observing things that were not real; and it was all the actions of the free-wheeling spirit's creative imagination, for I envisioned the most luminous divine rows of the swaying display of the Tree of Life. Sophistry, shall we say, is closely akin to the children's game of musical chairs! When the music stopped, O dear, you've just been adrift somewhere living it up on the other side of the life forces in duality. When we are mired within the mind-space complexity of everyday commuters; in evocative scenes of the presence time experiences walking, talking, and living among soulful spirit beings.

Wandering through this profundity of the psychological subconscious creative illusory has shepherded me. The dream state of surreality until the wokeness time in the warm confluence rays of the daylight cycle of temporal time period that transitions into the evening at dusk. It's so beautiful when dusk turns off the sun to the moon at nighttime. And in turn, again the morning sun marks the pinging noise distortions of our daily grind of hustling and bustling frivolities I imbibe as the activities of realtimes continuum moves in the polarized earth's spending every minute of the time measures life cycles turns through the hourglass of humanity beingness. A harmonic balance amid the *cacophony* distortions and the noisy daily grind of human activity with fast traffic symphony of commuters melded into noisy discordant of motor vehicles passing, and the others came to a full stop for a red traffic stoplight. They watched as the waves of people passed by each other; as some people entered or exited a retail or a commercial building.

While other ordinary people move asynchronously entering into public places. Some people are leaving from commercial workplaces activities that constitute the traffic waves. The daily human activities of crowds milling about in public spaces. Human activity is the energy of the life force that animates, it's derived from the same old spirit that pervades during a commuters' work-a-day time in the *asynchronous* daily grind. And as we are living beings, we experience the trials and tribulations as a separation from the universal unity derived from the intelligent, ineffable, infinite universal cosmic spirit energy. Yellow glowing candle light sets the mood fluttering on the mesmerizing faces, creating shadows of silhouettes by the candles light glow. Everyday *bon homies* warmed bodies engaged in the sun's above from the eastern western shore horizon. It's yet another new early morning for me. My spirit has come alive and lives in the Kavod rays of the earth's solar daylight turnstile duality of sun, and moonlight slowly fades away at dawn, waiting until the melodious male nightingale bird sings.

It's the beginning of another ordinary morning in every way; and meaning, no different from the previous day. I was awakened as I heard that sound of the familiar sound bellowing of the old hubris barnyard cock crowing three times. I knew that soon the sun was a precursor of dawn, followed by the sun to light up the sky crepuscular clouds *lucerne* sandisk that rises and slowly crosses the sky canvas then descends on the west coast ocean horizon, fades into the sunset over the horizon shoreline and brings darkness canvas of nighttime. It's that majestic radiant sunlight slowly ascending into the sky and peaks high at midday. This vainglorious divine that *succor* the poor and wealthy sustains with the providence of warm radiance movement across the covered sky cloud until it descends beneath the western shoreline horizon. Wittingly quiet your mind and drift off to sleep; awaiting an episode of smooth night voyage into the illustrative surreal realm of streaming mystique. The two hands of duality a dichotomy of night and day, always confluence diffusion across a transmutation where I was entering into the phenomenal *kaleidoscope* of the spiritual crystal light, with the harmonic vibration of luminous impulses of cosmic energy swirling around.

A dichotomy of night and day, always confluence diffusion across a transmutation where I was entering into the phenomenal kaleidoscope of the spiritual crystal light, with the harmonic vibration of luminous impulses of cosmic energy swirling around. The stairway that twisted buoyed my spirit upward. Everything was of vivid colors, likened to a perfect dream vision and my eyes mesmerized by the bright particles and light rays that were flashing, while spiritual essence twists upward. The infinite light of love felt as the luminous divine particle waves of rhythm harmonic vibration. I was swirling around and in patterns of aurora twisted and moving elixir, drifting like transformative clouds I envisaged.

With manifestation unfolding into fantastic, brilliant, erotic patterns my spirit invisaged while I drifted into the celestial oneiric nirvana. The quiet twilight encroaches upon the hot sunlight descending beneath the horizon metaphysics. It is my dreams that are always slowly fading the enchantment of the dream odyssey. A polarity spinning fast around its conic axis poles orbit. Movement derived from the primordial creative sacred principles and laws of cosmic manifestations coalesced of the illusion of rhythmic temporal reality. Earth living nature with the arrangement of the sunshine stands day and the moon by night dancing in orbit in the diurnal cycles turns ocean waves, spinning fast as the earth is always spinning around to bring sunlight and beautiful luminous moon light. A duality through a luminous gateway portal that buttresses the darkness dreamscape turnaround through the turnstile of the dreamweaver excursive realm. Much as is illustrative to imbibe in the realms of this esoteric universal cycle of the space-time continuum of in a binary tesalate reality and surreality. The dawn of darkness canvas yield when sun rises comes around in the turn around in cycle life experience. Yeah, there are many animated forms of recognizable embodiments. Humankind was born as units of separation from the *Neberdjer* as divine-human luminous souls with ups and downs is likened to the merry go around for the corporeal human vessel. So subtle a turn of time that comes and goes around and I can't feel the earth spinning without pauses.

The geosynchronous orbit of revolving planetary sphere rotation cycles experiencing transitory peregrinations drifting hither and thither; it's nature's universal cosmological canvas of infinite life force energy. Light to the darkness of duality, a carousel turns daylight into the dark of night.

I acknowledge another day of brilliant sunshine turning down at dusk to surrender to the western shore horizon. Presciently I am not aware of my dream state coalescing or that I had been adrift in the dreamweaver's fantastic oneiric surreal plane, where I admired the distant array of glinting stars scattered in the stillness of the majestically dark sky. It seemed so real as I stood in the moonlight. Might I say with a heart full of appreciation, gazing into the beautifully adorned mesmerizing eyes of my psychological inamorata yeah! For her presence to appear when daylight turns into a chance encounter with nirvana.

Where the spirit essence enters through the gateway crossing into the realm with soothingly calm lilting jazz sounds of oneiric idyllic accommodations of the dreamweaver's recursive entertainment.

Every morning preceding the night canvas never brings the same old dream; it ends and never again will it come around in the same place or the time and space! My eyes closed and my mind relaxed. My consciousness awareness is a vivid dream estate, a surreal atemporal alchemy that comes from the illusory of the moonlight. It's nighttime in the life cycle duality of the monthly daily calendar countdown to zero point of the time movement. Units of individual human beings with the divine energy field of the mind/body/spirit complex. Where I am one soul separated from the infinite creator who will rapture me into *anachronistic* places. We are all living spirits who are swept away into the sleep state to dream adrift, going upward into a marvelous infinity of the surreal realm of anachronistic places. We have no knowledge about where the spirit entertains me.

For it seems that I was aware, but didn't I care about where she compelled me to go! My spirit appreciated being in the world of randomly inspired serendipity. Caught up in blissful adorned enchantress eyes beguiled my heartfelt limerence that was my psychological illusion lost in the oneiric dimensions the dream cycles going hitherto and thither to places I had no remembrance.

My spirit essence adrift in itself fulfillment in the time-space continuum. I envisioned and experienced my presence residing in *anachronistic* places. As if I was there and animation in the universal language of the dream space, which I watched as the clock's longhand slowly ticked off seconds of the night cycle transitions around the clock face in equal measure of the space-time continuum. Every subtle tick-tock of the seconds turns the short and long hand track of the measure of the cycle of life without pause.

Life is confluence in synthesis with harmonic balance orbit cycle axis pole. Sunlight gives life. Moonlight glows as the oceans waves and the sweet waters of rivers flow with *rippling* waves that sound crested and wash upon the shoreline rhythmically. A perception insight of my clarity of the third eye vision, and to this a remarkable surreal illusory of my breathtaking fair lady. Captivated, I gazed at her perfect female form as a masterpiece portrait. A femme fatale seductress enchantress beguiled my eyes and drew me nigh. Everything there seemed stupendous opulence where well-dressed guests were milling about as the lilting smooth jazz tunes flowed. I sat and watched this graceful diva walk through this crowd of people until she finally approached the bar and took the empty barstool next to me.

In the midst of lively conversation and *shivoo*, her presence inflamed my heart with lemerance desire. With limerence and her urban affability, I imbibed up a full measure of this lovely *femme fatal's* showcase that was illustrious of a mysteriously beautiful goddess presence. My Kundalini conjugated into a total mind/body/spirit energy sensory complex. I was enamored with limerence; and yet indeed I had apprehended her breathtaking hourglass figure was a perfect complement to the provocatively elegant black dinner dress she wore; which was a perfect fit to her masterpiece female form and she was the epitome of style and grace that caught my eye. And lo, *ipso facto,* I knew she had captivated me when I gleaned her incredible spiritual eyes! Her regal style and affability, charm, and regal comportment; and yes, she was my first choice from the very first time our eyes met. That indeed it was a very special night meant for her and I to be struck by the jazz rhythm, and stately luxurious and ambiance that unfold magic that night.

Noticeably, she was queenly and personable as she was gracious when she entered this elegant palace hall. She looked so nice and quite fetching in her stunning attire and the sparkling karat diamond earrings she wore with poise. I saw her enter the room and continued to follow this gorgeous majestic looking seductress casually walk across the room as all eyes were on her. Her personna was closely akin to a lovely angelic vision. Her smile was so very beautiful, and her walk was a graceful refinement. She was the most beautiful female goddess who had set her big beautiful adorned spiritual eyes on me. We reciprocated smiles with mutual attraction. I blinked then rubbed my eyes, and with coyness she smiled with polite affability and was a very graciously charming regal enchanting femme fatale of engaging panache. I was besotted from the time I watched the lovely lady enter the grand affair, and each one she passed by, I heard the men exclamation, whoa as she walked into the hall! And you know I couldn't take my eyes away from her! She was turning heads of men who were mesmerized by her as she graced the grand splendid palace hall. What a pleasant delight to see this elegantly dressed lady that had the party-goers. When suddenly it occurred to me that She had cast her sultry adorned eyes to glean her beauty. You could see that she had charmed and this certain *je ne sais quoi*. Her august appearance I gleaned my lust full eyes upon her female form as followed by her sultry mesmerizing perfect figure that had beguiled me with limerence. I watched her from the time I saw her gracefully walk into the hall and stole through the crowd as she walked toward the bar and took the empty seat next to me. Like the lady she was, she smiled, and then slowly crossed her legs when she caught my eyes fixed on her. It was surreptitiously for me to greet her as a refined honorable gentleman of comportment. With genuine courtesy, affability, and my charming smile I entreated her to join me for a *potation*. Politely she agreed to enjoy each other's mutual conversation. Magic was pervading in the air coming into this wide open entrance way that was assigned to the stupendously beautiful open and spacious anti-chamber, where the cool breeze found its way into and through the fabulous appointed atrium. You see these amazing guests entering this glamorous interior space. So very wonderful and beautifully dressed socialites were having it large in this special place during the memorable time enfoldment of this dreamscape of merriment that ephemeral night odyssey. I envisaged a dream trance. When I was and envisaged this beautiful woman, in my dreamscapes animation. Yeah I was there looking around in appreciation of these vivid depictions on all sides with rhythmic entertainment that was a so incredibly fantastic sureality of human minds *ficto-sexual* surreal dream visions. One in a million encounters to get the chance to meet the aviator of the most stunning woman I had ever known. The one in a million lady for I envisaged w that was unforgettable ephemeral one-on-one enchanting of Heavenly mirth.

It was such a scene, there I was with this femme fatal, and casually I looked around the hall with this sultry diva who exemplified her *panache*. She had piqued my curiosity. Her perfume was sensual, her shimmering, long rust brown hair was flowing as it bounced on her sun tanned naked back.

You could observe that everyone had gleaned to take a full measured look at her hourglass form that showcased this evening dress that was a perfect fit to her masterpiece female form. An animated scene in cinematic slow motion showcased the refinement of a poised diva; a show-stopper who set the grand hall astir. Lo! She was so wildly good-looking. So very beautiful, like a warm glowing sunset; a calm fell over me with limerence and a tremendous joy and a pleasure mesmerized and captivated the others with a charismatic demeanor.

Smitten with a mysterious lady as I gleaned to and longingly admired her glorious adorable adorned eyesYeah there she was before my eyes; and I watched her enter this enchanting place. No one could take their eye off of her when she gracefully walked through the lively hall full of merrymaking in this high tone and opulence.

Without question she was a gorgeous *femme fatale* with high-tone, regal style, charming comportment that stirred up a fervent desire to know her. With decorum I wanted to make her my queen to be my only one-on-one. Like a flash of lightning she took my breath away! At that very instant I was compelled to get to know her. And there I was mulling in deep thoughts, but unbeknownst to me I was unaware of where I resided that night. Only that it all seemed so very real being there with this beautiful femme fatale which has been vivid and unforgettable when I revisit that time being in her presence in my daily morning mental focus in meditation. A remembrance of her was that female form that I envisaged within the interim time of my moment of reflection was with my inner peaceful calm meditation and tranquility of illusory solace transcendental episode dreams. And in this scene, my eyes were firmly fixed as I *imbibed* the visage of the perfect *female* form.

I imbibed all that I could see, and sensed my chest rise and fall synced to my rhythmically heart racing.

I was mesmerized as I respectfully gleaned the mysterious *femme fatale*. We engendered each other's eyes; and I was buoyant by her presence and ardent attractiveness. My eyes were fixed as I appreciated this marvelous illusory vision of the most beautiful woman I had known or seen sitting and sharing lively conversation! A regal goddess has stolen the hearts of many men who were beguiling men who were mesmerized by her lovely angelic aura of being in the presence of a beautiful *sweven*.

This place merriment was alive with smooth lilting mellifluous jazz tunes pervaded. I saw that She was a captivatingly beautiful *femme fatale*, and like a hot wildfire ablaze, I watched her slowly walk across the room as I watched her until she came to sit next to me at the bar! She was incredibly beautiful and sensing my look gave her a smile in appreciation of the moment our eyes met amid the merriment of high tone and lilting soft jazz tunes that melded perfectly within anachronistic place with demur soft ambient from the ceiling lined with the crystal glowing yellow ambient glowing light burning gave the appearance akin to the dancing shadows of the romantic *chandeliers* of demure candle lights flame burning had set the mood.

What remains of this psychological dream affair pervades within my thoughts as this unforgettable folly. Yes she was a delightful looking spirit *pleroma* with an adorable beautiful one on one love encounter. The serendipitous crossroads of the chance encounter with a one in a million *ficosexual* psychological love affair never blossomed beyond the memory, and my heart she set ablaze by the adorable *femme fatale*'s seductive like enchanting *sweven*.

I could not look away! I was mesmerized by her adorned spiritual eyes. In the quintessence her presence spurred a dulcet parlance that enlivened our mutual attractions for words inspired within the sensory cortex that romantic aura of my desire. Her enchantress' eyes had put a beguiling spell on me. This was my unforgettable dreamweaver's excursion that seemed so real. Enchantment that entertained my illusion of subconsciousness. I held tight to this remembrance. I had taken a full sip of this lovely golden ratio that had buoyant me up and imbued me with limerence. My rumination was a resplendent recall. Let me say that it's truly the stuff of my psychological vivid dreams. I am feeling buoyant with my thoughts of this mysterious lady. She was a femme fatales with adorned eyes who beguiled and spurred me amourious spirit-self with limerence. Appreciated myself being able to imbibe her aura as a moment of the psychological nudity of surreality. A lovely animated vision I experienced was a phycological mysterious beautiful femme fatale seduced me in the dreamweaver' surreal realm of exciting entertainment. I couldn't have resisted this feeling of pure *limerence*, as I felt my heart set ablaze. Was she not the most, beguilingly, exquisite-looking? I contemplated what I was feeling, compelling me to longingly glean her mesmerizing adorned eyes.

I was indeed smitten by this lovely lady, and buoyant with her enchantress eyes chilling in this mood of shivoo, and joyous merrymaking. There we gleaned to read each other's eyes. We exchanged smiles. She looked so beautiful in the glamorous black evening dress she wore.

This mysterious Lady was the *cynosure* of genuine desire, as my eyes imbibed of her gracefully female as she walked through the crowded grand hall of people of maryment, and I could see that all eyes were gazed upon her. As if a bolt of lightning struck me, with *limerence* our eyes met. With mutual attention we gleaned each other and smiled with a cursory look of affability and charm. When we were swept up in this scene of *shavoo* confabulation and generous reciprocal smiles and playful coyness while seated at the crowded bar. And just for a brief second, we said nothing; as we took slow sips of our favorite tinctured adult beverage. We had become comfortable being in that temporary lull when our ears could attend to and appreciate the musical, lilting jazz music permeating the perfect mood. This seductress mesmerized, she set my heart aflame! Her presence was closely akin to a true capstone *d' amore* supreme.

Yeah I felt smitten with her aura that complemented the most seriously beautiful spiritual eyes. Surely it was the way that she smiled. It was then that my clairsentience knew she had beguiled my eyes as we both imbibed each other's countenance. A showstopper with a *convivial* charming smile that was turning heads as she drew me nigh to this stunningly breathtaking femme fatale. Her *comeliness was* a mesmerizing golden ratio, with beautiful seductive adorned enchantress eyes. I was beguiled with feeling buoyant, I felt like she was the capstone d'amor with my *limerence;* and so beguilingly charming, she was a beautiful showstopper who drew me nigh! Her presence was the epitome of a blissful capstone feeling d'amore supreme. She was the the most beautifully appealing femme fatale with quite lovely adorned spiritual eyes drew me *nigh*.

I was so enthralled and totally besotted by the comeliness of this fair lady's beautiful adorned eyes that enfolded me with her graciousness. She was a very strikingly attractive and very lovely *femme Fatale with a charming* demeanor and a beautiful smile.

This mysterious *femme fatale* enamored me with her portrait like manifestation. Her long hair; her lovely smile; her beautifully adorned eyes, and oh yes, she looked so very *serendipitous* with her regal decorum and a charming compartment. We held each other's gaze. I was fascinated as I gleaned her presence. I could not look away as I fixed my eyes and watched her amaze everyone that gathered at the formal hall of the elite party socialites. What a marvelous crowd of regal high tone and *panache*. I watched as she walked in the room of merriment. She had posed like a runway fashion model when she moved toward the bar and sat down next to me. She was had fulsome presence indicative of this adorable charming *femme fatal,* and she was there alone. Briefly we exchanged smiles as a conscious acknowledgement. I could see that she was a heartbreaker. A sultry diva that compelled me to glean the and to look into her eyes my eyes upon her very beautiful, mesmerizingly adorned, seductively, and beguiling spiritual eyes. Her full lips were behind her stylish filigree veil of mystique enchantment. Then she smiled at me and turned away to observe the people gathered inside of the imperial hall full of mirth.

She had this air of comportment, being there among the hall of *shivoo* of my psychological illustrative festivity. Whereof I was captivated by the aura of the most beautiful female I apprehended in a surreal realm. What seems to be a mental clarity, was only the ephemeral avatar of this charmingly gracious and lovely femme fatale who had buoyed me up when I looked in to those adoration eyes whose stirred my desire for she!

I felt besotted being in this mysterious beautiful heartbreaker's immediate presence, for she was without one equal, and I knew that she was the only lady to be my one on one. She was the most gorgeous femme fatale with captivating affability and charm with decorum. And I did quickly apprehend that she was not real, but at

THE MIND, BODY, SPIRIT, AND STORYTELLING

all foolish in my mind. It was just my own spirit; and it had caused me to have the sense to appreciate being in the creative imagination and I drifted hither and thither in the pristine night illusory temporal reality. From the moment of zero time of falling asleep, we all are dreamers who are alive and we all dream until the time cycles between awake and asleep. Indulging my force of actions of free will is a human duty in the daylight vista of those glorious sun rays slowly drifting into dawn before nighttime.

Lo, it was the measure of time ticking without a pause, I had entered the turnstile after I closed my eyes when my head rested on the fluffy soft down pillow. Unbeknownst to me, my spirit had punched my ticket to the realm of entertainment, which fully accommodates the intellectual apprehension of the subconscious excursive thoughts envisaged. My energized spirit has shepherded my into the dreamweavers stupendously marvelous *anachronistic* episodes experienced this initiation into a time period of the ataraxia of the dynamics of the ubiquitously realm of the surreality; only that I was someplace I knew nothing about where my spirit drifted, going hither and thither, and buoyant in the grand palace hall slow sipping on my favorite neat tinctures adult beverage in the presence of a beautiful woman, straight trippin and chattering her up in this dreamweaver's psychological excursive serenity just living it up some places I have no recollection when I awakened from the dreamscape. The perception of wonder I envisaged stupendous things while going hither and thither within the Dreamweaver's beautiful, exclusively entropic illusory temporal reality drifting. I had fallen asleep. I did not feel as if my physical body was neither tired nor was I restless. I meandered in this subconscious spirit animated as I was dreaming, while asleep I ascended into the vaulted constellation of the and admired the starry cosmic sky cover.

The oneiric *astral plane*, unfolding a scenic mercurial surreal realm; stars across the purple atmosphere with blue clouds and the face of a full bright yellow luminous moon unframed a reverence of illustrative cosmic canvas that was enchanting. And I am quietly, reposefully dreaming alone with my pellucid spirit's intermittent introspection of my subconscious sensory perception as apprehension with a mind of clarity. I felt a sense of solace in an ebullient state of easiness and tranquility without gravity, I slowly drifted toward the mercurial excursive realm of the surreal fidelity into the dreamweaver's illusory. Whereas my cognition calmly drifted toward this lovely place that was quite breathtaking, awe-inspiring in every visual measure of mystical resplendent *astral metaphysical* spiteful vision into the *noumena* surreal realm.

Yeah, I experienced a fantastic episode. I felt as if I had entered into this and amid others spiritual souls who were standing or walking about in the ancient realm. What fantastic sweven-like picturesque peaceful scenes on all sides, brilliantly framed subconsciousness schemes. Having my consciousness aware in tune with my intelligent personalism, my clear sense of my soulful spirit consciousness, imbibed that blissful state of splendidness as the depictions of streaming episodic ephemeral surreal dream visions in another dimension.

A surreal utopian dreamscape of surreal apprehension of the illusory episodes I envisaged on all sides of the dreamweaver's creative episode of entertainment. All this I perceived as the actions of the spirit drifting into wonderfully ephemeral *anachronistic* places. Extemporaneously my smooth lines of dulcet words inspired her acknowledgment of my *d'amour*. This was a visceral psychological folly running away with me in a spectacular dream odyssey excursion like none other! The moments to remember within soothing tranquility that is the vibratory sounds was serenading my spirit's life force energy. Remember that I was hearing the flight attendant announce a call to all aboard! This was as if I had sat on board some unfamiliar, pristine sophisticated aerial vehicle for which I was perplexed and unknowing the intended flight destination of the forthcoming excursive dreamscape, only that I felt myself strapped in my seat, when I suddenly swept up and quickly zooming into a mysterious vortex and began experiencing calm, and seemingly unaware of the flight destination. Yet perceptible as my spirit essence was commonly relaxed, as my aura was buoyant while in space. I knew nothing of this flash of adrenaline rush.

For majestic scenes pervading in the *Akashic* realm of the transitory dream space continuum. This script was written and directed by the ineffable hand of the dreamweaver's mercurial creative odyssey voyage. My spirit was buoyant and, with free-will, drifted into the realm of the perfect nirvana of the lilting surreal enchantment of the kingdom of excursive mirthfulness going hither and thither. I was going about into the anachronistic places. Where the spirit drifts and goes zooming into the transportine mystical realm of wondrous conveyance of the dream sleep excursions of the brainwave the surreal.

Unwittingly I was shepherded through *transportine* progressive dreaming cycles fanciful fleeting scenes. Feeling buoyed, intoxicatingly laid back my mind pinging into a psychological ephemeral surreal realm unfolded within this quantum physics. Drift into the tranquility, before slowly falling into *anachronistic* period scenes, seemingly in another dimension walking there; it was a place that I had no remembrance of ever being or appeared there before. It was such a wonderful feeling, as I was looking around inside and admired the stylish elegance within this curiously remarkable depiction of the *anachronistic* places with such exquisite artistry of marvelous decorations. Whereas my body was reposed, my spirit calmly relaxed, adrift on board of a well-appointed space-age flying UFO spacecraft, while onboard seated in the quiet comfort of the cosmic vast volume of spacetime. With clairsentience of hindsight in a dream, there I was without a corporeal form, seemingly on board of the fantastic flight, acrossing the transpicuous constellation orbital kaleidoscopic arrays of mystical crystalline effulgence amid the scintillating constellation gleaming stars sparkles against the still dark canvas. And through the flight window and saw the incredibly remarkable constellation of an amazing galaxy. Looked and watched until I could see the bright arcing landing lights stretching towards a glowing portal that was a magnificent transportine Stargate. Then slowly we began to glide closer towards the final approach and descended down to the rows of colorful runway landing lights. The steady, subtle, ascending adrift with attraction upward in the spiraling quantum flashing straight lines of brilliance. The spirit guide causes the light of the galaxy Stargate portal to open up at another interim destination. here. I entered the realm of the celestial dreamscape peregrinations, someplace inside of the darkness of the duality in deep space sureality.

It was in this beautiful psychological creative dream nudity, engagement in confabulations with the most very beautiful *femme fatale* spiritual eyes were fixed and buoyant in the realm of the streaming consciousness. What a beautiful moon light I imbibed of everything that was on all sides. It was this rush of emotion that gave me a sense of delight and exuberance. She had a beautiful presence. Yes I recalled every little thing about her with *eidetic* clarity as I can't stop thinking about that night, when my essence captured and painted her vivid images that was so wonderfully unforgettable. I am reminded of this brilliant moon light array as it spurred my luminous buoyancy at that moment that was akin to drifting with my head in the mystical clouds, dynamic metaphysics realms volumetric orbital constellations in the space-time odyssey.

Yeah, I felt my spirit carry me into *anachronistic* places forever flashing upward through space odyssey toward the transportine pathway into the gravity of the spiraling, brightly lit Stargate, into the romantic sphere. The magic external empirical world of quiet beautiful night dreams.

Though my body was in bed, asleep in a recumbent stateSubconsciously my mind drifts me into somewhere beautiful, soft lilting music is playing in the peaceful realm of the oneiric illusory and frivolity within the constant of my own consciousness bias, mind/body/spirit complex?

Though the body is asleep in my bed, the mind is dreaming. My spirit essence was animated inside of this realm; a mysterious dimension in an anachronistic place. I was somewhere in a different world, one which was quite stupendous in every respect, and I knew nothing about it, except that I was there in a different place and with a different moonlight. Only that my soul was free from the diurnal daily vagaries of the empirical world reality. I tarried there in the presence of the most beautiful woman I have ever seen, and her voice was melodious with eyes that evoked a magic spell that consumed me.

Yeah, I was confabulating in this hall of glitz and glam in this surreal realm's ephemeral illusion of the spirit essence hosted my interim journey through the deep dream odyssey voyage turnstile of duality in the dreamweaver's in the space-time continuum. Peregrinations of my delusionary harmonic vibrations in balanced equilibrium. The transcendental psychological brief vision of the cinematic episode is closely akin to experiencing a cycle of vibrations in harmonic balance with the cosmic constellation mercurial wave life force effulgence. Such glitz and glamor was present on all sides; which seemed so very tangible and illustrative of things imbibed by the atemporal reality. And all the while my body was relaxed in the *recumbent* state of ataraxia. Whereof, my clarity perceives things, I envisaged while I was animated inside the nirvana of a mystical illusory realm of subconsciousness. This was a psychologically glorious multidimensional celestial vibratory universe of infinitely breathtaking bright stars, studded across the darkness of the night canvas, lying in the planetary sphere's magnificent constellation of gliding movement of the stars that shine like the glistening bright carat diamond. Adrift across the darkness alight with the sparkling stars over the vast *Akashic* field of subtle motion, I patiently relaxed as my soul entered *omphalos* astral spheres. The mystique of the mind's peregrinations into *anachronistic* places.

There I ventured beyond Earth's orbit beyond the terrestrial sphere; and channeled the gateway transient space destination to a Stargate portal and entered into the blissful *nirvana;* a utopian starry constellation space destination.

Dreamer's excursive descent into a psychological *Shangri-la* of dalliance of surreal odyssey; my physical body is lying asleep resting in my bed dreaming while my body of the soul travels in the anachronistic places of another dimensional realm. Calm and relaxed there I was flying aboard that large UFO Vermona when we had briefly hovered low and slowly as we were flying low I saw them waving as we flew past over the people's lands. They were awed by the remarkable idyllic places. A magnificently amazing visual depictions of the vast treasury of cosmic constellations confluence like beautiful colorful vivid cloud darkness; the scenic mystical colorful elixir of swirling arrangement of twisted mist. The subconscious mind accommodates thoughts and delighted my eyes to perceive wondrous feelings of excitement.

Smittened, I desirously and enamored with this sensory emotion as my mind imbibed this capstone d'Amor. Though my body was still reposed, the mind conjugated a parlance of my beautiful *dulcet* lines of affection. With a sense of perception, a self-realization embraced this vision. This was a conspicuous, surreal vivid streaming veins-like episode that unfolded. I was dwelling there amongst them, looking around within the rarified fresh air, pleasant sweet essence of mercurial, and felt that they could not see me. Paramore's beguiling presence gripped my soulful spirit as I longed to lift the red veil that could not conceal her beauty. She was a good-natured looking femme fatale of about thirty years. Her countenance was pleasant and the perfect ten for she was a well-dressed mysterious femme fatal with adorned gorgeous enchantress, big brown seductive eyes. I couldn't look away from her. I was filled with limerence in common parlance with my mellifluous poetic dulcet words captivated, resonated with reciprocating smiles, seemingly synced to the candle light fire, evoking a sparkle in her eyes. Her affability and charm intimated and abounded with my thoughts. The mirth and ambiance melded within this mercurial perfect harmony and, quite rhythmically, a stirring unity free of distortions from my mind, body, spirit complex.

This, I could apprehended, is tied to the melodiously synchronicity. Meaning that is to have infinity as a separated unity with the luminous divine free will actions, awakened to great remembrance olife subconsciousness. Unwittingly consciousness acquiescent subconscious illusory temporal reality. All fraught with ethereal blissful excursively visual fidelity floating within elevated subconsciousness.

Through permutations and going hither and thither. I lay in bed, asleep and dreaming. I knew nothing of this surreal peregrinations' transformation in mind, cognition, conjunction, and intersection drifting hitherto anachronistic places within the dimensions of the grand surreal realm of the dreamweaver's oneiric hermetic odyssey's animated entertainment and personifications of nature's intelligent infinity took me into the prodigious dreams episode. Whereof I drifted into the dreamweaver's tranquility of nirvana as surreal utopian scenes transitioned my spirit to anachronistic places that eased away pain from life's stress without entropic consciousness awakened.

THE MIND, BODY, SPIRIT, AND STORYTELLING

While in deep introspection, to acquire this reverence for the learning and teaching of the spiritual science principles of wisdom by the focus and emphasis on the Aten-Ra's Law of One theology of love via the philosophy of ancient Astronauts Anunnaki, Enki's sacred mystery schools, houses of lifegiving spiritual science daily inward meditation for I envisaged. In this state of calm meditation I imbibe a spiritual unity of well-being synced with myself that converges from the luminous divine conscious mind.

The illusory temporal reality of marvelous scenes of people animated within the epoch in scope, was seemingly alive in my spiritual dalliance. The liltingly magnificent dream visions I envisioned. As my emotions were touched by the limerence of my heartfelt emotions, being enamored and mesmerized; I gleaned, and took time to imbibe her full lips were accentuated by the red filigree veiled that partially covered her countenance.

That was a golden ratio. Smitten with amorous eyes I was bemused by Paramore's smooth quiet seduction; albeit, unlimited as infinite as an ephemeral epic voyage. In self-awareness within this dreamweaver's sidereal temporal reality. Quiet, fluid, sensual, conspicuous, and sprite-filly, ephemeral as pure fascinating narratives allegories of illusory temporal reality moving space/time. I was mesmerized, adrift in this oneiric *thespian* script. Yeah, I delivered prose with a romantic rhythm, with smooth affability of charming blarney romanticism. Being the stuff of mercurial spirit and intelligent matter, I had my self-awareness drifting into an *anachronistic*, symmetrical, illusory temporal reality. Empirical, quiet, brilliant, a splendid picturesque, as duality spun round a measured cycling of daylight, and the dark knight is ubiquitously manifesting everywhere.

My spirit essence is beguiled with my cause that animated me within this transcendental peregrination of the streaming illusory episode of the dynamic slender of Noumena of the darkness majestic dreamweavers spell that framed evocative scenes of the blissfulness of the space-time continuum as it enfolded with wonderful places in the surreal. realm. Unknowing and unaware of this transformation that was my separation from the existential form of my mind/body/spirit complex. But it was my soul in perfect form as I was feeling blissful in this place in which I was experiencing perfect harmony. Whereof I was in a psychological transformation abiding in this tranquil idyllic dreamscape. With beautiful rhythms of the night enjoined in and was replete with beautiful vivid depictions in the confluences of the spirit essence when I was present in a different light of fire of a remarkable place. I sensed myself adrift, poised against a moving cloud against the dark tapestry enhanced by the star-studded sky of colorful swirling rainbow clouds. While at a way station, I attended to the mounted digital *chyron* display crawling announcements screen. As I patiently sat there attentively watching teleportation announcements of the scheduled inbound flight arrivals and outbound departure calls, the oneiric voyages into the interior of space, I patiently waited to continue on my imperceptible transportine dreamtime excursion adrift through the sleep cycle dreaming during the turnstile episodes of the night journey unfolding through the uncoordinated destinations that can't be fully remembered. Contemporaneously buoyed as I unwittingly felt relaxed in flight. I was jubilant as my eyes apprehended such remarkable splendor. For this tranquility was beset on all sides; I felt *euphoria,* without worry or pain in the midst of a manifestation of a pellucid anachronistic scene on all sides. A surreal mellifluous sweven-like state. I longed to feel and squeeze this sweetie's perfect body tight. Yeah, I was beguiled by the enchantress's seductive adorned eyes. Calmingly caught up in the dreamweaver's turn-around of smooth lilting rhythmic sounds, and my *dulcet,* blarney serenaded and breached her boundaries. Serenity, I envisaged amid flicks of demur candle flames; ambiance conjugated my *lemerance* for a mysterious femme fatale's affability and decorum with my dulcet serenaded her in a surreal time-space continuum, which intimated the romantic mood.

    She was evocatively regal with scintillating complementary charming graciousness adorned spiritual eyes. She had a certain *je ne sais quoi.* And a subtle high tone closely resembling a perfect beautiful goddess. Being mesmerized, I gazed at her eyes with a capstone d'amore.

    From the very first glance at her lovely *countenance*, I beheld her amorous smile and I longed to lift up the silk vail to kiss her full lips. With coyness she had turned my carousel. Captivating ebullient inner sense of enchantment charmed and titillated within the aura of radiance. She stirred my heart with coy, flirting, jaunty, evocative enchantment drew me *nigh,* I was enticed with my own intoxicating sensation compelled me by her elegant demeanor. It was all an overwhelming sentiment of mutual desire and affection. She was a sophisticated femme fatale enchantress who was quite stunningly regal with panache. And she was fashionable in her stylish *raiment, bedecked with* complimentary articles of sparkling jewels.

Amid this crowded hall was this air of high tone with human spirit essence, full of joyful as I heard the peals of friendly banter and laughter and the airwaves of jubilant people partying, living it up in a grand stylish celebration of celestial mood merriment. And longingly, I gazed captivated by her lovely impeccable presence, the spiritual eyes. She was a mysteriously glamorous lady.

My eyes imbibed her countenance. I was enamored with this beautiful voluptuous woman who came to sit next to me. Yeah she was oh-so very fresh, regal, and full of life that inflamed the limerence. She was the perfect queen I desired to put up on a Royal pedestal right next to me. A posh enchantress captivated me and was the most gorgeous woman I have ever seen. So scintillating was her seductive aura that it was vibrant, as she was a charming fresh posh delight eye candy with that certain *je ne sais quoi!* A lonely seductive femme fatale's scintillating eyes was flirting with me! I was intoxicated and mesmerized by the most beautiful woman I know. She stayed on my mind, and I longed to peer deep into those unforgettable beautifully adorned spiritual eyes. I remember her eyes were as calm as inert water. That delighted limerence can *betoken* my thoughts of genuine happiness! I felt in my heart what my mesmerized eyes beheld her female form. The *etching vermilion* scarf was wrapped around her neck and draped loosely over her shoulder. With veiled countenance. The effulgence of dim, soft ambiance of delicate undulating yellow lighted candles fluttering was like unembodied spirits' mesmerized flickering ambience. All the romantic warmth of the flame illuminated the room. In this wondrous place, our eyes were fixed upon each other. Like whoa! With this reciprocating attraction, we gleaned each other, when she walked into the resplendent grand gathering of the free will spiritual dalliance.

From this auspicious moment, I knew my eternal happiness desired to reside. A fidelity that hides within the unity pure essence that is the true balance of oneness.

My heart beat was in sync with the mind, body, and spirit as a visible avatar of my likeness of beingness of a unity's total complex. One human form living together in the material external empirical world of events exists. In this sense I felt a sublime genuine supreme romanticism. For never before have my eyes envisaged, so wildly captivated and mesmerized! I stood there composed, with my eyes fixed upon her stunning female form, and so lovely lady sent my heart racing. I could see this external empirical world with clairvoyance looking into her beautiful adorned spiritual eyes. Before and hypnotized my gaze. Within that moment gleaned to imbibe a full sip of her, captivated my sensory imbibing her attractive golden ratio. She touched my mind, heart, body, and spirit and held my heartfelt emotions with a smile of mutual admiration and attraction.

My eyes gleamed upon that lovely vision of a mysterious presence of a beautiful seductress affability and charm. Dare I invite her to come into my space, for might I then entreat her with the most perfect solitary red rose bloom, symbolic of the capstone d' amore? Sentimental expression of love and to be loved by the most remarkably beautiful, stunningly *blithesome* female radiant aura of affability and charm. A showstopper that spurred my heartfelt desire, emotions *d'amore* arcing with *limerence*!

Yes, I indeed was attuned with my visceral and interminable sensory *d'amore* with genuine emotional feeling of true passion is a capstone love supreme. A fluttering of my heart; was I mesmerized by her beauty? To my delight I gleaned to appreciate this beautiful enchantress' big brown spiritual eyes longingly, for I had imbibed her and was captivated by her, quite stunning female perfection.

She was worthy of this impeccable monad red rose bloom that was the epitome of and symbolic of the purest of d'amore. One special perfect long solitary stem rose blossom emblematic of amorous psychological ficto-sexual love affairs of blissfulness; and enchanting romantic emotions that inflames and mesmerizes by the moon glowing against the dark canvas of night and the lighted sky full of scattered stars. A desirable seduction I felt blessed as I enjoyed being in the presence of she who I charmed to be my paramore long after her vision had unfolded me within heartfelt, torrid, scintillating psychological episode accommodation in the moonlight tranquility, and the rhythm of temporal magic dreams that glow within me.

To effervescent my heartfelt emotion that I entreat her with the most emblematic solitary red rose bud blossom. The desire in my eyes waxed with fervent adore, as mind and heart conjugated my dulcet parlance. I whispered within the streaming aura of quintessence. Feeling buoyed up into the clouds, and floating like a feather engaged in conversation; and I'm digging her affability and charm. Everything feels alright smiling and spending time enjoying the mood of syncretic mellifluous aura mesmerized by her urbane gorgeous charm.

All the while my body lay resting asleep in bed, dreaming. At the same time as my subconsciousness filled thoughts as I am dreaming of depictions, my eyes had envisaged these anachronistic scenes in harmonic vibration. Romanticism of the people confabulating the excursions of the dreamweaver's oneiric creative night odyssey dream travel to anachronist.

Hither and thither, I drifted upward. amid the moonlight tranquility delight and walk around anachronistic realm's mythology and the *seven Heaven of nirvana* psychological milieu existence of the pristine night canvas odyssey dreamscape dimension. Whereof, material illusory temporal reality of humankind's souls. People animated by the spirit that causes our actions to carry on living everywhere you look around. The luminous divine energy spark is imbibed in the breath of life, the myriad of material fulfillments without distortions. For the purified souls of humans was like a specter, before my eyes saw people entertain and delight themselves. A crystal-like vault of glowing stars glinted across this dreamy, imaginary vision of oneiric temporal reality. Outstanding scenery unfolds its wondrously transient delightful scenes with ephemeral enchantment. Seemingly to confluence thoughts of alluring visions entertains spirits within the realm of higher orbital plane dimension. This was an ornate domicile, with its dazzling grand royal palace with well manicured magnificent courtyard. I was buoyant and animated in the fantastic surreal realm, adrift into space oneiric dream frivolity. No consciousness awareness of illusory temporal reality; mind/body/spirit avatar complex is spiritual unity separation that is the essence of dreams and spiritual meditation.

So full of awe, buoyantly caught up inside of the dream maze fidelity. Bemusingly, I entered there and presupposed that I had appeared in some attractive place where spirit radiance mesmerized me. Whereas dreamy enchanting visions lie affluence, *mon cherie amor* comes flying with me tonight in space. Lovely romantic couples holding each other's hands, staring longingly into each other's eyes, were among the many touch-tone scenes, emblematic of mercurial enchanting mood.

Seemingly a real captivating consciousness awareness of my beingness transformation going beyond the existential terrestrial planet illusory reality of the present form of the mind, body, spirit complex of daily frivolities distortion streaming consciousness awareness of the space-time continuum as a reflection of a spiritual phenomenon when I appeared there. Alive in this confluence of the atemporal reality of being and having this incredible feeling, enjoy. I walked among the animated souls of happy people mingling beneath the cloud cover array of the band of bright stars light melding with friendly souls of lively *badinage* and human merrymaking. Sensuous harmonious vibes pervade the purest golden means with effervescent flora of sweet essence, aromatic qualities permeating the tranquility and stillness. Solitary yet charming as the red rose blooms, cultivating fields kissed by vainglorious thermal energy.

To this, might I place a gentle first intoxicating kiss upon her hand as oneiric dreams everything seems impeccable to entreat this *femme fatale* with this perfect long stemmed red rose bloom. One rose gift for the lady intrigued me with the perfect fresh cut long stemmed red rose blossom. One perfect solitary long stemmed freshly cut one perfect red rose bloom for only her delicate hand to hold. As I pondered and listened to the heart feeling as light as a feather, was my visceral feeling of d'amore.

Might I entreat her with a solitary beautiful longstim red rose bloom? A prodigious symbol of my genuine adoration that felt right. I scanned the field, selected a sentimental rose for only her hands to hold. One to entreat and breach her regal charm vision that had a hold on me; a captivating, picturesque beautiful journey, that *raptured* my soul and spurred my spirit to adrift from my physical form; as I was within this vibratory sounds of the human mind/body/spirit complex conjugated as my social complex. At night my body rests when I lie sleeping in a recumbent state, and spirit essence wandering in the dreamscape episode, as relaxing we my head lies quietly asleep dreaming in my bedroom in the recumbent form of ataraxia in the peaceful realm of comfort and solace. As my invisible essence was milling about into my *eidetic* memory of animated episodes of very beautiful anachronistic places for which was enchanting! Whereas everything appeared as if I was some other dimension. A magnificent architectural palace was a place that was completely unrecognizable. Yet there I felt my presence walking and mulled about. I watched as they engaged in reciprocal blathering, all smiled and preoccupied with each other's conversation.

They never noticed my presence amid this lilting air of mirth and merrymaking that was amusing to my soulful spirit essence. All the while I casually walked among them smiling among friendly souls chattering social conversation. In quietness, a clairsentient, I am in a new anachronistic higher plane of orbital tranquility.

It seems like no one there has even noticed my presence.

When suddenly lo! Then there's my presence standing within this context of the inspirational mystique asI gleaned all around. Besotted with amorous, everything before my vision I perceived was very unfamiliar and unrecognizable. But then suddenly I spied this beautiful, mysterious lady. I took a full glimpse of her and felt excited with my aim to make her my queen; she was the one for me when my spirit curiosity piqued. What a fabulously attractive femme fatal with stunning regal style. Her comportment and charisma could mesmerize and charm with adoration. I stood in this wonderful place and thought of myself as a recognizable manifestation my beingness elated to have been in her presence.

My curiosity was piqued with excitement; and I was not sure, but she seemed to be waiting there for me! Indeed, there had to be this ardent alluring endearing mutual attraction as I felt my heart racing.

We gleaned into each other's eyes. Bemused and feeling buoyant I looked around for some reassurances; her mesmerizing eyes had beguiled and drawn me nigh! In this surreal present space-time, I was captivated by her charming demeanor, affability, which complement her regal compartment. It made me appreciate my time in remembering this overnight spirit transportine dreamscape odyssey. My essence was an avatar communicating, walking, talking; as others danced, walked, and smiled in the company of others. Under vaulted hanging palace ceiling lights animated entities inside fantastic sensory dreamscapes of opulence tranquility. My spirit essence imbibed up the mood of lively ambiance scenes amid the peals of laughter, badinage, with the lilting jazz tunes flowing. Whereof this was me asleep in my bed dreaming of myself drifting to mysterious places, where I tarried there, gazing deep into her insouciance, vainglorious adorned spiritual eyes of a beautiful femme fatale's enchantress adorned spiritual eyes beguiled my emotions. The royal palace courtyard was replete with nature's aromatic floral scents showcasing the effervescent colorful flowers on all sides, pervading through the impeccable Royal palace garden landscape.

Everything in this place befits this elite royal palace, a beautiful palace courtyard so beautifully illustrated. People were elegantly dressed in high style imbibing the excellent cheer and mirthful happiness. Soothing rhythmic tunes filled. I then spied this wavefield with lively rows of the beautiful breathtaking rows of long stemmed red roses gently swaying. I appreciated the manicured garden panoramic view. An incredibly beautifully artistic arrangement in every conceivable manner with professional attention to the well-manicured royal palace and courtyard. I stood there for a moment and was awe struck by all the beautiful colorful garden landscape, which was a showcase of skilled artistry that complemented the massive tall construction of central buildings within the royal palace garden party guest in attendance who delighted themselves as they walked through the stately palace courtyard. As it was replete with the rimpling of lilting sound that emanated from a central position to hear the trickling water that crested inside of the huge marble pool of falling water. A natal nature and first breath came forth to life. I knew nothing of the fragrance of the pool of colorful lotus flowers, with lily pads floating in the fountain with the goldfish swimming about. A euphoric life of cathartic experiences of a soothing sensory encapsulated life scene for all to see. There I admired this wonderful scene with a full lunar lighted vista. Every scene enhanced underneath the bright moon light against the arrangement of glinting stars. In this space, cavalierly, I walked there with hubris and pondered this *paradisiacal* that pervaded with lively vivid scenes and soothing air romantic moods, replete within this *insouciance* of lively vibrations of mercurial manifestations in the beautiful pellucid visions of carefree animated human souls. Our bodies relaxed and lay asleep in bed resting. A dreamweaver streamed up animations of surreal streaming depicted alluringly entertainment of cinematic creative conterminous episodes scenes on all sides which I imbibed as lively experiences. And like me our cause being there was present and milling about in splendidly decorous fanciful opulence. Every firm step, I admired the beautiful fullness of life all around within this place of shivoo and joyous merrymaking. In this anachronistic oneiric place I strolled about somewhere across the grounds of *His Royal Majesty's* courtyard, a beautifully illustrated rose garden. My spirit perception is clearly psychological subconsciousness admiring the throngs of dreamers blathering contemporaneously.

Whereof, I observed it all with a bit of awesomeness, it was the action of my soulful spirit that had me buoyed with curiosity. I was aware of what my mind envisaged as my spirit traveled to the mystery of the oneiric surreal presence of this mysterious lady. She was seemingly flirting with me!

Her comeliness manifested a lovely golden ratio; her aura inviting me was a mutual attraction. I smiled sweetly and stared back gleaned my eyes upon the lovely and gracious female seductress. What a lovely woman with a beautiful countenance was almost concealed by the red satin scarf she wore; partially it masked her comeliness as worthy of a *monad* red rose bloom. And might I of chivalry and decorum akin to Middle ages, courtly love culled and cut the most perfect long-stemmed red rose bloom as a special gift for only her delicate hand to hold. For I longed to kiss her lips. When I paused briefly to look into her beautiful dorned spiritual brown eyes.

We both smiled as I long to kiss her perfect lips which she concealed beneath the bright red stylish filigree satin veil she wore. With a complementing scarf that was draped from her head around her neck. With my heart bemused, she was my only true desire for this courtly fervent amorous attraction. Then therein my sensory feelings and passion had imbued me, as I felt these mutual attractions bathed in the tranquility of the oneiric lunar light beneath the sky clouds and the sparkling bright stars were standing against the darkness.

With a flirtatious coy, and enjoy, we confabulated beneath the glowing lunar light was this warm night air of psychological nudity. I watched as the fireflies intermittently demure light flickering in the darkness of night canvas under the moon, I could still see the lunar light in her adorable adorned hazel eyes that beguiled and consumed me as my body lay asleep in bed, my fervent desire flowing as dulcet parlance as I had breached her boundary. With sincere desire are flirtatious badinage, streaming flirtatious badinage, and blarney spurred by two riven hearts melded into a harmonic balance, free from the weighted fetters and consternation elevated toward the light, love, and tranquility. The heart a fire touched d'amore; the spark of my spirit was like facets of the diamond-like stars glittering against a dark sky fleece that was still and in a reposeful calm aura.

This fitting a prodigious encapsulation was this red rosebud, sentimental capstone *d'amore*. Bountiful primordial warmth and grows a milieu tinctures with heartfelt romanticizing complexion; the long-stemmed red rose blooms. Dulcet parlance and verses breached her boundaries. Fresh charm spurred a smile upon Her full; an invitation symbolic of courtliness heartfelt d'amore.

An effervescent ubiquitous aura of bountiful, tiny, cool, nourishing, rejuvenating, tangential vital raindrops refreshments of life blessing the rose blooms and beautiful flowers of *His Royal Majesty's* palace courtyard. With the subtlety of the calm blue sky above, decried its neat raindrops to fall upon the swaying red blooms that grow under the radiant warm sunlight. A vainglorious fabulous vision where the delicately lined rows of beautiful cultivated fields of red blossoms swayed in the night air cool breeze. The loving radiance captivated me as if a spell constrained my senses' perception of a whimsical optical illusion's panoramic vista in this vibrant marvelous field of beautiful blooms gently swaying in the breeze. And as I stood there looking very composed, I was compelled to casually pan around to appreciate all of the of spectacular wonderland of the panoramic vista of such amazingly splendid grand view of the well-arranged and manicured bucolic garden courtyard, beautiful milieu of assorted blooms that were asynchronously swaying.

Undulating and fluttering with flickers, as the demure candlelights' effervescence, the perfect romantic mood, that melded into the nirvana fidelity of solace. Within this solemn tranquility and buoyed by the lady, I cut the perfect long stemmed red rose bloom. One sentimental long stemmed red rose, a symbolic capstone heartfelt exasperation of my d'amore's for the paramore's hand to hold. Within this carefree mood I strolled along with a splendid air of a regal gentleman from par excellence. Amongst all things, there I was, casually strolling about, surrounded by this treasury of stars glinting; and within me was this cool wind swept waves that came swaying across rows of the farmer's fields of red roses; and viz, as always, I cut one for only her hand to hold. And, ov *ovo*, I felt imbued by such visceral passion. Blood coursing my veins through a beating heart set on fire. For it's so true that from that first time my eyes gleamed upon her quintessential aura, now whenever my mind is in remembrance of us together, I revisited. I smile and think to myself that I have nothing else to long for, and if it takes a lifetime of one hundred and one nights I will dream in hopes of finding her. Though it is incredible folly, indeed. Yeah! But nevertheless I pursue this *de'javu*, when I never fail to *query* of the old dreamweaver with my same old salient question: have you seen her? And this folly was only a fleeting oneiric episode I try to let go of to no avail, as she is the indelible memory that I love to ruminate.

My eyes imbibed a full sip of her lovely and gracious charm was a mysterious beautiful woman with a stunning masterpiece female form; whereof my fervent heart soulful spirit mercurial essence arrested. Forever the delight in my heart is limerence, for she was the most beautiful woman I had ever the pleasure of to share a psychological wonderful reflection of this *atemporal* dream allusion as she was my one of a kind chance encounter in the surreal odyssey peregrinations. Albeit there, this *femme fatale* was this hologram like a psychological nudity and feeling bemuse and mesmerized by the allure that drew me nigh by the enchantress femme fatal. She was the most perfect looking of my psychological vision of an ephemeral enchantress within the surreal anachronistic dreamscape. This mysteriously satin-veil obscured her countenance and compelled my eyes to glean inside her adorned eyes beguilingly provocative had charmed the eyes and heartfelt adoration of many men. I was mesmerized by a femme fatale's adorned eyes, her gaze compelled me to a place I never planned to go. But what a desirously irresistible femme fatale who was the epitome of the golden ratio that was so redolent of the dream state of this remembrance, tinged with the smell of the dancing flame of undulating scented candle light fire fluttering and pervading the mood under the full moon light ambiance. Mesmerized within this celebratory scenic mood. While my eyes envisaged, my ears attended within this remarkably aura of high tone framed this *anachronistic* place of enchantment.

And all this magnificence was breathtakingly idealistic oneiric surreal streaming within this lovely *sylvan* retreat nestled in the countryside. This is the blissful moment in flight, adrift within the subconscious mind perception of this arcane in the peaceful realm. Going to places, then briefly hovered, slowly descended, soaring ever higher and zoomed in to the stars that glinted like diamonds, the darkness of the canvas that hosted the moonlight glow.

Dare I say this that I was unequivocally smitten by this mysterious beautiful woman who had buoyed me up into the dream space traveling flying *Vehmanna* that had taken me and quickly zoomed upwards into the distant star galaxy and it briefly hovered, and quietly and slowly descended, and softly touched down in somewhere I had never been consciously aware of the celestial surreal realm. With mercurial on all sides, I was there looking around. I was mesmerized within the scintillating episodic scene walking among the crowded hall of the spirit realm of the temporary dimensions of space-time replete with care free dreamers residing.

Splendid and peaceful with a confluence of fine melodiously rhythmic harmonious tunes whipped from inside of a private baronial residence. I strolled there amid ornate decor, walking upon the inclusive white stone pathways. On the wide stone walkway, she and I casually strolled without a purpose. We walked and marveled at seeing the stunning grand style architecture with very remarkably artistic ancient buildings construction. These decorative limestone buildings with colorful flowering plants that complemented the elegantly designed white washed limestone buildings that were conspicuously prominently featured in the magnificent courtyard and surrounding architectural palace structure that were attractive. I was filled with awe and somehow I sensed that I was somewhere far away from planet Earth. All the while I admired the scene of the most remarkably stunning showcases of beautifully looking architecture of this otherworld building construction.

Reflected on the exquisite well-crafted walls built by skilled Master Mason's baronial built royal palace castles and sun baked brick houses and replete with large ornamented incised geometrical patterns or figures carved in solid relief. I apprehended and beheld beautiful large ancient cisterns placed spaciously apart within the palace walkway, compliments by the stylishly perceptible Arabian cloisters of architectural buildings. A master Mason's skillful design was proprietary, reflecting this archetypal grand palace courtyard imperial medieval-style architecture.

These were the beautiful scenes I envisaged and admired. The intelligent creative elegantly designed tall buildings splendid sophisticated stylish features of decorative sculpture emphasized and all aspects accentuated with grand columns, well-manicured royal palace courtyard. Such panoramic views with those lovely displays with all kinds of different shades of ever-colorful flora artistically arranged beautifully complemented by a well-manicured garden and the perfect landscape. Every assorted manicured courtyard was carefully arranged with different varieties of flowering plants. That gently swayed by the subtle breeze in tandem, they stood out against the whitewashed stones' surface serpentine pathway. Within this wondrous air of high tone, floral fragrances pervaded beautiful displays.

Many colors of the aromatic scent of *myrtle* delighted the sensory serpentine along this magnificent grand courtyard surface pathway. Inside this spacious interior courtyard, the compound was arranged with many plethora and assortments of many varieties of colorful flowers and different types of different plant species. All were a perfect fit into the beautiful courtyard displayed in the tell-manicured grand royal courtyards. such are all the things in this my eyes had beheld the whole enfoldment of lovely breathtaking views.

The visible things in perspective of pure perfection; and this was appreciated as I was there casually walking within the tranquility of colorful flowers in a well-cultivated garden landscape of the royal courtyard milieu of magnificent *flora* and *fauna*. What a marvelous *paradisiacal-looking* magnificence amid peals of joyful laughter. Might I behold with this oneiric surrealism of consciousness, sublimely mesmerized by my own mental complex scenery and calm zenith of the peaceful feelings as I carried on my walk; and along the way, I lounged and carried on in my appreciation for the remarkable breadth of enchantment and solace.

The spirit consciousness peregrination enters into the visualization appearance in this *anachronist* decorous places I had never known. Straight up mind tripping on the arcane transformational epic time period. This brilliant *constellation of* glinting crystal star light, sparkling like bright carat diamonds, imperceptible *insouciance of* quiet oneiric surreal mood in moonlight. The stella canvas amid planetary stars' galaxies.

As I was there and walked among this crowd somewhere far beyond the boundary of the earthly firmament. A new realm of illusory temporal reality, in the cosmic canvas arrayed with dazzling brilliant shining stars. I was free of the earthly bounds of matter and gravity; I felt buoyed with euphoria; in illusory temporal reality my soul seemingly floated. It was the *euphoria* in space! My spirit consciousness adrift relaxed riding onboard a fantastic transient flight. Slowly we descended like a delicate bloom that suddenly moved waves upon the surface of water. My *dulcet* parlance, I whispered my words into her ear. Conspicuously this scarlet scarf draped her head and was wrapped around her neck.

For only her dazzling, very attractive eyes gazed upon me from behind the veil could not conceal Her countenance; that was a golden ratio. I couldn't look away. As had my gaze fixed upon her adorned sensuous spiritual eyes. Hand in hand together we walked beneath the glow of the romantic full moonlight.

Smiling, I felt my spirit presence in this creative infinity enjoyed the animation of my free will consciousness, devoid of the distortions of a dynamic field of the space and time continuum. Yeah! I was there with swagger, blathering with this beautiful lady, casually being among an episodic oneiric scene, with stylishly well dressed couples filled the hall with merriment and lively badinage with loud peals of joyous laughter was illustrative and indicative of a night of festivities of the high-tone elite spirit's that caused the actions and the mood with lilting smooth jazz tunes amid crowds of enlivened bon homies social gathering in time a dimension.

Being a free spirit and alive under a starry celestial constellation of friendly people and mirthful spirits having it large. Such was this magnificent scene I envisaged which my perceptive soul imbibed and admired the vibratory sounds of the human mind/body/spirit social complex that emanated from a magnificent fountain cascade into the fabulously arranged garden courtyard of the royal temple fortified palace. What a delightful appointment that complimented a perfect complementing mix of different colorful flower arrangements and that was the epitome of supreme courtyard garden on display. These were the so-called hightone of regal socialites of the material external empirical world of very *profligate means.* Feeling very buoyant, my spiritual noumena excursive essence caused me to glean around and mingle within the throngs of joyous merrymaking.

Beautiful well-dressed couples partying were talking, laughing, and smiling as they longingly gazed into each other's spiritual eyes. Yeah they were holding hands, dancing whilst others were smiling and socializing amid the *raucous* aura of merriment and *badinage*. I stood there listening and watching and listening as my spirit integrated with the impeccable opulent realm of higher-minded society of spiritually wonderful people smiling and *blathering*. They were all wearing very stylish suits and exquisitely designed dresses. All were polite, smiling with their ears and listening to *melliferous Kool* and *Klean* smooth soft melodious jazz tunes permeating the room set a mood of delightful dramatic easiness of pleasant crowded amid the grand taproom of smiling faces was the delightful sounds of *shivoo* and merrymaking. Some folks were slowly sipping on an adult tinctured beverage, and others were seated at tables dining and *alfresco*. Others were standing as some curiously milled about; they smiled, chatted, as well many slowly danced with joyous scenes that pervades the grand hall of the free spirit's evening of tremendous merrymaking.

My eyes imbibed this ambiance of candle lights, soft yellow fluttering mercurial serenading *sweven*-like, for couples who were holding hands and dining *alfresco* at a table for two underneath moonlight. Lighted aromatic scents of demure-burning candle flames fluttered. The delicate glowing yellow flame sets the mood of the fantastic feeling of peace that imitates ambiance from soft demure yellow candle lights fluttering glowing as her beautiful veiled countenance could not hide her friendly smile, as I envisaged in the universe of beautiful dreams!

What a delightful scene of this treasure of high-style socialites merrymaking. A pleasant decorum of party gatherers mingled among the people blathering. Feeling blissful, I appreciated the aura and charm that melted with the demure candlelight flames burning as lovers danced around on the ballroom floor. I appeared in the psychological enchantment of the spiritual realm going hither and thither into nondescript episodes. I stood there facing these huge magnificent golden pylons, I could see on each side of me. Ponderously in split infinity. Whereof I just marveled at the decorated stone palisades of the palace confines, which were flanked by the magnificent, well-fortified tall carved granite walls adorned perfectly breathtaking.

It was my spirit avatar of light force energy engaging other avatars that were there amid the wonderful mood of the stately class of royal *shivoo*. And with extrospection I was in some otherworld of entertainment. I took solace in the silent reverence that made me take a moment to pause and appreciate my living nature of the divine breathtaking milieu. With self-awareness I was in full appreciation of these blissful scenes with my eyes on all sides. The most beautiful captivating colorful flowers spurred by the sensory feelings of her smile I imbibed was with such a genuine trill and a delightful as was in full appreciation with awe to see this display majestic opulence. Everywhere I could see the beautiful manicured vine covered trestles flanked on both sides by me by the landscape of garden groves growing. With such a tremendous architectural design skills, with attention to detail was imbedded with *Leyland, Cypress, and long rows of sunbathing or the Poplar* and the graceful oak trees complementary view adjacent to the palace walls, surrounded by a fantastic homage to all of giant size, sturdy *spruce, cedar, and pine trees*.

There I walked through the grand central courtyard. It complimented the artistic designers' craftsmanship with elegance, well-armament vast, stylish, well-placed, equally spaced within the building accentuated with strategic placed cisterns' alignment decorated the colonnaded cloistered walkway, flanked by chestnut and oak trees accent complemented by the magnificently well-crafted constructed buildings displaying the Arabian style of professional architecture was built with skilled time honored geometric craftsmanship.

Such were the things that vividly appeared to me inside a mystical surreal anagnorisis of beautiful milieu streaming spectacles of olden shifting into anachronistic places. Demure burning yellow flames scented candle light flames flickering and fluttering in the gentle cool fresh breeze. Compelled to look around and admire such beauty, all the while thinking that this is the perfect life for me. Walking slowly I sense a warm feeling of calm radiance. Its aura infolded me with a feeling of love and in some place of stupendous things on all sides in this *atarax*, as I casually strolled through the picturesque royal garden courtyard.

Okay yeah, with a perfect red rose blossom, emblematic of d'amore's asynchronously swaying on all inside of the courtyard, was arranged along the pathway that grew everywhere. There were many beautifully designed colonnaded temple architectural buildings. Nothing seemed out of place with decorous ornamentation inside the interior. Everything delighted my senses. In appreciation of marvelous fine, well-placed pieces of priceless collection showcase impeccable artist things of the wealthy eccentrics who coveted all manner of the eclectic taste for the material.

Whereof, I admire everything in this grandiose elegant affair and I took a trek through many different winding paths, when from a distance I saw two massive pillars that flanked the arching gates entrance door as they slowly opened for me to enter without my touch. What I gleaned all around the richly decorated garden landscape and the signs of great artistic talent made me feel inner peace with calming quiet comfort and solace. In my solace continued to walk on the white stone pathway that as I meandered until I came to the view of tall sturdy ebony entrance doors, all inlaid with *lapis-lazuli* stones ostentatious gold trimmed doors that slowly opened. I entered and saw the spacious hall that accommodates well-dressed party goers. A spectacular decorative display of contrasts with marvelous colors to showcase skillful in time honored geometric craftsmanship. Things appeared as if I was so appreciative and beautiful opulence. And all of the well-dressed dreamers milled about in elegant high tone and style with very charming decorum, gracious, affability, and illustrative of high society exemplify regal charm and well-mannered class.

I was there among all other souls who were there, I walked among free spirited people with my propriety gait with swagger and I confabulated with these party gatherers. And yet it seemed as if no one could see me casually mingling and exchanging pleasant smiles among others in spiritual societies. Yet there I walked and mingled amid a cacophony of blathering, peals of laughter, and ruckus badinage. I admired the ease. I moved about amongst dazzling dreamers in demure flickering yellow ambiance of flickering romantic mood.

With etiquette and decorum, I stood among high tones and observed decorative elegance. Walked into the splendid and radiant stately appointed manor house. There upon an exquisitely designed black-and-white tessellated marble floor, I wondered about amid the opulence, jubilant, and cheerful dreamers blather and *peeled* laughter.

THE MIND, BODY, SPIRIT, AND STORYTELLING

It was a garden courtyard where elite guests held crystal glass in hand as they slowly sipped on their favorite tinctured adult beverages. With lively good chers and badinage which melded amid merrymaking of pealed laughter. Lighted yellow scented candles flickered beneath the vaulted decorous hall's stylish ceiling was palpable with romanticism. My emotions flickering like a demure candle flames undulated the ambiance of enchantment on friendly faces of fanciful dreamers! Impetuous, consumed and desirous I cling to the alluringly beautiful vision of the mysterious femme fatale's presence as I she was one of a kind without comparison. My heart was rhythmically beating while my eyes imbibed this measure of delightfulness. Whereas, I gleaned around this illustriously remarkable place of elegance and decorum. They were all ed in *exquisitely* stylish *period raiment*. My *clairsentient* was awakened as I abided in and among them that was ostensibly living it up in some places, in a realm that was unfamiliar far beyond my illusory temporal world reality. Nature's harmonic lilting melodious vibrations sound pinging into my ears, as my spirit essence shepard me along these peregrinations, going hither and thither into anachronistic epochal translucent episodes of entertainment I envisaged on all sides. Whereas, being compelled, I enter into this splendidly magnificent realm of spirits, animation, episodic scenes of merrymaking and shivoo showcased in the surreal realm. Whereas, I lie in bed and dream; I am sleeping while my subconscious is animated in my cinematic episodes of my the dreamscape visions. It was such a lovely and palpable psychological state of optically blissful illusory enchantment. And within the bright visage that I was drifting away within the dreamweaver's perception of my mind's harmonic wave vibrations in the illusory realm reality, buoyantly adrift into subconscious imagery space.

This was a pleasant voyage within this showcase of wondrously streaming of epic fabulous scenery and marvelous visions on all sides within this anachronistic place. I was not invited, yet my spirit en the stream-like in cinematic animation unfolding. What a surreality to behold? A wonderfully vivid depiction of streaming this opulence and wealth I imbibed with appreciation surrounding me was on all sides. Seemingly a proposition. Personification of desirability of the material temptation, or illusory temporal reality dynamic dimension. All I apprehended was owing to the dreamweavers ephemeral creative episodic streaming, a vivid narrative script pervading. Yeah, what lovely portraits of encapsulating optical and alluringly beautiful people were the enchantment that unfolded before me on all sides. A mercurial streaming epoch begins and soon recedes then fades back into the *akashic* field lucerne light waves causing animated living soulful spirit actions as incomprehensible as the constellation, sweven-like infinitely glinting against tranquil stillness of dark night canvas. Asynchronously as the night full of sounds sets the mood. The tangential concentric rippling waves glide over the water surface that crest ashore. The glorious prismatic Sun rays slowly emerged with its bright light. Steadily the bright sunlight rises and peaks through *crepuscular* clouds and moves slowly across from the eastern horizon toward the western ocean shoreline.

Where the time continuum transitions into dawn when the sun dimmed the majestic daylight. With which is superseded by the early lucerne morning light of another sunny day. It's this solar spectrum drifting on toward the western shore to enter the darkness of night. An episode of sensory mind, I was slowly drifting away, turned from dawn to dusk. In the daily rotating Earth plane, sunlight came again onto the eastern ocean shore horizon; depiction of nature's cycle of a golden mean. Such as the brightest luminous morning star. That cosmic transpicuous vibrant radiance bathed the animated and inanimate biosphere's milieu with bright sunshine rays. And this theme is about the perception of humankind; and our symbiotic of the all-pervasive consciousness of nature's laws of correspondence: so as above, so as below.

Whereof, I respect the living nature of the idyllic diurnal time measure, changing from darkness to light. The universe nebulae time zones void of the illusory conjugate into the nirvana of the enchantress's beautifully adorned spiritual eyes; in deep space I looked deep into a femme fatale's eyes that *inflamed my psychological de'amor*. I had gleaned to appreciate the beautiful lady, for her scarlet veil concealed a lovely countenance. Her beautiful spiritual eyes beguiled me with limerence. As I couldn't stop my gaze as longingly as if I was subjectively appraising a fine artist's masterpiece. A prized portrait of the perfect female form.

The epitome of graciousness, affability, impeccable and personable with a lovely face that titillated my sensory feelings, as I was mesmerized watching turning heads as she entered the glamorous affair. All men's eyes were fixed upon this gorgeous mystery woman with style and grace. Might I entreat her with the perfect solitary long stemmed red rose, I culled for only her hand to hold with my genuine fervent heartfelt adoration.

Yeah I am desirous within the lilting jazz tunes spurred by dulcet prose and the mellifluous smell as the aromatic red rose blossoms permeated from the beautiful palace garden courtyard. A solitary capstone rose bloom of my sentimental human emotion, a desire to kiss her hand. I was buoyed up as if I was in a swirling cloud slowly across the night sky. My mercurial spirit conjugated the ethereal aura of the scene I envisaged. Dim candle lit flames undulating.

The burning flame of candle light fire cast delicate dancing silhouettes of subtle titillating shadowy flickers. Ambience serenade's a warm regal charming faces smiling within the fantasy *anagnorisis*. Precisely a wondrous realm exists to showcase this vision of this crystal hologram-like surrealism and enchanting tranquility amid the unity of incomprehensible distortions pervading upon the mind, body, spirit complex in material reality is like the shifting sands shifting is the duality phenomenon of a psychological hourglass. This cosmic harmonic universal field of ubiquitous infinity, archival scenes of the dream illusions subconscious imagination exercise the thoughts of the mind's *peregrinations* starry *oneiric* illusory of mental complex depictions. Whereas daylight frivolity plays on while the body is in bed asleep resting.

Slowly the hands are ticking around the face of the time numbers. An intersection on my resurrection for several counting years merged from the day with the morning star that entered the twelve zodiac houses of the month, the celestial sign that begins in Aries to Taurus the bull will sail across the sky and move toward the dawn. The daily sun peaks and rises up from the eastern coastal shoreline horizon, slowly it travels upward slowly across the skydome and begins another cycle journey through the white clouds. Every day rolling down towards the western shore fades daylight into the mysterious night canvas of infinite fidelity.

Which underlies the lattice structure of the mind, body, spirit complex. The duality and cycles is a turnstile of nature's transmutative from the lunar light fades away with the sunrise and sunset. Vibrant physical illusion of my perception, my eyes imbibe up into my wonderful expressions. Free-flowing prose, I interpolate as my creative lilting animations merge my mind with poignant lines of reconciled affection. Dreamweaver's surreal night voyages conjugated the epic fanciful expressions entreaties with the sentimental rose symbolic of my genuine heartfelt capstone d'amore. For therein lie confabulations of flirtatious romanticism. Sensory vision and my heart racing, jaw dropping, mind blowing emotions felt real. This female's charming decorum seduction mesmerized me; captivated my spirit vision; she had set my heart ablaze! When I whispered dulcet words into her ear. This streaming utopian of the psychological illusory pervading amid very subtle melodious magnificent, I drifted inside that mercurial realm of lilting vibratory sounds of the human mind/body/spirit social complexes of merriment and badinage. Soothing soft jazz tunes created a vivid unforgettable mood of the framed optical social milieus. On the human animated spirit entities engaging in ephemeral activities of streaming conscious awareness of the dream excursive narrative in anachronistic places of which I had a great night. I was appreciating all of the depictions and sound of subtle rushing water enchanting mood melded with melodious cascading, emanating from the tranquility of nature, I beheld the harmonic vibration of this luminous psychological phenomenon of metaphysics effervescent all around for me to enjoy living, in nature's beautiful biosphere of fauna and flora, cavorting as they I looked around, and I tarried to apprehend in appreciation the scenic vista panoramic milieu. The spirit of the *Netjer* blows through the tall sturdy trees that grow on the mountain range and across the jungle forest canopy of dense vibrations, and by nightfall, streaming whispers of cool air is a welcome relief for the animals that call the hot desert plane home. Through every manifestation of nature's space

THE MIND, BODY, SPIRIT, AND STORYTELLING

of the planet Earth. It's the sacred waters and the fresh purified air we breathe; and the crystal life giving waters steadily flows streams through the tributaries.

Slowly it serpentines down from higher elevations with easy steady flows came rushing sound from mountains came to hear the water cascading, which enlivened the love of nature's beautiful panoramic pristine milieu vast life-sustaining providence as the lifeblood of this empirical world material existential reality. Our gift of the sense to appreciate the material world and the noumena geometric harmonic vibrations, and the melodious and discordant sounds we hear as a mind/body/spirit social complex. All of the birds, bees, animals, and the waterfowls who share this Earth we call our home. It paints a panorama of this vast manifestation of magnificent, captivatingly beautiful scenes of the symphony of the lilting enchantment of energizing harmonic vibrations of animated life amid the expansive vistas of a magnificently breathtaking perspective view of the energized biosphere canopy of dense forest, mountain, dales, and the spectacular lush green medals.

We enter into the peaceful melodious sound of the noisy birds' harmony chattering. Amid spectacular concert is the howling tranquility of the sublime quintessence melding with quiet comfort, solace for mental well-being and inner peace to achieve harmonic balance for my overall well-being. I enjoy the beautiful experiences of nature's animation in an illusory temporal reality interior plane. And within this symphonic life, an ephemeral place soothes and assuages weighted from my heart that felt the true and light ostrich feather of Egyptian mythological goddess Ma'at's spiritual theology guiding sacred principles of this arcane wisdom of the Law of One love teachings. And so like the *sepal* embraces the new red rose bloom I longed to wrap her warm vibrant body in my romantic embrace.

My sweetie was a psychological mysterious lady. I desired her to be a queen who would be my one-on-one fervent heartbeat d'amor. Two warm bodies embrace in the twisting conjugation of mutual adoration hands at play touching underneath the covers. Such radiance of two in fervent serenade.

HAKEEM R. JELANI

A special loving touch of sensual tender effervescence flowing. Surely as her adoring eyes titillate me entreating cupid's arrow to touch her sequestered heart. Whilst my rose bloom paints a vivid portrait that banishes recursive quotidian commute frivolities. For only she I desire to flow my purest heartfelt dulcet words for I to serenade her panache with my seductively tantalizing bedroom eyes of soothing gentle like charm, feeling as if I was feeling calm, and within this illusionary delight, I was there within the sense looking around.

A very gentle quintessential steadfast easiness of the liltingly *cacophony* of nature's melodie's symphony of lifestreaming within anachronistic vibratory sounds of the human mind/body/spirit social complexes of birds. The sound from the swift rushing waterfalls, cascading down from the tall mountains and high elevations settled in a lush vale in the milieu of the mountain ranges, serpentine the beautiful biosphere. I attune my consciousness to awareness of harmonic wave vibrations. Blissful journey through space-time fidelity was effervescence, radiance of metaphysical equilibrium. The cosmic universal planetary bodies of the Earth in is in rotating orbit with a twelve month cycle of the twelve month zodiac house's orbital wheel circulates through the Earth's constellation orbital cycles in imperceptibly motion, the moon turns the ocean waves in rotations. all-luminous divine energy forces are emblematic, and akin to the ataraxia of the symbolic nature of the solitary red rose blooms epitome my *d'amor*. The one genuine heartfelt sentimental emotion. *Oh mon cheri amor,* totally crushworthy, her smile, her hair, her dress, and the perfume was everything that complemented her charm. I gleaned longingly, feeling buoyantly bemused by the stunningly beautiful mysterious stylish lady.

Surely my eyes did imbibe up a full perception of her masterpiece female form. Her panache was gracious and alluring perception intimately dazzling in the yellow glow candle light permeated a romantic mood, mellifluous soft jazz melding that created the mood in the prevailing ambiance and my eyes could see the accentuated demure aromatic candles flames light flickering softly as some folks danced. All the while the clouds slowly move above in subtle motion

THE MIND, BODY, SPIRIT, AND STORYTELLING

show in the full moon as it waxes across the night. And soon the sun is ready to emerge over the eastern ocean shoreline horizon at dawn. And right on time the old dependable hubris country barnyard cock crows to announce the sun is coming to bring the shinelight. Slowly, I awaken to another blissful sunrise until the drifting sun will complete the daily flight across the sky.

When at dusk light turns down beneath the ocean cardinal horizon shoreline. And therein lies another cycle of life in the daylight transitions into dawn cycle to darkness, repeat cinematic streaming episodes where we are awake and sound asleep dreaming when the sun's warm daylight rays have yielded to nighttime ataraxia tranquility. A time for all to sleep in bed dreaming. I am in an interim stasis alive in quiet comfort, peace, and solace in a recumbent state of the repose spirit sleep cycle. In the grand scheme of the living spirit cycle, this is to be that intelligent infinity comes in equal measure. And in-turn the life cycle begins and it ends in the same place every day when the sun changes where the moonlight appears. Against the dawn canvas at twilight that quickly fades to pave the way for silent subtle harmonic rhythm, cycles the time-space continuum. And slowly in silence and equal measure, time is every unassuming tick-tock, moving around the clock face numbers. The Earth is spinning fast on its axis, daylight always comes again brings darkness. And the moon waxes and glows then fades away with the return of the new sunlight from the *crepuscular* clouds skydome by energy of the eastern horizon when sunlight appears every morning as it brings light. I could not let go as I sensed my bedroom was slowly coming into prominence for me to again wake up inside my bedroom. This allows me to enter my everyday all-pervasive consciousness.

We are the faces of humankind with an inextricable cycle of divine particle rays of life force energy derived from our birth into the daylight; and the darkness to rest our mind/body/spirit complex. Reposefully we sleep before a resurrection shortened by the passing of the luminous moon light which succumbs to the sun's daily resurrection. My eyes did perceive her veiled countenance showcase ebulliently illuminating effulgence.

Radiant, vainglorious, bright, remarkable sun rays shining down upon the earth at high noon and slowly drifting toward the occidental horizon as another day passes and moonlight rotation affects the of rhythmic vibrations of the Earth's moon turns the waters rippling that causes those cool mist to sprays of the lunar position affect upon the Earth surface. Illusory reality of appearance is just another day that comes forth, fades into a mental nebulous personal memory historical archives of experiences.

Yeah her magnificent figure had left its indelible essence in my mind. This is the profile of the infinity transcends the space-time continuum of the illusory temporal reality derived from the intelligence of luminous divine infinity. The one all infinite creator of intelligent geometry designs a master mind that rules by numbers. A magical ineffable excellent harmonic cosmic energy vibration, manifestation of illuminations of the vainglorious sunshine bathing the blooms in the fields of red rose gardens. Poses written by poets of the eons with sentimental passion en to the arcanum of old footprints that have long ago since faded away as the archetypal means that once upon a time was measured by the *rustic sundials, clip hydra*, visions of the sensory all fade like the sand of the *hourglass*, sifted in the units of the diurnal celestial orbital precinct; a turnstiles rotation of days to nights.

Life raindrops as refreshments of orchestrated falls upon all the vast plains, fields, and broad rolling country meadows, the radiant solar sunshine manifested in the life cycle of a metaphysical infinity into the mystical external empirical worlds, is emblematical of the perennial *pleroma*.

Illusory temporal reality underlies this salient point that elucidates my perception and observation of the profundity; a compendium of my prologue asserts that this was the vibrant life with many experiences of this plane of the terrestrial time-space continuum. And to this there exists a common universal cable communications system that underlies the fabric of the human social complex. A political struggle the message by which to influence the balance of power in the terrestrial world ruled by the elites expanding political gamesmanship via human conditions by the new are electronic information technology intrusive network communication systems of counting votes and individual entities that is the devil's playground wealth enterprise that is unfolding as the hand of governments. With a perfect long stemmed rose a serenade befitting the quantum surreal light-waves of moonlight. Developing is the illusory temporal reality inside the diuretic material cycle of dualities is nature's vibratory universe. These significant accounts of biblical historical events of the eastern sunrise and western sunset are awaiting to urge the new grand rebirth of its new bright rays of the new day sun that is the brightest morning star that rises in the eastern ocean shoreline horizon. Of which, slowly drift toward the geo Pacific *occidental* horizon shoreline.

In quiet stillness pervades the vaulted sky canvas, there, a lunar light fading away as signs of morning brings forth a moving light and slowly ticking. Serenity of the night silences my ears, attuned to the sound of the familiar acoustic echoing vibratory sound complexes of the stridently hubris country barnyard cock crowing piercing the tranquility of the new day at dawn. And as I slowly began to stir I lay there motionless listening to the mellifluous chirping cacophony of birds singing.

Must as always I sit up in bed and take a full breath of life and everything was becoming to the morning that revealed fresh dew that covered nature's biosphere. Awaken I adjusted my eyes; they are slowly becoming acclimated as my mental mind, body, spirit complex for my meditation of beautiful visions departed and entered into consciousness. The sounds of morning activities soon emerged with the bright warm sunshine. And again the morning light peeks up and steadily rises in the ocean's eastern shoreline. Light shines across the sky, the cover drifting across the blue sky and white clouds.

Sun is slowly disappearing beneath the rippling waves, sounds of ocean ebbs and flows rhymes rolling and crested against the sandy beach shoreline, the sun setting on the western horizon. valid for all who are the animated embodiment of physical human existence, aware of my own mind/body/complex of beingness. To this I enter the turnstile cloven cycle of the dream state spending night time fidelity in the surreality and to see the daylight yield to dusk turns into the darkness canvas for I to lie resting and quietly sleep transforms back into the rising morning sun arrival cycle into the new day. Truly seeking perfection within the realm of the light and becoming one with a pure heart of loving compassion; meaning what? I am awakened to live and seek spiritual transcendent upwards to be *mar haru* pure at heart.

    I am sleeping and dreaming of this as my body lies relaxed and calmly reposed until the early morning temporal reality of a new blessing of the day at dawn. The sunlight is slowly starting to peak and wax upon the canvas of darkness as moonlight is subdued.

    On a wind-blown field, such a beautiful scene of red roses swaying the tall flowers that have been transformed from the seeds sown and germinated blossoms being bathed in the warm energy growing is the providence of the intelligent infinite divine logos.

    My friends, nature is the genuine luminous divine primordial desire that is made to transpire in synchronization of the unity with the underlying wistfully visceral feeling of the heart of the self; the emotions and outward expressions of the *dulcet* intimations of sentimental attributions d'amor. A very emblematic as closely the fundamental symbolic capstone of my love heart's supreme manifestation is emblematic of my genuine arbor. There were many delicate red roses blooming in the well curated courtyard garden that was the epitome of the most perfect assortment in a beautiful landscape of colorful fauna that bathed in the sunlight swaying blooms. So I cut one perfect long stemmed red rose to be symbolic of my heartfelt fervent romantic emotions. A spirit of the self crush-worthy blush is the most symbolic of the long stem solitary red roses and is a passion emblematic of the truest *d'amore*. Might I must and apprehended the romantic serenity of the skylarks singing in flight. Whereof lilting soft jazz vibratory sound complexes were inviting a feeling of the ataraxia of quiet comfort and solace. Oneiric perception is closely akin to watching solitary dead leafs majestically floating down like raindrops that disturbed still calm water, causing the tangential concentric waves rings movements will slowly flow outward until they ebb on the ocean sandy beach shoreline and the soft muddy river-

THE MIND, BODY, SPIRIT, AND STORYTELLING

banks. Like the tiny animated calm concentric waves one by one, they gently ripple, rolling out atop the water surface.

We watch each slowly move outward and crests onto the shores of rivers and sandy beach shorelines. The rhythmic sound is soothingly cathartic. Elements of nature come forth in the ominous baleful vibration of sounds of the thunderous eminent thunder light against the dark sky clouds and the manifestation of shock and awe grace within the earthly realm. We can see flashing lightning and the sounds of rolling thunder. I felt reverence for the spirit of god's nature to provide rejuvenation, revitalization from torrential rainfall showers and maelstroms that bring forth heavy rain and baleful thunderstorms. Raindrops refresh the dry earth surface and give the tangential life rejuvenating raindrops. We are existential to the illusory world reality as a material embodiment that calmly reposes dreaming with encapsulated the spirit that is the cause of the *ephemeral oneiric* episodic scenes capstone my supreme d'amor.

A creative fantasy that set my mind adrift with a confluence perspective of the living human existence, I aim to encapsulate and incorporate my apprehensions like a touch from the cool tiny, trickling raindrops falling upon the long rows of beautiful lines of fresh growing red rose blossoms. The wind swept waves of many colorful rows of very majestic and beautiful living flora colors, and the delightful aromatic scents pervaded my sensory aura with fresh long stem red rose blooms enliven the moor with enchantment. It is illustrative of mystical harmonic vibrations touched by nature with the gentle breeze that gives the feeling of being in a calm state of euphoria, being beguiled as a heart succumbs to the seduction of an illicit paramour affair entanglement.

In this wondrous imperceptible motion in flight, my body asleep, while my eyes envisaged her beautiful female form that was intoxicatingly provocative when I looked into her adorable bedroom eyes. She was so mesmerizingly fresh. She was demure and wore a scarlet filigree veil that couldn't conceal her perfect full lips, complementing her lovely angelic countenance.

Mystery lady who could charm the eyes of men who looked at her lovely and gracious regal panache. And she wore a scarlet silk veil that could not hide her countenance that complimented her stunningly breathtaking hourglass figure that was turning heads as she was so fresh in the most incredible pleasing way! My limerence stirred up a fiery attraction when I looked at her worth a thousand dulcet words to whisper in her ear. A portrait of the panache of remarkable high style to compliment the fabulous black evening dress that was a perfect fit to her female form. I cast my eyes to gleaned respectively to move over Her magnificent masterpiece hourglass figure.

For in the moment I smiled and gazed upon her with a gentlemanly humble charming comportment. Yeah, I measured her fabulous female form that was a perfect ten. Periodically, I took small sips of my meat tinctured adult beverage; and we spent time confabulating from her scarlet *filigree* veil. Indeed she was a mysterious *femme fatale* with big brown adorned spiritual eyes that drew me nigh. I felt as if she had an incredible hold on my emotions. All went well as we were caught up in the jazz rhythms of shivoo and merrymaking. It's a perfect gathering of the soulful spirit essence of avatars mingling in the stupendous grand royal palace of dreamweavers surreality. A moment of transformation as she and I engaged in mutual delight I was besotted and she enamored me with her alluringly piercing spiritual eyes. With smooth charm and completed her captivating presence of a confluent synthesis with my gaze.

With body and mind in perfect harmony, one union as duality of cosmic equilibrium of the metaphorical wondrous heart of the self d'amour. This is the manifestation of flirtatious jaunty and comportment captivated by the stirring of emotions effervescence into a feeling of the fervent reciprocal mutual delight and attraction. For everything that is good, her female attributes fueled my vision. Yeah, to this a one-off chance encounter of delusion, is my folly was a wonderful moment is fully cemented within the night mood remembrance. Will she be the archetypal queen caught up in a fleeting one-on-one fanciful romantic capstone love supreme? I am seemingly there, surrounded by darkness, standing in this place, demure flicking romantic candle lights. I was looking around and took a slow sipped on my favorite neat adult tinctured beverage. Being so dignified with regal comportment, I admired the well-manicured royal palace courtyard's beautiful landscaped garden adorned with red rose blooms swaying. I felt like an ephemeral moment in my psychological perception that had never faded! It seemed like more than a dream folly.

It was so personal and inclined me to entreat her with a perfect solitary long stem red rose bloom worthy as a gift for her delicate hand to hold my purest adoration. For this was such a memorable moment when I cut the perfect luminous divine long stemmed red rose bloom. One special red rose bloom I selected and cut it from the courtyard of his Royal Majesty's well-manicured rose garden courtyard.

Luminous enlightenment feeling that I imbibed of the splendid *indecorous* grand opulence, delighted the mind, body, and spiritual complex. Although spirit had separated from my body's cubconscious awareness. The mind/body/spirit avatar complex calmed in subtle motion. I perceived my spirit's presence relaxed and became buoyant in flight as I drifted toward dream weavers' crossroad night odyssey dream travel to anachronist voyage. A space-time flight is drifting away into the anachronistic places in the mysterious, surreal realm. Of such, I long to remember that emblematic capstone of d'amor. This femme fatale set her beautiful adorned spiritual eyes that were pure 100 percent sentimental. Albeit a dreamer's excursion into the crystalline realm of *anachronistic* places, my spirit is outside of my human form, my body adrift within the wondrous realm of the most remarkable mystical opulence.

I was delighted and appreciated the presence of the most beautiful woman with her eyes fixed upon me! I was mesmerized when I felt a sudden urgency to entreat her with a capstone red rose bloom symbolical of d'amor. Enamored and in awe I watched as this lovely *femme fatale* gracefully walked crossed the room. I was there that night slow sipping on my adult beverage chilling among the bantering of refined dreamers as I saw her enter this most marvelous grand affair. Not knowing that it would all soon fade away. I am unwinding from the mind/body/spirit illusory odyssey excursion of this spectacular mercurial surreal realm. Yeah! This fleeting dreamweaver's prodigious episodes of merrymaking scenes animated beneath a starry night sky illumination en. The full moonlight and the subtle glinting stars unfold on the dark canvas into the psychological lilting sounds pervades and diffuse the encapsulating tranquility of streaming transporting episodes, through created the spirit enlightenment into esoteric mystery realm of the surreality of prodigious dreamweaver's Akashic field of the hidden halls of old archived records of my past life experiences.

My dream transient excursive flight was slowly fading. I woke up in bed with my private thoughts pervading my mind, I could not avoid the fact that I closed. Oh me, oh my *inamorata*, my *cherie amour*! My dearest and the most beautiful woman, for I long to feel up close as my lovely *inamorata*, my dearest *psychological* fairy lady, enlivened my spirit and bridged her boundaries of chivalry and courtly love.

Yeah, my illusory surreality was slowly fading from the surreal realm of this mercurial anachronistic of the psychological illusory nudity of the fluidity of the quiet comfort, with inner peaceful enchantress's spiritual eyes that was a total feeling of blissful dalliance of mutual feelings of easiness of the dreamweaver's night flight dream traveling epoch into anachronism in space odyssey in the dreamscape. Then like the sunlight rises at dawn, it also sets down at dusk. The mysterious beautiful femme fatale's alluring female form had begun to dematerialized right before my bemused eyes. When suddenly she turned away from me, and without a warning she said, goodbye! Like that her image was presciently redolent, as she had ever since lingered long past the clock's hands struck twelve. My psychological oneiric affair, I had never closed! Because in a flash her form was gone from my vision. And suddenly lo! It was no longer in the presence of this evanescent time-space. When before my eyes she quickly was gone!

There I knew that she had taken my breath away as she left my heart, feeling empty inside. And with only a remembrance was bemused and thinking about this lovely and charming lady. How in an instance, she was no longer a physical female avatar, I could tell that she was just gone! After all this was an illusory dream. Oh it seemed so very real she was extremely sweet. And when I find her again I ain't going to let her go. It was oh what, a night of magical blissful ataraxy reaching for the stars. And-so-it-goes. I had a dream when I met the most beautiful woman I know. An enchanting femme fatal's beautiful adorned mesmerizing eyes beguiled me with a feeling of *limerence*! Special memories of that fate of dalliance I revisit pervades my thoughts in this remembrance this early morning. For her in this quiet reflection, I muse upon her smile whenever I think of her lovely comeliness. Yet my limerence is folly because Her name I can't forget these beguiling, enchanting eyes. As I am left to cling to my intimate remembrance in my sentient spirit. Now I was no longer walking someplace amid the garden biosphere of colorful *fauna* and *flora*, flanked by fields of gorgeous flowers flanked by a dense mosaic of open and wooded biomes near a river nearby this Palace. There long rows of the *Willows*, sturdy *Oak, Chestnut of* tall rows of majestic tall swaying trees I admired.

This fantastic episodic stirring scene before my eyes without a moment to say goodbye, and lo! All that was blissful had slowly faded away from sub all-pervasive consciousness. Yeah, so very unsettling because I got the chance to close with a tender kiss.

Without continuation conjugations desist from the clarity of my free will spirit, which is the cause of my every living actions. It was this remembrance of a capstone feeling when I entered through the arcing gateway transporting bright colors of this gleaming crystal light portal.

And without my consent, these dreams' were a vivid cognition dissipated from the visual realm of the surreal episodic subconscious illusory temporal reality. The planetary sphere's entities of bright starry Heavenly bodies of the cosmic excursive dream body called me back into the plane of the external empirical world of illusory physical temporal reality. A realm of a Heavenly state we long to live beyond our constrictions; visual material illusory reality consciousness awareness is a transformation of spirit energy pervading within the realm of the dreamer's dalliance. Listening to the melodious tranquility of the early morning sound of hubris barnyard cock crowing three times had awakened me before daylight rises from my oneiric surreal excursions yielded to the breaking of dawn. As my eyes now have opened. I envisaged another early morning of the daylight sounds of reverie unfolding ticking frivolities.

I was besotted and in vivid remembrance of the lovely and gracious *femme fatale's* adorned spiritual eyes never dissipated; and she stays on my mind. Though without warning that beautiful charming enchantress stole my heart with one look into her big brown adorned spiritual seductively bedroom eyes that gleaned from behind her scarlet veil that complemented her beauty. I was hypnotized by her unforgettable seductive eyes. For her I felt that sense of a tender aura drifting away with imperceptible sublime motion. Buoyed and relaxed in the space constellation continuum.

Then we began to feel the spacecraft slowly approaching the Stargate portal mercurial constriction. Slowly descend down through the nebula cosmos pathway opening for my spirit avatar to enter an anachronistic conjugated mysterious realm. This nirvana was with intimate smooth rhythmic jazzy tunes that pervaded a lovely serenade that set the mood. I was there enjoying a merrymaking mood. Of which I walked among strangers. People who were standing next to me, I was feeling blessed; and then I smiled as my spirit was a separated unit entity in the transformation, whereof I was devoid of my physical human form.

Yet I see that I am awakened and animated living it up on the other side of this cloven infinity between temporal and the illusory surreality. As my body was asleep, dreaming in my bed, resting in a recombinant state. The calming aura was an incredible mercurial feeling of the essence of life, the animated and the calm resting recumbent state. I am no longer there inside of my familiar bedroom; and I was unaware that my head was asleep in bed, resting on the pillow at twenty degrees north by northeast, with my head lying upon a fluffy down pillow. Slowly my spirit self had entered into a higher level of the planetary dimension of the realm of the surrealism state. Yet all the while my body was still asleep resting in bed and dreaming. My *clairsentience* was unaware of the nirvana I appreciated being someplace I was quite unfamiliar. All the while dawn slowly rose upwards, emerging over the eastern coast ocean sunshine horizon shoreline. And as I was in this interning sunshine emerged into the sky. I was awakened and bemused by my eyes opening; and in my rush of beingness in temporal reality in the self in the remarkable oneiric blissful spiritual sojourn.

When I was wittingly partaking of the dreamweaver's magnificently stupendous *shivoo*, that swept me with limerence, besotted by the most beautiful femme fatale's enchantress adorned spiritually eyes beguiling. Her adorned spiritual eyes charmed by her lovely countenance.

For I decry let me drift away with She that beguiled me with my sensory *d'amor* and remembrance of this picturesque *oneiric* visions of the streaming enchantment of the excursive dream episodes. So I wondered to myself thinking: was she just a fanciful ephemeral, fleeting night was a psychologically folly. Yet, again dreaming of enchantingly blissful seductive eyes. Again, I sleep each night to search for her. Because I knew she was the only lady for me. I greeted folks with a polite, gracious smile and regal comportment with genuine humility. I respectfully greeted them and asked have you seen her? As always, my rumination of her concealed behind a scarlet filigree veil couldn't conceal her seductively adorned spiritual eyes. And you know, with lemorous, my eyes imbibed this wondrous *lucere* creative vision of folly beguiled by her presence in this *oneiric* space when the formosity of this unmatched beautiful enchantress eyes drew me nigh.

a dream odyssey unfolded this evocative tranquility of great delight. I am dreaming again. I tell myself that She was real. Everything that came before my vision was seemingly much more than fools folly. While I was seemingly imbibed of an alluringly beautiful excursive spiritual journey into the romantic *peregrinating* into the *anachronistic* places. Never had I realized that she was a lucid figment of the imagery of the dreamweaver's *oneiric* realm. The imaginary mind's fleeting dream vision. Though my remembrance is not knowing that I missed her felt real.

Today, again as I am with introspection in the bed dreaming, and recursively drifting hitherto thither as a hand in hand was a beautiful twist of the imagination of the mercurial realm of surreality. Yet each night I go on set for my fair lady to appear. Again, with my ruminations I revisit the dream folly, I imbibed her beautiful female form. Now in my physical present space-time continuum. I ruminate upon this lingering vivid picture, I can still remember seeing the way I looked into her unforgettable eyes when she smiled in appreciation in our mutual romantic gaze. And though she was an incredibly seductress, enchantresses adorned spiritual eyes inflamed my fervent heartfelt attention. With a feeling of nostalgic remembrance of being among the spiritual animated souls chattering and laughing with good cheer and mirth and amid merrymaking and the mercurial tranquility I beheld the visage of enchantment. In this luminous episodic surreal scene under mystical and the canvas sky, an array of billions of distant stars set against the universe. The fullness of the spectrum of my creative life forces an energetic manifestation of the love for and to be loved. The love vibration spurred by the intelligent force of the infinity cosmic harmonic vibrations. Whereas, the presentation of the time-space continuum is calm and asleep. Sentiently my spirit essence slowly conjugates the mind/body/spirit complex.

An individual separated unit of one's beingness of enthusiasm of my daytime temporal reality into mystical sojourns dream sequences, and from dusk to darkness turnstile and enter the transportine gateway portal of interim of dalliance. It terminates when the death throes come to a complete stop! When the spirit ceased to cause my actions each day to turn my carousel into the dawn horizon in the recumbent state, again I lay there in the dark quiet comfort no longer asleep, undisturbed and ruminating in the forenoon recalled that vivid dreamweavers tristful creative animation of the fanciful creative episodic voyage into the anachronistic surreal realm. Totally free forms in the mind, in separation from body as my spirit essence was the cause of the animation that was buoyant actions. And with fervent desire I gleaned my eyes on the most charming and gracious femme fatale's perfect hourglass figure. In this place we envisaged and I could see the candle light fire shadows as dancing silhouettes grace the countenance of my delight d'amor. So this again with another night dream in flight. Again I revisit the surreal realm. This heartbreaker harkened me back to remembrance of the most beguilingly adorned sultry eyes of a beautiful mysterious femme fatale. I didn't want to awaken from feeling buoyed as I could not stop thinking of her, I wondered whether she would once again materialize in another dream vision, just perhaps an illusory reality?

And you know what? My remembrance of her replays in the depiction is a repeat relay of this same old dream episode. It's that beautiful first time, now that is myself asking the same old salient question again: saying have you seen her? Silly of me clings steadfastly to that one spectacular dream sequence streaming scenes of subjective surreal episodes. Yeah! From what I envisaged, that dream vision I could not let go! Though nothing I tried rebuffed the magnificent thoughts of the mysterious presence of a beautiful goddess. Those full perfect lips, those beautiful adorned hazel eyes, and those amazing curvaceous hips. Again I remember the serenity in her adorned spiritual eyes glittered and with mischief and it was right then, with heartfelt *limerence,* she drew me nigh! But no! They could not have imbibed upon her charming, gracious, decorum, and effulgence.

All the while, my body was still asleep, dreaming. My spirit essence actions caused me to enter into the surreal realm scenes that unfold, where a femme fatale beguiled my eyes with enchantment delight. I apprehend an anachronistic places. The episode scenes streaming tranquility amid a lilting rhythmic mood.

My synapsis serenaded my brain waves with inner peace awareness and mental harmonic balance, quiet comfort, and a mood for tranquility and solace for a titillatingly torrid affair. Such mental depictions, was it folly of straight up tripping on within the alluring presence of the femme fatales *oneiric* seduction? This aura was a manifestation of a fervent heart with the folly of adoring infatuation. That one during that star light night odyssey. An ease of feeling alive in the ataraxia of quiet comfort and solace, adrift from the daylight *reveries.*

One special night, I imbibed this alluringly female form of a seductress's adorned eyes gaze into my eyes from behind her filigree silk scarlet veil; I was aware that I was desirous of her. My queen, my *mon-cheri amor* was a fair lady beguiled and mesmerized by my vision drew me nigh!

Ostensibly, unforgettable fanciful illusory for I am flummoxed with thoughts waves that conjure me back into the psychological state of oneiric illusory, temporal reality. The trustful dalliance of psychological illusory temporal reality, an enchanting scene of she appeared, and within this, my most remarkable, objectified full-on imagery of dreamy wonder in harmonic vibration. Slowly the morning light encroached and was emerging into dawn to wake up. Suddenly, right on time, I heard that familiar morning revelry sound that breaks the night tranquil, when the old country barnyard cock crows. It reminds me to rise again and go forth in other random events and frivolities. She was the most beautiful femme fatale who female form still pervades my mind as a stunning regal, avatar with impeccable comportment. Again I revisited the time when I was besotted by the most adorned spiritual beauty my eyes had ever seen. A one of a kind *monchari mi amor,* a lovely mysterious psychological femme fatale, I knew was my one on one *churri-sweet.*

Yeah she was the one queen of all others, whose perfect form I was pining for that surreptitiously I envisaged with heartfelt desire. The delightful reflection of the remembrance is of this one night of dalliance; a most treasured first night, my eyes behold and gaze upon her is a luminous divine vision of my ruminations with my solace in daily meditation. To think of her looked there before me. Her smile, it was the most complimenting indomitable *oneiric choori-sweet* enchantress's eyes was intoxicating. The dreamweaver's psychological dalliance was the epic night, relaxed in a recumbent state of in-flight subtle and quiet motion. Romantic charm and dazzlingly adorned, spiritual, adorable eyes and playful coy with sultry bedroom eyes she fixed upon me. I felt my heart beating fast. I imbibed to seal a visual remembrance of the mysterious femme fatal with sensuality. Brief ruminations flashed a psychological vision of the windswept fields of beautiful red roses blooming and swaying in subtle breeze. My daily remembrance harkens back to the dream odyssey, when I cut that particular long-stemmed perfect red rose bloom for her delicate hand to hold. Together that night we walked through the royal palace courtyard beneath a full moonlight for a swooning romantic tryst and the perfect occasion to entreat her with a red rose bloom for only her hand to hold. In the cool night air we talked, laughed between tender smiles hand in hand as we strolled in the glow of the full moonlight array of billions of distant stars that sparkled like highly prized brilliant karat diamonds, set in the dark sky canvas looming over the royal palace courtyard. A mystical wonderland of this phenomenon diffusion of life exists underneath the passing bands of fluffy white clouds and the sky adrift above the Earth light and dark shadowy silhouettes. A stupendous remembrance that I was in the nirvana of this spirit traveling my eyes in sync with the femme fatale casually cavorting with the graciously charming mysterious lady engaged in sexy communication of sheer delight on the lunar glow of moonlight. Within my spirit d'amore drifting through this oneiric realm of night canvas rhythm of temporal reality aglow, sailing across space, imperceptible motion under this dark vaulted skydome. Sacred wisdom is of the divine Law of One love of freewheel excursions of the realm of reality and the illusory surreal gateway turnstile! Again I revisit the dream excursion, into the animated dynamic dimension of night dreams with starry eyes. It was of brilliant gold, and as it appears I didn't know that my eyes were closed and my body was asleep in bed. The spirit of my cause my gleaned eyes on the enchantress's adorned beautiful countenance, a mercurial illusion was a very indelible moment. She was the one love for me. And so I had closed my eyes, zonked out as she beguiled and drew me nigh when I entered this fantastic night of the spirit's dream travel; never being aware that she was not real as I watched her ephemeral essence just fade from my vision into a full stop.

Yeah, again, it is another early morning rising to live among the unity of the distortions of the mind, body, spirit complex of experience in daylight illusory temporal reality. Yeah, it is clear that I have a broken heart; that is, the way to true love is seeming most elusive. It's another early morning with me laying in my quiet bedroom gazing at the coruscating sunlight rising with me in my private thoughts.

I am thinking about her big beautiful, seductive bedroom eyes that were scintillatingly fixated upon me. Yeah, who knows of the virtually unquenchable fanciful realm of the excursion into the illusion's dream sequence? Wonderful escape that is beyond the physical world reality of beingness into the mysterious illusory realm subconscious dimensions, and it's uniquely very personal to enter into

Dreamweaver's glorious beautiful streaming episodes. The confluence lilting serenity odyssey unfolds into an anachronistic space-time continuum. Maybe one night will be my ineffable chance encounter, meaning the moment to reconcile the folly of my *limerence* with a mental clarity of being in the illusory reality! But until the time comes when we meet again, I will continue to look for her to appear again before the hour of the morning time to awaken into the rising sunrise in the present timely continuum of reality. With futility, I could not cling to the oneiric solace in cinematic episodes scene in anachronistic places. I could do nothing but watch my passion fade along with the unforgettable beautiful adorned spiritual enchantress eyes drew me nigh. Though I am bemused and besotted with limerence for the femme fatale's eyes drew me nigh. A whirlwind dreamscape odyssey of folly was my limerence; she set my fiery heart ablaze.

It was all a dream odyssey dreamscape vision that was just my creative imagination into the illusory reality. It's just another morning with my innermost private thoughts. The mind, it has often been said, has an amazing ability to apprehend by introspection and extrospection and discern physical phenomena surrounding us on all sides of the living experience as humankind. While it is an irrefutable fact that explains the existence of the spiritual embodiment in the animated time-space continuum of our natural sciences as seen through the ability of the eyes to see the world of things we can touch, and that which our ear can hear. This is to say with the intelligence of the senses I can appreciate my extrospection. And so there are times in everyone's life for a private reflection to ruminate on the depictions of the life experiences within the formal affair within the streaming dream folly of the creative visions episodic. I observed the magnificent masterpiece of things designed architecture showcase the the most skilled master masons construction epitome of reminded creation inspired by the African Egyptians eponymous divine sun god Ra, Egyptian original revered symbol of the Anunnaki as he gained popularity as the pharaoh who brought learning and teaching of divine Law of One love social and moral precepts. With focus my thoughts and behavior, living life free of an everyday rollercoaster. But all the while living on the ground enjoying my walks beneath high life tightropes along the way. We must learn and be a preceptor of others to become attuned with the wisdom of the Law of One love of explaining my eclectic, *avant-garde prose*. My subconscious mental state, having visceral conviction inspired by the infinite Creator of the higher level of this spiritual realm. Seemingly forsaken, my heart was jettisoned. With only my remembrance of the subtle flight drifted away into a random air of high tone, such a perfect fit to see her radiance amid surreality that conjugated stupendously across the panorama of dark sky canvas against of majestic twinkle of billions of stars in harmonic balance. These visions resemble these anachronistic places. Again, the daily sun slowly descends, as twilight now awaits sunlight to wax the tranquility of moonlight.

She was indeed the most, you know she was a one of a kind heartbreaker—my stunningly beautiful, gorgeous femme fatale, who had beguiled me with limerence by this enchantress beautiful adorned spiritual eyes. She was a mysterious heartbreaker psychological mercurial avatar who had mesmerized me with limerence that drew me nigh! Yeah, it's her charming regal demure and aurora that had stirred up a fervent psychological playful coy with a high tone that spurred emotions that set my heart ablaze with the dream folly of unrequited love in the surreal illusory space continuum odyssey.

in stunned disillusionment and disenchanted from the psychological fanciful dream illusory: the surreal realm had harvested her presence in an instance! Quietly, before my wide eyes she faded. Presently the spirit conscious awareness I slowly attuned. I heard that piercing sound of the old barnyard country hubris cock crowing, waking me up from the Dreamweaver's *oneiric* state of nirvana. It's me again inside of my physical body. Awake, I lay there thinking in bed in a *recumbent* state of ataraxia by my consciousness. I am animated by spirit essence as a separate *oneiric* enchantment. Slowly the state of consciousness realizes that this was not an illusory *temporal reality* or my inner peace. No! Not at all! To continue on my peregrination to nirvana. Yeah, it's another mental tripping into anachronistic subconscious dream, excursive untethered free will, an external empirical world of wandering episodic night dream visions. Where living souls enter the fanciful realm of the temporary streaming surreal frivolities in space, and just as time is always, so too, I'll carry on the dream of her when I am sleeping in bed before the morning dawn.

With anticipation of a beautiful life waiting to come into fruition with mellow time at dusk into night transition of the turn of cycle streaming and the imagination to create wonderful dreams. Yes, I will keep on dreaming. Every night I will be dreaming and dreaming of them in search of her. But might dare to entertain the surreal as a therapeutic modality for the excursive crossing of the transportine into my imagination. A morning, when I might dare to reflect on the surreal as a therapeutic modality for the excursive crossing of the transportine into my imagination. Every morning I wake to find a visual objective reality, unlike all long and forgotten dream allusions.

She is now just a delightful remembrance of the objective surreal odyssey, being so unlike a dream episode. Only to realize no one is lying in bed next to me. So I ponder for a moment and ask the question: "Was it all just a silly dream of her running away from me: "Was it all just a silly dream of her running away from me? Again, I ask: "Was it all just a silly dream of her running away from me?"

The external psychological empirical world of my *xodó*, my muse! A fundamental *aphorism* that dovetails nicely with the pithy literary prose; and as they are poignant today and yesterday and quite befitting as tomorrow as the renowned author Stephen King's profound words I quote from his series, *Dark Tower*... *"long days and pleasant nights!*

The Divine Breath of the Four Cardinal Windswept Planet

Life in the spirit is by the winds of nature. Breathe in the
elixir of the illustrious luminous divine unity flowing.
We're a polarity manifestation of energy and unmanifested
ubiquitous omnipresent luminous divine primordial entities.
We are brilliant, luminous divine separate units living on the
new pure mercurial element flowing invisible life breaths.
Air is the life-giving breath, a confluence source pervading the
breezy convective diffusive swirling respiratory oxygen flows.
It's so essential is this vital and sustainable everlasting mercurial
hot and cold life-giving air system that flows everywhere.
Mercurial weather clouds drifting rain showers wet the ground;
as airfoils and gentle, serene wind gusts of invisible elements.
This air is pure ataxia streaming for I inhale and exhale, illustrious
divine leaves exchange the air that flows into the lungs.
Air cycles in through and out the nose. This sense is life synergistic
luminous divine-spirit pleroma, is by the cosmic flows.
Powerful air is streaming cool winds convention gusts is a
vainglorious divine providence from nature's refreshments.
Every breath taken is the ever living spirit pervasive as
precious air endued by the everlasting primeval universe.
The all monad vibrant is the hot and cold precious pure
rarified breath of life all Adam's inhaled and exhaled.
Pure air is the primordial element manifestation
symbolizing existential primordial life breath flowing.
The esoteric ubiquitin substance of life flows of the
magnificent breath for our luminous divine self.
Pure air inhaled and exhaled rhythmically convection
waves streamed the breath into my nose.

By every breath which I take a subtle rhythm
breathes into lungs, the air is exchanged.
God seeds blessed as the cedar trees' life spirit
is symbolic of ubiquitin air flows.
The cosmic harmonic balance frequency
vibrations underlie this serene element.
A streaming gust of peaceful air attests to Earth-
balanced invisible harmonic sounds.
All life flowing is twisting around winds as
convections, blowing keeps wildfire burning,
By the dent of convective energy airfoils changing
direction, they move freely turned by nature.
a refreshing invisible dynamic element as the four, air,
a dispensation, flows into sentient beings' lungs.
A rarefied air is luminous, divine inseparable from the all-
unity; omnipresence manifests itself everywhere.
Give me the clean air to breathe is a gracious gift of the
one infinity; the infinite creator brings the whirlwind.
That invisible element of air we breathe pervades flowing
into and out of the nostrils our lungs inhale and exhale.
Forever the wind is streaming as the breeze cools when the
raindrops fall. I take a clean breath of beneficent life.
Pure fresh streaming air sustains and maintains asynchronously
in through the nose as the lungs' rhythms flow.
Earth, water, fire and air. Give me the rarified air every
day; for I to breathe; invisible magnification lifeblood.
Air refreshment is the manifold invisible providence that
pervades oxygen flows streaming air over the planet into the
lungs exchange recycling. It is as subtle as the wind element,
vital energy that pervades my creative essence as fullness.
Everywhere temperamental, pervasive calm and destructive
vital to lungs. The air exchange we inhale and exhale is life.
This primordial element is a in nature refreshment by air
convection, the cosmic harmonic vibrations in equilibrium.
Cosmic gusts of winds churning streams in motion, and
winds blow in all four cardinal directions of the Earth.

THE MIND, BODY, SPIRIT, AND STORYTELLING

Baleful thunder clouds announce whirlwinds and torrential
raindrops by dint of the cosmic geomagnetical.
The stars in a Milky Way Galaxies deep dark black
holes; diffusive metaphysic imperceptible motion;
Bright stars lie resting against a dark cosmic canvas
harmonic vibrations in equilibrium,
Magnificent air a perfection of perceptible
creative harmonic oscillations,
Ruled winds change direction in sync to Earth's—cardinal points.
The gusting streams blow from four twisting wind directions.
Subtle East-West, a most irritating trade wind rotate stream.
Streaming powerful spinning tempest winds turn squalls overnight.
Swirling air twisted by the geo-quantum physics rotations every day.
Esoteric unpredictable ominous balmy
mild weather refreshing flowing;
fresh flowing invisible, gentle routine keeps
churning the air convection,
a precious air is streaming baleful winds at
high move waves to the shore.
Full luminous moon glow above Earth's the
darkness with sky clouds and stars,
Clouds movement against the sky, moon spurs-
waves, surfers ride waves to shore.
The living geosynchronous magnetic cosmic
universal spirit funnels the ebbs and flows.
Invisible refreshing air the trees reciprocate breath
as oxygen flowing through my nose,
All the sturdy trees are shedding dead leaves
by the dent of nature's dynamic force;
Life is the breath of air inhaled, and exhaled,
by the lungs is a gift Adam's life gift.
Forever and everywhere air flows, twists, and spins life refreshments.
Daily the human voices stream commentary narrative new on-air.
Daily front-page byline and dovetailing
tagline's daily news broadcast.

HAKEEM R. JELANI

A new media spur storylines propagated
skewed partisan agenda scripts.
Words flow across airwaves, and cable agendas
spur convoluted dust-ups to flow.
And so across media air-waves, broadcast signals
bellicose anchor's voices reverberate.
over airwaves run 24-7; 365 diatribes paid commercial
communications script streaming across
Where daily cable network communication network cycle
blitzes commentary reports expands across wide area
bandwidth. Moving as air blows churns in four cardinal
directions, and the Earth's spinning axis the clouds drift.
Elements of the southeastern and northeastern wind patterns
direction announcement broadcast the forecaster change.
Geo-external world winds correlate cardinal points' orbit spinning
axis; wind moves four wind directions; daily the air forecasters
announce direction changes on air. Four winds of cardinal
directions the powerful convections streaming blows turns the
wind cycles to twist and from north, south east, and west, first
wind directions spell: NEWS! Subtle rain showers pattern of
forecasters' predictions reporting the wind gusts bring us clean,
pure fresh breaths of primordial oxygenated pure air flows life for
sentient human beings and the animals. The mystical, spiritual
indispensable precious breezes and conventions of an invisible
element streaming the life. A luminous divine breathable air of this
vital lifeblood that lives in all things of the life is of creation we
have imbibed, from the power as a spirit flowing over with a studio
green light airwaves indomitable buzzwords saturate the listener's
ears via the airwaves. A weather forecast broadcast network services
streaming via the rolling partisan skewed agenda over chyron
streaming media channel messages by anchors target the airwaves!
Hats-off to the hubris egos of the tall towers of breathtaking
tall steel, concrete, and glass Towers of Babylon
Look there and you will see this egocentric exhibit of
people inhale and exhale this magnificent breath,

THE MIND, BODY, SPIRIT, AND STORYTELLING

God's presence as one primordial confluence thought sustainability of oxygen in through and out the nose. Invisible air flows everywhere everyday! Yet strangely essential to life, a new broadband target the ears. Sublime dog whistles partisan voices promulgates political bias script on air paid agenda sales message echo.
The air it forever changes spearhead new-age consumption demographic provisions of the economic sales bottom-line from production and consumption spurs sales growth by paid subscription. Revenue streaming bonanza from on-channel promotional schemes that dovetail tag buzz lines drive messages streams. The broadband on-air cable network channels propagate little scripts as cross waves of psychological tap-rooted living agendas, a wide-camera angle shot of the left-right intellectual one-up uncompromising political debate. The psychological arguments of dueling complex mental dyslexia. A long range camera lens of close-up camera view of lift and right-wing hyperbole back and forth ping-pong talking heads debates, network cable channel the air broadcasting entertainment views in wide angles and screenshots, the crawling chyron stream messages beneath the studio guests counterpoint dog whistles calls upon the audience to imbibe opinions. Spurious partisan erudition battleground of platitudinous dismal propaganda network broadcasting truthiness subtle propaganda messages hyperbolic political partisan social agenda on-air bylines. Geosynchronous wideband airwaves electronic communication commercialized online fishing line bandwidth. Creative illusory temporal reality is a profit or loss falsehood dichotomy. Allegorical tale narratives of unboundedness, as the story goes; a breath of pure rarefied air I inhaled like Adam. Owed is to praise for a gracious gift of life for humanity to breathe. Fresh air streaming rhythmically inhaled, exhaled, lungs breathed this fresh clean air in the nose. Infinitely a necessary refreshment, we inhale and expel the precious air life flows. Nature's laboratory whirlwind toss sailboats hither and thither,

HAKEEM R. JELANI

For swift gale four winds swirl and twist ubiquitously,
is my magnificent spiritual breath of life.
Air, essential and precious as the wind streams are
both subtle and very destructive to life.
I love to inhale the fresh breath air is infinitely
very essential for all life from to live.
The power of a life force air we breathe in
invisible precious life-giving elements.
The sentience of the natural air stream, I
inhale it and feel it touch my skin.
Airfoil's multiple directional waves blowing
steadily is my daily life breath.
Across the interior air convections of the
jet stream blow in all directions.
Yeah a daily news broadcast of a pattern system
that predicts ominous streams.
Planet Earth is turning up nature's wind blows
in cycles; fresh air the body can sense.
And by the dint **of** Earth lie harmonic vibrations
and crosswinds flow as seasons change.
Air abounds as wind flows everywhere as essential to
the inward spirit, body, and mind to imbibe.
Omnipresent potentate as in the breaths of air the eyes
can see it; cool breezes touch the skin's senses.
My precious mystical convectional wind twists force in
all directions; the hands can neither touch nor hold.
Fresh air is ever streaming, the life giving breath of air Adam
and Eve inhaled and exhaled is continuously flowing.
From everywhere this everlasting powerful air is so vital; a
unity—precious prana and chakras to the mind/body/spirit.
The mystical as the universality of everlasting life spirit prana.
Sustainable fresh air and green; a life alive in paradise.
Psychological metaphysical mind, body, spirit manifestation
of unity of the illusory world visual reality of the streaming
consciousness. Rhythmically life flows in through and out from
the nose and my lungs to breathe the precious vital ineffable

THE MIND, BODY, SPIRIT, AND STORYTELLING

primordial luminous divine air we inhale and exhale it. By every exchange of subtle invisible air flowing/streaming through every breath I take. I'm so blessed by the spirit animation. Another subtle breath of life air is essential for every living body; an existential living entity is awake and sleeps, air we inhale and exhale through the nose as the living spirit flowing.

Nature's Wildlife Kingdom Survival Lottery

Look out when the African lion pride is hungry. When they venture out to target the wild animals that graze the nature's safari landscape, that is when there is the foreshadowing of imminent strategic coordinated swift attack in the daily cycle that sustains, the regenerative forces of the infinite regenerative life cycle of the herds of Africa's vast arid landscape. While the large animal herds are casually eating grass to survive. It's an inevitable element of danger from the supreme apex lion pride is a dangerous beast of prey. The apex predator is roaming wide over the African interior plane to kill the gregarious timorous prey in the inevitable game of daily survival is the biosphere lottery. For there are so many deadly predators stocking *chary* game there is a dynamic relationship between the poignant manner of the predator and the prey as the lions and Sheep. A paradox posits the inevitable struggle within the life cycle. Where the paradox posits that inevitable struggle within the life cycle. Whether by day or night, one misfortune is another's means of survival that plays out for the prey animals that survive by grazing across nature's vast African plane. There is the whole animal kingdom, where survival is a struggle to exist. Wherein daily scenes of providence and bountiful finna and the flora of the animation genuine fear and courage. The inherent threat *of danger pervading nature's jungle rut without bias naturally plays out throughout the jungle plane's existential cycle of illusory temporal reality in the wildlife kingdom's survival lottery.* Together we see forms of existence amid fear that portends both the prey and predators have a common innate will to live; paradoxically carnivorous lions' instinct is to kill to satisfy hunger. Dynamic as the infinity is constantly expanding and twisting upwards and outwards. This lion's presence threatens and is a natural antipathies existence within the animal kingdom; and it

THE MIND, BODY, SPIRIT, AND STORYTELLING

plays out when danger from apex hungry lions' presence looms and kills the weak. When fear resides in the roaming herds that graze the African milieu. This steady *cacophony* of the noise distorts vibrations permeating through the temerarious grazing herds. Look there, and you will witness a living laboratory of plentiful scenes of animals in nature struggling to survive in this labyrinth of life and death, which plays out amid the African jungle biosphere. It's the luminous divine rhythmic cycle playing out across the African jungle safari landscape, where naked scenes unfold with a familiar chilling sound. An all too familiar inevitable scenario when the lion pride appears is the precursor to dreadful squeals of the *pusillanimous* prey's last soundbite of a melancholy cry entering the ear is the full stop. A sad bloody scene has stunned the mortified herds briefly paused from grazing.

No flowers or eloquent words are spoken, only a brief token moment of silence in reflection as they stood by idly in respect against the backdrop of the bellicose lion pride that grow as they jockeyed around the victim's body, blood soaked the earth red. Growling began while carnivorous lions gathered to feast as they all possessed their share of the fallen prey's sanguine carnage. Across the landscape, growls reverberate with bravado.

Upon the jungle safari plane of plentiful small and large various wildlife herds that graze wide over the African safari is amid the heat rays melded under the cacophony of sounds emanating from the large wild animal herds that move across the arid plane and sweltering sun heat. Amid the animation and sounds of the large grazing wildlife, free-ranging herds roam far and wide over the safari landscape, fear of the inevitable experienced episode. A survival killing plays out a daily dreadfully sad scene when death befalls one victim whose life of grazing among the herds enter the death throes of truncated one from herds to graze the sparse African safari plane. The lion pride has spied on their prey victim. Fear runs high amid the targeted pack that panicked under attack, as one culled victim becomes frantic with trepidation, tuned to sound, ready to dash as their ears scan nature's air.

They bristle with sentience and apprehension; they pause with fear. The fear and trepidation were palpable with uneasiness.

They sense there is danger looming as the predatory lions' pride approaches. While the herd becomes uneasy they realize that to run away from dangerous lions is a great idea. In a brief instant they freeze, and the sound of thundering herds of the panicked is a palpable thundering noise from the herd running to escape from the perceived that sent plumes of the stream dust cloud that leaves from the arid plane into the air.

A sense of uneasiness that all is not well, when suddenly the thundering hooves pounding the ground sending dust rising into the air and forming a dust cloud above the dry African Earth plane. A kill episode happens when the hungry pride hunts and kills one prey victim to survive, which is the scene that portends danger that certainty in the African sweltering heatwave. Fear of sudden and instant death is the threat that sends the herd's hearts racing rush of adrenaline and panic put upon the roaming herds that graze the vast African landscape unrelenting sweltering heat wave pervading plane. On the arid landscape this is a daily wear episode of nature sounds of impending death foreshadowing large thunder is a jungle rut. A loud racket foreshadows a death scene by the lion's ruthless aggression. The *craven* victim is killed and eaten by the lion pride who targeted one *timorous* prey whose life ended in the death throes! Such is the sacrifice in the primordial reality for the players who gamble is a fifty-fifty chance to live or die for animals who can stay alive in a deadly parlor survival lottery game where hungry lions' instinct is to kill. Survival is uncertain as the struggle to live is the scenario. Nature's law of survival plays in the jungle canopy every second of every hour during the day. The inevitable consumption mired in the jungle rut predation and existence is to live. The existential temporal reality of the dichotomy between life and death with the survival jungle lottery game; seemingly as it is closely akin to the game chance of the fifty-fifty spinning the roulette wheel. It's akin to the casino games of chance when the fallen victim loses to the lion's parlance game of the apex jungle predators being the house. At the onset of that one who brings death upon a craven victim; we see the herds stop, and watch as spectators that briefly pause and then continue to graze the physical landscape to survive in the jungle web. That showcase of the deadly daily life to death cycle of episodes that plays on as episodic senses of survival and predation.

    They are of the victim's social herd who are the living who are spared. Though they live to graze, they will again hear those loud bellicose lions' eerie, loud, dreadful deadly growling sound echo that sends them free of the death saga. Grazing herds are the target chary prey of the lions'. Large grazing animals herds roam far and wide eating with their ears attuned to dangerous killer lions, and awareness of untimely misfortune of one victim whose good blessings is to come to a full stop. Death ends a life that has succumbed to the natural law of the jungle life lottery game. None among the knowns who among the grazing beasts will hit the daily survival Lottery game. A life and death is an ironic wordplay with a clever twist on nature that depicts the hungry pride players of the survival of the fittest must kill to survive. This is the profile of the hard-bitten predatory lions who patiently wait to cull one among the potential grazing herds panicked and the lion pride launch a swift targeted one prey that is killed by well-coordinated full-on, flat-out fatal daily attack kill episode. A lion pride lies crouched as they harry the roaming herds. The lions are in close range and ready to attack one frightened chosen prey victim targeted. Looking around, they are uneasy with well-founded fear and trepidation. Each among the herd called upon their clairsentience as they calmed themselves from their nervous anticipation of what would come to be an impending episode of the horrifically, gashly death of a sanguine carnage. Waiting, they are the spectators who watch the saga. Pusillanimous grazing herds watch from the in awe of this bloody carnage playout. Amid the fear in sad eyes that looked on, and no one victim is culled from among the running herds one has fallen as the lion pride completes another kill episode, and there is not a sad eyes did the herd lose cry a sentimental teardrop when the fallen victims blood soaked the ground red and the disturbing sounds of panicked heads end with a reposeful scene of dread; and as the dusk settles, a lull of silent comes and goes as just another ordinary day for loss of life. One misfortune came death befalls one pusillanimous victim was culled from the large grazing herd who rebounds. They are ready to swiftly escape from any sign of impending dangerous threats that looms when the lion pride is ready to strike fear among the victims of the violence that is perpetuated by the daily rut of the death saga! As predictable as the time cycle that begins and ends in the same place daily. Amid this dynamic scenario lion prides kill to survive by their encroachments tactics and await their chance to survive. Stealthy and quietly, the lions waited patiently, and then with the saltiness from the stealth concealment, they swiftly the lions emerged with their tactile merciless attack on the head bolted straight away into a deadly chase. With patience poised and a burst of speed, they close in on their targeted chosen prey victim's who have no chance of surviving their vicious killing put upon the unwitting prey victim inevitable untimely death in jungle rut of the African survival scene of sanguine carnage. The predatory lion's spurs that deadly chase stirs up the dusty plumes to form a cloudlike contrails from the panicked herds and the prey that have been put to futile flight has no chance to escape these dangerous killers. Sprinter's deadly chase begins. Fear and cries in vain; panic spur a cacophony of asynchronous sounds. Wide eyes fixed, grazing was full, had panicked the large herds, stirring plumes of dusty clouds amid the arid African landscape. The swift lion's pride has spurred the deadly from the fleeing prey running to escape the inevitable jungle game is akin to a chance to win from the players as the winner of a fifty-fifty outcome that is closely akin to the roulette wheel that spins and stops on red or black. It's an African survival lottery of who lives or dies when the panicked herd loses another timorous prey dashed into an unchoreographed ballet dance of the survival rut, without forbearance from the apex predator's icy chilling stare. Inevitably a prey victim's life is swiftly truncated as the chase has played out as nature's is a naked struggle. Survival challenge is to evade death as a targeted victim of the lion pride encroachment and cull one among the fearful herds. Such plays out daily as the wildlife survival lottery. The lottery game of life and death scenes looms as the reality amid the animal Herds that roam and graze the wide landscape of the inevitable element of danger. Paradoxically a duality of the exuberance.

    With human birth is the life to live and the dichotomy amidst nature's cycle into death and regeneration of rebirth.

THE MIND, BODY, SPIRIT, AND STORYTELLING

Whereas timorous prey and intrepid apex lions interpolate a poignant illusory temporal reality spurs an inevitable scene. Nature predation fits into cycles of benevolent and malevolent duality underlying nature is a crucial dichotomy in daily life survival is a reciprocal tangled web. Inevitably, the targeted victim unwittingly will fall as another passing from life is another death that will call for one nominal untimely death. It's another fait-accompli of the understanding that all in nature's living garden will come face to face with death as a material energy of the mind/body/spirit complex experience between the material providence and consumption. Life struggles lie vital carnal consumption; a nominal daily victim lions execute as ironic lottery winners. This everyday illusory temporal reality of the jungle survival lottery is a nominal that before one unfortunate prey victim's life succumbs to truncation by this cruel, vicious necessary evil. Inevitable is to fall victim to the lion's daily eclectic cavernous menu, which denotes one generous inevitable feast as a sad tragedy. A fallen prey victim's body, a life sustainer for the audaciously intrepid hungry host, death is a consequence of the primal carnal consumption is a sad tragedy. Predators' existential survival against stealthiness lions roar with and they are showing their large deadly, sharp, and bloody powerful fangs. Haughty lions' pride sends cries that echo and reverberate across the African wildlife safari landscape; a circumstance of the life cycle that is inevitable when the those big cats strike fear and trepidation looms amid potential victims' plentiful grazing prey, one is to the targeted victim among the grazing herds of the African safari lottery game dichotomy of the is a cycle of life into death like the rising sun at dawn that sparsely covered landscape of luminous divine providence is a biosphere danger in landscape of earth replete with dreadful of violence play out as scene of consumption and as a predatory equilibrium follows a pattern of the killer lion pride steadily move in range ready to bring a death to the grazing herd. The approaching hungry predatory lion's pride lies hidden within the camouflage concealment of this African safari. Quietly stealth, lion pride steadily encroaches. Poised, they wait patiently, ready to bring death by jugular vein. Slowly lions waiting to spring attack hidden spurs a palpable fear and apprehension they senses danger looms palpable, beating hearts pound when bellicose safari lions pride draw near that sends hearts racing. A palpable fear resides among herds as lions swiftly launch their deadly attack is put forth upon one victim; futile cries die from the haughty lions that suddenly appear and swiftly attack and kill; and like a battle-hardened skilled army; they execute a daring, coordinated, swift, strategic battle charge that kills one unfortunate fallen victim. The hot African sun rays leave very few shaded covers from the blazing daily heat waves. Still roaming and grazing wide, large and small animals abound amid the iminent lions' pride. Watching and waiting patiently, these killers are devoid of urbane with indifference to socialized compassion. This another *fait accompli* for the victim who ran afoul with a face-to-face encounter with a hungry, hard-bitten lion's pride. There is a preeminent danger when the lion pride lies hidden waiting to kill to survive in the jungle web, it's a dichotomy between the duality of life morbidity.

The animation's illusory temporal reality jungle is the safari swathe of the physical landscape plane. Life is this providence existential to survival in life jungle danger web target the timorous prey victims body feeds the hungry host. It's a will to live that these audacious conquering lions launch swift brutal attacks from, brutal attacks from a concealment position. Palpable fear resides as they await the inevitable fatal curtain call that is the strategic attack.

Quietly in close range, intrepidly, patiently targets one fresh epicurean carnal delight lions the grazing herds. In an instance showing that powerful burst of speed, big cats emerge from their crouched positions set up as a targeted kill episode of death has befalls the one snared victim that succumbs to the powerful apex conquering Lions pride daily vicious attacks. A dreadful killing episode of the carnal epicurean's delight. One swift brutal blitz attack with big padded feet, deadly fangs kill straight away like men of war is akin to the lion's sharp teeth kill like a spearhead, when those sharp canine teeth are like arrowheads and sharp blades of swords. Moving herds unnerved and with frantic heartbeats racing, their ears now scanning; call upon clairsentience. Inevitably, a stealthy carnivorous lion's stealthy coordinated attack brings misfortune to that one chosen prey; a vicious fait-accompli fits a sanguine cycle. Values within life's

THE MIND, BODY, SPIRIT, AND STORYTELLING

union are replete with much diversity in all things abound within a crewel.

Life is this jungle illusory temporal reality of conspicuous consumption. A constant daily lottery underlies this vicious survival rut of ghastly sanguine carnage by predators panicked herds to hastily dashing across the safari landscape. Where the fear of the inevitable death saga scene comes to one unfortunate victim of the grazing wild animal herds when the presence of the spurs the timorous hightail straight away into the chase is palpable. When the lion pride launches into a skillful tactile maneuver that plays out, as this fatal chase quickly ends with panic, the victim's body is in the grip of lion's front paw hits the scurrying prey victim who falls and you hear the fatal squealing fall to the death throes. Another wildlife survival lottery game has ended to feed the hungry host. Inevitably one chosen victim to die will no longer graze amid the African physical plane, will have no time to say goodbye, and will depart the plentiful roaming herds. Another prey victim loses the life of the survival struggle. Which one will succumb to the throes of the survival lottery game. While the mendacious conquering lions growl, showing large sharp sanguine fangs that end the life of the *pusillanimous* victims, futile panic ends the horrible and dreadful squealing sound of the death saga. Yet another prey victim has been savivaged to feed the hungry host. As the air carries the baleful chilling lions' deadly growls that cause that reverberating bellowing sound of killing, who claim to be the undisputed winners of the *Wild Animal Survival Lottery*. The survival challenge is a daily drama scene of frantic herds grazing; dangerous predators target them. Inevitably the hunter-prey relationship, as the apex insensate lions pride has put forth a palpable fear amid the prey victims who are put to flight across the safari vast landscape. The jungle's wild animal prey are mired as the unwitting player, trapped in this deadly lottery game with misfortunate targeted prey, they will inevitably succumb to the death throes of the hungry conquering lion's jungle kingdom. An all too familiar recap of nature's daily episode of the victim's lifeless *sanguine* dead body, and to hear and see the lions pride leave little doubts about this savagery of the lottery game of life, it's an efficaciously vicious attacks that is the daily episodes that is the replay of the carnal safari lottery game of winners and the loser that is killed and eaten by the pride of proud, majestic, fear-inspiring, deadly hunting lions have been endowed with an instinct to kill for their prey to survive; and ergo, hungry must hunt and kill animals within the wildlife safari biosphere everyday to sustain their existence encounters in its nature's blueprint which playout where the predators of safari plane kill to survive, is the daily illusory reality. This being a survival jungle rut predatory and prey relationship within an environment where conquering lions are the strong that kill the meek to survive in nature's wildlife universe that reveals and conceal within this illusory temporal reality the vicious sounds of brutal ghastly carnage. Witness this disturbing experience of the experienced the fearful cries from the lions claws and long sharp teeth converge and one motionless dead body lies a prostate victim is savagely torn into pieces.

Yes, another victim has fallen to feed the apex killers. Another unceremonious death that has again fallen upon deaf ears. As the scene ends the same way, only a different victim killed as the herd witnessed another victim's life essence turned the Earth red. Inevitable is seen as another lifeless body ended with horrific dreaded sounds of frightful squeals that are painfully chilling naked episode playout.

Daily naturne's drama decry a narrative replay of benevolence as the providence of life survival *succors*. All life lies within natural balance is the fulcrum underlying this survival of the fittest of earth's temporal reality. What anature's succors from the daily struggle between nature's substance and providence in that play out is the cycle of life. There is always dread of death and the strong instinct and the irrepressible will to survive adrenaline rush pumping through the beating heart of the animal herds. The following blood is uneasy manifestations of fear and trepidation.

To all of the living death shall co whom it will be when neither a bell rings nor from the anyone's eyes that watch will one of them have a teardrop fall, another brief tense pause to mourn for the flow of bloodletting, the fallen victim's lifeless dead body is prostrated and being torn apart and savagely eaten and consumed. Another victim chosen among the panicked scattered herds one died. What a crucial

THE MIND, BODY, SPIRIT, AND STORYTELLING

end for the victim who hightailed it straight into the chase to lose to these deadly killers.

Again it's inevitable that another one bit the dust that had no chance. He has fallen to the death throes by the apex killers of the jungle when the safari lions launched a strategic targeted attack that eviscerated the unsuspecting objective of the chase. Life and death drama of high risk is seldom favorable to one timorous caravan victim that falls in the game of survival that plays out daily and is replete with sudden, unsuspecting, immediate death.

That reality underlies a microcosm of the wildlife web of the plane of the living, all fraught with magnificent figures's little life and death cycle that plays out an equation, which is a victim who loses at the roulette table when conquering lions appear. Life succumbs to predation is the deadly drama sustains and claims. Predictable as illusory temporal reality decry this lottery carousel, one is targeted amid heards falls. Inevitable is to bring a deadly chase as a dramatic display of the saga of gashly sanguinary scenes when death of one unwitting prey victim has fallen.

Haughty apex bellicose lion prides kill and growl as nature's equilibrium plays without bias.

Ostensibly being both essential to a survival cycle is a consequential yet necessary balance within a jungle universe. This daily drama as grazing prey struggle to survive against apex predators must hunt to survive.

Such as we can understand is a cruel scene in the atemporal illusory reality pervading the animal wild kingdoms' laboratory, which declares to one unwitting grazing victim of incapacitating, unsuspecting, cruel sacrifice. One petrified victim of dreadful sanguinary carnage. Grievously predictable deadly vicious orchestrated nominal attack by lions fits an eternal survival life cycle of the inevitable tortuous life and of, in turn, victorious, insensate, hungry apex conquering lion prides hunt to survive. Deadly, the lion's pride shows their long and sharp fangs when they kill and eat a victim who lives amid the bellicose growls. They are killers and they began jockeying around to claim and defend their share of a prostate victim to feast on the ghastly carnage.

Life is a dynamic experience of the survival and death episodes of nature as a jungle rut.

Inevitable is that life that is an sanguine episode of a lifeless victim's prostrate body is eaten by the apex lions role in nature's equilibrium weighing in the balance, always ends another life by their well-executed crafty ambush that slays a prey victim, an act of nature's survival challenge of life that is never gratuitous or personal. Targeted by the apex jungle predatory pride, deadly stealthiness has been put forth upon by a jungle victim that succumbed to the chase. Intrepid essay, conquering lions swift turn afoot, long siren teeth, and sharp deadly claws kill. Ergo, for the brave lions to win some prey, the victim's life is truncated in this vicious jungle rut. It's inevitable that without lamenting, those who are among the fortunate can hear loud blustering bellicose bravado as intimidating savage growls and roars fill the air; as life plays on, the lion's pride declares themselves the game winners. This is the microcosm that is an unframed snapshot of distorted illusory temporal reality that is. The survival instinct inherent in the predator and prey is to sustain the chary prey victim feeds. This probability is closely akin to the player's chance at the roulette wheel. A game of life plays out over Africa's safari landscape of large grazing herds roaming across the plane; they fear carnivorous predatory indisputable game winners in nature's wildlife survival kingdom lottery!

The Demure Candlelight Flames Enfolds And Entertains

In the interest of inner peace, awareness, and mental harmonic balance with quiet comfort, for all humankind, let's pause to attune to the harmonic sensory vibration enjoining yourself in conjugation with nature's well-founded laws, tenable logic and reason. To the Philistines, my aim here is to bring the knowledge that will wake you up. While at the same time, pique your curiosity and imbibe intelligent wisdom for all to acquire insights, sync to the inextricable profundity that underlies the common medium of mind, reason, and intellect that undergirds the cause of the human spirit's animated outward human behaviors. It's that vainglorious means of sacred wisdom of the Law of One (love) of mystery, spiritual science practiced in quiet daily meditation in the body/mind/spirit for my overall wellness and physical yoga postures designed to cultivate my spiritual focus. And with the evolution of the emergence into the new external empirical world into transformative development into the new age generation of conscious awareness. Peace and common purpose imbibe the spiritual wisdom of the Law of One love and sacred principles. A candlelight fire of light, life, through dialogue for the shared love for all humanity to benefit this new-age generation. Without divisive noise distortion, let's come to sit together to speak upon and ease the dichotomy of the social complex to confabulate about the means to create the framework to forge a solution for which we can move toward the future with parity. I am about positivity to the causes of community, economic, and social service activities, agendas utilizing partnerships cooperation without gratuitous acts of violence that indiscriminately with willful intent to burn down the commercial property of others. And where to learn and teach ways of sacred wisdom of the Law of One love principle of universal logic and reason that we might come to understand that this shall be our everlasting common medium of the mind of all bons hommes blessed by God. Together let's light a candle, attune to the quintessence of that demure delicate fluttering flame dancing in the rhythms and appreciate it mentally, soothing your spirit of yoga meditation as you imbibe visual scene of running waterfall cascading and flowing from a mountain range of high elevations, replete with free range animals, sounds of birds in harmony with beautiful tall trees that covered the dales and grassy meadows. A cathartic harmonic wave vibrations to disengage stressful noise distortion, pinging upon Earth present time-space continuum consciousness awareness.

Excursive mystical peregrinations from the earthly realm human experiences; to listen as perception has a pure vision by mere candlelight.

The surreal fanciful mercurial ondine spirits are intimate and put forth so we can apprehend the truth. To this is to understand the mystical symbolism of the esoteric realm of sprightliness replete with fleeting excursive transformations into an illusory world of creative episodic scenes, and unfolded seamlessly as a transformative voyage into marvelous places. Where sensory feelings undergird my perception, there behold this pure convergence of a tremendous synthesis of brief introspection. A perfect vision to go beyond terrestrial animated entropy abound as a magnificent joy and pain of illusory temporal reality. Esteemed young adults of this new age generation of human beings living homo sapiens might we all be a common genetic species, with our human aspirations as a separate unity; and the descendant of God! To be inspired by a spiritual movement, to come gather into everyone's mind space/time continuum for a new unified future all around. Let's sit down together to speak and muse about our common unity with ruminations upon our individual free will responsibilities as a conscious awareness. You are endued by a synthesis intrinsic, Neter, being in and of consciousness awareness with the ancient Law of One love of calmness of the mind, body, social complex. We are all humankind's souls and spiritual lattice structure that is a pervasive common medium of intelligent infinity

THE MIND, BODY, SPIRIT, AND STORYTELLING

with God's mindspace. A god scene of equilibrium with the primordial providence of the Earth, wind, fire, waters.

One unity of sustainable metaphysics synthesis of sunshine and rainfall brings forth transition cycles to new seasons of providence in coefficient equilibrium. Ephemeral glenting spriteful flames propositions the spirit to dance within this glowing tranquility intimates.

With validated introspections, meditate on this terrestrial material epoch derived from the luminous divine cosmic *Hermetic logos*.

My beloved magnificent figure's warm greetings go out to all of my fellow brethren and dearest, most lovely, and very gracious *inamorata*. Come! Let's all gather around and sit together and attune our thought distortions aligned with the infinite Creator's Law of One of the melodic sounds of nature's illustrious joyous remembrance, living in harmony within vainglorious spirits. Let the manifestations of spiritual unity in the luminous divine wisdom of the Law of One love, gracious gift of earthly things my abode from the highest Kavod.

For indeed, underlying visual optics entreat great imaginary minds to engender affinities for perspicuous lyrical prose and profundity appertains to nature's intrinsic abstruse aesthetic golden ratio archetypal aphorism of veritable perception of colors captivate and differentiate magnificent life derived from reflections of the solar rays showcase a great dichotomy of material and human perfections illusory temporal reality, and the beautiful treasury of the spiritual vibrations. Magnificent living soul, a spiritual figure quietly nestled amid the array of splendid living temporal reality beneath sky clouds' movement, a great, ubiquitous illusory temporal reality animation that permeates and space unity. The majestically vibrant depicts life's colorful multi-dimensional schemes as an empirical material reflection in aspects as accurate. Where daily, the radiance of sunlight rises into the sky, casting its heat rays refraction over the ebbs and flows. Therein, I presuppose, symbolically, the metaphors coalesce the empirical and emblematical tangible tangential synthesis; still, surface water appears, reflection staring at me is a duality; it's mirror imagery that has manifested in water material matter into the imaginary existential temporal reality. Look closely and see yourself as a fundamental complex visual arcane! Your life is the right gift! Yours to live, palaver, and to embrace each moment, basking under the warmth as the sun slowly descends beneath the horizon, scan the beautiful valleys and grand mountain peaks, you glean around to see demure lighted candle flames flutters burn after the twilight backdrop fades to the darkness falls. Come and let's all appreciate nature's *logos biosphere, a lush* and plentiful garden paradise of bucolic places imbued with lively scenic vistas peering into nature's cozy milieus. Cheers to all patrons and magnificently bons hommes of the new-age generation of sapiens! Come here, there, and attend as your spirit resides consciousness awareness of the laws of the material external empirical world. Let's sit down to meditate within the illusory imagination of the ebullience of the creative oneiric poets mystical realm of the nondescript excursive visualization onto the spiritual plane of the Akashic thoughts. For I am soaring high in meditation, peacefully hang gliding, seemingly drifting away into the realm of the surreal anachronistic places where the essence of yellow scented candles' flames burn and permeates the air of tranquility and solace; its soothing aromatic aroma melding amid charmingly fluttering peace. Delightful ambiance permeated to accentuate a touch of whisper of full palavering sounds within quotidian spotlights. Life-changing, uplifting, breathtakingly beautiful, quite rustic canvas, amid this lush baronial mountainous skyline fresh spring flowing.

Behold a demure alluring candlelight vaporous specter of the majestics shooting scene of a calming delicate flames. Yellow demure fluttering candles light set the mood of the ataraxia of quiet comfort and solace engenders and buoyant by the intrinsic mystery inherent to slow-burning undulations of the delicate candle light fire. This indeed is a demure, delightful, romantic, subtle flame that captivates with the purest form and the perfect of moods. Candle light inspires poignant emotions, palpable expressions that enjoins lilting sound and roses are romanticizing metaphors. The purest heartfelt rapturest human emotions. Seemingly quite emblematic of a palpable intimate moment, as a demure candle light flame undulating dance embrace. Light a scented candle and watch it slowly burn as you muse upon a powerful seduction that unveils, reveals, captivates illusory temporal

THE MIND, BODY, SPIRIT, AND STORYTELLING

reality. Muse, on its powerful lure of the affirmative capstone sentiments of the vibes and smooth rhythms of the lover's ultimate private candle light romantic serenades pervaded the spaces on all sides in the surreal realm mesmerize faces. Seemingly able to transcend space and illusion, it brightens the beholder's romantic vision, a passion felt within the lingering opacity of the subjective illusory as the empirical temporal reality. Things that bedazzle with the soft swaying candle flames that flutter in the dark canvas. Boldly it unveils the presence upon a vaporous illusion of shadowy twilight repose. Blissful candlelight titillates, mellifluously melding a permeating amorous of the pure genuine enchantment delight. Oh, the mystical daily sunlight glow and mesmerizing delicate soft allure is the power that burns as the yellow candle flame. Its undulations, captivating thoughts in whatever mood it touches my visceral sensory capstone emotions that dazzles the mind, enliven and warm my mood with heartfelt fidelity of quiet comfort and inspirational tranquility of the solace. Eyes that flirt with artistic perfection enlivens the intimate apprehended by the senses; it quickens the soulful spirit the parnassian butterflies spritely manifest that d'amore as pure passion, tranquility, and nirvana. Mental complexes imagine this musing on the shimmering glow of the soft candle light's flicks, swaying amid the breeze; its undulating flame entertains, my eyes mesmerized by this vainglorious sultry shimmering dance embrace. Surely genuine, heartfelt, cultured, sophisticated, and musingly poetic verses conflate hearts beating rhythmically; an essence of scented candle flames burning are the pages of nature's luminous divine laws. With a duality of illusory temporal reality and surrealism, we dream to escape our realm of physical work-day external empirical world's universe is a dichotomy. People's fugacious blathering love relationships, intimate d'amore. To present a specific emblematic gift of a solitary beautiful long-stemmed red rose bloom to epitomize a sensation that conjugates our two hearts like true lovers do, in the moonlight, dining alfresco by the slow flickering flame of dim burning fluttering of the dancing candlelight. Like the living nature, the lifeblood is flowing through our veins with every tender beating heart we live. A passion that blinds in shimmering shadows on beautiful faces, you are gingerly slowly sipping on a favorite tinctured adult intoxicating delightful libation spurred a genuine love in a cheerful heart imbued with the ambiance of burning scented candle flames.

    I stood there gazing into the eyes of an enchantress; an Amorously lovely face was conspicuously staring at me. Her adorned eyes, I gleaned, and smiled as I saw not a sign of nuance and delivered my dulcet charming poetic parlance of extemporaneous lines flowing. Caught in this moment of constellations unfolding fugacious amusement, it was a subtle seduction as alluring flickers of scented candlelight serenade the mood unbounded. And although seemingly prideful and insignificant, my pellucid palaver illusion of fanciful creative expressions as all convoluted risible notions display one's natural state of mind as you fly into anachronistic places. Sublimely ephemeral, before my eyes were remarkably beautiful garden pond with a large fountain a well-crafted ancient sundial, with a magnificent ancient Egyptian clepsydras nestled in amongst a multi-colorful stupendous array of trees verdant-green leaves and to see the flowers bloom in summer delighted me.

    With the gentlest touch of the wind as the plants swayed back and forth; like leaves of tall trees bathed in the bright warm sunlight rays by the wind directions, in the full moonlight breeze. Meaning that every flow of the life force energy is for a number of counting years.

    The demure inestimable candlelight interpolates flickering enchanting surreal moods that serenade. After all, the glowing candlelight flame unlocks the mystic veil. We are living in the plane of existence, the illusory empirical. The reality buttresses the surreal dreamscape into the nominal frivolity, effervescence that pierces the veil of quiet comfort, solace, and inner peaceful life in mind/body/spirit complex.

Summer Time, Birds, Butterflies, Night Flight Fireflies

Tiny life that spreads the wings flying in the luminous divine metaphysical phenomena, we see the beautiful birds in flight. Those wondrous tiny earth fireflies fly and the beautiful butterflies mesmerize me is a majestic sight for everyone to see. This dazzling spectacle is a marvelous display of majestic fireflies, asynchronous glints of tiny neon lights flashing rhythm of phenomenal existence in the temporal world, physical correspondence sun that sets at twilight dusk and showcases darkness. Magnificent, beautiful itinerant butterflies flutter about in daylight, they go about their search for sweet nectar flying on tangentially floating on colorful delicate wings. elegantly they move and land upon the bountiful swaying flowers of nature's lush picturesque colorful landscape green meadows. Gracefully they fly and land to extract the sweet nectar from nature's fields of colorful blooms that grow in the sunlight. With our eyes wide open, we perceive the elegance of the biosphere. Various tiny lives exist like fireflies and butterflies. We will acknowledge that in this realm of flight one flies by day, the other by night. Earthly life exists under a cloud-covered skydome. A lively panoramic place given by omnipotent forces of the most high Infinite Creator endued the succor in a Gardens in Eden. An archetypal blueprint of existential illusory temporal reality, a daily eternal life cycle like black and white dyads across nature, tiny life fluttering in flight under the moon, and warm rays of sunlight. By night, cover tiny swarming fireflies glint against the darkness as neon lights glow under a moonlit sky.

Tiny wings flutter to move about over the bountiful earth.
Symbolically as a reaction to the simple purity residing within
life's pervasive facets of the myriad creative constructions. Duality
exists within nature, which has a universal, eternal life cycle.
Whereas perfection abounds: the one is by daylight and
sound, and the other by darkness and is associated
with the harmful nature of evil powers, whereas the two shades
equate to this duality of life in excellent equilibrium.
And as the sun above will beneath the horizon, A nightlife awaits
to showcase ephemeral glints of swooning neon flying lights.
We wait for the butterflies in flight to amuse us in the daily
sunshine fluttering amid the marvelous arrays of flowers' by day.
Arrant butterflies in daylight on colorful wings bedazzle beholders'
eyes in the effulgent rays of sunlight. While arrant swooning night
fireflies flashlights animate twilight's sky canvas backdrop in repose.
On tiny wings they fly, a touchstone is derived: rustled
wings of spriteful young fireflies glow by night.
They are the colorful butterflies we see invite eyes to
behold a spectacle, that tiny life of optical amusement.
One flying by moonlight; one flying by sunlight. Two separate
spectacles of animated night fireflies swooning in darkness.
While those colorful wings of butterflies sedulously float in
search of nectar under rays of sunlight that warms the air.
Frivolously flying high over the vast majestic valleys, lush green
and fertile fields of rolling hillside dales, fresh meadow glistening
leaves covered with wet dew was so beautiful. Watch colorful
lighted fireflies and butterflies float amid nature's landscape,
Feeling buoyant, I was going about looking all around and
admiring a beautiful milieu that manifested a purity of calm.
So exceedingly delightful to watch giddy playful children
amused by the swarming fireflies asynchronously glowing.
It's the essence within all the fruits of nature's providence
of delightfulness. Watch as you observe the visible external
empirical world; its beautiful perfect harmony is separate,
and uniquely recognizable. This life we share is a luminous
divine unity with fireflies and butterflies captivated and

the mind's senses imbibe up this subtle amusement. Yeah, it's so close to the rhythmically swaying motion of the kite's tail undulating and floating on a majestic wind. Beautiful butterflies navigate through flowers is akin to watching fireflies and butterflies in inflight. Melancholy spirits neither feel right nor can it lift you higher; nothing like when watching lighted fireflies surf over the canvas of darkness unfolding with a beautiful glow all around you is like a delightfully zenithful feeling. Fireflies and butterflies arrest those maelstroms that tug on heartstrings tethered to kites calmly gliding on the gentle power of the wind; the leaves drift to the ground lie stretched beneath the clouds above move across the sky. Sunlight slowly passes into the twilight emerges forth with its affluent on the rhythmic, harmonic balance of foreshadowing daily earthly drama; I felt as if I was dreaming. As if this quiet touch of poetry descended from amongst the clouds; cascading like a taste of life's best nectar was like honey dew. Sensory as a flying kite floating on the wind, undulations of that undulating tethered tail of a kite soaring higher like the majestic free wings that are lifting the birds that are adrift and peacefully gliding through the windswept sky. You see the birds in flight; you watch them in awe. These beautiful birds are floating around, going higher as they drift in the subtle motion of the wind, and it's majestic to see them hovering above the Earth against the moving clouds and blue sky. Behold this envy spurred mankind's passion for human flight. A visible cosmic evolution and involution of creative consciousness and reflection of luminous divine recognizable wonderful cosmic external empirical world material illusory temporal reality. This visual creative spirit is the luminous divine god-self. The creative endued by all-luminous divine unity as material matters; things as separation become recognizable. The bequeathed his existence, buoyant in the ways of unknowing in search of nature's harmonic, geosynchronous sacred principles of the lifeforce balanced, as spiritual power and primeval energy burns like the purity of wisdom of the Law of One manifestation expressions are all

around us. It is there laying the truth that is the face of God! And there, too, you will observe life's creatures be recognizable in every form as creative existence from the ground. And as you look up above, scan the sky, and there you will surely admire the magnificent birds soaring higher as an adrenaline rush creates an incomparable feeling of incredible flight looking down. I watched full and majestic birds lift on the luminous divine spirit! With all the beautiful life fulfillment arrayed all around me. I stood close to the edge of the lakeshore vista and looked up and admired birds gently drift upward into the cool lovely ataraxis breezy mountains air gaze into the clear blue canvas white clouds. We see birds flying and seemingly carefree and detached as they look down into the earthly valleys, dells, glens, a city of concrete domicile amid a fauna and flora landscape. Seemingly, I was flying high above the ground, glancing down and admiring all of the beautiful things below. A moment of cosmic serenity looking down at the many things below that appeared very small.
My spirit-inspired by birds in flight seems
majestic, as my soul is now flying.
The people of Earth below walk in the luminous
divine particle waves in the warm, bright sun.
I watch birds vicariously gliding magnificent wings carrying them higher on the wind that keeps on lifting them higher. And seemingly moving higher, drifting across the sky clouds. Suddenly my spirit caused me to look up there, I am floating in the sky and feeling without the weight of my physical body complex. I am at peace flying high without my feet; I am flying high and seeing all of the tiny things below; I am flying higher and looking down low and feeling high untethered from my profile. A feeling that seems so right; you get this wonderful good peaceful feeling of calm came over me watching those birds gracefully gliding adrift, floating higher toward the clouds in spectacular flight. Mentally you perceive this visual image of birds that seemingly never care about where they're going. Unlike fireflies or beautifully colorful butterflies, birds sing melodious, soothingly sounding tunes.

THE MIND, BODY, SPIRIT, AND STORYTELLING

Before you know it, you are in the air, semi-transcending objective illusory temporal reality, soaring! Up there flying with eagles as I took in the skyline, and I was floating around and gliding around riding on the wind. It was incredible looking down and this felt so right as they were all looking up into the sky and waving at me from the earth below. Alive and in flight, I felt myself enjoying this peace of mind, and never wanting to come down. Visual things that come into existence live within an eternal life cycle of the human condition is wondrously full of tiny life that crawls, while some can spread their wings and fly up underneath this lively skydome. It's truly a beautiful "Garden of Eden." And no matter how high or how far they fly high above, they all lightly touch down in a metaphysical external empirical world that is the capstone and optics define the objective of the temporal world reality environment. Believe you are no longer bound, but buoyed above the vagaries and the quagmires, stressful daily illusory reveries. Life events pervades human consciousness as joy, pain, mental solace is an incomparable divine calm feeling with a sense of melancholy that is the common universal medium of the harmonic vibration of the human mind, body, spirit, complex!

Integrity And Honor
Above Reproach

To the philosophical neophytes who are the seekers of the spiritual light of God, these pearls of wisdom shall impart the integrity of my god's Law of One love, my being living in the service to myself—eternally existing as a soul gifted to me as a vibration derived from the eternal life force harmonic energy, waves of the highest essence of the vainglorious ineffable Kavod of the luminous divine spirit of the Shetaut Neter Neberdjer.

I'm uniquely different just as I am a separate soul entity like you, and viz., meaning that I am the embodiment of this material existential spirit, unity of incarnation, the transformation of my past other selves. The physical manifestation of the mind/body/spirit complex essence. The enthusiasm of my Ch'i is in sync with the Kundalini in harmonic balance with the infinite Creator spiritual science, Law of the Neter!

Yeah, my sentient human being ended existence, an incarnation derived from the luminous divine creative spirit energy, unknowing my meaningful life purpose, having free will. Responsibility to live a whole life with inner peace and mental stasis, blessed with harmonic conscious awareness, free of distortions. My illusory temporal reality. Both negative and positive spirit complex amid the agitated spur up tumult and chaos, going hither and thither alive inside the outer empirical world, as my clarion call consciousness is slowly ticking. A luminous divine spirit unity of natural free will animate manifolds of recognizable.

A mind/body/spirit complex imbibes in the consciousness to dream in the subconscious recumbent state.

Old worldwide river waves of misled unwittingly anesthetized victims cast aside, through life without foresight, and without it emerged into existence of the original prior lifesome have squandered-away. Our pathway is never a straight line or filled with life fulfillment of beautiful monumental events! Many pathways of life are straight-aways, with forks in roads that wind into curves, intersections and traffic stop lights controlled signals at the four way crossings into the serendipity. Through this turnstile of the dreams and the awakening into a life and in-turn, the sleep of the death recycled incarnation of the recumbent spiritual nature of the esoteric initiation of repose. Love and praise to the most high great infinite Creator. To always give high praise and thanks as intelligent spiritual sentient being, a living and blessed with the soul that appreciates inner, spiritual, temporal reality, for every time I breathe air that which I live. To free will and intellectual knowledge, enters the third eye of insight into anachronistic places through matutinal daily meditation of my mind/body/spirit complex, integrity is the essential thing in honor. My countenance abides by humility, civility of the Law of One unity, a spirit that causes my kind actions. The perceptions and knowledge of my manifestation as my spirit drives good or bad actions. Might our thoughts harken back to the primordial DNA blueprint and learn of the lifeblood of my living spirit? My nascence of old rebirth is a hidden mystery and derived from the luminous divine sacred primal spirit essence. I incarnated from holy water, an embryonic natal developing awake from nirvana into the visual temporal reality. My spirit radiated atomic neutrons and protons is a soulful life of mind, body; the luminous spirit is the essence. A tenuous lifestyle and arrested life's existence is the finite form. Life has for all a meaningful purpose that is not but it is in sync with the ubiquitous divine luminous Shetaut Neter, and that is that I am now fully awakened and aware of what I see is me. Myself peregrinations' to find the lighted pathway basking in the divine glory of the light, life, and to love the divine spiritual peacefulness of quiet comfort and solace. I am unaware of old prior eons of my visceral long-existing time periods; the mysteries concealed behind random closed doors. Now I patiently await a new life story to be unfurled and reveal that I am born naked and innocent. I'm a humbled unborn child, my soul resting in the ataraxia of quiet comfort and solace.

Life is the reality we have all been given to experience the benevolent life force energy by divine means. The will of the most high praise in humble reverence. God is everywhere you find quiet comfort and solace throughout our days of the warm light of sunny days and nights of dark lunar light until that first natal breath, as my eyes are now opened. With visionary clarity I scanned nature's beautiful vistas feature that tranquil melodious sound birds and the fast-moving flows streaming down through the panoramic view of Earth's scenic dales with the multiple fauna and flora that is the seeds of various life for effervesce with the fresh of the matutinal air and the wet dew covering the meadows, hillsides, and rugged foot traffic trails.

My genuine integrity with a pure heart and honor is my bond; and as my countenance is revealed with unwavering loyalty. A new regeneration coming forth into the human form of beingness that is a turn of life in the cycle and the blessed breath to enjoy having a new life peregrinations. The ephemeral realm of duality when light is the symbol of knowing, yet knowing nothing about the philosophical principles of sacred knowledge and wisdom insight. To cultivate honor and integrity, a moral flame of fire and light that fuels my guiding inner peace and worthy when weighed against the Egyptian goddess Ma'at's ostrich feather. And in perfect harmonic equilibrium, sync with the new world twenty-first-century high rise metropolitan epicenter of the new age economy. Not a life of crime or distortion of unreconciled chaos, repatriation into the time deficit repression of turpitude. Being constrained and unable to excavate the poverty of deprivation and the arrested development. Forsaken without a lifeline cannot extricate themselves out of dalliance with the slavery yoke are the rejected churlish folks of human society.

Human beings' existence is one of being a fleshly embodiment. The massive waves of the ignorance folks have yet to accept that as children of the human race, must realize that we all need to share and embrace the living social complex as a one love philosophy of our existence. Yet some human species have been anesthetized and polarized within/without. People have their beliefs rooted in a preferred Christian Gospel teachings of the religion of faith. While others adhere to spirituality which draws it inspiration from what they feel and show devotion and veneration for your god dichotomy between the transformation from the original Africans Kemetic origins of the ancient holy teachings of the canonical Bible of the ancient Coptic Churches of Christian occultic writing and the teachings spiritual principles of wisdom, derived from the Egyptian Goddess Maat' mythos forty-two laws of the sage. Teaching and learning the Kemetic mystery school temples of the sacred knowledge of esoteric wisdom of the Anunnaki titular gods of heaven. No disillusionment, because the hidden truth has been discovered that they came, and they landed. This ancient alien astronauts' vanguard fifty-man crew built and bequeathed culture and civilization on the Earth circa 450,000 years ago in ancient Mesopotamia (modern-day country of Iraq).

We explore the Bible in this context that which has been the mystery religion is the truth is no longer a confused state of conscious bias and misguided personalism of self-indulging bon homies of the teachings of religious falsehood misled away from the intransient waves of Africa's original Kemetic knowledge. No sense of influence from the learning and teaching of spiritual wisdom towards the African Egyptian practice of conscious awareness. Achieve and experience a recumbent state through the daily routine of yoga meditation. One's heart must be judged to be pure when weighed against the Egyptian priestess, Ma'at's ostrich feather. Our earthly existence is a tremendous and deep chasm; the weight of the external empirical world of the volatile streaming confluence of noise and explosive episodes of tumult is mired in the struggle for the power to assume control for material wealth (https://www.egyptconnection.com/42-laws-of-maat/).

This unity of the shared human inheritance is the evolution progress in the social complex. We there the entropy of destructive actions mired in this element's insanity pervasive as a jejune behavior, by those who are the lost and witting pawns that are the misled confused egos of this self-centered biased malcontent sociopathic denizen. They in the social culture without any motivation to spiral upward into the pathway towards spiritual fulfillment light of the one creator. Seemingly the callow walking dead lost souls among the social complex.

There are the elements of immoral and the evil soul of those who prey upon the malleable, the purveyors of cruel and unusual fetters aligned against the positives of the universal Neberdjer. There are those human beings of our species who have been misled, confused, and deceived; these are the lost that are poised and ready to sow their angry seeds, which fall prey to the seductive sway of evil deeds. Often they are mad, which is a predisposition inclined toward gratuitous sanguine violence against the construct of the status quo social complex of responsible action. Fractional, cultural, social-political right and left perennial rivalries escalating ad hominem lift and right-politician partisan brutal attacks permeate the social society toxic culture morality, ad-nauseam! A physical world of material things that are finite, while my soul is everlasting. To this, I attest to acknowledge that I am a living spiritual entity. But is it true for you too? Life is a mind/body complex is the unique separation from the vaingloriously, enigmatic, infinite unity. An esoteric numeric miracle that waxed the Earth satellite of Earth nine new moons as of each nascent, which is the light, life, and love.

It is the beginning and ending of marking the calendar day's specific date. Whereof it turns up rippling waves onto the shoreline. From the sunrise and sunset life recycles the living breath, I was born in the zodiac constellation of Taurus the bull. I slept growing in the womb until that natal date, knowing nothing of the sacred light of my incarnation. Life developed in the usual way until the recumbent state into the light of my development. The unborn embryonic child is conceived and developed, the mother's womb envelopes as the rose calyx is protected; inside, a child develops like the roses' anthesis of natal that happens in the early springtime. My beloved mother's body carried me; my embryonic spirit rested to the heart's rhythmic beat. I grew in quiet comfort Chi in harmonic balance, relaxing calm in visceral reflective solace. My eyes closed, so I knew nothing of the light, love, or future life for me. Yet my form changed while I calmly dreamed of resting inside the warm pool of my mother's sacred waters for nine lunar nights and sunny days until that natal date was certain; my initiation of that date of manifestation to live. My emotional tears pool in my mother's eyes to reflect tears of joy and pain as sounds of the cycle begin ticking until the end time; I know not when my present space-time continuum; I grew until that natal date is a full stop for me to incarnate.

My prior natal existence will have no consciousness awareness or remembrance of human embryonic embodiments. Only my innocent animated Chi; and my old prior being-ness have long been jettisoned before each rebirth into the cycle as the essence of mind/body/spirit complex incarnation and animation awaits. The gift of another life to experience the martial plane of the temporal reality, to experience love of myself, to be in God's service on earth for a finite number of counting years. Here I am growing and devoid of my old memories of the lost periods as a child of two parents to shepherd me in the light to serve with a pure heart endued by the infinite Creator of all existence. I am reposed and developing consciousness awareness as a gift of free will. Oh lord my eyes have seen the light of truth. Yet I have no remembrance of those prior ions that was before this incarnation into an illusory world reality. Though my eyes imbibe with sentience, I am amused by the sound of melodies and voices of human confabulating, it is a blessing that I can hear. Lo, I can't move my head to look around; I can not open my eyes to see the light, and I can't talk, so I will cry for my new mother to hold me. Somewhere deep within my consciousness, my other selves are archived and locked away from my present space-time continuum. Old pages of my previous life have been turned, my remembrance of which I can not revisit. For I have no cognitive comprehension of millions of past incarnations; they exist beyond the imaginary field of the dream state of the existential material world of the physical temporal reality of the space-time continuum. The nascent nature of life is derived from God's pages. The golden age of humanity historical data past epoch. No memories that harkens me back to when that olden times creator god Enki bequeathed the fate of earth's gregarious bon homies. We read of the beautiful allegory of Adam and Eve. We are all the descendants of children of the most high throne of god. Planet Earth is our home, the illusory duality realm of lunar nights and sunny days orbital cycle of temporal reality. The dichotomy between the generous free-will gift of conscious awareness. Humankind commune within the natural world of freewill is my consciousness awareness of my sound mind, body, spirit complex.

I of this life have woken up into the light, life, and love nature every minute of this diurnal time cycle of being. Save for some folks along the way of my life peregrination, there are many things to throw one's journey into chaos, tumult, in to face disorder. For they are, seemingly, awake—without having a clarity of understanding a purpose of beingness, in the present terrestrial time-space continuum. To observe that nothing is perfect; and many things in people's lives are not well!

You can be the judge of this personhood as their behavior, which exemplify the most indecorious shameful and despicable of those who draw the ire of the most despicable has been responsible for egregious offenses. Troubled souls of the wayward spirit, are closely akin to the walking dead who reside in the and among socialized complex are closely akin to the walking dead who reside in the and among social complex. They love the labyrinth of darkness. They do not fear the consequences associated with the transgressions of iniquity as actions put against the luminous spiritual principles of the unity of the universal forces of luminous divine nature. Life is derived from the unity of the Law of the One love, that is, by the vainglorious geometry of the cosmological grand divine principles of God as the metaphysical, harmonic, rhythmic vibrations of natural laws.

To those still asleep and dreaming awake, you will with no past remembrances of your peaceful realm of the restful nights of the dream excursions. For nine months, I slept as if I was not consciously aware of my beingness, as I was fully formed and grew I was quite comfortable in peace. Likened to outer covering, the calyx that surrounds and protects the undeveloped bloom of the beautiful red rose. I am resting in my inner peace without knowing or aware of my innermost thoughts, material embodiment of the mental harmonic balance; yet in this fetal position in a recombinant "stasis" until the clarion call to glory my incarnation of my spirit animation took its luminous divine breath and caused my free will to spur my actions. As life attests to its magnificent present to existence, quiet your thoughts as you stand in awe, listening to all of nature's soundtrack of the idyllic unframed living canvas.

Picture yourself just enjoying every moment learning to appreciate the precious days have a wonderfully beautiful day in the illusory realm of temporal reality. My embryonic ears hear words and sounds; I can not see. The melodious harmonic subtle light waves force energy pervades and sustainable providence of the bountiful fruit of the earth plane.

Awake positive thoughts towards a beautiful life journey toward the path to ultimate salvation. To be humble spirit essence with nuances to apprehend the clarity that underlying the luminous manifestation of the evanescent grace, beautiful life reflected in the Netjer's rolling mountain dales and is replete with panoramic vistas. Lilting sounds melded amid nature's pristine fresh flowing waters streaming cacophony as it slowly serpentines down through the tranquility of the colorful rolling mountain chains' panoramic landscape milieu. Luminous spirit of life that is abiding with the terrestrial landscape! People, of the living spirit, we are all separate entities who must know thyself as the children of the god.

THE MIND, BODY, SPIRIT, AND STORYTELLING

Learn to know that you must first serve thyself and be of service to the other selves; be humble, grow old and wise. Might all truth be everlasting love, peace, honor bring happiness for your beloved family ancestors spirit essence pervades conscious awareness. And may all life be blessed by the infinite creator gift of peaceful inner life, with spiritual freedom, physical health, and external empirical world peace. Thank you for taking this creative journey with me. And so might these prose resonate within the hearts and the minds with the light and love vibration, for every sentient being awaited my initiation by reincarnation into the earth plane!

Have yourself a wonderful blessed earth peregrination as a gift of life from the Kavod of the most high infinite Creator's luminous divine light. I leave now to continue living on the journey of love in the light energy of the one infinite Creator. One Great all unity. And as that tribal Indians and the Jamaican people shouted in praise says: Hey yah, Hey yah…Hey, Jah! Hey, Jahjah! The ubiquitous lord has manifested himself as the Neter that He has given unto the energetic spirit that dwells within me, awareness of my Chi in sync within the mind/body/spirit complex. The families of ttWithin the mind/body/spirit complex. The families of thIn sync within the mind/body/spirit complex.

Families of the social complex. To all of the human family social complex. To all of the human family, I here acknowledge in these words that they may bring you a spirit of inner peace, quiet comfort, peace, love, and the ataraxia life of mental solace that is a common medium of the human spirit entity in sync with the great infinite Creator god Adonai, meaning what? Reverence and praise given to the Highest all of gods of humankind.

Oh lord, Hallelujahs!

REFERENCES TO HYPERLINKS FOR THE PERSPICACIOUS ERUDITION OF THE KNOWLEDGE/FACTS

[1] https://www.ancient.eu/article/225/enuma-elish
[2] https://www.ancient.eu/article/225/enuma-elish
[3] afrikaisworke.com
[4] https://en.m.wikipedia.org/wiki/Anunnaki
[5] https://www.ancient-code.com/scientist-at-deathbed-makes-shocking-confessions-about-aliens
[6] http://www.ancient-code.com/nikola-tesla-ufos-an
[7] https://www.dralimelbey.com/metaphysics-and-the-end-of-religious
[8] https://godssecret.wordpress.com/2009/04/01/the-dropa-stones
[9] https://libguides.marquette.edu/c.php?g=36796&p=2974240
[10] https://www.faena.com/aleph/the-garden-of-eden-or-why-we-long-for-the-unknown
[11] http://www.talkgenesis.org/where-was-eden-located/; or at https://www.google.com/search?q=havilah
[12] https://en.m.wikipedia.org/wiki/Havilah
[13] https://www.britannica.com/browse/Philosophy-Religion
[14] https://en.m.wikipedia.org/wiki/Ancient_astronauts
[15] https://www.egyptianmysteries.org/what-do-neterians-believe-in-what-are
[16] https://www.amazon.com/Egyptian-Mysteries-1-Shetaut-Neter/dp/1884564410
[17] https://www.shamballaschool.org/articles/2018/9/4/the-black-rite-highest-initiation
[18] https://www.khanacademy.org/humanities/ancient-art-civilizations/ancient-near-east1/the-ancient-near-east.
[19] *www.Afrikaiswoke.com/anunnaki*

[20] https://exemplore.com/ufos-aliens/UFO-Evidence-Magnifies-Biblical-Story-of-ancient creation-The-Catholic-Kid-an
[21] https://enkispeaks.com/
[23] https://aalbc.com/books/bookinfo.php? https://aalbc.com/books/bookinfo.php?
[24] https://www.afrikaiswoke.com/Nephilim-of-the-bible
[25] *http://oracc.museum.upenn.edu/amgg/listofdeities/igigi/index.html*
[26] https://www.afrikaiswoke.com/anunnaki-in-africa/
[27] https://www.afrikaiswoke.com/book-of-enoch-civilization-anunnaki/
[28] https://www.publishersmarketplace.com/rights/display.cgi?no=15991
[29] https://www.google.com/amp/s/www.theafricareport.com/53429/zimbabwe-losing-millions-from-illicit-gol
[30] https://www.newsmax.com/newsmax-tv/ufos-jeremy-corbell-navy-space/2021/06/16/id/1025289/?ns_mail_uid=30bd680c-c2f8-49e0-bdad-4a0337bde4a6&ns_mail_job=DM228682_06162021&s=acs&dkt_nbr=0105026
[31] https://www.ancient-origins.net/history/eden-revisited-0012198
[32] https://smeekanadieus.com/post
[33] https://www.dralimelbey.com/metaphysics-and-the-end-of-religious-
[34] https://en.m.wikipedia.org/wiki/Spanish_Inquisition
[35] https://blogygold.com/garden-of-eden-found-how-archeologist-discovered-true
[36] https://www.ancient-origins.net/Myths-legends-asia/powerful-enki-epic-sumerian-Babylon
[37] https://yeyeolade.wordpress.com/2008/07/26/the-blackness-of-jesus-christ-again-found-on-a-white-site).
[38] https://en.m.wikipedia.org/wiki/Havilah
[39] https://interestingengineering.com/shedding-some-light-on-the-ancient-astronauts-theories.

ABOUT THE AUTHOR

HAKEEM R. JELANI

HAKEEM R. JELANI, graduated from Colorado Technical University (CTU) with a Masters of Science degree in Business Management. He is a military retiree and former active duty enlisted member of the United States Air Force, and has managed store operations while assigned to the Air force Commissary Service, or (AFCOMS), and with the new Department of Defense Agency, or (DeCA) in the contiguous United States and overseas in support of the worldwide mission. A recipient of the 1983, Air Force annual Commissary, Northeast Regional Outstanding Air Force Commissary Command award in the senior enlisted category. A 1984 graduate of McGuire Air Force-Fort Dix, Air Force Command Academy as senior student commander. During his illustrative twenty-four years was awarded one Air Force Achievement Medal, four Air Force Commendation Medals, and the Air Force Meritorious Service Medal. He is currently a resident of the Tampa Bay community. He enjoys long walks, reading, and cooking.

www.ingramcontent.com/pod-product-compliance
Lightning Source LLC
Chambersburg PA
CBHW031247230426
43670CB00005B/72